THE CAMBRIDGE HISTORY
OF ENGLISH LITERATURE

THE CAMBRIDGE HISTORY OF
ENGLISH LITERATURE

VOLUME II

THE END OF THE MIDDLE AGES

THE
CAMBRIDGE HISTORY OF
ENGLISH LITERATURE

EDITED

BY

SIR A. W. WARD

AND

A. R. WALLER

VOLUME II

THE END OF THE MIDDLE AGES

CAMBRIDGE

AT THE UNIVERSITY PRESS

1967

Published by the Syndics of the Cambridge University Press
Bentley House, 200 Euston Road, London, N.W.1
American Branch: 32 East 57th Street, New York, N.Y.10022

First edition	1908
Reprinted	1912
	1930
Cheap edition	1932 (text only)
Reprinted	1934
	1949
	1961
	1963
	1967

Printed in Great Britain
at the University Printing House, Cambridge
(Brooke Crutchley, University Printer)

PREFATORY NOTE

The Cambridge History of English Literature was first published between the years 1907 and 1916. The General Index Volume was issued in 1927.

In the preface to Volume I the general editors explained their intentions. They proposed to give a connected account of the successive movements of English literature, to describe the work of writers both of primary and of secondary importance, and to discuss the interaction between English and foreign literatures. They included certain allied subjects such as oratory, scholarship, journalism and typography, and they did not neglect the literature of America and the British Dominions. The History was to unfold itself, "unfettered by any preconceived notions of artificial eras or controlling dates," and its judgments were not to be regarded as final.

This reprint of the text and general index of the *History* is issued in the hope that its low price may make it easily available to a wider circle of students and other readers who wish to have on their shelves the full story of English literature.

CAMBRIDGE
1932

CONTENTS

CHAPTER I

PIERS THE PLOWMAN AND ITS SEQUENCE

FEW poems of the Middle Ages have had a stranger fate than those grouped under the general title of *The Vision of William concerning Piers the Plowman.* Obviously very popular in the latter half of the fourteenth century, the time of their composition, they remained popular throughout the fifteenth century, were regarded in the sixteenth by the leaders of the reformation as an inspiration and a prophecy, and, in modern times, have been quoted by every historian of the fourteenth century as the most vivid and trustworthy source for the social and economic history of the time. Yet their early popularity has resulted in the confusion of what is really the work of five different men, and in the creation of a mythical author of all these poems and one other; and the nature of the interest of the sixteenth century reformers has caused a misunderstanding of the objects and aims of the satire contained in the poems separately and collectively. Worst of all, perhaps, the failure of modern scholars to distinguish the presence of several hands in the poems has resulted in a general charge of vagueness and obscurity, which has not even spared a portion of the work remarkable for its clearness and definiteness and structural excellence.

Before taking up any of the problems just suggested, we may recall briefly certain undisputed facts as to the form of the poems. They are written throughout in alliterative verse of the same general type as that of *Beowulf* and other Old English poems, and, at first sight, seem to form one long poem, extant in versions differing somewhat from one another. As Skeat has conclusively shown in his monumental editions of the texts, there are three principal versions or texts, which he designates the A-text, the B-text and the C-text, or the Vernon, the Crowley and the Whitaker versions respectively. The A-text, or Vernon version, consists of three visions supposed to come to the author while sleeping beside a stream among the Malvern hills. The first of these, occupying the prologue and passus I—IV, is the vision of the field full of folk—a symbol of the world—and Holy Church and Lady Meed; the second, occupying passus V—VIII, is the vision of Piers the Plowman and the crowd of penitents whom he leads in search of Saint Truth; the third, occupying passus IX—XII, is a vision in which the dreamer goes in search of Do-well, Do-better and Do-best, but is attacked by hunger and fever and dies ere his quest is accomplished. The B-text and the C-text are successive modifications and expansions of the A-text.

Let us turn now from fact to theory. The two principal authorities, Skeat and Jusserand, though differing in details, agree, in the main, in the account they give of the poems and the author; and their account is very generally accepted. It is as follows. The author was William Langland (or Langley), born about 1331—2 at Cleobury Mortimer, 32 miles S.S.E. from Shrewsbury and 137 N.W. from London, and educated in the school of the Benedictine monastery at Malvern, among the hills S.W. of Worcester. Whether he was the son of freemen (Skeat's view) or of serfs (Jusserand's view), he was, at any rate, educated for the church and probably took minor orders; but, because of his temperament, his opinions, his marriage, or his lack of influential friends, he never rose in the church. At some unknown date, possibly before 1362, he removed to London and made a scanty living by singing masses, copying legal documents and other similar casual occupations. In 1362, he began his famous poems, writing first the vision of Lady Meed and the vision of Piers the Plowman.   Perhaps immediately, perhaps after an interval of some time, he added to these the vision of Do-well, Do-better and Do-best. This first version of these poems constitutes what is now called the A-text of *Piers the Plowman*. But, according to the current view, the author did not leave matters thus. Encouraged by the success of his work and impelled by his increasing indignation at the corruptions of the age, he took up his poem again in 1377 and expanded it to more than twice its original length. The lines of the earlier version he left essentially unchanged; but he inserted, here and there, additions of greater or less length, suggested now by some word or phrase of the original text, now by events in the world about him and his meditations on them; and he rejected the whole of the final passus, containing an imaginary account of his death, to replace it by a continuation of the vision of Do-well, Do-better and Do-best longer than the whole of the original version of the poem. The

A-text had contained a prologue and four passus (or cantos) of the vision of Lady Meed, four passus of the vision of Piers the Plowman and four passus of the vision of Do-well, Do-better and Do-best, or twelve passus in all, with a total of 2567 lines. The B-text runs parallel to this to the end of passus XI (but with 3206 lines instead of 2467), and then continues for nine more passus, making a total of 7242 lines. The author's active interest in his poem did not cease here, however, for he subjected it to another revision, about 1393 (according to Skeat) or 1398 (according to Jusserand). This revision is known as the C-text. Its relation to the B-text may be roughly stated as consisting in the insertion of a few passages, the rearrangement of a considerable number and the rewriting of a number of others with more or less change of content or of emphasis, but, on the whole, as involving no such striking differences from the B-text as exist between that and the A-text. This latest version numbers 7357 lines as against the 7242 of the second version.

Skeat and Jusserand ascribe to the same author another poem in alliterative verse, commonly known as *Richard the Redeless*, concerning the last years of the reign of Richard II. This poem, which, as we have it, is a fragment, was, Skeat thinks, written between the capture and the formal deposition of Richard in 1399, and was, perhaps, left unfinished by the author in consequence of the fate of the king.

The evidence relied upon to prove that all these poems were the work of a single author is entirely the internal evidence of the poems themselves, supposed similarity in ideas, style, diction, etc., together with the difficulty of supposing the existence, at, approximately, the same time, of several unknown writers of such ability as is displayed in these poems. Undoubtedly, the first impulse of any student of a group of poems related as these are is to assume that they are the work of a single author, and that any statements made in the poems concerning the personality and experiences of the dreamer are autobiographical revelations. Moreover, in this particular case, it will be remembered, each of the two later versions incorporates with its additions the preceding version; and, as the C-text, on account of the larger mass of material in it, has received the almost exclusive attention of scholars, the impression of the style and other literary qualities gained by the modern student has, necessarily, been a composite of the qualities of the three texts and not a distinct sense of the qualities of each and the differences between them.

Such differences do exist, and in the greatest number and variety. There are differences in diction, in metre, in sentence structure, in methods of organising material, in number and kind of rhetorical devices, in power of visualising objects and scenes presented, in topics of interest to the author and in views on social, theological and various miscellaneous questions. Some of these have, indeed, been observed and discussed by previous writers, but they have always been explained as due to such changes as might occur in any man's mental qualities and views of life in the course of thirty or thirty-five years, the interval between the earliest and the latest version. To the present writer the differences seem of such a nature as not to admit of such an explanation; and this opinion is confirmed by the existence of certain passages in which the authors of the later versions have failed to understand their predecessors.

This is, of course, not the place for polemics or for a detailed examination of all the problems suggested by the poems. Our principal concern is with the poems themselves as literary monuments and, if it may be, with their author or authors. But, for this very reason, it seems necessary to present the poems in such a way as to enable the student to decide for himself between the two theories of authorship, inasmuch as this decision carries with it important conclusions concerning the literary values of the poems, the mental qualities of the authors and the intellectual activity of the age to which they belong. Fortunately, such a presentation is precisely that which will best set forth the contents of the poems and their qualities.

Let us examine first the prologue and passus I–VIII of the A-text. This is not an arbitrary dismemberment of a poem. The two visions included in these passus are intimately connected with each other and definitely separated from what follows. At the beginning of the prologue the dreamer goes to sleep among the Malvern hills and sees a vision of the world in the guise of a field full of folk thronging a valley bounded on one side by a cliff, on which stands the tower of Truth, and, on the other, by a deep dale, in which, surrounded by a dark moat, lies the dungeon of Wrong. Within this valley begin the incidents of his first vision, and, though they range far, there is never any suggestion of discontinuity; at the end of the vision the dreamer wakes for only a moment, and, immediately falling asleep, sees again the same field of folk and another series of events unfolding themselves in rapid succession beneath the cliff with its high-built tower, until, finally, he wakes 'meatless and moneyless in Malvern hills.' The third vision, on the other hand, has no connection with Malvern hills; the dreamer sees nothing of his valley, with the folk and the tower and the dungeon; indeed, this is not a vision at all in the sense of the first two, but, rather, a series of dream-visits and dream-discussions, the like of which cannot be found in the first two visions. Skeat himself has recognised the close connection between the first two visions, and has suggested that the third may have been written after a considerable interval.

Each of the first two visions in the A-text is, contrary to the usual opinion, distinguished by remarkable unity of structure, directness of movement and freedom from digression of any sort. The author marshals his dream-figures with marvellous swiftness, but with unerring hand; he never himself forgets for a moment the relation of any incident to his whole plan, nor allows his reader to forget it, or to feel at a loss as to its meaning or its place.

We first see, with the vividness of the dreamer's own vision, the thronging crowd in the valley beneath the tower of Truth and hovering on the brink of the dark dale. People of all sorts are there—the poor and the rich, saints and sinners of every variety, living as they live in the world. Singly and in groups they pass before us, each noted by the poet with a word or a phrase that gives us their very form and pressure. Satire there is, but it is satire which does not impede the movement of the thronged dream, satire which flashes and plays about the object, revealing its inner nature by a word, an epithet, a brief phrase. We see the false beggars shamming for food and fighting at the ale-house, 'great lubbers and long that loth were to labour'; the friars, 'preaching the people for profit of their bellies'; the pardoner, surrounded by the crowd of ignorant believers, whom he deceives with his papal bull and his fair speech; and the corrupt priest, taking his share of the ill-gotten gains, while the bishop, who is not 'worth his two ears,' refuses to interfere. Then come a hundred lawyers in hoods of silk, ready to undertake any cause for money, but refusing 'to unloose their lips once for love of our Lord'; 'you could more easily,' says the poet, 'measure the mist on Malvern hills than get a mum of their mouths unless money were showed.' After them appears a confused throng of churchmen of all degrees, all 'leaping to London' to seek worldly offices and wealth. Wasters there are, and idle labourers 'that do their deeds ill and drive forth the long day with singing *Dieu save Dame Emme!*' Along with the satire there is commendation, now for the ploughmen who work hard and play seldom; now, of a higher sort, for pious nuns and hermits; now, for honest merchants; now, even for harmless minstrels who 'get gold with their glee.' But, neither satire nor commendation delays even for a moment our rapid survey of this marvellous motley crowd, or detracts from our feeling that, in this valley of vision, the world in miniature is visibly moving, living, working, cheating, praying, singing, crying for sale its 'hot pies,' its 'good geese and pigs,' its 'white wine and red.'

The author, having thus, in his prologue, set before us the vision first presented to the eyes of his mind, proceeds to interpret it. This he does characteristically by a further development of the dream itself.

A lovely lady comes down from the cliff and says to the dreamer:

> Son, seest thou this people, how engrossed they are in this confusion? The most part of the people that pass now on earth, if they have success in this world, care for nothing else; of other heaven than here they take no account.

The impression already made upon us by this strange majestic figure is deepened by the author's vivid comment, 'I was afeard of her face, fair though she was, and said, "Mercy, my lady; what is the meaning of this?"' The tower, she explains, is the dwelling of Truth, the Father of our faith, who formed us all and commanded the earth to serve mankind with all things needful. He has given food and drink and clothing to suffice for all, but to be used with moderation, for excess is sinful and dangerous to the soul. The dreamer enquires curiously about money: 'the money on this earth that men so fast hold, tell me to whom that treasure belongs.' 'Go to the Gospel,' she replies, 'and consider what Christ himself said when the people apposed him with a penny.' He then asks the meaning of the dungeon in the deep dale.

> That is the castle of Care; whoso comes therein may ban that he was born to body or to soul; in it dwells a wight named Wrong, the father of False, who seduced Adam and Cain and Judas. He is a hinderer of love, and deceives all who trust in their vain treasures.

Wondering who she is that utters such wisdom, the dreamer is informed that she is Holy Church. 'Thou oughtest to know me; I received thee first and taught thee faith, and thou didst promise to love me loyally while thy life should endure.' He falls upon his knees, beseeching her favour and begging her to teach him so to believe on Christ as to do His will: 'Teach me to no treasure but tell me this, how I may save my soul!'

'When all treasure is tried,' she declares, 'Truth is the best; it is as precious as God himself. Whoso is true of his tongue and of his deeds, and does ill to no man, is accounted to the Gospel and likened to our Lord. Truth is claimed by Christian and non-Christian; it should be kept by all. Kings and knights are bound by it, cherubim and seraphim and all the orders of angels were knighted by Christ and taught to know Truth. Lucifer and his fellows failed in obedience, and sinned by pride, and fell; but all who keep Truth may be sure that their souls shall go to heaven to be crowned by Truth; for, when all treasure is tried, Truth is the best.' 'But what is it? By what quality or power of my nature does it begin, and where?' 'Thou fool, it is a teaching of nature to love thy Lord dearer than thyself, and do no deadly sin though thou shouldst die. This is Truth, and none can teach thee better; it is the most precious thing demanded by our Lord. Love began by the Father and was perfected in the death of his Son. Be merciful as He was merciful, for, unless you live truly, and love and help the poor, you have no merit in Mass or in Hours. Faith without works is dead; chastity without charity is as foul as an unlighted lamp. *Date et dabitur vobis*, this is the lock of love that lets out my grace to comfort all sinful; it is the readiest way that leads to heaven.'

With this Holy Church declares that she can stay no longer, and passus I closes.

But the dreamer kneels and beseeches her, crying,

'Mercy, my lady, for the love of her that bore the blissful Babe that redeemed us on the cross; teach me to know False!' 'Look on thy left hand and see where he stands—both False and Favel (Duplicity) and all his whole house.' I looked on the left hand as the lady taught me; and I saw a woman wonderfully clothed, arrayed in furs the richest on earth, crowned with a crown no less costly than the king's, all her five fingers loaded with rings, with the most precious stones that prince ever wore. 'Who is this woman,' said I, 'thus richly attired?' 'That is the maiden Meed, who has often injured me. To-morrow will the marriage be made of her and False. Favel brought them together, Guile prepared her for it and Liar has directed the whole affair. I warn thee that thou mayst know them all, and keep thyself from them, if thou desirest to dwell with Truth in his bliss. I can stay no longer; I commit thee to our Lord.'

All the rich retinue that held with False was bidden to the bridal. Simony was sent for to seal the charters and feoff Meed with all the possessions of False and Favel. But there was no house that could hold the throng that came. In a moment, as if by some magical process, we see a pavilion pitched on a hill, with ten thousand tents set about it, for all men of all orders to witness the feoffment of Meed. Then Favel brought her forth, and Simony and Civil (Civil Law) stood forth and unfolded the charter, which was drawn up in due legal form and endowed the contracting parties with all the provinces of the seven deadly sins, 'to have and to hold, and all their heirs after, with the appurtenance of Purgatory, even to the torment of Hell; yielding, for this thing, at the year's end, their souls to Satan.' This was duly witnessed and delivered. But Theology objected to the wedding, because Meed was no bastard and should be wedded according to the choice of Truth.

The workman is worthy of his hire. False is no mate for her; she is of good birth and might kiss the king for cousin. Take her to London and see if the law will permit this wedding; and beware, for Truth is wise, and Conscience, who knows you all, is of his counsel.

Civil agreed, but Simony demanded money for his services. Then Favel brought forth gold, and began to bribe officers and witnesses; and all promised to go to London and support his claims before the court at Westminster.

The incident which follows is one of the best examples of the author's power of visualisation and of rapid narration unbroken by explanation or moralisation; for the moralising lines, unfortunately admitted into Skeat's text, which interrupt the narrative and tend to delay and obscure it, do not belong to the original, but are found in one MS only. To the rapidity and assurance with which the picture is developed is, perhaps, due in no small part the readiness with which we accept it and the vitality and solidity which these personified abstractions maintain throughout the dream.

'Then they lacked horses to carry them thither, but Favel brought forth foals of the best. He set Meed on a sheriff's back, shod all new, and False on a juror that trotted softly.' In like manner for each of the abstractions was provided some appropriate, concrete evil-doer; and, thus equipped, the fantastic crew immediately set out. But Soothness saw them well, and said little, but rode hard and came first to court. There he told Conscience, and Conscience reported to the king, all that had happened. 'Now, by Christ,' said the king, 'if I might catch False or any of his fellows, I would hang them by the neck.' Dread, standing at the door, heard his doom, and went wightly to warn False. At the news, the wedding party fled in all directions. False fled to the friars, Liar leaped away lightly, lurked through lanes, buffeted by many and ordered to leave, until pardoners had pity on him and received him as one of themselves. Then he was in demand: physicians and merchants and minstrels and messengers wanted him; but the friars induced him to come with them. Of the whole wedding party, only Meed durst stay, and she trembled and wept and wrung her hands when she was arrested.

In passus III the king orders that Meed shall be treated courteously, and declares that he himself will ask her whom she wishes to wed, and, if she acts reasonably, he will forgive her. So a clerk brought her to the chamber. At once people began to profess friendship for her and promise aid. The justices came, and said, 'Mourn not, Meed; we will clear thee.' She thanked them and gave them cups of clean gold and rings with rubies. Clerks came, and said, 'We are thine own, to work thy will while life lasts.' She promised to reward them all: 'no ignorance shall hinder the advancement of him whom I love.' A confessor offered to shrive her for a seam of wheat and to serve her in any evil. She told him a tale and gave him money to be her bedesman and her bawd. He assoiled her, and then suggested that, if she would help them with a stained glass window they were putting in, her name would be recorded on it and her soul would be sure of heaven. 'Knew I that,' said the woman, 'there is neither window nor altar that I would not make or mend, and inscribe my name thereon.' Here the author declares the sin of such actions, and exhorts men to cease such inscriptions, and give alms. He also urges mayors to punish brewers, bakers, butchers and cooks, who, of all men on earth, do most harm by defrauding the poor. 'Meed,' he remarks, 'urged them to take bribes and permit such cheating; but Solomon says that fire shall consume the houses of those who take bribes.'

Then the king entered and had Meed brought before him. He addressed her courteously, but said, 'Never hast thou done worse than now, but do so no more. I have a knight called Conscience; wilt thou marry him?' 'Yea, lord,' said the lady, 'God forbid else!' Conscience was called and asked if he would wed her.

Nay, Christ forbid! She is frail of her flesh, fickle, a causer of wantonness. She killed father Adam and has poisoned popes. She is as common as the cart-way; she releases the guilty and hangs the innocent. She is privy with the pope, and she and Simony seal his bulls. She maintains priests in concubinage. She leads the law as she pleases, and suppresses the complaints of the poor.

Meed tried to defend herself by charging that Conscience had caused greater evils. He had killed a king. He had caused a king to give up his campaign in Normandy.

Had I been the king's marshal, he should have been lord of all that land. A king ought to give rewards to all that serve him; popes both receive and give rewards; servants receive wages; beggars, alms; the king pays his officers; priests expect mass-pence; craftsmen and merchants, all take meed.

The king was impressed by this plea, and cried, 'By Christ, Meed is worthy to have such mastery.' But Conscience kneeled, and explained that there are two kinds of meed; the one, such as God gives to men who love him; the other, such as maintains evil-doers. 'Such as take bribes shall answer for it; priests that take money for masses have their reward on earth only. Wages is not meed, nor is there meed in the bargains of merchants.' He then illustrates the dangers of meed by the story of Saul and the Amalekites, and ends by declaring that Reason shall reign and govern realms; Meed shall no more be master, but Love and Humility and Loyalty shall rule, and Kind-Wit and Conscience together shall make Law a labourer, such love shall arise.

The king interrupted him and tried to effect a reconciliation between him and Meed, but Conscience refused, unless advised thereto by Reason. 'Ride forth and fetch Reason; he shall rule my realm,' replied the king. Conscience rode away gladly and returned with Reason, followed by Wit and Wisdom. The king welcomed Reason, and set him on the throne, between himself and his son; and, while they were talking together, Peace came, and put up a bill how Wrong had taken his wife, had stolen his geese, his pigs, his horse and his wheat, had murdered his men and beaten him. Wrong was afraid and tried to bribe Wisdom to plead for him. Wisdom and Wit told him that, without the help of Meed, he was ruined, and they took him to her. Peace showed the king his bloody head; and the king and Conscience knew he had been wronged; but Wisdom offered bail for Wrong and payment of the damages, and Meed offered Peace a present of gold; whereupon Peace begged the king to have mercy upon Wrong. The king swore he would not. Some urged Reason to have pity, but he declared that he would not

till all lords and ladies love truth, and men cease to spoil children, and clerks and knights are courteous, and priests practise what they preach, till the custom of pilgrimages and of carrying money out of the land ceases, till Meed has no might to moot in this hall. Were I king, no wrong should go unpunished or get grace by bribes. Were this rule kept, Law would have to become a labourer, and Love should rule all.

When they heard this, all held Reason a master and Meed a wretch. Love laughed Meed to scorn. The king agreed that Reason spoke truth, but said it would be hard to establish such government. Reason asserted that it would be easy. Whereupon the king begged Reason to stay with him and rule the land as long as he lived. 'I am ready,' said Reason, 'to rest with thee ever; provided Conscience be our counsellor, I care for nothing better.' 'Gladly,' said the king; 'God forbid that he fail; and, as long as I live, let us keep together!'

Thus ends passus IV, and, with it, the first vision. The style and the method of composition are, in the highest degree, worthy of note. The author, it will be observed, sets forth his views, not, after the ordinary fashion of allegorists, by bringing together his personifications and using them as mere mouthpieces, but by involving them in a rapidly moving series of interesting situations, skilfully devised to cause each to act and speak in a thoroughly characteristic manner. They do not seem to be puppets, moving and speaking as the showman pulls the strings, but persons, endowed each with his own life and moved by the impulses of his own will. Only once or twice does the author interrupt his narration to express his own views or feelings, and never does he allow them to interfere with the skill or sincerity of expression of the *dramatis personae*. His presentation has, indeed, the clear, undisturbed objectivity of excellent drama, or of life itself.

In the prologue, the satire, as has been observed, is all incidental, casual; the same is true of passus I; for these two sections of the poem are not essentially satirical. The first is a purely objective vision of the world with its mingled good and evil; the second is the explanation of this vision with some comment and exhortation by Holy Church, the interpreter. The satire proper begins with passus II, and, from there to the end of this vision, is devoted to a single subject—Meed and the confusion and distress which, because of her, afflict the world. Friars, merchants, the clergy, justices, lawyers, all classes of men, indeed, are shown to be corrupted by love of Meed; but, contrary to current opinion, there is nowhere even the least hint of any personal animosity against any class of men as a class, or against any of the established institutions of church or state. The friars have often been supposed to be the special object of attack, but, so far as this vision is concerned, they fare better, on the whole, than do the lawyers. The only notable order of fourteenth century society that escapes censure altogether is that of the monks. Of them there is no direct criticism, though some of the MSS include monks among those to whom Meed is common (III, 127—8). The possible bearing of this fact upon the social status of the author will be discussed later.

As to the style, no summary or paraphrase can reproduce its picturesqueness and verve. It is always simple, direct, evocative of a constant series of clear and sharply-defined images of individuals and groups. Little or no attempt is made at elaborate, or even ordinarily full, description, and colour-words are singularly

few; but it would be difficult to find a piece of writing from which
the reader derives a clearer vision of individuals or groups of
moving figures in their habit as they lived. That the author was
endowed in the highest degree with the faculty of visualisation is
proved, not merely by his ability to stimulate the reader to form
mental images, but even more by the fact that all the movements
of individuals and groups can be followed with ease and certainty.
Composition, in the larger sense of structural excellence, that
quality common in French literature, but all too rare in English,
and supposed to be notably lacking in *Piers the Plowman*, is one
of the most striking features of this first vision.

What has just been said of the qualities of the first vision is
true in equal degree of the second, *The Vision of Piers the Plowman*, properly so called, which occupies passus V—VIII. In outline
it is as follows :

At the close of the preceding vision, the king and his company
went to the church to hear the services. The dreamer saw them
enter, and awaked from his dream disappointed and sorrowful
that he had not slept more soundly and seen more. But, ere he
had gone a furlong, a faintness seized him, and he sat softly down
and said his creed; then he fell asleep and saw more than he had
seen before. He saw again the field full of folk and Conscience
with a cross preaching among them, urging them to have pity on
themselves and declaring that the pestilences were caused by their
sins, and that the great storm of wind on Saturday at even (15
January 1362) was a punishment for pride. Wasters were warned
to go to work; chapmen to cease spoiling their children; Pernel,
to give up her purfle; Thomas and Wat, to look after their frail
and extravagant wives; priests, to practise what they preached;
members of the religious orders, to keep their vows, lest the king
and his council should take possession of their property; pilgrims,
to cease journeying to St James, and seek St Truth. Then ran
Repentance and moved the hearts of all; William wept; Pernel
Proudheart prostrated herself ; Lecher, Envy, Covetousness,
Glutton, Sloth, Robert the Robber, all repented. The confessions
of the seven deadly sins (an accident has deprived us of the
confession of Wrath and of a portion of Envy's) follow one
another with breathless rapidity, and the climax is reached when,
in the words of the author, 'a thousand of men then thronged
together, crying upward to Christ and to His pure Mother to have
grace to seek St Truth—God grant they so may!'

With this passus v closes; but the movement of the narrative is uninterrupted. Some spurious lines printed by Skeat do, indeed, cause a semblance of at least a momentary delay; but the authentic text is better constructed.

There were few so wise, however, that they knew the way thither (*i.e.* to St Truth), but blustered forth as beasts over valleys and hills, till it was late and long that they met a person apparelled like a pilgrim, with relics of the many shrines he had visited. He had been at Sinai, Bethlehem, Babylon, Armenia, Alexandria and in many other places, but had never heard of St Truth, nor met a palmer seeking such a saint.

'By St Peter!' cried a ploughman, and put forth his head, 'I know him as well as a clerk his book; Conscience and Kind-Wit directed me to him and taught me to serve him ever. I have been his man these fifteen years, sowed his seed, kept his beasts, diked and delved and done his bidding in all things.'

The pilgrims offered him money to show them the way; but Piers, the ploughman, cried,

Nay, by the peril of my soul! I would not take a penny for the whole wealth of St Thomas's shrine; Truth would love me the less. But this is the way. You must go through Meekness till you come to Conscience-that-Christ-knows-that-you-love-him-dearer-than-the-life-in-your-hearts-and-your-neighbour-next. Then cross the brook Be-buxom-of-speech by the ford Honour-thy-father; pass by Swear-not-in-vain and the croft Covet-not, with the two stocks Slay-not and Steal-not; stop not at Bear-no-false-witness, and then will be seen Say-sooth. Thus shalt thou come to a court, clear as the sun; the moat is of Mercy, the walls of Wit, to keep Will out, the cornells of Christendom, the brattice of Faith, the roof of Brotherly Love. The tower in which Truth is is set above the sun; he may do with the day-star what him dear liketh; Death dare do naught that he forbids. The gate-keeper is Grace, his man is Amend-thou, whose favour thou must procure. At the gate also are seven sisters, Abstinence, Humility, Charity, Chastity, Patience, Peace and Generosity. Any of their kin are welcomed gladly, and, unless one is kin to some of these seven, he gets no entrance except by grace.

'By Christ,' cried a cut-purse, 'I have no kin there! And so said some others; but Piers replied, 'Yes; there is there a maiden, Mercy, who has power over them all. She is sib to all sinful, and, through help of her and her Son, you may get grace there, if you go early.'

Passus VII opens with the remark that this would be a difficult way without a guide at every step. 'By Peter!' replied Piers, 'were my half-acre ploughed, I would go with you myself.' 'That would be a long delay,' said a lady; 'what shall we women do meanwhile?' 'Sew and spin and clothe the needy.' 'By Christ!' exclaimed a knight, 'I never learned to plough; but teach me, and I will help you.' But Piers rejected his offer and bade him do only those services that belong to knighthood, and practise the virtues of a kindly lord. The knight promised to do so, and Piers prepared for his ploughing. Those who helped were to be fed. Before setting out on his journey, however, he wished to make his will, bequeathing his soul to God, his body to the church, his property to his wife to divide among his friends and his dear children.

Piers and the pilgrims set to work; some helped him to plough, others diked up the balks, others plucked weeds. At high prime (9 a.m.) Piers looked about and saw that some had merely been singing at the ale and helping him with 'hey, troly-loly!' He threatened them with famine, and the shirkers feigned to be lame or blind, and begged alms. 'I shall soon see if what you say is true,' said Piers; 'those who will not work shall eat only barley bread and drink of the brook. The maimed and blind I will feed, and anchorites once a day, for once is enough.' Then the wasters arose and would have fought. Piers called on the knight for protection, but the knight's efforts were vain. He then called upon Hunger, who seized Waster by the maw and wrung him so that his eyes watered, and beat the rascals till he nearly burst their ribs. Piers in pity came between them with a pease-loaf. Immediately all the sham ailments disappeared; and blind, bed-ridden, lame asked for work. Piers gave it to them, but, fearing another outbreak, asked Hunger what should be done in that event. The reply, which contains the author's view of the labour-problem, was that able-bodied beggars were to be given nothing to eat but horse-bread and dog-bread and bones and thus driven to work, but the unfortunate and the naked and needy were to be comforted with alms. In reply to a further question whether it is right to make men work, Hunger cited *Genesis, Proverbs, Matthew* and the *Psalms*. 'But some of my men are always ill,' said Piers. 'It comes of over-eating; they must not eat until they are hungry, and then only in moderation.' Piers thanked him, and gave him leave to go whenever he would; but Hunger replied that he would not go till he had dined. Piers had only cheese, curds, an oat-cake, a loaf of beans and bran and a few vegetables, which must last till harvest; so the poor people brought peascods, beans and cherries to feed Hunger. He wanted more, and they brought pease and leeks. And in harvest they fed him plentifully and put him to sleep. Then beggars and labourers became dainty and demanded fine bread and fresh meats, and there was grumbling about wages and cursing of the king and his council for the labour-laws. The author warns workmen of their folly, and prophesies the return of famine.

In passus VIII we are told that Truth heard of these things and sent to Piers a message to work and a pardon *a poena et a culpa* for him and his heirs. Part in this pardon was granted to kings, knights and bishops who fulfil their duties. Merchants, because of their failure to observe holidays, were denied full participation; but they received a letter from Truth under his privy seal authorising them to trade boldly, provided they devoted their profits to good works, the building of hospitals, the repairing of bridges, the aiding of poor maidens and widows and scholars. The merchants were glad, and gave Will woollen clothes for his pains in copying their letter. Men of law had least pardon, because of their unwillingness to plead without money; for water and air and wit are common gifts, and must not be bought and sold. Labourers, if true and loving and meek, had the same pardon that was sent to Piers. False beggars had none for their wicked deeds; but the old and helpless, women with child, the maimed and the blind, since they have their purgatory here upon earth, were to have, if meek, as full pardon as the Plowman himself.

Suddenly a priest asked to see Piers' pardon. It contained but two lines: *Et qui bona egerunt, ibunt in vitam eternam; qui vero mala, in ignem eternum.* 'By St Peter!' said the priest, 'I find here no pardon, but "do well, and have well, and God shall have thy soul; and do evil, and have evil, and to hell shalt thou go."' Piers, in distress, tore it asunder, and declared that he would cease to labour so hard and betake himself to prayers and penance, for David ate his bread with weeping, and Luke tells us that God bade us to take no thought for ourselves, but to consider how He feeds the birds. The priest then jested at the learning of Piers, and asked who taught him. 'Abstinence and Conscience,' said Piers. While they were disputing, the dreamer awoke and looked about, and found that it was noontime, and he himself meatless and moneyless on Malvern hills.

Here the vision ends, but passus VIII contains 53 lines more, in which the writer discusses the trustworthiness of dreams and the comparative value of Do-well and letters of indulgence.

In this second vision, the satire of passus V is very general, consisting, as it does, of a series of confessions by the seven deadly sins, in which each is sketched with inimitable vividness and brevity. It is significant of the author's religious views, and in harmony with such hints of them as he has given us elsewhere, that these confessions are not formal interviews with an authorised confessor, but, for the most part, sudden outcries of hearts which Conscience has wrought to contrition and repentance. The notable exceptions are the cases of Glutton and Sloth. Of these, the former has often been cited as one of the most remarkable pieces of *genre* painting in our early literature. It presents the veritable interior of an English ale-house in the fourteenth century, with all its basenesses and its gross hilarity.

Glutton is moved to repent, and starts for the church to confess, but, on his way thither, the ale-wife cries out to him. He says he is going to church to hear mass and confess. 'I have good ale, gossip; wilt thou try it?' He does not wish to drink, but asks if she has any spices to settle a queasy stomach. 'Yes, full good: pepper, peony, a pound of garlic and a little fennel-seed, to help topers on fasting days.' So Glutton goes in, and finds a crowd of his boon companions, Cis the shoemaker's wife, Wat the warrener and his wife, Tomkin the tinker and two of his men, Hick and Hodge and Clarice and Pernel and a dozen others; and all welcome him and offer him ale. Then they begin the sport called the New Fair, a game for promoting drinking. The whole day passes in laughter and ribaldry and carousing, and, at even-song, Glutton is so drunk that he walks like a gleeman's dog, sometimes aside and sometimes aback. As he attempts to go out, he falls; and his wife and servant come, and carry him home and put him to bed. When he wakes, two days later, his first word is, 'Where is the cup?' But his wife lectures him on his wickedness, and he begins to repent and profess abstinence.

As for Sloth, his confession, though informal, is not sudden, for the sufficient reason that he is too slothful to do anything suddenly.

The satire of passus VI and VII is directed principally, if not solely, against the labouring classes. In sentiment and opinion the author is entirely in harmony with parliament, seeing in the efforts of the labourers to get higher wages for their work only the unjustifiable demands of wicked, lazy, lawless vagabonds. In regard to the remedy, however, he differs entirely from parliament. He sees no help in the Statutes of Labourers or in any power that the social organisation can apply; the vain efforts of the knight when called upon by Piers for protection from the wasters (VII, 140 ff.) clearly indicate this. The only hope of the re-establishment of good conditions lies in the possibility that the wicked may be terrified by the prospect of famine, God's punishment for their wickedness, and may labour and live as does Piers Plowman, the ideal free labourer of the established order. The author is in no sense an innovator; he is a reformer only in the sense of wishing all men to see and feel the duties of the station in life to which they belong, and to do them as God has commanded.

Passus VIII is an explicit presentation of this idea, a re-assertion of the doctrine announced by Holy Church at the beginning of passus I and illustrated by all the visionary events that follow—the doctrine, namely, that, 'When all treasure is tried, Truth is the best.' The pardon sent to Piers is only another phrasing of this doctrine; and, though Piers himself is bewildered by the jibes of the priest and tears the pardon 'in pure teen,' though the dreamer wakes before the advent of any reassuring voice, and wakes to find himself hungry and poor and alone, we know authentically that there lies in the heart of the author not even the slightest question of the validity of his heaven-sent dreams.

The third vision, passus IX—XII of the A-text, differs from the first two, as has been said above, in very material respects. The theme is not presented by means of vitalised allegory; there are allegorical figures, to be sure, but their allegorical significance is only superficial, not essential; they engage in no significant action, but merely indulge in debate and disquisition; and what they say might be said by any one else quite as appropriately and effectively. Moreover, the clearness of phrasing, the orderliness and consecutiveness of thought, which so notably characterise the early visions, are entirely lacking, as are also the wonderful visualisation and vivid picturesqueness of diction. These differences are so striking that they cannot be overlooked by any one whose attention has once been directed to them. To the present writer they seem to justify the conclusion that in the third vision we have, not a poem written by the author of the first two, either immediately after them or even a few years later, but the work of a continuator, who tried to imitate the previous writer, but succeeded only superficially, because he had not the requisite ability as a writer, and because he failed to understand what were the distinctive features in the method of his model; but students of the poems have heretofore felt—without, I think, setting definitely before their minds the number and the character of these differences—that they were not incompatible with the theory of a single author for all the poems.

It is not intended to argue the question here, and, consequently, the differences will not be discussed further; but it may be of interest, to those who believe in a single author no less than to those who do not, to note, in addition, certain minor differences. The first writer seems not in the least interested in casuistry or theological doctrine, whereas notable features of the later passus are scholastic methods and interests, and a definite attitude towards predestination, which had been made by Bradwardine the foremost theological doctrine of the time, as we may infer from Chaucer and the author of *Pearl.* Indeed, the questions that interest the author of passus IX—XI are not only entirely different, but of a different order from those which interest the author of the first two visions.   Further, the use of figurative language is entirely different; of the twelve similes in passus IX—XI four are rather elaborate, whereas all the twenty found in the earlier passus are simple, and, for the most part, stock phrases, like 'clear as the sun,' only four having so much as a modifying clause.   The versification also presents differences in regard to the number of stresses in the half-line and in regard to run-on lines and masculine endings.   Some of these differences begin to manifest themselves in the last fifty-three lines of passus VIII; and it is possible that the continuator began, not at IX, 1, but at VIII, 131.   Of course, no one of the differences pointed out is, in itself, incompatible with the theory of a single author for all the passus of the A-text; but, taken together, they imply important differences in social and intellectual interests and in mental qualities and habits.   They deserve, therefore, to be noted; for, if the same person is the author of all three visions, he has at least undergone profound and far-reaching changes of the most various kinds, and no mere general supposition of development or decay of his powers will explain the phenomena.

We proceed, then, without further discussion, to examine the contents of the later passus.   Their professed subject is the search for Do-well, Do-better and Do-best, or, rather, for satisfactory definitions of them.   What were the author's own views, it is very hard to determine; partly, perhaps, because he left the poem unfinished, but partly, also, because the objections which, as a disputant, he offers to the statements of others seem, sometimes, only cavils intended to give emphasis and definiteness to the views under discussion.   It will be observed, however, that, on the whole, his model man is not the plain, honest, charitable labourer, like Piers, but the dutiful ecclesiastic.   Other topics that are clearly of chief interest to the author are: the personal responsibility of sane adults, and the vicarious responsibility of guardians for children and idiots; the duty of contentment and cheerful subjection to the will of God; the importance of pure and honourable wedlock; and the corruptions that have arisen, since the pestilence, in marriage and in the attitude of laymen towards the mysteries of faith, though Study, voicing, no doubt, the views of the author, admits that, but for the love in it, theology is a hard and profitless subject. There are also incidental discussions of the dangers of such branches of learning as astronomy, geometry, geomancy, etc.; of the chances of the rich to enter heaven; of predestination; and of the advantages as to salvation of the ignorant over the learned. A brief synopsis of these passus will make the method of treatment clearer.

Passus IX opens with the author roaming vainly about in his grey robes in search of Do-well, not in a dream, but while he is awake. At last, on a Friday, he meets two Franciscan friars, who tell him that Do-well dwells always with them. He denies this, in due scholastic form, on the ground that even the righteous sin seven times a day. The friars meet this argument by a rather confused illustration of a boat in which a man attempts to stand in a rough sea, and, though he stumbles and falls, does not fall out of the boat. The author declares he cannot follow the illustration, and says farewell. Wandering widely again, he reaches a wood, and, stopping to listen to the songs of the birds, falls asleep.

There came a large man, much like myself, who called me by name and said he was Thought. 'Do-well,' said Thought, 'is the meek, honest labourer; Do-better is he who to honesty adds charity and the preaching of sufferance; Do-best is above both and holds a bishop's crosier to punish the wicked. Do-well and Do-better have crowned a king to protect them all and prevent them from disobeying Do-best.'

The author is dissatisfied; and Thought refers him to Wit, whom they soon meet, and whom Thought questions on behalf of the dreamer (here called 'our Will.')

In passus X, Wit says that Duke Do-well dwells in a castle with Lady Anima, attended by Do-better, his daughter, and Do-best. The constable of the castle is Sir Inwit, whose five sons, See-well, Say-well, Hear-well, Work-well and Go-well, aid him. Kind, the maker of the castle, is God; the castle is Caro (Flesh). Anima is Life; and Inwit is Discretion (not Conscience), as appears from a long and wandering discussion of his functions. Do-well destroys vices and saves the soul. Do-well is the fear of the Lord, and Do-better is the fear of punishment. If Conscience tells you that you do well, do not desire to do better. Follow Conscience and fear not. If you strive to better yourself, you are in danger; a rolling stone gathers no moss and a jack of all trades is good at none. Whether you are married man, monk, canon, or even beggar, be content and murmur not against God. Do-well is dread, and Do-better is sufferance; and of dread and its deeds springs Do-best. As the sweet red rose springs from the briar, and wheat from a weed, so Do-best is the fruit of Do-well and Do-better, especially among the meek and lowly, to whom God gives his grace. Keepers of wedlock please God especially; of them come virgins, martyrs, monks, kings, etc. False folk are conceived in an ill hour, as was Cain. His descendants were accursed; and so were those of Seth, who intermarried with them, though warned against it. Because of these marriages, God ordered Noah to build the ark, and sent the flood to destroy Cain's seed. Even the beasts perished for the sin of these marriages. Nowadays, since the pestilence, many unequal marriages are made for money. These couples will never get the Dunmow flitch. All Christians should marry well and live purely, observing the *tempora clausa*. Otherwise, rascals are born, who oppose Do-well. Therefore, Do-well is dread; and Do-better is sufferance; and so comes Do-best and conquers wicked will.

In passus XI, Wit's wife, Study, is introduced. She rebukes him for casting pearls before swine, that is, teaching wisdom to those who prefer wealth. Wisdom is despised, unless carded with covetousness as clothiers card wool; lovers of Holy Writ are disregarded; minstrelsy and mirth have become lechery and bawdy tales. At meals, men mock Christ and the Trinity, and scorn beggars, who would perish but for the poor. Clerks have God much in the mouth but little in the heart. Every 'boy' cavils against God and the Scriptures. Austin the Old rebukes such. Believe and pray, and cavil not. Here now is a foolish fellow that wants to know Do-well from Do-better. Unless he live in the former, he shall not learn the latter.

At these words, Wit is confounded, and signals the author to seek the favour of Study. He, therefore, humbles himself, and Study is appeased, and promises to direct him to Clergy (Learning) and his wife, Scripture. The way lies by Sufferance, past Riches and Lechery, through Moderation of speech and of drink, to Clergy.

Tell him you were sent by me, who taught him and his wife. I also taught Plato and Aristotle and all craftsmen. But theology has troubled me much;

and, save for the love in it, it is naught.   Love is Do-well; and Do-better and Do-best are of Love's school.   Secular science teaches deceit, but theology teaches love.   Astronomy, geometry, geomancy, alchemy, necromancy and pyromancy are all evil; if you seek Do-well, avoid them.   I founded them to deceive the people.

The author goes at once to Clergy and his wife and is well received by them.   Clergy says that Do-well is the active life, Do-better is charity and Do-best is the clergy with benefices and power to help and possessions to relieve the poor.   Runners-about are evil; there are many such now, and the religious orders have become rich.   'I had thought kings and knights were best, but now I see that they are not.'   Scripture interrupts with the declaration that kinghood and knighthood and riches help not to heaven, and only the poor can enter.   '*Contra!*' says the author; 'Whoever believes and is baptised shall be saved.'   Scripture replies that baptism saves only *in extremis* and only repentant heathen, whereas Christians must love and be charitable.   Help, therefore, and do not harm, for God says, 'Slay not! for I shall punish every man for his misdeeds, unless Mercy intervenes.' The author objects that he is no nearer his quest, for whatever he may do will not alter his predestined end; Solomon did well and wisely and so did Aristotle, and both are in hell.

If I follow their words and works and am damned, I were unwise; the thief was saved before the patriarchs; and Magdalen, David, and Paul did ill, and yet are saved; Christ did not commend Clergy, but said, 'I will teach you what to say'; and Austin the Old said that the ignorant seize heaven sooner than the learned.

Passus XII opens with the reply of Clergy: 'I have tried to teach you Do-well, but you wish to cavil.   If you would do as I say, I would help you.'   Scripture scornfully replies, 'Tell him no more! Theology and David and Paul forbid it; and Christ refused to answer Pilate; tell him no more!'   Clergy creeps into a cabin and draws the door, telling the author to go and do as he pleases, well or ill.   But the author earnestly beseeches Scripture to direct him to Kind-Wit (Natural Intelligence), her cousin and confessor.   She says he is with Life, and calls, as a guide, a young clerk, *Omnia-probate*.   'Go with Will,' she orders, 'to the borough *Quod-bonum-est-tenete* and show him my cousin's house.' They set out together.

And here, it seems to me, this author ceased.   The remaining lines I believe to have been written by one John But.   They relate that, ere the author reached the court *Quod-bonum-est-tenete*, he met with many wonders.   First, as he passes through

Youth, he meets Hunger, who says that he dwells with Death, and seeks Life in order to kill him. The author wishes to accompany him, but, being too faint to walk, receives broken meats from Hunger, and eats too much. He next meets Fever, who dwells with Death and is going to attack Life. He proposes to accompany Fever; but Fever rejects his offer and advises him to do well and pray constantly.

Will knew that this speech was speedy; so he hastened and wrote what is written here and other works also of Piers the Plowman and many people besides. And, when this work was done, ere Will could espy, Death dealt him a dint and drove him to the earth; and he is now closed under clay, Christ have his soul! And so bade John But busily very often, when he saw these sayings alleged about James and Jerome and Job and others; and because he meddles with verse-making, he made this end. Now God save all Christians and especially king Richard and all lords that love him! and thou, Mary, Mother and Maiden, beseech thy Son to bring us to bliss!

Skeat originally ascribed to John But only the last twelve lines, beginning, 'And so bade John But.' It seems unlikely, however, that the 'end' which John But says he made refers to these lines only; certainly, it is not customary for scribes to use such a term for the supplications they add to a poem. And it is hard to conceive the motive of the author for finishing in this hasty fashion a poem which interested him, and which obviously had such immediate success. For these or similar reasons Skeat, later, admitted the possibility that the work of John But began seven lines earlier, with 'Will knew that this speech was speedy.' But the same reasoning applies to all the lines after l. 56, and an attentive reading of them will disclose several particulars at variance with the style or conceptions of the rest of the poem.

In closing our survey of the poems included in the A-text, we may note that, in their own day, they were not regarded as directed against the friars, for MS Rawl. Poet. 137 contains this inscription, 'in an old hand': *Hoc volumen conceditur ad usum fratrum minorum de observantia cantuariae.*

Let us turn now to the B-text. There is no reason to doubt the current view that it was written, in part at least, between June 1376 and June 1377. Tyrwhitt showed that the famous rat-parliament inserted in the prologue referred to the time between the death of the Black Prince and that of Edward III, and must have been written while men were anxious about the situation which then existed. The increased emphasis given to the pestilences in B, also points, as Skeat suggests, to a time not long after the pestilence of 1376. To these may be added the allusion to the drought and famine of April 1370 (XIII, 269—271) as 'not long passed.' No one, perhaps, believes that the whole of the B-text was written within the year indicated; but it has been generally assumed that the additions in the prologue antedate the rest of the B-text. For this assumption there is no reason except that the prologue is at the beginning of the poem. Two considerations suggest, though they by no means prove, that B, in his additions and insertions, did not always follow the order of the original poem. In the first place, in X, 115 is a promise of a discussion which occurs in XII. Any one who studies carefully B's methods of composition will find it easier to believe that B had already written XII when he thus referred to it, than that he purposely postponed a discussion. In the second place, it is hard to believe that such a writer as B, after becoming so thoroughly excited over political affairs as he shows himself to be in his insertion in the prologue, would have written the 4036 lines of his continuation of Do-well, Do-better and Do-best without again discussing them.

The author of the B-text, as we have seen, had before him, when he began his work, the three visions of the A-text. Whether he regarded them as the work of a single author is not our present concern. In his reworking of the poems he practically disregarded passus XII and changed the preceding eleven passus by insertions and expansions. Minor verbal alterations he also made, but far fewer than is usually supposed. Many of those credited to him are to be found among the variant readings of the A-text, and were merely taken over unchanged from the MS of A used as the basis.

Of the nine principal insertions made in the first two visions, six may be regarded as mere elaborations of the A-text, namely, the changed version of the feoffment, the confessions of Wrath, Avarice, Glutton and Sloth and the plea of Repentance. The other three, including the rat-parliament and the jubilee passages, are among the most important expressions of the political views of B, and will be discussed below. The insertions in the third vision, though elaborations of the A-text, are more difficult to characterise as to theme, on account of a tendency to rambling and vagueness sometimes almost degenerating into incoherency. The worst of them is the third (IX, 59—121), which ranges over indiscretion, gluttony, the duty of holy church to

fools and orphans; the duty of charity, enforced by the example
of the Jews; definitions of Do-well, Do-better and Do-best; waste
of time and of speech; God's love of workers and of those faithful
in wedlock.   A few lines translated from this passage may serve
to illustrate the author's mental processes, particularly his incapacity for organised or consecutive thinking, and his helpless
subjection to the suggestions of the words he happens to use.
They will also explain why students of these poems have found
it impossible to give a really representative synopsis of his work.
Let us begin with l. 88, immediately after the citation of the
brotherly love of the Jews:

The commons for their unkindness, I fear me, shall pay.   Bishops shall
be blamed because of beggars.   He is worse than Judas that gives a jester
silver, and bids the beggar go, because of his broken clothes.   *Proditor est
prelatus cum Iuda, qui patrimonium Christi mimis distribuit.*   He does
not well that does thus, and dreads not God Almighty, nor loves the saws of
Solomon, who taught wisdom; *Initium sapientiae, timor Domini:* who
dreads God does well; who dreads him for love and not for dread of
vengeance does, therefore, the better; he does best that restrains himself by
day and by night from wasting any speech or any space of time: *Qui offendit
in uno in omnibus est reus.*   Loss of time—Truth knows the sooth!—is most
hated on earth of those that are in heaven; and, next, to waste speech, which
is a sprig of grace and God's gleeman and a game of heaven; would never
the faithful Father that His fiddle were untempered or His gleeman a
rascal, a goer to taverns.   To all true tidy men that desire to work Our Lord
loves them and grants, loud or still, grace to go with them and procure their
sustenance.   *Inquirentes autem Dominum non minuentur omni bono.*   True-
wedded-living folk in this world is Do-well, etc.

As will be seen from this fairly representative passage, the
author does not control or direct his own thought, but is at the
mercy of any chance association of words and ideas; as Jusserand
well says, *il est la victime et non le maître de sa pensée.*

In the series of visions forming B's continuation of the poems,
the same qualities are manifest, and the same difficulty awaits the
student who attempts a synopsis or outline of them.   It is possible,
indeed, to state briefly the general situation and movement of
each vision, to say, *e.g.* that this presents the tree of Charity,
and this the Samaritan; but the point of view is frequently and
suddenly and unexpectedly shifted; topics alien to the main theme
intrude because of the use of a suggestive word; speakers begin
to expound views in harmony with their characters and end as
mere mouthpieces of the author; *dramatis personae* that belong
to one vision suddenly begin to speak and act in a later one as if
they had been present all the time; others disappear even more
mysteriously than they come.

Even the first of the added visions shows nearly all these peculiarities. At the beginning of passus XI, continuing the conversation of passus X, Scripture scorns the author and he begins to weep. Forgetting that he is already asleep and dreaming, the author represents himself as falling asleep and dreaming a new dream. Fortune ravished him alone into the land of Longing and showed him many marvels in a mirror called Mydlerd (*i.e.* the World). Following Fortune were two fair damsels, Concupiscencia-carnis and Covetyse-of-eyes, who comforted him, and promised him love and lordship. Age warned him, but Recklessness and Fauntelte (Childishness) made sport of the warning. Concupiscence ruled him, to the grief of Age and Holiness, and Covetyse comforted him forty-five years, telling him that, while Fortune was his friend, friars would love and absolve him. He followed her guidance till he forgot youth and ran into age, and Fortune was his foe. The friars forsook him. The reader expects to learn that this is because of his poverty, but, apparently, another idea has displaced this in the author's mind; for the reason given by him is that he said he would be buried at his parish church. For this, the friars held him a fool and loved him the less. He replied that they would not care where his body was buried provided they had his silver—a strange reply in view of the poverty into which he had fallen—and asked why they cared more to confess and to bury than to baptise, since baptism is needful for salvation. Lewte (Loyalty) looked upon him, and he loured. 'Why dost thou lour?' said Lewte. 'If I durst avow this dream among men?' 'Yea,' said he. 'They will cite "Judge not!"' said the author.

Of what service were Law if no one used it? It is lawful for laymen to tell the truth, except parsons and priests and prelates of holy church; it is not fitting for them to tell tales, though the tale were true, if it touched sin. What is known to everybody, why shouldst thou spare to declare; but be not the first to blame a fault. Though thou see evil, tell it not first; be sorry it were not amended. Thing that is secret, publish it never; neither laud it for love nor blame it for envy.

'He speaks truth,' said Scripture (who belongs not to this vision but to the preceding), and skipped on high and preached. 'But the subject she discussed, if laymen knew it, they would love it the less, I believe. This was her theme and her text: "Many were summoned to a feast, and, when they were come, the porter plucked in a few and let the rest go away."' Thereupon the author begins a long discussion with himself on predestination. It is obvious that such writing as this defies analytical presentation; and this is no isolated or rare instance. In certain passages where the author is following a narrative already organised for him, as in the rat-parliament of the prologue, or the account of the life of Christ in passus XVI, the rambling is less marked; but, if the narrative is long or elaborate, the author soon loses sight of the plan, as may be seen in the curious treatment, in passus XIX and XX, of the themes derived from *The Castle of Love.* In the instance last cited, the hopeless wandering occurs on so large a scale that it appears even in the synopses prepared by Skeat and others. Of the instances which disappear in synopsis, one of the most interesting is that of Activa-Vita, in passus XIII and XIV. Skeat's synopsis is as follows: 'Soon they meet with one Activa-Vita, who is a minstrel and seller of wafers. Patience instructs Activa-Vita, and declares that beggars shall have joy hereafter.' But the significant features are here omitted. Activa-Vita is the honest labourer, who provides bread for everybody, but, because he cannot please lords with lies and lewd jests, receives little reward. He is the friend and follower of Piers the Plowman. Yet, since he is Activa-Vita, in contact with the world, he is not spotless. The author therefore begins to tell us of the spots on Activa-Vita's coat, and, naturally, distributes them in the categories of the seven deadly sins. As soon as he enters upon this task he is perfectly helpless; he cannot control himself or his conceptions; and, consequently, he represents poor Activa-Vita as guilty of every one of the sins in its most wicked and vilest forms. The author of the C-text removed these passages to the confessions that followed the preaching of Conscience in the second vision, possibly, as Skeat thinks, in order to bring together passages of similar content and treatment, but, possibly, because such a contradiction in the character of Activa-Vita was too gross and glaring.

Recognising, then, the limitations with which every synopsis of the continuation by B must be received, we may say, briefly, that B adds seven visions, two and a fraction devoted to Do-well, two and a fraction to Do-better and two to Do-best. In the first (passus XI) there is no allegorical action; the dreamer meets various allegorical characters, such as Fortune, Recklessness, Nature and Reason, and hears them talk or talks himself either to them or to his readers. The subjects discussed are, as we have seen, very various; but chief among them are predestination, the value of poverty, incompetent priests and man's failure to follow reason as animals do. Following this, but not a vision, though it is distinguished from one only by the fact that the author is awake, is a long disquisition by Imaginative, containing views concerning the dangers and the value of learning and wealth very different from those expressed in A XI. The second vision begins with a dinner, given by Reason, at which are present the dreamer, Conscience, Clergy, Patience and a doctor of the church. Again there is no allegorical action; the dinner is only a device to bring together the disputants, who discuss theological subtleties. Following the dinner comes the interview with Activa-Vita described above. Conscience and Patience then instruct Activa-Vita to make amends by contrition and confession, and discuss at great length the benefits of poverty. The next vision is notable, though not unique, in containing a vision within a vision. In the first part (passus XV) Anima (also called Will, Reason, Love, Conscience, etc., an entirely different character from the Anima of A IX) discourses for 600 lines, mainly on knowledge, charity and the corruptions of the age due to the negligence of prelates; in the second part, when Anima, after describing the tree of Charity, says that it is under the care of Piers the Plowman, the dreamer swoons, for joy, into a dream, in which he sees Piers and the tree, and hears a long account of the fruits of the tree which gradually becomes a narrative of the birth and betrayal of Christ. At the close of this he wakes, and wanders about, seeking Piers, and meets with Abraham (or Faith), who expounds the Trinity; they are joined by Spes (Hope); and a Samaritan (identified with Jesus) cares for a wounded man whom neither Faith nor Hope will help. After this, the Samaritan expounds the Trinity, passing unintentionally to an exposition of mercy; and the dreamer wakes. In the next vision (passus XIX) he sees Jesus in the armour of Piers ready to joust with Death; but, instead of the jousting, we have an account of the crucifixion, the debate of the Four Daughters of God and the harrowing of hell. He wakes and writes his dream, and, immediately, sleeps again and dreams that Piers, painted all bloody and like to Christ, appears. Is it Jesus or Piers? Conscience tells him that these are the colours and coat-armour of Piers, but he that comes so bloody is Christ. A discussion ensues on the comparative merits of the names Christ and Jesus, followed by an account of the life of Christ. Piers is Peter (or the church), to whom are given four oxen (the evangelists) and four horses (the four fathers of the church) and four seeds to sow. A house, Unity, is built to store the grain, and is attacked by Pride and his host; but this is forgotten in the episodes of the brewer's refusal to partake of the Sacrament, the vicar's attack on the cardinals and the justification by the king and lords of their own exactions. The dreamer wakes and encounters Need, who gives him instruction very similar to that of Conscience in the preceding dream. Falling asleep again, he has a vision of the attack of Antichrist and Pride and their hosts upon Unity, which insensibly becomes an attack by Death upon all mankind, varied by certain actions of Life, Fortune, Sloth, Despair, Avarice and the friar Flattery. Conscience, hard beset by Pride and Sloth, calls vainly for help to Contrition, and, seizing his staff, starts out on a search for Piers the Plowman. Whereupon the dreamer wakes.

Some scholars have regarded the poem as unfinished; others, as showing by the nature of its ending the pessimism of the author. It is true that it ends unsatisfactorily, and that one or more visions might well have been added; but it may be doubted whether the author ever could have written an ending that would have been artistically satisfactory. He had, as we have seen, no skill in composition, no control of his materials or his thought. The latter part of the poem is supposed to be devoted in regular order to Do-well, Do-better and Do-best; but it may be said, without injustice, that these subjects determine neither the nature of the main incidents nor the manner in which they are developed, and that what the author himself would doubtless have cited as the supreme expression of his view of Do-well, Do-better and Do-best occurs early in the vision of Do-well—I mean, of course, the famous *Disce, Doce, Dilige*, taught to Patience by his leman, Love. He could never have been sure of reserving to the end of his poem the subjects with which he intended to end, or of ceasing to write at the point at which he wished to cease. It remains curious, nevertheless, and, perhaps, significant, in view of the continual recurrence in the work of B of invectives against the corruptions of the age, that the poem does end with the triumph of Antichrist, and that there is no hint, as in Kirchmayer's *Pammachius*, of preparations for his defeat and the coming of an age of endless peace and good.

The reader who has been impressed with what has been said about the vagueness and lack of definite organisation and movement in B's work may be inclined to ask, What merits are his and what claim has he upon our interests? The reply is that his merits are very great indeed, being no less than those rated highest by previous students of the poems—Skeat, Jusserand, ten Brink, Henry Morley and a host of others. The very lack of control, which is his most serious defect as an artist, serves to emphasise most convincingly his sincerity and emotional power, by the inevitableness with which, at every opportunity, he drifts back to the subjects that lie nearest his heart. Writing, as he did, without a definite plan and without power of self-direction, he touched, we may feel sure, not merely all subjects that were germane to his purpose, as a better artist would have done, but all that interested him deeply; and he touched most frequently those that interested him most. These subjects are, as is well known, the corruptions in the church, chiefly, perhaps, among the friars, but also, in no small measure, among the beneficed clergy; the dangers of riches and the excellence of poverty; the brotherhood of man; and the sovereign quality of love. To these should be added the idealisation of Piers the Plowman, elusive as are the forms which this idealisation often assumes. On the other hand, great as is the interest in political theory displayed by the author in the passages inserted in the prologue, this is not one of the subjects to which he constantly reverts; indeed, the only passage (XIX, 462—476) on this subject in the later passus touches it so lightly as to suggest that the author's interest in it at this time was very slight. The frequency with which subjects recur is, of course, not the only indication of the sincerity and depth of the author's interest; the vividness and power of expression are equally significant.

'Let some sudden emotion fill his soul,' says Jusserand, '....and we shall wonder at the grandeur of his eloquence. Some of his simplest expressions are real *trouvailles*; he penetrates into the innermost recesses of our hearts, and then goes on his way, and leaves us pondering and thoughtful, filled with awe.'

Such are:

And mysbede (mistreat) nou3te thi bonde-men, the better may thow spede.
Thowgh he be thyn underlynge here, wel may happe in hevene,
That he worth (shall be) worthier sette, and with more blisse,
Than thow, bot thou do bette, and live as thow sulde;
For in charnel atte chirche cherles ben yvel to knowe,
Or a kni3te from a knave,—knowe this in thin herte. VI, 46 ff.

For alle are we Crystes creatures, and of his coffres riche,
And brethren as of o (one) blode, as wel beggares as erles. XI, 192 ff.

Pore peple, thi prisoneres, Lord, in the put (pit) of myschief,
Conforte tho creatures that moche care suffren,
Thorw derth, thorw drouth, alle her dayes here,
Wo in wynter tymes for wanting of clothes,
And in somer tyme selde (seldom) soupen to the fulle;
Comforte thi careful, Cryst, in thi ryche (kingdom)! XIV, 174 ff.

The date usually assigned to the C-text is 1393—8. The only evidence of any value is the passage IV, 203—210, in which the author warns the king of the results of his alienation of the confidence and affection of his people. This, Skeat takes to be an allusion to the situation after the quarrel between the king and the Londoners in 1392; and, consequently, he selects 1393 as the approximate date of the poem, though he admits that it may be later. Jusserand argues that this local quarrel, which was soon composed, does not suit the lines of the poem as well as does the general dissatisfaction of 1397—9; and he, therefore, suggests 1398—9 as the date. Jusserand's view seems the more probable; but, even so early as 1386, parliament sent to inform the king that

si rex...nec voluerit per jura regni et statuta ac laudibiles ordinationes cum salubri consilio dominorum et procerum regni gubernari et regulari, sed capitose in suis insanis consiliis propriam voluntatem suam singularem proterve exercere, extunc licitum est eis....regem de regali solio abrogare.
(Knighton, II, 219.)

Of the changes and additions made by C we can here say very little, mainly for the reason that they are numerous, and small, and not in pursuance of any well-defined plan. There are multitudinous alterations of single words or phrases, sometimes to secure better alliteration, sometimes to get rid of an archaic word, sometimes to modify an opinion, but often for no discoverable reason, and, occasionally, resulting in positive injury to the style or the thought. Certain passages of greater or less length are entirely or largely rewritten, rarely for any important modification of view; never, perhaps, with any betterment of style. At times, one is tempted to think they were rewritten for the mere sake of rewriting, but many whole pages are left practically untouched. Transpositions occur, sometimes resulting in improvement, sometimes in confusion. Excisions or omissions may be noted which seem to have been made because C did not approve of the sentiments of the omitted passages; but there are other omissions which cannot be accounted for on this ground or on that of any artistic intention. The additions are all of the nature of elaborations or expansions and insertions. Some of these have attracted much attention as giving information concerning the life and character of the dreamer or author; these will be dealt with below. Others give us more or less valuable hints of the views and interests of the writer; such are: the passage accusing priests of image worship and of forging miracles; an account of the fall of Lucifer, with speculations as to why he made his seat in the

north; an attack on regraters; the long confused passage[1] comparing the two kinds of meed to grammatical relations. Still others modify, in certain respects, the opinions expressed in the B-text. For example, xv, 30—32 indicates a belief in astrology out of harmony with the earlier condemnation of it; the attitude on free-will in XI, 51—55 and XVII, 158—182 suggests that, unlike B, and the continuator of A, C rejected the views of Bradwardine on grace and predestination; several passages on riches and the rich[2] show a certain eagerness to repudiate any such condemnation of the rich as is found in B; and, finally, not only is the striking passage in B[3], cited above, in regard to the poor, omitted, but, instead of the indiscriminate almsgiving insisted upon by B, C distinctly condemns it[4] and declares[5] that charity begins at home—
'Help thi kynne, Crist bit (bids), for ther begynneth charite.'

On the whole, it may be said that the author of the C-text seems to have been a man of much learning, of true piety and of genuine interest in the welfare of the nation, but unimaginative, cautious and a very pronounced pedant.

The reader may desire a justification, as brief as possible, of the conclusion assumed throughout this chapter that the poems known under the title, *Piers the Plowman*, are not the work of a single author. So much of the necessary proof has already been furnished in the exposition of the different interests and methods and mental qualities displayed in the several parts of the work that little more will be necessary. The problem seems very simple: the differences pointed out—and others which cannot be discussed here—do exist; in the absence of any real reason to assume that all parts of this cluster of poems are the work of a single author, is it not more probable that several writers had a hand in it than that a single writer passed through the series of great and numerous changes necessary to account for the phenomena? To this question an affirmative answer will, I think, be given by any one who will take the trouble to examine separately the work of A (*i.e.* A, prol.—passus VIII), the continuator of A (A, IX—XII, 55), B and C—that is, to read carefully any passages of fifty or a hundred lines showing the work of each of these authors unmixed with lines from any of the others. In such an examination, besides the larger matters discussed throughout this chapter, the metre and the sentence structure will repay

[1] IV, 335. [2] XIII, 154—247; XIV, 26—100; XVIII, 21; XX, 232—246.
[3] XIV, 174—180. [4] X, 71—281. [5] XVIII, 58—71.

special attention. The system of scansion used will make no difference in the result; but that expounded by Luick will bring out the differences most clearly. It will be found that the writers differ in their conceptions of the requirements of alliterative verse, A being nearest to the types established by Luick, both in regard to stresses and secondary stresses and in regard to alliteration. This can be most easily tested by Luick's plan of considering separately the second-half-lines. Another interesting test is that of the use of the visual imagination. A presents to his own mind's eye and to that of his reader distinct visual images of figures, of groups of figures and of great masses of men; it is he who, as Jusserand says, 'excels in the difficult art of conveying the impression of a multitude.' A also, through his remarkable faculty of visual imagination, always preserves his point of view, and, when he moves his action beyond the limits of his original scene, causes his reader to follow the movement; best of all for the modern reader, he is able, by this faculty, to make his allegory vital and interesting; for, though the world long ago lost interest in personified abstractions, it has never ceased to care for significant symbolical action and utterance. On the other hand, B, though capable of phrases which show, perhaps, equal power of visualising detail, is incapable of visualising a group or of keeping his view steady enough to imagine and depict a developing action. The continuator of A and the reviser C show clearly that their knowledge of the world, their impressions of things, are derived in very slight measure, if at all, from visual sensations. These conclusions are not invalidated, but rather strengthened, by the fondness of B and C and the continuator of A for similes and illustrations, such as never appear in A.

Moreover, the number of instances should be noted in which B has misunderstood A or spoiled his picture, or in which C has done the same for B. Only a few examples can be given here. In the first place, B has such errors as these: in II, 21 ff. Lewte is introduced as the leman of the lady Holy Church and spoken of as feminine; in II, 25, False, instead of Wrong, is father of Meed, but is made to marry her later; in II, 74 ff. B does not understand that the feoffment covers precisely the provinces of the seven deadly sins, and, by elaborating the passage, spoils the unity of the intention; in II, 176, B has forgotten that the bishops are to accompany Meed to Westminster, and represents them as borne 'abrode in visytynge,' etc., etc. Worst of all, perhaps, B did not notice that, by the loss or displacement of a leaf between A, v, 235, 236, the confessions of Sloth and Robert the Robber had been absurdly run together; or that in A, VII, 71—74 the names of the wife and children of Piers, originally written in the margin opposite ll. 89—90 by some scribe, had been absurdly introduced into the text, to the interruption and confusion of the remarks of Piers in regard to his preparations for his journey. Of C's failures to understand B two instances will suffice. In the prologue, 11—16, B has taken over from A a vivid picture of the valley of the first vision:

> Thanne gan I to meten a merveilouse swevene,
> That I was in a wildernesse, wist I never where;
> As I behelde in-to the est an hiegh to the sonne,
> I seigh a toure on a toft, trielich ymaked;
> A depe dale benethe, a dongeon there-inne,
> With depe dyches and derke and dredful of sight.

C spoils the picture thus:

> And merveylously me mette, as ich may ʒow telle;
> Al the welthe of this worlde and the woo bothe,
> Wynkyng, as it were, wyterly ich saw hyt,
> Of tryuthe and of tricherye, of tresoun and of gyle,
> Al ich saw slepynge, as ich shal ʒow telle.
> Esteward ich byhulde, after the sonne,
> And sawe a toure, as ich trowede, truthe was ther-ynne;
> Westwarde ich waitede, in a whyle after,
> And sawe a deep dale; deth, as ich lynede,
> Wonede in tho wones, and wyckede spiritus.

The man who wrote the former might, conceivably, in the decay of his faculties write a passage like the latter; but he could not, conceivably, have spoiled the former, if he had ever been able to write it. Again, in the famous rat-parliament, the rat 'renable of tonge' says:

> I have ysein segges in the cite of London
> Beren biʒes ful briʒte abouten here nekkes,
> And some colers of crafty werk; uncoupled thei wenden
> Bothe in wareine and in waste, where hem leve lyketh;
> And otherwhile thei aren elles-where, as I here telle.
> Were there a belle on here beiʒ, bi Ihesu, as me thynketh,
> Men myʒte wite where thei went, and awei renne!
>
> B, *Prol.* 160—6.

Clearly the 'segges' he has seen wearing collars about their necks in warren and in waste are dogs. C, curiously enough, supposed them to be men:

> Ich have yseie grete syres in cytees and in tounes
> Bere byʒes of bryʒt gold al aboute hure neckes,
> And colers of crafty werke, bothe knyʒtes and squiers.
> Were ther a belle on hure byʒe, by Iesus, as me thynketh,
> Men myʒte wite wher thei wenten, and hure wey roume!

Other misunderstandings of equal significance exist in considerable number; these must suffice for the present. I may add that a careful study of the MSS will show that between A, B and C there exist dialectical differences incompatible with the supposition of a single author. This can be easily tested in the case of the pronouns and the verb *are*.

With the recognition that the poems are the work of several authors, the questions concerning the character and name of the author assume a new aspect. It is readily seen that the supposed autobiographical details, given mainly by B and C, are, as Jack conclusively proved several years ago, not genuine, but mere parts of the fiction. Were any confirmation of his results needed, it might be found in the fact that the author gives the names of his wife and daughter as Kitte and Kalote. Kitte, if alone, might not arouse suspicion, but, when it is joined with Kalote (usually spelled 'callet'), there can be no doubt that both are used as typical names of lewd women, and are, therefore, not to be taken literally as the names of the author's wife and daughter. The picture of the dreamer, begun by A in prologue, 2, continued by the continuator in IX, 1 and elaborated by B and C, is only a poetical device, interesting in itself but not significant of the character or social position of any of these authors. Long Will, the dreamer, is, obviously, as much a creation of the muse as is Piers the Plowman.

What shall we say of the name, William Langland, so long connected with the poems? One MS of the C-text has a note in a fifteenth century hand (but not early):

Memorandum, quod Stacy de Rokayle, pater Willielmi de Langlond, qui Stacius fuit generosus et morabatur in Schiptone under Whicwode, tenens domini le Spenser in comitatu Oxon., qui praedictus Willielmus fecit librum qui vocatur Perys Ploughman.

Another fifteenth century note in a MS of the B-text says: 'Robert or William langland made pers ploughman.' And three MSS of the C-text (one, not later than 1427) give the author's name as 'Willelmus W.' Skeat is doubtless right in his suggestion that the name Robert arose from a misreading of C, XI, 1; but he and Jusserand find in B, XV, 148:

I have lyved in londe, quod I, my name is long wille,

confirmation of the first note quoted above. It is possible, however, that this is really the source of the name. Curiously enough, this line is omitted by C, either because he wished to suppress it or because he did not regard it as significant. Furthermore,

Pearson showed pretty conclusively that, if the author was the son of Stacy de Rokayle (or Rokesle) of Shipton-under-Wychwood, his name, if resembling Langland at all, would have been Langley. If this were the case, Willelmus W. might, obviously, mean William of Wychwood, as Morley suggested, and be merely an alternative designation of William Langley—a case similar to that of the Robertus Langelye, alias Robertus Parterick, *capellanus*, who died in 19 Richard II, possessed of a messuage and four shops in the Flesh-shambles, a tenement in the Old Fish-market and an interest in a tenement in Staining-lane, and who may, conceivably, have had some sort of connection with the poems. It is possible, of course, that these early notices contain a genuine, even if confused, record of one or more of the men concerned in the composition of these poems. One thing, alone, is clear, that Will is the name given to the figure of the dreamer by four, and, possibly, all five, of the writers; but it is not entirely certain that A really meant to give him a name. Henry Bradley has, in a private letter, called my attention to certain facts which suggest that Will may have been a conventional name in alliterative poetry.

If we cannot be entirely certain of the name of any of these writers except John But, can we determine the social position of any of them? John But was, doubtless, a scribe, or a minstrel like the author of *Wynnere and Wastoure*. B, C and the continuator of A seem, from their knowledge and theological interests, to have been clerics, and, from their criticisms of monks and friars, to have been of the secular clergy. C seems inclined to tone down criticisms of bishops and the higher clergy, and is a better scholar than either the continuator of A (who translated *non mecaberis* by 'slay not' and *tabescebam* by 'I said nothing') or B (who accepted without comment the former of these errors). A, as has been shown already, exempts from his satire no order of society except monks, and may himself have been one; but, as he exhibits no special theological knowledge or interests, he may have been a layman.

In one of the MSS of the B-text occurs a fragment of a poem which is usually associated with *Piers the Plowman*. It has no title in the MS and was called by its first editor, Thomas Wright, *A Poem on the Deposition of Richard II*; but Skeat, when he re-edited it in 1873 and 1886, objected to this title as being inaccurate, and re-named it *Richard the Redeless*, from the first words of passus I. Henry Bradley has recently called attention to the fact that it was known to Nicholas Brigham in the first part of the sixteenth century as *Mum, Sothsegger* (*i.e.* Hush, Truthteller). There can be no doubt that this was, as Bradley suggests, the ancient title; for it is not such a title as would have been chosen either by Brigham or by Bale, who records it. The copy seen by Brigham, as it had a title, cannot have been the fragmentary copy that is now the only one known to us. Wright regarded the poem as an imitation of *Piers the Plowman*; Skeat undertook to prove, on the basis of diction, dialect, metre, statements in the text itself, etc., that it was the work of the same author. But claims of authorship made in these poems are not conclusive, as will be seen in the discussion of the *Ploughman's Tale*; and the resemblances in external form, in dialect, in versification, etc., on which Skeat relies, are not greater than might be expected of an imitator, while there are such numerous and striking differences in diction, versification, sentence structure and processes of thought from every part of *Piers the Plowman*, that identity of authorship seems out of the question. The poem, as has been said, is a fragment; and Skeat thinks that it may have been left unfinished by the author in consequence of the deposition of Richard. But the MS in which it is found is not the original, but a copy; and the prologue seems to imply that the poem had been completed when the prologue was written. The author professes to be a loyal subject and friendly adviser of Richard, but the tone of the poem itself is strongly partisan to Henry of Lancaster, and, curiously enough, nearly all the remarks in regard to Richard imply that his rule was entirely at an end. This latter fact is, of course, not incompatible with Skeat's view that the poem was written between the capture and the formal deposition of Richard, *i.e.* between 18 August and 20 September 1399. As to the form and contents of the poem, it is not a vision, but consists of a prologue, reciting the circumstances of its composition, and three passus and part of a fourth, setting forth the errors and wrongs of Richard's rule. Passus I is devoted to the misdeeds of his favourites. Passus II censures the crimes of his retainers (the White Harts) against the people, and his own folly in failing to cherish such men as Westmoreland (the Greyhound), while Henry of Lancaster (the Eagle) was strengthening his party. Passus III relates the unnaturalness of the White Harts in attacking the Colt, the Horse, the Swan and the Bear, with the return of the Eagle for vengeance, and then digresses into an attack upon the luxury and unwisdom of Richard's youthful counsellors. Passus IV continues the attack upon the extravagance of the court, and bitterly condemns the corrupt parliament of 1397 for its venality and cowardice.

The influence of *Piers the Plowman* was wide-spread and long-continued. There had been many satires on the abuses of the time (see Wright's *Political Poems* and *Political Songs and Poems*), some of them far bitterer than any part of these poems, but none equal in learning, in literary skill and, above all, none that presented a figure so captivating to the imagination as the figure of the Ploughman. From the evidence accessible to us it would seem that this popularity was due, in large measure, to the B-text, or, at least, dated from the time of its appearance, though, according to my view, the B-text itself and the continuation of A were due to the impressiveness of the first two visions of the A-text.

Before discussing the phenomena certainly due to the influence of these poems, we must devote a few lines to two interesting but doubtful cases. In 1897, Gollancz edited for the Roxburghe Club two important alliterative poems, *The Parlement of the Thre Ages* and *Wynnere and Wastoure*, both of which begin in a manner suggestive of the beginning of *Piers the Plowman*, and both of which contain several lines closely resembling lines in the B-text of that poem. The lines in question seem, from their better relation to the context, to belong originally to *Piers the Plowman* and to have been copied from it by the other poems; if there were no other evidence, these poems would, doubtless, be placed among those suggested by it; but there is other evidence. *Wynnere and Wastoure* contains two allusions that seem to fix its date at *c.* 1350, and *The Parlement* seems to be by the same author. The two allusions are to the twenty-fifth year of Edward III (1. 206), and to William de Shareshull as chief baron of the exchequer (1. 317). The conclusion is, apparently, inevitable that the imitation is on the part of *Piers the Plowman*. In *The Parlement* the author goes into the woods to hunt, kills a deer and hides it. Then, falling asleep, he sees in a vision three men, Youth, Middle-Age and Age, clad, respectively, in green, grey and black, who dispute concerning the advantages and disadvantages of the ages they represent. Age relates the histories of the Nine Worthies,

and declares that all is vanity. He hears the bugle of Death sum-
moning him, and the author wakes. In *Wynnere and Wastoure*
the author, a wandering minstrel, after a prologue bewailing the
degeneracy of the times and the small respect paid to the author
of a romance, tells how

> Als I went in the weste wandrynge myn one,
> Bi a bonke of a bourne bryghte was the sonne.
> . . . .
> I layde myn hede one an hill ane hawthorne besyde.
> . . . .
> And I was swythe in a sweven sweped belyve;
> Methoghte I was in a werlde, I ne wiste in whate ende.

He saw two armies ready to fight; and

> At the creste of a cliffe a caban was rered,

ornamented with the colours and motto of the order of the
Garter, in which was the king, whose permission to fight was
awaited. The king forbade them to fight and summoned the
leaders before him. There is a brilliant description of the em-
battled hosts. The two leaders are Wynnere and Wastoure, who
accuse each other before the king of having caused the distress
of the kingdom. The end of the poem is missing. Both poems
are of considerable power and interest in themselves, and are
even more significant as suggesting, what is often forgotten, that
the fourteenth century was a period of great and wide-spread
intellectual activity, and that poetical ability was not rare.

Not in the metre of *Piers the Plowman,* but none the less
significant of the powerful hold which the figure of the Plowman
obtained upon the English people, are the doggerel letters of the
insurgents of 1381, given by Walsingham and Knighton, and reprinted by Maurice and Trevelyan. Trevelyan makes a suggestion
which has doubtless occurred independently to many others, that
'*Piers Plowman* may perhaps be only one characteristic fragment
of a medieval folk-lore of allegory, which expressed for generations the faith and aspirations of the English peasant, but of
which Langland's great poem alone has survived.' One would like
to believe this; but the mention of 'do well and better' in the
same letter with Piers Plowman makes it practically certain
that the writer had in mind the poems known to us and not
merely a traditional allegory; though it may well be that Piers
the Plowman belonged to ancient popular tradition.

Next in order of time was, doubtless, the remarkable poem
called *Peres the Ploughmans Crede*, which Skeat assigns to 'not

long after the latter part of 1393.' The versification is imitated from *Piers the Plowman*, and the theme, as well as the title, was clearly suggested by it. It is, however, not a vision, but an account of the author's search for some one to teach him his creed. He visits each of the orders of friars. Each abuses the rest and praises his own order, urging the inquirer to contribute to it and trouble himself no more about his creed. But he sees too much of their worldliness and wickedness, and refuses. At last, he meets a plain, honest ploughman, who delivers a long and bitter attack upon friars of all orders, and, finally, teaches the inquirer the much desired creed. The poem is notable, not only for the vigour of its satire, but also for the author's remarkable power of description.

With the *Crede* is often associated the long poem known as *The Ploughman's Tale*. This was first printed, in 1542 or 1535, in Chaucer's works and assigned to the Ploughman. That it was not written by Chaucer has long been known, but, until recently, it has been supposed to be by the author of the *Crede*. The poem, though containing much alliteration, is not in alliterative verse, but in rimed stanzas, and is entirely different in style from the *Crede*. The differences are such as indicate that it could not have been written by the author of that poem. It has recently been proved by Henry Bradley, that very considerable parts of the poem, including practically all the imitations of the *Crede*, were written in the sixteenth century. These passages were also independently recognised as interpolations by York Powell and this was communicated privately to Skeat, who now accepts Bradley's conclusions. Bradley thinks that the poem may contain some genuine stanzas of a Lollard poem of the fourteenth century, but that it underwent two successive expansions in the sixteenth century, both with the object of adapting it to contemporary controversy. The relation of even the fourteenth century portion to *Piers the Plowman* is very remote.

Three pieces belonging to the Wyclifite controversy, which also bear a more or less remote relation to *Piers the Plowman*, are ascribed by their editor, Thomas Wright, to 1401, and by Skeat, who re-edited the first of them, to 1402. The first of them, called *Jacke Upland*, is a violent attack upon the friars by one of the Wyclifite party. By John Bale, who rejected as wrong the attribution of it to Chaucer, it is, with equal absurdity, attributed to Wyclif himself. There is some alliteration in the piece, which made Wright suppose it to have been originally written in alliterative verse. Skeat denies that it was ever intended as verse, and he seems to be right in this, though his repudiation of Wright's suggestion that our copy of the piece is corrupt is hardly borne out by the evidence. The second piece, *The Reply of Friar Daw Thopias*, is a vigorous and rather skilful answer to *Jacke Upland*. The author, himself a friar, is not content to remain on the defensive, but tries to shift the issue by attacking the Lollards. According to the *explicit* of the MS the author was John Walsingham, who is stated by Bale to have been a Carmelite. This piece is in very rude alliterative verse. *The Rejoinder of Jacke Upland*, which is preserved in the same MS with the *Reply*, is of the same general character as *Jacke Upland*, though, perhaps through the influence of the *Reply*, it contains a good deal more alliteration. None of these pieces has any poetical merit, but all are vigorous and interesting examples of the popular religious controversy of the day.

Very evidently due to the influence of *Piers the Plowman* is a short alliterative poem of 144 lines, addressed, apparently, to Henry V in 1415, and called by Skeat, its editor, *The Crowned King*. In a vision the author looks down into a deep dale, where he sees a multitude of people and hears a crowned king ask his commons for a subsidy for his wars; to the king a clerk kneels, and, having obtained leave to speak, urges him to cherish his people and beware of evil counsellors and of avarice. The piece is sensible and well written, but is entirely lacking in special poetical quality.

Of entirely uncertain date is an interesting allegorical poem called *Death and Liffe*, preserved in the Percy Folio MS. Its relation to *Piers the Plowman* is obvious and unmistakable. In a vision, closely modelled on the vision of the prologue, the poet witnesses a strife between the lovely lady Dame Life and the foul freke Dame Death, which was clearly suggested by the 'Vita de Do-best' of *Piers the Plowman*. In spite of its large indebtedness to the earlier poem, it is a work of no little originality and power.

In the same priceless MS is preserved another alliterative poem, which Skeat regards as the work of the author of *Death and Liffe*. It is called *The Scotish Feilde* and is, in the main, an account of the battle of Flodden. The author, who describes himself as 'a gentleman, by Jesu' who had his 'bidding place' 'at Bagily' (*i.e.* at Baggily Hall, Cheshire), was an ardent adherent of the Stanleys and wrote for the specific purpose of celebrating their glorious exploits at Bosworth Field and at Flodden. The poem seems to have been written shortly after Flodden, and, perhaps, rewritten or revised later. That the author of this poem, spirited chronicle though it be, was capable of the excellences of *Death and Liffe*, is hard to believe; the re semblances between the poems seem entirely superficial and due to the fact that they had a common model.

The influence of *Piers the Plowman* lasted, as we have seen, well into the sixteenth century; indeed, interest in both the poem and its central figure was greatly quickened by the supposed relations between it and Wyclifism. The name or the figure of the Ploughman appears in innumerable poems and prose writings, and allusions of all sorts are very common. Skeat has given a list of the most important of these in the fourth volume of his edition of *Piers Plowman* for the Early English Text Society.

We are accustomed to regard the fourteenth century as, on the whole, a dark epoch in the history of England—an epoch when the corruptions and injustices and ignorance of the Middle Ages were piling themselves ever higher and higher; when the Black Death, having devoured half the population of city and hamlet, was still hovering visibly like a gaunt and terrible vulture over the affrighted country; when noblemen and gentry heard in indignant bewilderment the sullen murmur of peasants awakening into consciousness through pain, with now and then a shriller cry for vengeance and a sort of blind justice; an epoch when intellectual life was dead or dying, not only in the universities, but throughout the land. Against this dark background we seemed to see only two bright figures, that of Chaucer, strangely kindled to radiance by momentary contact with the renascence, and that of Wyclif, no less strange and solitary, striving to light the torch of reformation, which, hastily muffled by those in authority, smouldered and sparkled fitfully a hundred years before it burst into blaze. With them, but farther in the background, scarcely distinguishable, indeed, from the dark figures among which he moved, was dimly discerned a gaunt dreamer, clothed in the dull grey russet of a poor shepherd, now watching with lustreless but seeing eye the follies and corruptions and oppressions of the great city, now driven into the wilderness by the passionate protests of his aching heart, but ever shaping into crude, formless but powerful visions images of the wrongs and oppressions which he hated and of the growing hope which, from time to time, was revealed to his eager eyes.

That the Black Death was a horrible reality the statistics of
its ravages prove only too well; that there was injustice and
misery, ignorance and intellectual and spiritual darkness, is only
too true; but the more intimately we learn to know the thirteenth
and fourteenth centuries, the more clearly do we see, not only
Grosseteste and Ockham and Richard of Armagh, but a host of
forgotten or nameless men who battled for justice, and kindliness,
and intellectual and spiritual light; and our study of the *Piers
the Plowman* cluster of poems has shown us that that confused
voice and that mighty vision were the voice and vision, not of
one lonely, despised wanderer, but of many men, who, though of
diverse tempers and gifts, cherished the same enthusiasm for
righteousness and hate for evil.

CHAPTER II

RELIGIOUS MOVEMENTS IN THE FOURTEENTH CENTURY

RICHARD ROLLE. WYCLIF. THE LOLLARDS

IT is often difficult to deal adequately with individual writers
in the Middle Ages. Both the general ideas and the literary
habits of the time tended to hide the traces of individual work.
Schools of thought were more important than their individual
members; at times, therefore, single thinkers or writers received
less than their due recognition because their achievements became
the common property of a school. Hence, we find it not always
easy to assign to any single writer his proper place in literary history,
and the difficulty is increased by medieval methods of composition.
Manuscripts were so widely copied, often with alterations and additions, that individual ownership was almost lost. Then, when in
later days men sought to trace the work and influence of individuals,
they ran two opposite risks: sometimes, they were likely to
under-estimate the individual's influence; sometimes, they were
likely to ascribe to one man tendencies and works which belonged
rather to his school. It is not surprising, then, that a great
deal still remains to be done in the publication and arrangement of manuscripts before a definite verdict can be given upon
some problems of early literary history. As might be expected,
moreover, this difficulty is most to be felt in some of the matters
nearest to daily life: where the feet of generations passed the
oftenest, traces of their forerunners were easiest lost. Richard
Rolle of Hampole and John Wyclif were men very different in
their lives and in their ecclesiastical standpoints, but the lives of
both illustrate these statements, and the same kind of difficulty
arises in respect of each of them. Much has been assigned to
them that was not really theirs: after this first mistake has been
repaired, it becomes possible to judge them more fairly. But, even
then, it cannot be done fully and finally until the materials have
been sifted and arranged.

By the fourteenth century, the north of England had long lost its former literary leadership, but its impulses had not quite died away, and the growing connection with Oxford, strengthened by the foundation of Balliol College (*c.* 1263), brought even outlying villages under the influence of great intellectual and religious movements. When Richard Rolle went up to Oxford, the friars, with their ideal of poverty, were still a powerful party there, although, before long, Fitz-Ralph was to attack their view of life ; and contests between realists and nominalists were the chief intellectual interests. The young student's connection with Oxford did not last long ; but it coloured the whole of his life, and his first writings were modelled upon academic forms. He must, also, have gone through much intellectual and spiritual trouble, if we may judge from the crisis that changed his life. But he took away with him from Oxford a sufficient knowledge of Latin, an acquaintance with, and some distaste for, the ordinary philosophical writers and, above all, a love of the Scriptures. By a regulation of Grosseteste, the first morning lecture had to be upon the Bible, which furnished the material for much of the teaching.

Richard Rolle was born, probably about 1300, although the exact date is unknown, at Thornton-le-Dale, near the old town of Pickering, if a note in one of the manuscripts concerning him is to be believed ; at Thornton-le-Street, if a modern conjecture, which places his birth nearer the scenes of his earliest activity, is to be accepted. When he was nineteen he came home from Oxford, eager, because he feared disaster to his soul, to follow the life of a hermit ; he asked his sister to meet him near his home and bring with her two of her frocks, a grey and a white, and, out of these, along with his father's hood, he made himself a rough and ready hermit's dress. Thus clad, he visited a church where worshipped the family of Dalton—two youths of which had known him at Oxford. On a second visit, he put on a surplice and, with the leave of the priest, preached an affecting sermon at Mass. The former undergraduates recognised him and asked him to their table at home. His father, a man of some substance, was known to the Daltons, and, struck by Richard's sermon and his earnestness, they settled him as a hermit upon their estate. Hermits were a common feature of medieval life : they were under episcopal control and received episcopal licence ; hence, they were often spoken of by bishops as 'our hermits'; indulgences were often granted to those who supported them, and they themselves often did useful service in the repair of roads and keeping up of bridges.

After a time—four years at least—he left his first cell for another at Ainderby, near Northallerton, where a friend of his, Margaret Kirby, lived in much the same way that he did. Another change brought him to Hampole, near Doncaster ; and here, kindly cherished by Cistercian nuns, he lived for the rest of his days. The end came 29 September 1349[1]—the year of the Black Death. So great had been his popularity that the nuns of Hampole sought his canonisation : an office for his festival—20 January —was composed (probably about 1331—2), and, later, a collection of miracles ascribed to his influence was made. Although not formally canonised, he was regarded as a saint ; and his reputation gave wider currency to his writings.

Rolle was not a priest, although, perhaps, in minor orders. If his spiritual advice was sought by many—especially by Margaret Kirby, the recluse of Ainderby, by another recluse at Yedingham and by nuns at Hampole—it was because of his spiritual insight rather than his position. He stood equally aloof from academic thought and general life—ecclesiastical and civil ; he wished to retire from the world and, by contemplation, reach a knowledge of God and an elevation of soul. Through the mystic stages of purgation and illumination, he reached, after two and a half years, the third stage, the contemplation of God through love. Here, he had an insight into the joys of heaven, and, in this stage, he passed through the *calor*, the warmth of divine love, which fired his being with effects almost physical ; then there came into his life the *canor*, the spiritual music of the unseen world, the whispering sound as of heaven itself ; and, together with these, he experienced the *dulcor*, the sweetness as of the heavenly atmosphere itself. If he mixed, at times, with the outside world, even with the rich of the world, if he jested, at times, as he went his way among them, this was not his true life, which was, henceforth, 'hid with Christ in God.' Even the company of his fellows was, at times, distasteful, for their objects were other than his ; yet he sought to win them over to love 'the Author.' Contemplative life had drawn him and set him apart ; but it had also given him his mission. He was to be to others a prophet of the mystic and unseen.

His first impulse had been to win the world to his system through preaching. There are traces of systematic attempts to gain influence over others, although not by forming an order or community ; but these ways of influencing others hardly sufficed him, for

---

[1] This is the date usually accepted, on fair evidence, but a manuscript correction by Henry Bradshaw, in a copy of Forshall and Madden, gives the date as 1348.

he found few like-minded with himself. It seems not improbable that he even came into collision with ecclesiastical authorities, for he preached as a free lance and from a particular point of view. Unrest, and the friction of awkward personal relations (for he was dependent upon the help of others) worked along with the difficulty of his general position to drive him from place to place. At last, his energy found a new outlet and he began to write. Short ejaculatory poems, then longer and more didactic works, were the natural expressions of his soul—and thus he found his true work in life. He describes the impulses which moved him 'if I might be able in some good way to compose or write something by which the Church of God might grow in divine delight.'

Rolle thus deserves a high place among the many poets of the religious life; and the forms he used, or, at times, elaborated, have a beauty answering to their thought. Intense personal feeling, sympathy and simplicity are their chief features. and thus, apart from their language, they appeal to all ages alike. Beginning with alliteration only, the author worked into rime. But followers, such as William Nassyngton, imitated him in poems hard to distinguish from Rolle's own; some versified editions of his prose works—such as that of the *Form of Living* (or *Mending of Life*)—were probably also due to Nassyngton. We thus come to a cycle of sacred poems, at once mystic and practical, all grouped around Rolle. At first purely local, they spread beyond south Yorkshire; copies were made in southern English, 'translated (says one MS) 'out of northern tunge into southern, that it schulde þe better be understondyn of men of þe selve countreye.' The *Psalms* had been to Rolle himself a source of inspiration and comfort; he had come to that constant intercourse with God, to that sense of personal touch with Him, in which even their most exalted language did not seem unreal or too remote. He could write: 'grete haboundance of gastly comfort and joy in God comes in the hertes of thaim at says or synges devotly the psalmes in lovynge of Jesus Crist.' His labour at the *Psalter* had a wide-reaching influence, and appears in many forms; a Latin commentary upon it is one of his most original works; and, in another of them, the Latin version is followed by an English translation, and a commentary; the last has been widely used and highly praised by pious writers of very different schools, but it is really a translation of Peter Lombard's commentary, and is, therefore, devoid of originality and personal touches. This commentary may not have been his only attempt at translation, as the English

version of *The Mirror of St Edmund* may also be his work. His
own prose is marked by flexibility and tender feeling fittingly
expressed. A metrical *Psalter*—apparently earlier in date—also
exists, and this, again, was largely copied, but it cannot be
ascribed with absolute certainty to Rolle himself.

From the date of the miracles at Hampole—1331 and thereabouts—a revival of Rolle's fame seems to have taken place, just
before the great Peasants' Revolt, and just when Lollard[1] influence
was spreading. To this coincidence is due the reissue of the
commentary upon the *Psalter* with Lollard interpolations and
additions. From various doctrinal inferences the date of this
reissue has been tentatively fixed as early as 1378, and its authorship
has been sometimes ascribed—although without reason—to Wyclif
himself. Against these Lollard interpolations the writer of some
verses prefixed to one MS complains :

> Copied has this Sauter ben of yvel men of Lollardy,
> And afterward hit has been sene ymped in with eresy ;
> They seyden then to lewde foles that it shuld be all enter
> A blessyd boke of hur scoles, of Richard Hampole the Sauter.

The writer of this particular MS claims that his copy, on the other
hand, is the same as that kept chained at Hampole itself. The
use made of Hampole's *Psalter*, and the quarrel raised over it,
illustrate its value. But originality cannot be claimed for it.

Rolle's activity was due to the wish to benefit his fellows, and
hence come a number of plain, practical treatises with religious
ends in view. His commentary upon the *Psalms* was written for
the edification of the same Margaret of Ainderby for whom he
wrote, in prose, *The Form of Living* ; his beautiful *Ego dormio*

---

[1] On the continent, the word Lollard was applied to Beghard communities and
men of heretical views in the thirteenth and fourteenth centuries. The name was
soon given to Wyclif's followers (see *Fasc. Ziz.* pp. 300 and 312 for its use oppro-
briously in 1382) : it is then applied to the poor priests. In Wright's *Political Songs*,
II, 243—4 we have an allusion to Oldcastle

> The game is noȝt to lolle so hie
> Ther fete failen fondement.
>
> . . . . . .
>
> Hit is unkyndly for a kniȝt,
> That shuld a kinges castel kepe
> To babble the Bibel day and niȝt.

Taken along with the gloss to Walsingham (*Hist. Angl.* I, 325) *hi vocabantur a
vulgo* Lollardi *incedentes nudis pedibus, vestiti pannis vilibus, scilicet de russeto*, the
word seems specially applied to street-preachers, or idlers in streets (*lollen*, to loll).
But the punning association with *lollium*, tares, appears in a song of about the year
1382 (*Pol. Songs*, I, 232), *in humo hujus hortuli* | ...*fecit zizania*, | *quae suffocant virentia*, |
velut frumentum lollia, | and Lollardi *sunt zizania*, | *spinae, vepres ac lollia.* This
fanciful derivation became popular.

et cor meum vigilat, a prose work which shows the influence of those pseudo-Dionysian writings that markedly affected both Grosseteste and Colet, was written for a nun of Yedingham; explanations of the *Canticles,* the Lord's Prayer and Commandments and some prayers in *The Layfolk's Massbook,* had the same object. His mysticism still left something practical in his character —so much so that, at times, he gave advice which, in spite of his assured orthodoxy, must have seemed, to some, unusual. Thus, he speaks of the error of taking too little food, in avoiding too much— and he never tries to impress upon all others the contemplative life he sought for himself. He saw that, for most of them, life must be active; he merely sought to teach them the spirit in which to live.

Of his attitude towards the church little need be said; he is a faithful and loyal son, although he keeps some freedom of speech. In a poem attributed to him, the impersonal *Pricke of Conscience*—a popular summary, in 9624 lines, of current medieval theology borrowed from Grosseteste and others, strong in its sense of awe and terror of sin, and firm in its application of ecclesiastical rules to the restraint and the pardon of sins—the abuses he condemns most strongly are those of individual licence and social life. If he had any quarrel with the church, it was rather with some of its theologians who did not share his philosophy than with its system or its existing development. When he spoke of God's 'loving-kindness in the gates of the daughter of Zion' he interpreted the gates as being the church, under whose shadow he dwelt.

His doctrine of 'love' was thus not purely mystical or remote from life: it overflowed into teachings of social righteousness, and the dignity of labour as a service before God; it made injustice and offences against love (charity) peculiarly hateful in his eyes. Yet he had no hatred of the rich or of riches, and, indeed, he had, at times, been even blamed for his friendship with the rich; it was merely against the abuse and misuse of riches he protested. Three things he held needful in daily life: that work should be honest without waste of time, that it should be done in freedom of spirit and that a man's whole behaviour should be honest and fair. There was thus in his teaching much that strengthened the democracy of the times, much that condemned the social and ecclesiastical conditions of the day. If, on the one hand, his judgment was *magna igitur est vita solitaria si magnifice agatur,* on the other hand, he realised for himself and taught to others the living power of Christian fellowship. He is as significant in the history of popular medieval religion as in that of medieval letters.

Although John Wyclif, like Rolle, was of northern origin, his life belongs altogether to Oxford and to national affairs. His northern background not only gave something to his character but also, probably, determined his career: his family had some connection with Balliol College, and it was the natural college for a Yorkshireman. At Oxford he came under the great influences which shaped himself and his work. But, between him and Rolle there were resemblances apart from the north and Oxford; each of them has a special place in the history of the English Bible as well as of the English tongue, and Biblical commentaries—probably due to Rolle—have been, at one time or another, ascribed to Wyclif. In both cases, assumptions have been made too readily before the existing works had been studied and classified: works such as *The Last Age of the Church* and *An Apology for the Lollards*—which could not possibly have been Wyclif's—have been put down as his. Until the Wyclif Society began its labours, his Latin works were mainly in manuscript, and, before they could be studied and compared with each other, the *data* for his life and character remained uncertain. Even now, there remain some points which it is wiser to leave open, but we know enough to say that certain traditional views and dates, at any rate, must be cast aside.

John Wyclif was born, according to Leland, at Ipreswel or Hipswell, near Richmond, in Yorkshire. His family took its origin from Wycliffe-on-Tees, and he himself is described in a papal document as of the diocese of York. The date of his birth is uncertain, but it is generally supposed to have been about 1320, and certainly not much later. The tradition which says that he went to Balliol College is probable, for we find him there as its Master in 1360. The university, which gained through papal provision some support for its learned sons, petitioned Urban V to grant Wyclif a canonry with prebend (or parish annexed) in York Minster. As an answer, he was appointed, by papal provision, to the prebend of Aust in the collegiate church of Westbury-on-Trym, in the diocese of Worcester (24 November 1362). And, on 26 December 1373, Gregory XI granted Wyclif leave to hold this prebend of Aust even after he had received a canonry with prebend in Lincoln, which he had been previously promised when a vacancy occurred. In his work *De Civili Dominio,* Wyclif apparently alludes to this latter appointment, and speaks, although without bitterness, of his being afterwards passed over for a young foreigner. Incidentally, it should be noticed that Wyclif was thus, as late as

1373, in good repute at the Curia; and, further, when he mentions the matter some years later (probably about 1377) he is not hostile to the pope.

The passage from the ranks of the learners to those of the teachers was better defined in medieval days than it is now, and it is important to know, therefore, that the date of Wyclif's doctorate (S.T.P., D.D. or S.T.M.) can now safely be placed about 1372. He could, after that, lecture upon theology, and, not long after his own day, this promotion was noted as a turning point in his teaching: it was then he was held to have taught at least the beginnings of heresy. Up to this time, his life had been mainly passed at Oxford, as boy (for undergraduates went up at an early age, and much elementary teaching, even in grammar, was given in the university), as pupil and as teacher, in arts before he taught theology. There is no evidence that he had taken much part in parish work, although he had held preferments, and the incidental dates that have come down to us, no less than the Latin writings lately edited, imply great activity in teaching. He would probably 'determine, and take his Bachelor's degree some four years after matriculation; in three more years he would take his Master's degree and 'incept' in arts, and, after some thirteen years more, in two stages, he could take his Doctor's degree and 'incept' in divinity. But, these periods might, of course, be prolonged in special cases; all the Fellows of Balliol, for instance, except six theological Fellows, were, until 1364, prohibited from graduating in theology; and, from some cause of this kind, Wyclif was, apparently, delayed in reaching his Doctor's degree. But his reputation as a lecturer had been made some years before; Masters of arts lectured to students specially under their care, while, just before his doctorate, a Bachelor of divinity could lecture upon 'the sentences.'

It is difficult for us to understand, not, indeed, the intellectual eagerness of the university, but its hold upon the country at large. From all parts of England, and from foreign countries too, youths were flocking to Oxford, where a new intellectual world opened itself to them. The fact that medieval thought and enquiry followed paths differing greatly from those we tread to-day sometimes hides from us the value of their intellectual training. Their material was, of course, limited, although not so limited as is sometimes thought: thus, although Wyclif, for instance, knew nothing of Greek beyond a few names and words, he had studied widely in natural science, of which Roger Bacon had left a tradition at Oxford. Their method had been originally formed to train the mind, in which it had once succeeded. By Wyclif's day, however, it had become too technical, and, far from helping thought, the scholastic method had become a cumbrous routine under which thought was cramped. The weight of the authorities whom he was expected to know, the knowledge which he had to accumulate, and the order in which his thoughts had to be arranged, checked a scholar's originality. Thus, the first reading of Wyclif's Latin works does not give one any idea of his mental vigour, for the thought has to be sifted out from under appeals to authorities and cumbrous apparatus. When that has been done, it is found, as a rule, that the thought is strong, tenaciously held and fearlessly applied. But, even then, we of to-day can hardly feel the power of Wyclif's personality. It was different in his own time, for these things were the medium through which minds influenced each other.

It is easy for us to understand the influence of Wyclif's English writings, and we are even likely to exaggerate it, but not so with his Latin works. In their case, we have to make the allowances spoken of above, and to remember, moreover, that, in the four-teenth century, men were almost ceasing to think in Latin; with Wyclif himself, the turn of expression, even in his Latin works, is English. It was not surprising, then, that even a scholar trained, as he had been, to regard Latin as the proper vehicle of deeper thought, should, in the end, turn from it to English; the old literary commonwealth of the Middle Ages was breaking up, to be replaced by a number of nations with separate ways of thought and a literature of their own. Wyclif's free use of English is, therefore, significant. In his double aspect, as standing at the close of a long series of Latin writers, and as an English writer early in the file, he belongs partly to the age that was going out, partly to the age that was coming in. But it would be a mistake to think that his democratic, popular impulses, shown by his choice of English and his appeal to a larger public, came to him solely from the national side. The modern conception of a scholar standing apart from the world, of a university professor working within a small circle and influencing a few select pupils, must be cast aside. For no place was more democratic than a medieval university: thither all classes came, and the ideas which were born in a lecture-room soon passed, as we have seen in the case of Rolle, to the distant villages of the north. When Wyclif threw himself upon a wider public than that of the university, he was, after all, only carrying a little further that desire to popularise knowledge and thought which was common to all medieval teachers. The habit of thinking in Latin, the necessity of writing in Latin, had been almost the only barriers to hinder any previous thinker from doing what Wyclif afterwards did. For him, those barriers hardly existed, and, hence, the passage from his lecture-room to the field of the nation was not so strange as it seems to us. The same impulses worked in both phases of his life; the great formative influences of his life were scholastic and academic, but this does not imply any isolation or intellectual aristocracy.

There were many great schoolmen whose works were known to him and to whom he owed his really great learning, but a few had specially influenced him. He belonged, like other great Englishmen, to the realists, who attributed to general ideas a real existence, and who were in the closest intellectual sympathy with the great fathers of the church, St Augustine above all others. The strife between them and the nominalists was bitter and prolonged, but, towards the close of the Middle Ages, the latter were victorious, and became, together with those who, as conceptualists, held their opinions in a slightly modified form, the prevalent school. Realism went out of fashion, and realists, Wyclif among them, were forgotten. To this cause, nearly as much as to the taint of heresy, was due the neglect into which he fell. But, at Oxford, in his day, the realists championed by Wyclif more than held their own. But for one nominalist, William of Ockham—the great Franciscan writer and advocate of the rights of the state—Wyclif had a great regard, and he refused to count him a heretic. Ockham had been a warm defender of the Franciscan doctrine of poverty—a doctrine which had a special charm for Wyclif—and, from it as a basis, had gone on to attack the existing constitution and power of the church. Wyclif, who, in his later years, followed the same course and took up the same position, owed him a certain intellectual debt.

But he owed even more to Grosseteste—'archi-doctor, 'Lincolniensis,' as he called him, and to Richard FitzRalph, 'Armaghanus,' archbishop of Armagh (1347—60). With the former, who had greatly influenced Oxford, Wyclif was in general philosophical agreement, and from him, possibly, learnt his great love of the Scriptures. From FitzRalph, who was chancellor of Oxford (1333), Wyclif drew the doctrine of dominion or lordship, to which, although carrying it somewhat further, he really added nothing. FitzRalph had reached his views through the controversy with the mendicants; he had come across them at Oxford; he knew the charges brought against them of enticing youngsters to join them; later, on his return from Ireland (1356), he found the controversy between them and the seculars peculiarly keen; he preached against them in London, and, afterwards, at Avignon (1357), he delivered his famous *Defensio Curatorum* on behalf of parish priests who suffered much from their encroachments. His *De Pauperie Salvatoris* not only dealt with the poverty of Christ (which, as he pointed out, was not mendicancy) but discussed 'lordship' and 'use.' In the end he made all 'lordship' depend on that of God, to whom all lordship belonged; man had once received as a loan from God an original lordship for himself; but this he had lost through sin, and a new relation had begun. There is, thus, a distinction between the lordship of the ideal state of innocency, and the conditional lordship found in the actual world. Only in so far as man serves God does he approach true lordship; so far as he is sinful, he forfeits his lordship. To use Wyclif's expression 'dominion is founded in grace,' and, as a consequence, a man in mortal sin cannot exercise lordship. But Wyclif did not follow FitzRalph blindly; for, while FitzRalph had gone on to condemn the poverty of the mendicant friars, Wyclif, until his last years, sympathised with the Franciscans, whose model his own 'poor priests' in some ways reproduced.

But this doctrine of dominion, excellently as it enforced responsibility towards God, was capable of much abuse. FitzRalph had carefully guarded it as an ideal, and his discussion of the civil state and property had moved in a different plane from that of his ideal conditions. But, as so often happens between a master and a scholar, Wyclif the scholar reproduces his master's outline in deeper colours and without the shades; hence, it was not always easy to see that his arguments applied merely to an ideal society. If his teaching was charged with favouring the Peasants' Revolt, and if, later, Lollards appeared to society as socialists, it was, largely, owing to Wyclif's unguarded expression of this doctrine of FitzRalph.

Wyclif's earliest writings are of a purely philosophical nature, and, of course, academic in origin and style. *De Logica, De Ente Predicamentali, De Materia et Forma, De Benedicta Incarnacione* and *De Composicione Hominis* are ordinary university lectures: in the case of the last it is probable that we have only the lecture-notes as they were delivered. They may be dated—not, of course, with certainty—from 1360 to 1370 or thereabouts. They give us Wyclif's philosophical basis, and show him as a follower of St Augustine, named after his master, 'Joannes Augustini.' Hence, also, came his views on predestination, upon which he had a friendly controversy with the logician Ralph Strode: his doctrine of the *presciti* (foreknown) remained unchanged throughout his life. Already, too, he denied the possibility of the annihilation of anything, a view which led him to his later denial of transubstantiation. His Latin works show how large a part these discussions, which both influenced others and gained him a great reputation in controversy, played in his life, and his chief opponents, with the exception of Wadford or Wodeford (probably a Franciscan), were monks. The abbot of Chertsey, for instance, came up to Oxford to draw him into a discussion, and many other opponents attacked him. Through these controversies, Wyclif's views, as to the wrongfulness of endowments (to which he ascribed all the evils of the church), as to the duty of the state and of lay authorities to enforce reformation by seizing church property, must have become widely known. But, probably, he had not yet made his entry into political life, and, certainly, he had not as yet any controversy with the mendicants. It is probable that Wyclif's *Determinatio*, printed by Lewis, containing a supposed account of a parliamentary debate upon papal taxation, belongs (as Loserth has pointed out) not to 1366—7 but to a date some ten years later. At the former date, it stands isolated in Wyclif's life; at the later date, it finds a fitting place in the controversy recounted in *De Civili Dominio* and *De Ecclesia*; the papal demand made upon England in 1366 was repeated in 1374, so that we are not restricted to the earlier date alone. Before 1374, also, great debates had taken place upon the taxation of the church for national needs, while the employment of churchmen in high secular offices —a question which caused the main struggle about the time, 1376—7, of the Good parliament—had been opposed by a strong court party since 1371. This 'lay-party' wished to lessen the power of ecclesiastics, and resented their appearance in politics. Hence, they welcomed Wyclif's attack on endowments. Wyclif's visit to Bruges (July 1374), as member of an embassy to discuss papal provisions, might deepen his interest in these questions.

A new parliament met 27 January 1377 and convocation assembled a little later (3 February). Wyclif, who had been asked up to London (22 September 1376) to help John of Gaunt and his party by his sermons, was now called before convocation to answer for his views, but what the charges against him were we can only infer from his writings: they probably arose out of his views as to ecclesiastical endowments. He appeared in his defence accompanied by John of Gaunt and Lord Percy, together with four mendicant friars. A quarrel between Courtenay, bishop of London, and John of Gaunt broke out, which led to a popular riot against the duke; and the proceedings against Wyclif were thus interrupted. But bulls—five in number—were now got from Rome against him: three were addressed to the archbishop of Canterbury, one to the king and one to the university of Oxford. Much discussion has arisen as to the originators of this attack. It was, largely, the result of the Oxford controversies, and was led by the monks; but some among the bishops—especially Brunton, bishop of Rochester—may have worked along with them; political dislikes embittered the controversy; and one reason why his enemies raised these controversies against him was, says Wyclif, their wish to get him deprived of his benefices. Eighteen errors were charged against him which centred in his views on endowments, but his assertions that the church in its censures and excommunications should conform to the law of Christ, and that churchmen should be subject to civil jurisdiction, were also brought against him. The complaints were thus concerned with the organisation and outside relations of the church rather than with its doctrines.

Both the young king Richard II and the parliament seemed to support him; and he now speaks of himself as *peculiaris clericus* of the king; he was consulted as to the action of parliament (which met 13 October 1377) with regard to the drain of money to Rome, and he also defended himself in a document addressed to parliament. Bishop Brunton had spoken in parliament, as early as February or March, of the expected bulls: they were dated 22 May 1377, but it was not until 18 December 1377 that the archbishop of Canterbury and the bishop of London—as commissioners appointed by the pope—began to move by requesting the university to enquire into the charges. The university resented the tone of the pope's bull to them, which had reproved their laxity in admitting heresy, and it was not thought lawful for the pope to order the imprisonment of anyone in England. But the archbishop's request to examine the truth of the charges was another matter. They made the investigation, during which they confined Wyclif to his rooms, and their verdict was that the doctrines, although capable of a bad construction, were not heterodox.

But Wyclif was further summoned before the two prelates at Lambeth—probably in February or March 1378. He had drawn up a defence of himself for transmission to the pope, which was sent through the hands of the bishops, and was also widely circulated in England, doubtless through the 'poor priests.' Once again, the proceedings were interrupted: a message from the princess of Wales stayed the trial, and the fickle and turbulent Londoners broke into the hall, this time on the side of Wyclif, and not on that of their bishop as before. He was, however, directed not to preach or teach the doctrines charged against him, which, although not judged erroneous, were likely to cause trouble. It is possible that the changed attitude of the Londoners was due to Wyclif's preaching among them, and, as a matter of fact, he did not obey the command of silence. In more ways than one, this year (1378) was a turning point in his life, and one of his larger Latin works, *De Veritate Sacrae Scripturae*, written at this very time, gives us unusual insight into his mind and feelings.

The election of Urban VI (7 April 1378) was followed (September 1378) by that of an anti-pope, Clement VII, and thus the barely ended sojourn at Avignon gave place to an even more disastrous schism. England supported Urban, and Wyclif, for a time, was loyal to him. But the many admitted ecclesiastical abuses, which others, besides Wyclif, freely pointed out, naturally grew greater during the schism, and the rivalry of two popes led to a wider discussion of ecclesiastical questions. The bishop of Norwich (Henry le Spenser) actually undertook (1382) the leadership of a crusade in Flanders proclaimed by Urban against Clement; indulgences were issued to all who shared in it; friars were specially active in furthering it, and the archbishop of Canterbury (Courtenay had now succeeded the murdered Sudbury) ordered prayers and a general collection for the expedition (April 1383). It is clear, both from Wyclif's Latin works (such as *Cruciata*) and from his English tracts, that the crusade, with its mingling of unchristian warfare, a keen struggle for power, the pursuit of wealth and the abuses of indulgences, turned him more strongly against the papacy. Henceforth, there was no reserve in his language, no moderation in his views: he regarded the pope as anti-Christ. But, by anti-Christ, Wyclif hardly meant the same that the prophetic school of later theologians mean. Anything opposed to the law of Christ was anti-christian, and, so far as he broke the law of Christ, a man might be anti-Christ; to be anti-Christ was thus, with Wyclif, a phase of character, and not a personal existence. Before 1378, he had used the expression of isolated acts, but, later, he came to hold the pope (though not the papacy) consistently and always anti-Christ. He no longer confined himself to the criticism of abuses; he questioned, at one time or another, the utility of every part of the church's system: sacraments, holy orders, everything was unessential. Far as this criticism went, it is probable that in it, and in the growing stress laid on preaching as the one essential of religion, lie Wyclif's chief affinities with later reformers. So strongly did he feel about the Schism and this crusade that the occurrence or omission of any reference to either is an accepted test of date for his works.

Wyclif's liking for the friars and their fundamental doctrine of poverty has already been mentioned. But he had also sympathy with their popular work, even if he thought it sometimes neglected or badly done. This feeling led him to institute his 'poor priests,' who must have begun their work while he was still at Oxford, probably about 1377, as they are certainly mentioned in works of 1378. Originally, they were priests living in poverty and journeying about the country, clad in simple russet, preaching as the Dominicans had done; later, some, if not most, of them were laymen; gradually, too, as his quarrel with the church authorities grew and he became estranged from his university, he demanded less learning from his poor priests; simple piety, a love of the Scriptures and a readiness to preach were all he asked from them. One unlearned man (*unus ydiota*) might, by God's grace, do more than many graduates in schools or colleges. There was nothing strange in the original idea of such a body, and it was only by an accident that Wyclif did not become the founder of a new order of friars. Before the end of his life they had spread his doctrines widely, and had met with great success, especially in the vast diocese of Lincoln, and in those of Norwich and Worcester. The districts which were centres of his teaching long remained centres of Lollardy, although the views of the later Lollards can hardly be held the same as his. For they changed his views upon property into a socialism discontented with existing government and the distribution of wealth; his denunciation of evils, which grew gradually more sweeping and subversive of ecclesiastical order, became, with them, a hatred of the whole church; his love of the Bible, and his appeal to it as the test of everything, too often became, with them, a disregard of everything but the Bible; his denial of transubstantiation, based upon philosophical reasoning, became, with them, a contempt for the Sacrament itself.

So far, we have seen Wyclif mainly critical and even destructive.

But there was also a strongly positive side to his teaching: his regard for the Scriptures and his frequent use of them in his writings (common with medieval writers, but very common with him) is best seen in his work *De Veritate Sacrae Scripturae*, which he was writing about 1378. He regarded Scripture as the test of everything, in comparison with which tradition had no force. It is impossible to trace fully the development of his views, but the medieval love of speculation and freedom of thought (which was not, as a rule, interfered with, unless it led to revolutionary action) carried him far: there is hardly anything in the constitution or worship or doctrine of the church which, in some of his latest works, was not questioned. Nevertheless, after leaving Oxford, he remained quietly working in his parish, following the ordinary round of a parish priest. It is to be noted, too, that in his English sermons he faithfully follows the church's choice of Epistles and Gospels, not casting it aside as did some later reformers. But the inconsistency between his life and his words is more apparent than real; the habit of hypothesis, of questioning, of making assumptions, was so ingrained in him that too much weight must not be assigned to all his statements, as if they expressed a deliberate and well-formed conviction. The world at large was, however, different from an academic audience, and many whom his works reached must have drawn practical inferences from them which Wyclif himself never drew. Still, as regards the church—poisoned as he held it to be by the endowments poured into its system first by Constantine and, since then, by others—his mental attitude was distinctly sceptical. His positive appeal to Scripture, however, was another thing; it was directed against the abuses of the time. But, among his opponents, men like bishop Brunton of Rochester also had a deep love for the Scriptures; the language often used as to ignorance or dislike of the Bible at the time is much exaggerated and mistaken, as the works of Rolle indicate. Nevertheless, there were some opponents of Wyclif whom he charged rightly with belittling the Scriptures. These criticisms were directed against the growing school of nominalists against whom Wyclif, as one of the latest medieval realists, fought vigorously, and whose influence had, in the end, the evil effects of which Wyclif complained.

It was this appeal to the Scriptures that gained Wyclif his name of *Doctor Evangelicus*. In the Bible he found a source of spiritual strength, an inspiration of moral energy as well as a guide to conduct. For these reasons he wished to spread its use. He pointed to other nations with translations of it in their own tongue and asked why England should not have the same: the faith should be known to all in the language most familiar to them. The same impulses that led him to found his poor priests made him wish to spread a knowledge of the Bible in England.

But in *De Veritate Sacrae Scripturae*, while there are already complaints that preaching is interfered with, there are no complaints that the Bible in the vernacular is prohibited: indeed, the history of the English translations before Wyclif show that such was not the case. We have already seen in the case of Rolle how translations were made for dwellers in religious houses; one of the independent versions—edited by Miss Paues—has an interesting prologue in which a 'brother' and 'sister' 'lewed and unkunnynge' ask a more learned 'brother' to teach them: 'I preye you pur charite to techen us lewed men trewlyche þe soþe aftur oure axynge.' The reply is 'Broþer, y knowe wel þat y am holde by Cristis lawe to parforme þyn axynge: bote naþeles we beþ now so fer y-fallen awey from Cristis lawe, þat ȝif I wolde answere to þyn axynge I moste in cas underfonge þe deþ.' The translation of the Bible into English was not prohibited, but the use now made of it was leading to a claim for stricter control. Much controversy, however, has arisen lately as to the share of Wyclif in the versions which go by his name. We have express statements by the chronicler Knighton—nearly contemporary and also anti-Wyclifite—and Hus—a little later (1411)—that Wyclif had translated the whole Bible into English. Archbishop Arundel, in a letter to the pope asking for Wyclif's condemnation, speaks (1412) of Wyclif having filled up the measure of his malice by the design to render the Scriptures into English; and a general tradition, the value of which may be much or little, confirms this statement. There are two 'Wyclifite' versions: one, a little earlier than the other, stiffer and inferior in style, closely following the Vulgate, from which both translations were made without the use of Greek. The prologues, some for the whole work, and some for commentaries upon individual books, are certainly Wyclifite in tone, although none of them can be assigned to Wyclif himself; specially important is the general prologue to the second version, giving an account of the writer's method of work; and the writer of this was certainly a Wyclifite. On the other hand, we have the curious fact that Wyclif himself never uses the translation that goes by his name. but gives an independent translation from the Vulgate. Too much, however, should not be made of this, for, no doubt, Wyclif knew the Latin better than the English, and he would, therefore, translate incidentally and afresh instead of referring to a manuscript : in acting thus he would be only following the usual course. More importance, however, belongs to a statement, made independently by Foxe and Sir Thomas More (in his *Dialogue*), that there were translations dating before Wyclif ; to which the latter adds that the whole Bible had been then translated by ' virtuous and well-learned men.' The whole question has been complicated by over-inference from actual statements on either side, by the ascription of everything Wyclifite to Wyclif himself, and by confusing two matters quite distinct—the existence of English translations and their permission or condemnation by the church.

We cannot cast aside the express association of a translation with the name of Wyclif ; his own works and feelings make such a translation probable, although they give us no express evidence. As to the part he himself took in it, nothing is known, although very definite statements are sometimes made. There were already in circulation many copies of isolated books of the Bible, and the whole of the New Testament could be read in English translations which had been made mainly for the inmates of monastic houses, especially for nuns ; the impulses which had produced these copies had been felt more in the north and the midlands than in the south, where French was understood and used down to a later date. Some of these earlier works, which prepared the way, may have been used by the Wyclifite translators ; among them are translations, such as one of the Apocalypse, and an English version (with preface) of the Latin *Harmony of the Gospels* by Clement of Llanthony, wrongly ascribed to Wyclif himself. But the Wyclifite versions were due to a more general impulse and were meant for a wider public. Their literary history needs much further study, and when criticism, textual and linguistic, has been further applied, some more certain conclusions may be drawn. But it does not appear likely that the statements made here will be largely affected.

As to Wyclif's fellow-workers, not very much is known. The names of two have come down to us—Nicholas Hereford and John Purvey. The former had worked with Wyclif at Oxford and is spoken of by the mendicants at Oxford in an appeal to John of Gaunt (18 February 1382) as their chief enemy ; he was then a Doctor, *paginae sacrae professor, et utinam non perversor*, words which may refer to his share in the translation. One of the manuscripts directly attributes the translation to Hereford, and the fact that it breaks off suddenly at *Baruch* iii, 20 implies a sudden interruption. Owing to tumults in the university, which had arisen out of his sermons (1381—2), he was summoned to appear in London, and was there excommunicated (1 July 1382). He appealed to Rome and went thither only to be imprisoned. Wyclif, in his *Opus Evangelicum*, which he was writing at his death, speaks indignantly of this imprisonment. In 1385, he escaped, and, in 1387, was back again in England: we find him, with Purvey and others, prohibited by the bishop of Worcester from preaching in his diocese. In 1391, he was promised protection by the king, and, in 1394, he became chancellor of Hereford, but, in 1417, he retired to be a Carthusian monk at Coventry.

So far as language is concerned, the revision ascribed to Purvey deserves higher praise than the first translation. John Purvey was born at Lathbury, near Newport Pagnell. In 1387, with Hereford, Aston, Parker and Swynderby, he was inhibited from preaching by the bishop of Worcester ; they were said to be leagued together in a certain college unlicensed and disallowed by law. He submitted and recanted his errors on 6 March 1401, and, in August of that year, became vicar of West Hythe, Kent; he held this post for two years, but, in 1421, we again find him in prison. He was the author of *Regimen Ecclesiae*, a work from which Richard Lavenham (1396) collected his errors. In his prologue to the Bible, he describes the method which he, 'a poor catiff lettid fro prechyng,' took for finding out the exact meaning and faithfully rendering it with 'myche travile, with diverse felawis and helperis.' But his work was far more than that of a mere scholar: he understands (and expresses in words that remind us of Colet) how a labourer at Scripture hath 'nede to live a clene lif, and be ful devout in preiers, and have not his wit occupied about worldli thingis'; only 'with good livyng and greet traveil' could men come to 'trewe understonding of holi writ.' The comparisons so often drawn between these two revisions make clear the superiority, in idiom and all that makes a language, of Purvey's revision. The earlier, ascribed partly to Wyclif, is the roughest of renderings, and its English is unlike that of Wyclif's sermons, which may, however, have undergone revision. But it must be repeated that the history of these early translations has yet to be deciphered and written; the literary tendencies of the Middle Ages, spoken of before, have thoroughly hidden from us the workers and much of their work. We can say that Wyclif, as the centre of the movement, was, probably, the source of its energy; more, we cannot assert as yet. It is likely that, when this history is made out, the importance of pre-Wyclifite translations, fragmentary and incomplete, will appear greater. It is also likely that we shall be led to assign less to individual labourers and more to successive labours of schools of writers. But the name of Wyclif will probably still be left in its old connection even if his individual share be uncertain or lessened.

This translation can claim to be the first complete rendering of the Bible into English; but it is quite possible that its effect upon the language has been sometimes over-estimated. The reason for this lies in its history and in the history of Wyclifism. For some years after 1381 or so, there is no hint of any hostility to the Scriptures on the part of ecclesiastical rulers; it is only Lollard preaching that is checked. The translation of Purvey is so far free from having any bias, that it has lately been even claimed for an authorised translation; MSS of it were certainly owned by obedient churchmen and by bishops themselves. Purvey does add a few simple glosses, but they are free from any party colour and are taken from Nicholas de Lyra (1340). His version seems to have superseded others, even the Vulgate itself; Henry Bradshaw stated that he had not come across a single Latin MS copied after its appearance. The question of prologues was a different matter; a Lollard prologue was often added to anything, as, for instance, to works of Rolle. But the church was not hostile to the translations themselves, nor did it forbid their being made. Lyndwood and Sir Thomas More both spoke to the fact that translations made before Wyclif were not prohibited nor forbidden to be read. Cranmer also said that 'if the matter should be tried by custom, we might also allege custom for the reading of the Scriptures in the vulgar tongue....For it is not much above one hundred years ago, since Scripture hath not been accustomed to be read in the vulgar tongue within the realm.' Archbishop Arundel himself praised queen Anne of Bohemia because of her love towards the Bible and her study of it, exceeding that of some prelates. The Wyclifite version did not become the property of a mere section of the people, such as the Lollards were. Possession of a copy of it, however, by a person not under religious vows, needed an ecclesiastical licence, which was freely granted. But the changed attitude of the church—the way in which it laid stress upon its right of controlling the reading of vernacular translations and was led to regard popular literature, when likely to supersede its own teaching, with suspicion—was due to the history of Lollardy.

The church, which had been so long the guardian of unity, found itself confronted by forces forming nations and tending to disruptions. To control and guide these forces would have been a noble work, but it was a work of supreme difficulty, not to be wrought by short-sighted or selfish men. To begin with, the church which recognised its duty of teaching the nation should have brought out an authorised version of its own. There is no proof that it ever tried to do this on a complete scale ; it was, indeed, content to use the Wyclifite versions, as it well might be, until the growth of Lollard prologues and commentaries made it suspicious. Thus, some of the Wyclifite MSS have the tables of lessons added, and some smaller MSS contain the Gospels and Epistles alone. The claim made by the Lollards that 'eche lewed man that schul be saved is a real priest maad of God' tended to weaken the power of the church, its power for good as well as for evil, and, naturally, made 'worldly clerkis crien that holy writ in Englische wole make cristen men at debate, and suggetis to rebelle against her sovereyns and therefor' ought not to be 'suffred among lewed men.' Medieval notions of freedom differed from our own, and, as a rule, freedom to do any special work was held to belong only to a corporation licensed for the purpose.

The danger of popular excitement was made pressing by the Peasants' Revolt. The appeal to a democratic public, the recognition of the simple layman's place in the church, the crusade against endowments and the growing criticism of ecclesiastical institutions, worked along with other causes of the rebellion, while Wyclif's exaltation of the power of king and state was lost sight of. His own sympathies, indeed, went strongly with the rebels. His 'poor priests' were charged with having incited to revolt, and Nicholas Hereford hurled back the charge at the friars. Friars and 'poor priests' were both parts of the large floating population which was all in a ferment, and there was probably some truth in the charges on both sides. If John Ball's confession that he had learnt his views from Wyclif be somewhat suspicious, it should still be remembered that Wyclif's revolutionary views on endowments had been before the world for some years. Both in Ball's confession and in a popular poem of the day, Wyclif's attack upon the doctrine of transubstantiation was connected with the general excitement. That attack stirred up many animosities new and old; it was the result of a gradual development of Wyclif's views, and it had important historical results.

There are three stages in Wyclif's views upon the Eucharist. First, a stage in which he accepts the current doctrine of transubstantiation, but holds it to be an exception to his other doctrine of the permanence and indestructibility of matter. This stage lasted until about 1370. But in *De Benedicta Incarnacione* (written before his doctorate in 1372) he is wavering as to what the changed substance is, and is inclined to leave the question aside as unnecessary to a simple 'pilgrim.' This being his position, he is not inclined to discuss the question overmuch. But when, about 1380 or so, he had reached a positive opinion, and maintained that the substance of bread remained, he felt bound to teach this, as he held, vital doctrine. Hence, this final stage is marked by great energy of utterance, and continual reference to the question. But the result of his latest view of the Eucharist, taught with much insistence and gradually made the centre of his system, was a controversy, in which he was opposed not only by his former enemies the monks, but by secular priests, and, lastly, by friars. With these last he had, indeed, been gradually breaking friendship; it had seemed to him that some of them, bound as they were to poverty, must sympathise with him and must, therefore, join him. In his disappointment he began to regard their law of life as hostile, like the law of monasticism, to the law of Christ; in his latest works, therefore, the friars are attacked with much bitterness. They, concerned, on their part, for their whole position, and, also, passionately believing in the central doctrine he now attacked, replied with equal vigour. His followers, too, who, possibly, may have hastened the quarrel, took their part in the strife. Hence, his teaching on this point seemed to overshadow all his other views. Thus, his system, as it was handed down to later years, attacked the papacy, the organisation of the church, monks and friars and overthrew the popular conception of the Mass. His positive teaching was forgotten; his followers kept merely to his love of the Scriptures and found practically no place for church organisation, for sacraments or rites; prayer, preaching and the reading of the Scriptures summed up, for them, the conception of the Christian faith.

An assembly of bishops and ecclesiastics was held at Blackfriars on 17 May 1382. The council, which was afterwards called 'the earthquake council' from its being interrupted in its session with 'earthdyn,' condemned some doctrines of Wyclif. He him-

self was not named in the decrees issued, but the bishops were
to excommunicate any one preaching the condemned doctrines, the
university was to prohibit their setting forth and the company
of those offending was to be avoided under pain of excom-
munication. After much discussion at Oxford, Wyclif was attacked,
and, like his supporters, was suspended from all scholastic duties,
by an order which was afterwards repeated by the king. But, of
his later life, and of the result of the proceedings against him,
we know little or nothing. A passage in his *Trialogus* seems to
imply that he was bound by some promise not to use certain
terms—*i.e.* substance of bread and wine—outside the schools. It
was supposed, at one time, that he, like his leading Oxford followers,
had recanted, but of this there seems no evidence. Just before
the earthquake council, he had presented a very bold defence of
his views to parliament, demanding not only freedom for his
opinions but their enforcement in practice. His boldness did not
leave him, but his influence in Oxford was at an end, and he lived
for the rest of his days at Lutterworth.

The sum of his work, Latin and English, in these last two years
(1382—4) is enormous, but there are traces of his utilising former
lectures ready to hand. To this time most of his undoubted English
writings belong, as does the *Trialogus*[1] in Latin, perhaps the best
known and most connected, although not most interesting, statement of his views. His struggle with the mendicants who opposed
him was now at its height, and his language was unmeasured;
we must suppose that much of what he said was put forth without
due consideration of possible dangers from its being misunderstood. But, in some of his later Latin works—especially his *Opus
Evangelicum*—notes of a growing calmness of mind may also be
heard beneath the controversies. He had always been inspired
by the warmest national feeling, and it was not at all strange
that he should, therefore, address the nation as he did; it is this
consciousness of the wide audience to whom he was speaking that
made his English writings distinctly different from any that had

---

[1] Wyclif used the form of dialogue also in the *Dialogus* (1379) between *Veritas*,
standing for Christ, and *Mendacium*, standing for Satan. But soon all characterisation
is lost, and Wyclif himself speaks throughout, the replies of *Mendacium* being short
and unworthy of his reputation. In *Trialogus* (about 1382) the form is handled
better; the characters are: *Alithia*, a *solidus philosophus*—Philosophy; *Pneustis*, a
captiosus infidelus—Unbelief; and *Phronesis*, a *subtilis theologus*—Theology: the first
lays down a proposition, to which the second objects, and, at length, the third sums
up. But *Pneustis* holds long silences, during which *Alithia* and *Phronesis* speak as
enquiring disciple and master. It may be noted that dialogue is also used in the
prologue and text of *A Fourteenth Century Biblical Version* (Miss Paues).

gone before. The nation that had proved its unity in the battle-field and in parliament was now, we may say for the first time, addressed as one body in popular literature. Neither in style nor in power, however, have his English works any special note of distinction. The style of his sermons ranks higher than the early version of the New Testament, commonly ascribed to him, and it would not be surprising to find that, like many other medieval works, they had undergone some revision by a faithful disciple. In these English works there is a strange mingling of simple directness and ruggedness; their true significance lies in their instinctive feeling for their large audience. Wyclif had proved his power over an academic world, democratic in itself, and so he easily passed to a more democratic public still; his conception of the state, and his experience of parliament, gave a peculiar vividness to the manner of his address, but an even higher quality gave it spiritual force.

For Wyclif had an intense reverence for the Incarnate Christ, *communis homo, unicus homo.* His realist mind made him unite Christ, as the type, with all Christian men. A like belief, worked out in practice, had been the strength of the early Franciscans, and hence had come Wyclif's original sympathy with them. In his later years, after he had parted from them, the same belief was the real basis of his popular appeal, and it was also connected with another characteristic of his last phase. After he had left Oxford, and the university had drifted, although reluctantly, away from his teaching, he came to undervalue learning; the simple, 'lewd' man, if a follower of Christ, could do all the educated man might do. This side of his teaching, which would naturally be exaggerated by the later Lollards, had a real theological basis in his intense desire to see the Christ in every man; an idea which, taught (1370—2) in *De Benedicta Incarnacione,* links together his earlier and later writings.

If we accept, as we probably should, the story told (1441) by John Horn, Wyclif's helper at Lutterworth, to Gascoigne, it is easier to understand his life after 1382. According to Horn, he was paralysed for his last two years, and this explains much. Silence had been enjoined upon him, and silence he had to keep; he was cited to Rome (this can be no longer doubted) and he could but refuse to go; he was *debilis* and *claudus,* the *Rex regum* had forbidden him to travel. He could still work at his writings without openly disobeying the order to be silent; and his 'poor priests' gave him a ready means of scattering them.

When we read in notes to some of the MSS of his works how they were copied in English villages by Bohemian scholars, as they moved from Oxford, to Braybrook, near Leicester, and then to Kemerton, near Evesham, places where Lollard influence was strong, it is easy to see how the crusade was carried on. But, with the growing severity of the persecution under the Lancaster kings, the whole Lollard movement was, as Erasmus says, 'suppressed but not extinguished.' 'It was,' as Gairdner has told us 'by no means an innocent attempt to secure freedom for the individual judgments ; it was a spirit that prompted the violation of order and disrespect to all authority.' It left behind it much discontent, an appeal to the Scriptures and to them alone and an exaltation of preaching above aught else; these traditions lingered on, especially in a few local centres, until Tudor days. But Wyclif himself was almost hidden by the loosely organised sect that claimed descent from him.

It is easy to understand why, under the circumstances, nothing more came of Wyclif's citation to Rome. Thus, the scholar, unexcommunicated, although, perhaps, bound by some promise, his feeble body consumed by this restless fire within, lived on in his quiet parish. Upon Holy Innocents' Day, 1384, the final stroke fell on him as he was hearing Mass, and, on St Sylvester's Day (31 December), he died. It is well known how his ashes were treated ; but the scanty remembrance of him left in England, contrasted with the activity of the Lollards, was, perhaps, more of a slight to his memory. At Oxford, few traces of his work were left. The university, although not without difficulty, was brought by archbishop Arundel under strict control, and, with the loss of its freedom, and the decay of the realist philosophy for which it had stood, Oxford lost much of its hold upon the nation : controversies such as Wyclif and his followers had raised destroy the atmosphere needed for study and intellectual life. It has been suggested that, owing to the decay of Oxford, Cambridge took its place ; such was certainly the result, although positive, as well as negative, reasons might be given for the growing reputation of the younger university.

Meanwhile, the suppressed activity of the Lollards lived on. The archbishop had used the ordinary episcopal powers of inquisition for heresy, which, in England, were never superseded by the inquisition, so that the earlier punishments of heresy by death took place under canon law. But, with the act *De Haeretico Comburendo* (1401), a new basis was given to the persecution, and the state, as usual, showed itself more severe than the church. The Lollard party in parliament was, at one time, strong, and, more than once, brought forward suggestions of sweeping changes and confiscation. But, with the condemnation for heresy of Sir John Oldcastle (Lord Cobham, by marriage) in 1413, it ceased to be coherent and effective. Oldcastle himself escaped, after a severe examination, and, until his execution for treason (1417), was a centre for disaffection and rumours of rebellion. Much popular ridicule, such as may be read in the political poems of the day, was thrown upon him, and some of it, by a curious change, was transferred to the Norfolk soldier Sir John Fastolf. The chief result of Oldcastle's life was, thus, a strangely confused impression upon literature, but his Lollardism had been driven back by Arundel's strong action and the wider sweep of domestic politics into the lowlier paths of the national life. The old centres of Lollardy, nevertheless, remained ; the activity of Lollard writers, in adding prologues to works already known and in copying or abridging them, went on. The work of Lollard schools, and the circulation of Lollard tracts—for the most part of little merit— had yet both a religious and a literary significance. They come mostly before us in trials, and isolated examples (such as the appeal to parliament in 1395, which, in its English dress, presented, in many slightly varying forms, originals possibly first composed in Latin) ; but a literature of this kind has often more effect than more ambitious and larger works. There always had been, before the days of Wyclif, this literature of lowly discontent. If, after his days, it was raised to rather a higher level, for a time a little invigorated, and nourished by vague memories, it had, nevertheless, no very precise connection with his teaching. The religious litera- ture of discontent lived on side by side with the more recognised literature of devotion. Tracts and sermons, handed about and read as treasured teachings to little gatherings, loosely copied and at times condensed, are difficult to classify, or to appreciate. But the exact relation of the later Lollard sect to Wyclif's doctrines, and its influence upon the reformation, are difficult and distinct historical problems. It is certain that, while like him in denying transubstantiation, the later Lollards were not like him in their positive view of the Eucharist ; his views upon endowment might reappear again and again in parliament, but had no permanent effect. If there was much floating discontent with the church, and still more with the abuses of the day, it is difficult to trace this to Wyclif's influence, and the same, probably, would have been found without him. In weight of learning, and power of argument, those who wrote against his views outmatched his English followers.

But, in Bohemia, the influence, which was denied Wyclif in England, was permanent and strong. It is sufficient to refer to Loserth, who has treated the whole question fully and with an adequate knowledge of both Wyclif and Hus. Bohemian students had been at cosmopolitan Oxford in the days of Wyclif himself, and the connection thus begun continued long. The whole Hussite movement in its beginning was Wyclifite, and was called so by its friends and enemies alike; Wyclif's influence was firmly established there even before 1403. His views became part of a national and university movement which, on its philosophical side, was also realist. Hus was simply a disciple of Wyclif, and his works were mainly copies of Wyclif's; this revival of Wyclifite teaching led to the condemnation of forty-five selected errors at the council of Constance (4 May 1415). But, when, in the early years of the reformation, the works of Hus were printed, and came into the hands of Luther and Zwingli among others, it was really Wyclif who was speaking to them. Everything seemed to work together in disguising the real influence Wyclif had exercised.

A survey, then, of Wyclif's life and works, as they can be estimated now, shows that much at one time assigned to him was not really his. He was the last of a school of philosophers, but, as such, his intellectual influence was not enduring; he was the first of a school of writers, but his literary influence was not great. His connection with our English Bible, difficult as it may be to state precisely, is, perhaps, his greatest achievement. His personality does not become plainer to us as his works are better known. Even his appearance is hardly known to us, for the portraits of him are of much later date and of uncertain genealogy. But Thorpe—an early Lollard and, probably, a disciple at Oxford—describes him as 'held by many the holiest of all in his day, lean of body, spare and almost deprived of strength, most pure in his life.' That he was simple and ascetic, quick of temper and too ready to speak, we hear from himself and can gather from his works. The secret of his influence, well suited to his day, whether working through the decaying Latin or the ripening English, lies in the sensitive, impulsive and fiery spirit of the Latin scholastic and English preacher, sympathetic towards movements and ideas, although not towards individual minds. But the medium through which that spirit worked belongs to an age that has passed away, and we cannot discover the secret of it for ourselves.

CHAPTER III

THE BEGINNINGS OF ENGLISH PROSE

TREVISA. THE MANDEVILLE TRANSLATORS

EARLY English prose had, of necessity, a practical character. To those who understood neither Latin nor French all proclamations and instructions, laws and sermons, had to be issued in English, while, for a long time, the official Latin of the accountant and the law clerk had been very English in kind, even to the insertion of native words with a case-ending appended. With the increasing importance of the commons in the fourteenth century, the proceedings of parliament itself began to descend to the vulgar tongue, which obtained a signal recognition when three successive parliaments (1362—4) were opened by English speeches from the chancellor. Furthermore, a statute, in 1362, ordered the pleadings in the law-courts to be conducted in English, though the cases were to be recorded in Latin, on the ground that French was no longer sufficiently understood. Political sentiment may have inspired this declaration, which was as much overstated as the plea of two of Henry IV's envoys that French was, to their ignorant understandings, as bad as Hebrew; for the yearbooks continued to be recorded in French, and in French not only diplomatic letters but reports to Henry IV himself were written. The use of that tongue, so long the medium of polite intercourse, did not vanish suddenly, but a definite movement which ensured its doom took place in the grammar schools, after the Black Death, when English instead of French was adopted as the medium of instruction. John Trevisa, writing in 1385, tells us that this reform was the work of John Cornwall and his disciple Richard Pencrich, and that, 'in alle þe gramere scoles of Engelond children leveþ Frensche and construeþ and lerneþ an Englische,' with the result that they learned their grammar more quickly than children were wont to do, but with the disadvantage that they 'conneþ na more Frensche than can hir lift heele'—and 'þat is harme for hem and þey schulle passe þe see and travaille in straunge landes.' Even noblemen had left off teaching their children French.

Before the close of the fourteenth century, therefore, it could no longer be assumed that all who wished to read would read French or Latin. There was a dearth of educated clergy after the Black Death; disaster abroad and at home left little inclination for refinement, and, when life was reduced to its essentials, the use of the popular speech naturally became universal. Thus, in the great scene of Richard II's deposition, English was used at the crucial moments, while, at the other end of the scale, king Richard's master cook was setting down his *Forme of Cury* for practical people. In the same way, on the continent, 'Sir John Mandeville' was writing in French before 1371 for the sake of nobles and gentlemen who knew not Latin, and there, as at home, Latin books and encyclopaedias were so far ceasing to be read that he could venture to plagiarise from the most recent. In England, the needs of students, teachers and preachers were now supplied in the vernacular by the great undertakings of John Trevisa, who translated what may be called the standard works of the time on scientific and humane knowledge—*De Proprietatibus Rerum* by Bartholomaeus Anglicus and Higden's *Polychronicon.* These great treatises are typically medieval, and the former a recognised classic in the universities. The minorite friar Bartholomaeus, who must have been born an Englishman, was a theological professor of the university of Paris, and his *De Proprietatibus Rerum,* an encyclopaedia of all knowledge concerned with nature, was compiled in the middle of the thirteenth century, possibly during his residence in Saxony, whither he was sent, in 1231, to organise the Franciscans of the duchy. Ranulf Higden was a monk of St Werburgh's, Chester, and wrote his *Polychronicon* about 1350. It is compiled from many authorities, and embraces the history of the entire world, from the Creation to Higden's own times; the different countries are described geographically, and all the favourite medieval legends in the histories of Persia, Babylon and Rome are introduced. There are many points in which Higden, Bartholomaeus and the later 'Sir John Mandeville' accord, revealing some common predecessor among the earlier accepted authorities; for the object of the medieval student was knowledge and no merit resided in originality: he who would introduce novelty did wisely to insert it in some older work which commanded confidence. Naturally, therefore, translations of books already known were the first prose works to be set before the English public, namely the two great works of Trevisa, and *The Travels of Sir John Mandeville,* a book which, under a thin disguise of pious utility, was really a volume of entertainment.

The translators of these works aimed at being understood by a wider class of readers than the audience of Chaucer or even of *Piers the Plowman.* The style, therefore, though simple, is by no means terse. Where any doubt of the meaning might arise, pairs of words are often used, after a fashion not unknown to the poets. This usage prevailed during the following century—and with some reason, for the several dialects of England still differed so much that a southern man could scarcely apprehend what Trevisa calls the 'scharpe slitting, frotynge and unschape' speech of York. The translators desired only to convey the meaning of their originals and their renderings are extremely free; they omit or expand as they choose, and this saves early English prose from the pitfall of Latinism, giving it a certain originality, though at the cost of tautology. Trevisa, in the introduction to *Polychronicon,* explains to his patron that though he must sometimes give word for word, active for active, passive for passive, yet he must sometimes change the order and set active for passive, or 'a resoun' (a phrase) for a word, but he promises that, in any case, he will render the meaning exactly. These translations became recognised authorities among the reading public of the fifteenth century and may reasonably be considered the corner-stones of English prose. All three were accepted as absolutely veracious; the adventures of Mandeville, the legends of *Polychronicon,* the fairy-tale science of Bartholomaeus, were taken as literally as their scriptural quotations or hints on health. The information, all the same, seems to be conveyed with an eye to entertainment; little effort of thought is required in the reader; paragraphs are short, statements definite and the proportion of amusing anecdote is only equalled by the trite moralising, couched in common-place phrases, which had become a required convention in a materialist age. Books were distributed to the public by means of professional scribes; but, since there lay no sanctity in exact phraseology, the translators themselves were at the mercy of copyists. Cheaper copies were sometimes produced by curtailing the text, or newer information might be added. Trevisa's *Bartholomaeus* was probably brought up to date by many a scribe, and the different MSS of his *Polychronicon,* though unaltered as to the narrative, present a variety of terms. Mandeville, too, appears in (probably) three distinct translations, the most popular of which was multiplied in shortened forms. It is, therefore dangerous to base theories upon the forms found in any one MS; for we can rarely be sure of having the actual words of the author. Often, though not always, the MS may be inconsistent with itself, and, in any case, few MSS of philological interest exist in many copies ; in other words, they were not popular versions, and, as most of the MSS are inconsistent with each other in spelling and in verb-forms, it seems that the general reader must have been accustomed to different renderings of sound. Caxton need hardly have been so much concerned about the famous 'egges or eyren.'

John Trevisa, a Cornishman, had made himself somewhat notorious at Oxford. He was a Fellow of standing at Exeter College in 1362, and Fellow of Queen's, in 1372—6, when Wyclif and Nicholas Hereford were also residents, at a time when Queen's was in favour with John of Gaunt, and, perhaps, a rather fashionable house. The university was then, like other parts of England, a prey to disorder. Factions of regulars and seculars, quarrels between university authorities and friars, rivalry amongst booksellers and a revolt of the Bachelors of arts, produced petitions to parliament and royal commissions in quick succession. Amongst these dissensions had occurred a quarrel in 'Quenehalle,' so violent that the archbishop of York, visitor of the college, had intervened and, in 1376, in spite of resistance and insult, had expelled the Provost and three Fellows, of whom one was Trevisa, 'for their unworthiness.' It is possible that Wyclifite leanings caused this disgrace; for the university was already in difficulties on the reformer's account, and both Exeter and Queen's are believed to have been to some extent Wyclifite, while Trevisa's subsequent writings betray agreement with Wyclif's earlier opinions[1]. The ejected party carried off the keys, charters, plate, books and money of their college, for which the new Provost was clamouring in vain three years later. Royal commissions were disregarded till 1380, when Trevisa and his companions at length gave up their plunder. No ill-will seems to have been felt towards the ejected Fellows, for Trevisa rented a chamber

---

[1] The old suggestion of Henry Wharton, rejected by Forshall and Madden, that Trevisa might be the author of the general prologue to the second Wyclifite Bible, has been lately repeated, on the ground of the likeness of their expressed opinions on the art of translation. But, apart from other arguments, the style is not Trevisa's, nor its self-assertion, nor its vigorous protestantism. Trevisa's anti-papal remarks are timid and he never finds fault with the secular clergy. The same principles of translation were in the literary atmosphere, and it is open to doubt whether Trevisa's scholarship would have been equal to the full and precise explanations of the prologue.

at Queen's between 1395 and 1399, probably while executing his translation of Bartholomaeus.   Most of his subsequent life, however, was spent as vicar of Berkeley in Gloucestershire and chaplain to Thomas, Lord Berkeley, reputed to have been a disciple of Wyclif. He also, like Wyclif, held a non-resident canonry of the collegiate church of Westbury-on-Trym. At some earlier date, Trevisa had travelled, for he incidentally mentions his experiences at Breisach on the Rhine, Aachen and Aix-les-Bains, but he had not seen Rome.

His two great translations were made at the desire of Lord Berkeley. *Polychronicon* was concluded in 1387, *De Proprietatibus* in 1398. He executed several smaller translations, including the famous sermon of archbishop FitzRalph, himself an Oxford scholar, against the mendicant orders, and, probably, a translation of the Bible now lost.

Trevisa was a man of wide reading rather than exact scholarship; his explanation of the *quadrivium* is incorrect, and his Latinity was far inferior to Higden's. But his robust good sense, his regard for strict accuracy and his determination to be understood, make him an interesting writer. He was fond of nature, he knew his *De Proprietatibus* well before he wrote it in English and he could even bring witness of additional wonders, told to him at first hand by trustworthy parishioners of Berkeley. Without historical acumen, he does not hesitate to level scathing criticisms at old writers, but, on the other hand, he sometimes clears away a difficulty by common sense. Why was Higden puzzled by the inconsistent descriptions of Alcluyd? was there not more than one Carthage, and is there not a Newport in Wales and another in the parish of Berkeley?

The explanations so frequently inserted in the text suggest that, though *Polychronicon* was translated in the first instance for Lord Berkeley, a wider public was in the maker's mind. His notes are usually brief:

Ethiopia, blew men lond; laborintus, Daedalus his hous; Ecco is þe reboundynge of noyse; Gode genius is to menynge a spirit þat foloweþ a man al his lyftime; Kent and Essex, Westsex and Mercia—þat is as hit were a greet deel of myddel Englond; theatres, places hiʒe and real to stonde and sytte ynne and byholde aboute: Tempe Florida, likynge place wiþ floures.

It is but seldom that he is absurd, as when he renders *matrones* by *old mothers*, or gives a derivation for *satirical*: 'som poete is i-clepede satiricus, and haþ þat name of satis, þat is inow, for þe matire þat he spekeþ of he toucheþ at þe fulle.' These lengthier notes, inserted 'for to brynge here hertes out of þouʒt' he always signs 'Trevisa.' We observe that he feels it advisable to explain in full a very simple use of hyperbole.

As a translator, many more slips in scholarship might be forgiven him for the raciness of the style. Neither in terms nor structure does it suggest the Latin, but the interpolated criticisms are less wordy than the translation. Trevisa expands his original, not because he is a poor Latinist but partly because he wishes to be understood, and partly from that pleasure in doublets which would seem to be a natural English inheritance. Sometimes the synonymous words are accepted catch-phrases, sometimes they evince pure pleasure in language. We always get 'domesmen and juges,' 'tempest and tene,' 'þis worlde wyde'[1]. Not that Trevisa is enslaved by alliteration; he uses it less as the work proceeds, save in the regular phrases ; but he loves balanced expression, and ruins Higden's favourite antitheses[2]. His picturesqueness is, perhaps, elementary, less that of an artist than of a child[3].

It is Trevisa's principle to translate every word: the Mediterranean is 'þe see of myddel erþe.' Even when he cannot understand a set of verses he doggedly turns them into a jumble of pure nonsense which he asserts to be rime, adding, candidly, 'God woot what þis is to mene.' The outspoken criticisms and occasional touches of sarcasm seem to betray a man impatient of conventions which he felt to be practical abuses, but scrupulously orthodox in every detail which could be held to affect creed. To the wonderful fable of the marble horses at Rome he appends the moral that it shows 'þat who forsakeþ all þyng forsakeþ all his cloþes, and so it foloweþ þat þey þat beeþ wel i-cloþed and gooþ aboute and beggeþ and gadereþ money and corn and catel of oþer men forsakeþ not al þing.' On the other hand, he is shocked that Gregory Nazianzen tells 'a ungodly tale of so worthy a prince of philosophes as Aristotle was.' A saying of the mythical Nectabanus: 'No man may flee his owne destanye' is thus stigmatised : 'Nectabanus seide þis sawe and was a wiiche, and þerfore it is nevere þe bettere to trowynge...for from every mishap þat man is i-schape in þis worlde to falle inne God may hym

[1] '*Limites* = þe meeres and þe marke, *afflixit* = dede hym moche woo and tene, *fortes* = stalworþe men and wight.' So too 'a pigmey boskeþ hym to bataile and array hym to fiȝt.'

[2] '*Figmenta gentilium, dicta ethicorum, miranda locorum,*' becomes 'feynynge and sawes of mysbileved and lawles men and wondres and merveillis of dyverse contrees and londes.'

[3] 'Ocean by clippeþ al þe erþe aboute as a garlond'; *antiquitas* = 'longe passynge of tyme and elde of dedes.'

save ȝif it is his wille.' To the charitable miracle recorded of
Dunstan and St Gregory who, respectively, prayed the souls of
Edwy and Trajan out of hell, he refuses credit—'so it myȝte seeme
to a man þat were worse þan wood and out of riȝt bileve.' At
least once, he deliberately modifies his author: Higden observes,
giving his reasons, that the Gospel of Matthew must, in a certain
passage, be defective; Trevisa writes that here St Matthew 'is
ful skars for mene men myȝte understonde.' Yet, though puncti-
liously orthodox, Trevisa has scant reverence for popes or for
fathers of the church, and none for monks and friars. Edgar, he
says, was lewdly moved to substitute monks for (secular) clerks:
and, in at least two of the early MSS, though not in all, a passage
distinctly Wyclifite is inserted in the midst of the translation:

and nowe for þe moste partie monkes beeþ worste of all, for þey beeþ to riche
and þat makeþ hem to take more hede about seculer besynesse þan gostely
devocioun...þerfore seculer lordes schulde take awey the superfluyte of here
possessiouns and ȝeve it to hem þat needeþ or elles, whan þey knowen þat, þey
beeþ cause and mayntenours of here evel dedes...for it were almesse to take
awey þe superfluite of here possessiouns now þan it was at þe firste fundacioun
to ȝeve hem what hem nedede.

Though this passage is not signed 'Trevisa,' its occurrence in the
copy which belonged to Berkeley's son-in-law Richard Beauchamp
suggests its authenticity. Trevisa was a positive man: he falls
foul of Alfred of Beverley for reckoning up the shires of England
'without Cornwall' and he cannot forgive Giraldus Cambrensis
for qualifying a tale with *si fas sit credere*.

The translation of Bartholomacus, also made for Lord Berkeley,
though doubtless as popular as the chronicle, has, perhaps, not
survived in so authentic a form; moreover, embodying the
accepted learning of the Middle Ages, it gave less scope for Trevisa's
originality. History anyone might criticise but novelty in science
was only less dangerous than in theology. The style of the original,
too, is inferior to Higden's; there are already duplicate terms
in plenty, and, though Trevisa contrived to increase them, he got
less opportunity for phrasing.

This encyclopaedia, in nineteen books, is a work of reference for
divine and natural science, intermixed with moral and metaphor.
Beginning with the Trinity, the prophets and angels, it proceeds
to properties of soul and body, and so to the visible universe. A
book on the divisions of time includes a summary of the poetical,
astrological and agricultural aspects of each month; the book
on birds in general includes bees, and here occurs the edifying
imaginary picture of these pattern creatures which was the

origin of so much later fable, including Canterbury's speech in
King Henry V. There are a few indications of weariness or haste
as Trevisa's heavy task proceeds, but it is especially interesting
for his rendering of scriptural quotations. Like the writers
of *Piers the Plowman* and like Mandeville, Trevisa expects
certain Latin phrases to be familiar to his readers, catchwords to
definite quotations ; but he translates the texts in full in a
version certainly not Wyclif's and possibly his own. Always
simple and picturesque, these passages cause regret for the loss
of that translation of the Bible, which, according to Caxton,
Trevisa made   Caxton's words in the *prohemye* to *Polychronicon*
imply that he had seen the translation ; but no more is heard
of it until the first earl of Berkeley gave to James II an ancient
MS 'of some part of the Bible,' which had been preserved (he
said) in Berkeley Castle for 'neare 400 years.' It probably passed
to the cardinal of York, and may have been that copy of Trevisa's
English Bible said once to have been seen in the Vatican catalogue,
but now unknown.

The dialogue between a lord and a clerk—Lord Berkeley and
John Trevisa—prefixed to *Polychronicon* is really Trevisa's excuse
for his temerity. It gives a somewhat humorous picture of the doubts
of the man of letters. Ought famous books and scriptural texts to
be put into the vulgar tongue ? Will not critics pick holes ? Lord
Berkeley brushes his objections aside. Foreign speech is useless to
the plain man : 'it is wonder that thou makest so febell argumentis
and hast goon soo longe to scole.' The clerk gives in, breathing a
characteristically alliterative prayer for 'Wit and wisdom wisely to
work, might and mind of right meaning to make translation trusty
and true.' He has only one question to put : 'whether is ʒou
lever have a translacion of þese cronykes in ryme or in prose ? '
We ought to be grateful for Lord Berkeley's reply :—'In prose,
for comynlich prose is more clere than ryme, more esy & more
pleyn to knowe & understonde.'

To be certain in any given instance exactly what words Trevisa
used is not always possible, for the four MSS which have been
collated for the Rolls edition of *Polychronicon* show a surprising
variety. Even in the same MS, old and new forms come close
together, as 'feng' and 'fong,' and other variations of past tenses
and participles, though the sentence is always the same[1].

---

[1] The same MS, which usually gives 'myncheon,' 'comlynge,' 'fullynge,' 'maw-
mette,' 'wood,' 'bytook,' 'dele,' gives, also, at least once, 'nonne,' 'alien,' 'bapteme'
and 'i-cristened,' 'idole,' 'madde,' 'took,' 'partye.' Prefixes are already disappearing:

Most of Trevisa's vocabulary is still in common use, though a
few words became obsolete soon after he wrote, for instance:
'orped,' 'magel,' 'malshave,' 'heled,' 'hatte,' which stand for
'brave,' 'absurd,' 'caterpillar,' 'covered,' 'called.' He uses 'triacle'
sarcastically for 'poison'—'Nero quyte his moder that triacle.'
He usually distinguishes between 'þewes' (manners) and 'manere'
(method) and between 'feelynge' (perception) and 'gropynge'
(touching). 'Outtake' is invariably used for 'except,' which did
not come into use until long after. Perhaps in 'Appollin,' as the
equivalent of Apollo Delphicus, we may recognise the future ap-
pellation of a later personage. Trevisa's translation needs only to
be compared with the bungling performance of the later anonymous
translator[1], in order to be recognised as a remarkable achievement
of fluency. Where Higden tried to be dignified, Trevisa was
frankly colloquial; this characteristic marks all his translations
and gives them the charm of easy familiarity. His use of the
speech of the masses is often vigorous—a 'dykere,' for a 'dead
stock,' the 'likpot,' for the 'first finger,' 'he up with a staff þat he
had in hond.' He had, too, a fine onomatopoeic taste : Higden's
boatus et garritus (talk of peasants) becomes a 'wlafferynge,
chiterynge, harrynge and garryge grisbayting'; and to this sense
of sound is, no doubt, owing the alliteration to which, though
southern by birth and education, he was certainly addicted—a
curious trait in a prose writer. His work would seem to have been
appreciated, the number of MSS still extant of *Polychronicon*
and its production by the early printers proving its popularity;
and his *Description of England* formed the model for later accounts.
The chroniclers of the sixteenth century who quoted from *Polychronicon* as from an unquestionable authority were, perhaps, not
altogether uninfluenced by the copiously vigorous style of this first
delineation of England and her story in native English.

The Travels of Sir John Mandeville had been a household
word in eleven languages and for five centuries before it was

we have 'to-sparpled' and 'to-schad' (*dispersus*), 'i-hilde' and 'i-schad' (*infusum*),
but few others. In the genitive, the separate 'his' is usual—'Austin his bookes,'
though we get 'the chirches roves'; the combination 'oon of Cristes nayles, our
lady smok and Seynt Symon his arme' gives all forms. The feminine, as a rule,
has no mark, though 'his' occurs twice, possibly by an error of the scribe ('Faustina
his body,' 'Latona his son'). Another translation of *Polychronicon*, made by an
anonymous hand, 1432—50, uses, by preference, the preposition 'of,' but 'his' had
even intruded into proper names. Trevisa expressly states that, in his day, Hernishowe
'is nowe Ern his hulle' and Billingsgate 'Belyn his gate.'

[1] Printed with Trevisa's in the Rolls edition.

ascertained that Sir John never lived, that his travels never took place, and that his personal experiences, long the test of others' veracity, were compiled out of every possible authority, going back to Pliny, if not further.

The Voiage and Travaile of Sir John Maundevile, knight. purported to be a guide for pilgrims to Jerusalem, giving the actual experiences of the author. It begins with a suitably serious prologue, exhorting men to reverence the Holy Land, since, as he that will publish anything makes it to be cried in the middle of a town, so did He that formed the world suffer for us at Jerusalem, which is the middle of the earth. All the possible routes to Jerusalem are briefly dealt with, in order to introduce strange incidents; and mention of saints and relics, interspersed with texts not always *à propos*, presses upon more secular fables. We pass from the tomb of St John to the story of Ypocras's daughter turned into a dragon; a circumstantial notice of port Jaffa concludes by describing the iron chains in which Andromeda, a great giant, was bound and imprisoned before Noah's flood[1]. But Mandeville's geographical knowledge could not all be compressed into the journeys to Jerusalem, even taking one *via* Turkestan; so, when they are finished, with their complement of legends from Sinai and Egypt, he presents, in a second portion of the book, an account of the eastern world beyond the borders of Palestine. Herein are lively pictures of the courts of the Great Cham and Prester John, of India and the isles beyond, for China and all these eastern countries are called islands. There is the same combination of the genuine with the fabulous, but the fables are bolder: we read of the growth of diamonds and of ants which keep hills of gold dust, of the fountain of youth and the earthly paradise, of valleys of devils and loadstone mountains. You must enter the sea at Venice or Genoa[2], the only ports of departure Sir John seems acquainted with, and go to Trebizond, where the wonders begin with a tale of Athanasius imprisoned by the pope of Rome. In the same way, all we learn of Armenia is the admirable story of the watching of the sparrow-hawk, not, says Sir John cautiously, that 'chastelle Despuere' (Fr. *del esperuier*) lies beside the traveller's road, but 'he þat will see swilk mervailes him behoves sum tym þus wende out of þe way.'

Both parts of the book have been proved to have been compiled from the authentic travels of others, with additions gathered from almost every possible work of reference. The journeys to

---

[1] Andromeda had become merged in Prometheus.   [2] Geen, Januenes.

Jerusalem are principally based upon an ancient account of the first crusade by Albert of Aix, written two-and-a-half centuries before Mandeville, and the recent itinerary of William of Boldensele (1336), to which are added passages from a number of pilgrimage books of the twelfth and thirteenth centuries[1]. The second half of Mandeville's work is 'a garbled plagiarism' from the travels of a Franciscan missionary, friar Odoric of Pordenone (1330), into which, as into Boldensele's narrative, are foisted all manner of details, wonders and bits of natural history from such sources as *The Golden Legend*, the encyclopaedias of Isidore or Bartholomaeus, the *Trésor* of Brunetto Latini, Dante's tutor, or the *Speculum* of Vincent de Beauvais (*c.* 1250). Mandeville uses impartially the sober *Historia Mongolorum* of Plano Carpini[2] or the medieval forgeries called *The Letter of Alexander to Aristotle*, and *The Letter of Prester John*; no compilation of fiction or erudition comes amiss to him. He takes no account of time; though he is quite up to date in his delimitation of that shifting kingdom, Hungary, many of his observations on Palestine are wrong by three centuries; a note he gives on Ceylon was made by Caesar on the Britons; some of his science comes, through a later medium, from Pliny; his pigmies, who fight with great birds, his big sheep of the giants on the island mountain, boast a yet more ancient and illustrious ancestry. The memory which could marshal such various knowledge is as amazing as the art which harmonised it all on the plane of the fourteenth century traveller, and gave to the collection the impress of an individual experience.

The genius which evolved this wonderful literary forgery sent it forth to fame from the great commercial city of Liège in the latter part of the fourteenth century. The unquestioned myth of its origin was that John de Mandeville, knight, of St Albans, had left England in 1322 to make the pilgrimage to Jerusalem; he afterwards travelled all over the world and, returning homewards in 1343, was laid up at Liège by arthritic gout and attended by a doctor, John *ad barbam*, whom he had previously met in Cairo. At the physician's suggestion he wrote, to solace his enforced dulness, a relation of his long experiences, which he finished in 1356 or 1357. Such is the statement given in the principal Latin edition; but neither the gout nor the physician

---

[1] Including *Pélerinaiges por aler en Iherusalem*, *c.* 1231, *The continuation of Wm. of Tyre* (1261), *Jacques de Vitry* (d. 1240) and others

[2] Papal emissary to Tartary in 1245.

are mentioned in the earliest MS now known, which is in French, dated 1371, and was originally bound up with a medical treatise on the plague by *Maistre Jehan de Bourgoigne autrement dit à la Barbe*, citizen of Liège, physician of forty years' experience, author (before 1365) of various works of science, of whose plague treatise several other copies still exist. Now, there was at this time resident in Liège a voluminous man of letters, Jean d'Outremeuse, a writer of histories and fables in both verse and prose. He told, in his *Myreur des Histors*[1], how a modest old man, content to be known as Jehan de Bourgogne or Jean à la Barbe, confided on his death-bed to Outremeuse, in 1372, that his real name was John de Mandeville, *comte de Montfort en Angleterre et seigneur de l'isle de Campdi et du chateau Perouse*, and that he had been obliged to fly from home in 1322 because he had slain a man of rank. Unluckily, Outremeuse's story only confounds Mandeville's own, as set forth in the Latin travels, and adds impossible titles to this knight turned doctor. Outremeuse also added that he himself inherited the old man's collection of foreign jewels and —damaging admission—his library. He quotes Mandeville sometimes in his own historical works; but he does not confess the use he makes of the genuine travels of friar Odoric—and neither did 'Mandeville.' According to Outremeuse, Sir John was buried in the church of the Guillemins, and there, by the end of the fourteenth century, stood his tomb, seen by several trustworthy witnesses in the succeeding centuries, adorned by a shield bearing a coat, which proves to be that of the Tyrrell family (fourteenth century), and an inscription differently reported by each traveller. Tomb and church were destroyed during the Revolution. At his birthplace, St Albans, the abbey boasted a ring of his gift, and, in course of time, even showed the place of his grave.

Whether John the Bearded really told Outremeuse that he was John de Mandeville of the impossible titles, or whether Outremeuse only pretended that he did, we cannot hope to ascertain. The puzzling point is the selection of so plausible a name: for there was a John de Bourgogne concerned, though not as a principal, in the troubles of Edward II, who had a pardon in 1321, revoked after Boroughbridge, 1322, when he fled the country. And there was a John de Mandeville, of no great importance, also of the rebellious party, who received a pardon in 1313, but of whom no more is known. The facts ascertained so far about the

---

[1] In Bk. 4, now lost, but copied, as to this entry, by Louis Abry, before 1720. See Nicholson. *The Academy*. xxx (1884), p. 261.

real author or authors of the *Travels* are: that he was not an Englishman; that he never visited the places he describes, or visited them without making any intelligent observation; that he wrote at Liège before 1371, and in French; that he was a good linguist and had access to an excellent library; that his intimate acquaintance with nearly all the works of travel and of reference then known implies long and diligent study hardly compatible with travelling; that he gauged exactly the taste of the reading public and its easy credence; and, finally, that he (or they) carried out the most successful literary fraud ever known in one of the most delightful volumes ever written. It would be curious if Liège contained at once two men so well read as Outremeuse and 'Mandeville,' both compiling wonder-books, secretly using the same basis, and not in collusion, and it is remarkable that the Latin version with its tale of the physician contains some adventures, not in the French and English versions, of Ogir the Dane, a hero on whom Outremeuse wrote an epic.

To the statements made by the author himself no credit need be attached. This greater than Defoe used before Defoe the art of introducing such little details as give to fictions the appearance of personal recollection. He is great on numbers and measurements not in his originals, on strange alphabets, some real, some garbled or 'not to be identified'; and, as his statements about himself cannot be verified, there is no more ground for believing that he visited Cairo and met Jean à la Barbe there, or was laid up at Liège with arthritic gout, than that he drank of the fountain of youth and knew the road to the earthly paradise. Similarly, the statement of the French MS that the author ought to have written in Latin, to be more concise, but preferred Romance as more readily understood by travelled gentlemen who could testify to his truthfulness, is to be accepted on the ground of internal evidence and because the Latin versions all betray a later date and a French original. That the writer was no Englishman, may be deduced from the absence of any local colouring, and from his ignorance of English distances, more surely than from the erroneous titles and coat of arms.

The Travels of Sir John Mandeville were translated into almost every European language, and some 300 MSS are said to be still in existence. The three standard versions are the Latin, French and English, all of which, as early as 1403, Mandeville was credited with having himself composed. Of the five known Latin versions, one[1] was far better known than the others; 12 copies of it survive,

---

[1] Warner's 'vulgate.'

and it was the basis of other translations. It contains the allusion to the physician. Not a very early version, it was made from the French, shortened in some respects, but with some interpolations. The French manuscripts are said to be all of one type and many copies remain; some of them were written in England for English readers, proving that, in the fifteenth century, the educated might still read French for pleasure. The best MS is the oldest, the French MS of 1371, once in the library of Charles V. Of English versions there seem to be three, represented by (1) the Cotton MS[1], (2) the Egerton MS[2] and (3) defective MSS[3]. The Cotton translation was the work of a midland writer who kept very closely to a good French original. The Egerton was made by a northerner who worked with both a Latin and a French exemplar, but whose French model must have differed from any now known, unless the translator, whose touch is highly individual, deliberately composed a free paraphrase. But the version popular in the fifteenth and sixteenth centuries was much shorter than either of these, being taken from some French MS which lacked pages covering nearly two chapters, while the translator, too dull to discover the omission, actually ran two incongruous accounts together and made nonsense of the words juxtaposed. The first printed edition corrected the error only very briefly. Though it is possible that this defective version, represented by several MSS, might come from the same original as the complete and superior Cotton MS, seeing that copyists not unfrequently shortened their tasks, the differences are so numerous that it seems, on the whole, easier to assume an independent hand. There is a curious variation in the dates assigned: the best French and Latin texts and the Cotton give 1322 for the pilgrimage and 1355 or 1357 for the composition of the book: the defective MSS and the Egerton put the dates ten years later, 1332 and 1366.

Of these three versions, the defective one is the least spirited, the Cotton is the most *vraisemblable*, owing to the fulness of detail and the plausibility with which everything appears to be accounted for, as it is in the French, while the Egerton is the most original in style and, though it omits some passages found in the Cotton, sometimes expands the incidents given into a more harmonious picture. The change of the impersonal 'men' to 'I,' the occasional emphatic use of 'he þis,' 'he þat' instead of the mere pronoun, the vivid comparisons—the incubator 'like a hous

---

[1] First printed 1725.   [2] Printed 1899 for the Roxburghe Club.
[3] Often printed 1499—1725.

full of holes'—and countless similar touches, give a special charm
to the tale in this version. So vigorous and native is the composition
that it scarcely gives the impression of a translation, and gallicisms,
such as 'þat ilke foot is so mykill þat it will cover and oumbre all
the body,' are rare exceptions. We find plenty of old and northern
words[1]. Slight hints of antipathy to Rome may be detected, and
there are some additions to the recital not found in other English
copies, in particular a legend of St Thomas of Canterbury, oddly
placed in Thule. The writer of this version so far identifies himself
with Sir John as to add to the account of the sea of gravel and the
fish caught therein an assertion that he had eaten of them himself.
It matters little that there are sundry inaccuracies of translation,
such as the rendering of *latymers* (Fr. *lathomeres* = interpreters)
by 'men þat can speke Latyne'; but the proper names are terribly
confused; we not only get 'Ysai' and 'Crete' for 'Hosea' and
'Greece,' or 'Architriclyne' as the name of the bridegroom at Cana,
but also other quite unintelligible forms. Indeed, the transforma-
tions of place-names might be worth while tracing: thus, the
town Hesternit appears in Latin as *Sternes ad fines Epapie*, in a
French version as *Ny e puis a fine Pape*, in Cotton as 'Ny and to the
cytie of fine Pape,' in Egerton as 'Sternes and to þe citee of Affyn-
pane.' The names of the Cotton version are far more accurate than
those of the Egerton, as its vocabulary and spelling are also less
archaic, but the translator sometimes errs by transferring the sound
of his French original; so, *poy d'arbres* becomes 'lytill Arborye,'
izles of Italy become 'hills,' and, with like carelessness, *porte du
fer* is turned to 'gates of hell,' *signes du ciel* to 'swannes
of hevene,' *cure d'avoir* to 'charge of aveer' (Egerton, 'hafyng
of erthely gudes'). The Cottonian redactor is strong in scientific
explanations and moral reflections, and, like his Egertonian brother,
must add his mite to the triumphs of the traveller; to the account
of the vegetable lamb he adds: 'Of that frute I have eten, alle
thoughe it were wondirfulle but that I knowe wel that God is
marveyllous in his werkes.'

This identification of themselves with Mandeville is partly the
cause of the high place which these three (or two) translators occupy
in the history of English letters. In all literary essentials their work
is original; tautology has disappeared; they find in their model

---

[1] 'Growe,' 'graven' (buried), 'warne' (unless), 'buse' (must), 'bese' (is), 'nedder'
(dragon or serpent), 'oker' (usury), 'umqwhile' (formerly), 'spire after' (ask for),
'mesells' (leprosy), 'salde wonder dere,' 'ga na ferrere,' 'to see on ferrum' (from
afar), 'mirkness umbelapped þe emperoure.'

no temptation to repetition or to jingling constructions and they add none; the narrative goes smoothly and steadily forward, with an admirable choice of words but without any phrasing, as different from the lavish colloquialism of Trevisa as from the unshapen awkwardness of the Wyclifite sermons. This natural style of simple dignity undoubtedly aids the genius of the original author in investing his fairy tales with that atmosphere of truthfulness which is the greatest triumph of his art. In the first place, Mandeville had the boldness not to be utilitarian, but to write with no other aim than entertainment. It is true that he professes to begin a manual of pilgrimage, but the thin disguise is soon cast aside, and the book could scarcely be mistaken for either a religious or a solidly instructive work. It was a new venture in literature—amusement had been hitherto the sphere of poets. And what vivifies the book, what marks it off from medieval tales like those of *Gesta Romanorum*, was also a new thing in prose : the sense of a human interest which is really the inspiring principle of the whole and forms out of scattered anecdotes a consistent story. The descriptions are of people and their behaviour, and in the midst is the quiet but discernible figure of Sir John himself. It was to the interest in human life that Mandeville appealed and this, in turn, he educated. He had, moreover, skilful devices for creating the feeling of reality : the wonders are sometimes accounted for by what appears a rational cause ; touches of criticism or personal reflection contradict the supposition of simplicity ; with equally circumstantial gravity he describes the trees which bear 'boumbe,' or cotton, and those which bear the very short gourds 'which, when ripe, men open and find a little beast with flesh and blood and bone, like a little lamb without wool.' Certainly, he was abreast of the most recent knowledge of his time in his account of the cotton-tree and in his assurance of the roundness of the earth. His readers, he says, witten well that the dwellers on the other side of the earth are straight against us, feet against feet, and he feels certain that by always going onwards one may get round the world, especially since Jerusalem is in the middle of the earth, as men may prove by a spear pight into the ground which casts no shadow at midday in the equinox. Then, as many journeys as it takes to reach Jerusalem, so many more will bring one to the edge of the world, after which one must proceed to India and other places on the underneath side ; 'I hafe oft tymes thoght on a tale þat I herd when I was ȝung' of a man who travelled till he reached an island where he heard one calling to plow oxen in words of his own tongue; 'but I suppose he had so long went on land and on see environunand þe werld þat he was commen in to his awen marchez' (Egerton). The author dovetails his bits of genuine information into his fictions with deft ingenuity. One of the means of proving a diamond is to 'take þe adamaund that drawez þe nedill til him by þe whilk schippe men er governed in þe sea' (Egerton), and, if the diamond is good, the adamant, 'that is the schipmannes ston' (Cotton) will not act upon the needle while the gem rests upon it. But Mandeville cannot refrain from heightening the marvellous stories culled elsewhere. To the account of the diamond, sufficiently strange in 'Ysidre' or 'Bertilmew,' to whose corroboration he appeals, he must needs add that 'þai growe sammen, male and female, and þai er nurischt with dew of heven...and bringes furth smale childer and so þai multiply and growez all way' (Egerton). He has often seen that they increase in size yearly, if taken up by the roots with a bit of the rock they grow on and often wetted with May dew. The source of this detail, as of the stories of Athanasius, of the man who environed the earth and of the hole in the Ark 'whare the fend ʒode out' when Noe said Benedicite, has not yet been discovered. Probably Mandeville invented them, as he did the details of the Great Cham's court: hangings of red leather, said Odoric—hangings made of panther skins as red as blood, says Mandeville; now, a panther, in those times, was reckoned a beast of unheard-of beauty and magical properties. Odoric expressly owned that he did not find such wonders in Prester John's land as he had expected from rumour; Mandeville declares that the half had not been reported, but that he will be chary of what he relates, for nobody would believe him. Such indications of a becoming reticence help to create the air of moderation which, somehow, pervades the book. The author's tone is never loud, his illustrations are pitched on a homelier key than the marvel he is describing—so of the crocodiles, 'whan thei gon bi places that ben gravelly it semethe as thoughe men hadde drawen a gret tree thorghe the gravelly places' (Cotton). It is a blemish on the grandeur of the Cham's court that 'the comouns there eten withouten clothe upon here knees.' Mandeville faces the probability that his readers may withhold belief: 'he þat will trowe it, trowe it; and he þat will noʒt, lefe. For I will never þe latter tell sum what þat I sawe...wheder þai will trowe it or þai nil' (Egerton). He discounts a possible comparison with Odoric by mentioning that two of his company in the valley of devils were

'frere menoures of Lombardye,' and artfully calls to witness the
very book that he stole from, 'the Lapidary that many men
knowen noght.' Not that he ever avowedly quotes, save, rather
inaccurately, from the Scriptures. The necessary conventional
dress of orthodoxy he supplies to his travels by the device of credit-
ing the mysterious eastern courts with holding certain Christian
tenets. The shrine of St Thomas is visited 'als comounly and
with als gret devocioun as Cristene men gon to Seynt James'
(Odoric said, St Peter's); Prester John's people know the Paternoster and consecrate the host.

Mandeville hopes that everyone will be converted; his tolerance
of strange creeds and manners is that of a gentle, not of a careless,
mind. The Soudan of Egypt—who, indeed, rebuked the vices of
Christianity after the fashion of Scott's Saladin—would have wedded
him to a princess, had he but changed his faith. 'But I thanke
God I had no wille to don it for no thing that he behighten me'
(Cotton). It is with such light touches that Sir John pictures himself. He is no egoist, nor braggart; we know nothing of his
appearance; he does no deeds of prowess himself 'for myn unable
suffisance'; his religion is that of ordinary men. He ventured,
duly shriven and crossed, down the perilous vale, full of treasure
and haunted by devils,

I touched none (he says) because that the Develes ben so subtyle to make a
thing to seme otherwise than it is, for to disceyve mankynde,... and also
because that I wolde not ben put out of my devocioun; for I was more devout
thaune than evere I was before or after, and alle for the drede of Fendes that
I saughe in dyverse Figures (Cotton).

Sir John, in short, reveals himself as a gentleman, filled with a
simple curiosity and with that love of strange travel which, he says,
is native to Englishmen, born under the moon, the planet which
moves round the world so much more quickly than the others.
He is honest and broad-minded, free from any taint of greed—
there is not a sordid observation in the whole book—and that he
ever comes to an end is due to his consideration for others, for
were he to tell all he had seen nothing would be left for other
travellers to say: 'Wherfore I wole holde me stille.'

CHAPTER IV

THE SCOTTISH LANGUAGE

EARLY AND MIDDLE SCOTS

THE history of the Scots vernacular is, in its earlier stages, a recapitulation of the tale of Northumbrian Old English and northern Middle English. It is, perhaps, too dogmatic to say, especially when the documentary evidence is so slight, that, in the earliest period, the language north of the Tweed was identical with that between the Tweed and the Humber; but we may reasonably conclude that the differences were of the narrowest. The runic verses of *The Dream of the Rood* on the cross at Ruthwell, Dumfriesshire, might have been cut on the shores of the Forth, or in Yorkshire. Later, though local differences may have been accentuated, chiefly by the intrusion at one point or another of Scandinavian or other words, the structural identity of the language in the two areas was maintained. The justice of this assumption appears when, in a still later period, we have an opportunity of comparison by written texts. It is unnecessary to point out the close kinship, in the fourteenth century, of the language of Barbour's *Bruce*, written in Aberdeen, with that of the writings of Richard Rolle, the hermit of Hampole, near Doncaster. The likeness is the more remarkable, if we accept the opinion that Barbour's text, in its extant form, was written out in the fifteenth century. It is, therefore, not only scientifically accurate to treat the language of the *Bruce* as northern English, but it is historically justifiable to call that language 'English.' To Barbour and his successors—till a change in political circumstance made a change in nomenclature necessary—their tongue is not 'Scots,' but invariably 'Ynglis,' or English.

The name 'Scots' or 'Scottish' has been applied to the language of the whole or part of the area of modern Scotland in such a variety of senses that some statement of the history of the term is a necessary preliminary to even the briefest outline.

Modern associations and modern fervour have too often obscured
the purely linguistic issues. In its original application, 'Scots' is
the speech of the Scottish settlers in Alban: that is, Celtic of the
Goidelic group, the ancestor of the present Scottish Gaelic. In
due course, the name was applied to the vernacular of the entire
area north of the dividing-line between the estuaries of the Forth
and Clyde. As this extension covered the eastern Pictish territory,
then under the rule of the kings of the Scots, it is possible that
some change was ultimately effected by the political association of
these several northern non-Teutonic communities. Whatever be
the outcome of speculation on this point, the only consideration
pertinent to our present purpose is that the speech of this wider
area was known as 'Scots' to all peoples south of the dividing-
line, whether Anglian settlers in the Lothians or Bretts (or
'Welsh') in Strathclyde.

When the limits of the 'Scottish' kingdom were enlarged
southward and had, in the thirteenth century, become identical
with those of modern Scotland, the name 'Scots' was no longer
applied to the language of the rulers. The process of amalgamation was, in every sense, an anglicisation, which became
more effective as the Scottish kings carried out their policy of
intruding Teutonic culture into the eastern fringe of their
ancestral 'Scotland.' Thus, when the wider political idea of a
'Scotland' takes shape, we find 'Ynglis' the name of the speech
of the 'Scottish' court and of the surrounding Anglian population
in the Lothians and Fife, and 'Scots' that of the speech of the
northern and western provinces. This alienation of the anglicised
Scot from the Gaelic Scot—illustrated in the story of Duncan and
Macbeth—was completed in the wars of independence, in which
the Teutonic or 'English' elements representing 'Scottish'
nationality were hampered in their resistance to the Anglo-
French civilisation of England by the vigorous opposition of
non-Teutonic Scots. When the struggle was ended and Teutonic
Scotland started on a fresh career of national endeavour, the
separation from the Celtic Scots was absolute. On the other hand,
certain elements of Anglo-French culture were readily assimilated.
The guiding factor was race. For some time after this, even at
the close of the fifteenth century, 'Scots' is the name for
the Gaelic speech of the north and west. By writers of Lothian
birth, this tongue is spoken of disrespectfully as the tongue of
'brokin men' and 'savages' and 'bribour bairdis.' These
Lothian men are Scots, willing subjects of the king of 'Scots,'

proud of their 'Scotland'; but they are careful to say that the language which they speak is 'Ynglis.'

Later, however, with the political and social advance of the kingdom and the development of a strong national sentiment during the quarrels with England, it came about, inevitably, that the term 'Ynglis' no longer commended itself to northern patriotism. It was the language of the 'auld enemy,' an enemy the nearest and the most troublesome. If these northerners were proud of Scotland and of being Scots, why might not their tongue be 'Scots'? In some such way the historian guesses at the purpose of sixteenth century literature in taking to itself the name of the despised speech of the 'bards,' and in giving to that speech the name of 'Ersch' or 'Yrisch' (Irish). The old reproach clung to the new title 'Ersch': and it was to be long before the racial animosity, thus expressed in the outward symbol of language, was to be forgotten in a more homogeneous Scotland. No better proof of this internal fissure can be found than in Dunbar's *Flyting with Kennedie*[1], which is, in first intention, an expression of the feud between the English east and the Gaelic west. If the poem be, as we are asked to believe, a mere bout of rough fun, it is none the less interesting as evidence of the material which gave the best opportunities for mock warfare.

This break with the family name and historic association indicates, in a blunt way, a more fundamental change in the language itself. The causes which produced the one could not fail to influence the other. For 'Scots,' erst 'Ynglis,' had, for some time, lived apart: during more than two centuries there had been little intercourse with England by any of the peaceful methods which affect language most strongly; closer association had been enforced with the unreconciled Gaels within its area or with new friends beyond; generally, a marked differentiation had been established between the civilisations north and south of the Tweed. These considerations, among others, prepare us for the changes which soon become evident, though they may not be very helpful in explaining the details of these changes. It may be that some of them were longer in the making than our study of the few extant documents of the earlier period has led us to believe. We lack evidence of the extent of Scandinavian interference in the northern Anglic dialect, structural and verbal, and we know too little of the Anglo-French influences resulting from the Norman culture which had grown up in the Lothians. Yet, while

[1] See Chapter x.

allowing for possibilities, or probabilities, of this kind, we may conclude that, on the whole, the literary language of Scotland down to the early fifteenth century was in close conformity with the usage of northern England. The texts of Barbour and Hampole force us to accept this. Any qualification which may be made must be due, not to the testimony of facts (for they are wanting), but to an acknowledgment of the general principle that languages and dialects change slowly and that the differences in the latter part of the fifteenth century (to which we are about to refer) are too fundamental to have taken shape of a sudden.

A change in the habit of the literary language is discernible from the middle of the fifteenth century. It is definite and of general occurrence; and it continues with but few variations, which are due to the idiosyncrasies of writers or the circumstances of publication, down to the opening decades of the seventeenth century. To this period (1450—1620) the name of 'Middle Scots' has been given. The title is not altogether satisfactory, but it is the best that has been found; and it is useful in suggesting the special linguistic phase which intervened between earlier and later (or modern) Scots. It is applied only to the literary speech. The spoken language pursued its own course and showed fewer points of difference from both the literary and spoken dialects of northern England. When the middle period closes, spoken Scots is again restored to something of the dignity of a literary medium. This is said advisedly, for diversity of dialect and the lack of a fixed orthography in Modern Scots are the denial of the main characteristics of a standard instrument. In Middle Scots, on the other hand, the linguistic peculiarities are, with the allowances already noted, uniform within the period, and deliberately followed.

The name 'Early Scots,' for the period ending *c.* 1450, is even less satisfactory than 'Middle Scots' for the next (from 1450 to 1620); but it will do no harm if it be understood to be the literary language of Teutonic Scotland during the century and a half before 1450, when such differentiation from early northern English as may be assumed, but cannot readily be proved, was established. The names 'Northumbrian' and 'Early Northern English' may be applied to the still earlier stages. Of 'Early Scots' the typical examples are Barbour's *Bruce* and Wyntoun's *Chronicle* : of Middle Scots the writings of Henryson, Dunbar, Douglas and Lyndsay. In a more exhaustive scheme it is convenient to have an intervening 'Early Transition Period'—say from 1420 to 1460—represented by such important works as *The Kingis Quair, Lancelot of the Laik,* and *The Quare of Ielusy.* The linguistic basis of these poems is Early Scots; but they show an artificial mixture with southern and pseudo-southern forms derived from Chaucer. Their language represents no type, literary or spoken; it is a bookish fabrication; but, though exceptional and individual, it has the historical interest of being the first expression of a habit which, in Middle Scots, was neither exceptional nor individual. In this transition period the foreign elements are exclusively Chaucerian: in Middle Scots, Chaucerian influence, though great and all pervading, is not the sole cause of the differences [1].

The statement that Middle Scots is uniform throughout its many texts must not be misunderstood. Full allowance must be made, in each case, for the circumstances of composition and production. Translations from Latin or French will show a larger percentage of Romance forms; a dream-poem will attract more Chaucerian words and phrases and tricks of grammar; a recension of a southern text or the writing of a Scot in exile in England will 'carry over' certain southern mannerisms; French printers in Paris, or Chepman and Myllar's English craftsmen in Edinburgh, will bungle and alter; and poets like Gavin Douglas will deal in archaisms which even an educated contemporary might not readily understand. Yet these exceptions, and others which might be named, but prove the validity of the general rule.

Middle Scots stands in marked contrast with Early Scots in phonology and orthography, in accidence, in syntax and in vocabulary and word-forms. It is not desirable to attempt even an outline of each of these in this short chapter. The reader who wishes further acquaintance is referred to the bibliography. The remaining pages will be devoted to brief consideration of the main causes of change and of their relative importance in the transformation of the dialect, especially in the matter of vocabulary. The persistence of certain popular misconceptions, or overstatements, of the indebtedness of Scots justifies some discussion of the question in this place.

An artificial dialect such as is used by the greater Middle Scots poets is, in some respects, unaffected by the processes which mould a living speech [2]. It draws from sources which are outside the natural means of supply; it adopts consciously and in accordance

---

[1] It may be well to add that these 'transition' texts are more strongly southern than are the later texts which continued the habit of borrowing.

[2] If the entire literature of the period (prose as well as verse) be considered, this impression of artificiality will, of course, be modified. This must always be so, even when eccentricity is more marked than it is in the present case. Yet we must not underestimate the importance of a habit which was, after all, followed by all Middle Scots writers who make any claim to literary style.

with a deliberately accepted theory of style. If it borrow the forms which come to all languages with the new things of the market-place, it does so advisedly, just as it recovers the older forms which have been lost to ordinary speech. Books are its inspiration, and the making of books is its end. In this way the literary conscious-ness of an age as it appears in writers like Henryson and Dunbar is an index to its linguistic habit. When poets show a new pride in the vernacular and are concerned with the problems of poetic diction and form, their admiration of the models of style takes a very practical turn. Scottish literature, in the full enjoyment of a new fervour, showed the effect of its enthusiasm in the fashion of its language. In it, as in the Italian and Burgundian, the chief effort was to transform the simpler word and phrase into 'aureate' mannerism, to 'illumine' the vernacular, to add 'fresch anamalit termis celicall.' This Crétinism was the serious concern of the Scottish poets for at least a century, and even of prose-writers such as the author of *The Complaynt of Scotlande*, or Abacuck Bysset, so late as 1622. In the later stages of Middle Scots, and especially in the prose, other influences were at work, but the tra-dition established during the so-called 'golden age' still lingered.

The chief modifying forces at work during the middle period are English, Latin and French. Others—say Celtic and Scan-dinavian—may be neglected, but the case for the former will be glanced at later.

The southern, or English, influence, which is the strongest, is exerted in three ways. It comes through the study of Chaucer and the English 'Chaucerians'; through religious and controversial literature; and, lastly, through the new political and social relations with England, prior to and following the accession of James VI to the English throne. The first of these is the most important. In a later chapter, attention is drawn to the debt of the Scottish 'makars' to the southern poet and his followers for the sentiment and fabric of their verse. The measure of that debt is not complete without acknowledgment to Chaucer's language. The general effect on Middle Scots of this literary admiration was an increase in the Romance elements. It may be taken for granted that the majority of words of Anglo-French origin which were incorporated at this time were Chaucerian; but it is not always easy to distinguish these words from the Anglo-French which had been naturalised in the early period. It must not be forgotten, especially in estimating the French contribution to Middle Scots (see *post*) that the most active borrowing from that quarter had been accomplished before this time. In

The Kingis Quair and *Lancelot*, which illustrate the first Chaucerian phase in Scots, the infusion is not confined to the vocabulary. Fantastic grammatical forms are common: such as infinitives in *-en* (even *-ine*), *weren* for *war*, past participles with *y-*, frequent use of final *-e*—all unknown and impossible to the northern dialect. In these cases there is no mistaking the writer's artifice and its source. Such freaks in accidence are hardly to be found in the poetry of James IV's reign ; though Gavin Douglas's eclectic taste allows the southern *ybound* and the nondescript *ysowpit*. In the verse of the 'golden age' it is the word, or tag, which is the badge of Chaucerian affectation. The prose shows little or nothing of this literary reminiscence. John of Ireland, whose writing is the earliest extant example of original Scots prose of a literary cast, speaks of 'Galfryde Chauceir' (by whom he really means Occleve), but exhibits no trace of his influence. When the Middle Scots prose-writer is not merely annalistic, or didactic, or argumentative, he draws his *aureat termis* from the familiar Latin. So, when *The Complaynt of Scotlande* varies from the norm, it is, in Rabelais's phrase, to 'despumate the Latial verbocination,' or to revel in onomatopoeia.

In the prose, the second and third English influences are more easily noted, and they are found towards the end of the period, when a general decadence has set in. Indeed, they are the chief causes of the undoing of Middle Scots, of breaking down the very differences which Chaucer, Latinity and (in a minor degree) French intercourse had accomplished. It is to be observed that the language of nearly all religious literature from the middle of the sixteenth century is either purely southern or strongly anglicised : it is worthy of special note that, until the publication of the Bassandyne Bible in 1576—9, all copies of the Scriptures were imported direct from England, and that the Bassandyne, as authorised by the reformed kirk, is a close transcript of the Genevan version. This must have had a powerful influence on the language, spoken and written. Even in Lyndsay, whose dialect is unmistakable, translated passages from the Vulgate are taken direct from the English text. The literary influence was strengthened by protestant controversialists, notably by Knox, perhaps the most 'English' of all Scottish prose-writers. This 'knapping' of 'sudroun' was one of the charges preferred against them by catholic pamphleteers —among others by John Hamilton, author of *Ane Catholik and Facile Traictise* (1581), who even saw treason in the printing of Scottish books at London 'in contempt of our native *language*.'

The third English influence, latest in activity, emphasised these tendencies. It is easy to trace in state documents and in the correspondence of the court the intrusion of southern forms. *Sal* and *shall*, *till* and *to*, *quhilk* and *which*, participles in *-and* and *-ing*, *-it* and *-ed*, jostle each other continually. The going of the court to England, and the consequent affectation of English ways, undid the artificial Middle Scots which had been fashioned at, and for, that court. Poetry was transferred, almost *en bloc*, as if by act of the British Solomon, to the care of the southern muse: all the singers, Alexander, Aytoun, Drummond and the rest became 'Elizabethan' in language and sentiment, differing in nothing, except an occasional Scotticism, from their southern hosts. When Scottish literature revives in the mid-seventeenth century, and in the next is again vigorous, its language is the spoken dialect, the *agrest termis* of the Lothians and west country[1].

That the Romance contribution to Middle Scots is large is obvious; that it is found in writings which are not mere *tours de force* of 'aureate' ingenuity is also obvious. But the sorting out of the borrowings according to their origin has not been so clear to amateurs of Scots etymology. There has been no lack of speculation, which, in its generally accepted form, must be seriously traversed.

The non-Teutonic elements (excluding Celtic) are Latin and French. An exaggerated estimate of the political and social intercourse with France, and a corresponding neglect or depreciation of the position of Latin in Scottish culture, have given vogue to a theory of French influence on the language which cannot be accepted without serious modification. The main responsibility for the popular opinion that Scots is indebted, inordinately, to French must rest with the late Francisque Michel's *Critical Inquiry into the Scottish Language, with the view of illustrating the Rise and Progress of Civilisation in Scotland* (1882). It may be true that, 'to thoroughly understand Scottish civilisation, we must seek for most of its more important germs in French sources'; but certain important qualifications are necessary.

The French element in Middle Scots represents three stages of borrowing: first, the material incorporated in the early period during the process of Anglo-French settlement in the Lothians; next, the material, also Anglo-French in origin, drawn from Chaucer and the 'Chaucerian' texts; and, finally, the material adopted from

---

[1] Some qualification is, of course, necessary in Ramsay's case. His antiquarian taste must be reckoned with by the philologer.

central French during the close diplomatic intercourse of the Scottish and French courts, and as a result of the resort of Scottish students to the university of Paris, and, later, of the national interest in Calvinistic protestantism. The last of these groups commends itself readily to the popular imagination : its plausibility is enforced by recalling the stories of the Scot abroad, of careers like Buchanan's, of the Quentin Durwards, and by pointing to the copies of French institutions in the College of Justice and the older universities. Yet, when all these are allowed for, the borrowings from this third source are the smallest in extent, and by no means important. From the second source, which is, in a sense, English (for the borrowings were already naturalised English words), the influx is much greater ; but from the first, certainly the greatest.

So far as the vocabulary is concerned, nearly all the Romance elements in Middle Scots which cannot be traced to the first or second, the Anglo-French or Chaucerian source, are of Latin origin. Even many of the borrowings which are French in form and derived through French were taken direct from the *rhétoriqueurs* because they yielded a ready-made supply of aureate terms and helped the purposes of writers who, like Gavin Douglas, had set themselves to cut and carve Latin for the betterment of the vernacular. It was of the nature of an accident that the media were French books. The forms appealed to the Latin-speaking, Latin-thinking Scot. Moreover, not a few of the words which are certainly French, such as the hackneyed *ashet* and *gigot*, belong to the period of Modern Scots ; others, as *attour, boule*, which appear to yield evidence of French origin, are 'English' dialectal forms. When Francisque Michel refers the child-word *bae* to the bleat in *Pathelin* we begin to understand what a Frenchified thing Middle Scots must have been ! Nor is it easy, even with the authority of another investigator[1], to allow a French origin to certain well-known eccentricities of grammar and syntax in Middle Scots— badges of that period and of no other—the indefinite article and numeral *ane*, in all positions ; the adjectival plural, *e.g. saidis, quhilkis* ; and the frequent placing of the adjective after the noun, *e.g. factis merciall, concepcioun virginale, inimy mortall.* The assumption that such a usage as *ane man* is an imitation of the French *un homme* is, in the first place, entirely unsupported by historical evidence ; secondly, it shows a grammatical interference in a place where intrusion is least likely, or hardly possible.

[1] See J. A. H. Murray's *Dialect of the Southern Counties of Scotland* (Historical Introduction).

In the case of the other alleged Gallicisms, criticism may be more constructive, for they may be explained (when they are not the outcome of verse necessity) as relics or reminiscences of Latin syntactical habit. The tradition of theological and legal Latin must be reckoned with ; and the fact that the adjectival plural is admitted to be first found 'in legal verbiage' is an important link in the evidence.

So far, we have assumed that the Romance influence which is not Anglo-French or Chaucerian comes through Latin rather than French. We may strengthen this position by pointing to the ascertained importance of Latin in the moulding of Middle Scots. There is, in the first place, the direct testimony of contemporary writers to the vitality of Latin, which stands in remarkable contrast with their silence on the subject of French borrowing. The circumstances of the writer and the nature of his work must, of course, be considered. It is to be expected that, in a translation from Latin, or in treatises on theology, political science, or law, the infusion will be stronger than in an original work of an imaginative or descriptive cast. This consideration may affect our conclusion as to the average strength of the infusion, but it does not minimise the importance of the fact that Middle Scots was liable to influence from this quarter. The testimony of such different writers as John of Ireland, Gavin Douglas and the author of *The Complaynt of Scotlande* is instructive. John excuses his Scots style because he was 'thretty ȝeris nurist in fraunce, and in the noble study of Paris in latin toung, and knew nocht the gret eloquens of chauceir na colouris þat men usis in þis Inglis metir.' Nor was he (we may be certain) the only Scot who, when it was a question of writing 'in the commoun langage of þis cuntre,' sought help from Latin, 'the tounge that [he] knew better.' Gavin Douglas allows the general necessity of 'bastard latyne, french, or inglis' to a progressive Scots, but he discusses the advantages of only the first, and shows that in his task of translating Vergil he must draw freely from Latin, if his work is not to be 'mank and mutilait' as Caxton's was. The author of *The Complaynt* says plainly that 'it is necessair at sum tyme til myxt oure langage vitht part of termis dreuyn fra lateen, be reson that oure scottis tong is nocht sa copeus as is the lateen tong.'

These confessions are amply supported by the texts. There we find not only words of unmistakable Latin lineage such as *translatory, praetermittit, caliginus,* but others used in their Latin sense, such as *prefferris* (excels), *pretendis* (aims at), and the like. Further, there is ample evidence of the process, at which Douglas clearly hints, that Latin was drawn upon without hesitation and without any attempt to disguise the borrowing. The word *mank* in the quotation already given is an illustration. It may be Old French (through Anglo-French), but its natural parent is *manc -us* Examples of direct association with Latin are plentiful : here, two must suffice. 'Withoutin more or delay' is plain *sine mora aut dilatione* : no imaginary French 'more' intervenes. Even at the close of the period a man may be described in kirk minutes as 'apt and idoneus to enter the ministry.' In accidence even, as in the uninflected past participle, *e.g. did fatigat, being deliberat, salbe repute*—a form which still lingers in Scottish legal style—the derivation from Latin is direct.

On the whole, therefore, the Romance material in Middle Scots, in so far as it is not Anglo-French, directly or mediately, is largely Latin. Central French is certainly represented in such words as *preaux* and *charpentier*, but they are in many cases ἅπαξ λεγόμενα or the liking of certain authors. To counterbalance this, it may be pointed out that in *The Complaynt of Scotlande*, that strange mosaic of verbatim translation from French with encyclopaedic digressions in Scots which are assumed to be original, the author is a more deliberate Latinist in the latter than he is when rendering the passages from the *rhétoriqueurs*. Here, again, it is the 'rhetorical' quality which attracts him to the French authors. He pays little heed to the French *timbre* of their work, and hastens, when he must be original, to find the closest imitation in diction of this sort.

Nou for conclusione of this prolog, i exort the, gude redar, to correct me familiarly, ande be cherite, Ande til interpreit my intention fauorablye, for doutles the motione of the compilatione of this tracteit procedis mair of the compassione that i hef of the public necessite nor it dois of presumptione or vane gloir. thy cheretabil correctione maye be ane prouocatione to gar me studye mair attentiulye in the nyxt verkis that i intend to set furtht, the quhilk i beleif in gode sal be verray necessair tyl al them that desiris to lyue verteouslye indurand the schort tyme of this oure fragil peregrinatione, & sa fayr veil.

And this writer dares to call these words 'agrest termis,' and to add that he 'thocht it nocht necessair til hef fardit ande lardit this tracteit vitht exquisite termis, quhilkis ar nocht daly vsit' and that he has employed 'domestic Scottis langage, maist intelligibil for the vulgare pepil.'

It has been argued that an additional cause of the differences between Early and Middle Scots is to be found in Celtic. Inter-action has been assumed because the Lowlander and Highlander were brought into a closer, though forced, association in a unified Scotland, or because the anti-English policy of the former, threw him back, no matter with what feelings, upon his northern and western neighbours. There are, however, serious objections to the general assumption and to the identification of many of the alleged borrowings from Celtic. In regard to the first, it must be kept in mind (*a*) that the only possible interaction, literary or otherwise, was with the Gaels of the west and south-west ; (*b*) that the inhabitants of Strathclyde and Galloway were, to a certain extent, Romanised Celts ; and (*c*) that race-antipathies, as shown in *The Flyting of Dunbar and Kennedie,* were a strong barrier to linguistic give-and-take, especially in grammatical structure and orthography. On the marches there would be borrowing of words, perhaps even breaking down of inflections and phonetic change. There is evidence of such effects in the initial *f* for *quh* (*hw*) of the pronoun, at the Aberdeenshire end of the 'Highland line'; but changes of this kind do not affect the literary standard, or every dialect of the spoken language.

The alleged contributions from Celtic are (*a*) verbal and (*b*) orthographic, perhaps phonological. The first are admittedly of the slightest, and are being gradually reduced. In the second a contingency is assumed which, as in the case of central French interference, was the least likely to happen. The closest intimacy is necessary before one language, especially that which is domi-nant, permits modifications of its grammatical and orthographic habit. Our chief authority on Lowland dialects[1] has described some of the salient variations of Middle Scots, 'in the form of words, and consequently in their written form,' as 'due mostly to Celtic influence.' While it may be admitted that Middle Scots was not 'founded upon precisely the same dialectic type as the written language of the early period,' it is by no means clear that *buik, moir, glaid*, etc. for older northern forms, the loss of *t* as in *direck*, or its addition as in *witht*, the inserted mute *l* in *chalmer* (or *chaumer*, as pronounced), *rolkis* (rocks) and *waltir* (water), the *t* in the past part. as *defamet*, or in the adverb, as in *frawart* —that any of these things are the result of the Lowlander's unconscious affectation of 'Ersch' speech. The *onus probandi* lies with the supporters of this view. At present no evidence has been produced : it will be surprising if it can be produced.

[1] *Dialect of the Southern Counties of Scotland.*

CHAPTER V

THE EARLIEST SCOTTISH LITERATURE

BARBOUR, BLIND HARRY, HUCHOUN, WYNTOUN, HOLLAND

As has been indicated in the preceding chapter, it is probable that, from a very early period in the English colonisation of Britain, an English dialect was spoken from Forth to Tweed, which was, in most respects, practically indistinguishable from that spoken between the Tweed and the Humber. Even along the north-eastern coast, English was soon the language of the little towns that traded by sea. Before 1124, the communities of Aberdeen, Banff, Elgin, Forres, Nairn and Inverness had formed themselves into a miniature Hanseatic league, on which David I conferred sundry privileges. The inland country behind these communities remained for long in the hands of a Gaelic-speaking people. In the north of Aberdeenshire there is evidence that the harrying of Buchan, carried out by Robert the Bruce, in 1308, as part of his vengeance on his enemies the Comyns, introduced the English language to the inland districts, for in local documents the names of persons change speedily after that date from Gaelic to English.

Of a Scottish literature before the wars of independence there is no trace. In the period preceding the death of Alexander III, in 1286, Scotland was so prosperous that it is difficult to believe no such literature existed. But, as the dialect of Scotland was not yet differentiated from that south of the Tweed, such a literature, unless it took the form of chronicles or was of a strictly local character, could not easily be identified. It is noticeable that there is no lack of literature of which the scene is connected with Scotland. The romance of Sir Tristram, which is associated with the name of True Thomas, the mysterious seer of Erceldoune, is preserved only in a dialect which is not Scots. Though the Gawain cycle appears in different forms in different dialects, all of them seem to be English. Yet Gawain, according to the legend, was prince of Galloway; and, as we shall see, there is some reason to connect some of these poems with a Scottish author. The contradiction, however, is more in appearance than in reality. If these poems were composed by a Scottish author, they were, undoubtedly, intended rather for recitation than for reading; and, even if they were meant to be read, a southern scribe would be certain to adapt the forms to his own dialect. This adaptation might be either intentional or unintentional. If intentional, the purpose would be to make the poem more easily intelligible to southern readers; if unintentional, it would typify the result which always ensues in all languages from the mechanical copying of an alien dialect.

In the Scots dialect itself, the political separation brought about by the wars of Wallace and Bruce produced considerable changes. The oldest fragments of the dialect are to be found in the phrases introduced for greater precision into the Latin laws of David I and his successors. In these we hear of *blodewit, styngisdynt, herieth* and so forth, for which, in the later Scots version, are substituted *bludewyt, stokisdynt, hereyelde*. Till Scotland has become again an independent kingdom, such words as these, and the vernacular glosses on the hard words in a Latin lease, are all that survive to us of the old Scottish tongue. Of early continuous prose there are no remains. The earliest poetry extant appears in the few musical and pathetic verses on the death of Alexander III, which have been quoted a thousand times:

> Quhen Alysandyr oure kyng was dede
>   That Scotland led in luve and le,
> Away wes sons[1] off ale and brede,
>   Off wyne and wax, off gamyn and gle;
> Oure gold wes changyd into lede,
>   Cryst born into Vyrgynyté
> Succoure Scotland and remede
>   That stad is in perplexyté.

Though preserved only by Wyntoun (*c.* 1420), they, no doubt, are not far removed from the original form of a hundred and fifty years earlier. In Fabyan's *Chronicle* are preserved some of the flouts and gibes at the English, baffled in the siege of Berwick and defeated at Bannockburn. But it is with Barbour, whose poem *The Bruce* is the triumphant chronicle of the making of the new kingdom of Scotland by Robert and Edward Bruce and the great 'James of Douglas,' that Scottish literature begins. As the national epic, coloured, evidently, to a large extent by tradition,

---

[1] abundance.

but written while men still lived who remembered Bannockburn and the good king Robert, it is entitled to the first place, even though conceivably some of the literature of pure romance be not less old.

In John Barbour, the author of *The Bruce*, we have a typical example of the prosperous churchman of the fourteenth century. As we may surmise from his name, he had sprung from the common folk. Of his early history we know nothing. We first hear of him in 1357, when he applies to Edward III for a safe-conduct to take him and a small following of three scholars to Oxford for purposes of study. By that date, he was already arch-deacon of Aberdeen, and, as an archdeacon, must have been at least twenty-five years old. He probably was some years older. He died, an old man, in 1396, and we may reasonably conjecture that he was born soon after 1320. In those days there was no university in Scotland, and it may be assumed that the archdeacon of Aberdeen was, in all probability, proceeding in 1357 to Oxford with some young scholars whom he was to place in that university; for the Latin of the safe-conduct need not mean, as has often been assumed, that Barbour himself was to 'keep acts in the schools.' The safe-conduct was granted him at the request of 'David de Bruys,' king of Scotland, at that time a captive in king Edward's hands; and Barbour's next duty, in the same year, was to serve on a commission for the ransom of king David. Other safe-conducts were granted to Barbour in 1364, 1365 and 1368; that of 1365 allowing him to pass to St Denis in France, while, in 1368, he was allowed to cross into France for purposes of study. In 1372 and 1373, he was clerk of the audit of the king's household; and, in 1373, also one of the auditors of the exchequer. By the early part of 1376, *The Bruce* was finished; and, soon after, we find him receiving by command of the king (now Robert II) ten pounds from the revenues of the city of Aberdeen. In 1378, a pension of twenty shillings sterling from the same source was conferred upon him for ever—a benefaction which, in 1380, he transferred to the cathedral of Aberdeen, that the dean and canons might, once a year, say mass for the souls of his parents, himself and all the faithful dead. With northern caution, he lays down careful regu-lations as to how the dean is to divide the twenty shillings among the staff of the cathedral, not forgetting even the sacrist (the name still survives in Aberdeen) who tolled the bell. Other sums were paid to Barbour by the king's order from the revenues of Aberdeen, and, in 1388, his pension was raised by the king, 'for his faithful service,' to ten pounds, to be paid half-yearly at the Scottish terms of Whitsunday and Martinmas. He died on 13 March 1396. Like Chaucer, he received from the king (in 1380—1) the wardship of a minor, who lived in his parish of Rayne in Aberdeenshire. On at least one of the many occasions when he was auditor of the exchequer, Sir Hew of Eglintoun, who, as we shall see, is also reputed a poet, served along with him.

Such are the simple annals of John Barbour's life, as known to us. For thirty-eight years at least he was archdeacon of Aberdeen, then, probably, one of the most prosperous towns in the realm. Fortunately for itself, it was far removed from the border, and had not suffered so severely as most towns in the wars of liberation, though it had been visited by all the leading combatants, by Wallace, by Edward I and by Bruce. The records of the city, unfortunately, do not begin till a few years after Barbour's death. There is, however, some reason to believe that Barbour was not alone in his literary activity. To the same district and to the same period belong the *Lives of the Saints,* a manuscript discovered in the Cambridge University Library by Henry Bradshaw, who assigned the authorship to Barbour himself. From Wyntoun we learn that Barbour was the author of other works which are now lost. In many passages he refers to themes treated of in a quasi-historical poem, *The Brut,* which clearly, in matter, bore a close resemblance to Layamon's poem with the same title. To Barbour, Wyntoun attributes, also, another lost poem, *The Stewartis Oryginalle,* which carried back the genealogy of the Stewart kings from Robert II of Scotland to Ninus who built Nineveh—a *tour de force* excelled only by another Aberdonian, Sir Thomas Urquhart, the translator of Rabelais, who carried the genealogy of his family back to Adam himself. It was perfectly well known that the Stewarts were a branch of the ancient English house of FitzAlan; but, in the bitter feeling against England which by this time had come to prevail in Scotland, it was, no doubt, desirable to find another and more remote origin for the Scottish royal family. The feeling which led to the production of this fabulous genealogy is vouched for by the author of the *Lives of the Saints* already mentioned, who tells us, in the life of St Ninian, that a paralytic English lord desired his squire, who had brought home a Scot as prisoner, to put a knife in his mouth with the blade outward, that he might 'reave the Scot of his life.' This lord, having been dissuaded from his deed of murder, and having listened to the advice of the prisoner that he should try a visit to St Ninian's shrine as a cure for his paralysis, finds the cure long in coming, and says that he might have known, if he had been wise, that a Scotsman of Galloway, as Ninian was, would never help an Englishman, and would prefer to make him ill rather than assist him to recover. The genealogy survives for us in the *History* of Hector Boece, where we are told that Fleance, the son of Banquo, had a son Walter, who became steward of Scotland—a genealogy which passed from Boece through Holinshed to Shakespeare.

To Barbour also has been attributed a poem on the *Siege of Troy*, translated from the popular medieval Latin *Troy Book* of Guido delle Colonne, of which two considerable fragments are preserved with Barbour's name in a manuscript in the Cambridge University Library. The second fragment is found also in a Douce MS in the Bodleian Library. There is no doubt that these fragments, which have been utilised to complete an imperfect copy of Lydgate's translation of Guido, are in the same metre as *The Bruce*, which is shorter than that of Lydgate. They are also, no doubt, in Scots, but, in all probability, they are in the Scots of the fifteenth, not of the fourteenth, century, and, in detail, do not resemble Barbour's undoubted composition. More recently, and with much more plausibility, George Neilson has contended that *The Buik of Alexander*, a Scottish translation from two French poems, is by the author of *The Bruce*. The similarities of phraseology between *The Buik of Alexander* (which exists only in a printed copy of about 1580, reprinted for the Bannatyne Club in 1831) and *The Bruce* are so numerous and so striking that it is impossible to believe they are of independent origin.

To return to *The Bruce*. This, the work by which the reputation of John Barbour stands or falls, dates from his later middle life. He must have been a man of between fifty and sixty before it was finished. It is in no real sense a history, for Barbour begins with the astounding confusion of Robert the Bruce with his grandfather the rival of John Balliol in claiming the crown. As Barbour's own life overlapped that of king Robert, it is impossible to believe that this is an accidental oversight. The story is a romance, and the author treated it as such; though, strange to say, it has been regarded from his own time to this as, in all details, a trustworthy source for the history of the period. So confident of this was Wyntoun, writing about a quarter of a century after

Barbour's death, that he says he will lightly pass over the details of Bruce's career because

> The Archedene off Abbyrdene
> In Brwyss his Buk has gert be sene,
> Mare wysly tretyde in-to wryt
> Than I can thynk with all my wyt.

Like any other hero of romance, Robert has no peer and no superior, though inferior to him and to him only are two other knights, James of Douglas and Edward Bruce. It is only natural, therefore, that, when he fights against the English, the English have much the worst of it, even when the odds are very much in their favour. But, though Barbour is an ardent patriot, he does his best to be fair, and, no doubt, the main historical events are related with good faith and as accurately as tradition allowed. The English are not all villains, the Scots are not all angels from heaven. For Maknab the traitor, who betrayed Christopher Setoun to the English, he reserves his bitterest indignation :

> In hell condampnyt mot he be. iv, 26.

All Barbour's resources are lavished upon the characters of king Robert and the good James of Douglas. Edward Bruce is a fine warrior, but attains not unto these first two for lack of self control (ix, 661 ff., xvi, 391 ff.). Had he had 'mesur in his deid' he might have equalled any warrior of his time, always excepted

> his brother anyrly[1]
> To quhom, in-to chevelry,
> I dar peir[2] nane, wes in his day. ix, 664 ff.

Douglas, too, is noble, but he is a darker spirit than king Robert and more cruel in his treatment of the English, for he has greater wrongs to revenge. Nothing becomes him better than his reply to king Robert's advice not to venture into Douglasdale :

> Schir, neidwais I will wend
> And tak auentur that God will giff
> Quhether sa it be till de or liff. v, 242 ff.

Barbour does not often draw full length portraits of his heroes; but, almost at the end of his poem, tells us how Douglas looked and what were his chief characteristics (xx, 511 ff.). The only other with whom he deals as fully is Sir Thomas Randolph, earl of Murray (x, 280 ff.). In both cases he praises, above all else, their hatred of treason (from which the Scots, both in the wars of Wallace and of Bruce, had suffered so much) and their love of loyalty. Douglas, he thinks, can be compared only with

---

[1] alone.   [2] compare.

Fabricius, who scorned the offer of Pyrrhus's physician to poison him.

The kindliness and humour of king Robert he illustrates by numerous instances—his delaying the army, in order that a poor laundress, too ill to be moved, may not be left behind to the mercy of Irish savages (XVI, 270 ff.); his modesty in declaring that he slew but one foe while God and his hound had slain two (VII, 484); his popularity among the country folk, when, disguised, he seeks a lodging and is told by the goodwife

> all that traualand ere
> For saik of ane ar velcom here,

and that one

> Gud kyng Robert the Bruce is he
> That is rycht lord of this cuntre. VII, 243 ff.

On occasion Barbour displays a dry, caustic humour characteristic of his country. Once on a time there were such prophets as David, Samuel, Joel and Isaiah,

> Bot thai prophetis so thyn are sawin
> That thair in erd now nane is knawin. IV, 685 f.

Of king Edward he remarks that

> Of othir mennis landis large wes he. XI, 148.

When O'Dymsy let out a loch in Ireland upon Edward Bruce's men, Barbour's comment is that though they lacked meat, they were well wet (XIV, 366).

Barbour does not often moralise; but, here and there, he turns aside from his narrative to express a general sentiment. The most famous passage of this kind is that on Liberty which, to Barbour, born when his country was just emerging from a life and death struggle for its independence, must have had a vividness beyond what the modern reader can realise. Truth to tell, the passage reads better as an extract than in its original setting, where it ends in a curious piece of medieval monkish casuistry.

> A! fredome is a noble thing!
> Fredome mayss man to haiff liking;
> Fredome all solace to man giffis:
> He levys at ess that frely levys!
> A noble hart may haiff nane ess
> Na ellys nocht that may him pless,
> Gyff fredome fail3he[1]; for fre liking
> Is 3harnyt[2] our all othir thing.
> Na he, that ay hass levyt fre
> May nocht knaw weill the propyrte,
> The angyr, na the wrechyt dome,
> That is cowplyt to foule thyrldome:

[1] fail. [2] desired.

> Bot gyff he had assayit it
> Than all perquer[1] he suld it wyt,
> And suld think fredome mar to pryss
> Than all the gold in warld that is. i, 225 ff.

Less well known is his praise of love as that which

> mony tyme maiss tender wychtis
> Off swilk strenthtis, and swilk mychtis
> That thai may mekill paynys endur. ii, 522 ff.

The tears of joy with which Lennox and his men welcome
Bruce and his followers, whom they meet half-famished among the
hills after they believed them dead, lead the poet on to a curious
disquisition on what makes men and women weep (iii, 596 ff.).
But, generally speaking, these γνῶμαι are confined to a single
verse such as

> Bot quhar god helpys, quhat may withstand? i, 456.

The changes and chances of the long-continued war brought
home to him very vividly the fickleness of fortune

> That quhile upon a man will smyle
> And prik him syne ane othir quhile. xiii, 633 f.

> Bot oft falȝies the fulys thoucht
> And wiss men's etling[2] cumis nocht
> Til sic end as thai weyn alwayis.
> A little stane oft, as men sayis,
> May ger weltir ane mekill wane.
> Na manis mycht may stand agane
> The grace of God, that all thing steiris. xi, 21 ff.

Barbour was not of the order whose 'eye in a fine frenzy
rolling, Doth glance from heaven to earth, from earth to heaven.'
He was a God-fearing churchman and statesman, who thought it
well to put on record his country's deliverance, before, in the in-
glorious days of Bruce's successors, its memory should have perished.
And what he aimed at he achieved. Like Scott, whose poetry he
inspired, he finds his metre so facile that, at times, he falls into the
merest commonplace. The battle of Bannockburn occupies an
altogether disproportionate space in the poem. Nevertheless,
the description of the battle is Barbour's masterpiece. He must
often have talked with men who had fought at Bannockburn; he
obviously had a very clear conception of the manner in which the
day was lost and won. In his narrative he combines the qualities
which Matthew Arnold assigns to the highest epic style ; he is
rapid in movement, plain in words and in style, simple in ideas
and noble in manner. The only one of these characteristics which
can be disputed is the last. But the description which follows

---

[1] thoroughly.   [2] endeavour.

speaks for itself. How it appealed to the most Homeric of
Barbour's admirers all readers of Scott's *Lord of the Isles* are
aware :

> And quhen schir Gelis de Argente
> Saw the king thus and his menȝe[1]
> Schape theme to fle so spedely,
> He com richt to the kyng in hy[2],
> And said, 'schir, sen that it is swa
> That ȝe thusgat ȝour gat will ga,
> Haffis gud day! for agane will I;
> ȝheit fled I neuir sekirly,
> And I cheiss heir to byde and de
> Than till lif heir and schamfully fle.'
> His brydill than but mair abaid[3]
> He turnyt, and agane he raid,
> And on schir Eduard the Brysis rout
> That was so sturdy and so stout,
> As dreid of nakyn thing had he,
> He prykit, cryand 'Argente!'
> And thai with speris swa him met,
> And swa feill speris on hym set,
> That he and horss war chargit swa
> That bath doune to the erd can ga;
> And in that place than slayne wes he.   XIII, 299 ff.

Barbour's achievement in his age and circumstances is
very remarkable. This is more vividly realised, if his work be
compared with the other national epic, Blind Harry's *Wallace*,
which, in its own country, secured a more permanent and more
general popularity than *The Bruce*. Till into the nineteenth
century, one of the few books in every cottage was the *Wallace*[4].
The causes of this popularity are to be sought in the fact that
Wallace, being more genuinely a Scot than Bruce, as time went
on, came more and more to be regarded as the national hero, and
his exploits were magnified so as to include much with which
Wallace had nothing to do. The very defects of Harry's poem
commended it to the vulgar. It professes to be the work of a
burel man, one without special equipment as a scholar, though it
is clear that Harry could at least read Latin. While Barbour's
narrative contains a certain amount of anecdotal matter derived
from tradition, and, on some occasions, deviates from the truth of
history, it is, on the whole, moderate, truthful and historical.
Harry's work, on the other hand, obviously is little but a tradition
of facts seen through the mists of a century and a half. Historians
are unable to assign to the activity of Wallace in his country's cause
a space of more than two years before the battle of Falkirk in

---

[1] following.   [2] in haste.   [3] without more delay.
[4] In the eighteenth century modernised by Hamilton of Gilbertfield.

1298. Harry, though nowhere consistent, represents his hero as fighting with the English from his eighteenth year to his forty-fifth, which is, practically, the period from the death of Alexander III to the battle of Bannockburn. But Wallace was executed in 1305. The contents of the work are as unhistorical as the chronology. If Barbour took care, on the whole, that Bruce should have the best of it, though recognising that he suffered many reverses, Wallace's path is marked by uniform success. Where Bruce slays his thousands, Wallace slays his ten thousands. The carnage is indiscriminate and disgusting. But, by the time that *Wallace* was composed, a long series of injuries subsequent to the wars of independence had engrained an unreasoning hate of everything English, which it has taken centuries of union between the countries to erase from the Scottish mind. Hence, the very violence of *Wallace* commended it to its readers. To the little nation, which suffered so severely from its powerful neighbour, there was comfort amid the disasters of Flodden or of Pinkie in the record of the doughty Wallace.

Of the author of this poem we know next to nothing. According to John Major (Mair) the historian, *Wallace* was written in his boyhood by one Henry, who was blind from his birth, and who, by the recitation of his poem in the halls of the great (*coram principibus*), obtained the food and clothing he had earned. The date of the composition of the poem may be fixed, approximately, with the clue supplied by Major, as 1460. In the treasurer's accounts various payments of a few shillings are entered as having been made to 'Blin Hary.' The last of these payments is in 1492. Harry probably died soon after. Sixteen years later, Dunbar, in his *Lament for the Makaris*, enters him in the middle of his roughly chronological list of deceased poets. From Major's account it is clear that Harry belonged to the class of the wandering minstrels who recited, like Homer of old, the deeds of heroes to their descendants. In Scotland, when the descendants of the heroes were no longer interested in such compositions, the bards appeared before humbler audiences; and many persons still alive can remember the last of them as, in the centre of a crowd of applauding yokels, he recited his latest composition on some popular subject of the day.

The sole manuscript of the poem, now in the Advocates' Library at Edinburgh, was written in 1488 by the same John Ramsay who, about the same time, wrote the two existing manuscripts of *The Bruce*. That he was a more faithful transcriber than he generally gets credit for having been, is shown by the well-marked differences

between the language of the two poems. While, in Barbour. hardly
a trace is to be found of the characteristic Scottish dropping of the
final *ll* in *all, small, pull, full*, etc., we find this completely developed
in *Wallace*, where *call* has to rime with *law, fall* with *saw*, etc.
Here also *pulled* appears as *powed*, while *pollis* is mistakenly put
for *paws* and *malwaris* for *mawaris* (mowers). As Harry was
alive at the time when Ramsay wrote the manuscript, it may have
been written from the author's dictation. Be that as it may, there
is nothing in Harry, any more than in Homer, to show that the
author was born blind. On the contrary, some of his descriptions
seem to show considerable powers of observation, though the
descriptions of natural scenes with which he prefaces several of
the books are an extension of what is found, though rarely, in
Barbour (*e.g.* v, 1—13, xvi, 63 ff.) and had been a commonplace
since Chaucer. The matter of his poem he professes to have
derived from a narrative in Latin by John Blair, who had been
chaplain to Wallace and who, if many of Wallace's achievements
are well nigh as mythical as those of Robin Hood, was himself
comparable in prowess to Little John   He was, however, a modest
champion withal, for Harry tells us that Blair's achievements were
inserted in the book by Thomas Gray, parson of Liberton. The
book is not known to exist; but there is no reason to doubt that
it had once existed. According to Harry (xi, 1417), its accuracy was
vouched for by bishop Sinclair of Dunkeld, who had been an eye-
witness of many of Wallace's achievements. But, either the book
from which Harry drew was a later forgery, or Harry must have
considerably embroidered his original; it is inconceivable that
a companion of Wallace could have produced a story widely
differing in chronology, to say nothing of facts, from real history.

But, when the poem has been accepted as a late traditional
romance, founded upon the doings of a national hero of whom little
was known, *Wallace* is by no means without merit. Harry manages
his long line with considerable success, and so firmly established
it in Scotland that the last romantic poem written in Scots—
Alexander Ross's *Helenore, or the Fortunate Shepherdess*—carries
on, after three centuries, the rhythm of Harry with the greatest
exactitude. There is no lack of verve in his battle scenes; but they
are all so much alike that they pall by repetition. The following
is typical (ii, 398 ff.). Longcastell (Lancaster), we are told,

> Hynt out his suerd, that was of nobill hew,
> Wallace with that, at hys lychtyn, him drew;
> Apon the crag with his suerd has him tayne;
> Throw brayne and seyne in sondyr straik the bayne.

The ferocity of Wallace is such that he says:

> I lik bettir to se the Sothren de
> Than gold or land that thai can giff to me.   v, 397 f.

Harry feels that the fame of his hero is a little dimmed by the
fact that he belonged only to the ranks of the smaller gentry, but
at once proclaims, like a greater successor, that the 'rank is but the
guinea stamp,' and strengthens his case by the example of the
knights of St John at Rhodes:

> Wallace a lord he may be clepyt weyll,
> Thocht ruryk folk tharoff haiff litill feill;
> Na deyme na lord, bot landis be thair part.
> Had he the warld, and be wrachit off hart,
> He is no lord as to the worthiness;
> It can nocht be, but fredome, lordlyknes.
> At the Roddis thai mak full mony ane
> Quhilk worthy ar, thocht landis haiff thai nane.   vii, 397 ff.

In Harry we find the same dry humour as in Barbour; but here
it is of a grimmer cast when the English are in question.   When
Wallace, to escape his enemies, had to disguise himself as a maid
spinning, Harry says quaintly

> he sat still, and span full connandly
> As of his tym, for he nocht leryt lang.   i, 248 f.

When their enemies were upon them,

> His falow Stewyn than thocht no tyme to bide.   v, 154.

When Wallace set the Englishmen's lodging on fire,

> Till slepand men that walkand[1] was nocht soft   vii, 440,

and on another occasion

> Quhar Sotheroun duelt, thai maid thair byggyngis hayt[2].
>   ix, 1692.

Even to Julius Caesar he applies a quip:

> Gret Julius, that tribute gat off aw,
> His wynnyng was in Scotland bot full smaw.   viii, 1339 f.

In his Chaucerian passages at the beginning of several books,
and in the apostrophe to Scotland in the last book (xi, 1109 ff.),
Harry employs those 'aureate' terms which, through the following
century, were to be a snare to Scottish literature.   But the use
of them proves that Harry was not, after all, a *burel* man.   Here
and there he makes pretensions to classical learning, and, like
Barbour, occasionally refers to the heroes of old romance, to

---

[1] waking.   [2] made their buildings hot.

Charlemagne at Roncesvalles, to king Arthur slaying the giant at Mont St Michel, to the Alexander story of Gawdyfer at Gaddris, also referred to by Barbour. He assumes that all men know Barbour's book; though, curiously enough, the name of Wallace is not once to be found in Barbour's poem. A still more recent writer is probably referred to in the apologue of the owl in borrowed plumes, which Stewart applies to Wallace, when angry because Wallace refused to let him lead the vanguard. For, only a few years before 1460, this story had been the subject of Holland's *Howlat*.

With the *Buke of the Howlat*, which is the proper title of this work, we pass from historical romance to the last type of the romance proper, with its metre founded on the old alliterative long line, but fashioned into an elaborate lyrical stanza of nine long verses of four beats and four short verses of two beats. The scheme is *ababababcdddc*, and no better example of its treatment in the *Howlat* can be found than the second stanza:

> This riche Revir dovn ran, but resting or ruf[1]
> Throwe ane forest on fold, that farly was fair
> All the brayis of the brym bair branchis abuf,
> And birdis blythest of ble on blossomes bair;
> The land lowne was and le[2], with lyking and luf,
> And for to lende by that laike thocht me levar,
> Becauss that thir hartes in heirdis couth huf[3],
> Pransand and prunȝeand, be pair and be pair.
> Thus sat I in solace, sekerly and sure,
> Content of the fair firth,
> Mekle mair of the mirth,
> Als blyth of the birth
> That the ground bure.

This is the commonest form of the metre, found also in *Golagros and Gawane* and in the *Awntyrs of Arthure at the Terne Wathelyne*, and, with a slight modification, in *Rauf Coilȝear*; while in the *Pistill of Susan* the ninth line is replaced by a 'bob' of one beat and two syllables like 'In Feere,' 'So sone,' etc.

The *Howlat* is preserved in two manuscripts, the Asloan, dating from about 1515, and the Bannatyne, written in 1568. The poem is between sixty and seventy years older than the earlier manuscript. It was composed, as the author tells us in the last stanza, in the 'mirthfull month of May' at Darnaway in the midst of Moray:

> Thus for ane Dow of Dunbar drew I this dyte,
> Dowit with ane Dowglass.

---

[1] pause.   [2] secluded and sheltered.   [3] abide.

In other words, it was written for Elizabeth Dunbar, Countess of Moray in her own right, whose first husband was one of the Douglas family that perished in the struggle with James II of Scotland, his eldest brother being that earl whom the king stabbed with his own hand. Pinkerton saw in the poem a satire on James II, a view which was entirely founded on a misreading of *crovne* for *rovme* in verse 984, and, with the restoration of the true reading, the theory falls to the ground. The poem, which introduces an elaborate account of the Douglas arms, must have been written before the final disaster to the Douglases at Arkinholm in 1455; for the unfortunate countess, no doubt with the intention of saving her lands, married, three weeks after the loss of her first husband, the son of the earl of Huntly, who was on the side of the king. As the arms of pope Nicholas V are described, the poem must be later than 1447, and, probably, before the murder of earl William by the king in 1452, as is shown by Amours in his edition for the Scottish Text Society. There seems to be no recondite meaning in the piece. The subject is the thrice-told tale of the bird in borrowed plumes, which gives itself airs and speedily falls to its former low estate. The owl, beholding himself in a river that flows through a fair forest, is disgusted with his own appearance and appeals to the pope of the birds, the peacock, against dame Nature. A summons is issued to the members of the council to convene. The author shows considerable ingenuity in finding names of birds and other words to suit his alliterative verse, and some humour in the parts which he assigns to the different birds. If it were necessary to search for hidden meanings, one might suspect that there was a spice of malice in representing the deans of colleges by ganders, and the archdeacon, 'that ourman, ay prechand in plane, Correker of kirkmen' by the claik, which is the barnacle goose, but also a Scots word for a gossip. It is a pretty fancy to make the dove 'rownand ay with his feir,' always whispering with his mate, a curate to hear whole confessions. The author, who was of the secular clergy, may have been well satisfied that

> Cryand Crawis and Cais, that cravis the corne,
> War pure freris forthward,
> That, with the leif of the lard,
> Will cum to the corne ʒard
> At ewyn and at morn. 191 ff.

When all are met, the unhappy owl is commanded by the pope to state his case; and, when this has been done, the pope calls upon his councillors to express their opinions. They proceed to do so in a manner with which Holland was no doubt familiar:

> And thai weraly awysit, full of wirtewe,
> The maner, the mater, and how it remanyt;
> The circumstance and the stait all couth thai argewe.
> Mony allegiance leile, in leid nocht to layne it[1],
> Off Arestotill and ald men, scharplie thai schewe;
> The Prelatis thar apperans[2] proponit generale;
> Sum said to, and sum fra,
> Sum nay, and sum ȝa;
> Baith pro and contra
> Thus argewe thai all.

Ultimately it is decided to consult the emperor—the eagle—and the swallow is despatched as herald with letters written by the turtle, who is the pope's secretary. The herald finds him 'in Babilonis tower,' surrounded with kings, dukes and other nobles, who, as is explained afterwards, are the nobler birds of prey. The specht or wood-pecker is the emperor's pursuivant and, as is the manner of pursuivants, wears a coat embroidered with arms. Then comes a long description of heraldic arms, including not only the emperor's but also those of Nicholas V, of the king of Scotland and, in greatest detail, of the Douglas family. More than a quarter of the poem is taken up with this dreary stuff, which was very interesting, no doubt, to Holland's patroness, but which ruins the poem as a work of art. The only interest it can have for the general reader is that in it is contained a version of the journey undertaken by the good Sir James with the heart of Bruce, which may be regarded as the official Douglas version, and which differs from that contained in the last book of Barbour's *Bruce*. Here, Douglas is represented as having journeyed to Jerusalem and as being on his way back when he perished fighting against the Moors in Spain; but there is no reason to doubt the correctness of Barbour's story that Douglas never travelled further than Spain[3]. The last third of the poem is occupied with a feast to which the pope invited the emperor and his courtiers. The bittern was cook, and the choir of minstrels consisted of the mavis and the merle, ousels, starlings, larks and nightingales. We have presented to us in full the hymn they sang in honour of the Virgin Mary, and a whole stanza is occupied with the names of the different musical instruments, which far outstrip shawms, sackbut and psaltery in obscurity. The visitors are entertained by the jay, who is a wonderful juggler. He makes the audience

---

[1] in language not to conceal it.   [2] opinion.

[3] It is, however, noteworthy that Boece adopts this version and not Barbour's.

see many wonderful things which do not really exist, among others the emperor's horses led off to the pound by the corncrake, because they had been eating 'of the corne in the kirkland.' The rook appears as a 'bard owt of Irland,' reciting much unintelligible Gaelic gibberish—such Gaelic bards no doubt were familiar enough at Darnaway in the fifteenth century—but is ignominiously routed by the jesters, the lapwing and the cuckoo, who then engage in a tussle for the amusement of the company. After grace has been said by the pope, it is agreed, at dame Nature's suggestion, that her supposed ill-treatment of the owl shall be remedied by grafting on the owl a feather from each of the birds. The owl, however, becomes so insolent in consequence, that Nature takes all the feathers from him again, much to his sorrow.

David Laing and Amours have diligently collected the little that is known as to the author of this *jeu d'esprit*. He is mentioned in various documents connected with the church and family of his patron. From these we learn that, in 1450, Richard de Holand was rector of Halkirk, in Caithness, in 1451, rector of Abbreochy in the diocese of Moray, and, like his contemporary Henryson, a public notary. In 1453, he was presented by the pope to the vacant post of chanter in the church of Moray. In 1457, after the fall of the Douglases, we find him in Orkney where, in 1467, he demits the vicarage of Ronaldshay. He seems to have joined the exiled Douglases in England, from which he was sent on a mission to Scotland in 1480, and, in 1482, along with 'Jamis of Douglace' (the exiled earl) and certain other priests 'and vther sic like tratouris that are sworne Inglismen, and remanys in Ingland,' he is excepted from a general amnesty.

Like this poem in form, but certainly of an earlier date, is a series of romances which cluster about the name of 'Huchoun of the Awle Ryale,' one of the most mysterious figures in our early literature. The earliest mention of him is to be found in Wyntoun's *Orygynale Cronykil*, written about 1420. Wyntoun, in describing king Arthur's conquests, remarks that 'Hucheon of the Awle Realle In til his Gest Historyalle' has treated this matter. Wyntoun feels it necessary to apologise for differing from Huchoun in saying that Leo and not Lucius Iberius was the Roman Emperor who demanded tribute from Arthur. He argues that he has good authority on his side, nor is Huchoun to be blamed:

> And men of gud discretioun
> Suld excuss and loif Huchoun,
> That cunnand wes in litterature.

> He maid the *Gret Gest of Arthure*
> And the *Anteris of Gawane,*
> The *Epistill als of Suete Susane.*
> He wes curyouss in his stile,
> Faire and facund and subtile,
> And ay to plesance and delite
> Maid in meit metyre his dite,
> Litill or ellis nocht be gess
> Wauerand fra the suthfastnes[1].

The verses which follow are vital for deciding what the nature of the *Gest Historyalle* or *Gret Gest of Arthure* was:

> Had he callit Lucyus procuratour
> Quhare he callit him emperour,
> It had mare grevit the cadens
> Than had relevit the sentens.

Clearly *cadens* is to be distinguished from rime, for, as Wyntoun's example shows, *procuratour* and *emperour* might rime together. The *Gest Historyalle* must, therefore, have been an alliterative poem, and all authorities are now agreed that the conditions are satisfied by the poem called *Morte Arthure* which is preserved in the Thornton MS of Lincoln Cathedral. In the *Morte Arthure*, not only is 'Sir Lucius Iberius' called 'the Emperour of Rome,' but the knights of the Round Table are called Duszepere; (or some variant thereof), which is evidently the origin of Wyntoun's Dowchsperys. As for the *Epistill of Suete Susane*, there can be no doubt that it is the poem preserved in five MSS under that title (with variations of spelling). What was the poem called the *Adventure* or *Adventures of Gawain*, the other work of Huchoun mentioned by Wyntoun? For this place there are several pretenders, the most plausible claim being, it seems, advanced for a poem surviving in three curiously different versions, *The Awntyrs off* [*of*] *Arthure at the Terne Wathelyne*, that is at Tarn Wadling, a small lake near Hesket in Cumberland, on the road between Carlisle and Penrith. As the story is mostly concerned with Gawain, his name might have appeared in the title no less justifiably than Arthur's.

Of none of these poems in their extant forms can it be said that the language is Scottish. Who, then, was Huchoun? Pinkerton, in the end of the eighteenth century, was the first to suggest that Huchoun was to be identified with the 'gude Sir Hew of Eglintoun,' enumerated amongst other poets in Dunbar's *Lament for the*

---

[1] Thus in the Wemyss MS (S.T.S. 1906), v. 4329 ff. The Cottonian MS, also printed in the S.T.S. edition, besides other variants gives the poet's name as Hucheon and reads *a* for *the* in 4332, *Awntyr* for *Anteris* in 4333, and in 4334 *The Pistil als of Suet Susane.*

Makaris. To this it has been objected that Huchoun is a familiar diminutive, and that, if the poet was the well known Sir Hew of Eglintoun, a statesman in the reigns of David II and Robert II, who was made a knight in 1342, and, later in life, was married to Egidia, step-sister of Robert II, Wyntoun was not at all likely to talk of him as 'little Hugh.' But George Neilson has shown that the name Huchoun was employed in solemn documents even of barons, and, therefore, might without disrespect be applied to a knight who was a king's brother-in-law. The name Hucheon has commonly survived in some districts as a surname, and must have been much commoner earlier, as is shown by the names Hutchinson and M'Cutcheon, which are merely the Lowland and the Highland forms of the same name. So far there is no difficulty. The explanation of the phrase 'of the Awle Realle' is more difficult, but Neilson's argument for the old view that it is simply the *Aula Regis,* an appropriate enough description for a knight who served for a period as justiciar, seems much preferable to any other that has been advanced. The more southern colouring of the dialect in his works is not sufficient proof of his English origin, for, where there are several manuscripts, the dialectal forms vary very considerably. Moreover, it would be strange that so fertile a writer should have no honour in the country of his birth, and should be talked of with respect and reverence in a country which was bitterly hostile. It is impossible here to enter fully into the elaborate and ingenious argument by which Neilson, in his *Huchown of the Awle Ryale,* not only supports the claim made by Wyntoun, but attempts to annex a whole cycle of other poems, which are ordinarily regarded as of English though anonymous origin, and which are discussed elsewhere[1]. For the present purpose, it is sufficient to say that there seems good evidence for the existence of a Scottish poet called Huchoun in the middle of the fourteenth century, and that, in all probability, he is to be identified with the statesman Sir Hew of Eglintoun, who was a contemporary, perhaps a somewhat older contemporary, of Barbour, who must have been at least twenty-one in 1342 when he was knighted, and who died about the end of 1376 or the beginning of 1377. It is noticeable that, on a great many occasions, Sir Hew of Eglintoun receives permission to travel to London under safe-conduct—a fact on which Neilson founds a plausible argument that he was a *persona grata* at the court of Edward III. This argument, if correct, would account for a more favourable attitude

[1] See volume I, pp. 320 ff.

towards England in his works than appears in Barbour's. In an alliterative poem scribes might change dialectal forms at their will, so long as they did not affect the alliteration or the number of syllables. In the rimed poems here attributed to Huchoun it is certain that the rimes are northern, though, in the fourteenth century, there was no distinction well enough marked to form a criterion of origin from north or south of the Border.

Panton and Donaldson, the editors for the Early English Text Society of the interminable *Gest Hystoriale of the Destruction of Troy* (it contains over 14,000 lines), were the first to point out that this unrimed alliterative translation of Guido delle Colonne's *Hystoria Troiana* must, from identity in style and phraseology, be attributed to the same author as *Morte Arthure*, though it had been copied from a Scottish original by a west midland scribe. Their opinion has been developed and confirmed by Neilson's work on Huchoun. As *Morte Arthure* is admittedly superior in execution to the *Gest Hystoriale* and as, unless it had some source still undiscovered or now lost, it is a very independent rendering of the story of Arthur as related in Books IX and X of Geoffrey of Monmouth's *Historia Regum Britanniae*, it may be used to illustrate the style of Huchoun. *Morte Arthure* begins with a rude demand from Lucius Iberius, emperor of Rome, for tribute from king Arthur. Arthur, after considering the matter with his council, comes to the conclusion that he has more right to the empire than Lucius has to tribute from him; he will, therefore, anticipate Lucius's threats of invasion by taking the field against him. Accordingly, he appoints Mordred to rule in his absence and charges him especially with the care of Waynour (Guinevere). Arthur himself crosses the Channel with his host, and, after an unpleasant dream, fights a great battle with a giant from Genoa 'engendered of fiends,' who lives on human flesh, has ravaged the Cotentin and, last of all, has carried off and slain the Duchess of Britanny. The author, who is excessively fond of alliteration, excels himself, in his description of the giant, by carrying on alliteration on the same letter through four consecutive verses; so that the first twelve lines (1074—85) make three stanzas of this sort, of which the last, as the least repulsive, may be taken as a specimen :

> Huke-nebbyde as a hawke, and a hore berde[1]
> And herede to the hole eyghn[2] with hyngande browes;
> Harske as a hunde-fisch[3], hardly who so luke͵,
> So was the hyde of that hulke hally[4] al ouer.

[1] hoary beard.	[2] hairy to the hollow eyes.
[3] rough as a dog-fish.	[4] wholly.

Hardly has Arthur had time to thank Heaven for his success in the combat, ere urgent messengers arrive from the marshal of France to say that he must have help at once against the emperor, who has entered the country and is carrying destruction far and wide. Sir Boice, Sir Gawain, Sir Bedivere and some others are hastily despatched to delay the emperor, who has brought with him all the powers of eastern heathenesse; and these knights, with the help of an ambuscade, win a victory. In the great battle which follows many noble deeds are done ; these are described with great vigour. Arthur himself with Collbrande (Excalibur) has a short way with his foemen :

> He clekys owtte[1] Collbrande, full clenlyche burneschte,
> Graythes hym[2] to Golapas, that greuyde moste,
> Kuttes hym euen by the knees clenly in sondyre.
> 'Come down' quod the kynge, 'and karpe to thy ferys[3]!
> Thowe arte to hye by the halfe, I hete the in trouthe!
> Thou sall be handsomere in hye[4], with the helpe of my Lorde!' 2123 ff.

The emperor himself perishes at the hands of Arthur, and his knights, having slaughtered the paynim till they are tired, fall upon the spoil, and help themselves, not only to 'hakkenays and horses of armes,' but to all kinds of wonderful animals, 'kamells and sekadrisses [whatever they may be], dromondaries,'

> Moylle3[5] mylke whitte, and meruayllous beste3
> Elfaydes, and arrabys, and olyfaunte3 noble. 2287 f.

And thus

> The roy ryall renownde, with his rownde table,
> One the coste of Costantyne by the clere strande3
> Has the Romaynes ryche rebuykede for euer. 2372 ff.

As a historical novel, which, in truth, it is, *Morte Arthure* passes rapidly from one scene to another of a different kind. On the battle follows the siege of Metz; on the siege, a single combat between Gawain and Sir Priamus, whose genealogy is remarkable —his father

> es of Alexandire blode, ouerlynge of kynges,
> The vncle of his ayele[6], sir Ector of Troye.

No sooner is Metz won with gallant chivalry than we are carried over the Alps with Arthur, who advances into Tuscany and halts 'in the Vertennon vale, the vines imangez.' There the 'cunningest cardinal' invites him to Rome to help the pope and to be crowned. But already fortune's wheel, which Arthur sees in a

[1] lugs out.
[2] advances in fighting trim.
[3] talk to thy mates.
[4] presently.
[5] mules.
[6] grandfather.

dreadful dream, is on the turn.   The king has passed the topmost
point of his glory, for Sir Cradok comes to tell that Mordred has
rebelled and has 'weddede Waynore.'   Forthwith the camp is
broken up, and they hurry homewards.   Mordred's allies, the
Danes, meet them at sea and a great naval battle is admirably
described.   The Danes are defeated, and, after landing, Gawain
meets Mordred in single combat and is slain.   It is the wicked
Mordred himself who in admiration declares,

> This was sir Gawayne the gude, the gladdeste of othire,
> And the graciouseste gome[1] that vndire God lyffede,
> Mane hardyeste of hande, happyeste in armes,
> And the hendeste[2] in hawle vndire heuen riche.   3876 ff.

Arthur vows that he will never rest till Gawain's slayer be slain.
So the last battle is joined.   Mordred keeps well behind his men
and changes his arms, but Arthur spies him and, after a great fight,
in which Arthur himself receives his death-wound, Mordred perishes
by Excalibur, a better death, says Arthur, than he deserved.
Arthur makes himself be carried in haste to the Isle of Avalon,
and, seeing there is no way but death, bequeaths the crown to
Constantine his cousin, orders Mordred's children to be slain and
makes a good end.

> I foregyffe all greffe, for Cristez luf of heuen,
> Ʒife Waynor hafe wele wroghte, wele hir betydde.   4324 f.

Like other poets, the author has drawn his battle scenes from
his own time.   Neilson has shown that the battle in France is
arranged like Crecy, and argues ingeniously that the sea-fight is
a poetical version of that fought off Winchelsea in 1350, while
other indications, more or less uncertain, lead him to fix the date
of the poem as 1365.

The *Pistill of Susan* is only a versified form of *The Story of
Susanna* in the Apocrypha, a story which both literature and art
show to have been very popular at the end of the Middle Ages.
The author is able to tell the tale in twenty-eight stanzas of
thirteen lines.   Like the later Holland, he discourages the reader
by the extraordinary amount of detail with which he feels it
necessary to describe the garden.   The advantage of mentioning
every tree and every vegetable of which he had ever heard is that
he is thus able to exercise more ingenuity in alliteration.   The
modern reader, however, hardly finds the same charm in

> The persile, the pasnepe, porettis[3] to preve...
> With rewe and rewbarbe, raylid on right.   107 f.

---

[1] man.   [2] most courteous.   [3] leeks.

Stanza xx, which describes the meeting of Susanna and her husband after she has been condemned, illustrates the versification and, if its form in the earliest (the Vernon) MS, of about 1380, be compared with that in the latest (the Ingilby), first published in Amours's edition for the Scottish Text Society and dating from about the middle of the fifteenth century, it will at once be clear how much change in a literary work may take place in a comparatively short time after the date of its composition. The Ingilby manuscript, though later than the Vernon and more corrupt, has, if Huchoun was a Scot, preserved the dialect better.

VERNON.

Heo fel doun flat in the flore, hir feere when heo fond,
Carped to him kyndeli, as heo ful wel couthe:
'I wis I wraththed the neuere, at my witand,
Neither in word ne in werk, in elde ne in ȝouthe.'
Heo keuered up on hir kneos, and cussed his hand:
'For I am dampned, I ne dar disparage thi mouth.'
Was neuer more serroful segge bi se nor bi sande,
Ne neuer a soriore siht bi north ne bi south;
      Tho thare
Thei toke the feteres of hire feete,
And euere he cussed that swete:
'In other world schul we mete.'
Seid he no mare.

INGILBY.

Sche fell flat to the flore whan sche hire [fere] fande,
And carped to him kyndely, as sche wele cowde:
'Sire, I wrethed ȝou neuer, at my witand,
Neythir in worde no in werke, in elde no in ȝowde.'
Sche couerde on hire knes, and kissid his hande:
'For I am dampned I ne dare disparage ȝour mowthe.'
Was neuer a sorowfuler syht be see no be sande,
Nor a dolefuler partyng be north ne be sowthe
      Als thore.
He toke the fetteres fro hir fete,
And ofte kyssyd he that swete:
'In other werld sal we mete.'
Sayde he no more.

Lastly, we come to the question of what Wyntoun meant by the *Anteris of Gawane*. Among the numerous Gawain poems the choice seems to be limited to either *The Awntyrs of Arthure* or *Golagros and Gawane*. There is, at this point, a further difficulty, for Dunbar tells us that, among the 'makaris,' death has carried away another writer on this subject:

> Clerk of Tranent eik he has tane
> That maid the anteris of Gawane.

Of Clerk (or, it may be, the clerk) of Tranent we know nothing but what Dunbar tells us, so that we are not aware whether it was one of the existing poems or a lost poem of which he was the author. It is equally possible to contend that the poem referred to by Wyntoun is lost. There is no certain criterion; but, on the whole, the probability is greater that the *Awntyrs of Arthure* is the older of the two works and may, therefore, be more reasonably assigned to the poet who was, presumably, the elder.

Arthur and his court go from Carlisle to Tarn Wadling to hunt. Queen Gaynour (Guinevere) is entrusted to Gawain; and, while they are in shelter from a storm, a ghost appears to them. Gawain goes forth with drawn sword to meet the phantom, which desires to speak with the queen, and, being permitted, tells her to take warning, for this is the lost soul of her own mother, who in life had broken a vow known only to herself and Guinevere. If masses are said for her soul she may yet be saved. In reply to Gawain, the spirit forecasts that, after a victory over the Romans, his doom will fall upon Arthur—the story of *Morte Arthure*. The figure disappears, the storm is over and all return and are told of the portent. They go to Randolf's Hall to supper, and there, during supper, a lady richly arrayed brings in a knight riding on horseback. It is Galeron of Galloway, who claims to fight for his lands, which have been given to Gawain. Arthur says they have no weapons now; but, on the morrow, Galeron shall have his claim to fight allowed. There is a long combat, in which both are wounded; but, ultimately, Galeron is defeated. The king interferes, Galeron receives back his lands and Gawain receives lands in Wales instead. When they have gone back to Carlisle and the combatants have been cured of their wounds, Galeron is made a knight of the Round Table and marries the lady who brought him into the Hall. Obviously, the adventures much more properly belong to Gawain than to Arthur. The story is in two scenes, which are connected in order of time, but not otherwise. It is told in fifty-five stanzas of thirteen lines each, constructed on a complicated system of rime, as the following example will show, and retaining the old alliterative form.

There are three manuscripts which differ very widely in their forms. The best is the Thornton MS at Lincoln. The Ireland MS, preserved at Hale in Lancashire, is in a very uncouth dialect, probably that of northern Lancashire. The Douce MS in the Bodleian Library is, clearly, the work of an Englishman of the Midlands copying northern forms. Neilson, the champion of

Huchoun, has not been slow to observe that the lands of Galeron
(418 ff.) are situated where Sir Hew of Eglintoun had his estates.
The story of the *Morte Arthure* is summed up in the following
stanza (XXIII):

> A knyghte salle kenly closene the crowne,
> And at Carelyone be crownede for kynge;
> That sege salle be sesede[1] at a sesone,
> That mekille bak and barete[2] tille Ynglande sall brynge.
> Ther salle in Tuskayne be tallde of that tresone,
> Ane[3] torne home a-ȝayne for that tydynge;
> And ther salle the Rownde Tabille losse the renowne,
> Be-syde Ramessaye fulle ryghte at a rydynge;
> And at Dorsett salle dy the doghetyeste of alle.
> Gette the, sir Gawayne,
> The baldeste of Bretayne;
> For in a slake[4] thou salle be slayne,
> Swylke ferly[5] salle falle[6].

The history of *Golagros and Gawane* is more obscure, for it is
known only from a pamphlet printed in 1508 by Chepman and
Myllar, the pioneers of printing in Scotland. Like the *Awntyrs of
Arthure*, there are two parts or scenes in the story. Arthur, once
upon a time, went on pilgrimage to the Holy Land accompanied by
all the knights of the Round Table. After a long march through
desolate hills and marshes, where their food gives out, they spy a
city in the distance. Kay is sent to ask permission to enter and
buy provisions; but, finding the gate open, enters a mansion and
seizes some birds which a dwarf is roasting on a spit. At the
outcry of the dwarf a knight enters, who, finding reproaches met
with temper, knocks Kay down. Kay, returning to the king,
advises him to go elsewhere. Gawain, however, suggests that
a better-tempered messenger might be more successful, and is
himself sent and kindly received. After feasting there four days,
they go on their way, and—though the poet forgets to mention the
fact—apparently their late host was Sir Spinagros, who now acts
as guide. By and by, they see a castle built by the side of the
Rhone; and king Arthur is surprised to hear from Spinagros that
the knight of the castle pays homage to no man. Arthur vows to
change all that on his return from Palestine. When he returns, he
proceeds to besiege the castle. On four successive days champions
are chosen, who fight with little success to either side. On the
fifth day, Golagros, the knight of the castle, takes the field himself,

---

[1] seat shall be seized.　　　　[2] strife.　　　　[3] And.
[4] hollow place.　　　　[5] Such marvel.
[6] Text according to Thornton MS, S.T.S. ed.

but is defeated by Arthur's champion Gawain. As Golagros declines to own defeat, preferring death to shame, Gawain is about to kill him, when Golagros asks Gawain to come into the castle as if he had been defeated; he will take care that Gawain's honour is not scathed by his action. Golagros asks his knights whether they would prefer that their chief, if vanquished, should still rule over them, or whether they would allow him to perish. As they say that they wish him to be chief in either case, he tells them what Gawain has done, and they set out to Arthur's camp, where Spinagros explains the situation. Golagros becomes liege man to Arthur; but, after nine days' feasting, Arthur releases him from homage before he departs.

The origin of the story is known. It is a free paraphrase of the French prose romance *Perceval le Gallois* by Chrétien de Troyes, or, rather, of a continuation of it.

The writer is best in his fighting scenes, of which the combat of Gaudifer and Galiot, the first champions of Arthur and Golagros, is a fair specimen (stanza XLIV).

> Gaudifeir and Galiot, in glemand steil wedis,
> As glauis glowand on gleid[1], grymly thai ride;
> Wondir sternly thai steir on thair stent stedis
> Athir berne fra his blonk[2] borne wes that tide.
> Thai ruschit up rudly, quha sa right redis;
> Out with suerdis thai swang fra thair schalk[3] side;
> Thair-with wraithly[4] thai wirk, thai wourthy in vedis,
> Hewit on the hard steill, and hurt thame in the hide.
> Sa wondir freschly thai frekis fruschit[5] in feir,
> Throw all the harnes thai hade,
> Baith birny[6] and breist-plade,
> Thairin wappynis couth wade,
> Wit ye but weir[7].

The poem is nearly twice as long as the *Awntyrs of Arthure*, containing a hundred and five stanzas. Of its date, nothing can be said definitely; for, without several manuscripts, we can know nothing of the tradition of the text. Its forms are more archaic than those of *Wallace*; but there is so large a proportion of traditional tags (necessitated by the alliteration) in the romances that this argument is not very conclusive; nor is there satisfactory proof that the *Awntyrs of Arthure* and *Golagros and Gawane*, though their vocabulary is often similar, are by the same hand.

One Scottish romance on the rival story survives. The Charlemagne cycle is represented by the quaint and amusing tale of

---

[1] swords glowing on coals. [2] horse. [3] *schalk* is probably corrupt.
[4] angrily. [5] men crashed together. [6] coat of mail.
[7] without doubt.

Rauf Coilȝear. The plot turns upon Charles finding a night's lodging incognito in the house of Ralph, the charcoal-burner. The king has lost his way and his suite in a storm. The scene is laid in the neighbourhood of Paris; but the whole story savours far more of Scotland than of France. The 'wickit wedderis amang thay myrk Montanis' ill agree with the surroundings of Paris. Rauf is a plain-spoken man and has his own views on many things, including good manners. He finds the king in the snow and gives him a hearty invitation to spend the night, but tells him that thanks are as yet unnecessary (stanza VII):

> 'Na, thank me not ouir airlie, for dreid that we threip[1],
> For I haue seruit the ȝit of lytill thing to ruse[2];
> For nouther hes thow had of me fyre, drink, nor meit,
> Nor nane vther eismentis for trauellouris behuse[3];
> Bot, micht we bring this harberie this nicht weill to heip
> That we micht with ressoun baith thus excuse;
> To-morne on the morning, quhen thow sall on leip,
> Pryse at the parting, how that thow dois;
> For first to lofe and syne to lak, Peter! it is schame.'
> The king said: 'In gude fay,
> Schir, it is suith that ȝe say.'
> Into sic talk fell thay
> Quhill thay war neir hame.

When they arrive at the hut, Rauf would have his guest enter before him. The guest wishes to give Rauf precedence, but Rauf

> said: 'Thow art vncourtes, that sall I warrand.'
> He tyt the King be the nek, twa part in tene[4];
> 'Gif thow at bidding suld be boun or obeysand,
> And gif thow of Courtasie couth, thow hes forȝet it clene.' 122 ff.

Rauf asks the king to take his wife Gyliane in to supper, and the king would again yield him precedence, but Rauf regards his ill manners as requiring stronger measures and hits him a blow under the ear that brings him to the ground. With true politeness, Rauf waits till his guest has finished his meal before he asks who he is. 'One of the queen's attendants, Wymond of the wardrobe,' says Charles, and offers to help to dispose of Rauf's charcoal at court. Rauf does not know where the court lies and does not like going where he is unknown, but is told that the king and queen are keeping Yule at Paris and Rauf need only ask for Wymond. The king spends a comfortable night, and, next day, offers to pay for his good cheer, but is told that even were he of 'Charlis cumpany, Chief king of Cheualry' payment would be refused. The following day, Rauf, taking Wymond at his

---

[1] quarrel. [2] praise.
[3] Plural of 'behoof' for sake of rime. [4] anger.

word, carries his charcoal in panniers to the court. The king had remembered his promise and had sent Roland out to fetch to the king whoever came that way. Roland orders Rauf to 'cast the creillis fra the Capill, and gang to the king'; but Rauf is not to break his promise to bring charcoal and offers to fight the knight in all his panoply, though he has but 'ane auld buklair and ane roustie brand,' and, as they are both busy to-day, challenges him to combat on the morrow. The king asks Roland whether he has done his command, and, finding that he has not brought Rauf, is annoyed. Rauf leaves his horse with the porter and passes into the court to look for Wymond, and, when he sees the king, recognises him as Wymond, though his clothes are different. Rauf is much disconcerted to think how he had treated the king; but Charles dubs him a knight, and appoints him Marshal of France.

The sole authority for the tale is a unique copy, printed by Lekpreuik at St Andrews in 1572 and now in the Advocates' Library, Edinburgh. But, as Gavin Douglas and Dunbar both refer to the story, it must have been well known by the end of the fifteenth century. Amours points out that its vocabulary is closely similar to that of *Golagros and Gawane*. It is almost a parody on the old romances; but the tale has plenty of movement and, what is lacking in the other romances, plenty of humour.

Along with it, Gavin Douglas mentions two other popular tales :

> I saw Raf Coilzear with his thrawin brow,
> Craibit Johne the Reif and auld Cowkeywis sow.
> *Palice of Honour*, p. 65 (Small).

John the Reeve, who is also mentioned by Dunbar, is printed in Laing's *Select Remains of the Ancient Popular Poetry of Scotland*, but is clearly an English work. The tale of Colkelbie's sow, also printed in the same work, is as clearly Scottish. The authority for it is the Bannatyne manuscript which was written in 1568. Colkelbie is in Stewarton in Ayrshire. Colkelbie (in Scotland the farmer or laird is, usually, called by the name of his estate) sells a sow for three pence. The first penny fell into a lake but was found by a woman who bought a pig wherewith to make a feast. But the pig escaped, and became a mighty boar. Near Paris, Colkelbie meets an old blind man who is being led by a beautiful damsel called Adria, finds a substitute, and carries off the damsel after giving the blind man the second penny. Adria grows up under the care of Colkelbie's wife and is ultimately married to his son Flannislie. This son is made a squire of the body-guard by the king of France and receives a grant of land which is called

Flandria (Flanders), from the names of Flannislie and Adria. With the third penny, Colkelbie, in Scotland apparently, buys twenty-four eggs to give at the baptism of the son of his neighbour Blerblowan. The mother of the child rejects the eggs, and Colkelbie gives them to one of his domestics, who raises from them such a stock of poultry that, in fifteen years, he is able to give a thousand pounds to his godson, who, ultimately, becomes immensely rich.

The story is divided into three parts, the metre of the first differing from that of the two others. From the numerous references to it, the story was obviously very popular, but it makes a sorry end to the old romances.

Of the other literature of this period, the *Lives of the Saints* and the *Chronicles*, there is not much to be said. The *Lives of the Saints*, which are contained in a single MS in the Cambridge University Library, extend to over 33,500 lines of the short couplet used by Barbour, to whom they have, no doubt incorrectly, been attributed. The MS is not the original and it would be difficult to locate their origin definitely by the language alone. But it is, I think, clear that they were intended for an Aberdeen audience. The lives, as a whole, are derived from the *Golden Legend* or the *Lives of the Fathers*, though, occasionally, other sources were employed; but two local saints Machar (Mauricius) and Ninian are included. Ninian, whose shrine was at Whithorn in Galloway, was a well known saint, but St Machar's reputation was purely local. His life was obviously compiled from local tradition and was inserted where it stands in the MS for local reasons. St Nicholas, a saint whose cult is very widely spread, is the patron saint of the great church of New Aberdeen, the city on the Dee; and it would only have occurred to a person with local knowledge to insert after the life of Nicholas the life of Machar, the patron saint of Old Aberdeen on the Don.

> Bot befor vthyr I wald fayne
> & I had cunnyng set my mayne
> sume thing to say of Sanct Moryse,
> that in his tym was ware and wis
> & in the erd of sic renown
> & als in hewine sa hye patron,
> of Aberden in the cite
> thru haly life was wont to be.   7 ff.

It is not clear whether all the lives are by the same author, though most authorities regard them as being so. The writer professes to be an old man, no longer equal to the duties of the

church. The date for the life of Ninian, at any rate, is clearly fixed
by a tale of how St Ninian saved a knight who had been betrayed
to the English, 'a ferly that in my tyme befel' (816); while, later,
he says (941):

> This wes done but lessinge
> Quhene Sir Davi Bruys ves kinge.

Besides the Aberdeen saints, knowledge of the north is postulated
by the story of John Balormy, born 'in Elgyn of Murrefe,' who,
having the 'worm in his shank' and knee, travelled on horseback
all the way to Whithorn, 'twa hundre mylis of Milavay,' and was
cured by St Ninian.

But the Scots of the fourteenth and fifteenth centuries did not
spend all their leisure in hearing and reading romances or the
lives of saints. They had an equal, or, if we may judge from the
number of extant manuscripts, a greater, interest in the chroniclers
of the past. With the earliest of these and, in some respects, the
most important of them we have but little to do, for they do
not write in the Scottish tongue. *Scalacronica* was compiled in
Norman-French by Sir Thomas Gray, of Heton in Northumberland,
while a prisoner in the hands of the Scots at Edinburgh, in 1355.
The valiant knight, ancestor of families still distinguished on the
Border, finding time hang heavy on his hands, put together from
the best sources at his disposal a chronicle from the beginning of
the world to his own time. For the period of the wars of independence it is a first-hand authority and, as the work of a man of
affairs, whose 'hands had often kept his head,' it has a value
distinct from that of the monkish chronicles. The next in order
of these records is *Scotichronicon*, the joint work of John of
Fordun and his continuator Walter Bower or Bowmaker, abbot of
Inchcolm in the Firth of Forth. Except for occasional quotations,
the work (in fourteen books) is entirely in Latin. The first five
books and some part of the sixth were completed by John of
Fordun, between 1384 and 1387, for he mentions that he had lately
received a genealogy from bishop Wardlaw, cardinal and legate,
and we know that bishop Wardlaw held those titles only during
those years. Fordun is generally said to have died in 1385, the
year in which his continuator tells us he himself was born. Of
Fordun, we know nothing save what is told us in various manuscripts of his works. He probably was born at Fordoun, in Kincar-
dineshire, whence he derives his name; and the statement in the
Black Book of Paisley, now in the British Museum, that he was
capellanus ecclesiae Aberdonensis, which is generally interpreted

'a chantry priest in the cathedral of Aberdeen,' is probable enough. If so, he was not only a contemporary but also a fellow citizen of Barbour. Fordun, undoubtedly, took great pains in collecting his materials by visiting monasteries in England and even in Ireland where chronicles were to be found. Unfortunately, he was able to complete his work only as far as the death of David I in 1153. The material with which his continuator worked was largely collected by Fordun. But Bower was a much less competent person than his predecessor. He was engaged upon the chronicle between 1441 and 1449, and brought down the history to the death of James I in 1437. He is garrulous, irrelevant and inaccurate. He interpolates passages into the part completed by Fordun, and he makes every important occurrence an excuse for a long winded moral discourse. When he has occasion to relate the unfortunate matrimonial experiences of David II, he feels it necessary to discuss the proper method of choosing a wife and to illustrate the problem with at least six passages from the Bible, and several more from Aristotle and the Christian fathers. He is able to fill the next chapter with rules for the proper management of a wife, illustrated by quotations from Solomon, St Paul, Varro and Valerius Maximus. Nearly two folio pages are required to state the unpleasant things to which a wicked woman is compared. Among these is the serpent, and this leads to an excursus on the serpent and two more chapters on the wicked woman:

> Till horsis fote thou never traist,
> Till hondis tooth, no womans faith. xiv. 32 f.

A single shorter chapter exhausts the good qualities of the female sex, and Bower is then able to return to Margaret Logie and the death of king David II. Even that patient age found the *taediosa prolixitas* of the abbot of Inchcolm more than it could endure, and he and others spent their time in making shorter manuals out of this vast and undigested mass.

Andrew of Wyntoun, who wrote his chronicle in Barbour's couplet and in the Scottish tongue, was an older contemporary of Walter Bower. He died an old man soon after 1420. Of him, as of the other contemporary chroniclers, we know little except that he was the head of St Serf's priory in Lochleven, and a canon regular of St Andrews, which, in 1413, became the site of the first university founded in Scotland. The name of his work, *The Orygynale Cronykil*, only means that he went back to the beginning of things, as do the others. Wyntoun surpasses them only in beginning with a book on the history of angels.

Naturally, the early part is derived mostly from the Bible, and *The Cronykil* has no historical value except for Scotland, and for Scotland only from Malcolm Canmore onwards, its value increasing as the author approaches his own time. For Robert the Bruce, he not only refers to Barbour but quotes nearly three hundred lines of *The Bruce verbatim*—thus being the earliest, and a very valuable, authority for Barbour's text. In the last two books, he also incorporates a long chronicle, the author of which he says he did not know. From the historical point of view, these chroniclers altogether perverted the early chronology of Scottish affairs. The iron of Edward I had sunk deep into the Scottish soul, and it was necessary, at all costs, to show that Scotland had a list of kings extending backwards far beyond anything that England could boast. This it was easy to achieve by making the Scottish and Pictish dynasties successive instead of contemporary, and patching awkward flaws by creating a few more kings when necessary. That the Scots might not be charged with being usurpers, it was necessary to allege that they were in Scotland before the Picts. History was thus turned upside down. Apart from the national interests which were involved, the controversy was exactly like that which raged between Oxford and Cambridge in the sixteenth century as to the date of their foundations, and it led to the same tampering with evidence. Wyntoun has no claims to the name of poet. He is a chronicler, and would himself have been surprised to be found in the company of the 'makaris.'

It was at the instance of 'Schir Iohne of Wemys' that he compiled his chronicle. The original scheme was for seven books, but the work was, later, extended to nine.

Wyntoun would not have been the child of his age and training did not the early part of his history contain many marvels. We hear how Gedell-Glaiss, the son of Sir Newill, came out of Scythia and married Scota, Pharaoh's daughter. Being, naturally, unpopular with the Egyptian nobility, he then emigrated to Spain and founded the race which, in later days, appeared in Ireland and Scotland. It is interesting to learn that Wyntoun identified Gaelic and Basque, part of the Scottish stock remaining behind in Spain,

> And Scottis thai spek hallely,
> And ar callyt Nawarry. II, 853 f.

And Simon Brek it was that first brought the Coronation Stone from Spain to Ireland. The exact date before the Christian era is given for all these important events.

When Wyntoun arrives at the Christian dispensation and the era of the saints, it is only natural that he should dwell with satisfaction on the achievements of St Serf, to whom his own priory was dedicated. St Serf was the 'kyngis sone off Kanaan,' who, leaving the kingdom to his younger brother, passed through Alexandria, Constantinople and Rome. Hence, after he had been seven years pope, his guiding angel conducted him through France. He then took ship, arrived in the Firth of Forth and was advised by St Adamnan to pass into Fife. Ultimately, after difficulties with the Pictish king, he founded a church at Culross, and then passed to the 'Inche of Lowchlewyn.' That he should raise the dead and cast out devils was to be expected. A thief stole his pet lamb and ate it. Taxed with the crime by the saint he denied it, but was speedily convicted, for 'the schype thar bletyt in hys wayme[1].' Wyntoun tells, not without sympathy, the story of that 'Duk of Frissis,' who, with one foot already in the baptismal font, halted to enquire whether more of his kindred were in hell or heaven. The bishop of those days could have but one answer, whereupon the duke said

> Withe thai he cheyssit[2] hym to duel,
> And said he dowtyt for to be
> Reprewit wnkynde gif that he
> Sulde withedraw hym in to deide[3]
> Fra his kyn til ane wncouthe leide[4],
> Til strangeris fra his awyn kytht,
> Qwhar he was nwrist and bred wp withe,
> Qwhar neuir nane was of his kyn,
> Aulde na ȝonge, mare na myn,
> That neuir was blenkyt withe that blayme.
> '[*Abrenuncio*] for thi that schayme,'
> He said, and of the fant he tuk
> His fute, and hail he thar forsuyk
> Cristyndome euir for to ta[5],
> For til his freyndis he walde ga
> Withe thaim stedfastly to duell
> Euirmare in the pyne of hel[6].

Good churchman as Wyntoun is, he is not slow to tell of wickedness in high places and duly relates the story of pope Joan, with the curious addition

> Scho was Inglis of nacion
> Richt willy of condicion
> A burges douchtyr and his ayre
> Prewe, pleyssande and richt fayr;
> Thai callit hir fadyr Hob of Lyne[7].

---

[1] v, 5230, Cotton MS, S.T.S. [2] chose.
[3] in death.   [4] a strange people.   [5] take.
[6] v, 5780 ff., Cotton MS, S.T.S.   [7] vi, 465, Cotton MS, S.T.S.

In this book (chap. 18) he also tells the most famous of all his stories—Macbeth and the weird sisters, and the interview between Malcolm and Macduff. But Wyntoun renders Macbeth more justice than other writers,

> 3it in his tyme thar wes plente
> Off gold and siluer, catall and fee[1].
> He wes in iustice rycht lauchfull,
> And till his liegis rycht awfull[2].

Birnam wood comes to Dunsinane, and Macbeth, fleeing across the Mounth, is slain 'in to the wod of Lumfanane[3].'

With all his credulity, Wyntoun, in the later part of his chronicle, is a most valuable source for the history of his country. To him and to Fordun we are indebted for most of our knowledge of early Scotland, since little documentary evidence of that period survived the wreck that was wrought by Edward I.

---

[1] sheep.　　　[2] Wemyss MS, 1929 ff., S.T.S.　　　[3] *Ibid.* 2310.

CHAPTER VI

JOHN GOWER

In spite of the progress which had been made in English literature by the middle of the fourteenth century, it still remained uncertain how far the cultured classes were prepared to accept English as an instrument of expression for the higher kinds of literature. With this uncertainty was bound up the question whether, out of all the provincial varieties which had existed during the Middle English period, a generally accepted literary form of English could arise—something which would stand towards the English dialects generally in the same relation that Dante's *volgare illustre, cardinale e cortigiano* held towards the dialects of Italy. Writers such as Robert of Gloucester and Robert of Brunne had addressed themselves distinctly to those who were unable to read French easily, and to whom even the new English of the day was difficult, because so much interlarded with French. They made occasional protests against the abnormal condition of things under which English, instead of being the speech of the whole nation, was degraded to the position of a language for the unlearned, but they hardly seem to have conceived that their labours should aim at removing this anomaly. It is true that a considerable amount of English verse had been produced which aimed at representing in the vulgar tongue the contents of the continental romances, and, consequently, may be supposed to have made an appeal to a more or less aristocratic audience. But we find little that suggests court influence in those English translations of French romances which abounded in the thirteenth and four-teenth centuries. Their tendency is towards a popular rather than a genuinely artistic verse form; and, when finally a school arose which worked to some extent on artistic principles, it was characterised more or less by a reversion to the old rule of alliteration. This carried with it a good deal of archaism of language; so that, notwithstanding the high poetical merit of such works as *Pearl* and *Sir Gawayne and the Grene Knight*, it was not possible that

they should form the basis of a poetical development which should
reconcile English and French tastes in literature. To accomplish
this reconciliation was pre-eminently the task of Chaucer, who,
however, in genius and in culture was so far in advance of his
generation that he can hardly be regarded as, in any sense, typical.
The mere fact that he alone of the poets of his time was capable
of being vitally influenced by Italian literature, by Dante and
Boccaccio, is enough to remove him from the common level.
If we desire to set before ourselves a picture of what we may,
perhaps, call the normal development of English literature in its
progress towards general acceptance, we ought rather, perhaps, to
direct our attention to the work of one who, in a certain sense,
stands by the side of Chaucer, though he is a man of talent only,
not of genius—the author of *Confessio Amantis.*

John Gower was a man of considerable literary accomplishments,
and, though not very deeply read, he was possessed of most of the
information which passed current as learning. He was master of
three languages for the purpose of literary expression, and he
continued to use French and Latin side by side with English even
in the last years of the century. As a man of culture, his attitude
towards English was at first one of suspicion, and, indeed, of rejection.
There is no evidence that he wrote his French ballades in the
earlier period of his career; but, unquestionably, his first work of
considerable extent was in French, the recently recovered *Speculum
Meditantis* or *Mirour de l'Omme.* His next venture was in Latin
elegiacs ; and it was not till nearly the last decade of the century
that, encouraged, perhaps, by the example of Chaucer, he adopted
English as his vehicle of literary expression. To the end, he was
probably doubtful whether a poet ought to trust to his English
works for a permanent reputation.

Gower was undoubtedly of a Kentish family : the arms on
his tomb are the same as those of Sir Robert Gower of Brabourne.
Some documents which have been cited to prove that John Gower
was a landowner in Kent probably refer to another person; but one
instrument, which undoubtedly has reference to the poet, describes
him as 'Esquier de Kent,' and it may be affirmed with certainty
that he was a layman. There is no evidence to prove that he led
the life of a country gentleman, but he was certainly a man of
some wealth, and was the owner of at least two manors, one in
Norfolk and the other in Suffolk, which, however, he leased to
others. It seems probable that, for the most part, he resided in
London, and he was personally known both to Richard II and to

the family of John of Gaunt. For some years in the latter part of his life he resided in lodgings assigned to him within the Priory of St Mary Overes, Southwark, of which house he was a liberal benefactor. He died at an advanced age in the year 1408, having lost his eyesight some years before this, and was buried in a magnificent tomb with a recumbent effigy, in the church of the Priory, now St Saviour's, Southwark, where the tomb is still to be seen, though not in its original state nor quite in its original position. He had been married in 1398, while living in the Priory, to one Agnes Groundolf, who survived him, but there are some indications in his early French work that the author had had a wife before this. That he was acquainted with Chaucer we know on good evidence. In May 1378, Chaucer, on leaving England for Italy, appointed Gower and another to act for him under a general power of attorney during his absence. A few years later, Chaucer addressed his *Troilus and Criseyde* to Gower and Strode, to be criticised and corrected where need was,

> O moral Gower, this book I directe
> To thee, and to thee, philosophical Strode,
> To vouchen sauf, ther nede is, to correcte,
> Of your benignetes and zeles gode.

Finally, Gower, in *Confessio Amantis*, pays a tribute to Chaucer as a poet of love in the lines which he puts into the mouth of Venus,

> And gret wel Chaucer, whan ye mete,
> As mi disciple and mi poete:
> For in the floures of his youthe
> In sondri wise, as he wel couthe,
> Of ditees and of songes glade,
> The whiche he for mi sake made,
> The lond fulfild is overal:
> Wherof to him in special
> Above alle othre I am most holde, etc.
>
> *Conf. Am.* viii, 2941* ff.

These lines were omitted in the later forms of the text, and upon this fact, combined with a supposed reference to Gower in the *Canterbury Tales*, as the author of immoral stories, has been founded the notion of a bitter quarrel between the two poets. But of this there is no sufficient evidence. The omission of the greeting to Chaucer may be plausibly explained on grounds connected with the mechanical circumstances of the revision of *Confessio Amantis*; and Chaucer's reference is, apparently, of a humorous character, the author of the not very decent tales of the miller, the reeve and the merchant taking advantage of his opportunity to reprove the 'moral Gower' for selecting improper subjects.

The development of Gower's political opinions may be traced in his writings, and especially in the successive alterations which he made in the text of *Vox Clamantis* and *Confessio Amantis*, as years went on and the situation changed. When *Vox Clamantis* was first written, no blame whatever was attached to the youthful king, who, at the time of the Peasants' rising, was only in his fifteenth year. In the earlier version of the poem, as now recovered from the Dublin and Hatfield MSS, we have, 'The boy himself is blameless, but his councillors are not without fault....If the king were of mature age, he would redress the balance of justice' (VI, 555* ff.), and again, 'I pray God to preserve my young king, and let him live long and see good days....O king, mayest thou ever hold thy sceptre with honour and triumph, as Augustus did at Rome....O flower of boyhood, according to thy worthiness I wish thee prosperity' (VI, 1167* ff.). In the later version of the first passage we have, written over erasure in the author's own copies, 'The king, an undisciplined youth, neglects the moral acts, by which he might grow from a boy to a man.... What he desires is desired also by his youthful companions; he enters upon the road, and they follow him....Older men too give way to him for gain, and pervert the justice of the king's court' (VI, 555 ff.). And the second passage runs as follows (in effect): 'The king is honoured above all, so long as his acts are good, but if the king is avaricious and proud, the people is grieved. Not all that a king desires is expedient for him: he has a charge laid upon him, and must maintain law and do justice. O king, do away with the evils of thy reign, restore the laws and banish crime: let thy people be subject to thee for love and not for fear' (VI, 1159 ff.). These alterations were evidently made while the king was still young, but at a time when he was regarded as fully responsible for the government. In 1390, when *Confessio Amantis* was first completed, and when the author's summary of his three principal works, which was appended to it, may be supposed to have been first written, the innocence of the king as regards the events of the year 1381 is still carefully asserted, and, from the manner in which the king is spoken of in the first edition of *Confessio Amantis* itself, both at the beginning and at the end of the poem, we know that the author had not yet abandoned his hope that the king, who even then was hardly more than three and twenty, might prove to be endowed with those qualities of justice and mercy which were necessary for a successful reign (VIII, 2970* ff.). Very soon, however, he saw reason to abandon these hopes; within a year, he composed an alternative version of his epilogue, in which his prayers for the king were changed into prayers for the good government of the land; and, finally, in 1392 or 1393, instead of the lines in the prologue in which reference was made to the king's suggestion of the work, he inserted others in which the book was said to have been written for England's sake, and was presented not to the king, but to his cousin Henry of Lancaster, to whose person the author had already transferred some of the hopes and aspirations which had previously centred in the king. It is probable that these changes were made in a few copies only, which either remained in the hands of the author, like the Fairfax MS, in which we can trace the actual process of the change, made by erasure and substitution of leaves, or were written for presentation to Henry himself, as is probably the case with the Stafford MS. By far the larger number of existing copies are of the earlier form. Gradually, Gower's spirit became more and more embittered, as the king's self-indulgence and arbitrary rule more and more belied his hopes of reformation; and in the final edition of his note upon his works, written after the fall of Richard, he omits all mention of the early events of the reign and of the king's youth and innocence, and represents *Vox Clamantis* as dealing generally with the evils of the time, for which the king is held primarily responsible by reason of his injustice and cruelty. Finally, in *Cronica Tripertita* the misfortunes which have overtaken Richard II are shown to be the natural consequences of a course of evil government and treachery, and in the English stanzas addressed to Henry IV the author's ideal of a king, as one who above all things should promote peace at home and abroad, is set forth with the enthusiasm of one who, after long waiting, at length sees his hopes for his country fulfilled.

The literary work of Gower is represented chiefly by those three books upon which the head of his effigy rests in St Saviour's Church, the French *Speculum Meditantis* (or *Speculum Hominis*, as it was originally called), the Latin *Vox Clamantis*, and the English *Confessio Amantis*. Let us first observe what he tells us himself of these works, in the Latin note already referred to, which is found, with variations, in most of the manuscripts:

Since every man is bound to impart to others in proportion as he has himself received from God, John Gower, desiring in some measure to lighten the account of his stewardship, while yet there was time, with regard to those mental gifts which God had given him, amid his labours and in his leisure composed three books for the information and instruction of others, in the form which follows.

The first book, written in the French language, is divided into ten parts, and, treating of vices and of virtues, as also of the various conditions of men in the world, endeavours rightly to teach the way by which the sinner who has trespassed ought to return to the knowledge of his Creator. And the title of this book is *Speculum Meditantis*[1].

The second book, metrically composed in the Latin language, treats of the various misfortunes which happened in England in the time of king Richard II, whence not only the nobles and commons of the realm suffered great evils, but the cruel king himself, falling from on high by his own evil doings, was at length hurled into the pit which he dug himself[2]. And the name of this volume is *Vox Clamantis*.

The third book, which was written in the English language in honour of his most valorous lord Henry of Lancaster, then earl of Derby[3], marks out the times from the reign of Nebuchadnezzar until now, in accordance with the prophecy of Daniel on the changes of the kingdoms of this world. It treats, also, in accordance with Aristotle, of the matters in which king Alexander was instructed by his discipline, both for the governance of himself and for other ends. But the chief matter of the book is founded upon love, and the infatuated passions of lovers. And the name appropriated to this work is *Confessio Amantis*.

The author conceives, then, of his literary work as essentially didactic in character, and of himself as fulfilling a mission in making use, for the benefit of his own generation, of the gifts which he has received. This, of course, was a quite usual standpoint. It was a didactic age, and Gower was fully in sympathy with the prevailing tendency to edification; but his books, on the whole, have a somewhat higher literary quality than might be supposed from his description of them.

The French work is placed first of these three books by the author, and, no doubt, it came first in the order of time. It contains evidence, however, that this was not his first literary essay, for he speaks in it of earlier poems of a light and amorous kind, the composition of which he now regrets[4]. It is not necessary to suppose that these *fols ditz d'amours* are identical with the *Cinkante Balades* which, near the close of his life, he dedicated to Henry IV. The passage referred to seems to speak of something lighter and in a more lyrical vein.

[1] In the first edition of this statement, the title is *Speculum Hominis*, corresponding to the French form *Mirour de l'Omme*.

[2] In the earlier form of the statement (1390), the author speaks of the insurrection made by the serfs against the nobles and gentry of the kingdom, and takes occasion to free the king from all blame by reason of his tender age. The form which is given above is, in fact, a reference to the later politics of the reign, rather than to the period dealt with in *Vox Clamantis*.

[3] In the earlier form 'at the instance of his lord...King Richard the second.'

[4] *Mirour de l'Omme*, 27,337 ff.

Speculum Meditantis has come down to us in a single copy, under the French title *Mirour de l'Omme.* For several centuries it disappeared from view and was supposed to have perished. 'Of the *Speculum Meditantis...*no trace remains,' wrote Courthope in the year 1895[1]. But in that very year a copy, slightly imperfect, was discovered in the Cambridge University Library, to which it had lately come by the sale of a private library ; and, though it bears no author's name, it has been identified with certainty by its correspondence with the author's description of his work, and by comparison of the style and substance with those of Gower's other works[2].

In this, the first of the three principal works, we have in its most systematic, and, consequently, its least attractive, form, the material which forms the groundwork also of the others. It is, in fact, a combination in one scheme of all the principal kinds of moral composition which were current in that age, the *Somme des Vices et des Vertus,* the *États des hommes,* and the metrical summary of Scripture history and legend. The scheme is of a very ambitious character. It is intended to cover the whole field of man's religious and moral nature, to set forth the purposes of Providence in dealing with him, to describe the various degrees of society and the faults specially charge-able to each class of men and, finally, to explain the method which should be followed by man in order to reconcile himself to the God whom he has offended by his sin. The author shows a certain amount of ingenuity in combining all this in a single scheme : he does not merely reproduce the current form of treat-ment, but aspires to a certain degree of literary unity, which distinguishes his work from that of writers like the author of the *Manuel des Pechiez.* Such works as this last were intended for practical purposes : Gower's poem aspires to be a work of literary art, however little we may be disposed to allow it that title. The following is the account which William of Wadington gives of his design at the beginning of the *Manuel des Pechiez* (the original of Robert of Brunne's *Handlyng Synne*), which, it must be remem-bered, has the form of a poem.

May the power of the Holy Spirit aid 'us to set forth the matters with regard to which a man should make his confession, and also in what manner

[1] *Hist. of English Poetry,* i, p. 308.
[2] See Macaulay's edition of Gower, Vol. i, pp. xxxiv—xli, and lxviii—lxxi. Previous enquirers had been misled by the expectation that the book, if found, would bear the title *Speculum Meditantis,* not sufficiently observing that this title was adopted long after its first production.

it should be made....First we will tell of the true faith, which is the foundation of our law....Then we will set down the commandments which all ought to keep; then the seven mortal sins, whence so many evils arise....Then you will find, if you please, the seven sacraments of holy Church....Then you will find a sermon on fear and how you ought to feel fear and love. You will then find a book on Confession which will be proper for everyone.

All this is strictly practical, and there is no attempt at artistic structure. Gower's work more nearly resembles such compositions as those of the Reclus de Moiliens, written at the end of the twelfth century in the same twelve-line stanza as he uses; but the *Mirour de l'Omme* is far more comprehensive, as well as more systematic, than the *Charité* or the *Miserere* of the Reclus. In his review of the estates of men, however, and especially in his manner of addressing the representatives of the various classes, when accusing them of their faults, Gower's work often strikingly resembles these well-known French compositions, with which, as well as with the *Vers de la Mort* of Hélinand de Froidmont, written in the same metre, he must, of course, have been acquainted. We may reasonably assume that the *Miserere* of the Reclus de Moiliens was one of Gower's principal models both of style and versification.

The general scheme of the *Mirour de l'Omme* is as follows.

Sin, the cause of all evils, is a daughter of the Devil, who, upon her, has engendered Death. Death and Sin, then intermarrying, have produced the seven deadly Vices; and the Devil sends Sin and her seven daughters into the world to defeat the designs of Providence for the salvation of Man. Temptation is sent as a messenger to Man, who is invited to meet the Devil and his council. He comes ; and the Devil, Sin and the World successively address him with promises. The Flesh of Man consents to be ruled by them, but the Soul expostulates with the Flesh, who is thus resolved upon a course which will ruin them both. The Flesh wavers, but is unable to give up the promised delights, until the Soul informs her of Death, who has been concealed from her view, and calls in Reason and Fear to convince her. The Flesh is terrified and brought back to Reason by Conscience, and thus the design of the Devil and Sin is, for the time, frustrated (1—750). Sin, thereupon, makes marriages between all her daughters and the World, so that offspring may be produced by means of which Man may be overcome. They all go in procession to the wedding. Each in turn is taken in marriage by the World, and by each he has five daughters, all of whom are described at length. The daughters of Pride, for example, are Hypocrisy, Vain Glory, Arrogance, Avantance, Disobedience, and so with the rest (751—9720).

They all make a violent attack upon Man, and he surrenders himself to them (9721—10,032). Reason and Conscience pray to God for assistance, and seven Virtues, the contraries of the Vices, are given in marriage to Reason, each of whom has five daughters, described, of course, in detail, as in the case of the Vices and their progeny (10,033—18,372).

A strife ensues for the conquest of Man. To decide who has gained the victory up to the present time, the author undertakes to examine the whole of human society from the court of Rome downwards; but he declares his opinion in advance that Sin has almost wholly prevailed (18,373—18,420).

Every estate of Man is passed in review and condemned; all have been corrupted and all throw the blame on the world (or the age) (18,421—26,604). The poet addresses the world, and asks whence comes this evil. Is it from earth, water, air or fire? From none of these, for all these in themselves are good. It is from Man that all the evils of the age arise. Man is a microcosm, an abridgment of the world, and, when he transgresses, all the elements are disturbed. On the other hand the good and just man can command the powers of the material world, as the saints have always done by miracles. Every man, therefore, ought to desire to repent of his sin and turn to God, so that the world may be amended. The author confesses himself as great a sinner as any man, but he trusts in the mercy of Jesus Christ. But how can he escape from his sins, how can he dare to come before God? Only by the help of Mary, Maid and Mother, who will intercede for him if he can obtain her favour (26,605—27,468). Therefore, before finishing his task, he will tell of her birth, her life and her death; and, upon this, he relates the whole story of the Virgin, including the Gospel narrative generally, and ending with her assumption, and concludes, as we have the book, with praises addressed to her under the various names by which she is called (27,469—29,945).

This, it will be seen, is a literary work with a due connection of parts, and not a mere string of sermons. At the same time it must be said that the descriptions of vices and virtues are of such inordinate length that the effect of unity is almost completely lost, and the book becomes tiresome to read. We are wearied also by the accumulation of texts and authorities, and by the unqualified character of the moral judgments. The author of the book shows little sense of proportion and little or no dramatic power.

In the invention of his allegory and in the method by which the various parts of his work are combined, Gower displays some originality. The style is uniformly respectable, though very monotonous. There are a few stories, but they are not told in much detail and are much inferior in interest to those of *Confessio Amantis*. Yet the work is not without some poetical merit. Every now and then we have a touch of description or a graceful image, which proves that the writer is not merely a moralist, but also, to some extent, a poet. The priest who neglects his early morning service is reminded of the example of the lark, who, rising early, mounts circling upward and pours forth from his little throat a service of praise to God. Again, Praise is like the bee that flies over the meadows in the sunshine, gathering that which is sweet and fragrant, but avoiding all evil odours. The robe of Conscience is like a cloud with ever-changing hues. Devotion is like the sea-shell, which opens to the dew of heaven, and thus conceives the fair, white pearl—an idea neither true to nature nor original, but gracefully expressed. Other descriptions also have merit, as, for example, that of the procession of the Vices to their wedding.

The most remarkable feature of the style, however, is the mastery which the writer displays over the language and the verse. The rhythm is not exactly that which properly belongs to French verse: it betrays its English origin by the fact that, though strictly syllabic, and, in that respect, far more correct than most of the French verse written in England, it is, nevertheless, also to some extent an accent verse, wanting in that comparative evenness of stress on accented and unaccented syllables alike which characterises French verse.

The author of the *Mirour* usually proceeds on the English principle of alternate strong and weak stress corresponding mainly to the accentual value of the syllables. Thus, when Gower quotes from Hélinand's *Vers de la Mort*, the original French lines,

> *Tex me couve dessous ses dras,*
> *Qui quide estre tous fors et sains,*

become, in Gower's Anglo-French,

> *Car tiel me couve soubz ses dras,*
> *Q'assetz quide estre fortz et seins;*

and the difference here is characteristic generally of the difference between French and English verse rhythm.

This is a matter of some importance in connection with the development of the highly artificial English metre employed by Chaucer, and also by Gower and Occleve, which depended precisely upon this kind of combination of the French syllabic principle with the English accent principle—a combination which, though occasionally effected earlier, was so alien to English traditions that it could not survive the changes caused in the literary language by the loss of weak inflectional syllables; and, therefore, in the fifteenth century, English metre, for a time, practically collapsed. In Chaucer's metre we see only the final results of the French influence; in the case of Gower the process by which the transition took place from the couplets of *Handlyng Synne* to those of *Confessio Amantis* is clearly exhibited.

As regards matter, the most valuable part of the *Mirour de l'Omme* is that which contains the review of the various classes of society, whence interesting information may often be drawn to illustrate the social condition of the people. This is especially the case as regards city life in London, with which the author is evidently familiar; and he describes for us meetings of city dames at the wine-shops, the various devices of shopkeepers to attract custom and to cheat their customers, and the scandalous adulteration of food and drink. The extravagance of merchants, the discontent and luxury of labourers, and the corruption of the law-courts are all vigorously denounced; and the church, in the opinion of our author, is in need of reform from the top to the bottom. Gower's picture is not relieved by any such pleasing exception as the parish priest of the *Canterbury Tales*.

The material which we find in the *Mirour de l'Omme* is, to a great extent, utilised again, and, in particular, the account given of the various classes of society is substantially repeated, in Gower's next work, the Latin *Vox Clamantis*. Here, however, a great social and political event is made the text for his criticism of society. The Peasants' rising of 1381 was, to some extent, a fulfilment of the prophecies contained in the *Mirour*, and it naturally made a strong impression upon Gower, whose native county was deeply affected, and who must have been a witness of some of its scenes. The poem is in Latin elegiac couplets, and extends to about ten thousand lines. The first book, about one-fifth of the whole, contains a graphic account of the insurrection, under a more or less allegorical form, which conveys a strong impression of the horror and alarm of the well-to-do classes. There is an artistic contrast between the beautiful and peaceful scene which is described at the opening of the work, and the vague horrors by which the landscape is afterwards darkened. The description of these events, especially so far as it deals with what took place in London, is the most interesting portion of the work; but it is quite possible, nevertheless, that this may have been an afterthought. The remainder is independent of it, and the second book begins in a style which suggests that, originally, it stood nearer to the beginning of the work. Moreover, in one manuscript[1] the whole of the first book is actually omitted, and no mention at all of the Peasants' rising occurs. In any case, the main substance of *Vox Clamantis* is an indictment of human society, the corruptions of which are said to be the cause of all the evils of the world. The picture which appears in several manuscripts of the author aiming his arrows at the world fairly represents its scope. The doctrine of the *Mirour* that Man is a microcosm, the evil and disorder of which affects the whole constitution of the elements, while the goodness of Man enables him to subdue the material world, is found again here; and the orders of men are examined and condemned much in the same way, except that the political portion is more fully and earnestly dwelt upon. Of the gradual development of Gower's political feelings we have already said something.

There is no need to dwell much upon the poetical style of Gower's Latin poems. Judged by the medieval standard, *Vox Clamantis* is fairly good in language and in metre, but the fact has recently been pointed out[2] that a very large number both of couplets and longer passages are borrowed by the author without acknowledgment from other writers, and that lines for which Gower has obtained credit are, in many cases, taken either from Ovid or from some medieval writer of Latin verse, as Alexander Neckam, Peter de Riga, Godfrey of Viterbo, or the author of *Speculum Stultorum*, passages of six or eight lines being often appropriated in this manner with little or no change. It is certain that Gower could write very fair Latin verse, due allowance being made for medieval licences, but we must be cautious in giving him credit for any particular passage. In the mean time we may observe that his contemporary account of the Peasants' rising has some historical importance; that the development of his political opinions, as seen in the successive revisions of *Vox Clamantis*, is of interest in connection with the general circumstances of the reign of Richard II; and that the description of social customs, and, particularly, of matters connected with the city of London, confirms the account given in the *Mirour*.

---

[1] Laud 719.
[2] See Macaulay's Gower, Vol. IV, p. xxxii, and the notes *passim*.

As regards the motives which determined Gower to the composition of a book in English, we have his own statement in the first edition of the book itself, that, on a certain occasion, when he was in a boat upon the Thames near London, he met the royal barge, and was invited by the king to enter it; that, in the conversation which ensued, it was suggested to him that he should write some new book, to be presented to the king; and that he thereupon adopted the resolution of composing a poem in English, which should combine pleasure and instruction, upon the subject of love.

It is not necessary, however, to assume that this incident, which was put forward by the author as a reason for the presentation of his book to Richard, was actually the determining factor of his decision to write in English. The years which followed the composition of *Vox Clamantis*, assuming it to have been produced about 1382, were a period of hitherto unexampled productiveness in English poetry. Chaucer, at this time, had attained almost to the full measure of his powers, and the successive production of *Troilus and Criseyde*, partly addressed to Gower himself, about 1383, and of *The Legend of Good Women*, about 1386, must have supplied a stimulus of the very strongest kind, not only by way of recommending the use of the English language, but also in suggesting some modification of the strictly didactic tone which Gower had hitherto taken in his larger works. The statement that to Gower's *Confessio Amantis* Chaucer owed the idea of a connected series of tales is quite without foundation. *The Legend of Good Women* certainly preceded *Confessio Amantis*, which bears distinct marks of its influence, and in *The Legend of Good Women* we have already a series of tales set in a certain framework, though the framework is slight, and no conversation connects the tales. Even if we suppose Chaucer to have been unacquainted with Boccaccio's prose, a supposition for which there is certainly some ground, he was fully capable of evolving the scheme of *The Canterbury Tales* without the assistance of Gower. On the other hand the influence of Chaucer must certainly have been very strong in regard to Gower's English work, which was probably composed in the years between 1386 and 1390, the latter year being the date of the completion of the first edition of the poem.

The most noteworthy point of *Confessio Amantis*, as compared with Gower's former works, is the partial renunciation by the author of his didactic purpose. He does, indeed, indulge

himself in a prologue, in which he reviews the condition of the
human race; but, at the beginning of the first book, he announces
the discovery that his powers are not equal to the task of setting
the world to rights :

> It stant noght in my sufficance
> So grete thinges to compasse,
> Bot I mot lete it overpasse
> And treten upon other thinges.

He avows, therefore, that, from this day forth, he intends to change
the style of his writings, and to deal with a subject which is of
universal interest, namely love. At the same time, he will not
wholly renounce his function of teaching, for love is a matter in
which men need very much guidance, but, at least, he will treat of
the subject in such a way as to entertain as well as instruct : the
book is to be

> betwen the tweie,
> Somwhat of lust, somwhat of lore.

Hence, though the form may suggest instruction, yet the mode
of treatment is to be popular, that is to say, the work is to consist
largely of stories. Accordingly, we have in *Confessio Amantis*
more than a hundred stories of varying length and of every kind
of origin, told in a simple and pleasing style by one who clearly
had a gift for story-telling, though without the dramatic humour
which makes Chaucer's stories unique in the literature of his time.
The framework, too, in which these stories are set, is pleasing.

The Lover, that is to say the author himself, is one who
has been long in the service of love, but without reward, and
is now of years which almost unfit him for such service.
Wandering forth into a wood in the month of May he feels
despair and wishes for death. The god and the goddess of love
appear to him; but the god passes him by with an angry look,
casting, at the same time, a fiery lance which pierces his heart.
The goddess remains, and to her he makes his complaint that he
has served long and received no wages. She frowns upon him,
and desires to know what service it is that he has done, and what
malady oppresses him. He professes readiness to reply, but she
enjoins upon him first a confession to be made to her priest Genius,
who, if he is satisfied, will give him absolution, and she will then
consider his case. Accordingly, Genius is summoned and Venus
disappears. The Lover, after some preliminary conversation, is
examined with regard to his sins against love, the examination
being arranged under the usual heading of the seven deadly sins

and their subordinate vices. The subdivision which we find in
the earlier books of *Confessio Amantis* is the same as that
which we have already encountered in Gower's *Mirour*: each sin is
regarded as having five principal offshoots; but, in the latter
half of the work, this regularity of subdivision is, to a great
extent, abandoned. In the case of each of the subordinate vices
the confessor sets forth the nature of the fault, and, at the
request of the Lover, illustrates his meaning by a story or by a
series of stories. In each case, after explanation of the nature
of the vice, a special application is made to the case of love, and
the stories illustrate either the general definition or this special
application, or both, no very clear line being drawn in many cases
between the two. The Lover, meanwhile, when he has at last been
made to understand the nature of the fault generally and also its
particular application to love, makes his confession or denial as
regards his love, and is further instructed or rebuked by the
confessor. By the general plan, one book should have been
devoted to each of the seven principal sins, Pride, Envy, Anger,
Sloth, Avarice, Gluttony and Lechery; but an additional book is
interpolated between the last two, dealing with quite irrelevant
matters, and, in general, there is much irregularity of plan in the
last four books, by which the unity of construction is seriously
marred. The ordinary conduct of the work may be illustrated
by a short summary of the second book, the subject of which is
Envy.

The first of the brood of Envy is Sorrow for another's joy. The
Lover confesses that he is often guilty of this in regard to his rivals,
and he is reproved by the tale of Acis and Galatea. He accepts
the rebuke and promises to offend no more. The second vice under
this head is Joy for another's grief. To this, too, the Lover pleads
guilty, and the odious character of the vice is illustrated by the
story of the traveller and the angel, in which one man preferred
to lose an eye in order that his fellow might lose both. The third
is Detraction, and here, too, the Lover admits that he has been in
some measure guilty. When he sees lovers come about his mistress
with false tales, he is sometimes moved to tell her the worst that he
knows of them. The confessor reproves him. By the Lover's own
account, his lady is wise and wary, and there is no need to tell her
these tales: moreover, she will like him the less for being envious.
The vice of Detraction is then illustrated by the tale of Constance,
who long suffered from envious backbiting, but whose love at length
prevailed. Then, again, there is the story of Demetrius and Perseus,

in which Perseus brought his brother to death by false accusations, but suffered punishment himself at last. The confessor passes then to the fourth vice, named False Semblant. When Envy desires to deceive, she employs False Semblant as her messenger. The Lover admits here, too, that he is guilty, but only in matters which concern his mistress. He thinks himself justified in gaining the confidence of her other lovers by an appearance of friendship, and using the knowledge which he thus obtains to hinder their designs. The confessor reproves him, and cites the case of the Lombards in the city, who feign that which is not, and take from Englishmen the profit of their own land. He then relates the tale of Hercules and Deianira, and how Nessus deceived her and destroyed him at last by False Semblant. Yet there is a fifth vice born of Envy, and that is Supplantation. The Lover declares that here he is guiltless in act, though guilty in his thought and desire. If he had the power, he would supplant others in the love of his lady. The confessor warns him that thought as well as act is sin, and convinces him of the heinousness of this particular crime by a series of short examples, Agamemnon and Achilles, Diomede and Troilus, Amphitryon and Geta, and also by the longer tale of the False Bachelor. This evil is worst when Pride and Envy are joined together, as when pope Celestine was supplanted by Boniface; and this tale also is told at length. The Lover, convinced of the evil of Envy, desires a remedy, and the confessor reminds him that vices are destroyed by their contraries, and the contrary to Envy is Charity. To illustrate this virtue the tale is told of Constantine, who, by showing mercy, obtained mercy. The Lover vows to eschew Envy, and asks that penance may be inflicted for that which he has done amiss.

In the other books, the scheme is somewhat similar, and, at length, in the eighth the confession is brought to a close, and the Lover demands his absolution. The confessor advises him to abandon love and to set himself under the rule of reason. He, strongly protesting, presents a petition to Venus, who, in answer, consents to relieve him, though perhaps not in the way that he desires. She speaks of his age and counsels him to make a *beau retret*, and he grows cold for sorrow of heart and lies swooning on the ground. Then he sees the god of love, and, with him, a great company of former lovers arrayed in sundry bands under the guidance of Youth and Eld. Youth takes no heed of him; but those who follow Eld entreat for him with Venus, and all the lovers press round to see. At length Cupid comes towards him and draws forth the fiery lance with which he had formerly pierced the Lover's heart; and Venus anoints the wound with a cooling ointment and gives him a mirror in which his features are reflected. Reason returns to him, and he becomes sober and sound. Venus, laughing, asks him what love is, and he replies with confusion that he knows not, and prays to be excused from attendance upon her. He obtains his absolution, and Venus bids him stay no more in her court, but go 'wher moral vertu dwelleth,' where the books are which men say that he has written; and so she bids him adieu and departs. He stands for a while amazed, and then takes his way softly homewards.

The plan of the work is not ill conceived; but, unfortunately, it is carried out without a due regard to proportion in its parts, and its unity is very seriously impaired by digressions which have nothing to do with the subject of the book. After the prologue, the first four books are conducted in a comparatively orderly manner, though the discussion on the lawfulness of war in the third can hardly be regarded as necessary, and the account of the discovery of useful arts in the fourth is too slightly connected with the subject. In the fifth book, however, a casual reference to Greek mythology is made the peg on which to hang a dissertation of twelve hundred lines on the religions of the world, while, in the sixth book, the discussion of Sorcery, with the stories first of Ulysses and Telegonus and then of Nectanabus, can hardly be regarded as a justifiable extension of the subject of Gluttony. Worse than this, the tale of Nectanabus is used as a pretext for bringing in as a diversion a summary of all earthly learning, the supposed instructions of Aristotle to Alexander, which fills up the whole of the seventh book[1]. The most important part of this is the treatise on Politics, under five heads, illustrated by many interesting stories, which occupies nearly four thousand lines. To this part of his work, which is absolutely irrelevant to the main subject, the author evidently attached great importance; and it is, in fact, another lecture aimed at the king, at whose suggestion the book was written, the author being unable to keep himself from improving the occasion. This proceeding, together with the great extension which has been given to Avarice in the fifth book, has the effect of almost entirely anticipating the proper contents of the eighth book. Nothing remains to be spoken of there except Incest, with reference to which the tale of Apollonius of Tyre is

---

[1] The statement, often repeated, that Gower is largely indebted to the *Secretum Secretorum* in this seventh book is quite inaccurate; very little is, in fact, drawn from this source. The *Trésor* of Brunetto Latini is a much more important authority.

told, and this, after all, has no sufficient bearing upon the subject to justify its inordinate length. It may justly be remarked, also, that the representation of the priest of Venus is full of absurd incongruities, which reach their climax, perhaps, when he is made to denounce Venus herself as a false goddess. In general, the characters of the moralist and of the high-priest of love are very awkwardly combined in his person, and of this fact the author shows himself conscious in several passages, as I, 237 ff. and VI, 1421 ff. The quasi-religious treatment of the subject was, no doubt, in accordance with the taste of the age, and there is a certain charm of quaintness both in this and in the gravity with which morality is applied to the case of love, though this application is often very forced. It must be admitted, also, that the general plan of the poem shows distinct originality, and, apart from the digressions and irrelevancies which have been noted, it is carried through with some success. The idea of combining a variety of stories in a single framework, with the object of illustrating moral truths, had become familiar in the literature of western Europe chiefly through a series of books which were all more or less of Oriental origin. Of these, the most important were the legend of Barlaam and Josaphat, the romance of the Seven Sages in its various forms and *Disciplina Clericalis*. With these, Gower, as we know, was acquainted, and also, doubtless, with various examples of the attempt to utilise such stories for definitely religious purposes in such edifying compositions as those of William of Wadington and Robert of Brunne. Moreover, Chaucer, in his *Legend of Good Women,* had already produced a series of stories in an allegorical framework, though the setting was rather slight and the work was left unfinished. The influence of Chaucer's work is apparent in the opening and concluding scenes of *Confessio Amantis,* and some suggestions were also derived from the *Roman de la Rose,* in which Genius is the priest of Nature, who makes her confession to him. But no previous writer, either in English or in any other modern language, had versified so large and various a collection of stories, or had devised so ingenious and elaborate a scheme of combination.

As regards the stories themselves, there is, of course, no pretence of originality in substance. They are taken from very various places, from Ovid (much the most frequent source), from the Bible, from Valerius Maximus, Statius, Benoît de Sainte More, Guido delle Colonne, Godfrey of Viterbo, Brunetto Latini, Nicholas Trivet, the *Roman des Sept Sages, Vita Barlaam et Josaphat,*

Historia Alexandri and so on[1]. Gower's style of narration is simple and clear; in telling a story he is neither tedious nor apt to digress. To find fault with him because he is lacking in humorous appreciation of character is to judge him by altogether too high a standard. He is not on a level with Chaucer, but he is distinctly above the level of most of the other story-tellers of his time, and it may even be said that he is sometimes superior to Chaucer himself in the arrangement of his incidents and in the steadiness with which he pursues the plot of his story. Gower is by no means a slavish follower of his authorities, the proportions and arrangement of his stories are usually his own, and they often show good judgment. Moreover, he not seldom gives a fresh turn to a well-known story, as in the Bible instances of Jephthah and Saul, or makes a pretty addition to it, as in the case of the tales from Ovid of Narcissus or of Acis and Galatea. His gift of clear and interesting narrative was, undoubtedly, the merit which most appealed to the popular taste of the day, and the plainness of the style was rather an advantage than a drawback.

The stories, however, have also poetical qualities. Force and picturesqueness cannot be denied to the story of Medea, with its description of the summer sun blazing down upon the glistening sea and upon the returning hero, and flashing from the golden fleece at his side a signal of success to Medea in her watch-tower, as she prays for her chosen knight. Still less can we refuse to recognise the poetical power of the later phases of the same story—first, the midnight rovings of Medea in search of enchantments (v, 3962 ff.), and again later, when the charms are set in action (4059 ff.), a passage of extraordinary picturesqueness. The tales of Mundus and Paulina and of Alboin and Rosemund, in the first book, are excellently told; and, in the second, the story of the False Bachelor and the legend of Constantine, in the latter of which the author has greatly improved upon his materials; while, in the third book, the tale of Canace is most pathetically rendered, far better than by Ovid. The fourth, which is altogether of special excellence, gives us Rosiphelee, Phyllis and the very poetically told tale of Ceix and Alceone; the fifth has Jason and Medea, a most admirable example of sustained narrative, the oriental story of Adrian and Bardus and the well-told romance of Tereus and Philomela. In the seventh, we find the Biblical story of Gideon

---

[1] Gower does not seem in any instance to have been indebted to *Gesta Romanorum*.

well rendered, the rape of Lucrece and the tale of Virginia. The long story of Apollonius, in the eighth book, is not one of Gower's happiest efforts, though it is often taken as a sample of his style owing to the connection with Shakespeare's *Pericles*. His natural taste for simplicity sometimes stands him in good stead, as in the description of the tears of Lucrece for her husband, and the reviving beauty of her face when he appears (VII, 4830 ff.), a passage in which he may safely challenge comparison with Chaucer. The ease of his more colloquial utterances, and the finished style of some of the more formal passages, are equally remarkable. As examples of the second quality we may cite the reflections of the emperor Constantine (II, 3243 ff.), the letters of Canace (III, 279 ff.) and of Penelope (IV, 157 ff.), the prayer of Cephalus (IV, 3197 ff.) and the epitaphs of Iphis (IV, 3674) and of Thaise (VIII, 1533 ff.).

In addition to the merits of the stories we must acknowledge a certain attractiveness in the setting of them. The conversation which connects the stories is distinguished by colloquial ease, and is frequently of an interesting kind. The Lover often engages the sympathy of the reader, and there is another character always in the background in whom we may reasonably be interested, that of the lady whom he serves. Gower, who was quite capable of appreciating the delicacy and refinement which ideal love requires, has here set before us a figure which is both attractive and human, a charming embodiment of womanly grace and refinement.

Passing from the substance of the poem to the language and versification, we remark, first, that the language used is, practically, the same as that of Chaucer, and that there is every reason to attribute this identity to the development, apart from the individual influence of either poet, of a cultured form of English speech which, in the higher ranks of society, took the place of the French that had so long been used as the language of literature and of polite society. This is not the place to discuss the development of modern English literary speech ; what we have to say in relation to Gower is that, by the purity and simplicity of his style, he earned the right to stand beside Chaucer as a standard authority for this language. *Sui temporis lucerna habebatur ad docte scribendum in lingua vulgari*, as Bale remarks; and it is worth noting that, in the syntax of Ben Jonson's *English Grammar*, Gower is cited as an authority more often than any other writer. It may be observed that, by Morsbach's test of a comparison with contemporary London documents, both Chaucer and Gower are shown to be more conservative of the full forms of inflection than the popular speech, and Gower is, in this respect, apparently less modern than Chaucer. He adopted a system of spelling which is more careful and consistent than that of most other Middle English authors, and, in general, he seems to have been something of a purist in matters of language.

With regard to versification, the most marked feature of Gower's verse is its great regularity and the extent to which inflectional endings are utilised for metrical purposes. We have here what we might have expected from the author's French verse, very great syllabic accuracy and a very regular beat, an almost complete combination of the accentual with the syllabic principle. As an indication of the extent of this regularity, it may be mentioned that in the whole of *Confessio Amantis*, which contains more than thirty-three thousand four-accent lines, there are no examples of the omission, so frequent in Chaucer, of the first unaccented syllable. Displacement of the natural accent of words and the slurring over of light syllables are far less frequent with Gower than with Chaucer, and in purity of rime, also, he is somewhat more strict. The result of Gower's syllabic accuracy is, no doubt, a certain monotony of rhythm in his verse; but, on the other hand, the author is careful so to distribute his pauses as not to emphasise the rime unduly. He runs on freely from one couplet to another, breaking the couplet more often than not in places where a distinct pause occurs, and especially at the end of a paragraph, so that the couplet arrangement is subordinated distinctly, as it is also by Chaucer, to the continuity of the narrative. The five-accent line is written by Gower in stanzas only, as in the *Supplication* of the eighth book and in the English poem addressed to Henry IV. In these it is a marked success, showing the same technical skill that we note elsewhere, with more variety of rhythm and a certain stately dignity which can hardly appear in the short couplet.

After *Confessio Amantis*, which seems to have assumed its final form in 1393, 'the sextenthe yer of King Richard,' Gower produced some minor Latin poems treating of the political evils of the times; and then, on the eve of his own marriage, he added, as a kind of appendix to *Confessio Amantis*, a series of eighteen French ballades on the virtue of the married state. After the fall of Richard II he produced three more poetical works, again in three different languages. In English, he wrote the poem already referred to, *In Praise of Peace (Carmen de pacis commendacione)* in fifty-five seven-line stanzas. In French, we have the series of ballades commonly known as *Cinkante Balades*, dealing with love according to the conventions of the age, but often in a graceful and poetical fashion. These may have been written earlier, but they were put together in their present form, as the author says, to furnish entertainment to the court of king Henry IV, and were dedicated to the king in two introductory ballades. It is clear that the feelings expressed are, for the most part, impersonal; sometimes the lover speaks and sometimes the lady, and the poems are evidently adapted to a diversity of circumstances. As poetry, they are much superior to those on marriage, and if they had been written in English, they would doubtless have been recognised as an interesting and valuable addition to the literature of the time. In Latin, the author sets forth his final view of contemporary history and politics in the *Cronica Tripertita*, a poem in leonine hexameters, in which the events of the last twelve years of the reign of Richard II are narrated, and the causes of his deposition set forth, as seen from the point of view of an earnest supporter of the Lancastrian party. As the title implies, it is in three parts, the first dealing with the events of the year 1387, and the proceedings of the appellants, the second with the year 1397, when Richard at length took vengeance on his opponents and the third with the deposition of Richard II and the accession of Henry IV. This work has no poetical merits, but a certain amount of historical interest attaches to it. Some minor Latin poems, including an epistle addressed to the king, also belong to this final period of Gower's literary life. Either in the first or the second year of the reign of Henry IV he became blind and ceased to write, as he himself tells us; and in the epistle to archbishop Arundel, which is prefixed to *Vox Clamantis* in the All Souls MS (*Hanc epistolam subscriptam corde deuoto misit senex et cecus Iohannes Gower*), he touchingly dwells upon the blessing of light.

That Gower, through the purity of his English style and the easy fluency of his expression, exercised a distinct influence upon the development of the language, is undoubted, and, in the fifteenth and sixteenth centuries, he was, on this account, uncritically classed with Chaucer. He is placed with Chaucer as an equal by the author of *The Kingis Quair*, by Occleve, by Dunbar, by Skelton and even by Sidney in *The Defence of Poesie*. But, in fact, though he may fairly be joined with Chaucer as one of the authorities for standard English, his mind was essentially formed in a medieval mould, and, as regards subject and treatment, he looks backwards rather than forwards. The modern note which was struck by Chaucer is almost entirely absent here. This medievalism, however, in itself has a certain charm, and there are qualities of this kind in *Confessio Amantis* which are capable still of giving genuine pleasure to the reader, while, at the same time, we are bound to acknowledge the technical finish of the style, both in the French and in the English poems. The author had a strong feeling for correctness of language and of metre, and, at the same time, his utterance is genuinely natural and unaffected. In his way he solved the problem of combining rhetorical artifice with simplicity of expression, and, if his genius moves within somewhat narrow limits, yet, within those limits, it moves securely.

CHAPTER VII

CHAUCER

OF the date of the birth of Geoffrey Chaucer we have no direct knowledge. But indirect evidence of various kinds fixes it between 1328, when his father, John Chaucer, was still unmarried, and 1346, before which date his own statement, at the Scroope-Grosvenor suit in 1386, of his age as 'forty years or more' would place it. Within this rather wide range, selection has, further, to be guided by certain facts to be mentioned presently; and, for some time past, opinion has generally adopted, in face of some difficulties, the date 'about 1340.' John Chaucer himself was a citizen and vintner of London, the son of Robert le Chaucer, who, in 1310, was collector of the customs on wine, and who had property at Ipswich and elsewhere in Suffolk. In 1349, John was certainly married to an Agnes whose maiden surname is unknown, who survived him and, in 1367, married again : therefore, unless she was the vintner's second wife, she must have been Chaucer's mother. The father seems to have had some link of service with the royal household, and the poet was connected with it more or less all his days. Probably he was born in Thames Street, London, where his father had a house at the time of his death in 1366.

We first hear of Chaucer himself (or, at least, of a Geoffrey Chaucer who is not likely to be anyone else) in 1357, when he received a suit of livery as member of the household of Edward III's son Lionel (afterwards duke of Clarence), or of his wife Elizabeth de Burgh. Two years later, he served in France, was taken prisoner at a place called 'Retters' (alternately identified with Retiers near Rennes, and with Rethel near Reims), but was liberated on ransom by March 1360—the king subscribing £16 (= over £200 now) towards the sum paid. Seven years later, on 2 June 1367, Edward gave him an annuity of 20 marks for life, as to *dilectus valettus noster*, and he rose to be esquire at the end of next year. Meanwhile, at a time earlier than that of his own pension, on 12 September 1366, another of half the amount had been granted to Philippa Chaucer, one of the damsels of the queen's chamber : and this Philippa, beyond reasonable doubt, must have been the poet's wife. If she was born Philippa Roet or Rouet, daughter of Sir Payn Roet, a Hainault knight, and sister of Katharine Rouet or Swynford, third wife of John of Gaunt, Chaucer's undisputed patronage by 'time-honoured Lancaster' would have been a matter of course. But we do not know Philippa's parentage for certain. There is also much doubt about the family that Geoffrey and Philippa may have had. The poet directly dedicates, in 1391, his *Astrolabe* to 'little Lewis my son,' who was then ten years old ; but of this son we hear nothing more. On the other hand, chancellor Gascoigne, in the generation after Chaucer's death, speaks of Thomas Chaucer, a known man of position and wealth in the early fifteenth century, as Chaucer's son : and this Thomas took the arms of Rouet late in life, while, in 1381, John of Gaunt himself established an Elizabeth Chaucer as a nun at Barking. Beyond these facts and names nothing is known.

Of Chaucer himself—or, at least, of a Geoffrey Chaucer who, as it is very important to remember, and as has not always been remembered, may not be the same in all cases—a good many facts are preserved, though these facts are in very few cases, if any, directly connected with his literary position. By far the larger part of the information concerns grants of money, sometimes connected with the public service in war, diplomacy and civil duties. He joined the army in France again in 1369 ; and, next year, was abroad on public duty of some kind. In 1372, he was sent to Genoa to arrange for the selection of some English port as a headquarters for Genoese trade, and must have been absent for a great part of the twelvemonth between the November of that year and of the next. On St George's day 1374, he began to receive from the king a daily pitcher of wine, commuted later for money. In the following month, he leased the gatehouse of Aldgate from the corporation, and, a month later again, was made controller of customs for wool, etc., in the port of London, receiving, in this same June, an additional pension of £10 a year from John of Gaunt to himself and his wife. Wardships, forfeitures and other casualties fell to him, and, in 1377, he went on diplomatic duties to Flanders and to France. In 1378, after the death of Edward III and the accession of Richard II, it is thought that he was again in France and, later in that year, he certainly went once more to Italy, in the mission to Bernabo Visconti of Milan. These duties did not interfere with the controllership; to which another, that of the petty customs, was added in 1382, and we have record of various payments and gifts to him up to the autumn of 1386, when he sat in parliament as knight of the shire for Kent, and gave evidence in the Scroope-Grosvenor case.

Then the tide turned against him. In the triumph of the duke of Gloucester and the eclipse of Gaunt during his absence in Spain, Chaucer lost his controllership; and it would appear that, in 1387, his wife died. In May, 1388, he assigned his pensions and allowances to another person, which looks like (though it cannot be said certainly to be) a sign of financial straits in the case of a man whose party was out of favour. But the fall of Gloucester and the return of John of Gaunt brought him out of the shadow again In July 1389, he was made clerk of the works to the king at various places; and, in the next year (when, as part of his new duty, he had to do with St George's chapel, Windsor), a commissioner to maintain the banks of the Thames. This latter post he seems to have retained; the clerkship he only held for two years. On 6 September 1390, he fell twice in one day among the same thieves, and was robbed of some public money, which, however, he was excused from making good. During parts of this year and the next, he held an additional post, that of the forestership of North Petherton Park in Somerset. In 1394 he received from Richard a fresh pension of £20 (say £300) a year. But, judging by the evidence of records of advances and protections from suits for debt, he seems to have been needy. In 1398, however, he obtained an additional tun of wine a year from Richard; while that luckless prince's ouster and successor, John of Gaunt's son, added, in October 1399, forty marks to the twenty pounds, making the poet's yearly income, besides the tun of wine, equal, at least, to between £600 and £700 of our money. On the strength of this, possibly, Chaucer (who had given up the Aldgate house thirteen years before, and whose residence in the interval is unknown) took a lease of a house in the garden of St Mary's, Westminster. But he did not enjoy it for a full year, and dying (according to his tomb, which is, however, of the sixteenth century) on 25 October 1400, was buried in Westminster Abbey, in the chapel of St Benedict, thus founding Poet's Corner. That he was actually dead by the end of that year is proved by the cessation of entries as to his pensions. Almost every known incident in his life has been mentioned in this summary, for the traditions of his residence at Woodstock and of his beating a Franciscan friar in Fleet street have been given up—the latter perhaps hastily. One enigmatical incident remains—to wit, that in May 1380, one Cecilia de Chaumpaigne gave Chaucer a release *de raptu meo.* There is, however, no probability that there was anything in this case more romantic or more shocking than one of the attempts to kidnap a ward of property and marry him or her to somebody in whom the kidnapper was interested—attempts of which, curiously enough, Chaucer's own father is known to have been nearly the victim. Otherwise, 'there is namore to seyn,' so far as true history goes. And it does not seem necessary to waste space in elaborate confutation of unhistorical traditions and assertions, which, though in some cases of very early origin, never had any basis of evidence, and, in most cases, can be positively disproved. They have, for some decades, passed out of all books of the slightest authority, except as matter for refutation ; and it is questionable whether this last process itself does not lend them an injudicious survival. It will be observed, however, that, in the authentic account, as above given, while it is possible that some of its details may apply to a Geoffrey Chaucer other than the poet whom we honour, there is not one single one of them which concerns him *as a poet* at all. There are, however, one or two references in his lifetime, and a chain, unbroken for a long time, of almost extravagantly laudatory comments upon his work, starting with actual contemporaries. Though there can be little doubt that the pair met more than once, Froissart's mention of him is only in reference to diplomatic and not literary business. But Eustache Deschamps, perhaps, on the whole, the foremost poet of France in Chaucer's time, has left a ballade of the most complimentary character, though, already anticipating the French habit of looking always at French literature first, it addresses him as *grant translateur*, which, beyond doubt, he was. In a certainly contemporary work of English prose, *The Testament of Love*, which, for sheer want of careful examination, was long attributed to Chaucer and which is now decided to be the work of one Usk, who was executed in 1388 by the Gloucester faction, Chaucer is spoken of with equal admiration, and his work is largely drawn upon. Scogan, another contemporary and a correspondent of his, celebrates him ; and a far more important person than these, the poet Gower, his personal friend, has left a well-known tribute. The two principal poets of the next generation, in England, Occleve and Lydgate, were, the former certainly, the latter probably, personal friends likewise : and, while both are copious in laudation, Occleve has left us a portrait of Chaucer illuminated on the margin of one of his own MSS. Throughout the fifteenth and early sixteenth century, the chorus of praise from poets, Scottish as well as English, continues unabated and uninterrupted. Caxton, though never executing a complete edition, repeatedly prints part of the works and is followed by others ; and, towards the middle of the sixteenth century, in a passage which writers on Chaucer have generally missed, Lilius Giraldus, one of the foremost humanists of Italy, in a survey of European letters, recognises the eminence of Chaucer in English.

We must, however, now make a further advance, and turn from the 'Chaucer' who figures in records, and the 'Chaucer' who is eulogised as a poet, to that other sense of 'Chaucer' which indicates the work, not the man—the work which gained for the man the reputation and the eulogy. Uncritically accepted, and recklessly amplified during more than three centuries, it has, since the masterly investigations of Tyrwhitt in the latter part of the eighteenth century, been subjected to a process of severe thinning, on principles which will be referred to again. Of external, or rather positive, evidence of early date, we have some, but not a very great deal—and that not of the most unexceptionable kind. The help of the MSS is only partial ; for no one of them is accepted by anyone as an autograph, and no one of them contains all the pieces which the severest methods of separation have left to Chaucer. But, in two of these pieces, which themselves as wholes are undoubted, there are lists, ostensibly by the poet, of his own works, and cross-references in other places. The fullest of these— the list contained in the palinode or retraction at the end of *The Parson's Tale* and *The Canterbury Tales* generally—has, indeed, been suspected by some, apparently without any reason, except that they would rather Chaucer had not repented of things of which, as it seems to them, he had no reason to repent. But, even in case of forgery, the forger would, probably, have taken care to be correct in his attribution. This list contains *Troilus*; *The book [House] of Fame*; *The book of the XXV Ladies [Legend of Good Women]*; *The book of the Duchess*; *The book of St Valentine's day of the Parliament of Birds [Fowls]*; *The Canterbury Tales* themselves, where the repentance extends only to those that 'sounen into sinne' ; *The book of the Lion*; and many others which he cannot remember, while *Boece* is specified as requiring

no repentance. All these exist except *The book of the Lion.*
Further, in the body of the *Tales,* in the introduction to *The
Man of Law's Prologue,* Chaucer is mentioned by name with an
unmistakably autobiographical humility, whether serious or humorous; and the *Legend* is again acknowledged under the general
title of 'the Seintes Legende of Cupyde.' Now, in the *Legend*
itself, there is another list of works claimed by the author in which
Troilus, The House of Fame, The book of the Duchess [*Death of
Blanche*], *The Parliament of Fowls* and *Boece* reappear, and *The
Rose, Palamon and Arcite* and divers smaller works named and
unnamed are added. This, however, does not exhaust the list of
contemporary testimony, though it may exhaust that of Chaucer's
own definite claim to the works specified. Lydgate, besides referring
to a mysterious 'Dant in English,' which some have identified
with *The House of Fame,* specifies the *A B C, Anelida and Arcite,
The Complaint of Mars* and the *Treatise on the Astrolabe.* But
there is another witness, a certain John Shirley, who seems to
have passed his first youth when Chaucer died, and not to have
died himself till the fifteenth century was more than half over.
He has left us copies, ascribed by himself to Chaucer, of the three
poems last mentioned as ascribed also by Lydgate, and of the
minor pieces entitled *The Complaint unto Pity, The Complaint of
Venus, Fortune, Truth, Gentilesse, Lack of Steadfastness* and the
Empty Purse. The epistles (or 'envoys') to Scogan and Bukton,
the Rosemounde ballade, *The Former Age* and one or two scraps
are also definitely attributed to the poet in early MSS.

This concludes the list of what we may, without too much
presumption, call authenticated works, or at least *titles,* which
is rather different. Not all even of these were printed by
Caxton or by his immediate successors; but Caxton gave two
editions of *The Canterbury Tales,* and added others of *Troilus
and Criseyde,* of *The Parliament of Fowls,* of *The House of
Fame,* etc., confining himself to, though not reaching, the limit
of the authenticated pieces. Pynson, in 1526, outstripped this by
including *La Belle Dame sans Merci.* It was not till 1532 that
the first collected edition appeared, under the care of William
Thynne, clerk of the kitchen to Henry VIII, who was assisted
by Sir Brian Tuke, and who, apparently, took great trouble to
consult all the MSS that he could lay hold of. This volume
occupies an important position and has recently been reprinted
in facsimile. It contains thirty-five several poems enumerated in
its table of contents, with a few short pieces which seem to have

been afterthoughts, and are of no mark or likelihood. One of these is actually assigned to Gower and one to Scogan, though it contains work of Chaucer. But the rest seem to have been considered Chaucer's by Thynne, though he excuses himself by a saving phrase. They are *The Canterbury Tales, The Romaunt of the Rose, Troilus and Criseyde, The Testament and Complaint of Cresseid, The Legend of Good Women, A Goodly Ballade of Chaucer, Boethius, The Dream of Chaucer,* [*The book of the Duchess*], *The Envoy to Bukton, The Assembly* [*Parliament*] *of Fowls, The Flower of Courtesy, The Death of Pity, La Belle Dame sans Merci, Anelida and Arcite, The Assembly of Ladies,* the *Astrolabe, The Complaint of the Black Knight, A Praise of Women, The House of Fame, The Testament of Love, The Lamentation of Mary Magdalen, The Remedy of Love, The Complaints of Mars* and *Venus, The Letter of Cupid, A Ballade in Commendation of our Lady, The Cuckoo and the Nightingale, Steadfastness, Good Counsel of Chaucer, Fortune, The Envoy to Scogan, Sapience,* the *Empty Purse* and a poem on *Circumstance*.

In 1542, a new edition of Thynne's collection appeared with one piece added, *The Plowman's Tale* (a piece of Lollardy not in the least like Chaucer), and a third followed, with alterations of order, in 1550. It was not long after this that [Sir] Thomas Wilson in his *Rhetoric* (1553) declared that 'the fine courtier will speak nothing but Chaucer.' In 1561, a fresh admission of new matter was made under the guidance of John Stow, the antiquary. The new pieces were chiefly short ballades, and the like, but one very important poem of length, *The Court of Love,* appeared for the first time; and, nearly forty years later, in 1597—8, Thomas Speght, in a fresh edition thought also to represent Stow, published another notable piece, *The Flower and the Leaf,* together with a new *Chaucer's Dream,* indicating also two other things, *Jacke Upland* and Chaucer's *A B C*. There were editions in 1602 and 1687; but nothing further of importance was added till the edition begun by Urry and published after his death in 1721. Here appeared *The Tale of Gamelyn, The Pardoner and Tapster,* an account of what happened after the pilgrims had reached Canterbury, and *The Second Merchant's Tale* or *Tale of Beryn*. 'The whole dissembly' of Chaucer's works, genuine and spurious, had now appeared except a very few short pieces, probably genuine, which have recently been unearthed. The process of wholesale agglomeration was ended; but it was some time before the inevitable reaction of meticulous scrutiny and separation was to begin.

In fact, though Dryden, at the very juncture of the seventeenth and eighteenth centuries, had, on all but metrical points, done the fullest justice to Chaucer, his own imitations had rather obscured the original ; and even Spenser fared better than his predecessor. Except Dryden himself, the last intelligent enthusiasts for Chaucer, who, up to Spenser's own death, had united the suffrages of all the competent, were Sir Francis Kynaston (an eccentric and minor but true poet, whose worship took the odd form of translating *Troilus* into Latin, keeping the rime royal) and the earl of Leicester, Algernon Sidney's elder brother (the 'lord Lisle' of the Commonwealth, but no regicide), who, as Dryden himself tells us, dissuaded him from modernising out of reverence for the original. By most writers, for the greater part of a century—Addison himself being their spokesman—Chaucer was regarded as an antiquated buffoon, sometimes coarsely amusing, and a convenient pattern for coarseness worse than his own. The true restorer of Chaucer, and the founder of all intelligent study of his work, was Thomas Tyrwhitt (1730—86), fellow of Merton College, Oxford, who, in 1775, published an edition of *The Canterbury Tales* with prefatory matter, and a glossary dealing with the whole subject. Tyrwhitt had no theory to serve and no arbitrary standard to apply ; but he had a combined knowledge of classical and medieval literature then probably unequalled in Europe, a correct ear, a sense of poetry and a singularly sane judgment strengthened and directed by legal training. He did not proceed by electing certain of the works to a position of canon and determining the reprobation of others by reference to this—a proceeding itself reprobated by the best principles of law, logic and literature. He knew, doubtless, that, although *The Canterbury Tales* themselves are Chaucer's beyond all reasonable doubt, no testimony that we have, from Lydgate's onward, authenticates any particular *form* of them like an autograph MS, or a modern printed book issued by the author. He knew also, doubtless, that it cannot be safe to assume that an author, especially in such days as Chaucer's, must have rigidly observed the same standards of grammar, diction and prosody at all times of his life—that, for instance, if we did so, we should, on the evidence of one edition of *The Essay of Dramatic Poesy*, assume that Dryden preferred to put the preposition at the end of the clause, and on that of another decide that he avoided this. He, therefore, proceeded on the only sound plan—that of sifting out, first, things certainly, and then, things probably, false—of gathering first the tares according to the advice of the parable

—and so, by successive degrees, winnowing a surer and purer wheat for garnering after it had been itself threshed and cleansed from offal and impurity.

The beginning of the process was easy enough : for some things had been expressly included by Thynne in the original collection as *not* Chaucer's, and these or others were, in some cases, known, practically beyond doubt, to be the work of actual and identified persons. Such was the case with Gower's and Scogan's verses above referred to, with Lydgate's *Tale of Thebes*, etc. and with the very remarkable and beautiful *Testament of Cresseid*, which, on the clearest internal showing, could not be Chaucer's, and which had been printed earlier as the work of the Scottish poet Henryson. *The Letter of Cupid* is not only acknowledged by Occleve, but actually dated after Chaucer's death ; and *La Belle Dame sans Merci* is not only attributed in MS to Sir Richard Ros, but is adapted from Alain Chartier, who belonged to the next century. Other pieces Tyrwhitt rejected for different reasons, all valid— *Gamelyn, The Plowman's Tale*, that of *Beryn, The Pardoner and the Tapster, The Lamentation of Mary Magdalen, The Assembly of Ladies*, etc.—while he brushed away contemptuously at a sweep 'the heap of rubbish' added by Stow. He left the following verse, besides *The Canterbury Tales*, the two undoubtedly genuine prose works and *The Testament of Love* (which he had evidently not had time to examine carefully):—*The Romaunt of the Rose, Troilus and Criseyde, The Court of Love, The Complaint unto Pity, Anelida and Arcite, The Assembly [Parliament] of Fowls, The Complaint of the Black Knight* (which had not then been identified as Lydgate's), the *A B C, Chaucer's Dream, The Flower and the Leaf, The Legend of Good Women, The Complaints of Mars* and *Venus* and *The Cuckoo and the Nightingale*, with nine shorter poems. It is, however, very important to observe that, though Tyrwhitt had read all these pieces for his glossary, he did not edit their text; and, therefore, cannot be taken as vouching fully for their authenticity. It is, for instance, pretty certain that if he had so edited *The Testament of Love* he would have discovered that it was not Chaucer's, whether he did or did not discover whose it actually was.

But great as was the service which Tyrwhitt did in sweeping out of the Chaucerian treasury much, if not all, of what had no business to be there, it was still greater in respect of the principal genuine treasure, which alone he subjected to thorough critical editing. It is quite astonishing, a century and a quarter after his work, to find how far he was in advance not merely of all his predecessors in the study of Chaucer but—in one of the most important points—of many who have followed. Whether it was in consequence of Chaucer's uniquely clear understanding of English versification as shown in his predecessors, or of his setting a standard too high for his contemporaries, or merely of a tyrannous change in the language, it is certain that even his immediate successors (in some cases actually contemporary with him) failed to reproduce the harmony of his verse in the very act of imitating it, and that following generations misunderstood it altogether. Some have thought that this misunderstanding extended even to Spenser ; but, while disagreeing with them as to this, one may doubt whether Spenser's understanding of it was not more instinctive than analytic. Dryden frankly scouted the notion of Chaucer's metre being regular : though it is nearly as much so, even on Dryden's own principles, as his own. Tyrwhitt at once laid his finger on the cause of the strange delusion of nearly three centuries by pointing out what he calls 'the pronunciation of the feminine *-e*' ; and, though in following up the hint which he thus gave, he may have failed to notice some of the abnormalities of the metre (such as the presence of lines of nine syllables only) and so have patched unnecessarily here and there, these cases are very exceptional. He may not have elaborated for Chaucer a system of grammar so complete and so complex as that which has been elaborated for him by subsequent ingenuity, to amend the errors of contemporary script. But his text was based upon a considerable collation of MSS in the first place ; in the second, on an actual reading— astonishing for the time when we remember that this also had to be mostly in MS—of Chaucer's English, as well as foreign, predecessors and contemporaries ; and, in the third, on careful examination of the poems themselves with, for guide, an ear originally sensitive and subsequently well-trained. Of the result, it is enough to borrow the—in the original—rather absurd hyperbole applied earlier to Kynaston's *Troilus* in the words 'None sees Chaucer but in Kynaston.' It was hardly possible for the ordinary reader to 'see Chaucer' till he saw him in Tyrwhitt ; and in Tyrwhitt he saw him, as far as *The Canterbury Tales* were concerned, in something very like a sufficient presentment.

But, just as Chaucer himself had gone so far beyond his contemporaries in the practice of poesy, that they were unable fully to avail themselves of what he did, so Tyrwhitt was too far in advance of the English scholarship of his age for very much use to be immediately made of his labours. For some half-century, or even longer, after his first edition, little was done in regard to the text or study of Chaucer, though the researches of Sir Harris Nicolas threw much light on the facts of his life. But the increasing study of Middle English language and literature could not fail to concentrate itself on the greatest of Middle English writers ; and a succession of scholars, of whom Wright and Morris were the most remarkable among the earlier generation, and Skeat and Furnivall among the later, have devoted themselves to the subject, while, of the societies founded by the last named, the Early English Text Society is accumulating, for the first time in an accessible form, the literature which has to be compared with Chaucer, and the Chaucer Society has performed the even greater service of giving a large proportion of the MSS themselves, with *apparatus criticus* for their understanding and appreciation. Complete agreement, indeed, has not been—and, perhaps, can never be expected to be—reached on the question how far grammatical and other variables are to be left open or subjected to a norm, arrived at according to the adjuster's construing of the documents of the period ; but the differences resulting are rarely, if ever, of strictly literary importance.

Meanwhile, the process of winnowing which Tyrwhitt began has been carried out still farther: partly by the discovery of authors to whom pieces must or may be assigned rather than to Chaucer, partly by the application of grammatical or other tests of the internal kind. Thus, *The Complaint of the Black Knight* was found to be ascribed to Lydgate by Shirley, a great admirer and student, as has been said, of Chaucer himself, and, apparently, contemporary with Lydgate during all their lives. *The Cuckoo and the Nightingale*—a very agreeable early poem —was discovered by Skeat to be assigned in MS to 'Clanvowe,' who has been sufficiently identified with a Sir Thomas Clanvowe of the time. *The Testament of Love*, one of the most evidently *un*-Chaucerian of these things when examined with care, has, in the same way, turned out to be certainly (or with strong probability) the work of Thomas Usk, as has been mentioned. Two other very important and beautiful, though very late, attributions allowed by Tyrwhitt, though in the conditions specified, have also been black-marked, not for any such reason, but for alleged 'un-Chaucerism' in grammar, rime, etc., and also for such reasons as that *The Flower and the Leaf* is apparently put in the mouth of a woman and *The Court of Love* in that of a person who calls himself 'Philogenet, of Cambridge, clerk,' to which we have not any parallel elsewhere in Chaucer. These last arguments are weak; but there is no doubt that *The Flower and the Leaf* (of which no MS is now accessible) to some extent, and *The Court of Love* (of which we have a single late MS) still more, are, in linguistic character, younger than Chaucer's time, and could only be his if they had been very much rewritten. These, and the other poems excluded, will be dealt with in a later chapter.

In these exclusions, and, still more, in another to which we are coming, very great weight has been attached to some peculiarities of rime pointed out first by Henry Bradshaw, the most important of which is that Chaucer never (except in *Sir Thopas*, where it is alleged that he is now parodying the Romances) rimes a word in *-y* to a word in *-ye* throughout the pieces taken as granted for his. The value of this argument must, of course, be left to the decision of everyone of full age and average wits; for it requires no linguistic or even literary knowledge to guide the decision. To some it seems conclusive; to others not so.

It has, however, been used largely in the discussion of the last important poem assigned to Chaucer, *The Romaunt of the Rose*, and is, perhaps, here of most importance. It is not denied by anybody that Chaucer did translate this, the most famous and popular poem in all European literature for nearly three centuries. The question is whether the translation that we have—or part of it, if not the whole—is his. No general agreement has yet been reached on this point even among those who admit the validity of the rime test and other tests referred to; but most of them allow that the piece stands on a different footing from others, and most modern editions admit it to a sort of 'court of the gentiles.' The two prose works, *The Tales, The Legend, Troilus, The House of Fame*, the *A B C, The Duchess*, the three *Complaints* (*unto Pity, of Mars* and *to his Lady*), *Anelida and Arcite, The Parliament of Fowls*, and some dozen or sixteen (the number varies slightly) of minor poems ranging from a few lines to a page or so, are admitted by all. Of these, some critical account must now be given. But something must first be said on a preliminary point of importance which has occupied scholars not a little, and on which fairly satisfactory agreement has been reached: and that is the probable order of the works in composition.

It has been observed that the facts of Chaucer's life, as known, furnish us with no direct information concerning his literary work, of any kind whatsoever. But, indirectly, they, as collected, furnish us with some not unimportant information—to wit, that in his youth and early manhood he was much in France, that in early middle life he was not a little in Italy and that he apparently spent the whole of his later days in England. Now, if we take the more or less authenticated works, we shall find that they sort themselves up into three bundles more or less definitely constituted. The first consists of work either directly or pretty closely translated or imitated from the French, and couched in forms more or less French in origin—*The Romaunt of the Rose, The Complaints, The book of the Duchess*, the minor ballades, etc. The second consists of two important pieces directly traceable to the Italian originals of Boccaccio, *Troilus and Criseyde* and *The Knight's Tale*, with another scarcely less suggested by the same Italian author, *The Legend of Good Women*, and, perhaps, others still, including some of *The Canterbury Tales* besides *The Knight's*. The third includes the major and most characteristic part of *The Tales* themselves from *The Prologue* onward, which are purely and intensely English. Further, when these bundles (not too tightly tied up nor too sharply separated from each other) are surveyed, we find hardly disputable internal evidence that they succeeded each other in the order of the events of his life. The French division is not only very largely second-hand, but is full of obvious tentative experiments; the author is trying his hand, which, as yet, is an uncertain one, on metre, on language, on subject; and, though he often does well, he seldom shows the supremacy and self-confidence of mature genius. In the Italian bundle he has gained very much in these respects: we hear a voice we have not heard before and shall not hear again—the voice of an individual, if not yet a consummate, poet. But his themes are borrowed; he embroiders rather than weaves. In the third or English period all this is over. 'Here is God's plenty,' as Dryden admirably said; and the poet is the steward of the god of poets, and not the mere interpreter of some other poet. He has his own choice of subject, his own grasp of character and his own diction and plot. He is at home. And it is a significant fact that we have references to other works in *The Tales*, but none to *The Tales* in other works. We may, therefore, conclude, without pushing the classification to a perilous particularity, that it is generally sound.

We now come, without further difficulty or doubt, to those parts of the works about which there is little or no contention; only prefixing a notice of the English *Romaunt of the Rose* with full reference to the cautions given previously. For this we have but one MS (in the Hunterian collection at Glasgow) and the early printed version of Thynne. The translation is very far from complete, representing only a small part of the great original work of Guillaume de Lorris and Jean de Meun, and it is not continuous even as it is. The usual practice of modern commentators has been to break it up into three parts—A, B and C; but, by applying to this division the rime and other tests before referred to, very different results have been reached. The solution most in favour is that Chaucer may not improbably have written A, may more or less possibly have written C, but can hardly have written B, which abounds in northern forms. It is, however, certain that he actually translated this very part, inasmuch as he refers to it in *The Legend*. Whatever may be the facts in these respects, there is a general agreement of the competent that, from the literary point of view, the whole is worthy of Chaucer and of the original. Of this original, the earlier or Lorris part is one of the most beautiful works of the Middle Ages, while the second or longer part by Jean de Meun is one of the shrewdest and most characteristic. The two authors were singularly different, but their English translator, whoever he was, has shown himself equal to either requirement, after a fashion which only a consummate man of letters could display—such a man for instance as he to whom we owe both the Prioress and the Wife of Bath. The soft love allegory of the earlier part, with its lavish description and ornament, is not rendered more adequately than the sharp satire and somewhat pedantic learning of the second. The metre is that of the original —the octosyllabic couplet—which was, on the whole, the most popular literary measure of the Middle Ages in English, French and German alike, and which had been practised in England for nearly 200 years. To escape monotony and insignificance in this is difficult, especially if the couplets are kept more or less distinct, and if the full eight syllables and no more are invariably retained. The English poet has not discovered all his possibilities of variation, but he has gone far in this direction. He has also been curiously successful in sticking very closely to the matter of his original without awkwardness, and, where he amplifies, amplifying with taste. English literature up to, and even after, the time is full of translation; is, indeed, very largely made up of it. But there is no verse translation which approaches this in the combined merits of fidelity, poetry and wit. The date is very uncertain, but it must be early; some, who think the poem may all be Chaucer's, connect it with an early possible sojourn of his in the north with the household of Lionel or his wife.

There are few data for settling the respective periods of composition of the early minor poems. If *The book of the Duchess* (Blanche of Lancaster, who died in 1369) be really of the earliest—and *The Complaint unto Pity* is not usually assigned to an earlier date—Chaucer was a singularly late-writing poet. But we may, of course, suppose that his earlier work is lost, or that he devoted the whole of his leisure (it must be remembered that he was 'in the service' in various ways) to the *Rose*. On the other hand, the putting of *The Complaint of Mars* as late as 1379 depends solely upon a note by Shirley, connecting it with a court scandal between Isabel of Castille, duchess of York, and John Holland, duke of Exeter—for which there is no intrinsic evidence whatsoever. From a literary point of view one would put it much earlier. With the exception of *The Parliament of Fowls*, which has been not unreasonably connected with the marriage of Richard II to Anne of Bohemia in 1382, internal evidence of style, metrical experiment, absence of strongly original passages and the like, would place all these poems before *Troilus*, and some of them at a very early period of the poet's career, whensoever it may have begun. Of the three which usually dispute the position of actual primacy of date, *The book of the Duchess* or *The Death of Blanche* is a poem of more than 1300 lines in octosyllables, not quite so smooth as those of *The Romaunt*, but rather more adventurously split up. The matter is much patched together out of medieval commonplaces, but has touches both of pathos and picturesqueness. The much shorter *Complaint unto Pity* has, for its special interest, the first appearance in English, beyond all reasonable doubt, of the great stanza called rime royal—that is to say, the seven-lined decasyllabic stanza rimed *ababbcc*, which held the premier position for serious verse in English poetry till the Spenserian dethroned it. The third piece, Chaucer's *A B C*, is in the chief rival of rime royal, the octave *ababbcbc*. The other he probably took from the French: it is noticeable that the *A B C* (a series of stanzas to our Lady, each beginning with a different letter of the alphabet in regular order), though actually adapted from the French of Deguileville, is in a quite different metre, which may have been taken from Italian or French. And one would feel inclined to put very close to these *The Complaint of Mars* and *A Complaint to his Lady*, in which metrical exploration is pushed even further—to nine-line stanzas *aabaabbcc*

in the first, and ten-line as well as *terza rima* in the second. These
evidences of tentative work are most interesting and nearly decisive in point of earliness; but it is impossible to say that the
poetical value of any of these pieces is great.

In *Anelida and Arcite* and *The Parliament of Fowls* this
value rises very considerably. Both are written in the rime
royal—a slight anachronism of phrase as regards Chaucer, since
it is said to be derived from the use of the measure by James I
of Scotland in *The Kingis Quair*, but the only distinguishing
name for it and much the best. To this metre, as is shown from
these two poems and, still more, by *Troilus*, Chaucer had taken a
strong fancy; and he had not merely improved, if not yet quite
perfected, his mastery of it purely as metre, but had gone far to
provide himself with a poetic diction, and a power of writing
phrase, suitable to its purely metrical powers. The first named
piece is still a 'complaint'—queen Anelida bewailing the falseness
of her lover Arcite. But it escapes the cut-and-dried character
of some of the earlier work; and, in such a stanza as the following:

> Whan she shal ete, on him is so hir thoght,
> That wel unnethe of mete took she keep;
> And whan that she was to hir reste broght,
> On him she thoghte alwey till that she sleep;
> Whan he was absent, prevely she weep;
> Thus liveth fair Anelida the quene
> For fals Arcite, that did hir al this tene—

the poem acquires that full-blooded pulse of verse, the absence of
which is the fault of so much medieval poetry. That it is not,
however, very late is clear from the curious included, or concluding,
Complaint in very elaborate and varied choric form. The poem
is connected with *The Knight's Tale* in more than the name of
Arcite.

It is, thus, the inferior of *The Parliament of Fowls*. This
opens with the finest piece of pure poetry which, if the order
adopted be correct, Chaucer had yet written,

> The lyf so short, the craft so long to lerne,
> Th' assay so hard, so sharp the conquering,
> The dredful joye, that alwey slit so yerne,
> Al this mene I by love, that my feling
> Astonyeth with his wonderful worching
> So sore y-wis, that whan I on him thinke,
> Nat wot I wel wher that I wake or winke;

and it includes not a few others, concluding, like Anelida, with a
lyric, shorter and more of the song kind, 'Now welcom somer,' in
roundel form. This piece is also the first in which we meet most

of the Chaucerian qualities—the equally felicitous and felicitously blended humour and pathos, the adoption and yet transcendence of medieval commonplaces (the dream, the catalogues of trees and birds, the classical digressions and stuffings), and, above all, the faculty of composition and handling, so as to make the poem, whatever its subject, a poem, and not a mere copy of verses.

As yet, however, Chaucer had attempted nothing that much exceeded, if it exceeded at all, the limits of occasional poetry; while the experimental character, in metre especially, had distinguished his work very strongly, and some of it (probably most) had been mere translation. In the work which, in all probability, came next, part of which may have anticipated *The Parliament of Fowls*, he was still to take a ready-prepared canvas of subject, but to cover it with his own embroidery to such an extent as to make the work practically original, and he was to confine it to the metre that he had by this time thoroughly proved—the rime royal itself.

In *Troilus and Criseyde*, to which we now come, Chaucer had entirely passed his apprentice stage; indeed, it may be said that, in certain lines, he never went further, though he found new lines and carried on others which here are only seen in their beginning. The story of the Trojan prince Troilus and his love for a damsel (who, from a confused remembrance of the Homeric heroines, was successively called Briseida and Griseida or Criseida) is one of those developments of the tale of Troy which, unknown to classical tradition, grew up and were eagerly fostered in the Middle Ages. Probably first sketched in the curious and still uncertainly dated works of Dictys Cretensis and Dares Phrygius, it had been worked up into a long legend in the *Roman de Troie* of Benoît de Sainte More, a French *trouvère* of the late twelfth century; these, according to medieval habit, though with an absence of acknowledgment by no means universal or even usual, had been adapted bodily a hundred years later in the prose Latin *Hystoria Troiana* of Guido delle Colonne. On this, in turn, Boccaccio, somewhat before the middle of the fourteenth century, based his poem of *Il Filostrato* in *ottava rima*; and, from the *Filostrato*, Chaucer took the story. Not more, however, than one-third of the actual *Troilus and Criseyde* is, in any sense, translated from Boccaccio, who is never named by the English poet, though he has references to a mysterious 'Lollius.' But such points as this last cannot be dealt with here.

What really concerns us is that, in this poem, Chaucer, though still playing the part of hermit-crab—in a manner strange to modern notions, but constantly practised in medieval times and by no means unusual in Shakespeare—has quite transformed the house which he borrowed and peopled it with quite different inhabitants. This is most remarkable in the case of Pandarus: but it is hardly less so in those of Troilus and Criseyde themselves. Indeed, in this poem Chaucer has not only given us a full and finished romance, but has endowed it with what, as a rule, medieval romance conspicuously lacked—interest of character as well as of incident, and interest of drama as well as of narrative. Discussions (which need not be idle and should not be other than amicable) have been, and may be, held on the question whether Chaucer himself is not a sixteenth-seventeenth century dramatist, and a nineteenth century novelist, who happened to be born in the fourteenth century: and *Troilus* is one of the first texts which lend themselves to this discussion. The piece is somewhat too long; it has (which amounts to much the same thing) too many digressions, and (again much the same thing) the action is too seldom concentrated and 'spirited up'—there is too much talk and too little happens. But these were faults so ingrained in medieval literature that even Chaucer could not entirely get rid of them: and hardly anyone before him had got rid of them to the same extent.

And if the comparative excellence of the story be great, the positive excellence of the poetry is greater. Of the rime royal stanza the poet is now a perfect master; and, if his diction has not acquired its full suppleness and variety of application, its dignity and its facility for the purposes to which it is actually applied leave nothing whatever to be desired. A list of show passages would be out of place here; it is enough to say that nowhere, from the fine opening to the far finer close, is the medium of verse and phrase other than fully adequate to the subject and the poet's intention. It is, on the whole, the weakest point of medieval poetry, that, with subjects of the most charming kind, and frequent felicities of sentiment and imagery, the verse lacks finish, and the phrase has no concentrated fire or sweetness. In *Troilus* this ceases to be the case.

Very strong arguments, in the absence of positive evidence, would be required to make us regard a work of such maturity as early; and the tendency has been to date it about 1383. Of late, however, attempts have been made to put it six or seven years earlier, on the strength, chiefly, of a passage in the *Mirour de l'Omme*, attributed to Gower and supposed to be itself of about 1376. Here it may be enough to say that, even if the passage be certainly Gower's and certainly as early as this, it need not refer to Chaucer's *Troilus* at all, or, at any rate, to any tale of Troilus that Gower knew Chaucer to have finished. That the poet, at this time still a busy man and having many irons, literary and other, in the fire, may have been a considerable time over so long a book, even to the length of having revised it, as some think, is quite possible. That, as a whole, and as we have it, it can be other than much later than the recognised 'early' poems, is, on sound principles of literary criticism, nearly impossible; the later date suits much better than the earlier both with what followed as well as with what went before[1].

In any case, Chaucer's position and prospects as a poet on the morrow, whenever this was, of his finishing *Troilus*, are interesting to consider. He had mastered, and, to some extent, transformed, the romance. Was he to continue this? Is it fortunate that he did not? Is not a *Lancelot and Guinevere* or a *Tristram and Iseult* handled *à la Troilus* rather to be deplored as a vanished possibility? It would appear that he asked himself something like this question; and, if the usually accepted order of his works be correct, he was somewhat irresolute in answering it—at any rate for a time, if not always. It is probable that, at any rate, *The Knight's Tale*, the longest and most finished constituent of the Canterbury collection, was begun at this time. It is somewhat out of proportion and keeping with its fellows, is like *Troilus* taken from a poem of Boccaccio's and, like *Troilus*, is a romance proper, but even further carried out of its kind by story and character interest, mixture of serious and lighter treatment and brilliancy of contributory parts. It seems not improbable that the unfinished and, indeed, hardly begun *Squire's Tale*, which would have made such a brilliant pendant, is also of this time as well as *St Cecily* and, perhaps, other things. But the most considerable products of this period of hesitation are, undoubtedly, *The House of Fame* and *The Legend of Good Women*. Neither of these is complete; in fact, Chaucer is a poet of *torsi*; but each is an effort in a different and definite direction, and both are distinguished remarkably from each other, from their predecessor *Troilus*, and from *The Canterbury Tales*, which, as an entire scheme, no doubt succeeded them.

The House of Fame is one of the most puzzling of Chaucer's

---

[1] See bibliography under Tatlock.

productions. There are divers resemblances to passages in Dante ('the great poet of Itaile,' as Chaucer calls him in another place), and some have even thought that this poem may be the 'Dant in English,' otherwise unidentified, which was attributed to him by Lydgate; but perhaps this is going too far. In some respects, the piece is a reversion—in metre, to the octosyllable; in general plan, to the dream-form; and, in episode, to the promiscuous classical digression: the whole story of the *Aeneid* being most eccentrically included in the first book, while it is not till the second that the main subject begins by a mysterious and gorgeous eagle carrying the poet off, like Ganymede, but not to heaven, only to the House of Fame itself. The allegorical description of the house and of its inhabitants is brilliantly carried on through the third book, but quite abruptly cut short; and there is no hint of what the termination was to be. The main *differentia* of the poem, however, is, besides a much firmer and more varied treatment of the octosyllable, an infusion of the ironic and humorous element of infinitely greater strength than in any previous work, irresistibly suggesting the further development of the vein first broached in the character of Pandarus. Nothing before, in this respect, in English had come near the dialogue with the eagle and parts of the subsequent narrative. It failed to satisfy the writer, however; and, either because he did not find the plan congenial, or because he found the metre—once for all and for the last time even as he had improved it—too cramping for his genius, he tried another experiment in *The Legend of Good Women*, an experiment in one way, it would seem, as unsatisfactory as that of *The House of Fame*, in another, a reaching of land, firmly and finally. The existence of a double prologue to this piece, comparatively lately found out, has, of necessity, stimulated the mania for arranging and rearranging Chaucer's work; but it need not do so in the very least. The whole state of this work, if it teaches us anything, teaches us that Chaucer was a man who was as far as possible removed from the condition which labours and 'licks' at a piece of work, till it is thoroughly smooth and round, and then turns it out to fend for itself. If two of Chaucer's friends had prevailed on him to give them each an autograph copy of a poem of his, it is much more probable than not that the copies would have varied—that that 'God's plenty' of his would have manifested itself in some changes. The work itself is quite unaffected by the accident of its double proem. Whether it was really intended as a palinode for abuse of women in earlier books

may be seriously doubted ; the pretence that it was is quite like
'Chaucer's fun,' and quite like the usual fashion of ushering in
literary work with some excuse, once almost universal and still
not quite unknown.   For the actual substance—stories of famous
and unhappy dames and damsels of old, who were, like Guinevere,
'good lovers'—he had precedents in two of his favourite authors,
Ovid and Boccaccio ; and this would have been more than enough
for him.   But, in handling them, he took a metre—which we cannot
say he had never used before, because we do not know the
exact dates of the original forms of *The Knight's Tale* and other
things, but—which had been sporadically and half-accidentally
practised in Middle English to no very small extent; which had
recently been used in France, where the single decasyllabic line
had been familiar ever since the dawn of French literature proper;
and of which, as it was, he had written many hundreds at the end
of his rime royal in *Troilus* and elsewhere.   This is the great
decasyllabic or heroic couplet; the 'riding rime' (not yet 'riding,'
as *Troilus* was not yet 'royal'); the ouster of the octosyllabic as
staple of English verse ; the rival of the stanza for two centuries,
and something like the tyrant of English prosody for two more ;
and still one of the very greatest of English metres for every
purpose but the pure lyric.

The work resulting is of the greatest interest, and has been,
as a rule, rather undervalued.   Tennyson judged better when he
made it the inspiration of one of the greatest of his own early
poems.   The prologue, in whichever form we take it, is the most
personal, the most varied and, perhaps, the most complete utterance
that we have from Chaucer as far as substance goes, though it is
not his most accomplished performance as art.   He is evidently at
a sort of watershed, looking before and after—but especially after—
at his own work.   The transitions of mood, and of attention to
subject, are remarkable.   In particular, that instantaneous shifting
from grave to gay, and from the serious to the humorous, which
puzzles readers not to the English manner born, and of which he,
Shakespeare and Thackeray are the capital representatives, pervades the whole piece like the iridescence in shot silk or in certain
enamels.   The allegory of the leaf and the flower ; the presence
of the god of love and his wrath with those who treat him lightly;
the intercession of the gracious lady Alcestis ; the poet's apology
and his determination to turn into English divers classical stories
as a penance, are all mixed up with descriptions of nature,
with innocent pedantry (which, in fact, determines the fashion

of the penance or for which the penance is an excuse) and with touches of temporal colour and respect of distinguished persons. All combine to make the thing unique. And both here and in the actual legends of the martyrs of love, from Cleopatra to Hypermnestra, the immense capacities of the metre are well manifested, though not, of course, either with the range or with the perfection of *The Canterbury Tales* themselves. It is very interesting to find that in this first essay in it he has had a presentiment of its great danger—monotony—and, though he has naturally not discovered all the preservatives, he is almost naïvely observant of one—the splitting of the couplet at a paragraph's end.

Still, that he was dissatisfied is evident, not merely from the incompleteness of the actual scheme, but from off-signs of impatience and discomfort in its course. The uniformity of subject, and the mainly literary character of the treatment required, obviously weighed on him. He 'wanted life and colour,' which here he could not give or, rather, which he could have given, but which he was anxious to apply to a larger and fresher scheme, a more varied repertory, and one which, above all, would enable him not only to take his models from the actual, but often, if not always, to give manners and character and by-play, as well as fresco painting from the antique, with a mainly sentimental connection of background and subject.

That he found what he wanted in the scheme of *The Canterbury Tales*, and that, though these also are unfinished (in fact not half-finished according to their apparent design), they are one of the greatest works of literature—everybody knows. Of the genesis of the scheme itself nobody knows anything. As Dickens says, 'I thought of Mr Pickwick': so, no doubt, did Chaucer 'think of' his pilgrims. It has been suggested—and denied—that Boccaccio, so often Chaucer's immediate inspirer, was his inspirer in this case also, by the scheme and framework of *The Decameron*. It is, indeed, by no means unlikely that there was some connection; but the plan of collecting individually distinct tales, and uniting them by means of a framework of central story, was immemorial in the east; and at least one example of it had been naturalised in Europe, under many different forms, for a couple of centuries, in the shape of the collection known as *The Seven Sages*. It is not necessary to look beyond this for general suggestion; and the still universal popularity of pilgrimages provided a more special hint, the possibilities of which it certainly did not require Chaucer's genius to recognise. These fortuitous associations—masses of drift-wood kept together for a time and then separated—offer almost everything that the artist, desirous of painting character and manners on the less elaborate and more varied scale, can require. Though we have little of the kind from antiquity, Petronius shows us the germs of the method; and, since medieval literature began to become adult in Italy, it has been the commonest of the common.

To what extent Chaucer regarded it, not merely as a convenient vehicle for anything that he might take a fancy to write, but as a useful one to receive anything of the less independent kind that he had already written, is a very speculative question. But the general tendency has been to regard *The Knight's Tale*, that of the *Second Nun* and, perhaps, others, as examples of this latter process, while an interesting hypothesis has been started that the capital *Tale of Gamelyn*—which we find mixed up with Chaucer's works, but which he cannot possibly have written—may have been selected by him and laid by as the subject of rehandling into a Canterbury item. But all this is guesswork; and, perhaps, the elaborate attempts to arrange the tales in a consistent order are a little superfluous. The unquestionable incompleteness of the whole and of some of the parts, the irregular and unsystematic character of the minor prologues and framework-pieces, alike preclude the idea of a very orderly plan, worked out so far as it went in an orderly fashion. In fact, as has been hinted above, such a thing is repugnant to Chaucer's genius as manifested not merely here but everywhere.

Fortunately, however, he was able to secure a sufficient number of happy moments to draw the main part of the framework—*The Prologue*, in which the plan of the whole is sketched, the important characters delineated and the action launched—without gap or lapse. For it would be short-sighted to regard the grouping of certain figures in an undescribed batch as an incompleteness. Some writers of more methodical disposition would, probably, have proceeded from this to work out all the framework part, including, perhaps, even a termination, however much liberty they might reserve to themselves for the inset tales. But this was not Chaucer's way. There have been controversies even as to the exact number of tales that he originally promises or suggests: and the incident of the canon's yeoman shows that he might very well have reinforced his company in numbers, and have treated them to adventures of divers kinds. In fact, the unknown

deviser of *The Pardoner and the Tapster*, though what he has
produced is quite unlike Chaucer in form, has been much less
out of the spirit and general verisimilitude of the whole work
than more modern continuators. But it is most probable that
the actual frame-stuff—so much of it as is genuine (for there are
fragments of link in some MSS which are very unlikely to be
so)—was composed by its author in a very haphazard manner,
sometimes with the tale he had in his mind, sometimes to cobble
on one which he had written more or less independently. The
only clear string of connection from first to last is the pervading
personality of the host, who gives a unity of character, almost as
great as the unity of frame-story, to the whole work, inviting,
criticising, admiring, denouncing, but always keeping himself in
evidence. As to the connection of origin between individual tales
and the whole, more hazardous conjectures in things Chaucerian
have been made than that the couplet-verse pieces were all or
mostly written or rewritten directly for the work, and that those
in other metres and in prose were the adopted part of the family.
But this can never be known as a fact. What is certain is that
the couplets of *The Prologue*, which must be of the essence of the
scheme, and those of most parts of it where the couplets appear,
are the most accomplished, various, thoroughly mastered verse
that we find in Chaucer himself or in any English writer up to
his time, while they are not exceeded by any foreign model unless
it be the *terza rima* of Dante. A medium which can render, as
they are rendered here, the manners-painting of *The Prologue*,
the comic monodrama of *The Wife of Bath* and the magnificent
description of the temple of Mars, has 'handed in its proofs'
once for all.

Whether, however, it was mere impatience of steady labour on
one designed plan, or a higher artistic sense which transcended
a mere mechanical conception of unity, there can be no doubt
of the felicity of the result. Without the various subject and
quality, perhaps even without the varied metre, of the tales, the
peculiar effect of 'God's plenty' (a phrase itself so felicitous that
it may be quoted more than once) would not be produced; and
the essential congruity of the tales as a whole with the mixed
multitude supposed to tell them, would be wholly impossible.
Nothing is more remarkable than the intimate connection between the tales and *The Prologue*. They comment and complete
each other with unfailing punctuality. Not only is it of great
importance to read the corresponding portion of *The Prologue*

with each tale; not only does each tale supply, as those of the
Monk and the Prioress especially, important correction as well
as supplement; but it is hardly fantastic to say that the whole
Prologue ought to be read, or vividly remembered, before reading
each tale, in order to get its full dramatic, narrative and pictorial
effect. The sharp and obvious contrasts, such as that of *The
Knight's Tale* with the two that follow, though they illustrate
the clearness with which the greatest English men of letters
appreciated the value of the mixture of tragedy or romance with
farce or comedy, are less instructive, and, when properly appreciated, less delightful, than other contrasts of a more delicate kind.
Such is the way in which the satire of *Sir Thopas* is left to the
host to bring out; and yet others, where the art of the poet is
probably more instinctive than deliberate, such as the facts that
nobody is shocked by *The Wife of Bath's Prologue* (the interruption by the friar and summoner is of a different character), and
(still more incomprehensible to the mere modern) that nobody
is bored by *The Tale of Melibeus.* Of the humour which is so
constantly present, it will be more convenient to speak presently
in a separate passage. It cannot be missed: though it may sometimes be mistaken. The exquisite and unlaboured pathos which
accompanies it, more rarely, but not less consummately, shown,
has been acknowledged even by those who, like Matthew Arnold,
have failed to appreciate Chaucer as a whole. But, on the
nature and constitution of that variety, which has also been
insisted on, it may be desirable to say something here and at
once.

It is no exaggeration or flourish, but a sound and informing
critical and historical observation, to say that *The Canterbury
Tales* supply a miniature or even microcosm, not only of English
poetry up to their date, but of medieval literature, barring the
strictly lyrical element, and admitting a part only of the didactic,
but enlarged and enriched by additional doses, both of the personal element and of that general criticism of life which, except
in Dante, had rarely been present. The first or *Knight's Tale*
is romance on the full, if not on the longest, scale, based on
Boccaccio's *Teseide,* but worked out with Chaucer's now invariable
idiosyncrasy of handling and detail; true to the main elements
of 'fierce wars and faithful loves'; possessing much more regular
plot than most of its fellows; concentrating and giving body to
their rather loose and stock description; imbued with much more
individuality of character; and with the presence of the author not

obtruded but constantly throwing a shadow. That it is representative of romance in general may escape those who are not, as, perhaps, but a few are, thoroughly acquainted with romance at large—and especially those who do not know that the man of the twelfth, thirteenth and fourteenth centuries regarded the heroes of the Charlemagne and Arthur stories, and those of antiquity, as absolutely on a par.

With the high seriousness and variegated decoration of this romance of adventure and quality contrast the two tales that follow, one derived from a known *fabliau*, the other, possibly, original, but both of the strict *fabliau* kind—that is to say, the story of ordinary life with a preferably farcical tendency. If the morals are not above those of the time, the nature and the manners of that time—the nature and manners no longer of a poetic Utopia, localised, for the moment, in France or Britain or Greece or Rome or Jerusalem or Ind, but of the towns and villages of England— are drawn with a vividness which makes their French patterns tame. What threatens a third story of this same kind, *The Cook's Tale*, is broken off short without any explanation after about fifty lines—one MS asserting that Chaucer 'maked namore' of it. *The Man of Law's Tale*, the pathetic story of the guiltless and injured Constance, returns to a favourite romance-motive and treats it in rime royal—the most pathetic of metres—while *The Shipman* falls back on the *fabliau* and the couplet. But Chaucer was not the man to be monotonous in his variety. The next pair, *The Prioress's Tale* and Chaucer's own *Sir Thopas*, indeed, keep up the alternation of grave and gay, but keep it up in quite a different manner. Appropriately in every way, the beautiful and pathetic story of the innocent victim of Jewish ferocity is an excursion into that hagiology which was closely connected with romance, and which may even, perhaps, be regarded as one of its probable sources. But the burlesque of chivalrous adoration is not of the *fabliau* kind at all : it is parody of romance itself, or, at least, of its more foolish and more degenerate offshoots. For, be it observed, there is in Chaucer no sign whatever of hostility to, or undervaluation of, the nobler romance in any way, but, on the contrary, great and consummate practice thereof on his own part. Now, parody, as such, is absolutely natural to man, and it had been frequent in the Middle Ages, though, usually, in a somewhat rough and horseplayful form. Chaucer's is of the politest kind possible. The verse, though singsong enough, is of the smoothest variety of 'romance six' or *rime couée* (664664 *aabccb*); the hero is 'a

very parfit *carpet* knight'; it cannot be proved that, after his long
preparation, he did not actually encounter something more terrible
than buck and hare ; and it is impossible not to admire his determination to be satisfied with nobody less than the Fairy Queen to
love *par amours*. But all the weak points of the weaker romances,
such as *Torrent* and *Sir Eglamour*, are brought out as pitilessly
as politely. It is one of the minor Chaucerian problems (perhaps
of as much importance as some that have received more attention),
whether the host's outburst of wrath is directed at the thing as a
romance or as a parody of romance. It is certain that uneducated
and uncultivated people do not, as a rule, enjoy the finer irony ;
that it makes them uncomfortable and suspicious of being laughed
at themselves. And it is pretty certain that Chaucer was aware of
this point also in human nature.

Of *The Tale of Melibeus* something has been said by a hint
already. There is little doubt that, in a double way, it is meant
as a contrast not merely of grave after gay, but of good, sound,
serious stuff after perilously doubtful matter. And it is appreciated accordingly as, in the language of Tennyson's farmer,
'whot a owt to 'a said.' But the monk's experience is less happy,
and his catalogue of unfortunate princes, again strongly indebted
to Boccaccio, is interrupted and complained of, not merely by the
irrepressible and irreverent host but by the knight himself—the
pattern of courtesy and sweet reasonableness. The criticism is
curious, and the incident altogether not less so. The objection
to the histories, as too dismal for a mixed and merry company, is
not bad in itself, but a little inconsistent considering the patience
with which they had listened to the woes of Constance and the
prioress's little martyr, and were to listen (in this case without
even the sweetmeat of a happy ending) to the physician's story
of Virginia. Perhaps the explanation is meant to be that the
monk's accumulation of 'dreriment'—disaster heaped on disaster,
without sufficient detail to make each interesting—was found
oppressive: but a subtler reading may not be too subtle. Although
Chaucer's flings at ecclesiastics have been exaggerated since it
pleased the reformers to make arrows out of them, they do exist.
He had thought it well to atone for the little gibes in *The Prologue*
at the prioress's coquettishness of way and dress by the pure and
unfeigned pathos and piety of her tale. But he may have meant
to create a sense of incongruity, if not even of hypocrisy, between
the frank worldliness of the monk—his keenness for sport, his
objection to pore over books, his polite contempt of 'Austin,'

his portly person—and his display of studious and goody pessimism. At any rate, another member of the cloth, the nun's priest, restores its popularity with the famous and incomparable tale of the Cock and the Fox, known as far back as Marie de France, and, no doubt, infinitely older, but told here with the quintessence of Chaucer's humour and of his dramatic and narrative craftsmanship. There is uncertainty as to the actual order here; but the Virginia story, above referred to, comes in fairly well, and it is noticeable that the doctor, evidently a good judge of symptoms and of his patients' powers of toleration, cuts it short. After this, the ancient and grisly but powerful legend of Death and the robbers strikes a new vein—in this case of eastern origin, probably, but often worked in the Middle Ages. It comes with a sort of ironic yet avowed impropriety from the pardoner: but we could have done with more of its kind. And then we have one of the most curious of all the divisions, the long and brilliant *Wife of Bath's Prologue*, with her short, and by no means insignificant but, relatively, merely postscript-like, tale. This disproportion, and that of the prologue itself to the others, seems to have struck Chaucer, for he makes the friar comment on it; but it would be quite a mistake to found on this a theory that the length was either designed or undesigned. *Vogue la galère* seems to have been Chaucer's one motto: and he let things grow under his hand, or finished them off briefly and to scale, or abandoned them unfinished, exactly as the fancy took him. Broadly, we may say that the tales display the literary and deliberately artistic side of his genius: the prologues, the observing and dramatic side; but it will not do to push this too hard. *The Wife of Bath's Prologue*, it may be observed, gives opportunity for the display of reading which he loves, as well as for that of his more welcome knowledge of humanity: the tale is like that of Florent in Gower, but the original of neither is known.

The interruption by the friar of *The Wife of Bath's Prologue*, and a consequent wrangle between him and the summoner, lead to a pair of satiric tales, each gibing at the other's profession, which correspond to the earlier duel between the miller and reeve. The friar's is a tale of *diablerie* as well as a lampoon, and of very considerable merit; the summoner's is of the coarsest *fabliau* type with a farcically solemn admixture. There is no comment upon it; and, if *The Clerk's Tale* was really intended to follow, the contrast of its gravity, purity and pathos with the summoner's ribaldry is, no doubt, intentional. For the tale, introduced by some pleasant rallying from the host on the clerk's shyness and silence, and by a most interesting reference of the clerk's own to 'Francis Petrarch the laureate poet,' is nothing less than the famous story of Griselda, following Petrarch's own Latin rendering of Boccaccio's Italian. Some rather unwise comment has been made (in a purely modern spirit, though anticipated, as a matter of fact, by Chaucer himself) on the supposed excessive patience of the heroine. But it is improbable that Griseldas ever were, or ever will be, unduly common ; and the beauty of the piece on its own scheme and sentiment is exquisite. The indebtedness to Boccaccio is still more direct, and the *fabliau* element reappears, in *The Merchant's Tale* of January and May—with its curious fairy episode of Pluto and Proserpine. And then romance comes back in the 'half-told' tale of the squire, the 'story of Cambuscan bold' ; which Spenser did not so much continue as branch off from, as the minor romances of adventure branch off from the Arthurian centre ; of which Milton regretted the incompleteness in the famous passage just cited ; and the direct origin of which is quite unknown, though Marco Polo, the French romance of *Cléomadès* and other things may have supplied parts or hints. The romantic tone is kept up in *The Franklin's Tale* of Arviragus and Dorigen, and the squire Aurelius and the philosopher-magician, with their strange but fascinating contest of honour and generosity. This is one of the most poetical of all the tales, and specially interesting in its portrayal—side by side with an undoubted belief in actual magic—of the extent of medieval conjuring. *The Second Nun's Tale* or *Life of St Cecily* is introduced with no real link, and has, usually, been taken as one of the poet's insertions of earlier work. It has no dramatic or personal interest of connection with the general scheme ; but this is largely made up by what follows—the tale of the follies and rogueries of alchemy told by the yeoman of a certain canon, who falls in with the pilgrims at Boughton-under-Blee, and whose art and mystery is so frankly revealed by his man that he, the canon, 'flees away for very sorrow and shame.' The exposure which follows is one of the most vivid parts of the whole collection, and shows pretty clearly either that Chaucer had himself been fleeced, or that he had profited by the misfortunes of his friends in that kind. Then the host, failing to get anything out of the cook, who is in the drowsy stage of drunkenness, extracts from the manciple *The Tale of the Crow* and the reason that he became black—the whole ending with the parson's prose tale, or, rather, elaborate treatise, of penitence and the seven deadly sins. This, taken from both Latin and French originals, is introduced by a verse-prologue in which occur the lines, famous in literary history for their obvious allusion to alliterative rhythm,

> But trusteth wel, I am a southren man,
> I can nat geste *rum, ram, ruf* by lettre,

and ending with the 'retraction' of his earlier and lighter works, explicitly attributed to Chaucer himself, which has been already referred to.

Of the attempts already mentioned to distribute the tales according to the indications of place and time which they themselves contain, nothing more need be said here, nor of the moot point whether, according to the host's words in *The Prologue*, the pilgrims were to tell *four* stories each—two on the way to Canterbury and two on the return journey—or *two* in all—one going and one returning. The only vestige we have of a double tale is in the fragment of the cook's above referred to, and the host's attempt to get another out of him when, as just recorded, the manciple comes to the rescue. All these matters, together with the distribution into days and groups, are very problematical, and unnecessary, if the hypothesis favoured above be adopted, that Chaucer never got his plan into any final order, but worked at parts of it as the fancy took him. But, before speaking shortly of the general characteristics of his work, it will be well to notice briefly the parts of it not yet particularised. *The Parson's Tale*, as last mentioned, will connect itself well with the remainder of Chaucer's prose work, of which it and *The Tale of Melibeus* are specimens. It may be observed that, at the beginning of *Melibeus*, and in the retraction at the end of *The Parson's Tale*, there are some curious fragments of blank verse.

The prose complements are two :—a translation of Boethius's *de Consolatione*, executed at an uncertain time but usually associated in general estimate of chronology with *Troilus*, and a short unfinished *Treatise on the Astrolabe* (a sort of hand-quadrant or sextant for observing the positions of the stars), compiled from Messahala and Johannes de Sacrobosco, intended for the use of the author's 'little son Lewis,' then (1391) in his tenth year, and calculated for the latitude of Oxford. Both are interesting as showing the endeavour of Middle English prose, in the hands of the greatest of Middle English writers, to deal with different subjects. The interest of the *Astrolabe* treatise is increased by the constant evidence presented by the poems of the attraction exercised upon Chaucer by the science of astronomy or astrology. This, so long as the astrological extension was admitted, kept its hold on English poets and men of letters as late as Dryden, while remnants of it are seen as late as Coleridge and Scott. It is an excellent piece of exposition—clear, practical and to the purpose ; and, in spite of its technical subject, it is, perhaps, the best prose work Chaucer has left us. But, after all, it is a scientific treatise and not a work of literature.

The translation of Boethius is literature within and without— interesting for its position in a long sequence of English versions of this author, fascinating for a thousand years throughout Europe and Englished by king Alfred earlier and by queen Elizabeth later ; interesting from the literary character of the matter; and interesting, above all, from the fact that Chaucer has translated into prose not merely the prose portions of the original, but the 'metres' or verse portions. These necessarily require, inasmuch as Boethius has fully indulged himself in poetic diction, a much more ornate style of phrase and arrangement than the rest—with the result that we have here, for the first time in Middle English, distinctly ornate prose, aureate in vocabulary, rhythmical in cadence and setting an example which, considering the popularity both of author and translator, could not fail to be of the greatest import- ance in the history of our literature. Faults have been found with Chaucer's translation, and he has been thought to have relied almost as much on a French version as on the original. But one of the last things that some modern scholars seem able to realise is that their medieval forerunners, idolaters of Aristotle as they were, appreciated no Aristotelian saying so much as that famous one 'accuracy must not be expected.'

The remaining minor verse, accepted with more or less agree- ment as distinguished from 'Chauceriana,' which will be dealt with separately, requires but brief mention. Of the ballade *To Rose- mounde*, *The Former Age*, the *Fortune* group, *Truth*, *Gentilesse* and *Lack of Steadfastness*—though none is quite without interest, and though we find lines such as

<blockquote>The lambish peple, voyd of alle vyce[1],</blockquote>

which are pleasant enough—only *Truth*, otherwise known as *The Ballad of Good Counsel*, is unquestionably worthy of Chaucer. The note of vanity is common enough in the Middle Ages ; but

---

[1] *The Former Age.*

it has seldom been sounded more sincerely or more poetically than here, from the opening line

> Flee fro the prees, and dwelle with sothfastnesse

to the refrain

> And trouthe shal delivere it is no drede;

with such fine lines between as

> Hold the hye wey, and lat thy gost thee lede.

The *Envoys*, or personal epistles to Scogan and Bukton, have some biographical attraction, and what is now called *The Complaint of Venus*, a translation from Otho de Granson, and the wofully-comical *Empty Purse*, are not devoid of it; the elaborate triple roundel (doubted by some) of *Merciles Beaute* is pretty, and one or two others passable. But it is quite evident that Chaucer required licence of expatiation in order to show his genius. If the reference to 'many a song and many a licorous lay' in the retraction is genuine and well-founded, it is doubtful whether we have lost very much by their loss.

The foregoing observations have been made with a definite intent to bring the account of this genius as much as possible under the account of each separate exercise of it, and to spare the necessity of diffuse generalisation in the conclusion; but something of this latter kind can hardly be avoided. It will be arranged under as few heads and with as little dilation upon them as may be; and the bibliography of MSS, editions and commentaries, which will be found in another part of this volume, must be taken as deliberately arranged to extend and supplement it. Such questions as whether the Canterbury pilgrimage took place in the actual April of 1385, or in any month of the poetical year, or whether it is safe to date *The House of Fame* from the fact that, in 1383, the 10th of December fell on a Thursday, the day and month being given by the text and the day of the week being that of Jove, whose bird carries the poet off—cannot be discussed here. Even were the limits of space wider, the discussion might be haunted by memories of certain passages in *The Nun's Priest's Tale* and elsewhere. But some general points may be handled.

One such point of some importance is the probable extent and nature of Chaucer's literary instruction and equipment. He makes, not exactly a parade in the bad sense, but a very pardonable display of knowledge of that Latin literature which was the staple of the medieval library; and, of course, he illustrates the

promiscuous estimate of authorities and values which is charac
teristic of his time. But the range of his knowledge, from the
actual classics (especially Ovid) downwards, was fairly wide, and
his use of it is generally apposite. In French, at least the French
of his own day, there can be no doubt that he was proficient, not
only as being *grant translateur*, but as taking subjects and forms
freely from what was still the leading literary vernacular of Europe
generally, though it had now been surpassed by Italy, so far as
individual accomplishment went. Nor, though the evidence is
less positive, can there be any reasonable doubt that he was
acquainted with Italian itself. A man of Chaucer's genius could,
no doubt, pick up a great deal of knowledge of Italian literature
even without, and much more with, the assistance of his Italian
visits. His mere reference to the 'laureat clerk Petrarch,' or to
Dante, 'the great poet of Italy,' would not prove very much
as to the exact extent and nature of his acquaintance with
them. But the substance of *Troilus*, and of *The Knight's*
and *Clerk's Tales*, and of *The House of Fame*, proves everything that can be reasonably required. It may be rash, especially considering how very uncertain we are of the actual
chronology of his works, to delimit periods of French and periods
of Italian influence too rigidly. But that these influences
themselves exist in Chaucer, and were constantly exerted on
him, there is no doubt at all. Much less attention has been
paid to his acquaintance with existing English literature; and
doubt has even been cast as to his possession of any. This is
ultra-sceptical, if it be the result of any real examination of the
evidence; but it is, probably, in most cases, based on a neglect or
a refusal to consider that evidence itself. That Chaucer had no
scholastic instruction in English (such as, no doubt, he had in
French and, possibly, in Italian) we know, indeed, for certain, or
almost for certain, inasmuch as his contemporary, Trevisa, informs
us that English was not used in schools, even for the purpose of
construing, till later. And it is, of course, certain that he makes
little direct mention of English writers, if any. He knew the
romances, and he makes them the subject of satiric parody in
Sir Thopas; he knew (a point of some importance) the two
modes of alliteration and rime, and refers to them by the mouth
of one of his characters, the parson, in a fashion capital for literary
history. But there is little else of direct reference. A moment's
thought, however, will show that it would have been very odd
if there had been. Although Chaucer's is very far from being

mere court-poetry it was, undoubtedly, composed with a view to court-readers ; and these, as the passage in Trevisa shows, were only just becoming accustomed to the treatment of English as a literary language. There were no well-known named authors for him to quote ; and, if there had been, he could have gained none of the little nimbus of reputation for learning which was so innocently dear to a medieval writer, by quoting them. That, on the other hand, he was thoroughly acquainted, if only by word of mouth, not reading, with a great bulk of precedent verse and, probably, some prose, can be shown by evidence much stronger than chapter-and-verse of the categorical kind. For those who take him—as he has been too seldom taken—in the natural evolution of English poetry and English literature, there is not the slightest need to regard him as a *lusus naturae* who developed the practice of English by the study of French, who naturalised by touch of wand foreign metres and foreign diction into his native tongue, and who evolved 'gold dewdrops' of English 'speech' and more golden bell-music of English rhythm from Latin and Italian and French sources. On the contrary, unprejudiced study will show that, with what amount of actual book-knowledge it is impossible to say, Chaucer had caught up the sum of a process which had been going on for some two centuries at least and, adding to it from his own stores, as all great poets do, and taking, as many of them have done, what help he could get from foreigners, was turning out the finished product not as a new thing but as a perfected old one. Even the author of *Sir Thopas* could not have written that excellent parody if he had not been to the manner born and bred of those who produced such things (and better things) seriously. And it is an idle multiplication of miracles to suppose that the verse—the individual verses, not the batched arrangements of them—which directly represents, and is directly connected with, the slowly developing prosody of everything from Orm and Layamon to Hampole and *Cursor Mundi*, is a sudden apparition—that this verse, both English and accomplished, is fatherless, except for French, motherless, except for Middle and Lower Latin, and arrived at without conscious or even unconscious knowledge of these its natural precursors and progenitors.

Of the matter, as well as of the languages, forms and sources of his knowledge, a little more should, perhaps, be said. It has been by turns exalted and decried, and the manner of its exhibition has not always been wisely considered. It has been observed above, and the point is important enough for emphasis, that we must not look in Chaucer for anything but the indiscriminateness and, from a strictly scholarly point of view, the inaccuracy, which were bred in the very bone of medieval study ; and that it would be hardly less of a mistake to expect him not to show what seems to us a singular promiscuousness and irrelevancy in his display of it. But, in this display, and possibly, also, in some of the inaccuracies, there is a very subtle and personal agency which has sometimes been ignored altogether, while it has seldom been fully allowed for. This is the intense, all-pervading and all but incalculable presence of Chaucer's *humour*—a quality which some, even of those who enjoy it heartily and extol it generously, do not quite invariably seem to comprehend. Indeed, it may be said that even among those who are not destitute of the sense itself, such an ubiquitous, subterranean accompaniment of it would seem to be regarded as an impossible or an uncanny thing. As a matter of fact, however, it 'works i' the earth so fast' that you never can tell at what moment it will find utterance. Many of the instances of this are familiar, and some, at least, could hardly fail to be recognised except by portentous dulness. But it may be questioned whether it is ever far off; and whether, as is so often the case in that true English variety of the quality of which it is the first and one of the most consummate representatives, it is not mixed and streaked with seriousness and tenderness in an almost inextricable manner. '*Il se moque,*' says Taine of another person, '*de ses émotions au moment même où il s'y livre.*' In the same way, Chaucer is perpetually seeing the humorous side, not merely of his emotions but of his interests, his knowledge, his beliefs, his everything. It is by no means certain that in his displays of learning he is not mocking or parodying others as well as relieving himself. It is by no means certain that, seriously as we know him to have been interested in astronomy, his frequent astronomical or astrological lucubrations are not partly ironical. Once and once only, by a triumph of artistic self-restraint, he has kept the ludicrous out altogether—in the exquisite *Prioress's Tale,* and even there we have a sort of suggestion of the forbidden but irrepressible thing in

As monkes been, *or elles oghten be.*

Of this humour, indeed, it is not too much to say (borrowing Coleridge's dictum about Fuller and the analogous but very different quality of wit) that it is the 'stuff and substance,' not merely of Chaucer's intellect, but of his entire mental constitution. He can, as has been said, repress it when art absolutely requires that he should do so ; but, even then, he gives himself compensations. He has kept it out of *The Prioress's Tale* ; but he has indemnified himself by a more than double allowance of it in his description of the prioress's person in *The Prologue*. On the other hand, it would have been quite out of place in the description of the knight, for whom nothing but respectful admiration is solicited ; and there is no need to suspect irony even in

And though that he were worthy, he was wys.

But in *The Knight's Tale*—which is so long that the personage of the supposed teller, never obtruded, may be reasonably supposed forgotten, and where the poet almost speaks in his own person— the same writ does not run ; and, towards the end especially, we get the famous touches of ironic comment on life and thought, which, though they have been unduly dwelt upon as indicating a Voltairian tone in Chaucer, certainly are ironical in their treatment of the riddles of the painful earth.

Further, it is desirable to notice that this humour is employed with a remarkable difference. In most great English humorists, humour sets the picture with a sort of vignetting or arabesquing fringe and atmosphere of exaggeration and fantasy. By Chaucer it is almost invariably used to bring a higher but a quite clear and achromatic light on the picture itself or parts of it. The stuff is turned rapidly the other way to show its real texture ; the jest is perhaps a burning, but also a magnifying and illuminating, glass, to bring out a special trait more definitely. It is safe to say that a great deal of the combination of vivacity and veracity in Chaucer's portraits and sketches of all kinds is due to this all-pervading humour ; indeed, it is not very likely that any one would deny this. What seems, for some commentators, harder to keep in mind is that it may be, and probably is, equally present in other places where the effect is less immediately rejoicing to the modern reader ; and that medieval pedantry, medieval catalogue-making, medieval digression and irrelevance are at once exemplified and satirised by the operation of this extraordinary faculty.

That the possession of such a faculty almost necessarily implies command of pathos is, by this time, almost a truism, though it was not always recognised. That Chaucer is an instance of it, as well as of a third quality, *good* humour, which does not invariably accompany the other two, will hardly be disputed. He is not a sentimentalist; he does not go out of his way for pathetic effect; but, in the leading instances above noted of *The Clerk's* and *Prioress's Tales*, supplemented by many slighter touches of the same kind, he shows an immediate, unforced, unfaltering sympathy which can hardly be paralleled. His good humour is even more pervading. It gives a memorable distinction of kindliness between *The Wife of Bath's Prologue* and the brilliant following of it by Dunbar in *The Tua Mariit Wemen and the Wedo* ; and it even separates Chaucer from such later humorists as Addison and Jane Austen, who, though never savage, can be politely cruel. Cruelty and Chaucer are absolute strangers ; indeed, the absence of it has brought upon him from rather short-sighted persons the charge of pococurantism, which has sometimes been translated (still more purblindly) into one of mere courtliness—of a Froissart-like indifference to anything but 'the quality,' 'the worth,' as he might have put it himself. Because there is indignation in *Piers the Plowman*, it is thought that Chaucer does not well *not* to be angry : which is uncritical.

This curious, tolerant, not in the least cynical, observation and relish of humanity gave him a power of representing it, which has been rarely surpassed in any respect save depth. It has been disputed whether this power is rather that of the dramatist or that of the novelist—a dispute perhaps arguing a lack of the historic sense. In the late sixteenth or early seventeenth century, Chaucer would certainly have been the one, and in the mid-nineteenth the other. It would be most satisfactory could we have his work in both avatars. But what we have contains the special qualities of both craftsmen in a certain stage of development, after a fashion which certainly leaves no room for grumbling. The author has, in fact, set himself a high task by adopting the double system above specified, and by giving elaborate descriptions of his personages before he sets them to act and speak up to these descriptions. It is a plan which, in the actual drama and the actual novel, has been found rather a dangerous one. But Chaucer discharges himself victoriously of his liabilities. And the picture of life which he has left us has captivated all good judges who have given themselves the very slight trouble necessary to attain the right point of view, from his own day to this.

Something has been said of the poetic means which he used to work this picture out. They were, practically, those which English poetry had been elaborating for itself during the preceding two or three centuries, since the indrafts of Latin or Romance vocabulary, and the gradual disuse of inflection, had revolutionised the language. But he perfected them, to, probably, their utmost possible point at the time, by study of French and Italian models as regards arrangement of lines in groups, and by selecting a diction which, even in his own time, was recognised as something quite extraordinary. The old delusion that he 'Frenchified' the language has been nearly dispelled as regards actual vocabulary; and, in points which touch grammar, the minute investigations undertaken in the case of the doubtful works have shown that he was somewhat more scrupulous than were his contemporaries in observing formal correctness, as it is inferred to have been. The principal instance of this scrupulousness—the management of the valued final -*e*, which represented a crowd of vanished or vanishing peculiarities of accidence—was, by a curious consequence, the main cause of the mistakes about his verse which prevailed for some three centuries; while the almost necessarily greater abundance of unusual words in *The Prologue*, with its varied subjects, probably had something to do with the concurrent notion that his language was obsolete to the point of difficulty, if not to that of unintelligibility. As a matter of fact, his verse (with the exception of one or two doubtful experiments, such as the nine-syllabled line where ten should be) is among the smoothest in English; and there are entire pages where, putting trifling differences of spelling aside, hardly a single word will offer difficulties to any person of tolerable reading in the modern tongue.

It is sometimes complained by those who admit some, if not all, of these merits in him that he rarely—a few would say never—rises to the level of the highest poetry. Before admitting, before even seriously contesting, this we must have a definition of the highest poetry which will unite the suffrages of the competent, and this, in the last two thousand years and more, has not been attained. It will, perhaps, be enough to say that any such definition which excludes the finest things in *Troilus and Criseyde*, in *The Knight's* and *Prioress's Tales* and in some other places, will run the risk of suggesting itself as a mere shibboleth. That Chaucer is not always at these heights may be granted: who is? That he is less often at them than some other poets need not be denied; that he has access to them must be maintained. While as to his power to communicate poetic grace and charm to innumerable other things less high, perhaps, but certainly not always low; as to the abounding interest of his matter; as to the astonishing vividness in line and idiom of his character-drawing and manners-painting; and,

above all, as to the wonderful service which he did to the forms
and stuff of English verse and of English prose, there should be
no controversy; at least the issue of any such controversy should
not be doubtful.

One afterthought of special interest may perhaps be appended.
Supposing Skeat's very interesting and quite probable conjecture to be true, and granting that *The Tale of Gamelyn*
lay among Chaucer's papers for the more or less distinct
purpose of being worked up into a Canterbury 'number,' it
is not idle to speculate on the probable result, especially in
the prosodic direction. In all his other models or stores of
material, the form of the original had been French, or Latin, or
Italian prose or verse, or else English verse or (perhaps in rare
cases) prose, itself modelled more or less on Latin or on French.
In all his workings on and after these models and materials, his
own form had been a greatly improved following of the same
kind, governed not slavishly, but distinctly, by an inclination
towards the Latin-French models themselves in so far as they
could be adapted, without loss, to English. Pure unmetrical
alliteration he had definitely rejected, or was definitely to reject,
in the famous words of the Parson. But in *Gamelyn* he had,
or would have had, an original standing between the two—and
representing the earliest, or almost the earliest, concordat or com-
promise between them. As was observed in the account given of
Gamelyn itself in the chapter on Metrical Romances[1], it is, generally
speaking, of the 'Robert-of-Gloucester' type—the type in which
the centrally divided, alliterative, non-metrical line has retained its
central division but has discarded alliterative-accentual necessity,
has taken on rime and has adopted a roughly but distinctly
metrical cadence. If, however, we compare *Gamelyn* (which is
put by philologists at about 1340) with Robert himself (who probably finished writing some 40 years earlier) some interesting
differences will be seen, which become more interesting still in
connection with the certainly contemporary rise of the ballad
metre of four short lines, taking the place of the two centre-
broken long ones. Comparing the *Gamelyn* execution with that
of Robert, that, say, of the *Judas* ballad and that of the earliest
Robin Hood pieces and others, one may note in it interesting
variations of what may be called an elliptic-eccentric kind. The
centre pin of the verse-division is steady; but it works, not in a

[1] Volume I, p. 298.

round socket proportionate to itself so much as in a kind of
curved slot, and, as it slips up and down this, the resulting verse
takes curiously different, though always homogeneous, forms. The
exact 'fourteener,' or eight and six without either lengthening or
shortening, is not extremely common, but it occurs often enough.
More commonly the halves (especially the second) are slightly
shortened; and, not unfrequently, they are lengthened by the
admission of trisyllabic feet. There is an especial tendency to
make the second half up of very short feet as in

Sik | ther | he lay |

where an attempt to scan

Sik ther | he lay

will disturb the whole rhythm; and a tendency (which forewarns
us of Milton) to cut the first syllable and begin with a trochee as
in the refrain beginning

Litheth and listeneth

in

Al thi londe that he hadde

and so on. While, sometimes, we get the full anapaestic extension

The frankeleyn seyde to the champioun: of him stood him noon eye.

And, in the same way, the individual lines indicate, in various
directions, the settlement of the old long line towards the decasyllable, towards the alexandrine, towards the 'fourteener' and
towards the various forms of doggerel, themselves giving birth to
the pure four-anapaest line which we find in the early sixteenth
century. Now the question is: 'Would the necessary attention to
these metrical peculiarities, implied in the process of (in Dryden's
sense) "translation," have produced any visible effect on Chaucer's
own prosody?' Nor is this by any means an idle question. That
Chaucer was a great *mimic* in metre, we know from *Sir Thopas*,
where he has exactly hit off the namby-pamby amble of the
'romance six' in its feeblest examples. Now this romance six
is very near to the ballad four—some have even guessed that the
latter is a 'crushed' form of it, though this is, perhaps, reversing
the natural order of thought. Would Chaucer have tried the
ballad four itself—regularising and characterising it as he did
other metres? Or would his study of the extremely composite and
germinal kind of verse in which, as has been shown, *Gamelyn* is
written, have resulted in the earlier development of some of these
germs?

The question, let it be repeated, is by no means idle. That the developments actually took place in the next century and a half, at the hands of lesser men, shows, conclusively, that they might have taken place, and probably would, at the hands of a greater one earlier. But: 'Ought we to be sorry that they did *not*?'—though again not idle, is a very different question and one to which the answer should probably be 'No' and not 'Yes.'

For the impending linguistic changes, which ruined Chaucer's actual decasyllable in the hands of his actual successors, would probably, have played even greater havoc with freer and looser measures, if he had attempted them. And if he had made a strict eight and six, as he did a strict eight eight six in *Sir Thopas*, the danger of rigid syllabic uniformity being regarded as the law of English prosody—a danger actual for centuries—would have been very much increased. As it was, these half-wildings of verse continued to grow in their natural way, without being converted into 'hybrid perpetuals' by the skill of any capital horticulturist. They remained in striking contrast to the formal couplets and stanzas: reliefs from them, outlets, escapes. It did not matter if they were badly done, for they carried no weight as models or masters: it mattered supremely if they were well done, for they helped to tune the national ear. They were in no vituperative sense the *corpora vilia* in which experiment could be freely and inexpensively made: though the experiments themselves were sometimes far from vile. Therefore, one need not weep that Chaucer let *Gamelyn* alone. He would have given us a delightful story, but the story is full of delight for competent readers as it is. If he had made it into 'riding rime' it would not have been better, as such, than its companions. If he had made it into anything else it might have been a doubtful gain. And, lastly, the copy might, as in so many other cases, have killed the original. Now, even for more Chaucer, of which we fortunately have so much already, we could not afford to have no *Gamelyn*, which is practically unique.

CHAPTER VIII

THE ENGLISH CHAUCERIANS

THE influence of Chaucer upon English poetry of all dialects, during the entire century which followed his death, and part, at least, of the next, is something to which there is hardly a parallel in literature. We have to trace it in the present chapter as regards the southern forms of the language : its manifestation in the northern being reserved for separate treatment. But, while there is absolutely no doubt about its extent and duration, the curiously uncritical habit of the time manifests itself in the fact that, after the very earliest period, not merely Gower, who has been dealt with already, but a third writer, himself the first and strongest instance of this very influence, is, as it were, ' co-opted ' into the governance which he has himself experienced ; and Chaucer, Gower and Lydgate are invoked as of conjoint and nearly equal authority. So with Lydgate we must begin.

It was no part of the generous and spontaneous, if not always wisely allotted, adoration which the Middle Ages paid to their literary masters to indulge in copious biographical notices of them ; the rather numerous details that we possess about Chaucer are almost wholly concerned with him as a member, in one way or another, of the public service, not as a poet. Now Lydgate (though his membership of a monastic order would not, necessarily, have excluded him from such occupations) seems, as a matter of fact, to have had nothing to do with them ; and we know, in consequence, very little about him. That his name was John, that he took, as was very common, his surname from his birthplace, a Suffolk village, but just on the border of Cambridgeshire, and that he was a monk of the great Suffolk abbey of St Edmund's Bury, are data ; he was, in fact, and even still is, from habit or affectation, spoken of as 'the monk of Bury,' as often as by his own name. But further documentary evidence is very slight and almost wholly concerned with his professional work ; even his references to him-

self, which are by no means unfrequent, amount to little more than
that he had not so much money as he would have liked to have,
that he had more work than he would have liked to have and that
he wore spectacles—three things not rare among men of letters—
besides those concerning the place of his birth and his entry into
religion at fifteen years of age. Tradition and inference—sometimes
the one, sometimes the other, sometimes both—date his birth at
about 1370 and assign Oxford as the place of his education, with
subsequent studies in France and Italy. He seems, at any rate, from
his own assertion in an apparently genuine poem, to have been at
Paris perhaps more than once. His expressions as regards 'his
mayster Chaucer' may, possibly, imply personal acquaintance.
Formal documents exist for his admission to minor, subdiaconal,
diaconal and priest's orders at different dates between 1388—9 and
1397. He (or some other John Lydgate) is mentioned in certain
documents concerning Bury in 1415 and 1423, in which latter
year he was also elected prior of Hatfield Broadoak. Eleven years
later, he received licence to return to the parent monastery. He
had divers patrons—duke Humphrey of Gloucester being one.
References to a small pension, paid to him jointly with one John
Baret, exist for the years 1441 and 1446; and it has been thought
that a reference to him in Bokenam's *Saints' Lives* as 'now existing' is of the same year as this last. Beyond 1446, we hear
nothing positive of him. It is thus reasonable to fix his career
as lasting from *c.* 1370 to *c.* 1450.

If this be so, his life was not short : and it is quite certain that
such exercises of his art as we possess are very long. The enormous
catalogue of his work which occurs in Ritson's *Bibliographia
Poetica*, extending to many pages and 251 separate items, has
been violently attacked : it certainly will not stand examination
either as free from duplicates or as confined to certain or probable
attributions. But it was a great achievement for its time; and it has
not been superseded by anything which would be equally useful to
whoever shall desire to play Tyrwhitt to Lydgate's Chaucer. Until
quite recently, indeed, the study of Lydgate was only to be pursued
under almost prohibitive difficulties ; for, though, in consequence of
his great popularity, many of his works were issued by our early
printers, from Caxton to Tottel, these issues are now accessible
only here and there in the largest libraries. Moreover they—and it
would seem also the MSS which are slowly being brought in to
supplement them—present, as a rule, texts of an extreme badness,
which may or may not be due to copyists and printers. Till

nearly the close of the nineteenth century nothing outside these MSS and early prints was accessible at all, except the *Minor Poems* printed by Halliwell for the Percy Society, and the *Story of Thebes* and other pieces included among Chaucer's works in the older editions down to Chalmers's *Poets*. During the last fifteen years, the Early English Text Society has given us *The Temple of Glass, The Secrets of the Philosophers* (finished by Burgh), *The Assembly of Gods, The Pilgrimage of the Life of Man,* two *Nightingale Poems, Reason and Sensuality* and part of the *Troy Book*; while the Cambridge University Press has issued facsimiles of Caxton's *The Churl and the Bird* and *The Horse, the Sheep and the Goose*, reprinted earlier for the Roxburghe Club. These, however, to which may be added a few pieces printed elsewhere, form a very small part of what Lydgate wrote, the total of which, even as it exists, has been put at about 140,000 lines. Half of this, or very nearly half, is contained in two huge works, the *Troy Book* of 30,000 lines, and *The Falls of Princes*, adapted from Boccaccio, his most famous and, perhaps, most popular book, which is more than 6000 lines longer. *The Pilgrimage of Man* itself extends to over 20,000 lines and the other pieces mentioned above to about 17,000 more. The remainder is made up of divers saints' lives—*Our Lady, Albon and Amphabel, Edmund and Fremund, St Margaret, St Austin, St Giles* and the *Miracles of St Edmund*—varying from five or six thousand lines to three or four hundred; another allegorical piece, *The Court of Sapience*, of over 2000; poems less but still fairly long bearing the titles *Aesop, De Duobus Mercatoribus, Testament, Danse Macabre*, a version of *Guy of Warwick, December and July* and *The Flower of Courtesy*; with a large number of ballades and minor pieces.

The authenticity of many of these is not very easy to establish, and it is but rarely that their dates can be ascertained with anything like certainty. A few things, such as the verses for queen Margaret's entry into London, date themselves directly; and some of the saints' lives appear to be assignable with fair certainty, but most are extremely uncertain. And it does not seem quite safe to assume that all the shorter and better poems belong to the earlier years, all the longer and less good ones to the later.

The truth is that there is hardly any whole poem, and exceedingly few, if any, parts of poems, in Lydgate so good that we should be surprised at his being the author of even the worst thing attributed to him. He had some humour: it appears fairly enough in his best known and, perhaps, best thing, the very lively little poem called *London Lickpenny* (not 'Lackpenny' as it used to be read), which tells the woes of a country suitor in the capital. And it appears again, sometimes in the immense and curious *Pilgrimage*, a translation from Deguileville, which undoubtedly stands in some relation—though at how many stages nothing but the wildest guessing would undertake to determine—to *The Pilgrim's Progress* itself. But this humour was never concentrated to anything like Chaucerian strength ; while of Chaucerian vigour, Chaucerian pathos, Chaucerian vividness of description, Lydgate had no trace or tincture.

To these defects he added two faults, one of which Chaucer had never exhibited in any great measure, and from the other of which he freed himself completely. The one is prosodic incompetence ; the other is longwinded prolixity. The very same reasons which made him an example of the first made his contemporaries insensible of it ; and, in Elizabethan times, he was praised for 'good verse' simply because the Elizabethans did not understand what was good or what was bad in Middle English versification. Fresh attempts have recently been made to claim for him at least systematic if mistaken ideas in this respect ; but they reduce themselves either to an allegation of anarchy in all English verse, which can be positively disproved, or to a mere classification of prosodic vices, as if this made them virtues. The worst of Lydgate's apparently systematic roughness is a peculiar line, broken at the caesura, with a gap left in the breaking as in the following,

> For specheles nothing mayst thou spede,

or,

> Might make a thing so celestial.

This extraordinary discord, of which some have striven to find one or two examples in Chaucer, is abundant in Lydgate and has been charitably connected with the disuse of the final -e —in the use of which, however, the same apologists sometimes represent Lydgate as rather orthodox. Unfortunately, it is not, by a long way, the only violation of harmony to be found in him. That some of his poems—for instance, *The Falls of Princes*—are better than his average in this respect, and that some, such as *The Story of Thebes*, are worse, has been taken as suggesting that the long-suffering copyist or printer is to blame ; but this will hardly suffice. Indeed, Lydgate himself, perhaps, in imitation of Chaucer, but with reason such as Chaucer never had, declares that at one time (' as tho ') he had no skill of metre. It is enough to say that. even in rime royal, his lines wander from seven to fourteen syllables, without the possibility of allowing monosyllabic or trisyllabic feet in any fashion that shall restore the rhythm ; and that his couplets, as in *The Story of Thebes* itself, seem often to be unaware whether they are themselves octosyllabic or decasyllabic— four-footed or five-footed. He is, on the whole, happiest in his ostensible octosyllabics—a metre not, indeed, easy to achieve consummately, but admitting of fair performance without much trouble, and not offering any great temptation to excessive irregularity.

Unluckily, this very metre tempted Lydgate to fall into what is to most people, perhaps, his unforgivable fault—prolixity and verbiage. It has, now and then, enticed even the greatest into these errors or close to them : and Lydgate was not of the greatest. But it shows him, perhaps, as well as any other, except in very short pieces like the *Lickpenny*.

He is, accordingly, out of these short pieces and a few detached stanzas of his more careful rime royal, hardly anywhere seen to more advantage than in the huge and curious translation from Guillaume de Deguileville which has been referred to above. Its want of originality places it at no disadvantage ; for it is very doubtful whether Lydgate ever attempted any work of size that was not either a direct translation or more than based upon some previous work of another author. This quaint allegory, with absolutely nothing of Bunyan's compactness of action, or of his living grasp of character, or of his perfect, if plain, phrase, has a far more extensive and varied conglomeration of adventure, and not merely carries its pilgrim through preliminary theological difficulties, through a Romance-of-the-Rose insurrection of Nature and Aristotle against Grace, through an immense process of arming which amplifies St Paul's famous text into thousands of lines, through conflicts with the Seven Deadly Sins and the more dangerous companionship of the damsel Youth—but conducts him to the end through strange countries of sorcery and varied experiences, mundane and religious. Thus, the very multitude and the constant phantasmagoric changes of scene and story save the poet from dulness, some leave of skipping being taken at the doctrinal and argumentative passages. In the ' Youth' part and in not a few others he is lively, and not too diffuse.

Scarcely as much can be said of the still longer version of Guido delle Colonne's *Hystoria Troiana*, which we possess in some 30,000 lines of heroic couplet, with a prologue of the same and an epilogue in rime royal. To say that it is the dullest of the many ver· sions we have would be rash, but the present writer does not know where to put his hand upon a duller, and it is certainly inferior to the Scots alliterative form, which may be of about the same date. Part of its weakness may be due to the fact that Lydgate was less successful with the heroic couplet than, perhaps, with any other measure, and oftener used his broken-backed line in it. But the poem was twice printed, huge as it is, and was condensed and modernised by Heywood as late as 1614.

The theme of the *Tale of Troy*, indeed, can never wholly lack interest, nor is interest wanting in Lydgate's poem. In this respect he was more successful with the yet again huger *Falls of Princes* or *Tragedies of John Bochas*. But this, also, was popular and produced a family more deplorable, almost, than itself (with one or two well known exceptions) in *The Mirror for Magistrates* of the next century. Its only redeeming point is the comparative merit, already noticed, of its rime royal. To this we may return: a few words must now be said of some other productions of Lydgate. For what reason some have assigned special excellence to *Reason and Sensuality*, and have, accordingly, determined that it must be the work of his poetic prime, is not very easy to discover. It is in octosyllables, and, as has been said, he is usually happier there than in heroics or in rime royal ; it is certainly livelier in subject than most of his works ; and it is evidently composed under a fresher inspiration from the *Rose* itself than is generally the case with those cankered rose leaves, the allegoric poems of the fifteenth century; while its direct original, the unprinted *Échecs amoureux*, is said to have merit. But, otherwise, there is not much to be said for it. Its subject is a sort of cento of the favourite *motifs* of the time— Chess; Fortune (not with her wheel but with tuns of sweet and bitter drink); the waking, the spring morning and garden; Nature; the judgment of Paris ; the strife between Venus and Diana for the author's allegiance ; the Garden of Delight and its dangers; and the Forest of Reason, with a most elaborate game of chess again to finish—or, rather, *not* to finish, for the piece breaks off at about its seven-thousandth line. It is possible that the argument of earliness is correct, for some of the descriptions are fresh and not twice battered as Lydgate's often are ; and there seems to be a certain zest in the writing, instead of the groaning weariness which so frankly meets the reader halfway elsewhere.

The Temple of Glass, partly in heroics, partly in rime royal, is one of the heaviest of fifteenth century allegorical love-poems, in

which two lovers complain to Venus and, having been answered
by her, are finally united. It is extremely prosaic ; but, by sheer
editing, has been brought into a condition of at least more
systematic prosody than most of Lydgate's works. *The Assembly
of Gods* is a still heavier allegory of vices and virtues presented
under the names of divinities, major and minor, of the ancient
pantheon, but brought round to an orthodox Christian conclusion.
The piece is in rime royal of the loosest construction, so much
so that its editor proposes a merely rhythmical scansion.

By far the best and most poetical passages in Lydgate's vast
work are to be found in *The Life of Our Lady,* from which Warton
long ago managed to extract more than one batch of verses to
which he assigned the epithets of 'elegant and harmonious' as
well as the more doubtful praise of 'so modern a cast.' It is
possible that these citations and *encomia* are responsible for the
good opinion which some have formed of the poet ; but it is to
be feared that they will wander far and wearily among Lydgate's
myriads of lines without coming upon the equals of

> Like as the dewe discendeth on the rose
>   In silver drops,

or,

> O thoughtful herte, plonged in dystresse,
>   With slomber of slouthe this longe winter's night—
> Out of the slepe of mortal hevinesse
>   Awake anon! and loke upon the light
>   Of thilke starr;

or,

> And he that made the high and crystal heven,
>   The firmament, and also every sphere;
>   The Golden ax-tree and the starres seven,
> Citherea so lusty for to appere
> And redde Marse with his sterne here.

The subject which never failed to inspire every medieval poet who
was capable of inspiration has not failed here.

The best of Lydgate's *Saints' Lives* proper appears to be the
Saint Margaret ; it is very short, and the innumerable previous
handlings of the story, which has intrinsic capabilities, may have
stood him in good stead. On the other hand, the long *Edmund
and Fremund,* in celebration of the saint whom the poet was
more especially bound to honour, though spoken of by some
with commendation, is a feeble thing, showing no skill of narration.
It is not in quite such bad rime royal as Lydgate can sometimes
write ; but, even here, the plangency of which the metre is capable,

and which would have come in well, is quite absent; while the poem is characterised throughout by the flattest and dullest diction. The two *Nightingale* poems are religious-allegorical. They are both in rime royal and average not more than 400 lines each.

The beast-fable had something in it peculiarly suitable to Lydgate's kind of genius (as, indeed, to medieval genius generally) and this fact is in favour of his *Aesop* and of the two poems (among his best) which are called *The Churl and the Bird* and *The Horse, the Sheep and the Goose.* Of these two pieces, both very favourite examples of the moral tale of eastern origin which was disseminated through Europe widely by various collections as well as in individual specimens, *The Churl* is couched in rime royal and *The Horse* in the same metre, with an envoy or *moralitas* in octaves. Both are contained, though not completely, in Halliwell's edition of the minor poems. The actual *Aesop*—a small collection of Aesopic fables which is sometimes assigned to Lydgate's earliest period, perhaps to his residence at Oxford—is pointless enough, and contrasts very unfavourably with Henryson's. But the remainder of these minor poems, whatever the certainty of their attribution, includes Lydgate's most acceptable work :—*London Lickpenny* itself ; the *Ballade of the Midsummer Rose*, where 'the eternal note of sadness' and change becomes musical even in him ; the sly advice to an old man who wished for a young wife ; the satire on horned head-dresses ; *The Prioress and her Three Suitors*; the poet's *Testament*; the sincere 'Thank God of all' and others.

The Complaint of the Black Knight, for long assigned to Chaucer, though not quite worthy of him, is better than most of Lydgate's poems, though it has his curious flatness ; and it might, perhaps, be prescribed as the best beginning for those who wish to pass from the study of the older and greater poet to that of his pupil.

Lydgate has not lacked defenders, who would be formidable if their *locus standi* were more certain. The fifteenth century adored him because he combined all its own worst faults, and the sixteenth seems to have accepted him because it had no apparatus for criticism. When, after a long eclipse, he was in two senses taken up by Gray, that poet seems chiefly to have known *The Falls of Princes*, in which, perhaps by dint of long practice, Lydgate's metrical shortcomings are less noticeable than in some other places, and where the dignity and gravity of Boccaccio's Latin has, to some extent, invigorated his style. Warton is curiously guarded in his opinions; and a favourable judgment of Coleridge may, possibly, be regarded as very insufficiently based. The apologies of editors (especially those who are content with systematised metre, however inharmonious) do not go very far. On the whole, though Ritson's condemnation may have been expressed with characteristic extravagance and discourtesy towards the 'voluminous, prosaic and drivelling monk,' nobody can dispute the voluminousness in the worst sense, and it is notable that even Lydgate's defenders, in proportion as they know more of him, are apt to 'confess and avoid' the 'prosaic' and to slip occasionally into admissions rather near the 'drivelling.' It is to be feared that some such result is inevitable. A little Lydgate, especially if the little be judiciously chosen, or happily allotted by chance, is a tolerable thing : though even this can hardly be very delectable to any well qualified judge of poetry. But, the longer and wider that acquaintance with him is extended, the more certain is dislike to make its appearance. The prosodic incompetence cannot be entirely due to copyists and printers ; the enormous verbosity, the ignorance how to tell a story, the want of freshness, vigour, life, cannot be due to them at all. But what is most fatal of all is the flatness of diction noticed above—the dull, hackneyed, slovenly phraseology, only thrown up by his occasional aureate pedantry—which makes the common commoner and the uncommon uninteresting. Lydgate himself, or some imitator of him, has been credited with the phrase 'gold dewdrops of speech' about Chaucer. He would hardly have thought of anything so good ; but the phrase at least suggests an appropriate variant, 'leaden splashes,' for his own.

The inseparable companion in literature of Lydgate is Thomas Occleve or Hoccleve ; whether this companionship extended to life we do not know, though they may, perhaps, have had a common friend in Chaucer, whose portrait adorns one of Occleve's MSS, and of whom he speaks with personal warmth. This portrait is one chief reason which we have for gratitude to Occleve ; but it is not the only one. In the first place, we have from him what seems to be at least possibly autograph writing, a contribution to our knowledge of the actual language and metre of the work which (though one cannot but wish it came from Chaucer himself) would, if certain, be of the greatest value. In the second place, he has added, by some autobiographical confidences which make him (in a very weak and washed out way, it is true) a sort of English and crimeless Villon, to the actual picture of his times that we have in Lydgate's *Lickpenny*. His surname is supposed, as that of his fellow Lydgate is known, to be a place-name, and the nearest form is that of Hockliffe or Hocclyve in Bedfordshire. But both Ock- and Hock- are common prefixes all over the south and the midlands, while -cleve and -cliff are equally common suffixes. In a *Dialogue*, he appears to assign his fifty-third year to the twelve-month just before Henry V's death in 1422 : so that he must have been born about 1368. In another poem, some ten years earlier, the *De Regimine Principum*, he says that he had been ' twenty years and four' in the office of the Privy Seal, which gives us another date—say 1387—for his entrance there at the very probable age of nineteen or so. He is also mentioned as actually a clerk in a document apparently of that year. He thought of taking orders, but did not : though, in 1399, he received a pension of £10 till he should receive a benefice (without cure of souls) of double the value. Various entries of payments of this pension exist, and also of office expenses. In 1406, he wrote the curious poem above referred to, *La Male Règle*, in which he begs for payment and confesses a long course of mild dissipation. His salary was very small: under £4, apparently. He seems at one time to have lived at Chester's inn in the Strand, and to have married about 1411, being then over forty. About five years later, he was out of his mind for a time. In 1409, his pension had been increased to £13. 6s. 8d. Not till 1424 did he get a benefice—at least, a ' corrody ' or charge on a monastery—but we do not know the amount. And how long he enjoyed this we also do not know. Tradition, rather than any positive authority, extends his life as long as Lydgate's or (if he was born earlier) a little longer, and puts his death also at about 1450. But it is difficult to say how much of this is due to the curious and intangible fellowship which has established itself between the two poets. This fellowship, however, did not, at the time, carry Occleve into the position assigned to Lydgate by subsequent versifiers ; nor did it assure him equal attention from the early printers. We are, indeed, even yet, in considerable uncertainty as to the extent of his work that is in existence : some of what he probably wrote having not yet been printed, while some of the things printed as his are doubtful. This uncertainty, however, does not extend to a fairly large body of work. The most important piece of this is *De Regimine Principum* or *Regiment of Princes*, addressed to Henry prince of Wales, and extending in all to some 5500 verses. Not more than 3500 of these contain the actual advice,

which is on a par with the contents of several other poems
mentioned in this chapter—partly political, partly ethical, partly
religious, and based on a blending of Aristotle with Solomon.
The introduction of 2000 verses, however (the greater part of which
consists of a dialogue between the poet and a beggar), is less
commonplace and much more interesting, containing more biographical matter, the address to Chaucer, a quaint wail over the
troubles of the scribe and other curious things. Next to this
in importance come two verse-stories from *Gesta Romanorum*,
The Emperor Jereslaus's Wife and *Jonathas*; the rather piquant
Male Règle with the confessions above referred to; a *Complaint*
and *Dialogue*, also largely autobiographical; and a really fine *Ars
Sciendi Mori*, the most dignified, and the most poetical, thing
that Occleve has left us. We have also a number of shorter poems,
from ballades upwards, some of which are datable, and the dating
of one of which at about 1448 by Tyrwhitt is the nearest approach
to warrant for the extension of the poet's life to the middle of the
century.

There is no doubt that Occleve—like Pepys and some other,
but not all, talkers about themselves—has found himself none
the worse off for having committed to paper numerous things
which any one but a garrulous, egotistic and not very strong-
minded person would have omitted. Nor can it exactly be
counted to him as a literary merit that he does not seem to have
been at all an unamiable person. Nor, lastly, is his wisdom in
abstaining from extremely long poems more than a negative
virtue. Yet all these things do undoubtedly, in this way and that,
make the reading of Occleve less toilsome than that of Lydgate;
though the latter can, on rare occasions, write better than Occleve
ever does, though he is immeasurably Occleve's superior in
learning and industry and though (again at his best) he is
slightly his superior in versification. Though lesser in every
other sense, one merit Occleve may claim—that he has some
idea how to tell a story. Neither *Jereslaus* nor *Jonathas* is
lacking in this respect; and though, of course, they are not original,
neither is anything of Lydgate's in this kind that we know of.
In aureateness or heavily pompous diction, there is not much
to choose, though Lydgate knows a little better how to make use
of his ornaments. Prosodically, the chief difference seems to be that
Occleve has the actual number of syllables that should be in a
verse rather more clearly before him, though he is, perhaps,
Lydgate's inferior in communicating to them anything like

poetic rhythm. He generally uses rime royal, but, like almost all these poets, varies it, occasionally, with octaves. Neither couplet seems to have had strong attraction for him.

Of the poems not yet noticed, that to Sir John Oldcastle, written about 1415 and some five hundred lines long, has a certain historical interest and something of the actuality which Occleve often manages to communicate. Every now and then, too, it stumbles on a vigorous line, as in

> The fiend is your chief: and our Head is God.

Indeed, Occleve, seldom good at a sustained passage or even stanza, does, sometimes, hit off good single lines. This piece is in octaves; *The Letter of Cupid to Lovers* is of about the same length and also of some merit. It is imitated, of course—in this case from Christine de Pisan. *The Mother of God*, once assigned to Chaucer, is rather better than *The Complaint of the Virgin*: but the latter is certainly translated and the former probably so. A curious contrast, but one quite in Occleve's usual manner, to the serious and woful ballades to which we are accustomed, is to be found in that to Sir Henry Sommer, chancellor of the exchequer, in reference to a club dinner to be held by a certain society called the 'Court of Good Company,' and, apparently, to be mainly provided by the said Sir Henry. To the same person are addressed a poetical petition for the payment of arrears of salary, and a punning roundel, 'Somer, that rypest mannes sustenance.' These are, in fact, the things which make Occleve, no matter what his technical shortcomings, refreshing, for it is certainly, in verse even more than in prose, better to read about good fellowship or even about personal troubles than to be compelled to peruse commonplaces on serious subjects, put without any freshness in expression and manner. Even Wordsworth might, in such a case, have preferred 'personal talk.'

The task of continuing one of Lydgate's last and most prosaic works was taken up by a younger writer, Benet or Benedict Burgh, from whom we have some other things. Burgh is said to have had his education at Oxford, and, probably, had his extraction from Essex, where he was, in 1440, made rector of Sandon. He was also tutor in the Bourchier family, and successively rector of Sible Hedingham, archdeacon of Colchester, prebendary (1477) of St Paul's and canon of St Stephen's at Westminster, which latter benefice he held at his death in 1483. Besides his completion of *The Secrets of the Philosophers*, which seems to have been done

to order, we have a poem of Burgh's in praise of, and addressed
to, Lydgate himself, *A Christmas Game, Aristotle's A B C* and
a version of the famous distichs attributed to Cato, which was
printed by Caxton separately, before he attempted his own translation. The last piece has been spoken of as showing versification
superior to that of Burgh's other work, but this is only partially
true. His favourite metre is rime royal, which he manages with
all the staggering irregularity common to English poets of the
fifteenth century, and not fully explicable by the semi-animate
condition of the final -*e* and some other things of the kind. Burgh's
earlier equivalents for the so-called decasyllable vary numerically
from seven syllables to fourteen : no principle of metrical equiva-
lence and substitution being for the most part able to effect even a
tolerable correspondence between their rhythm, which is constantly
of the following kind :

> When from the high hille, I mean the mount Canice.
> > *Poem to Lydgate*, i, 45.

> Secunde of the persone the magnificence royale.
> > *Secrets*, i, 1558.

The opening verses (which probably gave rise to the opinion
above recorded) of *Cato* are more regular, the author having had
by this time about thirty years' practice and having attained a
certain Occlevian power of counting on his fingers. But he relapses
later and we have lines like these

> Mannes soule resembleth a newe plain table
> In whiche yet apperith to sight no picture
> The philosophre saith withouten fable
> Right so is mannes soule but a dedly figure
> Unto the tyme she be reclaimed with the lure
> Of doctrine and so gete hir a good habit
> To be expert in cunnyng science and prouffit. Bk. i, st. 2.

Even here may be noticed that strong tendency towards the
alexandrine which is notable in all the disorderly verse of this
time, and which attempted to establish and regularise itself in the
poetry of the earlier Elizabethans, making its last and greatest
effort in *Polyolbion*.

There is no poetry in Burgh : there could not well be any ; and
there is, and there could be, as little in George Ashby, clerk of the
signet to queen Margaret of Anjou, who, being imprisoned in the
Fleet, *c.* 1461—3, for debt and other causes which he makes more
obscure, wrote there fifty rime royal stanzas of reflection and

self-condolence on his state. At a more uncertain time, but in his own eightieth year, he composed, in the same metre, a longer poem on the *Active Policy of a Prince*, intended to instruct the ill-fated son of Margaret and Henry before they 'stabbed [him] in the field by Tewkesbury.' A yet larger collection, in the same stanza but detached, of more 'sayings of the philoshers' is also attributed to Ashby : didactic verse being particularly dear to that troubled and gloomy century. The sense is sound and often shrewd enough, showing the rather Philistine and hard but canny temper of the later Middle Ages ; and the verse is not so irregular as in some of Ashby's contemporaries. But it is not illumined by one spark of the divine fire. As none of these versifiers is everywhere accessible, a single stanza, fairly average in character, may be given :

> Yf ye cannot bringe a man by mekenesse,
> By swete glosyng wordes and fare langage,
> To the entente of your noble highnesse,
> Correcte him sharpely with rigorous rage,
> To his chastysment and ferful damage.
> For who that wol nat be feire entreted
> Must be foule and rigorously threted.

To the same rime royal division—as a later member of it, but still partly before 1500—belongs Henry Bradshaw, a monk of St Werburgh's abbey at Chester (his native place), who has left a large life of his patroness, extending to those of Etheldreda and Sexburga, and a good deal of profane history of Chester and Mercia at large. It thus has a variety and quality of subject contrasting favourably with the didactic monotony of the works just mentioned ; and it is not specially unreadable so far as treatment is concerned, while students of literary history will be interested to find that the author, paying the invariable compliment to Chaucer and Lydgate, omits Gower, but substitutes his own contemporaries,

> To pregnant Barclay now being religious,
> To inventive Skelton and poet-laureate.

Bradshaw died in 1513: and his poem was printed by Pynson eight years later. In prosody it is one of the most remarkable documents as to the complete loss of grip which had come upon English verse. It has been charitably suggested that, in place of Chaucerian decasyllable, Bradshaw retains the 'old popular long line,' whatever that may be. To which it can only be replied that if he did not mean decasyllables he constantly stumbles into

them; and that, elsewhere, his lines are neither like those of
Robert of Gloucester, nor like those of *Gamelyn*, but frank
pieces of prose rimed at the end and cut anyhow to a length
which is, perhaps, on the average, nearer to that of an alexandrine
than to any other standard, but almost entirely rhythmless. If he
is not quite so shambling as some of his predecessors and contemporaries, he is, throughout, steadily pedestrian. His verse,
perhaps as well as anything else, makes us understand the wrath
of the next generation with 'beggarly *balducktoom* riming.'

A still more noteworthy set of instances of the all-powerful
attraction of rime royal, and a curious and not uninteresting
section of the followers of Chaucer, is provided by the fifteenth
century writers in verse on alchemy. This following is of substance, as well as in forms, as the mention of *The Canon's Yeoman's
Tale* is sufficient to show. And there is the further noteworthy
point that each of the two chief of these writers follows one
of Chaucer's main narrative measures, the couplet and rime
royal.

These are George Ripley (called 'Sir' George merely as a
priest) and Thomas Norton, both of whom, by their own testimony,
wrote in the eighth decade of the fifteenth century, and who, by
tradition though not certainly, were connected as master and
pupil. Of neither is much known; and of Ripley scarcely anything except that he was an Augustinian and canon of Bridlington
—the connection with Chaucer's canon being again interesting.
His principal English work, *The Compound of Alchemy or the
Twelve Gates*, was, as the author tells us, written in the year 1471,
and was printed 120 years later by Ralph Rabbards. Ashmole,
who reprinted it (after, as he says, comparison with several MSS)
in his *Theatrum Chemicum* of 1652, included therein several
minor verse-pamphlets on the same subject, attributed to the
same author—the most interesting being an English preface, in
octosyllabic rime royal of tolerable regularity, to his *Medulla
Alchemiae*, written five years later than *The Compound*, and
dedicated to archbishop Nevill. *The Compound* itself is spoken of
by Warton (delusively enough, though he explains what he means
or, at least, indicates his own laxness of speech) as 'in the
octave stanza.' As a matter of fact, it consists of a *Titulus
Operis* and a dedication to Edward IV, both written in octaves,
and of a body of text, prologue, preface and the twelve gates
('Calcination,' 'Solution,' etc., up to 'Projection') in rime royal.

The first stanza of this preface is no ill example of the

aureate language and of the hopelessly insubordinate metre common at this time:

> O hygh ynccomprehensyble and gloryous Mageste,
> Whose luminos bemes obtundyth our speculation,
> One-hode in Substance, O Tryne-hode in Deite,
> Of Hierarchicall Jubylestes the gratulant gloryfycation;
> O pytewouse puryfyer of Soules and puer perpetuation;
> O deviant fro danger, O drawer most deboner,
> Fro thys envios valey of vanyte, O our Exalter!

It was common, however, to overflow in this manner at the beginning of a poem; and the bulk of Ripley's text is more moderately phrased, though there is not much more to be said for the metre. Even the final distichs, which, in rime royal, un-doubtedly did a great deal to help on the formal couplet, are exceedingly lax and, sometimes, as in

> I am a master of that Art
> I warrant us we shall have part,
>
> (Ashmole, p. 157),

purely octosyllabic. The matter, allowing for the nature of the subject, is not ill set forth; and Ripley evidently had the true experimental spirit, for he records his failures carefully. Of less interest are the shorter pieces attributed to him besides the *Medulla* Preface—his *Vision* in about a score of fairly regular fourteeners, his *Scroll*, or the verses in it in irregular octo-syllables, sometimes approaching 'Skeltonics,' and one or two others in the same metre, extending instead of contracting itself.

Of Thomas Norton, who dates his own *Ordinall of Alchemy* at 1477, a little more is known or supposed to be known. Ashmole's statement that 'from the first word of his Proeme and the Initial Letters of the six following chapters (*discovered by acromonosyllables and syllabic acrostics*) we may collect the author's name and place of residence,' which has sometimes been quoted without the parenthesis, is thus misleading, for you must take the first syllables, not the first letters, to make

Tomas Norton of Bristo.

And the identification of the master whom he tells us he sought at the age of twenty-eight and from whom he learnt alchemy, is conjectural, though it was, most probably, Ripley.

He is generally supposed to have been the son of a Norton who was a very prominent citizen of Bristol, being bailiff in 1392, sheriff in 1410, mayor in 1413 and M.P. pretty continuously from 1399 to 1421; while the alchemist himself is thought to have sat for the city in 1436. Whether all these dates are not rather far from 1477 is a point merely to be suggested.

The Ordinall is written in exceedingly irregular heroic couplets, often shortening themselves to octosyllables,

> He was, and what he knew of schoole
> And therein he was but a fool,

and sometimes extending themselves or their constituent lines after the fashion of

> Physicians and Appoticaries faut [*make mistakes in*] appetite and will.

Indeed, if Ascham was really thinking of *The Ordinall* when, in *The Scholemaster*[1], he ranks 'Th. Norton, of Bristow' with Chaucer, Surrey, Wyatt and Phaer as having made the best that could be made of the bad business of riming verse, it merely shows how entirely insensible he was to true English prosody. Still, Norton is not quite uninteresting, because he shows, even more than Lydgate, how many hares at one time the versifiers of this period were hunting when they seemed to be copying Chaucer's couplet. Indeed, in some respects he is the earliest writer to exhibit the blend of which Spenser nearly made a very great success in the *February* of *The Shepheards Calender*, and, in a less degree, in *May* and *September*—this blend, however, being, in Norton's case, no doubt, not at all consciously aimed at, but a mere succession of hits and misses at the couplet itself. He sometimes achieves very passable Tusserian anapaestics,

> Her name is Magnesia, few people her knowe,
> She is found in high places as well as in low,

extending himself in the very next line almost to a complete fourteener,

> Plato knew her property and called her by her name,

and in a line or two contracting to

> That is to say what this may be.

The matter is less clearly put than in Ripley; and, though neither can be called a poet, the master is rather less far from being one than the scholar. But Norton's greater discursiveness may make his work more attractive to some readers, and the story of Dalton and Delves in his second chapter reads like a true anecdote.

Great as was the attraction of rime royal, it was not likely quite

[1] p. 289, ed. W. Aldis Wright, *Cambridge English Classics.*

to oust the older favourite, the octosyllabic couplet, which, it has
to be remembered, could also boast the repeated, if not the final,
patronage of Chaucer, and that (which was almost as influential)
of Lydgate, while the third great influence, Gower, was wholly
for it. No practitioner of this time, however, attained the ease
and fluency of *Confessio Amantis* as a whole or came anywhere
near the occasional vigour of its best parts, while the slip-shod
insignificance of the measure at its worst found constant victims.
The so-called romance (really a didactic poem) of *Boctus and
Sidrac* by Hugh de Campden, who is supposed to represent
the first half of the century, may stand as a representative
of this, while the *Legends of the Saints* by Osbern Bokenam,
copied by, or for, a certain Thomas (not Benet) Burgh, in 1447,
are written entirely in Chaucerian decasyllabic verse, differently
arranged as regards line group, but fairly regular in the line itself
—much more so, indeed, than the average verse of the time. This
regularity, however, is compensated by an extraordinary failure to
attain even the slightest tincture of poetic style and sentiment.
Bokenam, a Suffolk man, and using some dialectal forms, was an
Augustinian friar. But there is little doubt that he must have
been a pretty constant student of Chaucer himself, as we know he
was of his contemporary and countryman Lydgate.

Though there may seem to be 'nothing but low and little' in
this account of the known or, at least, named writers in southern
English verse during the fifteenth century, yet some satisfaction is,
no doubt, to be extracted by a true, and not impatient or ignorant,
lover of English poetry, in every part and period of its long and
important development. But there is probably no period in the
last seven hundred years which yields to such a lover so little
satisfaction as this. In comparison with it, the period preceding
Chaucer is a very 'Paradise of Dainty Devices.' It ought not to be
neglected, because it is necessary to the understanding of the
whole story, and is, perhaps, the most remarkable illustration in
that story of the French proverb about falling back to make a
better spring. But its attractions are almost wholly the attractions of instruction; and the instruction is seldom that which
the writers desired to give, pedagogic as they often were.

To the most attractive, if also the most puzzling, part
of it, we may now come. There can be no doubt that, putting
ballads, carols and the like aside, no verse in southern English,
from 1400 to 1500 or a little later, has anything like the
literary and poetical merit or interest which attaches to the

best of the doubtful 'Chauceriana' themselves. These pieces have, during the last generation, been rather unfortunate: for some Chaucer-students, in their fear of seeing them readmitted to the canon, have, as it were, cast them out altogether and refused to have anything to do with them, while even those who have admitted them to a sort of court of the gentiles have seemed afraid of paying them too much attention. This seems irrational, and it is certainly unlucky; for more than one or two of these pieces possess poetical merit so considerable that their authors, when discovered, will have to be put above any writer previously mentioned in this chapter. *The Plowman's Tale*, which falls quite out of Chaucerian possibility from its substance and temper, has already been handled with its begetter the *Vision*, and many of the smaller pieces are sufficiently disposed of with Tyrwhitt's label of 'rubbish.' But *The Tale of Beryn* or *Second Merchant's Tale*, with the preliminary adventures of the Pardoner; *La Belle Dame sans Merci*, ascribed to Sir Richard Ros; *The Cuckoo and the Nightingale*, ascribed to Sir Thomas Clanvowe; *The Flower and the Leaf*, *The Assembly of Ladies* and *The Court of Love* are well entitled to notice here, and at least three of them deserve the commendations suggested above, whosoever wrote them and at whatsoever time between the possible limits of *c.* 1390—*c.* 1550 they may have been written.

The professed sequels to *The Canterbury Tales* themselves are shut off from the rest of the last group by a formal peculiarity, the neglect of which, by those who composed them and those who admitted them, is a curious indication of the uncritical attitude of the time. All *The Canterbury Tales* proper are written in very strict metre, regularly handled. *The Merchant's Prologue and Tale* are in a peculiar doggerel, half-way between the fourteeners or run-on ballad measure of *Gamelyn,* and the much more doggerellised medium of the early interludes. Not unfrequently the lines can be forced into decasyllables; but the only satisfactory general arrangement is that of 'the queen was in her parlour' with a more or less strong stop in the middle. This metre or quasi-metre Chaucer never uses or approaches in any of the works certainly, or even in those probably, his; and it is, of course, unlikely that he should have arranged in it 'prologue' matter which, in every one of the other numerous cases of its occurrence, is in irreproachable 'riding rime' or decasyllabic couplet. The single MS—the duke of Northumberland's—relied on for the tale is put at before 1450, but we have no other indication of origin, personal or temporal. The most curious thing, however, is that the unknown author, while making this singular blunder as to his form—a blunder which he could only have exceeded by going directly in the teeth of the disclaimer of alliterative rhythm in *The Parson's Prologue* —is not by any means so un-Chaucerian in matter and temper. The prologue, which is a fairly lively account of how the pilgrims occupied themselves when they reached Canterbury, busies itself especially with the adventures of the pardoner and his beguilement by an insinuating but treacherous 'tappestere' or barmaid. The substance of this is not looser than that of *The Miller's* and *Reeve's Tales*, and the narrative power is by no means inconsiderable. As for *The Second Merchant's Tale*, which starts the homeward series, it is a story (drawn from a French original) of commercial adventure and beguilement in foreign parts which, though rather long and complicated, by no means lacks interest or, again, narrative power, and fully deserves the pains spent upon it by Furnivall, Clouston and others in the Chaucer Society's edition; indeed, it is to be regretted that it is not included in Skeat's edition of Chaucer and Chauceriana. But Chaucer's own it cannot possibly be—any more than *Gamelyn* itself, which was, possibly, its model.

The other pieces, though of various literary merit, all obey, in measure and degree, the rules of regular metre. The least good of them is *La Belle Dame sans Merci*, translated from Alain Chartier (who, beyond all doubt, wrote the original after Chaucer's death), and now attributed, on MS authority, to Sir Richard Ros, who may have written it about the middle of the fifteenth century or a little later. It is partly in rime royal, partly in octaves, and is a heavy thing, showing the characteristic, if not the worst, faults of that *rhétoriqueur* school, of which Chartier was the precursor, if not the actual leader.

Very much better is *The Cuckoo and the Nightingale*, sometimes also called *The Book of Cupid God of Love*, which, as a MS has the quasi-signature of '*explicit* Clanvowe,' is assigned to a certain Sir Thomas Clanvowe, a Herefordshire gentleman, of whom we find mention in the very year after Chaucer's death (1401), as well as seven years earlier and three later. It is, therefore, practically Chaucerian in date if not in authorship, being the only one of these pieces which can be brought so close to him. And it is, accordingly, very noteworthy as showing that all writers of the time did not adopt the severe rime system attributed to

Chaucer himself in the matter of the final -*e*, while Clanvowe's use of that suffix within the line is also different. The poem is one of great attractiveness—quite independently of the fact that Milton evidently refers to it in an early sonnet. It is written in an unusual metre—a quintet of decasyllables of rimed *aabba*—which has no small harmony; and, numerous as are the pieces which deal with May mornings and bird-songs, it may keep its place with the best of them, while it has an additional hold on literary history as suggesting one of the earliest of possibly original Middle English poems—*The Owl and the Nightingale.* There is some idea that it may have been written in connection with the marriage of Henry IV to Joan of Navarre.

Of the three pieces which remain, one, *The Assembly of Ladies*, was rejected by Tyrwhitt and is of considerably less literary merit and interest than the other two, though, by some of those who are most certain of these not being Chaucer's, it is considered to be by the same author as *The Flower and the Leaf.* All three, it may be observed, are in rime royal. *The Assembly*, for which we have two MSS as well as Thynne's edition of 1532, purports, as does *The Flower and the Leaf*, to be written by a woman. It is of the allegorical type, and contains elaborate descriptions of the house and gardens of Loyalty, with a porter Countenance, a guide Diligence and so forth. There are references to the (Chaucerian) stories of Phyllis and Demophoon, of Anelida and Arcite, etc. The descriptions of dress are very full; but the poem comes to no particular end. It has all the character of having been written by an ardent and fairly careful student of Chaucer who possessed no poetical gift. The rimes, the grammar and the use of the final -*e* digress considerably from the standard adopted as Chaucerian. But the fact is that, as Tyrwhitt saw, there is no reason for attributing this poem to him. It is quite evidently—to anyone fairly skilled in literary criticism proper—a school copy, and not by any means a very good one.

The case is different with the two others, *The Flower and the Leaf* and *The Court of Love.* To begin with, the positive external evidence in their favour is of the weakest kind—is, indeed, next to non-existent. Of *The Flower and the Leaf* we have no MS whatsoever, though one is said to have been heard of; and it was not even admitted to the printed works till 1597—8 by Speght. *The Court of Love* had been printed by Stow in 1561, and we have, apparently, the MS which he used; but there is no other, and this would not appear to be much older than the date of the print.

Yet, further, it is evident that, if either poem was written anywhere near Chaucer's time, it must have been considerably tampered with by scribes. In *The Court of Love*, particularly, there is a remarkable jumble of archaic and modernised forms, which has led some to think that it was forged by a writer who actually had Thynne's *Chaucer*, as well as works by Lydgate and other Chaucerians before him.

It will be observed that this is rather a dangerous argument, because it admits the strongly Chaucerian character of the poem: and, indeed, this may be asserted of both pieces. They are, in fact, so good and so Chaucerian that it is not too much to say that, between Chaucer himself and Wyatt (whose manner they do not in the least resemble), we know of no southern English poet who could have written either, and must place two *anonymi* at the head of the actual list. But, in face of the philological difficulties above stated, and of the fact that there is absolutely no internal claim to Chaucerian authorship—the 'daughter,' who is spoken to in *The Flower*, is unnamed, and the author of *The Court* styles himself 'Philogenet, of Cambridge, clerk'—it is impossible to pronounce them Chaucer's. Yet it must be pointed out that the arguments against his authorship from the feminine attribution in *The Flower* are absolutely valueless. Pushed to their legitimate and logical conclusion, they would lead us to strike out *The Wife of Bath's Prologue*, had it survived alone of *The Canterbury Tales*. We do not know in whose mouth the author intended to put the piece any more than we know who that author was. Nor is the stress laid on description of dress much better. Was Sir Piercie Shafton a lady, or John Chalkhill of *Thealma and Clearchus* fame? It may be added that *The Flower and the Leaf* is conjecturally put at about the middle of the fifteenth century and *The Court of Love* at some half-century or even three-quarters of a century later. But these dates are, admittedly, guess-work.

What is not guess-work is the remarkable excellence of the poems themselves, which have been too seldom considered of late on their own merits, apart from polemical and really irrelevant considerations. When we take *The Flower and the Leaf* in the only text which we possess—not as vamped up to a possible or impossible Chaucerian norm—we find in it more than a trace of that curious prosodic vertigo which seems to have beset the whole fifteenth century. There is not only uncertainty about the use of the final -*e* as a syllable, and a vacillating sense of its value; but, though the decasyllable is not extended in the wild fashion which we find from Lydgate downwards, it is often cut short, sometimes to the Chaucerian, and even the Lydgatian, 'nine'—sometimes to a frank dimeter. But these shortcomings, most of which are, at least possibly, scribal, do not interfere with the general smoothness of the metre; nor do a few infelicities of diction (such as the comparison of grass to 'green wool') interfere with its attractiveness, in that respect also unusual for its time, undue aureation and undue beggarliness being equally avoided. Still, the great charm of the piece is a certain nameless grace of choice, arrangement and handling of subject. The main theme, which has some connection with the story of Rosiphele in *Confessio Amantis*, and which, in another way, is anticipated by Chaucer himself in *The Legend of Good Women*, is an allegory—not, perhaps, exactly of chastity and unchastity, but of something like the Uranian and Pandemic Venus, adjusted to medieval ideas and personified by Diana and Flora respectively. Each of these has her train of knights and ladies devoted to the Leaf (regarded as something permanent), and the Flower (gay, but passing) and wearing liveries of green and white. The lady who tells the tale beholds the processions and sports of the two parties and the small disaster, which, in the shape of a sudden squall of wind and rain, tarnishes the finery of the Flower party, and drives them and their queen to take shelter with the lady of the Leaf under her greenery. The piece is not long—less than 600 lines—and its scheme is quite common form: sleeplessness, early rising, walk abroad and the like; but there is a singular brightness and freshness over it all, together with a power of pre-Raphaelite decoration and of vivid portraiture—even of such action as there is—which is very rare. Indeed, out of Chaucer himself and the original beginning of Guillaume de Lorris in the *Roman de la Rose*, it would be difficult to find anything of the kind better done.

For literary history, the interest of the poem is, of course, increased by the fact that Dryden, having no doubts about its being Chaucer's, took it for the canvas of one of his 'fable' translations, and reproduced it with remarkable success on the different system which he brought into play. But this neither adds to, nor lessens, its intrinsic merit. It may, however, be added that, though simpler and less pedantic, it has strong points of likeness to *The Kingis Quair*, and that, after a long and careful reading, it gives the impression of having, though complete in

itself, been probably intended by its author, if not exactly as a
continuation of other pieces in a larger whole, at any rate as a
production to be taken in connection with them. This impression,
however, may be individual and arbitrary. The question of its
merit is a different one.

In *The Court of Love*, on the other hand, we are, at any rate
as to prosody, out of what has been called the 'period of
staggers'; and, perhaps, this is a stronger argument for a late
origin than some that have been advanced on that side—though
it opens fresh difficulties. The rime royal here is of an accomplishment, an assured competence, which we do not find elsewhere
in southern English in any writer between Chaucer and Sackville.
The stanzas are frequently run on—not a common thing with this
metre, and, on the whole, not an improvement, because it destroys
the rest-effect of the final couplet. But, in themselves, and in the individual lines, there is plenty of spring and cadence. The language
is of a somewhat composite kind, showing aureation; and faults
are found with the grammar, while a great deal of indebtedness
to Lydgate has been urged. But, in fact, all these poets, and
Chaucer their master, had a community of goods in the matter of
phraseology. What is undeniable is that 'Philogenet,' if really
'of Cambridge, clerk,' adds one to its nest of singing birds that
even the university of Spenser, Milton and Dryden cannot afford
to oust. He may be an interloper or a coiner, but his goods are
sound and his standard pretty high. The title of the piece—if the
obvious pitfall of mistaking the reference as being to the half-
fabulous, half-historical *cours d'amour* be avoided—speaks it
plainly enough. The poet strays to the palace of Citherea (near,
of course, the mount, instead of the isle, of 'Citheree') finds
Alcestis and Admetus vice-king and queen there; and makes
interest with a lady of the court, one Philobone, who had been
a friend of his. She shows him over the palace, where he
beholds and rehearses at great length the statutes of love, some
of which are hard enough and, in fact, mere counsels of perfection.
He makes solemn profession, and is assigned as 'servant' to a
beautiful damsel, named Rosiall, whose heart is yet untouched
and by whom he is received with the proper mixture of cruelty and
kindness. After this he is once more consigned to Philobone to
see the rarities of the place. Various allegorical personages and
scenes pass before him: the most famous and beautiful of which is
the picture of those who have wilfully denied themselves love.
After a gap (of which there are more than one in the poem) Pity,

who has been lying tranced in a shrine, rises and bids Rosiall be gracious to him; and the piece, which comes a little short of 1500 lines, ends with a charming, if not entirely original, bird chorus to the initial words of favourite psalms and passages of Scripture, the nightingale choosing *Domine labia*, the eagle *Venite* and the throstle cock *Te deum amoris*, while the peacock appropriately delivers *Dominus regnavit*.

The mere descriptions here are a little less artistic, and the atmosphere and colouring of a less dewy freshness than in *The Flower and the Leaf*; but a much larger range of qualities is brought into play. The actual narrative power, which is apt to be wofully wanting in these allegorical poems, is not small; and there is some character both about Philogenet and about 'little Philobone,' though Rosiall, naturally, has not much to do save smile or frown in look and speech. Further, there is not a little humour, and the whole is distinctly free from the invertebrate character of the usual fifteenth century poem; while, if we look to the parts, very few stanzas out of the more than two hundred lack the salt or the sweetness which are both constantly wanting at this time. But there is no doubt that the episode of the repentant ascetics and the conclusion are the choicest parts of the poem; and that neither of them ought to be absent from any full and representative collection of specimens of English poetry. The special quality of the stanza, its power of expressing passion and complaint, is thoroughly well brought out in the *Regrets*, and it is very noteworthy that the running-on, which was commented on above as a mistake, is not attempted in these places. It is, however, quite certain, even from this passage, that the sole MS is not the original.

The conclusion, besides its intrinsic beauty, has (if it actually be late) the interest of being one of the latest examples of a habit which began quite early in Middle English, of mixing Latin phrases, chiefly of the Scriptural kind. This became specially popular in the late fifteenth century just before it died out; and we have remarkable examples of it both from Skelton and Dunbar. But in them it usually shows itself by taking whole lines of Latin, not, as here, by interweaving scraps. The effect of the mixture is curiously pleasing, if a little fantastic, and gives a kind of key to the rhetorical attraction, in prose and poetic style, of the intermixture of words of Romance and other origin.

Taking it altogether, if *The Court of Love* is to be placed within the sixteenth century, we must regard it as the latest piece of

purely English poetry which exhibits strictly medieval characteristics in a condition either genuine or quite astonishingly imitated
—the very last echo with us, putting aside examples in Scots, of
the actual music, the very last breath of the atmosphere, of *The
Romance of the Rose.* That it should have been written by
Chaucer, in its present state, is philologically impossible; that, in
any form, it was his, there is no evidence whatever to show. But
that it is good enough as literature to have been his, and strangely
like him in temper and complexion, may be laid down as a critical
certainty.

CHAPTER IX

STEPHEN HAWES

In the closing years of the fifteenth century and the opening years of the sixteenth, the English language was still in that stage of transition in which it had been for about a century. The final -*e*, influential for much that is good in Chaucer and for much that is bad in his successors, had now fallen into disuse in the spoken language and accentuation, especially of words borrowed from foreign tongues, was unstable. These, and other linguistic developments, beginning at different times in different localities and proceeding with varying rapidity, made it a matter of considerable difficulty for the men of Henry VII's reign to understand the speech of another shire than their own, or the English of an older age.

In literature, too, the age was, in England, an age of transition; for with the end of other currents of medieval activity came the end of what had been the main stream of medieval literature. Popular poetry and morality plays flourished, history written in English made tentative efforts, but the court poetry of the Chaucerian tradition came to a stop in Stephen Hawes, who, amid the men of the new age, stands out as a survivor of the past, one born an age too late. He felt his solitariness, and in his most important work, *The Passetyme of Pleasure*, chap. xiv, he lamented that he remained the only faithful votary of true poetry. And, if we bear in mind his idea of poetry as essentially allegorical and didactic, we must allow that he had good cause for his lament. When we omit Skelton as standing apart in a niche of his own, we see that, though many songs and ballads of unknown authorship and—if one view be correct—those Chaucerian poems, *The Flower and the Leaf*, *The Assembly of Ladies*, *The Court of Love*, belong to this period, Hawes occupies a position of peculiar isolation. In this dearth of poets, it need not surprise us that a Frenchman, the blind Bernard André of Toulouse, author of *Les Douze Triomphes de Henry VII*, a poem in which the labours of Hercules form a framework for the king's exploits, was created poet laureate by Henry VII, who preferred French literature to any other.

Hawes is supposed to have been born in the county of Suffolk, where the name was common. The date of his birth is uncertain. In *The Passetyme*, he more than once identifies himself with the hero, who, in one passage, is said to be thirty-one years old. The poem was written, according to Wynkyn de Worde, in 1505—6; and, if Hawes himself was then thirty-one years of age, we get 1474—5 as the date of his birth—an inference quite consistent with our other information. He was educated at Oxford and afterwards visited several foreign universities. His acquirements, linguistic and literary, recommended him to Henry VII, whose household he entered as groom of the chamber. Anthony à Wood states that the king's favour was gained by Hawes's facetious discourse and prodigious memory: he could repeat most of the English poets, especially Lydgate. Entries in the public records show that, in 1506, Hawes was paid ten shillings for 'a ballet that he gave to the king's grace.' From Henry VIII's accounts we learn that in January 1521 'Mr Hawse' was paid £6. 13s. 4d. for a play. The play is unknown, but the writer may be Stephen Hawes. He died before 1530, for he is mentioned as dead in a poem belonging to that year, written by Thomas Feylde, *The Controversy between a Lover and a Jay*:

> Yonge Steven Hawse, whose soul God pardon,
> Treated of love so clerkely and well,
> To rede his workes is myne affeccyon,
> Whiche he compyled of La bell Pusell,
> Remembrynge storyes fruytfull and delectable.

Besides *The Passetyme*, Hawes wrote *The Example of Virtue*, in 1503—4[1], as we learn from Wynkyn de Worde's edition; *The Conversion of Swearers*, before 1509; *A Joyful Meditation to all England of the Coronation of Henry the Eighth*, 1509; and *The Comfort of Lovers*, date unknown. No manuscript of any of these seems to have been preserved. Of other works

---

[1] Some have assumed that *The Example of Virtue* was composed after *The Passetyme of Pleasure*, the date of which is given by Wynkyn de Worde as 1505—6. But we have the same authority for dating *The Example* as 1503—4. See the following extract from the copy of Wynkyn de Worde's edition of 1512, in the Pepysian library, Cambridge.

'This boke called the example of vertue was made and compyled by Stephen hawys one of the gromes of the moost honorable chaumber of oure soverayne lorde kynge Henry the .vii. the .xix. yere of his moost noble reyne and by hym presented to our sayd soverayne lorde.' (Fol. iii.)

attributed to Hawes, only one merits notice. Bale mentions a *Templum Chrystallinum*, and Warton regards Lydgate's *Temple of Glass* as by Hawes, though admitting himself puzzled because Hawes includes it in his list of Lydgate's poems, given in *The Passetyme*, chap. XIV. Hawes's writings bear out Bale's remark that his whole life *quasi virtutis exemplum fuit*.

With the exception of the Gobelive episode, which is in decasyllabic couplets, *The Passetyme* is in rime royal and contains about 5800 lines, divided into forty-five chapters. The hero, Graund Amour, is the narrator. Having entered on the way of the active life, he met Lady Fame. She described the excellences of La Bel Pucell, with whom he fell in love. He set off to the tower of Doctrine, where he saw an arras portraying his future life, and began his instruction under Lady Grammar. Here Hawes inserts a denunciation of the sloth and gluttony of his contemporaries. Then Graund Amour visited Logic, and, next, Rhetoric. Rhetoric, or the art of poetry, is elaborately discussed under the divisions of invention, disposition, elocution, pronunciation and memory. Hawes praises the old poets, defends allegory, attacks ignorance and sloth and finally eulogises Chaucer, Gower and Lydgate.

After listening to Arithmetic, Graund Amour went to Music, with whom was La Bel Pucell. He had the ineffable happiness of dancing with her, but lacked courage to tell his love. Advised by Counsel, he visited the lady in her garden. A 'disputation' followed, in which the commonplaces of medieval love-making are presented with freshness and vivacity. Graund Amour won his lady, but her friends carried her off to a distant land. Before setting out for it, the hero was instructed by Geometry and Astronomy. At the tower of Chivalry, he was trained in arms by Minerva and knighted by Melizius. Then he met a foolish dwarf, whose first words: 'when Icham in Kent Icham at home' showed his origin. He was Godfrey Gobelive, a despiser of women. Graund Amour and he came to a 'parliament' held by Venus, who despatched a letter urging La Bel Pucell to be kind.

Graund Amour now encountered a giant twelve feet high, with three heads, which he, at last, cut off. Three ladies hailed him victor, and Perseverance brought a gracious message from La Bel Pucell. Then he had to fight a seven-headed giant, fifteen feet high, wielding an axe seven yards long, whom, after a fierce conflict, he overthrew. Passing through a dismal wilderness, he caught a glimpse of La Bel Pucell's palace on an island infested by

the fire-breathing monster, Privy Malice. Blinded by its fire and
smoke, torn by its claws, Graund Amour was preserved by an
unguent given him by Pallas. The monster burst asunder, and
La Bel Pucell's palace became visible. The lovers were married
by Lex Ecclesiae, and lived many years in happiness. But Age
glided in, and with him Policy and Avarice. Death at last summoned Graund Amour away. Then follows a pageant of allegorical
personages—Fame, Time and Eternity. In conclusion Hawes
apologises for his ignorance; prays that bad printing may not
spoil his scansion; and expresses his hope of imitating the moral
writings of Lydgate.

Much of the contents of the other poems is found in *The
Passetyme* in only slightly varied form.

The Conversion of Swearers contains an exhortation from
Christ to princes and lords to cease swearing by His blood,
wounds, head and heart. It is, in short, a versified sermon. The
metre is the seven-line Chaucerian stanza, except a fantastic
passage in form as follows:

Se
Ye
Be
    Kind,
Again
My payne
Retcyne
    In Mynde;

and so on the metre goes, increasing to lines of six syllables
and decreasing again to words of one syllable. It is an early
example of shaped verses, which, in later days, take the form of
Pan's pipes, wings, crosses, altars, pyramids, gridirons and frying-
pans, and are to be found even in the days of George Herbert's
Temple.

*A Joyful Meditation to all England of the Coronation of
Henry the Eighth,* in the seven-line Chaucerian stanza, has little
to distinguish it from any other coronation poem. We may note,
however, that Hawes finds an apology for Henry VII's avarice in
the plea that he was amassing wealth to be ready for war—a view
which has been taken by modern historians. He urges the people
to be loyal and patriotic. He appeals also to Luna, as mistress of
the waves, and to the Wind-god to inspire Englishmen to chase their
enemies and—with words that anticipate *Ye Mariners of England*
—to sweep the sea in many a stormy 'stour.'

The Example of Virtue is written in the seven-line Chaucerian

stanza, except the description of the arming of the hero, where
decasyllabic couplets are used, and it is divided into fourteen
chapters. It tells how Youth, conducted by Discretion, sailed
over the sea of Vainglory and reached a fair island ruled by four
ladies, Nature, Fortune, Courage and Wisdom. Youth and Discretion, admitted by the warder Humility into the ladies' castle,
visited them in turn. Fortune was great and glorious, but unstable. Courage was powerful and famous, but Death was stronger.
Wisdom had the greatest attraction for Youth, who entered her
service and received much instruction. Nature possessed great
loveliness, but, behind her, was the grim visage of Death. Youth
and Discretion were present at a disputation in which each of the
four ladies urged her claims to be considered the highest in worth.
The umpire Justice bade them cease disputing and combine to
secure man's happiness.

Wisdom advised Youth to marry Cleanness. To be worthy
of her, he must be led by Discretion, and must not give way to
frailty or vainglory. Youth then passed into a wilderness, moon-
less and sunless. There, he triumphed over the temptations of
Sensuality, a fair lady mounted on a goat, and of Pride, a pleasant
old lady on an elephant. After emerging from the maze of worldly
fashion, he met Wisdom, who, with Discretion, brought him to a
stream crossed by a bridge as narrow as the ridge of a house.
Passing over, he arrived in the land of Great Grace, where lived
the king of Love and his daughter Cleanness. Before Youth could
win his bride, he must overcome a marsh-infesting dragon with three
heads, the world, the flesh and the devil. For this conflict he was
armed with 'the whole armour of God,' described by St Paul.

After a hard-won victory, Youth, now sixty years of age, was
renamed Virtue, and was married to Cleanness by St Jerome,
while, all around, were troops of allegorical ladies—Prayer, Penitence, Charity, Mercy; fathers of the church and saints such as
Bede and Ambrose; and the heavenly hosts with Michael and
Gabriel. St Edmund the martyr-king and Edward the Confessor
led the bride to the marriage feast. Finally, after Virtue had
been shown the sufferings of the lost in hell, all the company
ascended to heaven. The poem ends with a prayer that the union
of the Red Rose and the White may grow in all purity and
virtue; and with Hawes's usual address to Chaucer, Gower and
Lydgate.

In choice of theme, in method of exposition and in mode of
expression, Hawes has a limited range. He repeatedly insists

that every poet should be a teacher ; and he always presses his own lessons home, especially the lesson to eschew sloth. In his two long poems, he has the same didactic aim—to portray a man's struggle to attain his ideal : moral purity in *The Example of Virtue*, worldly glory in *The Passetyme of Pleasure*, the former being fuller of moralising than the latter. *The Passetyme*, which was composed after *The Example*, exhibits greater skill in treatment and possesses more human interest. Both poems belong to the same type of allegory, and are worked out on similar lines. They have a number of incidents in common, as crossing seas to reach the loved one, and killing a foe with three heads. Several of the personified abstractions are the same in both, as Fortune, Justice, Sapience or Wisdom, Grace, Perseverance, Peace, Mercy, Charity, Contrition. In all his poems, Hawes has certain pet ideas, which he puts forward again and again with little variation in phraseology : as eulogies of Chaucer, Gower and Lydgate ; apologies for rude diction and want of poetic power ; declarations that poets keep alive the memory of the great, and conceal moral instruction under 'cloudy figures.'

This sameness renders it unnecessary to examine all Hawes's poems in detail. We shall be able to appreciate the quality of his work even though we restrict ourselves, for the most part, to *The Passetyme of Pleasure*. It is an allegory of human life, couched in the form of a chivalrous romance, with the addition of a strong dash of scholastic learning and theology, and is in the line of such works as the *Roman de la Rose*, the allegories of Chaucer, Gower and Lydgate, Dunbar's *Goldyn Targe* and *Dance of the Sevin Deidlie Synnis*, Douglas's *King Hart*, Sackville's *Induction*, Googe's *Cupido Conquered* and Spenser's *Faerie Queene*. What Hawes did was to make a new departure, and, in working out his didactic allegory, emphasise the element of chivalrous romance. This suited his age, for, after the collapse of the feudal baronage in the wars of the Roses, came a revival of chivalry, though rather of the outward show than of the inward reality, of courtiers and carpet knights rather than of chivalrous warriors. Later, it blazed out in the Field of Cloth of Gold. The attempted revival in Henry VII's day explains the passage in *The Passetyme*, chap. XXVI, where Graund Amour is admonished to renew the flower of chivalry now long decayed, and in the dissertation of king Melizius, chap. XXVIII, on the true meaning of the chivalrous idea. Caxton, too, in *The Order of Chivalry*, recommends the reading of Froissart, and of tales about king Arthur's

knights, as likely to resuscitate chivalry. Hawes, however, with all
his advocacy of knighthood, insists more on the *trivium* and
quadrivium, less on the training that produced the men pictured
in Chaucer's knight and squire.

The long and complicated allegory of *The Passetyme* is
managed with much success. The personified abstractions are
selected and fitted in with no little dexterity. But it need
cause no surprise that we feel the details tiresome and obscure :
it may be that often details which seem obscure are pictorial and
not didactic. In the construction of the poem there are curious
slips ; in fact, the design seems to have been altered while it was
being worked out. Graund Amour, chap. IV, is shown an arras
picturing his journey and adventures till he wins his lady. What
he sees does not exactly coincide with what afterwards happens.
The arras does not show the meeting of the lovers in the tower of
Music, chap. XVII. More than once, after the hero saw the arras,
he is represented as doubtful of his ultimate success, *e.g.* chap. XVII.
Perhaps Hawes discovered—his readers certainly discover—that
the foreknowledge of the final result removes the feeling of suspense
and spoils the interest of the story. Again, Graund Amour and
La Bel Pucell come to a perfect understanding in the garden and
plight their troth, chap. XIX. Yet, later, chaps. XXIX ff., the
garden scene is entirely ignored ; and the conventional plan that
makes Venus the intermediary to persuade the lady to take pity on
her lover is employed. Nor is the allegory always consistent ; but
that is a trifle, for even in *The Pilgrim's Progress* lynx-eyed critics
have detected inconsistencies. In *The Passetyme*, inconsistency
often arises from the exigency of the narrative. We recognise the
aptness of the allegory when the perfect knight has as his companions the knights Truth, Courtesy, Fidelity, Justice, Fortitude,
Nurture and such like : that is, possesses the qualities symbolised
by those knights. Soon, however, they bid him farewell, not because he has lost those traits of character, but because the narrative
requires that he shall fight his battles alone. The greyhounds
Grace and Governance are, in spite of their names, conventional
figures : when stirring events are in progress they drop into the
background. Sometimes an abstraction, which has been already
employed in one connection, is reintroduced in another, and even
an incongruous, connection. Envy, for example, is one of the
giant's seven heads and is cut off by Graund Amour ; but it reappears as one of the contrivers of the metal monster. Like other
allegories, *The Passetyme* is marred by the fact that the characters

talk and debate too much, and act too little. And it must be
admitted that the personification of the seven sciences makes
dreary reading nowadays. Hawes himself found it difficult to
turn his expositions of learning into musical form. His stanzas on
the noun substantive, chap. v, must surely be among the most
unpoetical passages of all metrical writing. Four lines will be
sufficient to quote.

> The Latyn worde whyche that is referred
> Unto a thynge whych is substancyall,
> For a nowne substantyve is wel averred,
> And wyth a gender is declynall.

We have seen that Hawes was reputed a man of wide learning,
and his writings bear this out. He was familiar with the Bible
and with theological books. The influence of the wisdom-
literature of the Old Testament and the Apocrypha is manifest
in the prominent part assigned to Wisdom and Discretion in *The
Example of Virtue*. The conclusion of the same poem is crowded
with saints and martyrs, while Augustine and Bernard are quoted
in *The Conversion of Swearers*. The exposition of the sciences in
The Passetyme, though not free from slips, of which he was himself
aware, shows that he had studied the text-books of the *trivium*
and *quadrivium*. It was not, however, the intellectual value
of those studies that appealed to him so much as their moral
influence. Rhetoric and music, he says, produce not only order
in words and harmony in sounds, but also order in man's life and
harmony in his soul. Hawes was thoroughly versed in the romantic
and allegorical writings of the preceding generations. He appeals
to Caxton's *Recuyell of the Histories of Troy*, and, speaking of
Arthur, he evidently refers to Malory's *Morte d'Arthur* as a
familiar book. Whether or not Hawes possessed the powerful
memory attributed to him, his methods, illustrations, turns of phrase,
continually remind us of the *Roman de la Rose*, of Chaucer—
Troilus and Criseyde for example—of Gower's *Confessio Amantis*,
of Lydgate—especially *The Temple of Glass*. His indebtedness to
these three poets he frequently acknowledges; and it may be
summarily illustrated. The prayer at the end of *The Passetyme*,
that the scansion may not be marred by bad printing and that
the poet's intention may be manifest, is, in idea and phrasing,
closely modelled on a passage near the conclusion of Chaucer's
Troilus. *Troilus*, which Hawes often cites, is also his original for
the lovers' meeting in the temple of Music and for their sorrowful
parting, chaps. XVII, XIX. Gower's *Confessio* supplies the fabliaux

about Aristotle and Vergil, and the tradition that Evander's daughter devised the principles of Latinity, chaps. XXIX, V. *The Passetyme* resembles *The Temple of Glass* in being partly in rime royal, partly in decasyllabic couplets. Again, the dazzling brightness of the tower of Doctrine and the impossibility of gazing at it till clouds covered the sun, chap. III, Hawes borrowed, diction and all, from Lydgate's description of the crystal fane. The gold vine with grapes of rubies in the roof of the same tower comes from Mandeville. Hawes evidently had *The Court of Sapience* also in his mind. The prison in the tower of Chastity, chap. XXXII, is a distant and pale reflection of Dante's *Inferno*. Finally, Hawes appears to have drawn, directly or indirectly, from Martianus Capella's *de Nuptiis Philologiae et Mercurii*, the well known text-book of the Middle Ages.

Living though Hawes did at the opening of a new age, and having studied abroad at the time when the study of the classics was reviving in western Europe, he still shows the characteristic marks of medievalism. His writings abound in long digressions, irrelevances, debates, appeals to authority, needless repetitions, prolix descriptions. One glaring instance of prolixity occurs in *The Passetyme*, chap. XLII, where the sum and substance of a seven-line stanza on Pride can be adequately expressed in the six words, 'Why is earth and ashes proud?' Hawes also exhibits want of proportion. More than one-eighth of *The Passetyme* is devoted to the exposition of Rhetoric, with two digressions. Again, he jumbles together ideas and associations of various ages, and fails to appreciate the difference between his own age and classical times. Anything characteristic of an earlier age and not of his own, he transmutes, like other medieval writers, into something of his own days that seemed analogous. Thus, Plato is 'the cunning and famous clerk'; Joshua is a 'duke'; the centaur-king Melizius is the founder of feudal chivalry and is conversant with St Paul's epistles; Minerva[1] and Pallas are spoken of as distinct—the former being instructor in arms at the court of Melizius, the latter being the goddess. Vergil, too, is the magician. Hawes employs the familiar medieval machinery—the May morning, Fortune and her wheel, the seven deadly sins, astronomical lore, and he firmly believes that all poetry is allegory. In his defence of poets, *The Passetyme*, chap. IX, he maintains that it is because the revilers of poetry cannot discover the moral under the allegory that they fail to appreciate poetry. Equally medieval is he in holding that poets should always have

[1] So Dunbar, *Goldyn Targe*, l. 78, makes Minerva and Pallas two goddesses.

a lesson to teach. So strongly does he hold this, that to those who write without a moral he would almost deny the name of poet. He bewails the dearth of moral poets in his own day: most versifiers, he says, waste their time in 'vaynful vanyte,' composing ballades of fervent love, 'gests' and trifles without fruitfulness[1].

Hawes never outgrew those views of poetry and never thoroughly rid himself of the traditional conventions. Sometimes he forgets them, and then he is at his best. His style becomes animated or graceful; his diction shakes itself free from the load of aureate terms. At times his fine rhetoric—'aromatyke fume' he calls it—is very cumbrous and disfiguring: as in *The Passetyme*, chap. XXXVIII,

> Her redolente wordes of swete influence
> Degouted vapoure moost aromatyke,
> And made conversyon of complacence;
> Her depured and her lusty rethoryke
> My courage reformed, that was so lunatyke.

He uses also the words 'pulcritude,' 'facundious,' 'tenebrous,' 'sugratife,' 'exornate,' 'perdurable' and 'celestine.' He frequently runs riot in the rhetorical figure of epanaphora, as in *The Passetyme*, chap. XXI, where each line of one stanza begins 'Where lacketh mesure,' while in another, 'Without mesure wo worth' occurs seven times. In spite of pedantry, however, Hawes manages to write passages of poetic beauty and sweet tenderness. Such passages are found in the garden scene, where Graund Amour woos La Bel Pucell, *The Passetyme*, chap. XVIII. There, allegory disappears; and, though we meet with verbiage and stiffness, we cannot miss the beating of human hearts, the eager passion of the man, the coyness of the maid, coyness that ends in complete surrender. Allegory is again dropped in the episode of Godfrey Gobelive, *The Passetyme*, chaps. XXIX, XXXII. There, Hawes is a keen observer of contemporary life, which he describes at first hand. If the rest of the poem with its personified abstractions may be reckoned akin to the morality plays, this episode is in tone a comic interlude. It exhibits also a change then beginning among the abstractions of the moralities, a change destined to develop in comedy. Godfrey Gobelive and his ancestors, Davy Dronken-nole, Sym Sadle-gander, Peter Pratefast, are not allegorical shadows but living personalities. Such alliterative nicknames are parallel to the Tom Tosspot and Cuthbert Cutpurse of the moralities, to Tibet Talkapace and Davy Diceplayer of the comedies.

---

[1] *The Passetyme*, chap. XIV.

So, too, Godfrey's Kentish tongue, his Kentish home, his grandfather's voyage up the Thames in search of a wife, which give a touch of reality to the narrative, find parallels in the moralities : *e.g.* in *The World and the Child*, where Folly describes his adventures in Holborn and Southwark. Godfrey has humour of the rough type seen in *Gammer Gurton's Needle* : his great-grandmother, for example, is praised for cleanliness, because, when she had no dishclout, she wiped the dishes with her dog's tail.

The Passetyme of Pleasure and *The Example of Virtue* belong to the group of allegorical poems culminating in *The Faerie Queene* ; and it is generally agreed that Hawes influenced Spenser. Opinions, however, differ as to the extent of this influence. On the one hand E. B. Browning calls *The Passetyme* one of 'the four columnar marbles, the four allegorical poems, on whose foundation is exalted into light the great allegorical poem of the world, Spenser's *Faery Queen.*' On the other hand, Saintsbury admits only a faint adumbration of *The Faerie Queene* in *The Passetyme* and *The Example* : 'its outline without its glorious filling-in, its theme without its art, its intellectual reason for existence without any of its aesthetic justification thereof. It is not improbable that Spenser did know Hawes ; but, if so, he owed him a very small royalty.' The extent of this influence, or indebtedness, is easy to overstate and very difficult, or, rather, impossible, to prove. Mere coincidences may readily be mistaken for borrowing. It does not follow that, when two writers speak in very similar terms of the seven deadly sins, one has borrowed from the other. For, from the time of *Piers the Plowman*, the seven deadly sins had appeared again and again in allegory, in morality play and in pageant : they are found, too, along with other miscellaneous information, in that perpetual almanac, *The Kalendar of Shepherds*. It seems better, then, simply to enumerate points of resemblance —grouped together they make a striking list—than to attempt to define where the limit of Spenser's indebtedness to Hawes should be fixed.

Hawes's main idea is to describe the discipline a man must undergo and the obstacles he must surmount to attain moral purity, in *The Example*, or win worldly glory, in *The Passetyme*. Spenser states that his general aim is 'to fashion a gentleman or noble person in virtuous and gentle discipline.'

Spenser follows the lead of Hawes in adopting the paraphernalia of chivalry as allegorical symbolism. The knights of *The Faerie Queene* put into practice what Melizius enunciates in

The Passetyme as the underlying idea of chivalry—not fighting in every quarrel, but fighting for the truth or for the common-weal, and helping widows and maidens in distress. Some of Melizius's knights, as, for instance, Courtesy and Justice, appear among Spenser's paladins.

It is after hearing a description of La Bel Pucell's surpassing beauty and worth that Graund Amour falls in love and determines to win his ideal. Spenser represents Arthur as having 'seen in a dream or vision the Faerie Queene, with whose beauty ravished, he, awaking, resolved to seek her out.'

Graund Amour in *The Passetyme*, Youth in *The Example*, and Spenser's Red Cross Knight wear the same armour, the Christian soldier's panoply described by St Paul, whose *Epistle to the Ephesians* is expressly referred to in each of the three instances.

In *The Example* there is a dragon with three heads—the world, the flesh and the devil—which must be defeated before Lady Cleanness is won; and the Red Cross Knight must overcome the same three foes before he wins Lady Una.

Lechery, in *The Example*, is a fair lady riding on a goat, and, in *The Faerie Queene*, a man upon a bearded goat. In the former poem, Pride is an old lady in a castle on an elephant's back, in the latter, a lady in a coach drawn by peacocks. Hawes writes of the park of Pride, Spenser of the garden of Pride.

When fighting with the seven-headed giant, Graund Amour leaps aside to evade the stroke of the ponderous axe, which then crashes into the ground three feet and more. In a similar way, Orgoglio's club misses its mark and ploughs three yards into the ground.

Humility is warder of the castle in *The Example*, and porter of Spenser's house of Holiness.

The claim asserted by Mutability in Spenser's fragmentary seventh book resembles Fortune's claim to universal rule, as set forth by Hawes in both his poems.

Envy, Disdain and Strangeness contrive Hawes's monster Privy Malice; Spenser's blatant beast, Slander, is urged on by Detraction and Envy.

The list of resemblances might be extended, but to no purpose; and of the many verbal coincidences one must suffice. Spenser (Book v, canto xi, stanzas 55, 56) makes Artegall say to Burbon:

> Die rather than do aught that mote dishonour yield.
> . . . .
> Fie on such forgery!
> Under one hood to shadow faces twain:
> Knights ought be true, and truth is one in all.

With this, compare three passages from *The Passetyme*. Minerva exhorts Graund Amour:

> And rather deye in ony maner of wyse,
> To attayne honour and the lyfe dyspyse,
> Than for to lyve and remayne in shame. Chap. XXVIII.

Fortune is described as a lady of pride and of perfect excellence,

> But that she had two faces in one hode. Chap. XXVII.

Sir Truth says that he guards the door of the chamber of chivalry,

> That no man enter into it wrongfully,
> Without me, Trouthe, for to be chivalrous. Chap. XXVIII.

Hawes employs the Chaucerian seven-line stanza almost exclusively. Exceptions have already been noted—the fantastic *tour de force*, and several passages in decasyllabic couplets. It must be set down to his defective sense of metrical fitness that he used rime royal so extensively. However suitable that measure is for serious and pathetic subjects, it is less suitable for much of Hawes's work, a great part of *The Passetyme*, for instance, where a metre of superior narrative capacity is required. For continuous narrative, Hawes found the compartment nature of rime royal inconvenient, and, consequently, sentences often overflow the stanza. In one instance, a whole stanza is occupied by the modifying parts of the sentence, while the main predicate is pushed into the next stanza, which, because the printer, or somebody else, blundered, happens to begin another chapter[1]. In using decasyllabic couplets for the humorous Godfrey Gobelive scenes, Hawes proves himself not wholly insensible to metrical fitness. It is possible that he employed the two metres in the same poem in imitation of Lydgate's *Temple of Glass*. If so, he missed Lydgate's tolerably constant distinction of couplet for narrative, stanza for lyrical parts.

When we read a passage from Hawes, we feel that his verse is possessed of a strange hobbling gait; and when we seek to scan the lines, we are likely to become bewildered. Some of the lines, it is true, scan quite correctly; at times, they have a flow and cadence which competent critics have likened to the music of Spenser, as

> I sawe come ryding in a valey farre
> A goodly ladye, envyroned about

---

[1] *The Passetyme*, chaps. XXXIII, XXXIV.

> With tongues of fyre as bright as any starre,
> That fyry flambes ensensed alway out.
> *The Passetyme*, Chap. I;

or

> Was never payne, but it had joye at last. Chap. XVII.

But we are not to expect to find in Hawes the artistic splendour of Spenser. Indeed, most of his lines are inartistic and unmusical. We must remember, however, that the non-existence of a critical edition of Hawes renders it uncertain how far we may justly lay the blame on the writer. The text is undoubtedly corrupt, and Hawes was justified in praying that bad printing might not spoil his scansion[1]. The following corrupt line does not show metre spoiled, but is given because it can be corrected from *The Passetyme* itself. We read in a stanza dealing with Gluttony,

> The pomped clerkes with foles delicious, Chap. XLII,

which, in the context, is absolutely without meaning. A correction is easily got from the line in chap. v,

> The pomped carkes wyth foode dilicious.

In chap. XXXIII three riming lines end thus : 'craggy roche,' 'hye flackes,' 'tre toppes,' where the natural emendation[2] is 'rockes,' 'flockes.' But, even then, 'flockes,' 'toppes,' is assonance and not rime[3]. Taking the text, however, as we have it, we must conclude that Hawes possessed a very defective ear. This must be said, even after allowance has been made for the difficulty which Chaucer's successors had in imitating his versification with words of changed and changing, not to say chaotic, pronunciation. The difficulty was a very real one for those who in diction and metre were slavish imitators of Chaucer. When Chaucer used an expression like 'the yonge sonne' or 'smale fowles' with final -e sounded, he was following grammatical usage and current pronunciation. But after these endings ceased to be sounded, such expressions had a different metrical value. Not knowing their rationale, Chaucer's imitators adopted the

---

[1] *The Passetyme, ad fin.*

[2] Made by Skeat, *Specimens of Eng. Lit.* p. 119 (6th ed.).

[3] Another example of assonance is 'loked' 'toted,' chap. XIX. Other curious, weak, or faulty rimes are 'slomber' 'wonder'; 'muche why' 'truly'; 'moved' 'hoved' 'i-tuned'; 'fooes' 'schooles'; 'carbuncles' 'solacious'; 'appese' 'suppose'; 'lylly' 'prety' 'body'; 'engraved' 'amased'; 'tassel' 'fayle'; 'joye' 'waye'; 'approcheth' 'requireth.' When necessary, Hawes writes 'rigorious' instead of 'rigorous,' and he delights to match a word like 'thing' with any termination '-ing,' or 'stable' and 'fable' with '-able.'

final -*e* as a metrical licence, and only at haphazard did their use
of it coincide with its etymological origin. Hawes neglects the
final -*e*, when, for example, he rimes 'mette' with 'great,' *The
Passetyme*, chap. XIX; he observes it in such lines as

> You can not helpë in the case I trow, *Ibid.*;

and he adds it without historical justification,

> A! tourë! tourë! all my joye is gone. Chap. XX.

The shifting accent is made use of, especially in words of French
origin; and we find both accentuations in the same stanza, sometimes even in the same line, as

> Mesure mesureth mesure in effecte. Chap. XXI.

This line also exemplifies the alliterative repetition of allied words
or of forms of the same word. Those licences are comparatively
harmless. Others disfigure the Chaucerian decasyllabic, whether
in stanza or couplet, and tend to ruin all its harmony. Lines of
four feet are common. Some are regular octosyllabics, as

> Alas! what payne and mortall wo. Chap. XXXI.

Others have an additional final syllable, as

> And on my way as I was riding, Chap. XXXI;

or a trisyllabic foot, as

> Whose hart ever inwardly is fret, Chap. XXXV;

or two trisyllabic feet and consequently ten syllables, as

> His good is his God, with his great ryches. Chap. XLII.

Again, lines of five feet occur with an unaccented syllable omitted
at the caesura, a device which produces an awkward break, as

> The minde of men chaungeth as the mone. Chap. XVIII.

Hawes may have learned this from Lydgate, in whose works
Schick says it is more used than anywhere else. The numerous
trisyllabic feet which Hawes, influenced, perhaps, by the freedom
of versification in the popular poetry of his day, introduced into
the seven-line stanza, spoil its rhythm, as

> In the toure of Chyvalry I shall make me stronge. Chap. XIX.

Alexandrines are frequently found: some regular, others with one
or two trisyllabic feet, which lengthen out to thirteen or fourteen
syllables, as

> The hye astronomier, that is God omnipotent. Chap. XXII.

Consequently, the same stanza may contain lines of different lengths riming together. This gives the impression of jolting, and suggests doggerel with its grotesque effect in serious poetry, as

> In my maternall tonge opprest with ignoraunce, Chap. xxv,

riming with

> He shall fynde all fruytfull pleasaunce.

Instead of seven lines, one stanza has six, chap. XVII; another only five, chap. XVIII. Instead of the regular rime sequence, *ababbcc*, we find, chap. XVIII, *ababccc*; chap. XXVIII, *ababbcb*; chap. XXXIV, *abalbbb*.

Hawes is not a creator of familiar quotations. We find in him much sound sense, much homely wisdom, on such themes as the fickleness of fortune, the certainty of suffering, the seven deadly sins, the transitoriness of the world,

> worldly joye and frayle prosperitie
> What is it lyke, but a blast of wynde? Chap. XLV.

We meet with gnomic lines, as

> Who spareth to speke he spareth to spede. Chap. XVII.

But he did not produce passages memorable for choice diction and for harmony of sweet sounds, passages familiar as household words; for the well-known couplet which is the earliest form, perhaps the original form, of a favourite sixteenth century saying, is solitary in its splendour. It occurs in Graund Amour's epitaph, *The Passetyme*, chap. XLII. Death, says Hawes, is the end of all earthly happiness; the day is followed by the dark night,

> For though the day be never so longe,
> At last the belles ringeth to evensonge.

And with that we may take leave of Hawes, who, as a rule and, often, to an exaggerated extent, continues the defects of the fifteenth century poets—confused metre, slipshod construction, bizarre diction—defects which did not disappear from English poetry till it was influenced by the literary masterpieces of Italy. and of ancient Greece and Rome.

CHAPTER X

THE SCOTTISH CHAUCERIANS

It is a critical tradition to speak of the fifteenth century in Scotland as the time of greatest literary account, or, in familiar phrase, 'the golden age of Scottish poetry.' It has become a commonplace to say of the poets of that time that they, best of all Chaucer's followers, fulfilled with understanding and felicity the lessons of the master-craftsman; and it has long been customary to enforce this by contrasting the skill of Lydgate, Occleve and their contemporaries in the south, with that of James I, Henryson, Dunbar and Gavin Douglas. The contrast does not help us to more than a superficial estimate; it may lead us to exaggerate the individual merits of the writers and to neglect the consideration of such important matters as the homogeneity of their work, and their attitude to the older popular habit of Scottish verse[1].

We must keep in mind that the work of the greater Scottish poets of the fifteenth century represents a break with the literary practice of the fourteenth. The alliterative tradition dragged on, perhaps later than it did in the south, and the chronicle-poem of the type of Barbour's *Bruce* or the *Legends of the Saints* survived in Henry the Minstrel's patriotic tale of Wallace and in Wyntoun's history. With James I the outlook changes, and in the poems of Henryson, Dunbar, Douglas and some of the minor 'makars' the manner of the earlier northern poetry survives only in stray places. It is not that we find a revulsion from medieval sentiment. The main thesis of this chapter will be that these poets are much less modern than medieval. But there is, in the main, a change in literary method—an interest, we might say, in other aspects of the old allegorical tradition. In other words, the poetry of this century is a recovery, consciously made, of much of the outworn artifice of the Middle Ages, which had not yet reached, or hardly reached, the northern portion of the island. The movement is artificial and experimental, in no respects more remarkably so than in the deliberate moulding of the language to

[1] See Chapter XI.

its special purpose[1]. Though the consciousness of the effort, chiefly in its linguistic and rhetorical bearings, may appear, at first glance, to reveal the spirit of the renascence, it is nevertheless clear that the materials of this experiment and much of the inspiration of the change come from the Middle Ages. The origin is by no means obscured, though we recognise in this belated allegorical verse the growth of a didactic, descriptive and, occasionally, personal, habit which is readily associated with the renascence. We are easily misled in this matter—too easily, if we have made up our minds to discover signs of the new spirit at this time, when it had been acknowledged, more or less fully, in all the other vernacular literatures of Europe. Gavin Douglas, for example, has forced some false conclusions on recent criticism, by his seeming modern spirit, expressed most strikingly in the prologue to the fifth book of his translation of the *Aeneid*:

> Bot my propyne coym fra the pres fuit hait,
> Unforlatit[2], not jawyn[3] fra tun to tun,
> In fresche sapour new fro the berrie run.

The renascence could not have had a better motto. Yet there should be little difficulty in showing that Douglas, our first translator of Vergil, was, perhaps, of all these fifteenth century Scots, the gentlest of rebels against the old-world fancies of the Courts of Love and the ritual of the Rose.

The herald of the change in Scottish literary habit is the love-allegory of *The Kingis Quair*, or King's Book. The atmosphere of this poem is that of *The Romance of the Rose*: in general treatment, as well as in details, it at once appears to be modelled upon that work, or upon one or more of the many poems directly derived therefrom. Closer examination shows an intimacy with Chaucer's translation of the *Romance*. Consideration of the language and of the evidence as to authorship (to which we refer elsewhere[4]) brings conviction that the poem was the direct outcome of study, by some northerner, of Chaucer's *Romaunt* and other works. It was fortunate for Scots literature that it was introduced to this new genre in a poem of such literary competence. Not only is the poem by its craftsmanship superior to any by Chaucer's English disciples, but it is in some respects, in happy phrasing and in the retuning of old lines, hardly inferior to its models. Indeed, it may be claimed for the Scots author, as for his successor, in the *Testament of Cresseid*, that he has, at times, improved upon his master.

---

[1] See Chapter IV.   [2] fresh-drawn.   [3] dashed.
[4] See note in Bibliography; also Chapter IV.

The Kingis Quair (which runs to 1379 lines, divided into 197 'Troilus' stanzas, riming *ababbcc*) may be described as a dream-allegory dealing with two main topics—the 'unsekernesse' of Fortune and the poet's happiness in love. The contradiction of these moods has led some to consider the poem as a composite work, written at different times : the earlier portion representing the period of the author's dejection, real or imaginary, the latter that of the subsequent joy which the sight of the fair lady in the garden by his prison had brought into his life. One writer[1] has expressed the opinion that the poem was begun at a time when the poet 'had little to speak of beyond his past misadventures'; and, while allowing that it may have been 'afterwards partially rewritten,' he finds evidence of its fragmentary origin in the presence of sections which 'have absolutely nothing to do with the subject.' For these reasons, he disallows Tytler's division (1783) of the poem into six cantos, which had held in all editions for a full century (down to 1884), because it assumes a unity which does not exist. This objection to the parcelling out of the text may be readily accepted—not because it gives, as has been assumed, a false articulation to a disconnected work, but because it interferes unnecessarily with that very continuity which is not the least merit of the poem. The author, early in the work (st. 19), calls upon the muses to guide him 'to write his *torment and his joy.*' This is strong evidence by the book in its own behalf, and it is not easily discredited by the suggestion that the line 'may have been altered afterwards.' If there be any inconsistency observable in the poem, it is of the kind inevitable in compositions where the personal element is strong. In the earlier allegory, and in much of the later (if we think of the Spenserian type) the individuality of the writer is merged in the narrative : in *The Kingis Quair*, on the other hand, a striking example of the later dream-poem which has a direct lyrical or personal quality, greater inconsequence of fact and mood is to be expected. Whether that inconsequence be admitted or not by the modern reader, we have no warrant for the conclusion that the work is a mosaic.

The poet, lying in bed 'alone waking,' turns to the pages of *Boethius*, but soon tires of reading. He thinks of Fortune and recalls

> In tender 30uth how sche was first my fo
> And eft my frende.

---

[1] Skeat : *Kingis Quair* (see bibliography).

He is roused by the matins-bell, which seems to say 'tell on, man, quhat the befell.' Straightway he resolves 'sum newë thing to write,' though he has in his time spent ink and paper to small purpose. He begins his tale of early misfortune with an elaborate metaphor of a ship at the mercy of the elements; then narrates how the actual ship in which he was sailing from his own country was captured by the enemy, and how he was sent into confinement. From his window, he looks upon a fair garden and hears the love-song of the birds. This song, which is given as a *cantus*, prepares the reader for the critical passage of the poem in which the poet sees the lady who from that moment brings sunshine into his life:

> And there-with kest I doun myn eye ageyne,
> Quhare as I sawe, walking under the toure,
> Full secretly new cummyn hir to pleyne,
> The fairest or the freschest yong[ë] floure
> That euer I sawe, me thoght, before that houre;
> For quhich sodayn abate, anon astert
> The blude of all my body to my hert. XL.

When the lady, unconscious of her lover's prayer, departs, she leaves him the 'wofullest wicht,' plunged again in the misery from which her coming had raised him. At night, tired out, he dreams that he is carried high into the heavens to the house of Venus. The goddess receives him graciously, but sends him with Good Hope to Minerva for further advice. This, the learned goddess gives, with quotations from *Ecclesiastes* and observations on pre-destination; and she sends him, as he is 'wayke and feble,' to consult Fortune. He returns to earth, and, passing by a plain, stocked, in the conventional way, with all kinds of animals, he meets again his guide Good Hope, who takes him to Fortune's citadel. He finds the dame, and sees the great wheel. This is described to him, and he is ordered to take his place upon it.

> 'Fare wele,' quod sche, and by the ere me toke
> So ernestly, that therewithall I woke.

Distracted by the thought that all may be but a vain dream, he returns to the window from which he had seen the lady. To him comes a turtle-dove with a sprig of gillyflower, bearing the tidings, inscribed in gold on the edges, that, in heaven, the cure of all his sorrow is decreed. The poem concludes with the lover's hymn of thanks to each and every thing which has con-tributed to his joy, even to the castle-wall and the 'sanctis marciall' who had guided him into the hands of the enemy;

and, lastly, he commends his book to the poems ('impnis') of his masters Gower and Chaucer, and their souls to heaven.

A careful examination of this well-constructed poem will show that, to the interest of the personal elements, well blended with the conventional matter of the dream-poem, is added that of its close acquaintance with the text of Chaucer. It is not merely that we find that the author knew the English poet's works and made free use of them, but that his concern with them was, in the best sense, literary. He has not only adopted phrases and settings, but he has selected and retuned lines, and given them, though reminiscent of their origin, a merit of their own. Sometimes the comparison is in favour of the later poem, in no case more clearly than in the fortieth stanza, quoted above, which echoes the description, in *The Knight's Tale*, of Palamon's beholding of Emilie. The lines

> And ther-with-al he bleynte, and cryde 'a!'
> As though he stongen were unto the herte,

are inferior to the Scot's concluding couplet. The literary relationship, of which many proofs will appear to the careful reader, is shown in a remarkable way in the reference at the close to the poems of Gower and Chaucer. This means more than the customary homage of the fifteenth century to Chaucer and Gower, though the indebtedness to the latter is not textually evident. The author of *The Kingis Quair* and his Scottish successors have been called the 'true disciples' of Chaucer, but often, it must be suspected, without clear recognition of this deep literary appreciation on which their historical position is chiefly based.

The only MS text of *The Kingis Quair* is preserved in the Bodleian Library, in the composite MS marked 'Arch. Selden. B. 24,' which has been supposed to belong to the last quarter of the fifteenth century. It is there described in a prefatory sentence (fol. 191) as 'Maid be King Iames of scotland the first callit the kingis quair and Maid quhen his Maiestie Wes In Ingland.' This is confirmed in the Latin *explicit* on fol. 211. The ascription to James I, king of Scots, remains uncontroverted. A recent attempt[1] to place the text later than *The Court of Love*, has led to a careful sifting of all the evidence, actual and circumstantial, with the result that the traditional view has been established more firmly, and something beyond a suspicion raised that, if there be any borrowing, *The Court of Love* is the debtor. The story of the

---

[1] See bibliography.

poem is James's capture in March 1405, his imprisonment by the English and his wooing of Joan Beaufort. There is no reason to doubt that the story was written by James himself, and the date of composition may be fixed about the year 1423. During his exile the king had found ample opportunity to study the work of the great English poet whose name was unknown in the north, and whose influence there might have been delayed indefinitely. This literary intimacy enhances the autobiographic interest of *The Kingis Quair*.

The influence of Chaucer is hardly recognisable in any of the other works which have been ascribed to James, unless we accept a recent suggestion that fragment B (ll. 1706—5810) of the *Romaunt* was written by him[1]. The short piece of three stanzas, beginning 'Sen trew Vertew encressis dignytee' is unimportant; and the 'popular' poems *Peblis to the Play* and *Christis Kirk on the Grene*[2], if really his, belong to a genre in which we shall look in vain for traces of southern literary influence. The contrast of these pieces with *The Kingis Quair* is, indeed, so marked as to have led many to assume that James cannot be the author of both. This is, of course, no argument; nor does the suggestion that their tone sorts better with the genius of his royal successor, 'the Gudeman of Ballengeich,' count for much. On the other hand, the identification of *Peblis to the Play* with the poem *At Beltayne*, which Major ascribes to James, and the acceptance of the statement in the Bannatyne MS that he is the author of *Christis Kirk*, must be counterbalanced by the evidence of language and prosody, which appear to point to a later origin than the first decades of the fifteenth century.

The Kingis Quair represents the first phase of Scottish Chaucerianism, in which the imitation, though individualised by the genius of its author, is deliberate and direct. Even the personal and lyrical portions do not destroy the impression that the poem is a true birth of the old allegory. In other words, allegory is of the essence of the conception: it is not introduced for the sake of its interpretation, or as a decorative aid. In the second stage, as disclosed in the poems of Henryson, Dunbar and Douglas, we recognise an important change. Some of the pieces appear to have the old outlook and the old artistic purpose; yet, even in these, the tone is academic. They are breaking away from the stricter and more self-contained interest of the literature of the *Rose*; they adapt both sentiment and style to more individual, or

---

[1] See bibliography.   [2] See Chapter xi.

national, purpose, and make them subservient to an ethical thesis. Yet Chaucer remains the inspiring force, not merely in turns of phrase and in fashion of verse, but in unexpected places of the poetic fabric. Even as late as the mid-sixteenth century, in such a sketch as Lyndsay's *Squyer Meldrum*, we are, at times, reminded of the vitality of Chaucerian tradition.

Of Robert Henryson, in some respects the most original of the Scottish Chaucerians, we know very little. He is described, on the title-page of the earliest extant edition of his *Fables* (1570) as 'scholemaister of Dunfermeling.' His birth has been dated about 1425. A 'Master Robert Henryson' was incorporated in 1462 in the university of Glasgow, which had been founded in 1451. The entry states that the candidate was already a licentiate in arts and bachelor in decrees. It is probable, therefore, that his earlier university education was received abroad, perhaps at Paris or Louvain. His mastership at the Benedictine abbey grammar-school in Dunfermline and his notarial office (if he be the Robert Henryson who witnesses certain deeds in 1478) would lead us to infer that he was in lower orders. His death, which may have taken place about 1500, is alluded to in Dunbar's *Lament for the Makaris*[1]. There are no dates to guide us in tracing the sequence of his poems, and the internal evidence is inconclusive. Yet we cannot be far out in naming 1450 as the earlier limit of the period during which they were composed.

Henryson's longest and, in some ways, his best work is his *Morall Fabillis of Esope*. The material of the book is drawn from the popular jumble of tales which the Middle Ages had fathered upon the Greek fabulist; much of it can be traced directly to the edition of Anonymus, to Lydgate's version and to English Reynardian literature as it appeared in Caxton's dressing. In one sense, therefore, the book is the least original of Henryson's works; but, in another, and the truer, it may take precedence of even *The Testament of Cresseid* and *Robene and Makyne* for the freshness of its treatment, notably in its adaptation of hackneyed *fabliaux* to contemporary requirements. Nor does it detract from the originality of presentation, the good spirits, and the felicity of expression, to say that here, even more than in his closer imitations of Chaucer, he has learnt the lesson of Chaucer's outlook on life. Above all, he shows that fineness of literary taste which marks off the southern poet from his

[1] *post*.

contemporaries, and exercised but little influence in the north even before that later period when the rougher popular habit became extravagant.

The *Fables*, as we know them in the texts of the Charteris print of 1571 and the Harleian MS of the same year, are thirteen in number, with a general prologue prefixed to the tale of the Cock and the Jewel, and another introducing that of the Lion and the Mouse. They are written in the familiar seven-lined stanza, riming *ababbcc*. From the general prologue, in which he tells us that the book is 'ane maner of translatioun' from Latin, done by request of a nobleman, he justifies the function of the fable

> to repreue the haill misleuing
> Of man, be figure of ane uther thing.

And again he says,

> The nuttis schell, thocht it be hard and teuch,
> Haldis the kirnell, and is delectabill.
> Sa lyis thair ane doctrine wyse aneuch,
> And full frute, vnder ane fein3eit fabill.
> And clerkis sayis, it is richt profitabill
> Amangis eirnist to ming ane mery sport,
> To licht the spreit, and gar the tyme be schort.

As the didactic element is necessarily strong in the fable, little may be said of its presence in Henryson's work, except, perhaps, that his invariable habit of reserving all reflections for a separate *moralitas* may be taken as evidence of the importance attached to the lesson. Earlier English fabulists, such as Lydgate, mixed the story and the homily, to the hurt of the former. Henryson's separation of the two gives the narrative greater directness and a higher artistic value. Indeed, the merit of his *Fables* is that they can be enjoyed independently and found self-satisfying, because of the contemporary freshness, the unfailing humour, and the style which he weaves into familiar tales. The old story of the sheep in the dog's skin has never been told in such good spirits; nor is there so much 'character' in any earlier or later version of the Town and Country Mouse as there is in *The Uponlandis Mous and the Burges Mous*.

In his treatment of nature he retains much of the traditional manner, as in the 'processional' picture of the seasons in the tale of the Swallow and the other Birds, but, in the minor touches in the description of his 'characters,' he shows an accuracy which can come only from direct and careful observation. His mice, his frog with

> hir fronsit[1] face,
> Hir runkillit cheikis, and hir lippis syde[2],
> Hir hingand browis, and hir voce sa hace[3],
> Hir logerand[4] leggis, and hir harsky[5] hyde,

his chanticleer, his little birds nestling in the barn against the storm, even his fox, are true to the life. It is, perhaps, this realism which helps his allegory and makes it so much more tolerable to the modern reader. There is, too, in his sketches more than mere felicity : he discloses, again and again, that intimacy and sympathy with nature's creatures which we find fully expressed in Burns, and, like his great successor, gently draws his readers to share the sentiment.

Orpheus and Eurydice, based on *Boethius*, may be linked with the *Fables* in type, and in respect of its literary qualities. The *moralitas* at the close, which is irksome because of its undue length, shows that the conception is similar: the title *moralitas fabulae sequitur* indicates that the poet was unwilling to let the story speak for itself. This, however, it does, for it is well told, and it contains some lyrical pieces of considerable merit, notably the lament of Orpheus in ten-lined stanzas with the musical burden 'Quhar art thow gane, my luf Erudices ?' or 'My lady Quene and luf, Erudices.' Even in the processional and catalogue passages, in which many poets have lost themselves or gone aground, he steers a free course. When he approaches the verge of pedantic dulness in his account of the musical technicalities which Orpheus learnt as he journeyed amid the rolling spheres, he recovers himself, as Chaucer would have done,

> Off sik musik to wryte I do bot dote,
> Tharfor at this mater a stra I lay,
> For in my lyf I coud nevir syng a note.

In *The Testament of Cresseid*, he essays the bold part of a continuator. Having turned, for fireside companionship on a cold night, to the 'quair'

> Writtin be worthie Chaucer glorious
> Of fair Cresseid and lustie Troylus,

he meditates on Cresseid's fate, and takes up another 'quair' to 'break his sleep,'

> God wait, gif all that Chauceir wrait was trew.
> Nor I wait nocht gif this narratioun
> Be authoreist, or fenȝeit of the new,
> Be sum Poeit, throw his inventioun
> Maid to report the Lamentatioun

---

[1] 'frounced,' wrinkled.   [2] wide.   [3] hoarse.   [4] loosely hanging.   [5] rugged.

> And wofull end of this lustie Cresseid;
> And quhat distres scho thoillit, and quhat deid!

After this introduction, he proceeds, obviously on a hint from Chaucer's text, to give the sequel to the Diomede episode. Chaucer had prayed each 'lady bright of hewe,'

> That al be that Criseyde was untrewe,
> That for that gilt she be not wrooth with me.
> Ye may hir gilt in othere bokes see;
> And gladlier I wol wryten, if yow leste,
> Penelopëes trouthe and good Alceste.
> *Troilus*, v, ll. 1774—8;

and he had chivalrously passed on to the closing scene in the tragedy of Troilus. Henryson supplements this with the tragedy of Cresseid. Cast off by Diomede, the distressed woman retires to an oratory and prays to Venus and Cupid, till she falls into an ecstasy. She dreams of her judgment by Saturn, that she shall be stricken with disease, and shall drag out her days in misery. She awakes, to find that she is a leper. A child comes to tell her that her father bids her to supper. She cannot go; and her father appears by her side, and learns how Cupid has taken his vengeance upon her. Sad at heart, he grants her wish to pass straightway with 'cop and clapper' to the spital. There, in a dark corner, she 'chides her dreary destiny.' On a day there passes Troilus and his company in triumph; and the lepers beg for alms.

> Than upon him scho kest up baith her ene,
> And with ane blenk it come in to his thocht
> That he sum tyme hir face befoir had sene,
> Bot scho was in sic plye he knew hir nocht;
> Yit than hir luik into his mynd it brocht
> The sweit visage and amorous blenking
> Of fair Cresseid, sumtyme his awin darling.

He trembles, and changes colour, but no one sees his suffering. To Cresseid he throws rich alms, and passes on. The lepers marvel at his affection for 'yone lazarous'; and Cresseid discovers that her friend is Troilus. Not the least effective part of the poem is that which contrasts the sensitiveness of the lovers; or the concluding passage in which the penitent Cresseid makes her testament, and a leper takes her ring from her corpse and carries it to Troilus.

> He swelt for wo, and fell doun in ane swoun;
> For greit sorrow his hairt to birst was boun:
> Siching full sadlie, said, ' I can no moir,
> Scho was untrew, and wo is me thairfoir!'

The felicity of the simple style of the next stanza is unmistakable—

> Sum said he maid ane tomb of merbell gray,
> And wrait hir name and superscriptioun,
> And laid it on hir grave, quhair that scho lay,
> In goldin letteris, conteining this ressoun:
> 'Lo, fair ladyis, Cresseid of Troyis toun,
> Sumtyme countit the flour of womanheid,
> Under this stane, late lipper, lyis deid.'

The thirteen shorter poems which have been ascribed to Henryson are varied in kind and verse-form. The majority are of a reflective cast, dealing with such topics as Want of Wise Men, Age, Youth, Death, Hasty Credence and the like—topics which are the delight of the fifteenth century minor muse. There are allegorical poems, such as *The Bludy Serk*, with the inevitable *moralitas*, a religious piece on the annunciation, and *A Prayer for the Pest*. Two of the poems, the pastoral dialogue of *Robene and Makyne* and the burlesque *Sum Practysis of Medecyne*, deserve special mention for historical reasons; the former, too, for its individual excellence. The *estrif* between Robene (Robin) and Makyne (Malkin) develops a sentiment, thus expressed in the girl's own words—

> The man that will nocht quhen he may
> Sall haif nocht quhen he wald——

which is probably an echo of the *pastourelles*. In literary craftsmanship, the poem excels its later and more elaborate analogue *The Nut Brown Maid*. The older and simpler language, and the ballad *timbre* (which runs throughout many of Henryson's minor poems) place *Robene and Makyne* almost entirely outside Chaucerian influence. This is even more obvious in *Sum Practysis of Medecyne*; and, for this reason, some have doubted Henryson's authorship. The divergence is, however, no evidence against the ascription. Taken with the pieces of the same type which are known to be by his contemporaries, it gives us an earlier link in the chain of popular alliterative (or neo-alliterative) verse which resisted the Chaucerian infusion and was destined to exert a strong influence upon later Scottish poetry. These burlesque pieces in Henryson, Dunbar and Douglas and, later, in Lyndsay (in each case a single and disconnected effort) appear to have been of the nature of experiments or exercises in whimsicality, perhaps as a relief from the seriousness or more orderly humour of the muse. The roughness in tone resembles that of the 'flytings,' in which it is intentional, and, in many cases, without parallel in English literature. The persistence of this form throughout the century. and in places least expected, may supply an argument for James I's authorship of *Peblis to the Play* and *Christis Kirk on the Grene*. At least, the dissimilarity between these and the *Kingis Quair* would not, did other reasons not intervene, disprove that they came from the same pen[1].

William Dunbar has held the place of honour among the Scottish 'makars.' It may be that his reputation has been exaggerated at the expense of his contemporaries, who (for reasons now less valid) have not received like critical attention. Scott's statement that he is 'unrivalled by any which Scotland ever produced' strikes the highest note of praise, and is, perhaps, responsible for much of the unvaried appreciation which has followed. Russell Lowell's criticism has arrested attention because it is exceptional, and because it is a singular example of extravagant depreciation. It has, however, the indirect value that it prompts us to test our judgments again, and weigh the value of such popular epithets as 'the Scottish Chaucer' and 'the Scottish Skelton.' There is generally a modicum of truth in easy titles of this kind, though the essence of the epithet is too often forgotten or misunderstood.

Of the personal history of William Dunbar, we have only a few facts; and of the dates of his writings or of their sequence we know too little to convince us that any account of his literary life is more than ingenious speculation. As Dunbar appears to have graduated bachelor of arts at St Andrews in 1477, his birth may be dated about 1460. Internal evidence, for the most part indirect, points to his having survived the national disaster at Flodden, perhaps till 1520. Like Kennedy, his poetic rival in the *Flyting*, Gavin Douglas and Lyndsay, and, indeed, like all the greater poets from James I, with the exception of the schoolmaster of Dunfermline, he was connected with the court and, like most of them, was of noble kin. These facts must be kept in mind in a general estimate of the courtly school of Scottish verse, in explaining its artificialities and in understanding the separation in sentiment and technique from the more popular literature which it superseded for a time. This consideration supplies, among other things, part of the answer to the problem why the national or patriotic note, which is strongly characteristic of later writers, is wanting at a period when it might be expected to be prominent. In preceding work, with the exception, perhaps, of *Wallace*, the appeal to history is in very general terms; during 'the golden age,' when political forces were active and Border memories might have stirred the imagination, the poets are wholly absorbed in the literary traditions of romance, or in the fun and the disappointments of life at court; only in the mid-sixteenth century, and, first, most unmistakably in the French-made *Complaynt of Scotlande*, do we find that perfervid Scotticism which glows in later literature[1].

Dunbar's kinship with the house of Dunbar did not bring him wealth or place. After his college course he became a novice, subject to the strict rule of the Observantines of the Franciscan order. He appears, however, to have fretted under the restraint of his ascetic calling. In a poem entitled *How Dumbar wes desyrd to be ane freir* he makes frank confession of his difficulties, and *more suo* describes the exhortation to him to 'refuse the world' as the work of the devil.

> This freir that did Sanct Francis thair appeir,
> Ane feind he wes in liknes of ane freir;
> He vaneist away with stynk and fyrie smowk;
> With him me thocht all the houshend he towk,
> And I awoik as wy[2] that wes in weir[3].

He found some relief in the roving life of a friar, and he appears to have spent a few years in Picardy and other parts of France, where he certainly was in 1491 with Bothwell's mission to the French court for a bride for the young James IV. There, among the many Scots then haunting Paris, he may have met Gavin Douglas, Elphinstone, bishop of Aberdeen, Hector Boece and John Major; but the Sorbonne, where they were to be found, had, probably, few attractions for him. It is tempting to speculate that the wild life of the faubourgs and the talent of Bohemians like François Villon (whose poems had just been printed posthumously, in 1489) had the strongest claims upon the restless friar. It has been assumed, not without some plausibility, that there are traces in the Scot's poems of direct French influence, in other and deeper ways than in the choice of subjects which Villon had made his own. By 1500, he was back in Scotland, no longer an Observantine, but a priest at court, pensioned by the king, and moving about as a minor official in royal business. The title

---

[1] See also Chapter XI. [2] man. [3] fear (doubt).

'rhymer of Scotland,' in the English privy council accounts during the sojourn in London of the Scottish embassy for the hand of Margaret Tudor, has been taken by some to mean that, beyond his being the poetical member of the company who praised London in verse[1], he was recognised to some extent as laureate. Of his literary life, which appears to have begun with his association with the court in 1500, we know nothing beyond what the poems tell us indirectly; but of the sentiment of his age, as seen by a courtier, we have the fullest particulars.

Dunbar's poems fall into two main divisions—the allegorical and occasional. Both show the strength of Chaucerian tradition, the former in a more immediate way, the latter (with full allowance for northern and personal characteristics) in the continuance of the satirical, moral and religious themes of the shorter poems of Chaucer's English followers. There is, however, a difference of atmosphere. Dunbar's work is conditioned by the circumstance that it was written by a courtier for the court. Poetry had fallen, as has been hinted, into close association with a small royal and aristocratic coterie. But life at court, though it showed a political and intellectual vigour which contrasts favourably with that of earlier reigns, and had grown more picturesque in serving the exuberant taste of the 'redoubted roye,' was circumscribed in its literary interests, and, with all its alertness, added little or nothing to the sum of poetic endeavour. The age may have been 'golden'; it was not 'spacious.' Literary consciousness, when it existed, turned to the romantic past or to the old ritual of allegory, or to the re-editing, for contemporary purposes, of plaints of empty purses, of the fickleness of woman, of the vanity of the world and of the lack of piety; or it was absorbed in the merely technical task of illuminating or aureating the 'rude' vernacular[2]. If, however, the area was not enlarged, it was worked more fully. From this experience, at the hands of writers of great talent, much was gained for Scottish verse which has the appearance of newness to the literary historian. What is, therefore, outstanding in Dunbar, is not, as in Henryson, the creation of new genres

---

[1] Beginning 'London, thou art of townes A *per se*,' and with 'London, thou art the flour of Cities all,' as the burden of each stanza. The poem is, with all its conventionality of phrase, of considerable historical interest.

[2] Cf. the address to Chaucer, Gower and Lydgate in the well-known stanzas of the *Goldyn Targe* (ll. 253—270). There, the praise is of Chaucer's 'anamalit termis celicall,' and of the light which he brought to 'oure Inglisch' (*i.e.* Lowland Scots). And the praise of Gower and Lydgate is that by their 'sugarit lippis and tongis aureate' and 'angel mouthis most mellifluate' they have illumined the language and 'our-gilt oure speche, that imperfyte stude.'

or fresh motives. Compared with Henryson, Dunbar shows no advance in broad purpose and sheer originality. He is, apart from all question of vocabulary, more artificial in the stricter historical sense; and he might have deserved no better from posterity than Lydgate and Occleve have deserved had he not suppled the rhythms and added life and humour to the old matter.

Dunbar's debt to Chaucer is less intimate and spiritual than Henryson's or king James's. He could not have given us the after-tale of Cresseid, or caught so clearly the sentiment of the master in a new *Quair*. Chaucer is, to him, the 'rose of rethoris all' (as every poet of the century admitted), but he follows him at a distance and, perhaps, with divided affection for the newer French writers. Still, the Chaucerian influence is there, though the evidence of direct drawing from the well of English is less clear.

The Goldyn Targe has the simple *motif* of the poet's appearance (in a dream, on a conventional May morning) before the court of Venus, where he endeavours to resist the arrows of dame Beauty and her friends with the aid of Reason's 'scheld of gold so schene.' He is wounded near to death and taken prisoner. Then he knows that the lady is 'lustiar of chere': when she departs, he is delivered over to Heaviness. As she sails off, the noise of the ship's guns wake him to the enjoyment, once more, of the May morning and the singing birds. The allegory is of the simplest; the contemporary didacticism has hardly invaded it, and the abstractions which the poet introduces are in closer kinship with the persons of courtly allegory than with the personages in the moralities of the period. A similar theme appears in his well-known short poem, *Sen that I am a presoneir* (sometimes known as *Beauty and the Prisoner*); but there didactic and personal elements have been added. It is probable that criticism has been over busy in seeing references to the king, to his liaison with Margaret Drummond and to her suspicious death. In *The Thrissil and the Rois*, the intrusion of the *moralitas* is at once obvious. The setting is heraldic: the theme is the marriage of James IV and Margaret Tudor. The familiar machinery of the dream-poem is here; but the general effect is that of an elaborate prothalamium. It is an easy stage from this poetic type to the pageant and masque; but in the single example of Dunbar's 'dramatic' endeavour—in the fragment of *The Interlude of the Droichis Part of the Play*—the allegory is used merely to enhance the whimsicality of the design.

In Chaucer's simpler narrative manner, we have the tale of *The Freiris of Berwik*, dealing with the old theme of an untrue

wife caught in her own wiles. The ascription of this piece to
Dunbar has been doubted, but there is nothing in it unworthy
of his metrical art or his satiric talent. The *Tretis of the Tua
Mariit Wemen and the Wedo*, which is certainly his, echoes the
gossip of the Wife of Bath, but it speaks with a freedom from
which Chaucer would have shrunk. Its antique line and alliteration connect it formally with the popular poetry which Chaucer
parodied and undid ; yet the association is remote. For it is
essentially a literary exercise, perhaps a burlesque *pastiche* to
satisfy the romantic fashion of the court. The art of this remarkable poem is always conscious. In the fierce thrusts of sarcasm,
in the warping of words, uncouth and strong, we seem to see the
personal satisfaction of the craftsman in his triumph of phrase
and line.

> I haue ane wallidrag, ane worme, ane auld wobat carle,
> A waistit walroun, na worth bot wourdis to clatter;
> Ane bumbart, ane dron bee, ane bag full of flewme,
> Ane skabbit skarth, ane scorpioun——

So hurtle the words in this dialogue on matrimonial risks. In
some respects, it is difficult to differentiate this *tour de force* from
a 'flyting'; but the husbands are not present, and may not (if they
could) meet the torrents of abuse.

In considering the satirical and occasional poems of Dunbar,
which constitute at once the greater and more important portion
of his work, it is well, in the first place, to see how far the
Chaucerian influence holds. Here, at least, it is difficult to allow
the aptness of the title 'the Scottish Chaucer,' unless it mean
nothing more than that Dunbar, by analogical compliment, has the
first place in Early and Middle Scots, as Chaucer has in Middle
English. It cannot mean that he shows Chaucer's spirit and outlook, as Henryson has shown ; nor that Dunbar is, in these satirical
and occasional pieces, on which his wider reputation rests, a
whole-hearted pupil in the craft of verse. The title would have
appeared more fitting in his own day, when his appeal to contemporaries (apart from any acknowledged debt to his forerunner)
was of the same technical kind which Chaucer had made to his ;
but a comparison, nowadays, has to take account of other matters.
Both poets are richly endowed with humour : it is the outstanding
quality of each ; but in no respect do their differences appear
more clearly. Here, Dunbar is unlike Henryson in lacking the
gentler and more intimate fun of their master. He is a satirist in
the stronger sense ; more boisterous in his fun, and showing, in his
wildest frolics, an imaginative range which has no counterpart

in the southern poet. His satirical powers are best seen in his *Tidings from the Session,* an attack on the law courts, and in his *Satire on Edinburgh,* in which he denounces the filthy condition of the capital; in his verses on his old friends the Franciscans, and on the flying friar of Tungland who came to grief because he had used hens' feathers; in his fiercer invectives of the *General Satire* and *The Epitaph on Donald Owre*; and in the vision of *The Dance of the Sevin Deidlie Synnis.* The last is one of the best examples of Dunbar's realism and literary cunning in suiting the word and line to the sense, as in the description of Sloth—

> Syne Sueirnes, at the secound bidding,
> Come lyk a sow out of a midding,
> Full slepy wes his grunʒie[1]:
> Mony sweir[2] bumbard[2] belly-huddroun[3],
> Mony slute daw[4] and slepy duddroun[5],
> Him serwit ay with sounʒie[6].

In all, but especially in the *Dance,* there is not a little of the fantastic ingenuity which appears in his more purely comic sketches. And these again, though mainly 'fooleries,' are not without satirical intention, as in his *Joustis of the Tailʒeour and the Sowtar* and his *Black Lady,* where the fun is a covert attack on the courtly craze for tourneys. Of all the pieces in this category, his *Ballad of Kynd Kittok* best illustrates that elfin quality which relieves his 'busteous' strain of ridicule. The waggish description of the thirsty alewife, her journey on a snail, her arrival in heaven and her sojourn there till, desiring a 'fresh drink,' she wanders forth and is not allowed to return, her going back to her ale-house and the poet's concluding request—

> Frendis, I pray ʒou hertfully,
> Gif ʒe be thristy or dry,
> Drink with my Guddame, as ʒe ga by,
> Anys for my saik——

strike a note, of which the echoes are to be often heard in later northern verse[7]. There is more than an accidental likeness between this roguish request to the reader and the close of Burns's *Address to the Deil* and *The Dying Words of Poor Mailie.* The reach of Dunbar's fancy is at its greatest in *The Interlude.* There, in his description of Fyn, he writes—

> He gat my grauntschir Gog Magog;
> Ay quhen he dansit, the warld wald schog[8];
> Five thousand ellis ʒeid in his frog[9]
> Of Hieland pladdis, and mair.

---

[1] face (snout)   [2] lazy.   [3] glutton.   [4] dirty slut.   [5] sloven.
[6] care, attention.   [7] See Chapter xi.   [8] shake.   [9] 'frock,' tunic.

> ȝit he was bot of tendir ȝouth;
> Bot eftir he grewe mekle at fouth[1],
> Ellevyne myle wyde met[2] was his mouth,
> His teith was ten ell sqwair.
> He wald apon his tais stand,
> And tak the sternis doune with his hand
> And set them in a gold garland
> Above his wyfis hair.

This is a triumph of the grotesque on the grand scale which the creator of Gargantua would have admired, and could not have excelled. Something of the same quality is seen in his wild picture of the birth of Antichrist in mid-air, in his *Vision*, which opens with the customary dream-setting and gives no hint of this turn in the poet's fancy.

Of lyrical, as of strictly dramatic, excellence, there is little in Dunbar. His love poems are few and, taken as a whole, undistinguished. His religious and moral verses, the one of the hymn type, the other on the hackneyed themes of Good Counsel, *Vanitas vanitatum* and (when he is cheery in mood) Blitheness, deserve commendation for little beyond their metrical facility. They are too short to be tedious to the modern reader. He uses the old device of the 'testament' to good purpose in the comic poem on the physician Andrew Kennedy; and, here again, his imagination transforms the old convention. In all Goliardic literature there is nothing to excel this stanza:

> A barell bung ay at my bosum,
> Of varldis gud I bad na mair;
> *Et corpus meum ebriosum*
> I leif onto the toune of Air;
> In a draf mydding for euer and ay
> *Ut ibi sepeliri queam,*
> Quhar drink and draff may ilka day
> Be cassyne *super faciem meam.*

In *The Dance*, already referred to, Dunbar works up the familiar material of the *Danse Macabre*. In his *Flyting of Dunbar and Kennedie* (his poetic rival Walter Kennedy[3]) we have a Scottish example of the widely-spread European genre in its extremest form. It remains a masterpiece of scurrility. The purpose of the combatants in this literary exercise was to outdo each other in abuse, and yet not to quarrel. It is hard for the most catholic modern to believe that they kept the peace, though Dunbar speaks kindly of his 'friend' in his *Lament*. The indirect value of *The Flyting* is great—linguistically, in its vocabulary of invective;

---

[1] *lit.* 'in fullness (fulth).'　　　[2] measure.　　　[3] *post.*

biographically, for it tells us more of the poet than we derive
from any other source; historically, in respect of its place in
the development of this favourite genre in Scots, and its testimony
to the antipathies of Celtic and Lowland civilisations in the early
sixteenth century[1]. A like indirect interest attaches to *The
Lament for the Makaris*, which Dunbar wrote 'quhen he was
seik.' It is a poem on the passing of human endeavour, a *motif*
which had served the purpose of scores of fifteenth century laments.
If it was written under the influence of Villon's master ballades,
praise must be allowed to Dunbar that he endenised the Frenchman's art with some success. The solemn effect of the burden,
Timor mortis conturbat me, occasional happy turns, as

> He takis the campioun in the stour,
> The capitane closit in the tour,
> The lady in bour full of bewte;
> *Timor Mortis conturbat me*

and a sense of literary restraint give the piece distinction above
the average poem of this type. Much of its reputation nowadays
is as a historical document, which tells us nearly all that we
know of some of Dunbar's contemporaries. He names his greater
predecessors, and, properly, puts Chaucer first on the roll.

Dunbar, we have said, has been called the 'Scottish Skelton.'
There is some justice in the likening, but the reasons are not
consistent with those which give him the title of the 'Scottish
Chaucer.' His allegiance to Chaucer is shown in literary reminiscence, whether of *motif*, or phrase, or stanza—a bookish reminiscence, which often helps us to distinguish the fundamental
differences in outlook. There is a spiritual antithesis; but there
are textual bonds. With Skelton, on the other hand, who must
have been the borrower, had any contact been possible, he stands
in close analogy, in two important respects. In the first place,
both poets, in their unexpected turns of satire and in their
jugglery of words, anticipate the Rabelaisian humour in its intellectual audacity and inexhaustible resource. Whether in wider
excursions of fancy, or in verbal orgies, such as in the *Complaint to the King*—

> Bot fowll, jow-jowrdane-hedit jevellis,
> Cowkin-kenseis, and culroun kewellis;
> Stuffettis, strekouris, and stafische strummellis;
> Wyld haschbaldis, haggarbaldis, and hummellis;
> Druncartis, dysouris, dyvouris, drewellis,
> Misgydit memberis of the dewellis; *etc.*

[1] See Chapter IV.

we are constantly reminded of the rector of Diss, and often of the historian of Gargantua and his son Pantagruel. In the second place, their metrical purposes have much in common. The prosodic variety of both is always our first impression—of Dunbar, without parallel in range and competence in any English writer before his time. The interest of the matter in him, as in Skelton, is that the variety is not the effect of mere literary restlessness, but the outcome of experiment to extend the capabilities of English verse in counterpart to what was being done by 'aureation' and other processes for poetic diction and style. If Dunbar's prosodic cunning were less remarkable, and if Skelton's so-called 'doggerel' were even less palatable than it is to those who take a narrow view of this problem of English, the endeavour of both poets. and of the Scot in particular, would lose none of its historical value. Dunbar borrows from all quarters, chiefly from Chaucer, but also from older popular forms, and from French models found in that other Bohemian genius, François Villon. Yet he is not a mere copyist: his changes in the grouping of the lines in the stanza, his varying the length of the verses and his grafting of one form upon another, are evidence of the literary artist at work. It is useless to attempt to illustrate this by selection from the hundred and one poems which are ascribed to him, for a selection cannot disclose his kaleidoscopic ingenuity. The remarkable range and resource of his technique and the vitality of his imagination must redeem his work in the eyes of the most alien modern of the charges which have been brought against the art of Lydgate and Occleve. His was not the heavy-headed fancy of a moribund medievalism. The explanation of the difference may be, after all, largely personal. Only so far is he of the renascence. The chief interest to us lies in the old things which he has chosen and recast, as genius may do at any time, whether the age be 'dark' or 'new.'

If no serious effort has been made to claim Dunbar as a child of the renascence, except in respect of his restlessness, in which he shows something of the human and individual qualities associated with that movement, his contemporary Gavin Douglas has been frequently described as the embodiment the fullest and also the first among Scottish poets, of the principles of neo-classicism. A critic of high consideration has recently said that 'no poet, not even Dante himself, ever drank more deeply of the spirit of Virgil than Gavin Douglas.' Others who consent to this

have laid stress on the fact that Douglas was the first translator of
a great verse classic into the vernacular. If this conclusion were
as just as it is, at first sight, plausible, Douglas could have no
place, or only a very minor place in this chapter, which assumes
a fundamental homogeneity in medieval method, in most respects
incongruent with the literary intention of the new learning.

Like Dunbar, Douglas was of good family, and a cleric ; but he
had influence and fortune which brought him a large measure of
worldly success. He had become a dignitary of the church when
the erst-friar was riming about the court and writing complaints
on his empty purse. Unlike Dunbar, he had no call to authorship.
His literary career, if we may so speak of the years when all
his work was written, is but a part of a busy life, the early
experience of a man destined to lose his leisure in the strife
of politics. He was the third son of Archibald, fifth earl of
Angus, the 'great earl,' better known as 'Bell-the-Cat.' He was
born *c.* 1475, and completed his early training in 1494, when
he graduated at St Andrews. In 1501, after spending some
time in cures in Aberdeenshire and the Lothians, he became
provost of the collegiate church of St Giles in Edinburgh,
his tenure of which partly synchronised with his father's civil
provostship of the capital. Between this date and 1513 (that
defining year in all Scottish biography of this period) he did all
his literary work, *The Palice of Honour, King Hart, Conscience*
and the translation of the *Aeneid,* begun early in 1512 and printed
in 1553. Other writings have been ascribed to him—a translation
of Ovid (though, in one place, he speaks of this work as a task
for another), plays on sacred subjects and sundry *Aureae
orationes* ; but none are extant, and we have his testimony (in
the 'Conclusion' of the *Aeneid*), which may be accepted as valid,
that he made Vergil his last literary task.

> Thus vp my pen and instrumentis full 30yr
> On Virgillis post I fix for evirmore,
> Nevir, from thens, syk materis to discryve:
> My muse sal now be cleyn contemplatyve,
> And solitar, as doith the byrd in cage;
> Sen fer byworn is all my childis age,
> And of my dayis neir passyt the half dait
> That natur suld me grantyn, weil I wait.

His later history is exclusively political, a record of promotions
and oustings. He was bishop of Dunkeld from 1516 to 1520, when
he was deprived of his see because he had gone to the English
court for aid in the Douglas-Albany quarrels. Two years later, he

died of plague in London, in the house of his friend lord Dacre. Just before his death, he had sent to another friend, Polydore Vergil, material for the latter's *History*, by way of correction of Major's account, which Vergil had proposed to use.

The Palice of Honour, Douglas's earliest work, is an example, in every essential sense, of the later type of dream-poem, already illustrated in the *Goldyn Targe*. It is, however, a more ambitious work (extending to 2166 lines); and it shows more clearly the decadence of the old method, partly by its over-elaboration, partly by the inferior art of the verse, partly by the incongruous welding of the pictorial and moral purposes. The poem is dedicated to James IV, who was probably expected to read between the lines and profit from the long lesson on the triumph of virtue. The poem opens in a 'gardyne of plesance,' and in May-time, as of yore. The poet falls asleep, and dreams of a desert place 'amyd a forest by a hyddeous flude, with grysly fische.' Queen Sapience appears with her learned company. This is described by the caitiffs Sinon and Achitophel, who wander in its wake. Solomon, Aristotle, Diogenes, Melchisedech and all the others are there and are duly catalogued. The company passes on to the palace. Then follow Venus and her court with Cupid, 'the god maist dissauabill.' The musical powers of this company give the poet an opportunity for learned discourse. We recall several earlier passages of the kind, and especially Henryson's account in the *Orpheus*. Douglas's remark,

> Na mair I vnderstude thir numbers fine,
> Be God, than dois a gukgo[1] or a swine,

almost turns the likeness into a plagiarism from his predecessor. The procession of lovers moves the poet to sing a 'ballet of inconstant love,' which stops the court and brings about his arrest. His pleas that 'ladyis may be judges in na place' and that he is a 'spiritual man' avail nothing; he is found guilty. Reflecting sorrowfully on what his punishment may be, he sees another procession approach, that of the muses with their court of poets. Calliope pleads for him, and he is released on condition that he will sing in honour of Venus. Thereafter, the poet proceeds to the palace, in companionship with a nymph, bestowed by Calliope. They pass through all countries and by all historic places, and stop for festivity at the well of the muses. Here Ovid, Vergil and others, including Poggio and Valla, recite by command before the company. The palace lies beyond on a

---

[1] cuckoo.

rock of 'slid hard marbell stone,' most difficult of ascent. On
the way up, the poet comes upon the purgatory of idle folk. The
nymph clutches him by the hair and carries him across this pit to
the top, 'as Abacuk was brocht in Babylone.' Then he looks
down on the wretched world and sees the carvel of the State
of Grace struggling in the waters. After a homily from the nymph
on the need of grace, he turns to the palace, which is described
with full architectural detail. In it, he sees Venus on her throne ;
and he looks in her mirror and beholds a large number of noble
men and women (fitly described in a late rubric as a 'lang cathalogue'). Venus observes her former prisoner, and, bidding him
welcome, gives him a book to translate.

> Tuichand this buik perauenture ȝe sall heir
> Sum tyme eftir, quhen I haue mair laseir.

So it would appear that Douglas had his *Aeneid* then in mind.
Sinon and Achitophel endeavour to gain an entrance. Cati-
line, pressing in at a window, is struck down by a book thrown by
Tully. Other vicious people fail in their attempts. Then follows a
description of the court of the prince of Honour and of secretary
Conscience, comptroller Discretion, ushers Humanity and True
Relation and many other retainers. The glories of the hall
overcome the poet, who falls down into a 'deidlie swoun.' The
nymph ministers to him, and gives him a thirteen-stanza sermon
on virtue. Later, she suggests that they should take the air in
the palace garden. When following her over the tree-bridge
which leads to this spot, the poet falls out ouir the heid into
the stank adoun,' and (as the rime anticipates) 'is neir to droun.'
Then he discovers that all has been a dream. A ballad in commendation of honour and virtue concludes the poem.

The inspiration of the poem is unmistakable; and it would
be easy to prove that not only does it carry on the Chaucerian
allegory, but that it is directly indebted to

> Geffray Chauceir, as A *per se* sans peir
> In his vulgare,

who appears with Gower, Lydgate, Kennedy, Dunbar and others
in the court of poets. There is nothing new in the machinery
to those who know the *Rose* sequence, *The House of Fame*
and *The Court of Love*. The whole interest of the poem is
retrospective. Even minor touches which appear to give some
allowance of individuality can be traced to predecessors. There
is absolutely nothing in *motif* or in style to cause us to suspect
the humanist. Douglas's interest in Vergil—if Venus's gift be

rightly interpreted—is an undiscriminating interest which groups the Mantuan, Boccaccio and Gower together, and awards like praise to each. He introduces Ovid and Vergil at the feast by the well of the muses, much as they had been introduced by the English poets, though, perhaps, with some extension of their 'moral' usefulness, as was inevitable in the later type of allegory. The *Palice of Honour* is a medieval document, differing from the older as a *pastiche* must, not because the new spirit disturbs its tenor.

Of *King Hart*, the same may be said, though it must be allowed to be a better poem, better girded as an allegory, and surer in its harmony of words. Its superiority comes from a fuller appreciation of Chaucerian values : it cannot be explained, though some have so considered it, as an effect of Vergilian study. There is not the faintest trace of renascence habit in the story of king Heart in his 'comlie castle strang' and of his five servitors (the senses), queen Pleasance, Foresight and other abstractions. The setting and sentiment recall the court of the prince of Honour in the *Palice of Honour*; and that, again, repeats the picture of the court of the palace in all the early continental versions of the *cours d'amour*.

Conscience is a four-stanza conceit telling how the moral sense has grown dull in men. 'Conscience' they had ; then they clipped away the 'con,' and had 'science' and 'na mair.' Then, casting off 'sci,' they were left with 'ens,'

> Quhilk in our language signifies that schrew
> Riches and geir, that gart all grace go hens.

Douglas's translation of the twelve books of the *Aeneid* and of the thirteenth by Mapheus Vegius is his most interesting work, apart from the question how far his tone is Vergilian in the stricter humanistic sense. In respect of the thirteen prologues and supplementary verses of a more personal character, it may be said to be more original than the so-called 'original' allegories. Not all of these are introductory to the 'books' to which they are attached ; and those which are most pertinent are concerned with the allegory of Vergil's poem. Some may be called academic exercises, which may have been written at odd times, and, perhaps, for other purposes. A picture of a Scottish winter, which has been often quoted, introduces book VI ; another, of May, book XII ; and another, of June, book XIII. The subjects may have been suggested by the time of the year when the poet reached these stages in translation ; if they were deliberately introduced for pictorial relief, they are the nearest approach to renascence habit in the whole work and in all Douglas's writings. A *tour de force* in the popular alliterative stanza, not without suspicion of burlesque intention, is offered as the appropriate preface to the eighth book:

> Sum latit lattoun, but lay, lepis in laud lyte;
> Sum penis furth a pan boddum to prent fals plakkis,
> Sum goukis quhiil the glas pyg grow full of gold jit,
> Throw cury of the quentassens, thocht clay mugis crakis;
> Sum warnour for this warldis wrak wendis by his wyt;
> Sum trachour crynis the cunje, and kepis corn stakis;
> Sum prig penny, sum pyk thank wyth privy promyt;
> Sum garris wyth a ged staf to jag throw blak jakkis.
> Quhat fynjeit fayr, quhat flattry, and quhat fals talis!
>> Quhat misery is now in land!
>> How mony crakyt cunnand!
>> For nowthir aiths, nor band,
>> Nor selis avalis[1].

This audacious break in the web of the *Aeneid* may have served some purpose of rest or refreshment, such as was given by the incongruous farce within the tedious moralities of the age; but it is not the devising of a humanist. The dialogue between the translator and Mapheus Vegius, in the thirteenth prologue, follows the medieval fashion, which was familiar before Henryson conversed with Aesop about his *Fables*. The first, or general, prologue is the most important, and is frequently referred to for evidence of Douglas's new outlook. The opening homage to Vergil is instructive.

> Laude, honor, prasingis, thankis infynite
> To the, and thi dulce ornate fresch endite,
> Mast reuerend Virgill, of Latyne poetis prince,
> Gemme of ingine and fluide of eloquence,
> Thow peirles perle, patroun of poetrie,
> Rois, register, palme, laurer, and glory,
> Chosin cherbukle, cheif flour and cedir tree,
> Lanterne, leidsterne, mirrour, and A *per se*,
> Master of masteris, sweit sours and springand well.

It is not difficult to underline the epithets which have done good service in the Chaucerian ritual. Indeed, were we to read 'Chaucer' for 'Virgill' and 'English' for 'Latyne' in the third line, we should have a straightforward 'Chaucerian' passage, true in word and sentiment. But Chaucer is really not far away. Douglas names him ere long, and loads him with the old honours, though he places him second to Vergil. The reason for this is

---

[1] Glossarial notes to this passage would be too numerous and too speculative for this place. Those who are familiar with this genre know that strict verbal interpretation is hardly possible, and that any serious attempt towards it may disclose little but a pedantic misunderstanding of the poet's intention.

interesting. Chaucer, in telling the story of Dido in *The Legend of Good Women*, had said,

> I coud folwe, word for word, Virgyle,
> But it wolde lasten al to long a whyle.

This, Douglas politely disputes, especially as Chaucer had said, rather 'boldly,' that he followed Vergil in stating that 'Eneas to Dido was forsworne.' Douglas is careful to disprove this, because it distorts Vergil's purpose to teach all kind of virtue by the consistent goodness of his hero, and to point out (as Henryson seems to have thought in his *Cresseid*) that Chaucer 'was ever, God wait, wemenis frend.' We are a long way from Vergil here; as we are when the poet complains that Caxton's translation does not do justice to what is hidden 'under the cluddes of dirk poetry.' Douglas makes a more plausible claim to be a modern in a further objection that Caxton's translation (taken from a French version) is bad, that it is out in its words and its geography, and marred by omissions; in quoting Horace on the true method of rendering a foreign author; and in urging the advantages to vernacular style from the reading of the Latin poet. Yet, after all, his aim was to make Vergil's book a literary bible, as Boccaccio's and Chaucer's were. He desires to be thanked by schoolmasters and by 'onletterit' folk, to whom he has given a new lesson[1]; he joins St Gregory's opinion with Horace's; he sees a Christian purpose in his work, and he prays for guidance to Mary and her Son, 'that heavenlie Orpheus.' His Vergil is, for the most part, the Vergil of the dark ages, part prophet, part wizard, master of 'illusionis by devillich werkis and coniurationis.' These, he confesses, are now more rare for 'the faith is now mair ferme'; but the circumstances should have been allowed for by the dullard Caxton. When he returns in the prologue to the sixth book to chide those who consider that book but full of 'gaistis and elriche fantaseis' and 'browneis and bogillis,' he says of Vergil—

> As tuiching hym, writis Ascencius:
> Feill of his wordis bene lyk the appostillis sawis;
> He is ane hie theolog sentencius,
> And maist profound philosophour he hym schawis.
> Thocht sum his writis frawart our faith part drawis,
> Na wondir; he was na cristin man, per de;
> He was a gentile, and leifit on payane lawis,
> And зit he puttis ane God, Fadir maist hie.

So it would appear, only too clearly, from these interesting

---

[1] *Directioun* and *Exclamatioun.*

prologues, that Douglas's literary attitude was not modern, and that he is not even so much a Janus-poet as his position and opportunities would warrant. When we separate him from his literary neighbours, it must be as a dilettante.

Probably, the main interest of the translation, and of most of Douglas's work, is philological. No Scot has built up such a diction, drawn from all sources, full of forgotten tags of alliterative romance, Chaucerian English, dialectal borrowings from Scandinavian, French, Latin. No one is harder to interpret. Literary merit is not wanting; yet, in those passages, and especially in his *Aeneid*, which strike the reader most, by the vigorous, often onomatopoeic force of the vocabulary, the pleasure is not what he who knows his Vergil expects, and must demand. The excellence of such a description as that of Acheron—

> With holl bisme[1], and hiduus swelth wnrude,
> Drumlie of mud, and scaldand as it wer wod[2],
> Popland[3] and bullerand[4] furth on athir hand
> Onto Cochitus all his slik[5] and sand,

is not the excellence of the original. We are sometimes reminded of Stanyhurst's later effort, in which, however much we may admire the verbal briskness in the marshalling of his thunder and storm passages, we feel that all 'wanteth the trew *decorum* of Vergilian sentiment. The archaic artifices, the metrical looseness and the pedestrian tread, where Vergil is alert, destroy the illusion. Still, if we may not give Douglas more than his due, we must not give him less. His *Aeneid* is a remarkable effort, and is gratefully remembered as the first translation of a great classical poet into English, northern or southern.

Douglas's work, considered as a whole, expresses, in the amplest way, the content of the later allegorical literature. He has lost the secret of the older devices, and does not understand the new which were about to usurp their place. He has not the artistic sense of Henryson, or the resource of Dunbar. His pictorial quality, on which so much stress has been laid by some who would have him to be a modern, is not the pagan delight, nor is its use as an interpretation of his mood after the fashion of the renascence. Some passages which have been cited to prove the contrary are but copies from Henryson and earlier work. In him, as in Hawes (to quote a favourite metaphor of both) 'the bell is rung to evensong.' If Lyndsay and others in the next period still show Chaucerian influence, with them it is a reminiscence, amid the turmoil of the new day.

---

[1] abysm. [2] mad, wild. [3] 'bubbling.' [4] roaring, 'boiling.' [5] slime, wet mud.

The minor contemporaries of Henryson, Dunbar and Douglas add nothing to our sketch of Middle Scots poetry. What information we have of these forgotten writers is derived from Dunbar's *Lament for the Makaris*, Douglas's *Palice of Honour* and Lyndsay's *Testament of the Papyngo*. Historians have probably exaggerated the extent and importance of this subordinate literature[1]. It is true we know little of the authors or of their works, but what we do know shows that to speak of 'nests of singing birds,' or to treat Dunbar as a kind of Shakespearean eminence overtopping a great range of song, is amiable hyperbole. What is extant of this 'Chaucerian' material lies in the lower levels of Lydgate's and Occleve's work. The subjects are of the familiar fifteenth century types, and, when not concerned with the rougher popular matter, repeat the old plaints on the ways of courts and women and on the vanity of life. Walter Kennedy, Dunbar's rival in *The Flyting*, and the most eminent of these minors, has left five poems, *The Passioun of Christ, Ane Ballat in praise of Our Lady, Pious Counsale, The Prais of Aige* and *Ane agit Manis invective against Mouth-thankless*. His reputation must rest on the *Flyting* rather than on the other pieces, which are conventional and dull; and there only because of the antiquarian interest of his 'billingsgate' and his Celtic sympathies[2]. With Kennedy may be named Quintyne Schaw, who wrote an *Advyce to a Courtier*.

In a general retrospect of this Chaucerian school it is not difficult to note that the discipleship, though sincere, was by no means blind. If the Scottish poets imitated well, and often caught the sentiment with remarkable felicity, it was because they were not painful devotees. In what they did they showed an appreciation beyond the faculty of Chaucer's southern admirers ; and, though the artistic sense implied in this appreciation was dulled by the century's craving for a 'moral' to every fancy, their individuality saved them from the fate which befel their neighbours. Good as the *Testament of Cresseid* is, its chief interest to the historical student is that it was written, that Henryson dared to find a sequel to the master's well-rounded story. Douglas's protest in the general prologue to his *Aeneid*, though it fail to prove to us that Vergil was much more to him than Chaucer was, shows an audacity which only an intelligent intimacy with the English poet could allow. The vitality of such appreciation, far from undoing the Chaucerian tradition, gave it a fresh lease of life before it yielded, inevitably, to the newer fashion.

[1] For the non-Chaucerian elements see next chapter.   [2] See Chapter IV.

CHAPTER XI

THE MIDDLE SCOTS ANTHOLOGIES: ANONYMOUS VERSE AND EARLY PROSE

STRONG as was the Chaucerian influence on the Scottish poets during the fifteenth and sixteenth centuries, it by no means suppressed or transformed what may be called the native habit of Scottish verse. That influence came, as has been shown, from the courtly side; it was a fashion first set by the author of *The Kingis Quair*—in its treatment of the language and in its literary mannerisms, a deliberate co-operation with the general European effort to dignify the vernaculars. It did much, but it came 'ate; and, being perhaps too artificial, it yielded, in due course, to another southern influence, more powerful and permanent. Were the Chaucerian makars of the fifteenth and sixteenth centuries and their successors in the seventeenth century to be taken as the sole representatives of northern literature, it would be hard to account for the remarkable outburst of national verse amid the conventionalities of the eighteenth. Chaucer and the Elizabethans do not explain Ramsay[1] and Fergusson and Burns: and these writers are not a sudden dialectal sport in the literary development. It is the object of this chapter to show that the native sentiment which has its fullest expression in these 'modern' poets was always active, and that the evidence of its existence and of its methods is clear, even during that period when the higher literary genius of the country was most strongly affected by foreign models. The vitality of this popular habit has been shown in the most courtly and 'aureate' verse of the so-called 'golden age.' Even in those passages in which the poets may be suspected of burlesquing this habit—whether by direct satire or in half-conscious repetition of Chaucer's dislike of 'rum ram ruf'—the acknowledgment is significant. The thesis of this chapter is, therefore, to supplement what has been said parenthetically of this non-Chaucerian 'matter.' It deals with those pieces which lie outside the work of the

---

[1] See Chapter IV, p. 95, note.

'Chaucerians,' for the most part with those anonymous poems which have been preserved in the greater anthologies of the sixteenth century. The interest of this body of literature is complex—in sentiment, in choice of subject, and, not least, in verse technique.

No literature has been better served than Scottish has been by the industry of early anthologists. The all-important Cancioneros have not done more for Spanish ; and they lack the exclusive and exhaustive value of the Scottish collections. For the latter preserve not only all that is known of the work of some of the greatest poets, but, also, a large body of minor verse, without which we should have formed but a poor estimate of contemporary taste, and without which we should have lost the perspective of later literature. These anthologies are representative in the truest sense. They were written out by men who were, first and foremost, collectors and antiquaries, who show no critical obsession, no desire to select and honour what may have appealed most to their individual taste. Their books are historical documents, which must be interpreted by historical methods[1].

The importance of this fugitive 'popular' literature is made clear in the references by the more 'academic' writers. Dunbar's *Lament for the Makaris* derives part of its bibliographical value from its record of poets who owed little or nothing to 'noble Chaucer, of makaris flour.' Though Gavin Douglas, in his *Palice of Honour*, names but Kennedie, Dunbar, and Quintine [Schaw] as the Scottish companions of the world's poets, yet in the 'lang cathalogue of nobyll men and wemen,' he tells us—

> I saw Raf Coilȝear with the thrawin brow,
> Craibit Johne the Reif, and auld Cowkewyis sow ;
> And how the wran came out of Ailssay ;
> And Peirs Plowman that maid his workmen fow ;
> Greit Gowmakmorne and Fyn Makcoul, and how
> Thay suld be goddis in Ireland as they say ;
> Thair saw I Maitland vpon auld Beird Gray,
> Robene Hude, and Gilbert with the quhite hand,
> How Hay of Nauchtoun flew in Madin land.

The list of tales, 'sum in prose and sum in verse,' and popular songs in the oft-quoted passage in the *Complaynt of Scotlande*, is—though a mere list, and, as it were, the table of contents to a more elaborate Asloan or Bannatyne MS—evidence of the highest value. Nor is the ascription of this wide taste in literature to a band of merrymaking shepherds—however

---

[1] For an account of these collections, see bibliography.

'academic' these pastoralists may be—without significance. Further interest is derived from the fact that the *timbre*, colour, idiosyncrasy (whatever we may call it), which constitutes the internal interest of this material, is represented in the works of the 'Chaucerian' poets. The evidence of this, to which we have already referred[1], is not less instructive whether the poetic intention be to burlesque courtly fashions or to escape for a time from the ceremonies of the aureate muse.

To the reader of this miscellaneous verse there are but few rewards of 'literary' pleasure. It is easy to agree with Pinkerton's caustic note on the last lines of *Rowllis Cursing*—

> This tragedy is callit, but dreid,
> Rowlis cursing, quha will it reid—

'he might have put a point of interrogation at the close[2].' We are here less concerned with aesthetic and individual merits than with the historical importance of the whole body. At the same time, it may be maintained that, but for the accident of anonymity, some of the pieces might well take their place in the works of Dunbar or Scott and do them no dishonour. We excuse Henryson's *Practysis of Medecyne* less as a lapse of genius than as an illustration of the dues which the best of Chaucerians had to pay at times to rough popular taste.

It is difficult to classify this miscellaneous verse and prose—the foundlings of the fifteenth and sixteenth centuries—according to the traditional scheme of types, and in dull analogy with the groups into which contemporary southern literature may be conveniently divided. Not only are the 'kinds'—lyrical, satirical, allegorical and the like—merged into each other in a perplexing way, but their differentiation may tempt us to overlook that Scottish idiosyncrasy in which the entire critical interest of the matter may be said to rest[3]. Further, when we apply the term 'popular' to this body of literature, we must guard against using it in the sense familiar in the controversy on the origins of the ballads. It is to be understood, in the main, as 'native,' in opposition to the more affected style of the makars; but, at the same time, with 'artifice' and 'literary tradition' of its own. Its appeal to us is the appeal of Allan Ramsay and his greater successors—the protest of vernacular habit against alien literary fashion.

---

[1] See Chapter x.

[2] The Hunterian Club text has taken the suggestion seriously.

[3] There are, of course, 'non-Chaucerian' contributions to the miscellanies which are not Scottish. The Bannatyne MS, for example, contains verses by John Heywood.

As in these later writers, the prevailing sentiment is that of the farm and burgh 'wynd'—a sentiment always robust and unreserved, finding expression in the revel of country fairs and city taverns, and carrying from both, to our modern sense, the mingled odours of the field and kennel. The two best known examples of this 'rustic' muse are *Peblis to the Play* and *Christis Kirk on the Grene*. These are, in theme and form, companion-pieces, and might well be, according to a persistent tradition, by the same author. Reference has been made to the claims set up in behalf of James I[1]. Some would ascribe the poems to James V because their popular character suits better the character of the 'Gudeman of Ballengeich' than of the author of *The Kingis Quair*. It has been shown that the assumption of inappropriateness in style is invalid as an argument against authorship by James I, and that there are certain difficulties of date which stand in the way of the claim for his successor. That James I may have been the author is an allowance of some importance in studying the entwined relationship of the Chaucerian and the 'popular' verse during the period.

The theme of these poems is the rough fun of a village festival or 'wappinshaw,' such as has been made familiar by Geikie's pencil. The main impression is that of wild spirits: there is plenty of movement, but no story, or coherence in the effects. Incidentally, there are passages which, for descriptive directness, rank with the best in the 'Dutch' manner, but their success comes from the sheer verve of composition rather than from cunning in the treatment of detail.

> To dans thir damysellis thame dicht[2],
>   Thir lassis licht of laitis[3];
> Thair gluvis wer of the raffell[4] rycht,
>   Thair schone wes of the straitis[5];
> Thair kirtillis wer of lynkome[6] licht,
>   Weill prest with mony plaitis.
> Thay wer so nys[7] quhen men thame nicht[8],
>   Thay squeilit lyk ony gaittis,
>   So lowd,
> At Chrystis kirk of the grene that day.

In exact parallel with this are the opening stanzas of *Peblis to the Play*, describing the morning fuss among the country wenches; but with this additional touch—

> 'Evir, allace!' than said scho,
>   'Am I nocht cleirlie tynt[9]?

---

[1] See Chapter x.   [2] made ready.   [3] manner, behaviour.
[4] roe-skin.   [5] ?coarse cloth (woollen).   [6] Lincoln.
[7] 'nice.'   [8] came near.   [9] lost, undone.

> 'I dar nocht cum 3on mercat to,
> I am so evvil sone brint.
> Amang 3on merchandis Maj-drest so[1]!
> Marie! I sall anis mynt[2]—
> Stand of far, and keik þaim to[3],
> As I at hame wes wont,'
> > Quod scho,
> Of peblis to the play.

The likeness is preserved throughout, in the rough love-making, the coarse farce of the upset cadger, the wild dancing and quarrelling (told at great length in *Christis Kirk*), and in the introduction of certain popular types, such as the miller and the piper. Everybody is at fever-heat: the louder the women's voices and the harder the blows, the better the fun.

> The wyvis kest vp ane hiddouss yell,
> Quhen all thir yunkeris yokkit[4];
> Als ferss as ony fyrflaucht fell,
> Freikis[5] to the feild thay flokkit;
> The cairlis[5] with clubbis cowd vder quell[6],
> Quhill blud at breistis out bokkit[7]:
> So rudly rang the commoun bell,
> Quhill all the stepill rokkit,
> > For reird[8],
> At Chrystis kirk of the grene.

When the 'rush' of the verse slackens, it sometimes gains in literary felicity, as in this excellent stanza—

> Than thai come to the townis end
> Withouttin moir delay,
> He befoir, and scho befoir,
> To see quha wes maist gay.
> All þat luikit þame upon
> Leuche fast at þair array:
> Sum said þat þai wer merkat folk,
> Sum said the quene of may
> > Wes cumit
> Of peblis to the play.

Here, too, there is movement, but the pace is comfortable. This is partly effected by the happy redoubling of phrase. Even in the noisier *Christis Kirk* the gentler song-note comes in, as in these lines—

> Off all thir madynis myld as meid
> Wes nane so gympt[9] as Gillie;
> As ony ross hir rude[10] wes reid,
> Hir lyre[10] wes lyk the lillie——

---

[1] (Sibbald's emendation).   [2] try, venture.   [3] peep at them.
[4] engaged (in conflict).   [5] men.   [6] attacked each other.
[7] burst, spurted.   [8] clamour.   [9] 'jimp.' graceful, neat.
[10] ruddy parts of the complexion, cheeks and lips; contrasted with 'lyre.' the white skin.

a striking anticipation of the opening verse of Henry Carey's immortal ballad[1]. Occasional literary merit of this kind, or wealth of illustration to the antiquary of social manners, are less important than the evidence which these poems yield of the abiding rusticity of the northern muse, and of its metrical habit. It is, as has been said, not hard to find hints of this homely quality in the greater makars, even in their most artificial moments: here we have in all their fulness, the setting, the actuality, the humour, the coarseness so familiar in later northern literature. Not less important—and for retrospective reasons too—is the complicated verse-form. The exact manipulation of the intricate stanza, with its lines of varying length, its richness in rime and alliteration, may well impress the reader who comes fresh to the subject as the work of some master-craftsman ; but the frequency with which it occurs at this time, as well as earlier and later, shows that it was no *tour de force*. It supplies one of the most important links in the 'formal' transition from the older northern romance to the later northern ballad. We appear to trace the earlier stages of the process in the riming alliterative romances, from the long irregular stanza of such a poem as *Sir Gawayne and the Grene Knight,* through the thirteen-lined stanza of *The Buke of the Howlat* or *The Pistill of Susan,* and the eleven-lined stanza as shown in *Sir Tristrem.* There is no chronological intention in this statement of descent: we may find here, as we find in the history of the early dramatic forms of English literature, as much parallelism and analogy as derivation. But the point is that the habit of these 'popular' fifteenth and sixteenth century poems—the alliteration, rime and, above all, the breaking away in the 'bob'—is an 'effect of antiquity.' This stanzaic form represents the permanent native element which is lost, or almost lost, for a time during the 'Chaucerian' ascendancy. Recognition of this fact gives a new meaning to the stray examples in the verse of the makars, and almost compels the critic to look upon the accredited manner of the 'golden age' as an exception and 'accident.' History confirms this ; for when aureation and other fashions had passed, the reviving vernacular broke forth anew in the old forms. Further, in this stanza we are not merely in close association with the older romance forms ; in it we have both the

[1] Of all the girls that are so smart,
There's none like pretty Sally:
She is the darling of my heart,
And she lives in our alley.
Sally in our Alley.

timbre and measure of the ballad. This is not the place for the discussion of the vexed question of the relationship of romance and ballad. Whatever conclusions be reached, or whatever general principles be assumed, the data here supplied towards the prosodic history of the 'popular' ballad are significant. The actual form of the *Christis Kirk* stanza, however it may stand to that of the ballad and other forms, lived on, and again and again, in the vernacular revival, was the medium for the retelling of rustic frolic[1].

Another example of this type is *Sym and his Brudir*. It is, in intention, a good humoured satire on church abuse, in a tale of two palmers in St Andrews; but the adventures of these arrant beggars are on the same lines as those of the yokels in the pieces already discussed, and the appeal to the reader is identical. Here too, when the people come to the 'brother's' wedding—for

> quhair that Symy levit in synnyng
> His bruder wald haif ane bryd——

there is the like rough 'justing,' wild chasing on horseback, dashing down in the dirt, and general noise. Even the literary setting at the end of the poem is deliberately restless, for the poet, after describing how the brother's 'mowth was schent' in the scrimmage, adds—

> He endis the story with harme forlorne:
> The nolt begowth[2] till skatter,
> The ky ran startling to the corne.

The rustic habit is shown more happily in *The Wyf of Auchtirmuchty* and *The Wowing of Jok and Jynny*, both in stanzas of eight lines with four accents, riming respectively *ababcdcd* and *ababbcbc*. In the former, a husbandman tired after a wet day's work at the plough, and out of humour at finding his wife

> baith dry and clene,
> And sittand at ane fyre, beikand bawld[3],
> With ane fat sowp, as I hard say,

arranges that he shall change places with her. Disaster upon disaster falls upon the amateur 'housewife,' until he declares

> Quhen I forsuk my plwche[4],
> I trow I bot forsuk my seill[5];
> And I will to my plwch agane,
> For I and this howss will nevir do weill.

---

[1] Occasionally with minor modifications, which do not affect the type, or disguise its ancestry.

[2] began.

[3] lit. 'warming herself boldly, or bravely.'

[4] plough.

[5] happiness, 'good.'

The theme is obviously old, but the treatment by the unknown makar (for the ascription in a later hand in the Bannatyne MS to Moffat has no warranty) is fresh and lively. The kernel of the tale is the enumeration of the misguided man's misfortunes, which fulfils the same purpose of cumulative farce as the rushing and sprawling in *Peblis to the Play* and *Christis Kirk on the Grene.* In the matter of prosodic relationship to the rimed alliterative poems on the one hand and to the ballads on the other, the text supplies interesting evidence of the 'echo' or 'iteration' between, and within, the stanzas. We take, for example, the concluding lines of the seventh stanza and the opening lines of the eighth—

> Bot than or he come in agane,
> The calfis brak lowss and sowkit the ky.
>
> The calvis and ky being met in the lone, *etc.*

Or, in the eleventh and twelfth—

> The first that he gat in his armis
> Wes all bedirtin to the ene.
>
> The first that he gat in his armis
> It was all dirt vp to the eine.

Or, very fully, throughout the ninth stanza—

> Than to the kyrn that he did stoure,
> And jwmlit[1] at it quhill[2] he swatt:
> Quhen he had jwmlit[1] a full lang houre,
> The sorow crap[3] of butter he gatt.
> Albeit na butter he cowld gett
> ʒit he wes cummerit with the kyrne,
> And syne he het the milk our hett,
> And sorrow spark[3] of it wald ʒyrne[4].

In these passages we have the true ballad *timbre* and the familiar devices.

The *Wowing*[5] *of Jok and Jynny*[6] is an early treatment of the theme which Burns has refashioned in *Duncan Gray.* There is a strong family likeness between the opening of the 'second setting' by Burns and that of the *Wowing*—

> Robeyns Jok come to wow our Jynny,
> On our feist evin quhen we were fou.

Much of the intended humour of the piece lies in the list of Jynny's 'tocher-gud' or dowry and in the complementary inventory

---

[1] stirred, churned.   [2] till.   [3] 'sorry a bit.'
[4] thicken.   [5] wooing.
[6] Bann. MS. No. CL. An unwarranted ascription to John Clerk has been marked out in the MS.

which John gives to prove that he is a worthy suitor—a 'fouth o'
auld nick-nackets,' after the heart of Captain Grose. Here again,
the fun comes from the 'rush' of detail and the strange medley of
worthless treasures.

> I haif ane helter and eik ane hek,
> Ane cord, ane creill, and als ane cradill,
> Fyve fidder[1] of raggis to stuff ane jak,
> Ane auld pannell of ane laid sadill,
> Ane pepper-polk maid of a padill,
> Ane spounge, ane spindill wantand ane nok,
> Twa lusty lippis to lik ane laiddill;
> To gang to gidder Jynny and Jok.

It will be observed that the use of alliteration is frequent.

In all these pieces, dealing in some way with rustic wooing
and matrimony, there is a burlesque element, but this must be
distinguished from the subtler, more imaginative, and more
literary type of burlesque which constitutes the second permanent
characteristic of Middle and Modern Scots poetry. Examples have
been noted in the preceding chapter on the work of the greater
makars, and especially in the *Ballad of Kynd Kittok* and the
Interlude of the Droichis Part of the Play. What Gavin Douglas
wrote of Vergil's sixth book,

> All is bot gaistis and elriche fantasies,
> Of browneis and of bogillis full this buke,

might well be said of this strange set of Middle Scots poems.
We must not seek, with the sententious bishop, for any allegory
or moral purpose in these whimsicalities. Some of these are,
perhaps, mere burlesques of romance-tradition, most are but
'dremis and dotage in the monis cruik.'

The short tale of *Gyre Carling* (in three stanzas of the riming-
alliterative type, with the bob) relates how this mother-witch, who
dwelt in 'Betokis bour' and fed on Christian men's flesh, was loved
by Blasour, her neighbour 'on the west syd.'

> For luve of hir lawchane[2] lippis, he walit and he weipit;

and he gathered a crowd of moles to warp down her tower. But
the unresponsive lady cudgelled him well (as St Peter served
Kynd Kittok) until he bled 'a quart off milk pottage inwart.'
She laughed, and, after the manner of Gog Magog's spouse in the
Interlude of the Droichis Part, ejaculated North Berwick Law in
her mirth. Then the king of Faery, with his elves and all the dogs
from Dunbar to Dunblane and all the tykes of Tervey (which

---

[1] fother.   [2] laughing.

might well be Topsy Turvy land!), laid siege to the fair; but she transformed herself into a sow and went 'gruntling our the Greik Sie.' There, in spite, she married Mahomet or Mahoun, and became queen of the Jews. She was sadly missed in Scotland; the cocks of Cramond ceased to crow, and the hens of Haddington would not lay.

> All this langour for lufe befoirtymes fell,
>   Lang or Betok wes born,
>   Scho bred of ane acorne;
>   The laif[1] of the story to morne
>   To ȝow I sall tell.

This piece might well be by Dunbar.

Another love-tale of fairyland is told in *King Berdok*. This 'grit king of Babylon'

> dwelt in symmer in till ane bowkaill[2] stok;
> And in to winter, quhen the frostis ar fell,
> He dwelt for cauld in till a cokkill schell.

A 'stalwart man of hairt and hand,' he wooed for seven years Mayiola, or Mayok, the 'golk[3] of Maryland'; and yet 'scho wes bot ȝeiris thre.' This 'bony bird' had but one eye, and her 'foir-fute wes langar than hir heill.' Berdok set out to ravish the 'golk,' and, finding her milking her mother's kine, cast her in a creel on his back. On his return, his load proved to be but a 'howlat nest, full of skait birdis[4].'

> And than this Berdok grett
> And ran agane Meyok for to gett.

But the king of Faery was now in pursuit, and the lover took refuge in a 'killogy[5].' With the assistance of the kings of the Picts and Portugal, Naples and Navern (Strathnaver), the lord of Faery laid siege. The attackers mounted guns and fired at Berdok with bullets of raw dough. Jupiter prayed Saturn to save the lover by turning him into a toad; but Mercury transformed him into a bracken bush.

> And quhen thay saw the buss waig to and fra,
> Thay trowd it wes ane gaist, and thay to ga;
> Thir fell kingis thus Berdok wald haif slane;
> All this for lufe, luveris sufferis pane;
> Boece said, of poyettis that wes flour,
> Thocht lufe be sweit, oft syiss it is full sour.

It is not necessary to hold with Laing that this piece was intended

---

[1] rest. [2] cabbage. [3] cuckoo.
[4] 'Dungbirds,' a name applied to the Arctic gull.
[5] The entrance or recess of a kiln, to help the draught.

as a burlesque of some popular 'gest' or romance : the comic elfin intention may be accepted on its own merits.

There is more of direct parody in the interlude of the *Laying of Lord Fergus's Gaist*, beginning

> Listis lordis, I sall ȝow tell
> Off ane verry grit mervell,
> Off Lord Ferguss gaist,
> How mekle Schir Andro it chest[1]
> Vnto Beittokis bour.

It indulges, amid its satire of the ritual of exorcism, in the quaintest fancy.

> Suppois the gaist wes littill
> Ȝit it stall Godis quhittill[2];
> It stall fra peteouss Abrahame
> Ane quhorle[3] and ane quhum quhame[4];
> It stall fra the carle of the mone
> Ane pair of auld yrn schone;
> It ran to Pencaitlane
> And wirreit ane auld chaplane.

Its allusions to 'Colkelbeis Feist' and 'St Bettokis Bour' would establish its kinship, even if its manner did not make this evident.

Lichtounis Dreme helps us a little to the secret of this 'skimble-skamble' verse. The rimer asks 'Quha douttis dremis ar bot phantasye?' and proceeds :

> My spreit was reft, and had in extasye,
> My heid lay laich into this dreme but dout;
> At my foirtop my fyve wittis flew out,
> I murnit, and I maid a felloun mane[5]:
> Me thocht the King of Farye had me tane,
> And band me in ane presoun, fute and hand,
> Withoutin reuth, in ane lang raip of sand :
> To pers the presoun wall it was nocht eith[6],
> For it wes mingit and maid with mussill teith,
> And in the middis of it ane myir of flynt;
> I sank thairin, quhill I wes neir hand tynt;
> And quhen I saw thair wes none uthir remeid,
> I flychterit[7] vp with ane feddrem of leid.

He rambles on, telling of his escape to 'mony divers place,' and at last to Peebles and Portjafe. Then he sailed in a barge of draff to Paradise.

> Be we approchit into that port in hye,
> We ware weill ware of Enoch and Elye,
> Sittand, on Yule evin, in ane fresch grene schaw,
> Rostand straberreis at ane fyre of snaw.

---

[1] chased.	[2] knife.	[3] whorl.	[4] 'nick-nack.'
[5] moan.	[6] easy.	[7] fluttered.	

Like Gog Magog's kin in Dunbar's interlude, he makes free with
the interlunar spaces. Later in the poem, when telling how he
desired to leave the moon, he says:

> Bot than I tuke the sone beme in my neif[1]
> And wald haif clumin[2], bot it was in ane clipss[3];
> Schortlie I slaid, and fell upoun my hips,
> Doun in ane midow, besyde ane busk of mynt;
> I socht my self, and I was sevin yeir tynt[4],
> Yit in ane mist I fand me on the morne.

We need not follow his adventure with the Pundler and the three
white whales which appeared at the blast of the 'elriche horne.'
The conclusion is suggestive. When Lichtoun *monicus*[5] awakes,
he asks:

> Quhair, trow ye, that I was?
> Doun in ane henslaik[6], and gat ane felloun fall,
> And lay betuix ane picher and the wall.

And he adds:

> As wyffis commandis, this dreme I will conclude;
> God and the rude mot turn it all to gud!
> Gar fill the cop, for thir auld carlingis[7] clames
> That gentill aill is oft the causs of dremes.

Another wife, in later verse, warned her Tam how by 'bousing at
the nappy' he would be 'catch'd wi' warlocks in the mirk.

In the bacchanalian quality shown in different ways in these
rustic sketches and elfin dream-poems we have a third tradition
of Scottish verse. It would, of course, be vain to seek a complete
explanation of the eighteenth century convivial muse in the
historical evidences of a literary habit—as vain as to estimate
the general effect of Burns's work as an editorial modification of
old material; but the testimony of historical continuity, in theme,
in attitude and in technique, is too strong to be overlooked in
a survey of Scottish literature. The more thorough and connected
the survey is, the clearer will it appear that the rusticity, the wild
humour and the conviviality are not more the idiosyncrasies of
Burns and his fellow poets than the persistent, irrepressible
habits of the literature itself. Criticism has been too willing
to treat pieces like Burns's *Scotch Drink* as mere personal
enthusiasm.

The best of all the Middle Scots convivial verse is Dunbar's
Testament of Mr Andro Kennedy[8], but some of the anonymous
pieces in the collections deserve mention. *Quhy sowld nocht*

---

[1] fist, hand.   [2] climbed.   [3] eclipse.   [4] lost.
[5] So signed in the MS.   [6] In a poultry-yard: say, 'in the mire.'
[7] women.   [8] See Chapter x.

Allane honorit be? is a sprightly 'ballat' on 'Allan-a-Maut,' *alias*
John Barleycorn.   By a misreading of the subscription in the MS
—'Quod Allane Matsonis suddartis[1]'—the poem has been given
to one Watson.   It tells the history of 'Allan' from his youth, when
he was 'cled in grene,' to his powerful manhood.

> The grittest cowart in this land,
> Fra he with Allane entir in band[2],
> Thocht he may nowdir gang nor stand,
> ʒit fowrty sall nocht gar him flie:
> Quhy sowld nocht Allane honorit be?

'Allane' too

> is bening, courtass, and gude,
> And servis ws of our daly fvde,
> And that with liberalitie;
> Quhy sowld nocht Allane honorit be?

The theme is familiar in Burns's *John Barleycorn,* itself based
on an older popular text.   Another in the Bannatyne MS, in
eleven-lined stanzas, and signed 'Allanis subdert,' anathematises
the bad brewer and praises the good.

> Quha hes gud malt, and makis ill drynk,
> Wa mot be hir werd!
> I pray to God scho rott and stynk
> Sevin ʒeir abone the eird.

And another piece 'I mak it kend, he that will spend,' in the same
collection, is, appropriately, given to 'John Blyth,' a fellow-reveller
with Allan's jolly-boys.

> Now lat ws sing with Chrystis blissing,
> Be glaid and mak gude sound:
> With an O, and ane I, now or we forder found[3],
> Drink thow to me, and I to the,
> And lat the cop go round.

In the foregoing groups we find the representative and historical
qualities of the national verse, the *timbre* of Scotticism : in the
large residue of anonymous pieces in the collections we encounter
the familiar fifteenth and sixteenth century southern types.

Fabliaux, in the manner of the *Freiris of Berwik*[4], are not
numerous.   The *Thrie Priestis of Peblis* is a long didactic tale,
or set of tales, with a politico-social purpose, kin in spirit with
Lyndsay's verse, or the prose *Complaynt of Scotlande,* or the
fragmentary recension of the *Talis of the Fyve Bestis* in the
Asloan MS.   The truer note of the *fabliau* is struck in the tale

---

[1] 'subjects.'   [2] join company.
[3] 'before we farther go.'   [4] See Chapter x.

of *The Dumb Wyf,* in which a dumb woman is, by her husband's desire—and to his own undoing—made to speak.

> The leist deuill that is in hell
> Can gif ane wyff hir toung;
> The grittest, I ȝow tell,
> Cannot do mak hir dum.

There is, throughout the collections, no lack of cynical fun at the expense of woman, according to the lively tradition of *The Romance of the Rose,* and not a little of that severer satire and audacious double meaning which we find in Dunbar[1]; occasionally, as in *Sic Perrell in Paramouris lyis,* and invariably with sober warning rather than satirical purpose, the verse-makers discuss 'menis subtell slicht.' There is church satire, too, in *Sir John Rowllis Cursing,* a tedious invocation of 'Godis braid malisoun' upon those who stole Sir John's five fat geese and other fowls. The anathema is so paralysing in its fulness that it is well the writer becomes merciful at the close and prays

> Latt nevir this sentence fall thame vpone,
> Bot grant thame grace ay till forbeir
> Resset or stowth[2] of vthir menis geir;
> And als agane the geir restoir
> Till Rowle, as I hafe said befoir.

There is not much to choose between a 'cursing' and a 'flyting.'

Of historical and patriotic verse there is little. The fragment of the *Ring*[3] *of the Roy Robert*[4] (ascribed to Dean David Steill in the Maitland folio) recalls *Bruce* in metre and *Wallace* in sentiment. In the *Talis of the Fyve Bestis,* the second or 'Hartis Tale' is devoted to praise of Wallace for his defence of Scotland 'fra subiectioun of Saxonis blud'; and, in the Scots recension of the *Nine Nobles*[5], the last in the list of great men is Robert the Bruce, who 'venkust the mychty Kyng | Off England, Edward, twyse in fycht.' There is, too, in the Maitland folio, a short defence of the Scots, which is an extract from Wyntoun's *Chronicle.* The plea for the peasant, familiar in the *fabliaux* of *Rauf Coilȝear* and *John the Reeve,* in Lyndsay's *John the Commonweill,* and in the prose *Complaynt of Scotlande* is represented here and there, as in *John Uponlandis Complaint* and *Few may fend for falsett*[6].

---

[1] Cf. Sempill's *Ballat on Margret Fleming, callit the Fleming Bark in Edinburcht,* his *Defence of Crissell Sandelandis,* and another on three women 'being slicht wemen of lyfe and conversatioun.' This type of poem is by no means rare in Scots.

[2] theft.   [3] reign.   [4] Robert III.

[5] In the Edinburgh University copy of Fordun.   [6] In the Bannatyne MS.

In all these pieces the literary interest yields to the historical and antiquarian : but in the love poems and lyrics it is of more account. Some of these are hardly inferior to the known work of Alexander Scott and others represented in these collections; and they may, indeed, prove to be theirs. The love lay *Tayis Bank*, in the common ballad measure, arranged in eight-lined stanzas, is curiously deliberate in its mixture of the alliterative and aureate styles. The 'mansuet Mergrit, this perle polist most quhyt,' who is the object of the poet's admiration, has been identified with Margaret Drummond, the mistress of James IV before his marriage with Margaret Tudor. The nature-setting, though happy, is conventional; and the poet's praise of the lady is always ceremonious and distant.

> This myld, meik, mansuet Mergrit,
> This perle polist most quhyt,
> Dame Natouris deir dochter discreit,
> The dyamant of delyt,
> Neuir formit wes to found on feit
> Ane figour moir perfyte,
> Nor non on mold that did hir meit
> Mycht mend hir wirth a myte.

When she departs, the poet is not sorrowful as the author of the *Kingis Quair* was. He appears to take comfort from the artistic propriety of her going into a wane 'most hevinly to behold.' He tells us that he admired the beauty of that place 'as parradyce but peir,' and adds

> And I to heir thir birdis gay
> Did in a bonk abyd.

Here, certainly, is the reserve of the professional makar. *The Murning Maiden* is on a higher level, in respect of directness and technical accomplishment; and, though it is not without traces of alliterative and allegorical convention, it is never artificial. It is no exaggeration to say that, in all our Middle English literature, there is no poem more plainly human and simple. A forlorn maiden, wandering in a wood in 'waithman weir[1],' encounters a man (the writer of the lyric) who, after listening to her soliloquy of sorrow, asks her why she trespasses with bow and arrows. She answers:

> Thocht I walk in this forest fre,
> Withe bow, and eik with fedderit flane[2],
> It is weill mair than dayis thre
> And meit or drink ʒit saw I nane.
> Thocht I had neuer sic neid
> My selffe to wyn my breid.
> ʒour deir may walk, schir, thair alane:
> ʒit wes never na beistis bane;
> I may not se thame bleid.

---

[1] huntsman's dress. [2] arrow.

Sen that I neuer did ȝow ill,
It wer no skill ȝe did me skaith.
ȝour deir may walk quhair euir thai will:
I wyn my meit be na sic waithe[1].
I do bot litill wrang,
Bot gif I flowris fang.
Giff that ȝe trow not in my aythe[2],
Tak heir my bow and arrowis bayth,
And lat my awin selffe gang.

She refuses the frank terms which he offers, and insists on remaining in the forest, a 'woful weycht[3],' with her bed

full cauld,
With beistis bryme[4] and bauld.

The forester, touched by her sorrow, vows he will not consent to her wild plan.

In to my armes swythe
Embrasit I that blythe[5],
Seyand, 'sweit hairt, of harmes ho[6]!
Found[7] sall I neuer this forrest fro,
Quhill ȝe me confort kyth.'

Than knelit I befoir that cleir[5],
And meiklie could hir mercye craiff,
That semlie than, with sobir cheir,
Me of hir gudlynes forgaif.
It wes no neid, I wys,
To bid us vther kys;
Thair mycht no hairtis mair joy resaif,
Nor ather could of uther haif;
This[8] brocht wer we to blis.

Of other pieces of this genre mention may be made of *The Luvaris Lament* (ascribed by Bannatyne to Fethe or Fethy), with the burden—

Cauld cauld culis the lufe
That kendillis our het,

and *In May in a Morning*, reminiscent, in its form, of the riming alliterative poems. Though *Welcum to May*[9] continues the traditional 'courtly' manner and the aureate diction of the makars (*e.g.* 'saufir firmament,' 'annammellit orient,' 'beriall droppis,' and the like), it shows a change in the point of view. It may be extravagant to discover more than a renascence appreciation of nature in the poem, yet these lines are not merely conventional:

Go walk vpoun sum rever fair,
Go tak the fresch and holsum air,
Go luk vpoun the flurist fell,
Go feill the herbis plesand smell.

---

[1] hunting.   [2] oath.   [3] wight.   [4] fierce.   [5] 'fair one,' maid.
[6] pause.   [7] go.   [8] thus.   [9] Beginning. 'Be glad al ȝe that luvaris bene.'

Another lyric, beginning *Quhen Flora had ourfret the firth*, works up the commonplaces about the merle and mavis, and does not shrink from aureation.

> Scho is sa brycht of hyd and hew,
> I lufe bot hir allone I wene;
> Is non hir lufe that may eschew
> That blenkis of that dulce amene.

So, too, *O Lusty May, with Flora quene* proclaims its kinship in such a phrase as 'preluciand bemis.' The *Song of Absence*, which Pinkerton wrongly attributed to James I[1], is more lively in its verse. Its irregular lines recall the movement of the 'rustic' stanza; but these are steadied by the ballast of such phrases as the 'hait canicular day' or the 'sweet mow redolent' of the beloved. Evidence of this 'aureate' habit is so persistent in the minor love poems in the collections that they must be grouped with the courtly poetry of the period.

Finally, there is the didactic and religious verse of the collections. Little of this is, however, anonymous; and rarely, if ever, may it be described as 'popular.' Engrained as the ethical habit appears to be in Scottish literature—so deeply, indeed, as often to convey the impression of unrelieved seriousness—it is not in any strict sense an idiosyncrasy of pre-reformation verse. In her reflections on life's pains and aspirations, Scotland but conformed to the taste of her neighbours. If she appear, after the sixteenth century, to ponder more upon these things—or, let us say, less upon others—she does so under stress of a combination of special circumstances, rather than in indulgence of an old habit or incurable liking.

An additional interest, philological rather than literary, attaches to the Asloan collection from the fact that it contains a number of prose passages, which are among the earliest remains of Scots prose, other than legal and official documents. That there should be any vernacular prose, whether official or quasi-literary, at the beginning of the fifteenth century is almost surprising, when we consider the place held by Latin in the intellectual life, even in the commercial relationships of renascence Scotland[2]. The plea for a native medium is hardly urged before the middle of the sixteenth century; and then it is only occasional, and, as in Lyndsay's *Exclamatioun to the Redar*, apologetic,

---

[1] *Ancient Scottish Poems* (1786), II, 425. See Chapter x of this volume.
[2] See Chapter IV.

because of the stress of reformation conflict. It was probably but rarely that a Scot excused his 'Ynglis' on the grounds stated by the earl of March in his letter to Henry IV of England[1]. We know that Scots was used in public documents in the late fourteenth century. In the Bute MS of Laws six of the twenty-five pieces are in the vernacular; so too are the parliamentary records from the reign of the first James. But neither in these nor in the texts represented in the Asloan MS can we discover any half-conscious effort of style, such as marks the beginnings of fifteenth century prose in England.

The earliest examples[2] of vernacular prose are the translations of Sir Gilbert Hay, or 'of the Haye,' dated 1456, and preserved in a single volume now in the collection at Abbotsford. They are (1) *The Buke of the Law of Armys*, or *Buke of Bataillis*, based on the French of Honoré Bonet, (2) *The Buke of the Order of Knichthood*, following *L'Ordre de Chevalerie* and (3) a version of the pseudo-Aristotelian *Government of Princes*. To which of these the entry in the Asloan MS ('The Document of Schir Gilbert Hay') refers is not known, for the portion of the MS which contained the text has been lost. Of more originality, but with small claim as literature, is the long treatise on political wisdom and rule of life for a prince, by John of Ireland, rector of Yarrow and quondam confessor to James III and Louis XI of France. The text, labelled *Johannis de Irlandia Opera Theologica*, is preserved in the Advocates' Library. A long extract from John's writings stands first in the Asloan MS ('On the Passioun,' etc.); and we have clues to his authorship of other vernacular treatises of a semi-theological character which are not extant. The place of his prose in the history of the language has been discussed in another chapter[3]. The contents of the *Portuus of Noblines* in the Asloan MS, and (in part) in the Chepman and Myllar prints, are explained by the fuller title, 'The wertuis of nobilnes and portratours thairof &c. callit the Portuus and matynnis of the samin.' This piece is a dull discussion, in a series of homilies, on Faith, Loyalty, Honour and the other virtues. It purports to be a translation by Andrew Cadiou from the French. The *Spectakle of Luf* or *Delectatioun*

---

[1] It 'ys mare cleir to myne understandyng than latyne or Fraunche' (1400). Cf. Chapter IV.

[2] Perhaps we should say the earliest important examples; for the short fifteenth century tracts, *Craft of Deyng*, *The Wisdom of Solomon* and *The Vertewis of the Mess*, preserved in the Cambridge University MS, Kk. I. 5, may be earlier. Their interest is, however, entirely philological. See the edition by J. Rawson Lumby, E.E.T.S. 1870.

[3] See Chapter IV.

of Wemen, translated from the Latin, is an exhortation, in the conventional dialogue-form, 'to abstene fra sic fleschly delectatiounis quhilk thow callis luf.' The reader is informed in the conclusion that the translation was finished at St Andrews on 10 July 1492, by G. Myll, 'ane clerk, quhilk had bene in to Venus court mair than the space of xx ʒeiris, quhill (he adds) I mycht nocht mak the seruice that I had bene accustomyd to do; quharfor I was put out of hir bill of hushald.' *The Schort Memoriale of the Scottis corniklis for addicioun*, an account of the reign of James II, is of no literary pretence.

Early in the sixteenth century, Murdoch Nisbet wrote out his version of Purvey's recension of Wyclif's translation of the New Testament. It anticipates the Bassandyne Bible by half-a-century; but it does not appear to have been circulated. It remained in manuscript till 1901. Its mixture of northern and southern forms gives it considerable philological interest. After it, we may name Gau's *Richt Vay* (a translation from Christiern Pedersen), Bellenden's *Livy* and *Scottish History*, the patchwork translation called *The Complaynt of Scotlande*, Winzet's *Tractates*, bishop Leslie's *History of Scotland*, Knox's *History* and Buchanan's *Chamaeleon*, Lindesay of Pitscottie's *History*, the controversial writings of Nicol Burne and other exiled Catholics and king James VI's early effort on versification (*Ane Schort Treatise*); but the consideration of these belongs to a later chapter. The professional *Rolment of Courtis*, by Abacuck Bysset, though of the seventeenth century (1622), represents the aureate style of Middle Scots and is the last outpost of that affectation in northern prose.

CHAPTER XII

ENGLISH PROSE IN THE FIFTEENTH CENTURY

I

PECOCK. FORTESCUE. THE PASTON LETTERS.

THE work of popularising prose was a slow and humble process. In the 'century of the commons' literature was consistently homely. Works of utility—books of manners and of cookery, service books and didactic essays, as well as old romances copied and modernised and chronicles growing ever briefer and duller—familiarised the middle classes with books. Dictionaries prove the spread of study; and, though verse was more popular reading than prose, countless letters and business papers remain to show that soldiers, merchants, servants and women were learning to read and write with fluency. The House of Commons and the king's council now conducted business in English; and, in the latter part of the century, politicians began to appeal to the sense of the nation in short tracts. In the meantime, the art of prose writing advanced no further. The Mandeville translations mark its high tide, for even *The Master of Game*, the duke of York's elaborate treatise on hunting, was, save for the slightest of reflections—'imagynacioun (is) maistresse of alle werkes'—purely technical. A fashionable treatise, as the number of manuscripts proves, it was, in the main, a translation of a well known French work; it is chiefly interesting for its technical terms, mostly French, and as witness to the excessive elaborateness of the hunting pleasures of the great.

Save for the solitary and unappreciated phenomenon of Pecock, Latin, for the greater part of the century, maintained its position as the language of serious books. The other two learned men of the time wrote first in Latin, and seem to have been driven to use English by the political ascendency of a middle-class and unlettered faction. The praises of Henry V are recorded in Latin; nearly two dozen Latin chronicles were compiled to some seven in English; the books given by the duke of Gloucester and the earl of

Worcester to the universities were in Latin, and so were the volumes purchased by the colleges themselves.

John Capgrave, the learned and travelled friar of Lynn in Norfolk, was the best known man of letters of his time. His reputation was based upon comprehensive theological works, which comprised commentaries upon all the books of the Bible, condensed from older sources, besides a collection of lives of saints, lives of the *Famous Henries* and a life of his patron, Humphrey, duke of Gloucester. All these were in Latin. But he composed in English, for the simple, a life of St Katharine in verse and one of St Gilbert of Sempringham in prose, as well as a guide for pilgrims to Rome and a volume of *Annals,* presented to Edward IV.

Capgrave's chronicle, so far as originality goes, makes some advance on Trevisa, being a compilation from a number of sources with an occasional observation of the writer's own. He seems to have regarded it in the nature of notes: 'a schort remembrauns of elde stories, that whanne I loke upon hem and have a schort touch of the writing I can sone dilate the circumstaunces.' Valuable historically, as an authority on Henry IV, it also attracts attention by the terseness of its style. It 'myte,' says the author, 'be cleped rather Abbreviacion of Cronicles than a book'; but graphic detail appears in the later portion, dealing with Capgrave's own times. It is he who tells us that Henry V 'after his coronacion was evene turned onto anothir man and all his mociones inclined to vertu,' though this is probably in testimony to the peculiar sacredness of the anointing oil. Capgrave was a doctor in divinity and provincial of his order, the Austin Friars Hermit; he was extremely orthodox, violently abusive of Wyclif and Oldcastle, an apologist of archbishops, yet, like other chroniclers, restive under the extreme demands of the papacy.

Even apart from his signal achievement in literature, the lively character and ironical fate of Reginald Pecock must attract interest. A learned man and original thinker, he was yet astoundingly vain. Though Humphrey of Gloucester was his first patron, he was raised to the episcopate by the party which ruined the duke, and shared that party's unpopularity. An ardent apologist of the newest papal claims and of the contemporary English hierarchy, he was, nevertheless, persecuted by the bishops and deserted by the pope. Finally, his condemnation on the score of heretical opinions was brought about by the malice of a revengeful political party.

Reginald Pecock was a Welshman, a student in the university of Oxford, where he became a fellow of Oriel and took holy orders. He was early celebrated for his finished learning and, before 1431, Humphrey, duke of Gloucester, it seems, drew the rising man to London where, in that year, he was made Master of Whittington College near the Tower, the recent foundation of the famous mayor.

London was still thick with Lollards, and it became Pecock's lifelong aim to overcome their heresy by persuasion. Before ten years were passed he had issued a number of books or pamphlets to cope with those which the heretics were pouring forth. In 1444, he was made bishop of St Asaph, and he was so active in his diocese, in preaching and in other ways, as to rouse opposition. He had not, however, withdrawn from the public life of London; and, in 1447, he preached a sermon at Paul's Cross which provoked much antagonism. He defended episcopal non-residence and neglect of preaching on the ground that the conduct of the ecclesiastical organisation was a prior duty; but he also justified papal 'provisions' to benefices and the payment of annates to Rome upon grounds most displeasing to the English hierarchy. He put the substance of his discourse in writing[1] and gave it to his friends. Yet not only the populace but many scholars, clergy and friars called him a heretic. His apology was controverted from Paul's Cross by the celebrated Millington, Provost of King's, Cambridge, and archbishop Stafford, though personally friendly, was obliged to investigate Pecock's opinions. Pecock was not censured; but his translation to Chichester on the murder of Moleyns perhaps marked him as a member of the court party who might conveniently be thrust into a thankless post of danger. The mob hated him as one of Suffolk's friends, and he had the distinction of mention in the lively ballad on the duke's death, *The Dirge of Jack Napes*. As a privy councillor and trier of petitions, Pecock took his share in the unpopular work of government, but he continued to put forth short popular books against the Lollards and, at length, a complete and reasoned work, *The Repressor of overmuch blaming of the clergy*. This elaborate book, which its author thought would destroy Lollardy and prevent further criticism of the hierarchy, brought about his ruin.

A hollow truce was then (1457) subsisting between the two political parties; one of Pecock's latest pamphlets, addressed to Canynge, mayor of London, contained allusions to disturbances which the Yorkist mayor chose to consider seditious. He accordingly laid

[1] *Abbreviatio R. Pecock.*

the tract before the council. An outcry was raised at once by the politicians, and Pecock's theological adversaries seized the moment to accuse him of heresy. Archbishop Bourchier, allied with the Yorkist faction, conducted the examination promptly. Nine of Pecock's works were, in one day, inspected and reported upon by twenty-four divines, who can hardly have been placated by the claim of the accused 'to be judged by his peers' in erudition. After several interviews, Pecock was formally condemned, and the archbishop, in a conventionally fraternal speech, bade him choose at once between recantation and death by fire. Apparently confounded by the charge of heresy, Pecock at length replied: 'it is better to incur the taunts of the people than to forsake the law of faith and to depart after death into hell-fire and the place of torment.' According to his own principles, indeed, submission to the authority of the church was all that was open to him. A public recantation was exacted, and at Paul's Cross, before a great crowd whose ferocity, excited by the spectacle of the solitary bishop beside the bonfire, rose so high that they would fain have flung him into it, Pecock handed fourteen of his works ('that cost moch goodes') to the executioner to be burned, and recited a full recantation in English in his peculiar repetitive style. After a vain attempt to obtain protection from the papacy, Pecock was committed to a dreary imprisonment for life in Thorney abbey; and there, a year or two later, he died.

It is not hard to see why the bishops repudiated their self-appointed champion. Immeasurably their superior in learning as in argument, his conceit galled them, his assertion of the feudal authority of the pope cut at the roots of hierarchical independence; he had treated the friars with contempt, and his mode of defending the condition of the church was felt to be dangerous. One of the charges against him was that he wrote on great matters in English; another, that he set the law of nature above the Scriptures and the sacraments: in truth, Pecock's attempt to defend the ecclesiastical system by an appeal to reason was a negation of the principle of authority upon which it rested, and a superficial reading of *The Repressor* might give the impression that the author minimised the importance of the Bible.

The Repressor was the climax of Pecock's endeavours to conquer the Lollards on their own ground. Corporal punishment he allowed to be lawful in the last resort; but he held it the duty of the clergy to reclaim heretics by reasonable argument. To attempt this thoroughly, Pecock, in *The Repressor*, first stated

clearly what were the erroneous 'trowings' of the Lollards, and
then proceeded to reason against them instead of crushing them
by merely quoting a mass of authority. Unhappily, this fair
statement of his adversaries' case proved a two-edged weapon,
for his own replies were sometimes of a kind so casuistical
as to provoke irritation. Again, Pecock's excellent arguments
from history and theological literature made little impression
upon contemporaries almost as ignorant as they were biassed,
while his philosophical reasoning not only was beyond their grasp,
but was suspected of being a greater danger than the Lollardy it
controverted. To reason of religion at all, and in the vulgar
tongue, was a crime; to reason with heretics appeared to admit
that they had some kind of case; worst of all, in those intolerant
times, was Pecock's tolerance.

The book is clearly arranged in five parts, each divided into
chapters, and a short prologue sets forth the purport and plan,
namely, to defend eleven points of 'governances of the clergy'
condemned by 'some of the common people.' Part I deals with
the Lollard position in general, while the succeeding parts defend
the arraigned practices by special arguments. Part I is the most
important and shows by how great a distance Pecock was in
advance of his age. Could his methods have been adopted by
the English hierarchy, the ecclesiastical revolution of the next
dynasty would, perhaps, never have occurred, and Hooker would
have been forestalled by a century.

Pecock finds the heresies of the Lollards to arise from three
fundamental errors in their method of thinking; when these are
relinquished, the way will be clear for constructive explanation.
The Lollards assume the New Testament to be the origin of
religion and morality, holding no ordinance to be binding unless
grounded, that is originating, in Scripture; secondly, they maintain
that every pious Christian can instinctively discover the full
meaning of Scripture; and, last, they assert that this pious Christian
is then justified in scorning any reasoning or expounding by
scholars and churchmen.

These theses of 'the lay party' are to be disproved not by
counter-quoting of texts, but by reasoning; and Pecock, therefore,
enters first upon a brief explanation of the method of logical
argument: 'Wolde God it (logic) were leerned of al the comon
people in her moderis langage for thanne thei schulden therbi
be putt fro myche ruydnes and boistousness which thei han now
in resonyng.'

Pecock declares that Scripture was not intended to reveal to man any of the moral laws which he had already discovered by 'law of kind,' *i.e.* light of nature. Scripture, in fact, assumes that men recognise the moral law, and if it were possible that any apparent discord should subsist between the words written in 'the outward book of parchemyn or of velym' and 'the doom of resoun write in mannis soule and herte,' then must the written words be interpreted to accord with reason, not reason glosed to accord with the writing. It is actually worse to undervalue this 'inward Scripture' than to undervalue the Bible itself. Because Scripture enforces many points of morality, we are not to regard the book as the foundation of the moral law—any more than men of London say, when men of the country upland bring branches of trees from Bishop's wood and flowers of the field for the citizens to array their houses with at midsummer, that these branches grew out of the carts or the hands of the bringers. It follows that neither the truths of moral philosophy nor corollaries deduced from either philosophy or the law of nature are 'grounded' in Scripture. To ask of any ordinance or custom so deduced by philosophy or common sense: 'where fyndist thou it groundid in Holi Scripture?' is as far beside the mark as to ask of a conclusion of grammar: 'where findist thou it groundid in tailour craft? or of a point of sadler craft where findist thou it groundid in bocheri?' Much that is needful for us to know is left for us to discover by reason and experience: 'I preie thee, Sir, seie to me where in Holi Scripture is ʒouen the hundrid parti of the teching upon matrimonie which y teche in a book mad upon *Matrimonie* and in the firste partie of *Cristen religioun*?' Nor does Scripture give a hundredth part of Pecock's teaching upon usury in *The filling of the four tables*, and yet these books he considers full scanty to teach all that is needful to know upon matrimony and usury. He concludes that pilgrimages, the use of images in churches, or the endowments of the clergy, are not to be condemned because they are not expressly ordained in Scripture.

That the members of the lay party overvalue the authority of Scripture Pecock generously grants to be due to the excellent effect on their minds of studying it. Precious, indeed, is the effect; but to hold the Bible, therefore, for the sole rule of truth, is as if one should endeavour to live entirely upon that necessary of life, honey. The lay party will, however, allege that reason is fallible; to which Pecock answers, that so may eyesight or hearing sometimes prove deceptive, and yet we cannot see or hear save with eye and ear; while the dangers of fallacious reasoning are minimised by a learned clergy, whose gathered knowledge enables them to expound the whole meaning of Scripture. Another safeguard, he avers, we have in the infallibility of syllogism; let reason proceed on this method and she cannot err: 'for if y be siker and suer in my reason that no man is in the chirche of Seint Poul at Londoun, and that the bischop of London is a man, y may be sekir and sure that the bischop of London is out of the chirche of Seint Poul at London, thou3 alle aungels in heven wolde seie the contrarie.'

As for the second 'trowing' of the Lollards—that every humble Christian can sufficiently interpret Scripture—they can easily recognise its falseness by their own divisions. Do not the Bible-men already distinguish parties, some as doctor-mongers, some opinion-holders, some neutrals? Hath not Bohemia experienced the doom of 'ech kingdom devidid in hem silf'? To interpret Scripture aright is evidently difficult, therefore should learned men be consulted; not that every preacher or wearer of a doctor's cap is competent to expound, and grievous it is to find so little attention paid to the serious scholar who 'flotereth not so ofte aboute the eeris of the lay peple as dooth the feet of preaching.'

The third 'trowing' of the lay party—that, having (as they assume) attained to the knowledge of Scripture, they should pay no further attention to the arguments of clerks—is as bad as the Mohammadan law which punishes the man who reasons about his faith, whereas truth is ready to come to the light and be confirmed: it is but 'countirfeet goold' which abides not the fire.

This mistaken endeavour to make Scripture the sole rule of life springs of ignorance and want of thought. Where does Scripture say that the New or Old Testament 'schulde be writt in Englisch tunge to lay men or in Latyn tunge to clerkis'; where.

that men schulden make ale or beer of whiche so myche horrible synne cometh myche more than of setting up of ymagis or of pilgrymagis?...without ale and beer and without sidir and wijn and meeth, men and women myte lyve ful long and lenger than thei doon now, and in lesse jolite and cheerte of herte forto bringe hem into horrible grete synnes——

and yet the laity think these drinks quite permissible, *i.e.* lawful, *i.e.* right. Would that those women who make themselves so wise in the Bible and 'so coppid of speche a nentis clerkis' might wear none of their fine 'coverchefis of lynnen or of silk of whiche so miche synne cometh' till they could find scriptural warrant for them!

Illustration is among Pecock's strong points—homely, striking and tersely worded, but too often adding a provocation. He had the unlucky art of selecting an irritating topic: 'If the king of England dwelt in Bordeaux and should send a noble letter to the judges exhorting them to impartial justice,' was one of his illustrations, when the nation was frantic over the loss of Gascony and not a law-court was freely held.

The second part of *The Repressor* takes point by point the lay party's objections to the church and proves, to the author's satisfaction, that the arraigned customs are not only unforbidden by Scripture, but that each rests upon good grounds. Even if a good custom, such as the use of images, be abused, the abuse is not serious, for nobody makes literal idols of images, taking them to be gods. Besides, scriptural warrant exists for them in the practice of Laban and of Micah and the Levite.

The necessity of vindicating every ecclesiastical practice compels Pecock to have recourse, sometimes, to casuistry; and his justification of the practice of the mendicants who only touched money with a stick, or of those who deserted necessitous parents to save their own souls in a convent, is not pleasant. But he was unconscious of any weakness in his case; to him, logic was everything; 'prove' is his favourite word; he believed men were convinced by logic. Nor was it to the details of his case that his enemies objected. His appeal to reason was the real crime, and his criticism was hardly less weakening to the rule of authority. To nullify the current moral of a fable connected with the donation of Constantine, he proved the fabulousness of the famous donation itself, imprudently adding that the evils ascribed to the wealth of the church arise from the appointment, nowadays, of unfit persons to bishoprics. He had the audacity to declare that a statement of St Jerome's was probably not true. He pointed out a discrepancy between Eusebius and pseudo-Damasus, and decided, on historical grounds, for Eusebius. It could only be expected that he would have to face the charge of denying the authority of Scripture and of the Fathers of the church. The prelates were little likely to think well of a man who dragged their practices to the bar of criticism.

Pecock's smaller works seem to have pursued the same plan of facing the heretic on his own ground. In *The Book of Faith* he discards the axiom that the Church cannot err, because the Lollards would not admit it, and proceeds on the supposition that she might. But, if the Church should err, this would not excuse the laity from obedience, for she would fail only after having done all that was humanly possible to find the truth much more than an individual could do. God would not blame her members for such unavoidable error. Nor hath any man proved, neither ever can, his own trowing to be true contrary to the Church. He must submit, then, to her wisdom, which, if not absolutely infallible, is relatively enormously greater than that of any individual. But the prelates accused Pecock of declaring that the catholic church was liable to error.

It is certain that Pecock was sincere in his bold arguments, and that he believed himself to be refounding the ecclesiastical structure. Whether his works were as widely read as he believed we cannot tell. He intended them for the lay party, *i.e.* the Lollards, and made his books as brief as possible, because they were necessary for every man to study. In *The Donet* he seems (like some later apologists) to have tried to find the necessary minimum of belief and to frame a creed which all would accept, paving his way by the assertion that the apostles' creed was only named after the apostles, not compiled by them. *The Poor Men's Mirror* was a selection or skeleton made from *The Donet* in the hope that even the poor would purchase so cheap and necessary a book. Many other productions Pecock names in a self-satisfied manner in *The Repressor*; yet, when his orthodoxy was suddenly challenged, he replied that he would not be responsible for works more than three years old, for many had been copied and circulated without his consent and might be incorrect. As this limit would exclude nearly all his works save *The Repressor*, Pecock either knew the accuracy of copyists to be notoriously poor, or was entering a disingenuous plea. His enemy, Gascoigne, declares that he was always changing his mind and disavowing his former statements.

At all events, Pecock had some following of young men, probably at Oxford, where, though the university had promptly renounced him and expressed penitence for permitting heresy to flourish, his books were still being burned as late as 1475, having been overlooked, said the apologetic authorities, in very obscure corners. That they should be even then hidden and remembered implies a more than superficial effect; yet there are very few copies now existing. Most of his works have perished altogether, and, after the Tudor reformation, Reginald Pecock was considered a martyred protestant and received the mistaken eulogy of Foxe.

The Repressor is so clearly written that the achievement of its author is hardly realised at first in its magnitude. Pecock had to find or make terms for conveying abstract ideas and philosophical distinctions; yet it is but seldom that he betrays the difficulty and states that he uses a word in two senses (*e.g. leeful* for 'permissible' and 'enjoined'). His wide command of terms is not that of a man conversant only with theological literature; many of his more unusual words are to be found in Chaucer or in *Piers the Plowman*[1], while others seem to be of recent importation and a few, even, of his own invention[2].

Perhaps it is significant of the materialism of the age that Pecock so seldom indulges in metaphor; 'to *lussche* forth texts,' 'a *coppid* (crested) woman' are simple, but he felt obliged more than once to explain elaborately, as did Trevisa, the nature of figurative language where one would have thought the meaning self-evident[3].

The only drawback to Pecock's style, for a modern reader, is his tendency to pleonasm. The reason already suggested does not cover nearly all the instances of double, or even triple, expressions. Pecock is not wholly free from the old love of

---

[1] *Carect, apposid, approprid, aliened*, etc.

[2] *Corrept, correpcioun* = rebuke, distinguished from *correction* = punishment, *coursli* = in course of nature.

Probably the difficulty lay less in finding abstract terms than in making precise distinctions: *deliciosite, cheerte, carpentrie, bocheri* give no pause; nor the active use of verbs: to *feble*, to *cleree* (make clear); nor the host of adverbs and adjectives composed by *-li, -ose, -able*: *manli* = human, *cloistrose, contrariose, plentuose, makeable, doable, kutteable, preachable*, *i.e.* of a text, etc. Not that his words have all survived: yet *coursli, overte* and *netherte, aboute-writing, mynde placis* = shrines, a *pseudo*, a *reclame* = protest, are good terms.

On the other hand Pecock could not be sure that a word would be restricted to a particular use, that readers would seize the opposition of *graciosli* to *naturali*, the distinction between *correcte* and *correpte, orologis* and *clocks* (dials and mechanical clocks), *lete* and *lette* (permit and hire out, hinder), *jollite*, with a bad signification, and *cheerte*, a neutral term. A few words which already bore a twofold meaning Pecock accepted for both senses: *religiose* (conventual or pious), *persoun* (person or parson), *quyk* (alive or speedy, but *quykli* has the modern meaning), *rather* (more or earlier), etc. Like earlier writers he often couples the elder and newer words: *undirnome* and *blamyd, rememoratiij* and *minding signs, wiite* and *defaute, skile* and *argument*, but, as the work progresses, he uses oftener *skile, minding sign* and *undirnome*. He has no preference for the new-fangled, his aim is to be understood; if a few of Trevisa's or Capgrave's obsolescent words disappear and *feng* or *fong* or *bynam, fullynge, out-take*, are replaced in *The Repressor* by *take* or *took, baptym, no but*, yet Pecock prefers *riall, beheest, drenched, hiled*, to the unfamiliar *regalle, promissioune, drownede, couered*, though these last are to be found already in the anonymous translation of *Poly-chronicon* (see *ante*, p. 78). We find that some of the old prefixes so common in Trevisa, *by-* and *to-*, appear no longer, while the hitherto rare preposition is frequent in *underling, undertake* and *undirnym* (Trevisa seldom ventured upon *undirneþe*). The opposition of a *yeer of dearth* to one of *greet cheep*, and the use of *doctour-monger, guest-monger*, suggest the modern signification.

[3] *E.g.* Vol. I, pp. 151, 162.

balanced phrases, nor, perhaps, from the turn for quasi-legal forms affected in his age. He repeats *the seid, the now rehercid* tiresomely, and rejoices in triplicates: *so mich fonned, masid and dotid: ech gouernaunce or conuersacioun or policie which Holi Scripture werneth not and forbedeth not.* This tendency, however, is most noticeable in the early and more dialectical portions of *The Repressor*, while the very contrast between the full precision of the arguments and the colloquial turn of the examples gives a pleasing sense of variety. The spelling is, as a rule, consistent, and is noteworthy for a system of doubling the vowels to give a long sound: *lijk, meenis, waasteful,* etc. It is probable that the extant copy of *The Repressor* was executed under Pecock's immediate supervision, to be handed to the archbishop.

Sir John Fortescue, the intrepid chief justice of Henry VI and the earliest English constitutional lawyer, occupies, in the sphere of political literature, a position not unlike that of Pecock in religious controversy. But the larger part of his works, which aim at justifying the title of the house of Lancaster, are in Latin. The arguments of the smaller tracts are historical; but his large work, *De Natura Legis Naturae*, is, mainly, philosophical. In this book the actual claim of Henry VI is made to rest upon the large foundation of that law of nature which resolves the succession to all kingdoms. He discovers three 'natural' kinds of government: absolute monarchy (*dominium regale*), republicanism (*dominium politicum*) and constitutional monarchy (*dominium politicum et regale*). The right of the Lancastrian house, therefore, is bound up with the English constitution. Even when he reaches the second part of the book and deals with the struggle then being waged, Fortescue keeps to an abstract form of argument. 'Justice' is to settle the claim to a kingdom in Assyria preferred by three personages, the brother, daughter and daughter's son of the deceased monarch. The reader reflects on Edward III, but Fortescue throws over the claim to France and the settlement of Scotland; there is no inheritance through a female, and 'Justice' assigns the kingdom to the brother.

Such an attempt to solve the problem of the time by referring it to a general law is something in the manner of Pecock. The consideration of the 'natural' forms of government and the decision that the constitution of England is a *dominium politicum et regale* became, with Fortescue, a firm conviction. Though the cause he had at heart, and for which he risked fortune and life and went into exile, was not advanced by his reasoning but hopelessly crushed by the cogent arguments of archery and cannon, he was able to exercise a perhaps not unsatisfying activity in the composition of two works which might teach Englishmen better to understand and value that noble constitution to which the Yorkist conqueror certainly paid little enough attention. His book *De Laudibus Legum Angliae* was written 1468—70, and, like its predecessor, was meant for the use of the young prince Edward, whose education Fortescue seems to have had in charge, and who sustains a part in the dialogue. His travels with the fugitive royal family had shown the observant chief justice something of Scottish, and more of French, modes of government. As he compares the French absolute system with the noble constitution of England, his philosophy becomes practical, and he endeavours to apply theory to the actual conduct of government, giving us by the way pictures of the life and the law courts of England as he had known it.

But Tewkesbury field left the Lancastrians without a cause, and Fortescue could do no more than bow to the inevitable and lay before the new sovereign *de facto* his last treatise upon his favourite subject. It is in English. The house of York, possibly from lack of learning as well as from a perception of the importance now pertaining to the common people's opinions, always dealt with politics in the vulgar tongue. The treatise, sometimes entitled *Monarchia*, and sometimes *The Difference between an Absolute and a Limited Monarchy*, combines a eulogy of the English theoretical system of government with advice for its practical reformation. It was probably finished in 1471 or a little later, though there are reasons for thinking that it was originally intended for Henry VI. Fortescue again distinguishes between the two kinds of monarchy, absolute and constitutional, and praises the advantages of the latter. Not that an absolute monarch is necessarily a tyrant: Ahab offered Naboth the full price for the vineyard.

The all important question for a constitutional king is revenue, and with this his subjects are bound to provide him : 'As every servant owith to have is sustenance off hym that he serveth so ought the pope to be susteyned by the chirche and the kyng by his reaume.' The expenses of the English king are of three kinds ; (1) 'kepynge of the see,' provided for specially by the nation in the poundage and tonnage duties, 'that the kynge kepe alway some grete and myghty vessels, ffor the brekynge off an armye when any shall be made ayen hym apon the see. Ffor thanne it shall be to late to do make such vessailes'; (2) ordinary royal charges, household, officials, etc.; (3) extraordinary, including ambassadors, rewards and troops on a sudden necessity: there is no thought of a permanent army. The dangers of royal poverty and overgreat subjects are pointed out, with examples discreetly taken from French and old English history. How shall the revenue be increased? Not by direct taxes on food, as abroad, 'his hyghness shall have heroff' but as hadd the man that sherid is hogge, much crye and litel woll.' Let the king's 'livelode' come of his lands: as did Joseph in Egypt, on the plan which yet keeps the 'Saudan off Babilon' (Cairo) so wealthy. (Is this a reminiscence of Mandeville?) It is a method within the king's competence, for an English king can never alienate his lands permanently; which, says the philosophic judge, only proves his supreme power: 'ffor it is no poiar to mowe aliene and put away, but it is poiar to mowe have and kepe to hym self. As it is no poiar to mowe synne and to do ylle or to mowe be seke, wex old or that a man may hurte hym self. Ffor all thes poiars comen of impotencie.'

The danger of impoverished subjects is discussed next. Poor commons are rebellious, as in Bohemia. A poor nation could not afford to train itself in marksmanship as the English all do at their own costs. Why, then, do not the poverty-stricken French rebel? Simply from 'cowardisse and lakke off hartes and corage, wich no Ffrenchman hath like unto a Englysh man.' The French are too cowardly to rob: 'there is no man hanged in Scotland in vij yere to gedur ffor robbery....But the English man is off another corage,' for he will always dare to take what he needs from one who has it. Fortescue glories in the prowess of our sturdy thieves. An interesting plan for forming the council of salaried experts, to the exclusion of the great nobles, brings the little book to a close, with a prophetical 'anteme' of rejoicing, which a grateful people will sing when Edward IV shall on these lines have reformed the government and revenue. A quaint postscript seems to deprecate the possible distaste of king Edward for the parliamentary nature of the rule described.

Fortescue had to make his peace with the new king by retracting his former arguments against the house of York. This he did in the form of a dialogue with a learned man in a *Declaration* upon 'certayn wrytyngs...ayenst the Kinges Title to the Roialme of Englond,' wherein, not without dignity, he admitted fresh evidence from the learned man and declared himself to have been mistaken. This, and a few other and earlier Latin pamphlets, are of purely historical interest. His last work was, probably, the dialogue between *Understanding and Faith*, a kind of meditation upon the hard fate of the righteous and the duty of resignation.

The works of Pecock and Fortescue were destined to appeal rather to later generations than to their own contemporaries whose tastes were better served by books more directly didactic and less controversial, whether these were of the purely devotional type or pseudo-devotional compilations of tales with arbitrary applications. Of this latter sort the most famous example is *Gesta Romanorum*. Devotional literature, as distinct from the Wyclifite and controversial literature, for nearly a century and a half derived from the school of mystics, the spiritual descendants of Richard Rolle of Hampole. Their great master is Walter Hylton, an Augustinian canon of Thurgarton in Nottinghamshire, whose beautiful *Ladder of Perfection* supplied both system and corrective to Rolle's exuberance of feeling.

That English mysticism was practical and missionary was doubtless due to Rolle; and the example he set of copious writing in the vernacular was followed by his disciples, whose tracts, sermons and meditations, whether original or translated from the Fathers, helped to render the language of devotion more fluent than that of common life. When the life of the recluse had become once more an honoured profession, the phraseology of mysticism was readily understood by the special circle to which it appealed. Hylton's works are far more modern than Rolle's, both in matter and expression. They were favourites with the early printers and are still read in modernised form. The lofty thought and clear insight, the sanity, the just judgment of *The Ladder of Perfection* or *The Devout book to a temporal man* are not more striking than the clarity of the style. Hylton's language has not, perhaps, a very wide range, but he renders abstract and subtle thoughts with ease. Careful explanations are made of any fresh term; pairs of words and phrases, though very frequent, are scarcely ever tautologous, nor is alliteration noticeable. Biblical language occurs less often than might be expected, but illustration is common and ranges from simple comparison ('as full of sin as a hide or skin is full of flesh') to complete metaphor, whose significance he evidently expects his readers to grasp readily. Thus, when he likens the progress of the soul to a pilgrimage to Jerusalem, he adds, 'Jerusalem is as moche as to saye as a syght of peace, and

betokeneth contemplacyon in parfyte love of God[1].' Or he speaks
of meekness and love, the prime virtues of the recluse's life, as two
strings, which, 'well fastened with the mynde of Jesu maketh good
accorde in the harpe of the soule whan they be craftely touched
with the fynger of reason ; for the lower thou smytest upon that
one the hyer sowneth that other[1].' In almost every respect
Hylton presents a contrast to his contemporary Trevisa.

An incidental remark in *The Ladder*—'this readest thou in
every book that teacheth of good living' bears witness to a considerable body of literature of which only fragments have come
down to us. Chief among them is the well-known *Revelations of
Divine Love* by the anchoress Juliana of Norwich, a work of
fervent piety, pre-eminent in the graces of humility and love.
Juliana's meditations upon her vision evince her acquaintance
with Hylton, and, probably, with other religious writers. Such
study was, indeed, a duty strictly enjoined upon recluses by the
Ancren Riwle. More than once she uses Hylton's actual words
when developing the same ideas : 'the soul is a life,' they both
reiterate, and Juliana terms its inalterably pure essence, or spirit,
as distinguished from the sense-perceptions, its *substance*, in a
manner reminiscent of older scholars[2]. Apparently, she was not
acquainted with the translation of à Kempis, made in the middle
of the century, and again translated for the Lady Margaret.

Wholly different in kind are the moralised skeleton tales, by no
means always moral in themselves, of the famous *Gesta Romanorum*,
the great vogue of which is witnessed by the fact that the Anglo-
Latin recension assigned to the end of the fourteenth century was
being continually copied in the fifteenth, and that an English
translation then appeared, popularising this source-book of future
literature, beside the English *Legenda Aurea*, which, half-original,
half-translation, belongs to the same period.

---

[1] Wynkyn de Worde's edition.

[2] Juliana's date is hardly certain. Only two late MSS are now known, B.M. Sloane
2499, said to belong to the seventeenth century, and Paris, Bibl. Nationale 30, said to
be a sixteenth century copy (cf. Miss Warrack's preface to her edition of Juliana).
According to these she was born in 1342, saw the vision in 1373, wrote her account of
it about 1393, and was still living in 1442. (Cf. *The Examination of William Thorpe*,
which demands the belief that he, too, lived to be nearly a hundred, as used to be
assumed also of Hylton and of Juliana Berners.) It is generally stated that Juliana
describes herself as unable to read, but this is an error. The Paris copyist calls her
'a symple creature unlettyrde'; but 'a simple creature' is a term of humility:
the author of the prologue to the Wyclifite Bible so describes himself: 'unlettered'
may only mean no great scholar. The Sloane manuscript alters this word to 'that
cowde no letter.' But the *Revelations* do not require the ascription of such a miracle
to enhance their value.

Much akin to *Gesta* was another old classic of the Middle Ages, *Secreta Secretorum*, three translations of which were executed in the fifteenth century, one, by James Yonge in 1422, hailing from the English Pale in Ireland. It is a work which ranks high among medieval forgeries, professing to be no less than an epistle on statesmanship addressed by Aristotle to his pupil Alexander the Great. No doubt the public found its medley of astrological and medical rules and elementary precepts on cleanliness and decency the more impressive for its profound advice to 'avoid tyranny,' or to husband resources 'as the ampte getys liflode for winter,' or not to trust in one leach alone, for fear of poison, but to have at least ten. The clumsy attempt to express more or less abstract ideas in English is interesting as a sort of foil to Pecock's achievement. The Anglo-Irish version partakes of the nature of a political appeal. The terror inspired in the Pale by O'Dennis or MacMorough is plainly set forth, as illustration to the original, and the earl of Ormonde is besought to remember Troy when he captures rebels, 'trew men quelleris,' and to destroy them 'by the thow sharpe eggis of your swerde...rygoure of lawe and dyntes delynge.' Save for the uncouth spelling, the composition is not very different from translations penned in England.

Yonge's use of modern illustration is but one among many indications of the interest which the middle classes were beginning to feel in the political events of their own days, and, to satisfy it, a group of contemporary chronicles appeared, more interesting to the historian than to the student of letters.

With the increase of popular agitation, the dull monastic Latin chronicles withered away and were succeeded by a few in the vernacular. Though these, in their earlier portions, are meagre translations from the popular compendium called the *Brute* (French or Latin or English[1]) or from the *Eulogium* (Latin), the writers often become individual when dealing with their own times. The restrained indignation of the monk of Malmesbury or Canterbury who made the *English Chronicle* (1347—1461) at the incompetence which produced the civil war invests his concise record with real dignity, homely as is his vocabulary. But his political judgment does not temper his readiness to accept the circumstantial legends of the day, and two pages of his little work are given to a graphic story of a ghost, futile and homely as only a fifteenth century ghost could be.

In contrast with this, or with the more staid *Cronycullys of*

---

[1] English translation by J. Maundeville, Rector of Burnham Thorpe, in 1435.

Englonde may be set the more scholarly composition of the Lancastrian Warkworth, Master of Peterhouse, Cambridge, who took
pains to preserve his chronicle for future readers. His picture of
the final loss of the royal cause[1] has the dignity of tragedy.
He sees retribution in the falls of princes and points the moral
pithily: 'suche goodes as were gadirde with synne were loste
with sorwe'—'perjury schall nevere have bettere ende withoute
grete grace of God.' He is clear in style and a little addicted
to the usual pleonasms ('wetynge and supposynge,' 'excitynge
and sturing,' 'a proverb and a seyenge,' etc.).

Some short contemporary accounts bear the character of
official reports, or news letters, *e.g. The History of the Arrivall*
(1471), *Rebellion in Lincolnshire* (1470), *Bellum apud Seynt
Albons* (1455). They are couched in the wearisome formalities
of semi-legal documents, like the proclamations of the time. Poor
as the expression was, men at least felt it needful to be articulate.
The productions of Richard duke of York are probably the
worst.

A specimen of something very different from these stilted
pamphlets survives in the note-book of William Gregory, a skinner
of London, who became mayor in 1461. In it he entered ballads
and rules of medicine, notes on the chase, the weather, etc.,
besides a city chronicle. There are several of these, of which
Fabyan's is the best; all are extremely meagre, but Gregory's
account of his own days reflects the cheerfulness of a man who
has weathered hard times successfully, and it has the freedom
of a private diary. Not only are there hints of a humane
pity, then rare, for the misfortunes of 'meek innocents' or of a
brave old soldier, but touches of humour quite as unusual. Though
a fifteenth century writer, he jokes: the description of Cade's
'sympylle and rude mayny' is really comical, weening they had
wit and wisdom to guide all England just because they had
gotten London by 'a mysse happe of cuttynge of ii sory cordys
that nowe be alteryde.' They entrenched, like soldiers, but they
kept not discipline, 'for als goode was Jacke Robyn as John at
the Noke, for alle were as hyghe as pyggsfete.' He may tag
the proper moral over 'thys wrecchyde and fals trobely worlde';
but he tells how the earl of Wiltshire, held the handsomest knight
in England, 'set the king's banner against a house end and fought
manly with the heels, for he was afeared of losing of beauty'; how
a preacher at Paul's Cross once preached the truth before the

---

[1] He chronicled the events of 1461—71.

king, but all the great reward he had was riding of eightscore mile in and out, and all his friends full sorry for him; how Sir Andrew Trollope cut a joke ; how the mayor strove to collect supplies for queen Margaret, but the mob, learning its destination, pillaged the convoy; it was Sir John Wenlock's cook who attacked the victuals, 'but as for the mony I wot not howe hit was departyd, I trowe the pursse stale the mony.' If he makes but the briefest mention of the famous tournament of lord Scales, he does 'aftyr heryng'—'ax of em that felde the strokys, they can telle you best.'

Still less to be considered as literature, yet even more interesting in themselves, are the private letters which prove that ordinary people were conversant with pen and ink without intervention of scribes: 'Mastresse Annes, I am prowd that ye can reed Inglyshe wherfor I prey yow aqweynt yow with thys my lewd hand[1].' Even the correspondence addressed to Henry IV and Henry V, the latter very considerable in quantity, was certainly not all done through secretaries ; and it is of interest to notice that Henry IV appears to have preferred to be addressed in French. Chance has preserved a private letter from one of Henry V's soldiers[2] to his 'felous and frendys, describing how 'alle the ambassadors that we dele wyth ben yncongrue, that is, in olde maner of speche in Englond, "they ben double and fals,"' and they had made the king a *beau nient*, or cypher. He is fain of peace and begs his friends to pray that he may soon come 'oute of thys unlusty soundyour's lyf yn to the lyf of Englond.'

Though the epistles of the learned are usually couched in Latin, provost Millington and bishops like Grey and Bekynton could be extremely forcible in English, and even the university of Oxford addressed English to the House of Commons[3], to great ladies and even, sometimes, to noblemen. A kind of testimonial to the famous Sir John Talbot, then lord lieutenant of Ireland, was addressed to Henry V by all the principal inhabitants of the Pale in very careful English, urging his claims upon the king in respect of his energy against 'your Irishe Enimies and English Rebels.' The corporate towns, too, were accustomed to send missives to one another or to the great nobles; but the compositions of the town clerks, *e.g.* of Caerleon or Youghal, are on a different plane from those of the universities.

---

[1] Paston Letters, No. 588.   [2] 1420.   [3] 1439.

The famous collection of letters and business papers preserved by the Pastons furnishes a detailed picture of three
generations of a well-to-do Norfolk family, their friends and
enemies, their dependents and noble patrons. At first John
Paston and his devoted wife Margaret, afterwards their sons,
are the leading correspondents, and the cares of property form
the topic. John Paston inherited from his father, a worthy judge,
considerable estates and was ambitious of acquiring more ; but
the cupidity of the nobles of the district kept him in continual
difficulties. The old judge used to say that 'whosoever should
dwell at Paston should have need to know how to defend himself,'
and had placed his sons to study at the inns of court, since the
only help against violence lay in the intricacies of the law, with
which every age, class and sex was acquainted. The letters,
accordingly, trace the endeavours of John Paston, and, after him,
of his sons, to form such a combination of royal favour, local
intrigue and bribery as to procure effective legal protection
against those who seized their manors by armed force. This
main thread of interest is interwoven with every sort of business.
We should scarcely gather that the crown of England lay in the
scales of civil war. What the correspondence reveals is a state
of anarchy in which jurymen are terrorised, gentlemen of repute
waylaid by ruffians after church or market, or even dragged
from the Christmas dinner at home to be murdered by the way-
side; when a sheriff professedly friendly dare not accept a bribe,
because he cannot safely take more than £100 (*i.e.* over £1000
present value), and lord Moleynes (Paston's foe) is a great lord
who can do him more harm than that; when the duke of Suffolk's
retainers attack dame Margaret in her husband's house with
bows and handguns, pans of fire and scaling ladders, break in the
gates, undermine the house-front, cut asunder the great timbers
and carry the courageous woman forth to watch them destroy it.

In the midst of such turmoil, business is conducted regularly.
We see the squires and their stewards incessantly riding to and
fro, letting farms and holding manor courts, attending markets
or elections at Norwich, trying to curry favour at the court of
the duke of Norfolk, complimenting the duchess or giving her
waiting-woman a jewel, above all visiting London, where lawyers
may be found and, possibly, the appointment of sheriff or under-
sheriff manipulated. Letters come by messengers, with plate
and money concealed in parcels ; sometimes tokens are mentioned,
for a seal might be stolen—'by the token that my mother hath

the key but it is broken.' Countless commissions are given for grocery or dress. Treacle 'of Genoa' is sought whenever sickness is rife, cinnamon and sugar, dates and raisins 'of Coruns' must be priced to see if they be 'better cheap' than in Norwich. If Paston once orders a doublet 'all of worsted for the honour of Norfolk'—'which is almost like silk'—his wife prays that he will do his cost on her to get something for her neck, for she had to borrow her cousin's device to visit the queen among such fresh gentlewomen, 'I durst not for shame go with my beds.'

The family acts together, like a firm, against the rest of the world; husband and wife are working partners, mother and brothers can be counted on to take trouble; the confidential servants are staunch, and not one seems to have betrayed his master, though gratitude is not a marked trait of the next generation. Nor does it seem surprising that the daughter, Margery, neglected as her upbringing had been—Paston had grudged outlay on his elder children—should have fallen in love with the steward, Richard Calle, and, after two years of home persecution, insisted that she had betrothed herself to him and would marry him— 'to sell kandyll and mustard in Framlyngham,' as her angry brother cried. Her mother immediately turned her out of the house and left her to the reluctant charity of a stranger. Every relationship of life, indeed, was of the commercial nature: marriages were bargains, often driven by the parents without intervention of the persons concerned, as had been the case with John and Margaret. The wardship of children was purchased, as a speculation. 'There is a widow fallen,' writes one brother to another, or, 'I heard where was a goodly young woman to marry...which shall have £200,' or, 'whether her mother will deal with me.' Paston's hard old mother, dame Agnes, sends to ask at the inns of court if her son Clement 'hath do his dever in lernyng,' and, if not, to pray his tutor to 'trewly belassch hym tyl he will amend, and so did the last maystr and the best that evir he had, att Caumbrege'[1]. The tutor's fee was to be ten marks. Several of the lads went to Cambridge, one to Oxford and one to Eton, where he stayed till he was nineteen; the inns of court came later, for some at least; then, one was placed in the household of the duke of Norfolk for a time, and another remained long in the service of the earl of Oxford, the one courteous nobleman of this correspondence.

---

[1] Forty years earlier it needed a royal writ to compel the Cambridge students to attend lectures.

Daughters were merely encumbrances, difficult to marry with little dowry, expensive to bring up in the correct way by boarding with a gentle family. Keeping them at home was a disagreeable economy. Dame Agnes so maltreated her daughter Elizabeth, beating her several times a week, and even twice in a day, forbidding her to speak to anyone, and taunting her, that her sister-in-law besought Paston to find her a husband. 'My moder...wold never so fayn to have be delyvered of her as she woll now.' Parental authority was so unquestioned that, years after Paston's death, his sons, grown men, and one, at least, married, were boarding with their mother and treated like children. Dame Margaret leaned on her chaplain, one James Gloys, and quarrels were picked to get John and Edmund out of the house. 'We go not to bed unchidden lightly.' 'Sir James and I be tweyn. We fyll owt be for my modyr with "thow proud prest" and "thow proud sqwyer."' The priest was always 'chopping' at him provokingly, but 'when he hathe most unfyttynge wordys to me I smylle a lytyll and tell hym it is good heryng of thes old talys.' Thus (1472) writes John, a husband and father, to his elder brother, also named John, a young knight about court in London[1].

With this younger generation a rather lighter tone becomes apparent in the letters. Sir John was of a somewhat shallow and unpractical character, his brother a man of high spirits and good temper; and it would seem as if, after Towton field, the dead weight of terrorism had begun to lighten. The decade after 1461 was less anarchical than that which preceded it, and the young men sometimes have leisure for slighter concerns than sales and debts, lawsuits and marriage bargains. Sir John took an interest in books, his brother in hawking, and he merrily threatens his elder 'to call upon yow owyrly, nyghtly, dayly, dyner, soper, for thys hawk,' which he suggests might be purchased of a certain grocer 'dwelling right over against the well with 2 buckets' near St Helen's. When Sir John at length sends a poor bird, it is with admirable temper that the disappointed brother thanks him for his 'dylygence and cost...well I wot your labore and trowbyll was as myche as thow she had ben the best of the world, but...she shall never serve but to lay eggys.' Sir John had a better taste in the points, laces and hats about which his brothers and he were so particular. Their friendliness is the most amiable thing in the letters. The one sign of parental affection

[1] Letters, Nos. 697, 702.

in them comes from the younger John, who was sent in the princess
Margaret's train (1468) to the court of Charles the Bold. ('I hert
never of non lyek to it save Kyng Artourys cort.') He is anxious
about his 'lytell Jak' and writes home 'modyr I beseche yow that
ye wolbe good mastras to my lytell man and to se that he go to scole.'
Humour was, apparently, invented in London, for the brothers and
their town friends have many a jest, crude as these often are. Sometimes we have a touch of slang—'He wolde bear the cup evyn,
as What-calle-ye-hym seyde to Aslake' (*i.e.* be fair). 'Put in
hope of the moon schone in the water.' If the tailor will not
furnish a certain gown, 'be cryst, calkestowe over hys hed (? a
double caul) that is schoryle (churl) in Englysche, yt is a terme
newe browthe up with my marschandis of Norwych,' says John the
younger, who addresses his knightly brother as 'lansmann' and
'mynher,' and jests on having nearly 'drownke to myn oysters,'
i.e. been murdered. Many a good colloquial expression rarely
found its way into literature, 'to bear him on hand' is common
for 'to accuse'; 'cup-shotten,' 'shuttle-witted' are good terms[1].

The scanty notices, during the fifteenth century, of the making
and selling of books no more indicate a general lack of them
than the names of Fortescue and Pecock represent the literature
in demand. The monasteries had long ceased to supply the
market, and professional scribes were employed. The stationers'
guild, in existence much earlier, was incorporated in 1403, and
had a hall in Milk street. 'Paternoster Rewe' was well known.
In Oxford, scribes, parchmenters, illuminators and bookbinders
were distinct from stationers before 1373, and, apparently, in
Cambridge also. Other book centres were Bury and Lincoln,
where king John of France had made purchases of many expensive
books in the preceding century, and, probably, several other
cathedral or scholastic cities had store of books. Prices were
stable, and materials cheap: in the fourteenth century a dozen
skins of parchment cost 3*s.*, through most of the fifteenth century a
quaternion of parchment was 3*d.* and the writing of it 16*d.*, *i.e.* 2*d.*
a page, but small-paged books could be copied at 1*d.* the page.
Sometimes a limner charged by the number of letters, at 1*d.* or
4*d.* the hundred, according to quality, no doubt. Legal documents
were paid for at special rates. The trade does not seem to have
been very remunerative, for the scrivener who did a good deal

---

[1] A curious instance of the fluid state of the vocabulary is the use by nearly all the
colloquial writers of *me*, short for *men*, or *they*—'*causeth me to set the lesse be us*'—
while scholarly writers are beginning to use it for *I*, *meseemeth*, etc.

of copying for Sir John Paston writes from sanctuary to beg for payment and would be grateful for the gift of an old gown. At the universities, however, regulations may have succeeded in 'protecting' the scribes. As early as 1373, Oxford reduced 'the excessive number of booksellers' by forbidding outsiders who were bringing volumes of great value from other places, to expose any books for sale at more than half-a-mark — cheap text-books they might sell, but the university stationers were not to have their accustomed profits taken from them by competition. Not that students usually possessed their own books, though William Paston sent to London for his brother's 'nominal' and 'book of sophistry'; the tutors or the stationers loaned or hired out books at regular charges. Certainly, the large Latin volumes made for the colleges were much more expensive than Paston's purchases. These handsome folios and quartos, as a rule, cost from 40*s.* to 50*s.*, always calculated in marks (13*s.* 4*d.*), and were, usually, standard theological works, although Peter-house[1], which ventured upon books of natural science and a Vergil, seems to have smuggled FitzRalph's revolutionary sermon into the works of Augustine, and Ockham's *Defensor* into a commentary. Prices, of course, varied according to the beauty of the volume, a primer for a princess might cost 63*s.* 6*d.*, one Bible cost 'not over 5 mark, so I trowe he wyl geve it,' while another cost but 26*s.* 8*d.* Several of the Pastons had books and were chary of lending them; Anne possessed *The Siege of Thebes*, Walter, *The Book of Seven Sages*, John mentions *The Meeting of the Duke and the Emperor*, and Sir John had a library of English books.

These books are of different kinds, and often, as then was usual, included various works by several hands—the volume which contained two of Chaucer's poems contained also Lydgate's *The Temple of Glass* and *The Grene Knight*. Another included *The Dethe of Arthur begynyng at Cassabelaun*, *Guy of Warwick*, *Richard 'Cur de Lyon'* and a *Chronicle to Edwarde the iii.* One was didactic, comprising a book about the mass, *Meditations of Chylde Ypotis*[2] and the *Abbey of the Holy Ghost*, a recent devotional work. Several are old fashioned ballads—*Guy & Colbronde* (an Anglo-Norman tale), *A Balade of the Goos* (probably Lydgate's). *Troylus* appears alone, and *De Amicitia* was lent to William of Worcester, Fastolf's ill-requited scholar-servant, who

---

[1] The catalogue names eighteen different scriveners.
[2] A medieval form of Epictetus.

afterwards translated it. One book is mentioned as 'in preente,' *The Pleye off the Chess*[1].

Sir John, indeed, was in the fashion in patronising literature and the drama, for he complained that one of his servants whom he had kept 'thys three yer to pleye Seynt Jorge and Robin Hod and the Shryff off Notyngham' had suddenly deserted him : 'he is "goon into Bernysdale,"' like the sturdy outlaw in the ballad to which this is an early allusion. But his taste is still medieval: romances of the old kind were shortly to go out of fashion. Up to the close of the century, however, such books, along with useful manuals of all kinds, were, evidently, plentiful enough, as may be gathered from the number of scriveners and their poor pay; Sir John Paston had bought his volume of chronicle and romances from 'myn ostesse at The George,' and one or two had been given by his friends; even the niggardly Fastolf had translations executed for him, like the Lady Margaret or the duchess of Burgundy; literature had become an amusement.

---

[1] Cf. Catalogue in No. 869, Paston Letters.

CHAPTER XIII

THE INTRODUCTION OF PRINTING INTO ENGLAND AND THE EARLY WORK OF THE PRESS

WITH the advent of printing, books, from being expensive and the property of the few, became cheap and were scattered far and wide. The change was gradual, for an increased demand for books could not grow up at once; but, by the time printing was introduced into England, the art was widespread and books were freely circulated. From a study of the productions of the various presses of different countries can be determined, more or less accurately, the general requirements of the reading public. This is especially the case in England, where no books were printed for exportation. It is proposed, therefore, in the present chapter to examine the work produced by the earlier English printers as a means of ascertaining the general literary taste of the period in this country.

It was soon after the year 1450 that the first products of the new art appeared at Mainz. In 1465, two German printers, Sweynheym and Pannartz, migrated to Italy, setting up a press at Subiaco and moving, two years later, to Rome. Switzerland followed soon after Italy, and, in 1470, the first French press began work at Paris. In all these cases, the first printers had been Germans. The northern Netherlands, which have persistently claimed to be the birth-place of printing, have no authentic date earlier than 1471, when two native printers began work at Utrecht. Belgium and Austria-Hungary follow in 1473 and Spain in 1474. There are thus eight European countries which precede England, and at no less than seventy towns were printers at work before Caxton started at Westminster. So, too, as regards the quality and quantity of books produced, England takes but a poor place, the total number of books of every kind, including different editions printed here before the end of the fifteenth century, only reaching the total of about three hundred and seventy. On the other hand, it must be remembered that the literary value of the books printed in England is high; for, unlike other countries, most of the productions of the press are in the vernacular.

William Caxton, our first printer, was born in the weald of Kent between the years 1421 and 1428, probably nearer the earlier date. The weald was largely inhabited by descendants of the Flemish clothmakers who had been induced by Edward III to settle in that district, and this would, no doubt, have a certain effect on the English spoken there, which Caxton himself describes as 'broad and rude.' He received a good education, though we are not told where, and, having determined to take up the business of a cloth merchant, was apprenticed, in 1438, to Robert Large, one of the most wealthy and important merchants in London and a leading member of the mercers' company.

Here Caxton continued until the death of Large, in 1441, and, though still an apprentice, appears to have left England and gone to the Low Countries. For the next few years we have little information as to his movements; but it is clear that he prospered in business for, by 1463, he was acting as governor of the merchant adventurers. In 1469, he gave up this post to enter the service of the duchess of Burgundy, and, in the leisure which this position afforded him, he turned his attention to literary work. A visit to Cologne in 1471 marks an important event in Caxton's life, for there, for the first time, he saw a printing press at work. If we believe the words of his apprentice and successor Wynkyn de Worde, and there seems no reason to doubt them, he even assisted in the printing of an edition of *Bartholomaeus de Proprietatibus Rerum* in order to make himself acquainted with the technical details of the art.

A year or two after his return to Bruges, he determined to set up a press of his own and chose as an assistant an illuminator named Colard Mansion. Mansion is entered regularly as an illuminator in the guild-books of Bruges up to the year 1473, which points to Caxton's preparations having been made in 1474. Mansion was despatched to obtain the necessary type and other materials, and it appears most probable that the printer who supplied them was John Veldener of Louvain. Furnished with a press and two founts of type, cut in imitation of the ordinary book hand, Caxton began to print.

The first book printed in the English language was the *Recuyell of the Histories of Troy*, issued, about 1475, at Bruges. The French original was compiled in the year 1464 by Raoul le Fevre, chaplain to Philip, duke of Burgundy; and, four years later, Caxton began to translate it into English, but, disheartened, as he tells us in his prologue, by his imperfect knowledge of French, never having been in France, and by the rudeness and broadness of his English, he soon laid the work aside. Encouraged by Margaret duchess of Burgundy, he, later, resumed his task and finished the work in 1471. His knowledge of French was not perfect, as may be seen from occasional curious mistranslations, but his position must have required an adequate knowledge of the language. So, too, with his English. His education had been good, and he had served as apprentice with one of the most prominent of London citizens; so that he had every opportunity to acquire good English and lose his provincialisms. Nearly all his literary work consisted of translations, but, to most of his publications, he added prologues or epilogues which have a pleasant personal touch, and show us that he had one valuable possession, a sense of humour.

His *Recuyell of the Histories of Troy* was a popular book at the Burgundian court, and Caxton was importuned by many famous persons to make copies for them. The copying of so large a book was a wearisome undertaking; so Caxton, remembering the art of printing which he had seen in practical use at Cologne, determined to undertake it on his own account and thus be able to supply his patrons with copies easily and rapidly. Accordingly, about 1475, a printed edition was issued, followed, shortly, by Caxton's translation from two French versions of the *Liber de ludo scacchorum* of Jacobus de Cessolis, made by Jean Faron and Jean de Vignay. Caxton, in his *Game and playe of the Chesse*, made use of both these versions, translating partly from one and partly from the other. The last book he printed at Bruges was the *Quatre dernieres choses*.

In 1476, Caxton returned to England and set up his press at Westminster in a house with the sign of the Red Pale, situated in the precincts of the abbey. In the two years following his arrival, he issued a large number of books, though very little from his own pen. We have it on the authority of the printer Robert Copland, who worked for Wynkyn de Worde, Caxton's assistant and successor, and who might himself have been with Caxton, that the first products of the Westminster press were small pamphlets. Now this description exactly applies to a number of tracts of small size issued about this time. These are Lydgate's *Temple of Glass*, two editions of *The Horse, the Sheep and the Goose* and *The Churl and the Bird*; two editions of Burgh's *Cato*, Chaucer's *Anelida and Arcite* and *The Temple of Brass*, the *Book of*

Courtesy and the *Stans puer ad mensam.* From what we know
of Caxton's tastes, these are just such books as he would be
anxious to issue. The first two large books which he printed were
The History of Jason and Chaucer's *Canterbury Tales.* The
History of Jason was translated by Caxton from the French
version of Raoul le Fevre, and undertaken immediately he had
finished the *Recuyell of the Histories of Troy* and *The Game of
Chess.*

On 18 November 1477, was finished the printing of the *Dictes
and Sayings of the Philosophers,* the first dated book issued in
England. The translator, Anthony Wodville, earl Rivers, while
on a voyage to the shrine of St James of Compostella, in 1473, was
lent by the famous knight Lewis de Bretaylles a manuscript of *Les
ditz moraulx des philosophes* by Guillaume de Tignoville. With
this, the earl was so pleased that he borrowed the volume and, on
his return to England, set about the translation. This, when
finished, was handed to Caxton to 'oversee.' He revised the book
with the French version and added an amusing epilogue, pointing
out that the earl, for some reason, had omitted the remarks of
Socrates concerning women, which he, therefore, had added himself.

In the following February, Caxton printed another translation
by earl Rivers, *The Moral Proverbs of Christine de Pisan,* a
small tract of four leaves. At the end is a short epilogue in verse,
written by Caxton himself, giving some details as to the author,
translator and date of printing. Another translation by earl
Rivers appeared in 1479, entitled *Cordyale, or the Four last things.*
This was rendered from the *Quatre dernieres choses,* a French
version of the *De quattuor novissimis* made by Jean Mielot,
secretary to Philippe le Bon in 1453.

Two editions of *The Chronicles of England* were printed in 1480
and 1482. This was the history known as *The Chronicle of Brute,*
edited and augmented by Caxton himself. The *Polychronicon*
of Higden was also issued in 1482, Caxton revising Trevisa's
English version of 1387, and writing a continuation, bringing down
the history to the year 1460, this continuation being the only
piece of any size which we possess of Caxton's original work.

In 1481, no less than three of his own translations were printed
by Caxton, *The Mirror of the World, Reynard the Fox* and *The
History of Godfrey of Bologne.* The origin of the first named is
obscure; but the English translation was made from a French
prose version by 'Maistre Gossouin,' which, in its turn, was rendered
from a French version in metre made, in 1245, from an unknown

Latin original. *Reynard the Fox* was, apparently, translated from the Dutch version printed by Gerard Leeu at Gouda in 1479.

About 1483, *The Pilgrimage of the Soul* and Lydgate's *Life of our Lady*, were issued, and, also, a new edition of *The Canterbury Tales*. Caxton's prologue to this book is extremely interesting, and shows in what great esteem he held Chaucer and his writings. He observes that, some six years previously, he had printed an edition of *The Canterbury Tales* which had been well received. One of the purchasers, however, had pointed out that in many places the text was corrupt, and that pieces were included which were not genuine, while some which were genuine were omitted. He had added that his father possessed a very correct manuscript which he much valued, and he offered, if Caxton would print a new edition, to obtain the loan of it. This Caxton undertook to do and issued the new edition, which, unlike the earlier one, contains a series of woodcuts illustrating the various characters. About the same time were also issued Chaucer's *Troilus and Criseyde*, and *House of Fame*, and, in September 1483, Gower's *Confessio Amantis*.

The Golden Legend, Caxton's most important translation, was finished, if not printed, in 1483. In his second prologue, the printer tells us that, after beginning his translation, the magnitude of his task and the probable great expense of printing had made him 'halfe desperate to have accomplissd it,' had not the earl of Arundel come forward as a patron. With this assistance, the book was, at last, finished. In its compilation, Caxton used three versions, one French, one Latin and one English. The French original can be clearly identified with an early printed edition without date or place, for Caxton has fallen into several pitfalls on account of the misprints which occur in it; for example, in the life of St Stephen, the words *femmes veuves* have been printed *Saine venue*, which the translator renders 'hole comen' in spite of the words making no sense.

In 1484, four more books translated by himself were printed by Caxton: *Caton, The Book of the Knight of the Tower*, Aesop's *Fables* and *The Order of Chivalry*. *The Book of the Knight of the Tower* is a translation of the work written, in 1371, by Geoffroi de la Tour Landry, for the instruction of his daughters, a medley compiled from the Bible, *Gesta Romanorum* and the chronicles of various countries. The next year saw the issue of three books, *The Life of Charles the Great, The History of Paris and Vienne* and, most important of all, Sir Thomas Malory's *Morte d'Arthur*.

The Life of Charles the Great was translated from an anonymous
French version compiled at the request of Henry Bolomyer, canon
of Lausanne, the *Paris and Vienne* from the French version made
by Pierre de la Seppade of Marseilles early in the fifteenth century.
Both these books are now known only from single copies.

The compilation of the *Morte d'Arthur* was finished in 1469,
but of the compiler little is known save the name. He is generally
believed to be the Sir Thomas Malory of Newbold Revell in
Warwickshire who died in 1471. No manuscript of the work is
known, and, though Caxton certainly revised it, exactly to what
extent has never been settled. The prologue to this book is,
perhaps, the best and most interesting piece of writing the printer
ever composed, and still remains one of the best criticisms of
Malory's romance. Of the popularity of the book we have striking
evidence. Of Caxton's edition two copies are known, of which
one is imperfect. The second edition, printed by Wynkyn de
Worde in 1498 is known from one copy only, which is imperfect,
while the third edition, also printed by de Worde is, again, only
known from one imperfect copy. It may well be, considering
these facts, that there were other intervening editions which have
entirely disappeared.

While Caxton was busily at work making and printing his
translations, he did not neglect other classes of books which were
in demand. His position near the abbey would turn his attention
to service-books, and, of these, he printed a large number. One of
the first books he issued was a *Sarum Ordinale*, and this he advertised by means of a little handbill fixed up in prominent places.
Of *Books of Hours* he issued at least four editions. Besides
these, he printed the *Psalter, Directorium Sacerdotum* and some
special services to add to the breviary. The larger service-books
he does not seem to have attempted. These were always of a
highly ornamental character and his own types and material,
intended simply for ordinary work, were not equal to the task.
In 1487, when there was a demand for an edition of the *Sarum
Missal*, he gave a commission for the printing to a Paris printer
Guillaume Maynial, but added to it his own device.

The Royal Book and *The Book of Good Manners* were the
next two of Caxton's translations to be printed. The first is a
translation of *La Somme des Vices et des Vertus*, the latter of *Le
livre des bonnes meurs* by Jacques Legrand. *The Book of Good
Manners*, issued in 1487, was a popular book and was reprinted at
least four times before the close of the century.

The Fayttes of Arms, the next of Caxton's translations to be printed, was issued in 1489. It was undertaken at the express desire of Henry VII, who himself lent the manuscript, now in the British Museum, from which the translation was made. The authorship is generally ascribed to Christine de Pisan.

About this time, two very popular romances were issued, *The History of the Four Sons of Aymon* and *The History of Blanchardyn and Eglantine*. The first, of which manuscripts are common, was printed in French as early as 1480, at Lyons, and it was, no doubt, from this edition that Caxton prepared his translation. The second was translated at the request of Margaret, duchess of Somerset, from a manuscript of the French version, which she had purchased from Caxton himself many years previously. In this translation, Caxton has adhered to his original far more nearly than is usual in his translations, rendering word for word in the closest manner.

The *Eneydos*, translated in 1490 and printed about the same time, is not in any way a translation of the *Aeneid*, but, rather, a romance founded on it. Caxton's version was translated from a French version, probably the work called *Le livre des Eneydes*, printed at Lyons, in 1483, by Guillaume le Roy. The printer's preface is a most interesting piece of writing, for Caxton sets out at length his views and opinions on the English language, its changes and dialects. He points out how rapidly it was altering. 'And certaynly our langage now used varyeth ferre from that whiche was used and spoken when I was borne.' The difference in dialect is illustrated by a story of a London merchant who asked a woman in 'Forland' for some eggs, and was met with the answer that she could not speak French, but she understood when asked for 'eyren.' The different styles of speech are contrasted, and Caxton ends up as might have been expected, 'And thus bytwene playn, rude, and curious I stande abasshed, but in my judgemente the comyn termes that be dayli used ben lyghter to be understonde than the olde and auncyent englysshe.' In order to make the style as correct as possible, Caxton obtained the assistance of John Skelton to revise the book for the press.

One other translation by Caxton remains to be noticed, the *Metamorphoses* of Ovid. He speaks of this work, along with some others, in the introduction to *The Golden Legend*, and, since all the others were printed, we may presume that this was also. No trace of a printed copy remains, but there is in the Pepysian library a manuscript of the last six books with the colophon

'Translated and finished by me William Caxton at Westminster the twenty second day of April, the year of our Lord 1480, and the twentieth year of the reign of king Edward the fourth.' This, like the rest of Caxton's books, was rendered from the French.

In 1491 he died, having just completed a translation of St Jerome's *Lives of the Fathers*, which was printed by his successor in 1495.

It is impossible for many reasons to consider the books issued by Caxton as quite representative of the popular demand. His position was entirely different from that of the ordinary printer or publisher. The best part of his life had been spent abroad in business connected with the woollen trade, he had risen to a high position and was, doubtless, a man of very considerable wealth. When he settled in England as a printer, he was able to consult his own tastes in the matter of what he should print, and this clearly lay in the direction of English poetry and prose romances. The reading public was not then very large, and Caxton directed rather than followed the popular taste. A third of the books he printed were translations made by himself, and he carefully edited all that he printed. At the same time, it cannot be supposed that he neglected the popular demand. He printed service books for the clergy, school books and statutes, but his own interest lay elsewhere. In especial, he was an admirer of Chaucer. He took pains, as we have seen, in the printing of his works, and expressed his admiration and appreciation in several prologues and epilogues. He did even more, for, as we learn from the epilogue to *Boethius*, he placed a memorial tablet to the poet in Westminster Abbey.

Soon after Caxton began to print in Westminster, presses were set up in 1478 at Oxford, and, about 1479, at St Albans. Naturally, the books issued at Oxford were mainly scholastic, and, of all the books printed there in the fifteenth and early sixteenth century, but one is in English. This was an edition of the *Liber Festivalis* of John Mirk, issued in March 1486—7. It is not a mere reprint of Caxton's edition issued in 1483, but has many points of difference ; and, when Caxton printed his second edition, about 1491, he copied this version in preference to his own.

The St Albans press, like that of Oxford, was mainly employed on learned works. Of the eight books issued, the first six are in Latin; but the last two are in English.   The first, *The Chronicles of England*, printed about 1485, is mainly founded on Caxton's earlier editions, but with interpolations relating to the popes and other ecclesiastical matters.   Its compiler and printer was, as we learn from a later edition, 'sometime schoolmaster of St Albans'; but his name is unknown.

The last book from this press is well known under the title of *The Book of St Albans*.   It contains three treatises, the first on hawking, the second on hunting and the last on coat-armour or heraldry.   Much has been written about the authorship of this book, which is probably not all from one hand.   The part on hunting, which is in verse, ends with the words '*Explicit* Dam Julyans Barnes in her boke of huntyng,' and this is generally considered to refer to a somewhat mythical Juliana Berners, traditionally prioress of the nunnery of Sopwell near St Albans. The treatise on heraldry is expressly said to have been translated and compiled at St Albans, and is probably derived, in great part, from a work on the same subject written, in 1441, by Nicholas Upton and dedicated to Humphrey, duke of Gloucester.   Whatever part dame Juliana Berners may have taken in the compilation of *The Book of St Albans*, it is certainly not an original work, and the greater part of the books on hawking and hunting are derived from the *Venerie de Twety*, a work composed early in the fourteenth century.   The work on fishing, which was added to succeeding editions of the book, appears, from internal evidence, to have been originally composed in English.

The first London press, started in 1480 by John Lettou under the patronage of William Wilcock, a wealthy draper, produced only two Latin books, a commentary on the *Metaphysics* of Aristotle by Antonius Andreae and an exposition on the *Psalms* by Thomas Wallensis.   When, later, Lettou printed in partnership with William de Machlinia, they issued nothing but law-books, and it was not until about 1483, when Machlinia was at work by himself, that books in English were printed in London.   One of the earliest was the *Revelation of St Nicholas to a monk of Evesham*.   It was composed in 1196; but the author is unknown.   In an abridged form, it is found in Roger of Wendover's *Flores Historiarum* under the year 1196.   It is a curious religious allegory, treating of the pilgrimage of a soul from death through purgatory and paradise to heaven.   The monk, conducted by St Nicholas, is taken from place to place in purgatory, where he meets and converses with persons of various ranks, who relate their stories and their suffering. From purgatory he advances slowly to paradise, and finally reaches the gates of heaven; after which he awakes.

The later press of Machlinia issued few English books. Among them came a reprint of *The Chronicles of England* and three editions of a *Treatise of the Pestilence*, a translation of the *Regimen contra pestilentiam* of Benedict Canutus, bishop of Westeraes, in Sweden. These can certainly be dated about 1485, in which year London was visited by the plague. One other interesting book was issued by Machlinia, entitled *Speculum Christiani*. It is a curious medley of theological matter in Latin, interspersed with pieces of religious poetry in English. The authorship has been ascribed to a certain John Watton, but the book, without the English verse, was also printed abroad. The verse, though spoken of by Warton as poor, is, occasionally, quite good; and the hymn to the Virgin, reprinted in Herbert's *Typographical Antiquities*[1], is a simple and charming piece of writing, reminiscent of an earlier period. The second part of the book consists, mainly, of an exposition on the Lord's prayer, while the third contains selections taken from the works of St Isidore.

With the death of Caxton, the character of the English press changed. Both Wynkyn de Worde, his successor, and Richard Pynson, the only other printer then at work in England, were practical printers only, depending on their business for their livelihood, and had to follow, not direct, the popular demand. De Worde especially seems to have been without initiative, most of his early work consisting of reprints and, for a year or two, his press was almost idle. A foreign printer, Gerard Leeu of Antwerp, took advantage of this period of inactivity and printed four books for the English market. Three were mere reprints of Caxton's books, *The History of Jason*, *The History of Paris and Vienne* and *The Chronicles of England*; but the fourth is unknown in any other English version. This is the *Dialogue or communing between the wise king Solomon and Marcolphus*, a widespread and popular story, of which there are versions in many languages. The English version is translated from the Dutch, but there is no clue to the translator. The story tells of the various questions put by Solomon, which are answered by the rustic wit of Marcolphus, and of the various ruses and quibbles by means of which he escaped the punishments designed for him by the king. As the other three of Leeu's books are reprints of Caxton's editions, it is just possible

[1] i, pp. 113—4.

that there may have been an English printed edition of it also; but, if so, no trace of it remains.

About 1503, another Antwerp printer, Adraien van Berghen, printed a book for sale in England, which goes under the name of Arnold's *Chronicle*. Richard Arnold, the compiler, was a merchant trading with the Low Countries and his work is a miscellaneous collection of stray facts relating to the city of London, copies of charters, examples of business letters, lists of mayors and bailiffs, of London churches and quaint recipes; it is, in fact, the commonplace book of a man with antiquarian tastes. Its chief fame is derived from its including, inserted between a list of the tolls of Antwerp and the difference between English and Flemish coinage, the famous ballad of *The Nut Brown Maid*. A second edition of the *Chronicle* was issued in which the lists were brought down to 1520.

When William de Machlinia ceased printing, probably about the year 1488, his place was taken by Richard Pynson, a Norman, who had been educated at the university of Paris. His first object was to print law-books, and here his knowledge of French would be of great use; but he also issued works of general interest. Before November 1492, when his first dated book was issued, he had printed a Latin grammar, an edition of *The Canterbury Tales* and a version of *The Goste of Guy*.

The Canterbury Tales is an exact reprint of Caxton's second edition, and was probably issued before Caxton's death in 1491. The short preface, a most confused and involved piece of writing, shows that Pynson was not thoroughly acquainted with the English language, and it is rare to find him making use of it.

The Goste of Guy must have been a most interesting book; but, unhappily, all that remains of it are two small fragments of a leaf, containing altogether twelve lines. On comparison with manuscripts of the poem, it is clear that the printed version was very much abbreviated and bore about the same relation to them as the early printed editions of such books as *Sir Beves of Hamtoun* or *Guy of Warwick* bear to their earlier manuscripts. The manuscripts of *The Goste of Guy*, both in prose and verse, are, apparently, derived from a northern English prose original. The version in verse is placed by Schleich in the second quarter of the fourteenth century. The Pynson fragment is quite independent of any of the known English versions, and is valuable as evidence of a lasting interest in the subject. A short Latin version was printed towards the close of the fifteenth century at Cologne; and this may be more nearly connected with the version printed by Pynson. In June 1493, Pynson issued the first edition of *Dives and Pauper*, by Henry Parker, a Carmelite monk of Doncaster, who died in 1470. The work, which is an explanation of the ten commandments, points out the duties of the rich towards the poor, and begins with a treatise on holy poverty.

In the following year, Pynson issued an illustrated edition of Lydgate's *Falls of Princes*, translated from Boccaccio; and, in 1495, an edition of the *Hecyra* of Terence the first printed of a set of the plays issued between 1495 and 1497. It is probable that these were printed for William Horman for use at Eton; and other books, such as *Dialogus linguae et ventris* and one or two grammars bearing Horman's initials, were issued about the same time.

Pynson seems to have had little enterprise in printing English books; and, besides those already mentioned, he only issued six in the fifteenth century which were not mere reprints. He must be credited with the first edition of *Mandeville's Travels*, and of *The History of Guy Earl of Warwick*. The remaining four are small poetical pieces of a few leaves each. The earliest, *The Life of St Margaret*, is only known from a fragment. The next is *The Epitaph of Jasper Tudor, Duke of Bedford*. The poem ends '*Quod Smerte maister de ses ouzeaus*'; but it is generally ascribed to Skelton. The duke died in 1495, and the book was printed very shortly afterwards. *The Foundation of the Chapel of Walsingham* gives an account in verse of the miracle which led to the building of the shrine in 1061, and may have been printed for sale to the pilgrims who travelled there. The remaining piece is *The Life of St Petryonylla*.

The sixteenth century shows slight advance. In 1503, Pynson published a translation of *Imitatio Christi*, by William Atkynson, to which was added a spurious fourth book, translated from the French by Margaret, countess of Richmond and Derby. Nothing further of interest was issued until 1509, when Barclay's translation of *The Ship of Fools* appeared. Barclay seems to have been a favourite author with Pynson, who printed many of his works. In 1511, appeared *The Pilgrimage of Sir Richard Guilforde*, a most interesting account of a journey to the holy land, written by his chaplain. A good deal of the book is compiled from earlier guide-books; but there are several pieces of picturesque writing, especially the account of the death and burial of Sir Richard at Jerusalem.

In 1516, Fabyan's *Chronicles* were printed, the first of the series of modern chronicles. The work was compiled by Robert Fabyan, sheriff of London, who died in 1512. It is a compilation from previous writers of the history of England from the days of Brutus, but the earlier parts are very superficial. The later parts are only valuable where they touch on matters which came under his own personal observation; but much matter relating to London is given in detail.

In the same year was issued the *Kalendar of the new legend of England,* a work treating of the lives of British saints.

Soon after this date, Pynson, as king's printer, found much of his time occupied in printing more or less official works and books relating to political affairs; and English books of this period are few. Between 1523 and 1525, he completed the printing of the most important of his publications, the translation of the *Chronicle* of Froissart by John Bourchier, Lord Berners—a work of great bibliographical interest on account of the several variations in the first edition. Its publication introduced a new style of historical writing; but it seems to have met with little success and was but once reprinted before the nineteenth century. Berners's love of romance led him to translate three books from French and Spanish, *Huon of Bordeaux, The Castle of Love* and *The History of Arthur of Little Britain,* to which reference is made elsewhere[1]. Pynson's later work was mainly confined to books in Latin and treatises on law; English books printed by him are rare and, usually, mere reprints. In fact, during his whole career, he did not issue one English book for ten issued by de Worde. His taste was for serious literature, and he was the favourite publisher for such learned writers of England as chose to have their books printed in this country. He was heavily handicapped by want of type. He had a fair Latin fount, but hardly any Greek; so that scholars preferred to send their work to foreign printers such as Froschover or Froben, who had not only adequate type and good correctors, but were well situated for publishing the books at the various local fairs, the then recognised centres for circulating books. If success in business may be taken as a sign of popular approval, Pynson, with his learned books and the official income derived from his work as king's printer, stood no chance against Wynkyn de Worde, with his romances and poetical tracts; for, as we know from the subsidy rolls, de Worde was by far the richer man.

Wynkyn de Worde, who succeeded to Caxton's press and

[1] See Chapter XIV, p. 339.

material, published very little during the first few years, being contented with a few reprints. In 1495, he issued a translation of the *Vitae Sanctorum Patrum* of Jerome. This translation was the work of Caxton and was only finished, as de Worde writes in the colophon, on the last day of his life. It was rendered from the French edition printed at Lyons in 1486; but, as might have been expected, it attained little popularity and was never reprinted.

About this time, de Worde published an English version of '*Bartholomaeus de Proprietatibus Rerum,* made by John Trevisa.' The printer, or some one under his direction, has added an epilogue which contains some curious details as to the beginning of Caxton's career as a printer, and also the information that the book was the first to be printed on English-made paper. The year 1496 saw the issue of new editions of *Dives and Pauper* and *The Book of St Albans,* the latter being enlarged with a third part containing the treatise of *Fishing with an angle,* a book which would seem to be the work of a practical fisherman, is much more modern in feeling than many books of the same class issued at a later date and differs much in style from the other treatises. The fourth edition of Chaucer's *Canterbury Tales,* printed in 1498, again clearly shows de Worde's carelessness as a printer and the absence of editorial work on his books. A large portion of *The Monk's Tale* is omitted; and, though the printer, when he discovered this, inserted an extra printed leaf, still, much is missing. Though not skilful as a printer, de Worde was not idle: before the close of the fifteenth century, he had issued at least one hundred and ten books. A large number were reprints and many others of no literary interest, such as grammars, service-books and law-books; but, among the remainder, are some worthy of notice. The *Contemplacyon of sinners,* written by a monk, William Touris, and an illustrated edition of *Mandeville's Travels* were issued in 1499. Among the undated books are several romances, *Beves of Hamtoun, Guy of Warwick* and *Robin Hood*; the works of John Alcock, bishop of Ely; some curious religious works such as *The Doctrinal of Death, The Miracles of Our Lady, The Rote or mirror of Consolation, The Twelve profits of tribulation.* There is also one work of Skelton, *The Bowge of Court,* a satire on the court manners of the time, and a book which, from the number of editions, appears to have been popular, *The History of the Three Kings of Cologne,* a translation of the *Historia trium regum* of John of Hildesheim.

We have no evidence that de Worde did anything in the way of editing or translating; but he had in his employ assistants who were able to translate from the French. Chief among these was Robert Copland, who was responsible for the translation of the *Kalendar of Shepherds, The mirror of the Church, Helyas Knight of the Swan* and *Kynge Appolyn of Thyre,* while he frequently added short prologues and epilogues in verse to the books he printed for de Worde. Copland printed also several books on his own account, two, at least, being of his own composition. These are *The Hye Way to the Spyttell Hous* and *Iyl of Braintford's Testament.* The former, though it cannot lay claim to any merit, is curious on account of its matter. It purports to be a dialogue between Copland and the porter of an almshouse, in the course of which they criticise all the applicants for charity as they pass, and discuss the various frauds and deceits practised by thieves and beggars, and, incidentally, the vices and follies which have brought them to ruin. The second piece is very inferior to the first, and coarse even for the period.

Another translator, an apprentice to Wynkyn de Worde, was Henry Watson, and his first work was a prose translation from the French of *The Ship of Fools.* This work must have been done directly for the press, since it is said in the prologue to have been undertaken at the request of Margaret, countess of Richmond, the king's grandmother. This must have been after 21 April 1509, and the finished book was published on 6 July. His other translations were *The Church of Evil Men and Women* and *Valentine and Orson.* The first is from a French version of a work by St Augustine. Another translation by Watson from the French was *The History of Olyver of Castylle and the fayre Helayne,* issued in 1518. In the prologue, the translator speaks of the cheapness of books owing to the invention of printing. Andrew Chertsey, of whom nothing is known, also translated a considerable number of books for de Worde. His earliest translation was *The Ordinary of Christian men,* which, like all his other books, was taken from the French. Among them may be mentioned *The Lucydarye, The Flower of commandments of God, The Treatise of the Passion of Christ, The Craft to live well and to die well,* a complete translation of a book from which Caxton had already translated extracts under the title of *The Art of good living and good dying.*

A good idea of the ordinary demand for books may be obtained by examining the publications of Wynkyn de Worde in the year 1509.

This was the busiest year of his career, for, no doubt, the funerals of Henry VII and the countess of Richmond, and the coronation of Henry VIII, would bring large crowds to London. Altogether, he issued twenty-five books and these, again, can be arranged in an almost exact order. Up to 21 April, he had published five, a York *Manuale*, an edition of the *Manipulus Curatorum* and editions of *The Gospel of Nicodemus*, *The Parliament of Devils* and *Richard Cœur de Lion*. Between 21 April and 12 July, the busiest time, he issued eleven ; four grammatical books, two editions each of Fisher's *Sermon on the seven penitencial psalms* and *Funeral sermon on Henry VII*, the prose version of *The Ship of Fools* and two works by Stephen Hawes, *The Passetyme of Pleasure* and *The Conversion of Swearers*. During the rest of the year he printed seven—two service-books, a grammar, Hawes's *Joyful meditation...of the coronation of...Henry VIII*, Fisher's *Mourning Remembrance*, and two anonymous books, *The Fifteen Joys of Marriage* and *The Seven Sheddings of the blood of Jesu Christ*. Two more books belong to this year which cannot be placed in any group, a service-book, and *The rule of the living of the bretherne and systars*.

The publications of this year are the most miscellaneous of any, and, very soon, the taste began to change. New romances continued to be published for some years : *King Apolyn of Tyre* and *The Birth of Merlin* in 1510, *The History of King Ponthus* in 1511, *The History of Helias, Knight of the Swan* in 1512 and *Oliver of Castile* (probably a reprint of a lost earlier edition) in 1518. Yet a gradual but marked change was taking place. Educational books and books on religious subjects became more and more in demand. The influence of scholars like Erasmus and the general revival of letters in the one case, and the growth of the reformation and the influence of the 'new learning' in the other, were beginning to produce effects. In Wynkyn de Worde's second busiest year, 1532, out of eighteen books, six were scholastic, eleven religious and the remaining one a romance, *The History of Guystarde and Sygysmonde*, translated from the Latin by William Walter.

William Walter, 'servant' to Sir Henry Marney, chancellor of Lancaster from 1509 to 1523, translated at least three books. *Guystarde and Sygysmonde* is a version in seven-lined stanzas taken, probably, from the Latin version of Boccaccio's story made by Leonardo Aretino. This, like so many of de Worde's books, was edited by Robert Copland, who added some verses of his own. Though the earliest edition known is dated 1532, there must, most probably, have been an earlier one. Another of Walter's books, *The Spectacle of Lovers*, though spoken of as 'newly compiled,' is, apparently, a translation; while the last, *The History of Titus and Gesippus* is, also, translated out of Latin.

In 1521, de Worde printed a book of carols, of which only a fragment is known. It contains the well known carol on the bringing in of the boar's head beginning 'The boar's head in hand bring I,' still sung on Christmas day in Queen's College, Oxford, and another carol on hunting.

After this year, we find hardly any new English books printed; the revival of letters was beginning to make itself felt, and half the produce of the press consisted of educational books. So much had the demand for this class of book increased that de Worde sometimes printed three or four editions of one grammar in the course of a year.

Among some two hundred undated books issued from this press there are many of great interest; but, unfortunately, many are known only from fragments, and very many more from single copies in private libraries, and, therefore, difficult of access. As examples of such books may be mentioned the metrical romance of *Capystranus*, *The Complaint of the too soon married*, *The Complaint of the too late married*, *The Complaynte of the Heart*, Feylde's *Controversy between a lover and a jay*, *The Fifteen joys of marriage*, *The Jest of the Miller of Abingdon*, *The Pain and sorrow of evil marriage* and many other small metrical pieces, all of which are in private hands.

The total number of books at present known to have been issued by Wynkyn de Worde in the sixteenth century is about six hundred and forty. Of these, more than two hundred were merely small school-books, about one hundred and fifty service-books and religious treatises and the same number of poems and romances; the remainder consisting of chronicles, law-books, accounts of passing events and other miscellaneous books.

The productions of the minor printers of the period show little originality, though, here and there, we come across books which had not already been issued by de Worde or Pynson. Julian Notary, who printed between 1496 and 1520, issued, out of some forty books, only five not previously printed. The earliest of these, *The Gospel of Nicodemus*, printed in 1507, evidently suited the popular taste and was very frequently reprinted. Besides this there are two small poetical tracts, *The mery geste of a Sergeaunt and Frere*, by Sir

Thomas More, and *A mery gest howe Johan Splynter made his testament*. This last tells how John Splynter, rent-gatherer at Delft and Schiedam, having neglected his private concerns for the sake of his professional business, was treated with contempt by the nuns who employed him, but who, hoping to obtain as a legacy the chest which he pretended was full of money, kept him in comfort for his life. Pepwell, between 1518 and 1523, printed eight books ; *The Castle of Pleasure*, by W. Neville, *The City of Ladies*, by Christine de Pisan, *The Dietary of ghostly health*, are all, probably, reprints from editions printed by Wynkyn de Worde. Another book contains several religious pieces printed together, some of which had not been issued before. Among them are the treatise named *Benjamin*, written by Richard of St Victor, *The life of St Katherine of Senis, The book of Margery Kempe, ancresse of Lynn, The treatise of the Song of angels* by Walter Hylton and others.

Richard Faques, out of a total of about twenty books, printed three or four of interest. Two are ballads relating to the battle of Flodden. Another is a curious and hitherto unnoticed work, entitled *The booke of the pylgrymage of man*. The preface runs 'translated from *Le Pelerinage de l'homme* of late drawen into prose by dane William Hendred, Priour of Leomynstre, and now newly at the specyal commandement of the same father reverent I have compyled the tenure of the same in metre, comprehended in XXVI chapitours.' The book is written in highly alliterative seven-lined stanzas, but there is no clue to the name of the compiler. The date of the printing of the book may be put down to about the year 1515; but no authorities mention prior William Hendred, so the exact date of his translation cannot be determined.

Among John Rastell's productions, for the most part legal or religious, are a few of a totally different nature. In 1526, he issued *The merry jests of the widow Edith*, written by Walter Smith. This is the story in verse of the many tricks played by Edith, the daughter of John Haukin and widow of Thomas Ellis, on various persons, innkeepers, tradesmen and the servants of Sir Thomas More and the bishop of Rochester. She was still alive when the book was written ; and the author, Walter Smith, was, very probably, a stationer of that name in London and a neighbour of Rastell. The poem itself is coarse and of no merit, but interesting on account of its references to contemporary persons. The other book of the same year is *The Hundred merry Tales*, of which the unique copy is at Göttingen. Rastell was in the habit of giving performances of plays at his own house; and to this we may attribute his printing several interludes and plays by Medwall, Skelton and Heywood.

One other book by this printer is worthy of notice, *The Pastime of People*. This is a short chronicle, carried up to the year 1530 and, apparently, compiled by Rastell himself, which contains some curious statements on recent events. It contains also full-page portraits of the kings of England.

The only other among all the minor printers of the period to show any originality in his choice of publications was John Skot. He issued, about 1535, a curious religious imitation of the celebrated ballad of *The Nut Brown Maid*, entitled *The newe Notbrowne mayd upon the passyon of Cryste*, and also printed two editions of *Every-man*, a morality of exceptional literary merit, closely connected with the Dutch *Elckerlijk*, written by Petrus Dorlandus towards the close of the fifteenth century.

Another cause militating against the production of much good work by these minor early printers was the smallness of their resources. They had practically no capital, and, without good type and illustrations, could not venture upon the production of a large work. A fount of type discarded by some other printer, and a small collection of miscellaneous and worn wood-blocks, were their sole stock. They could thus only work on small books, and had, moreover, to choose those which, by previous publication, had proved to be popular.

Reference has been made before to the attempt, very soon after Caxton's death, to produce English books abroad for sale in this country. At the beginning of the sixteenth century, this attempt was renewed with greater success.

Antoine Verard, the famous French publisher, attempted, about 1503, to issue books for the English market. In that year, he issued *The Kalendar of Shepherds* and *The Art of good living and dying*. The former became a very popular book, and at least sixteen editions were issued in the sixteenth century. It is a translation of the *Calendrier des Bergers*, of which there are many early French editions, and is an extraordinary collection of miscellaneous matter, 'a universal magazine of every article of salutary and useful knowledge.' The language of this first edition is even more curious than its contents; for the translator was, manifestly, a young Scotchman with a very imperfect knowledge of French. It has been suggested that this version was intended for sale in Scotland; but this is hardly probable, since the language would have been as unintelligible to the Scottish as it was to the English reader. In 1506, Pynson issued a new edition revised from the 'corrupte englysshe' of the earlier; and, in 1508, Wynkyn de Worde published a new translation made by Robert Copland, who definitely speaks of the language of the first as Scottish; and this final translation was frequently reprinted.

The Art of good living and dying, a translation from *L'Art de bien vivre et de bien mourir*, was also translated by the same hand; and of it, again, a new translation made by Andrew Chertsey was issued by Wynkyn de Worde in 1505. The third of Verard's books, but, probably, the earliest published, is the first edition of Alexander Barclay's translation of Gringore's *Chasteau de labour*, which may have been printed under Barclay's own supervision when he was staying in Paris. It is known only from fragments, but was fortunately reprinted, once by Pynson and twice by Wynkyn de Worde.

Another very remarkable foreign printed book, clearly translated by a foreigner, is *The Passion of Christ*. The strangeness of the language is evident from the first sentence 'Her begynnythe ye passion of dar seygneur Jesu chryste front ye resuscytacion of lazarus and to thende translatet owt of frenche yn to englysche the yer of dar lorde. M.v.cviii.' The book, said to have been translated at the command of Henry VII, was evidently printed in Paris, probably by Verard and is illustrated with a number of fine wood-cuts copied from a series by Urs Graf published at Strassburg. The name of the translator is not known; but many of the words point to a native of the Low Countries.

Soon after the beginning of the sixteenth century, an Antwerp bookseller and stationer, John of Doesborch, began to print books in English for sale in this country. These range in date from about 1505 to about 1525 and are good evidence of what a speculative printer considered most likely to appeal to popular taste. The earliest is a religious tract on the subject of the last judgment, entitled *The Fifteen Tokens*, a translation by the printer from some Dutch version of a part of *L'Art de bien mourir*. There are four small grammars of a kind in common use, but the majority are story-books. These are *The Gest of Robyn Hode, Euryalus and Lucrece, The Lyfe of Virgilius, Frederick of Jennen, Mary of Nemmegen, Tyll Howleglas* and *The Parson of Kalenborowe*. With the exception of the first two, all are translations from the Dutch. Douce, without apparently any reason, suggested Richard Arnold, the compiler of Arnold's *Chronicle*, as the translator; but the work was more probably done by Lawrence Andrewe, who was then living in Antwerp and was afterwards a printer in London. The remaining English books issued by Doesborch are very miscellaneous. There are two editions of the *Valuation of gold and silver*; a work on the pestilence; two tracts relating to expeditions against the Turks; another, on the wonderful shape and nature of beasts and fishes; and, lastly, what is generally considered the first English book on America, *Of the new lands found by the messengers of the King of Portugal named Emanuel.* Only a single leaf of the book, describing a voyage made in 1496, relates to America; the rest is compiled from various sources such as the *Tractatus de decem nationibus christianorum*, appended to the *Itinerarius* of Johannes de Hese, and a Dutch book, also printed by Doesborch, *Van Pape Jans landendes.*

The printers of Antwerp always continued to be connected with the English book trade; but the year 1525, which saw the cessation of John of Doesborch's press with its popular little books, witnessed also the publication at Worms of Tindale's *New Testament*, which marks an entire change in the character of the books printed abroad. After this time, the foreign presses issued nothing but religious and controversial books, the work of refugees whose religious or political opinions had made them outcasts from their own country. The reformation seems to have dealt a blow at both books of amusement and books of education, and story-books and grammars almost ceased to be published.

In taking a general survey of the English press during the first fifty years of its existence, several points stand out very prominently. One, in especial, is the comparative scarcity of books by contemporary writers. Skelton, who flourished during this period, is very badly represented, and Stephen Hawes but little better. But, when we consider how very many of these early books have come down to our time only in single copies or even fragments out of an edition of some hundreds, it is only natural to suppose that a great number must have utterly disappeared. This would be especially the case with small poetical books and romances; but others, of which copies might have been expected to be preserved, are lost. There is no trace of *The epitaph of the King of Scotland*, written by Petrus Carmelianus and 'stuffed full of womanly abuse,' which, according to Erasmus, was printed by Pynson in 1513. Of the several books relating to the impostures of the Maid of Kent which are known to have been printed, not a fragment now remains. Perhaps their popularity was the cause of their destruction. It seems impossible that writings on contemporary events could escape being printed. For instance, Dunbar's poem 'London thou art the flower of cities all,' composed on his visit to London in 1501 and circulated in manuscript, is just what an enterprising printer would have seized upon. Yet we have no evidence of its existence in a printed form. The popular demand was for reprints of older works and translations of French poems and romances; there is hardly any genuine original work printed in the period.

Another point which has been commented upon is the entire absence of any classical books. Apart from books evidently intended for school use, such as *Cicero pro Milone*, printed at Oxford about 1483, and the *Terence* printed by Pynson in 1495—7, the only book to which we can point is Pynson's edition of *Vergil*, printed about 1520. But the reason here is not far to seek. There were no restrictions on the importation of foreign books, and English printers could not possibly compete either in accuracy and neatness or in cheapness with the foreign productions of this class. Very wisely they left them alone. Thus, the output of the English presses show rather the popular, than the general, demand. To discover this, it would be necessary to find a day-book or ledger of some London bookseller similar to that of John Dorne the Oxford bookseller of 1520. This latter. being the accounts of a bookseller in a university city, furnishes no fair criterion of general taste; though, even at the fairs where the most general trade was done in books, his English books formed but a small proportion of his sales.

The seeming neglect by the age of the work of its own more important writers is balanced by the precipitancy of modern writers, who have hitherto skipped from Skelton to Surrey without a pause, entirely ignoring the minor authors and translators whose books supplied the main reading of the English public.

CHAPTER XIV

ENGLISH PROSE IN THE FIFTEENTH CENTURY

II

Caxton. Malory. Berners

ALTHOUGH the introduction of printing brought about no sudden renascence, it accelerated and strengthened, under the direction of Caxton, the drift of the current of our fifteenth century literature; and this places our first printer in a position wholly different from that of his more mechanical successors. Caxton was quick to discern the direction in which taste was tending and, himself helping to direct that taste, he ignored the old metrical romances, favourites for long, preferring to satisfy the chivalric-romantic fashion of the times by prose translations from French works of already established repute. That romances of the kind of *The Four Sons of Aymon*, or *Paris and Vienne* were destined to disappearance early in the next century in no way neutralises their importance as a step in English literature. They handed on material not disdained by Spenser, they formed a link between medieval and modern romance and, from among them, has survived an immortal work, Malory's *Morte d'Arthur*.

We might have supposed Caxton's publication of Chaucer to have been epoch-making, had it not had to wait for long before kindling any fresh torch; but there is no evidence that it roused in others the enthusiasm felt by its editor. In truth, the men of that age, who had but just emerged from a long and sordid war, were not, and could not be, poetical; and, save for the poems of Chaucer and Lydgate, Caxton held firm to prose.

His publications, excluding church service-books and practical manuals, fall into three groups: didactic works, romances and chronicles. Of the last—large and, doubtless, costly—three proved sufficient; of romances, he issued ten or eleven, probably for the courtly class of readers; while, of moral and didactic works, for the most part small and cheap, he provided no less than twenty-nine, not counting *Reynard the Fox*, and the *Golden Legend*,

which partake of the entertaining element at least equally with
the instructive. As several of these books and tracts went into
two editions, they were, evidently, in considerable demand with the
general public; but the tinge of utility is upon them, and they have
not the literary interest of the larger works.

As has been observed already, the greater part of Caxton's
output was translated. Tudor prose, like that of the earlier period,
was chiefly fashioned on French models, to which we owe nearly
all the prose masterpieces of the epoch, and a proportionate debt of
gratitude. But Caxton found another quarry in fifteenth century
prose, and in the case of both English and French material he
acted as editor, translating with the same freedom as his predecessors, and 'embellishing the old English' of Trevisa or of *The
Golden Legend.*

Caxton had lived so long abroad that he probably found more
difficulty than other writers in selecting the most suitable words to
employ; and it is difficult to believe that one hand alone turned
out so large a mass of literature as he did, any more than it
manipulated the printing-press unaided. Nevertheless, his translations must, like his press, be reckoned as having the stamp of
his authority, though others, probably, helped. A comparison
of his editions of *The Golden Legend, Polychronicon* and *The
Knight of the Tower* with the original English versions leaves the
older prose easily first. Again and again, the modern reader will
find the word rejected by Caxton more familiar than its substitute;
again and again, Caxton's curtailments, inversions, or expansions
merely spoil a piece of more vigorous narrative. This is particularly evident in *The Knight of the Tower*, which Caxton seems
to have translated entirely afresh, unaware of the older version,
whose superiority is remarkable. And in his original and interesting prefaces we may, perhaps, see how it was he went wrong.
He appears to have been desirous of avoiding the colloquially
simple manner of earlier writers, and to have felt his way towards
the paragraph, working out, in those prefaces for which he had
no French exemplar, a somewhat involved style. He is fond of
relative sentences, and sometimes piles them on the top of each
other without finishing the earlier ones: 'Which thing when
Gotard had advertised of and that he bare so away the bread, but
he wist not to whom ne whither, whereof he marvelled and so did
all his household[1].' He mixes direct and indirect speech; he uses
the redundant *which*: 'I fynde many of the sayd bookes, whyche

---

[1] *Life of St Rocke*, in *Golden Legend*, No. 154, tr. by Caxton.

writers have abrydged it and many thynges left out.' Only
when he has plain statements to convey, as in his continuation
of the *Chronicle*, or an anecdote to relate, such as the tale of the
dean and the poor parson in the epilogue to Aesop, does he become
direct; but then he is, sometimes, almost as vigorous as Latimer
himself. In this power of writing with a naïve vivacity, while
deliberately striving after a more ornate manner, Caxton belongs
to his age. He provides, as it were, a choice of styles for his
readers.

The mannerisms of the Middle Ages are still noticeable in
Caxton's work : in his irrepressible moralising, his quotations
from old authority, his conventional excuse for writing a book
(to keep himself from idleness, which is the nurse of sin), his
arrant inaccuracy as to names, his profession of incapacity 'to
smattre me in suche translacions'; but his definite claim to have
embellished the older authors, his quiet pride in his own authorship and the interest taken therein by his noble patrons, his
conscious appreciation of language, are of the new world, not of
the old. The days of anonymous compiling are over ; and, henceforth, not the substance, alone, but its form will challenge
attention. Prose is no longer to be merely the vehicle of information, but conscious literature.

Caxton's largest and most popular book, *The Golden Legend*, is,
also, the most medieval in kind. It may almost be called a
cyclopaedia of traditional sacred lore, comprising not lives of the
saints only, but explanations of the church service and homilies
upon the feast days, as well as a shortened but complete chronicle,
Lombard in origin, to A.D. 1250. The public decidedly preferred
it to Malory or Chaucer, and it went through edition after edition.
For one thing, it was a long recognised classic; for another, it
presented the favourite mixture of morality combined with entertainment. Many of the lives are copies from earlier English
versions, more or less 'mollified' by their editor. Those of French
saints are a new, and often slipshod, translation. Others are
compiled from the three renderings (Latin, English and French)
and from further sources such as *Polychronicon* and *Josephus*,
and practically form a new version. With regard to the merit of
these, opinions will differ. It may be true that Caxton's *Becket*,
for example, presents a more compact story than the original ; on
the other hand, the incessant curtailment has spoiled the charming
incident of the Saracen princess. Caxton, moreover, altered the
usual arrangement of the *Legend* to insert a series of lives of

Old Testament heroes, and it is a vital question in estimating
his rank as a prose writer whether these lives are to be
reckoned his own or not. They are so far superior to the mere
translations that one of his critics takes it for granted they must
be his own; another, that they must come from an earlier
English version now lost. The MSS of the old version now
remaining to us contain none of these Old Testament lives save
Adam, from which the Caxtonian version differs entirely. The
earlier *Adam*[1], except for the usual legendary interpolations,
is strictly Biblical in language, adhering closely, at first, to the
revised Wyclifite version, afterwards, to the first Wyclifite version;
whereas Caxton's *Adam* is, in the main, a sermon, and the succeeding lives, though they follow the Bible closely as to incident,
are much shortened as to wording, and not distinctively reminiscent of the Wyclifite versions; indeed, they afford more points of
resemblance to the later phraseology. If it can be supposed that
Caxton actually rendered them into English himself, his literary
powers here rose to a pitch far higher than he attained at any
other time[2].

Like *The Golden Legend*, the *Morte d'Arthur*, the publication
of which holds a chief place in Caxton's work, looks back to the
Middle Ages. Based on translation, a mosaic of adaptations, it is,
nevertheless, a single literary creation such as no work of Caxton's
own can claim to be, and it has exercised a far stronger and longer
literary influence.

If, as is possible, Malory was the knight of Newbold Revell,
he had been a retainer of the last Beauchamp earl of Warwick, he
had seen the splendours of the last efforts of feudalism and had
served in that famous siege of Rouen which so deeply impressed
contemporary imagination. Apparently, he was a loyalist during the
Civil Wars and suffered from Yorkist revenge; his burial in the
Grey Friars may, possibly, suggest that he even died a prisoner in

---

[1] In Lambeth MS, 72.

[2] The English MSS of *The Golden Legend* (for which see Pierce Butler, bibliog.
cap. XII), end with a kind of appendix on Adam and Eve and a sermon on the five
wiles of Pharaoh. The Lambeth MS (No. 72) adds a long account of the three kings
of Cologne, probably the legendary history often issued separately. Though this
MS contains only one hundred and sixty-two chapters to compare with the one
hundred and seventy-nine of MS Harl. 4775, it contains several English saints not
included in the latter or the parallel MS Addit. 11,565. Caxton has not got all of
them: he omits *Frideswide*, *Chadd* and *Bride*, but those he has are nearly all exactly
like the older version, except *K. Edmund*, which he evidently obtained from some
source we do not know.

Newgate. In any case, he must have died before the printing of his immortal book, which comes to us, therefore, edited by Caxton, to whom, possibly, are due most of the lacunae, bits of weak grammar and confusions in names. Nevertheless, the style seals the *Morte d'Arthur* as Malory's, not Caxton's. It is as individual as is the author's mode of dealing with the material he gathered from his wide field. This material Malory several times says he found in a French book—*the* French book—but critics have discovered a variety of sources. It is in the course of the story that the multiplicity of sources is at times discernible—in the failure of certain portions to preserve a connecting thread, in the interruption of the story of Tristram, in the curious doubling of names, or the confusion of generations—the style reveals no trace of inharmonious originals. The skilful blending of many ancient tales, verse and prose, French and English, savage and saintly, into a connected, if but loosely connected, whole is wrought in a manner which leaves the *Morte*, while representative of some of the nobler traits of Malory's century, in other respects typical neither of that nor any particular epoch, and this is an element in its immortality.

If such an ascetic purity and rapt devotion as glows in the *Grail* story was practised among the mystics, such a fantastic chivalry portrayed by Froissart, such a loyalty evinced by a Bedford or a Fortescue, yet the *Morte* assumes the recognition of a loftier standard of justice, purity and unselfishness than its own century knew. These disinterested heroes, who give away all they win with the magnanimity of an Audley at Poictiers, these tireless champions of the helpless, these eternal lovers and their idealised love, are of no era, any more than the forests in which they for ever travel. And, if the constant tournaments and battles, and the castles which seem to be the only places to live in, suggest a medieval world, the total absence of reference to its basic agricultural life and insistent commerce detach us from it again, while the occasional mention of cities endows them with a splendour and remoteness only to be paralleled in the ancient empire or in the pictures of Turner.

Medieval stories were, naturally, negligent of causes in a world where the unaccountable so constantly happened in real life, and a similar suddenness of adventure may be found in tales much older than this. Malory, however, on the threshold of an age which would require dramatic motive or, at least, probability, saved his book from the fate of the older, unreasoned fiction by investing it with an atmosphere, impossible to analyse, which withdraws his figures to the region of mirage. This indescribable conviction of magic places Malory's characters outside the sphere of criticism, since, given the atmosphere, they are consistent with themselves and their circumstances. Nothing is challenged, analysed or emphasised; curiosity as to causation is kept in abeyance; retribution is worked out, but, apparently, unconsciously. Like children's are the sudden quarrels and hatreds and as sudden reconciliations. The motive forces are the elemental passions of love and bravery, jealousy and revenge, never greed, or lust, or cruelty. Courage and the thirst for adventure are taken for granted, like the passion for the chase, and, against a brilliant and moving throng of the brave and fair, a few conceptions are made to stand forth as exceptional—a Lancelot, a Tristram, or a Mark. Perhaps most skilful of all is the restraint exercised in the portrayal of Arthur. As with Shakespeare's Caesar and Homer's Helen, we realise Arthur by his effect upon his paladins; of himself we are not allowed to form a definite image, though we may surmise justice to be his most distinct attribute. Neither a hero of hard knocks nor an effective practical monarch, he is not to be assigned to any known type, but remains the elusive centre of the magical panorama.

The prose in which is unfolded this scarcely Christianised fairy tale—for the *Grail* was to Arthurian legend something as the Crusades to feudalism—is, apparently, of a very simple, almost childlike, type, with its incessant 'so—and—then,' but, unlike mere simplicity, it never becomes tedious. There is a kind of cadence, at times almost musical, which bears the narrative on with a gradual swell and fall proportioned to the importance of the episodes, while brevity, especially at the close of a long incident, sometimes approaches to epigram. But the style fits the subject so perfectly as never to claim attention for itself. A transparent clarity is of its essence. Too straightforward to be archaic, idiomatic with a suavity denied to Caxton, Malory, who reaches one hand to Chaucer and one to Spenser, escaped the stamp of a particular epoch and bequeathed a prose epic to literature.

Tudor prose owes its foundations to three men of affairs who took to literature late in life. Next to Caxton and Malory stands Sir John Bourchier, Lord Berners. Like Malory, he was an active soldier, but, unlike him, a well known and prosperous man, a politician and courtier. He belonged to the influential Bourchier clan, Yorkists till the death of Edward IV, and had earned and experienced the gratitude of Henry VII. But he had the less good fortune to attract the favour of Henry VIII, and, late in life, suffered from that monarch's customary harshness. It was partly to solace his anxieties while captain of Calais, as well as 'to eschew idleness, the mother of all the vices,' that he executed the series of translations which secure to him the credit of a remarkable threefold achievement. Berners was the first to introduce to our literature the subsequently famous figure of Oberon, the fairy king; he was the first to attempt in English the ornate prose style which shortly became fashionable; and he gave to historians at once a new source-book and a new model in his famous rendering of the *Chronicles of Froissart.*

Lord Berners was peculiarly well fitted to execute this translation. He had himself been active at the siege of Terouenne and on the Field of the Cloth of Gold, where Henry VIII regarded himself as, in some sort, reviving the glories of old; he had visited the Spanish court of Charles V and knew something of that of France. He so thoroughly entered into the spirit of his original as to make his work rather an adoption than a translation. In his hands history is still near akin to fiction, but rather to the heroic romance than to the well worn marvels of ancient chronicles. If these remind us of *Gesta Romanorum* or of Sir John Mandeville, Froissart, in the dress of Berners, may be paralleled with Malory. Sir John of Hainault champions the cause of queen Isabel as would a knight of Arthur; and from orthodox romance comes the fancy picture of Bristol, the well closed city on the good port of the sea, which beats round its strong castle. While the old chronicles are wearisome, Berners conveys all the vigour and freshness of Froissart in his descriptions and conversations. Both the human interest and the chronicler's personal attitude towards it are preserved. Berners is in full sympathy with Froissart's aristocratic spirit, which places the violence of a duke of Britanny or a count of Foix on a plane above criticism though not beyond sympathy, and bestows a contemptuous pity on the crestfallen burghers of Bruges and a lofty disdain on the upstart pride of Ghent. In language, Berners follows the excellent method of earlier translators: 'In that I have not followed myne authour worde by worde yet I trust I have ensewed the true reporte of the sentence of the mater.' And he varies his narration pleasantly by a not unskilful use of inversion.

But the *Froissart* of Berners taught something further to the Tudor historians, of the value of well proportioned detail and occasional quotation of witness in impressing the sense of actuality. It can hardly be said that Hall and Holinshed, the most ambitious of Tudor historians, borrow much from Berners in style; but it is evident that the new model influenced their aims and methods quite apart from its value as a new mine of information.

In *Arthur of Little Britain* and *Huon of Bordeaux*, Berners took up the prose tale, or romance, of the ordinary medieval type, most of the incidents in which are of the wildly absurd order. But the favourite of the two, *Huon*, is remarkable for its unusual pair of heroes. The uncouthness of Charlemagne and his court is in odd contrast to the conventional pictures of Arthur, and the whole romance is treated on a different and lower level, whether because it represents a fourteenth or even thirteenth century story, or because some folk-tale influence had been at work upon it. Huon himself is apt to remind us of the ignobly born simpleton heroes of German peasant story, and he is a bad simpleton. He runs headlong into danger, not from extravagance of knightly daring but out of stupidity, or greed, or childish impatience. He complains querulously, tries to deceive his benefactor Auberon and has no notion of either gratitude or morality. For instance, Auberon has warned him never to tell a lie, but, so soon as the paynim porter of Babylon asks whether he be a Saracen, 'Yea,' replies Huon promptly, and then reflects that Auberon will surely not be angry at such a lie, 'sen I did it not wilfully but that I forgat it!' It is only when he has committed some offence against the fairy that Huon prides himself upon being a Christian : his Saviour ought to shield him from the wrath of Auberon. And yet this perjured simpleton is incongruously represented as the only creature 'sinless' enough to be able to drink from Auberon's magic horn.

Auberon himself is half-way to being the fairy of poetry ; 'a dwarf of the fairy' is he, child of a fairy mother, 'the lady of the isle' and a mortal father, Julius Caesar (who, in the Middle Ages, obtained the same magical reputation as Vergil). Auberon, therefore, is mortal, he can weep, he falls sick ; but he is never of more stature than a child of three years, and his magical powers are so absolute that he has only to wish, and his will accomplishes itself. He knows all that passes afar as he rules in his fairy capital, Momure, for he is a civilised fairy with a knowledge of politics. He is a much better Christian than Huon, and, when he dies, his corpse is buried in an abbey and his soul is carried to heaven by an innumerable company of angels.

Huon of Bordeaux was so popular as to obtain a reissue in 1601, modernised as to wording and adorned as to style[1]. As Berners wrote it out, the English is extremely straightforward, and bears hardly more trace of the graceful fluency of his *Froissart* than of the novel experiment its translator was shortly to assay.

To a modern reader, it appears, at first sight, wonderful that the most popular work of the translator of Froissart should have been his rendering of a verbose, didactic book by the Spanish secretary of Charles V, Antonio de Guevara, an author whose involutions of language rapidly captivated fashionable taste in Spain, France and England. Berners has the credit of first introducing him and his style to English readers in *The Golden Book of Marcus Aurelius*, which so much delighted the polite world that it went through fourteen editions in half a century. The substance of this volume of tedious letters and trite reflections Guevara pretended he had discovered in an old MS, claiming for himself only the merit of bestowing 'style' upon the emperor's writing.

The desire to treat composition as itself an art was beginning to be felt in England, as in other countries, and Berners must have already paid attention to that peculiar manner of writing which, vigorously introduced by translations of which his own was the earliest specimen, was to receive its distinctive epithet from its most perfect example, *Euphues*.

The prefaces of Berners to his *Froissart* are his first experiments in the ornate, and not much more successful, though more lavish, than the earlier groping of Caxton. 'As said is'; 'I pray them that shall default find,' result from his preference of inversion to direct speech, and relative pronouns are a puzzle to him.

Yet perhaps these elaborate prologues are but a fresh outburst of the native love of double terms which hampered every prose writer between Chaucer and Malory. The national bent to cumulative expression must have been a good preparation to the reception of the new style when it came, by the means of translated Guevara, in a flood. What was wanting was the art to weave the customary repetitions of thought, the synonyms, antitheses and alliterative combinations into a balance and harmony of sentences. To this, neither Berners nor his nephew and literary disciple Sir F. Bryan had attained. A comparison of his *Golden Book* with North's rendering of it, *The Dial of Princes*, exhibits the crudity of the efforts of Berners in this style. He can faithfully reproduce the repetitions and run the slight idea to death, but the 'sauce of the said sweet style,' as his nephew terms it, lacks savour.

[1] Cf. Sidney Lee's list in his edition of *Huon*, E.E.T.S.

CHAPTER XV

ENGLISH AND SCOTTISH EDUCATION. UNIVERSITIES AND PUBLIC SCHOOLS TO THE TIME OF COLET

In an age innocent of historical criticism, champions of Oxford and Cambridge, waging a wordy war for the honour of prior foundation, referred the establishment of their respective universities to Alfred and to Sigebert. In these days, the historians of both are content to look to the twelfth century as the birth period, not only of the English university, but of the university of Paris from which English university life drew its early inspiration.

When the twelfth century drew to a close, Paris was the English academic metropolis. Already, indeed, there were masters and students in Oxford. What was the attraction which drew them to a town that had no well based claims to high antiquity, and was, otherwise, of little consequence, it is impossible now to point out with certainty. Looking to the history of continental universities, analogy would seem to demand, as the nucleus of the concourse, a cathedral or a monastic school. But Oxford was not a bishop's seat; its diocesan was posted in far distant Lincoln. And, if monks provided or salaried the first Oxford teachers, they wholly failed to obtain, or, at any rate, to retain, control over the rising university; there is not the slightest trace of monastic influence in the organisation or studies of the earliest Oxford of historic times. The cloister school of St Frideswide may well have charged the atmosphere with the first odour of learning; but its walls at no time sheltered the university soul.

Certain, however, it is that, in the first half of the twelfth century, a number of famous names are connected with Oxford teaching. It may be that if, as Gervase of Canterbury testifies, Vacarius taught civil law at Oxford, in 1149, he did not lecture as an Oxford master, but as a member of the train of archbishop Theobald. But Theobaldus Stampensis, as a recent historian[1] has pointed out, in letters written between 1101 and 1117 styles

[1] Rashdall. *Universities of Europe in the Middle Ages*, ii, 333.

himself master in Oxford; Robert Pullen, afterwards cardinal and the author of *Sententiarum Libri Octo*, is stated, on good authority, to have taught in Oxford in 1133; and, when in 1189 Giraldus Cambrensis read his *Topographia Hibernica* at Oxford, 'where the most learned and famous of the clergy of England were then to be found,' he entertained 'all the doctors of the several faculties and such of their pupils as were of greater fame and repute.'

In the story of this last incident we have clear indications of an existing and of an organised Oxford university.

Modern research points to the year 1167 as the date of the birth of Oxford as a *studium generale*, and offers a chain of circumstantial evidence to connect it with an expulsion of alien students by the Parisian authorities and the contemporary recall by Henry II, then engaged in the contest with Becket, of all clerks holding English cures[1]. However this may have been, the last few years of the twelfth century furnish abundant proof of the presence in Oxford of students in considerable numbers.

In 1192, Oxford, according to Richard of Devizes, could barely maintain her clerks. In 1197, the great abbot Samson of Bury entertained a large company of Oxford masters. When the troubles of 1209 burst upon the university, scholars to the number—according to Matthew Paris—of three thousand dispersed in various directions.

It is to this last occasion that the Oxford historian[2] refers the appearance of Cambridge as a *studium generale*.

The story is characteristic of the times. An Oxford clerk kills a woman—accidentally, as it is afterwards said. But the culprit flees. The town authorities search the dwelling wherein he lodged, and, in his absence, arrest two or three of his companions, who are perfectly innocent of the offence, if such it be. King John, however, is in the middle of his famous quarrel with the pope, and is ready to wreak his vengeance on any clerk. On the king's instructions, the innocent prisoners are hanged. In combined fear and indignation, the Oxford masters proclaim a suspension of studies; and the scholars scatter. Some merely retreat to Reading; others migrate further afield. Some go to Paris; some to Cambridge.

Cambridge, as a town, dates back to the days of the Roman occupation of Britain, when it represented the intersection of two great military highways and a consequent guard-post. William I made it his base for attack upon Ely, and pulled down eighteen of

[1] Rashdall, Chap. xii.   [2] *Ibid.* ii, 349.

its 387 dwelling-houses to secure a site for a castle which should command the passage of its important ford. Henry I erected it into a borough corporate. The establishment of a great fair at Barnwell about 1103 and the settlement of Jews in 1106 denote a growth of trade and population. At what date students first found their way to its narrow streets, and what was the attractive force compelling them thither, it is, as in the case of Oxford, impossible, absolutely, to determine. Cambridge, like Oxford, was not a cathedral city; and the wealthy priory of Barnwell, founded about 1112, lay well away from the district in which the students congregated. A story of early lectures by a party of monks despatched by Joffred, abbot of Crowland, to his manor of Cottenham is, by internal evidence, demonstrated to be a late invention. It is not until the first quarter of the thirteenth century that genuine history records the presence in Cambridge of a concourse of clerks; it is in 1231, when the Parisian scholars were returning to their former quarters after the famous secession of 1229, that we obtain our first clear proof of the existence in the English fen town of an organised society of masters and students. In that year (3 May) a royal writ commands the sheriff of the county to proclaim and, if need be, take and imprison certain pretended clerks in Cambridge *qui sub nullius magistri scholarum sunt disciplina et tuitione;* he is to expel within fifteen days any clerk who is not under the control of a responsible master. At the same time, a second writ addressed to the mayor and bailiffs recites that *Satis constat vobis quod apud villam nostram Cantebr. studendi causa e diversis partibus tam cismarinis quam transmarinis scholarium confluit multitudo,* and enjoins that the hostel rents chargeable to scholars shall be fixed *secundum consuetudinem Universitatis* by two masters and two good and lawful men of the town.

The Oxford *suspendium clericorum* of 1209 had at least reinforced the numbers of the Cambridge scholars. In 1229, a riot in Paris led to a similar migration of students from the metropolitan university. Henry III issued an invitation to the migrants to come over into England, and settle 'in what cities, boroughs and villages they pleased to choose'; and Cambridge shared with Oxford in the benefits of the Parisian exodus.

Henceforward, Oxford and Cambridge advance on parallel lines, Oxford enjoying the advantage of a start of fifty years.

The Oxford *suspendium* came to an end in 1214 under the terms of a settlement arranged by the papal legate, Nicholas of Tusculum. A legatine ordinance subjected to penance the executioners of the unfortunate victims of 1209 and, in true medieval fashion, imposed a heavy mulct upon the townsmen, present and future. It further required that a clerk arrested by townsmen should be forthwith surrendered on the demand of the bishop of Lincoln, or the archdeacon or his official, or 'the chancellor or whomsoever the bishop of Lincoln shall depute to the office.' And the rents of halls were to be taxed by a joint board of four burghers and four clerks. Here we have the record of the beginnings of a privileged academic society. The first task of an infant university is, necessarily, the organisation of its constitution. That work was begun in Oxford before 1214. In a very real sense the university of Oxford was a 'republic of letters.' The Oxford constitution, as it reveals itself in the course of the thirteenth century, is, essentially, democratic. The centre of its organic life is the assembly of masters. For the distribution of her members into four nations, as at Paris, Oxford substituted a division into northerners and southerners; Scottish students combined with English north countrymen to form the *boreales*, whilst Welshmen, 'Marchmen' and Irishmen were ranked with the *australes*. The two proctors were the elected mouthpieces of the two divisions. The supreme legislative authority was the entire body of masters of all faculties assembled in the 'great congregation'; where the proctors brought forward proposed statutes, counted the votes and announced decisions. A 'lesser congregation' of regents, *i.e.* of actually teaching masters, of all faculties, passed graces affecting studies or dealt with minor finance; while a yet narrower assembly of regents in arts supervised the grant of the magisterial licence to teach, and elected the proctors for the year.

The titular head of the university was the chancellor. It was round this officer that the struggle for university liberties was destined to be waged.

The first antagonists of the scholars were the townsmen. Grasping burgher householders demanded unconscionable rents or cheated the students in the sale of supplies; mayor and bailiffs asserted an eager jurisdiction over peccant clerks. The scholars had recourse to the ecclesiastical arm; and the legatine ordinance of 1214 marks their first decisive victory. In the taxors of hostels they obtained their tribunes against exaction, and, in the chancellor 'or whomsoever the bishop of Lincoln shall depute to the office,' they secured a resident protector against arbitrary arrest.

The chancellor was, in 1214, apparently, not, as yet, a regularly appointed officer. Grosseteste, who, at a subsequent date, exercised the functions of the office, was, in style, merely *rector scholarum.* When the chancellor appears as the occupant of a permanent office, it is as the bishop's officer. He was chosen, indeed, from amongst the masters; but it was the bishop who appointed. He was, in fact, an ecclesiastical official, who wielded the weapon of the church's censure, whether for the needful discipline of the scholars or for their protection against the venom of the town.

Supported by king and bishop, the chancellor secured, step by step, his position in and against the town. By successive royal writs he obtained the confirmation of the system of conjoint taxation of lodgings; the expulsion of irregular clerks ; and the use of the town prison and of the castle cells for the confinement of his domestic recalcitrants. By a series of charters he secured the limitation of the interest chargeable by Jews on the debts of scholars; his own right of jurisdiction in actions of debt in which one party was a clerk; and the right to take part in the assize of bread and beer. In 1255, he laid the foundation of a more extensive jurisdiction over laymen. In 1275, a royal writ gave him cognisance of all personal actions wherein either party was a scholar. When, in 1288, a royal bailiff engaged in altercation with the chancellor, the indiscreet layman lost his office. In 1290, the jurisdiction of the chancellor was defined by parliament as covering all crimes committed in Oxford when one of the parties was a scholar, except pleas of homicide and *mayhem.* The ranks of privileged persons included, with clerks proper, their attendants (*familias*), and all writers, parchment-makers, illuminators, stationers and other craftsmen who were employed exclusively by scholars.

In the struggles for these liberties the university employed the weapon forged by the Roman *plebs* of old. Between 1260 and 1264, seceding masters formed a *studium* at Northampton, and, at a later date (1334), a similar concourse at Stamford[1] threatened the well-being of Oxford.

On St Scholastica's Day 1354, a tavern brawl between innkeeper and dissatisfied customers gave rise to a fierce three days' 'town and gown,' wherein countrymen from the outskirts reinforced the

---

[1] So late as the first quarter of the nineteenth century every candidate for an Oxford degree was required to take an oath not to lecture at Stamford. Rashdall, II, 398.

burghers. The chancellor was shot at; inns and halls were looted; scholars were slain; books were destroyed. The friars, coming forth in solemn procession to play the part of peace-makers, were maltreated. The scholars of Merton alone were able to resist a siege, thanks to the strength of their walls.

But the blood of scholars became the seed of fresh university privileges. The university declared a general suspension of studies, and the town was put under interdict. A royal commission made short work of its task. Mayor and bailiffs were imprisoned; the sheriff was dismissed; an annual penance was imposed on the burghers; and the chancellor's prerogative was increased by the transfer to him of no inconsiderable share of the local government.

Yet once more, in 1405, the university, in amplification of a charter of Richard II, secured the right of trial before its own steward of a privileged person indicted for felony. The victory over the town was now complete.

At Cambridge, in like fashion, although without the accompaniment of serious bloodshed, the university developed its constitution; and a long series of royal writs and parliamentary enactments fortified the chancellor against the burghers. A great riot in 1381—the year of Tyler's insurrection—when the townsmen sacked Bene't College and burnt charters and title-deeds, was the Cambridge St Scholastica's Day. The privileges of the Cambridge chancellor, though ample and, to the town, sufficiently galling, fell short of the fulness of those of his Oxonian fellow-officials; and the Cambridge constitution differed in some details from the Oxford model.

Meanwhile, bishop's officer as he was in origin, the chancellor, in Cambridge, as in Oxford, had, with the episcopal countenance, first shaken himself free from the control of other episcopal officials; and then, in alliance with the archbishop and with the pope, successfully challenged the authority of the diocesan himself. The contest against minor ecclesiastical officials is best illustrated by the award issued in 1276 by bishop Hugo de Balsham in the dispute between the archdeacon of Ely and the Cambridge scholars, who had denied the jurisdiction of the archidiaconal court, and in a contemporary discussion between the Cambridge chancellor and the 'Master of Glomery,' in whom we may recognise the master of local grammar schools, who was a nominee of the archdeacon. The award is conceived in the spirit at once of liberal policy and of strict justice. He adjudges that all disputes in which a 'glomerel' is defendant shall be decided by the *Magister Glomeriae*; he thus enjoying the same privilege as that possessed by the other masters, of deciding the suits in which his students were involved. But this minor jurisdiction shall not extend (1) to the taxation of houses, or (2) to serious offences calling for imprisonment or expulsion from the university; in which cases the chancellor shall adjudicate. A scholar plaintiff may appeal to the chancellor from the decision of the *Magister Glomeriae*; but in disputes between two glomerels the chancellor shall have no right of intervention, except in the two above cited cases. Persons doing services exclusively for scholars shall enjoy the privileges of scholars, and shall rank as exempt from the control of the archdeacon. Rectors, vicars, parish chaplains and others in the service of local churches shall be held subject to the archdeacon; but clergy residing in Cambridge merely for the purposes of study shall be exempt. Hugo concludes by approving and confirming a statute issued by the chancellor and masters which provides

that no one should receive a scholar who has not had a fixed master within thirteen days after the said scholar had entered the university, or who had not taken care that his name had been within the time aforesaid inserted in the matriculation book of his master, unless the master's absence or legitimate occupation should have prevented the same[1].

It may be that the equity of this decision and the consequent absence of local friction helped to preserve from attack for a long period that jurisdiction of the bishop himself, which Hugo clearly reserved. Moreover, Hugo himself was the founder of Peterhouse, the oldest Cambridge college; he, and a long line of his successors as diocesans, not only took an enlightened interest in the well-being of the scholars, but were enrolled among their most conspicuous benefactors; and the propinquity of Cambridge to Ely gave little opportunity for the unnoted nursing of rebellious projects. Certain it is that the bishop of Ely continued to exercise a regular jurisdiction over the university down to the date of the Barnwell Process in 1430. And then the chancellor, John Holbroke, master of Peterhouse, and his advisers turned against their diocesan and, at the same time, against his metropolitan, the engine of the framers of the forged decretals. They submitted to the papal arbitrators at Barnwell Priory, and secured a favourable verdict on, a bull of Honorius I and a like asserted document of Sergius I, which declared the exemption of the university of Cambridge from all archiepiscopal, episcopal or other ecclesiastical control. Henceforward, the university was not only a regularly recognised and organised body, orderly, legislative and possessed of

[1] Trans. in Mullinger, Vol. i, p. 226.

peculiar powers—in a word, a privileged corporation; but it was independent of other control than that of king, parliament and pope.

Oxford reached the same end gradually and more rapidly. Lincoln was far removed from the university town. Between the university and bishop Grosseteste, a former *rector scholarum* and an enthusiastic patron of learning, the relations were of the most friendly order; but under his immediate successor disputes began. Prolonged vacancies in the see assisted the scholars in the establishment of their independence. The position of the bishop was, indirectly, sapped by the successive royal amplifications of the rights of the chancellor in the town. In 1280, the privileges of the chancellor were strongly asserted against bishop Oliver Sutton, the grant of probates of scholars' wills being, *inter alia*, claimed. The contention was boldly put forward that, even in spiritual matters, the jurisdiction of the diocesan was only 'in defect of the chancellor,' or by way of appeal in the last resort (*in defectu cancellarii et universitatis*). In a provincial synod, Oliver's episcopal brethren, with their metropolitan, were induced to side with the university against his lordship of Lincoln. In future, an appeal was to run from the chancellor's court to the regent congregation; thence, finally, to the great congregation.

In 1350, an application to the pope resulted in the reduction to a mere formality of the episcopal confirmation of the Oxford chancellor, and, in 1368, its necessity was, by the same authority, entirely abrogated. In 1395, a bull of Boniface IX exempted the university from the jurisdiction of all archbishops, bishops and ordinaries, and, when, in 1411, archbishop Arundel, in pursuit of his anti-Lollard crusade, attempted a visitation of Oxford, St Mary's was fortified against him, and swarms of armed scholars compelled his retreat. In this instance, the university acted with more legality than discretion. The king took up the cause of his offended kinsman; the chancellor and proctors were summoned to London and compelled to resign; and, when the university decreed a cessation and boldly re-elected the deposed officers, pope John XXIII ruined the defences of the scholars by revoking the bull of Boniface. Parliament confirmed their defeat by a declaration of the archbishop's right of visitation. It was not until 1479, after the extirpation of Lollardism, that, by means of a bull of Sixtus IV, the university recovered the lost ground. Meanwhile, the scholars had learned a lesson in policy; the chancellorship was erected into a permanent office and conferred upon a powerful court prelate or noble; a vice-chancellor annually nominated by the chancellor assumed the functions of the resident head.

The peace of both universities was, from time to time, disturbed by serious domestic broils. Irish students raised commotions; the struggles of north and south well-nigh assumed the proportions of petty civil wars, and called for the interference of the king. Disputes, more interesting from the educational standpoint, were excited by the presence of monks and friars. When the successive barbarian irruptions burst upon western Europe, learning had taken refuge in the monasteries. It might have been anticipated that, on the return of brighter days, scholarship would emerge with the Benedictines. Within limits this, indeed, had been the case. The Benedictines never lost their love of letters, and their schools were long and deservedly in high repute. The Benedictine monasteries and the episcopal schools together preserved the useful arts of writing, illuminating and music, and in the Latin tongue held the avenue to ancient stores of knowledge. But the Benedictine scheme of education was directed exclusively to the requirements of the religious life. The Benedictines had their schools in Oxford and Cambridge before the rise of the two universities; but it was not until after the coming of the mendicants[1] that they were roused to play an active part in English university life.

In 1217, within two years after the foundation of their order, the Dominicans planted a settlement in Paris; in 1221 they invaded Oxford; and in 1274 they were in Cambridge. They were followed at Oxford in 1224 by the Franciscans, who, at the same time, appeared in Cambridge. Entering in the guise of mendicants, they speedily became possessed of valuable property, and, within fifty years of their first appearance, their magnificent buildings were the envy of the scholars of both universities. Carmelites, Augustinians and White Canons imitated the example of the Black and the Grey Friars, and their convents lined the streets of the two university towns. Franciscans and Dominicans alike flung themselves with enthusiasm into university life.

In the first quarter of the twelfth century Irnerius, the father

---

[1] Already, in 1278, the Benedictine priory of Durham had begun to despatch clerks to study in Oxford; and, before the end of the thirteenth century, the site of Durham Hall was acquired. The Benedictines of St Peter's at Gloucester established in 1283 at Oxford a Hall for the accommodation of thirteen students of their order; and, eight years later, the numbers of the students of Gloucester Hall were increased by a combined effort of other southern Benedictine convents. In 1334, a Bull of Benedict XII required that each Benedictine society should send up one monk in twenty with a fixed allowance to pursue higher studies in some university.

of the glossators, had laid the foundations of the fame of Bologna as a school of civil law. Accursius had emulated him at Florence. Vacarius, attempting to follow the example at Oxford, was, thanks to the jealousy of the canonists, silenced by Stephen. In 1144, the Benedictine Gratian published at Rome the famous *Decretum*, in which he provided the students of canon law with a *Corpus Juris* worthy to rank with the *Pandects* of Justinian. At Oxford, the opposition of the canonists to the civil law was soon exchanged for ardent pursuit, and doctors graduated as *utriusque juris*.

Meanwhile (*c.* 1160) Peter Lombard, archbishop of Paris, attempted to render to theologians the service which Gratian had rendered to the canonists. Applying to such subjects as the Trinity, free will, original sin, the sacraments, the resurrection of the dead and final judgment, the methods of a strict dialectic, he developed a scientific theological system. His *Sententiae* became the standard theological text-book of the Middle Ages. The mendicants, invading the seats of Parisian teachers, endeavoured to ally with Christian doctrine an Aristotelian philosophy which had trickled through the schools of Jews and Saracens. They thus became the leading exponents of scholasticism.

At Oxford, the Franciscans Duns Scotus and William of Ockham emulated the fame won for the Dominicans at Paris by Albertus Magnus and Thomas Aquinas. Grosseteste, before his elevation to high office, lectured in the Oxonian Franciscan school, where he had as pupil Adam Marsh, destined to be Hugo de Balsham's competitor for the see of Ely. Friar Bungay became head of the Franciscan convent in Cambridge, where Humphry Necton, a Carmelite, took the D.D. degree in 1259. The glory of the Grey Friars culminated in Roger Bacon (*c.* 1214—94). Skilled in all the recognised studies of his age, he, in opposition to prevailing ideas, though remaining a schoolman, pointed to the study of languages and mathematics as affording the true basis for a sound system of education, and incurred amongst his contemporaries and succeeding generations the lasting suspicion of tampering with the illegitimate by leading the way in the pursuit of natural science.

As a rule, the schoolmen did not amass knowledge, but trained ability ; the real value of their discussions lay in their development of the art of expression, in the fostering of agility of thought and subtle distinction : in a word, in the development of pure dialectical skill. Logic was their contribution to the world's future. Chaucer's Clerk of Oxenford had 'unto logik longe y-go.'

It was not their studies but their ambition which lost to the mendicants the favour of the medieval universities. Starting as assailants of the abuses of the older orders, within a very few years they furnished to the world a still more striking spectacle of moral degradation ; and the barefooted friars rivalled the Cistercians as pure epicureans.

> I fond there freres, Alle the foure ordres
> Prechynge the peple, For profit of hemselves;
> Glosed the gospel, As hem good liked;
> For coveitise of copes, Construwed it as thei wolde.

So Piers the Plowman, voicing the experience of the nation at large. In the universities, whilst claiming the rights, the friars strove to shirk the duties, of the non-professed scholar. 'It was their object to create an *imperium in imperio*, and, while availing themselves of these centres as fields of propagandism, they were really intent on the creation of a rival if not of a hostile authority.' A fierce struggle ensued. Already, in 1300, the chancellor of Cambridge, Stephen de Haselfield, as the outcome of a brawl, excommunicated the friars, two of whom were expelled from the university. On an appeal to the pope, the friars secured the honours of the field ; but the university authorities returned to the fray. In 1336, a university statute forbade the friars to admit into their orders any scholar under 18. Two years later, a similar statute was passed in Oxford. In 1359, the Cambridge houses enacted that two members of the same convent of mendicants should not incept in the same year. An appeal to parliament went in their favour, and, in 1365, the friars actually obtained a papal bull dispensing, in their case, with the statutory requirement of actual regency in arts before the assumption of the degree of D.D. The mendicants in both universities had outstayed their welcome a full century before Chaucer launched at them the shafts of his humour, the Piers Plowman poems lashed them with invective, or Wyclif, himself a distinguished schoolman, poured forth on them the vials of his vituperation. In the foundations of both Walter de Merton and Hugo de Balsham, admission into a religious order was expressly declared incompatible with membership of a college society. With these two names and with the rise of colleges we reach a new stage in English university history.

How was the throng of medieval scholars maintained ? Many of the students could and did support themselves. The lecturers were for generations maintained by the *collectae* of their auditors. The fees levied for graces, the dues collected from the principals of halls and keepers of acts and various academic contributions and fines, all predicate a paying *clientèle*. Not infrequently, as it would seem, a wealthy scholar defrayed the charges of a more needy companion. When the colleges began to admit pensioners, these paid highly for their accommodation, and in proportion to their rank. Henry Beaufort at Peterhouse, in 1388—9, paid the sum of twenty shillings as *pensio camerae*, while a humbler contemporary paid 6*s*. 8*d*. There were scholars in both universities who ruffled it after the manner of courtiers; who affected lovelocks, red hosen and long shoes; who wore rings 'for vain glorying and jettyng, pernicious example and scandal of others'; and otherwise in their attire came within the compass of the sumptuary provincial constitution issued by archbishop Stratford in 1342. But Chaucer's typical clerk was of another mould. The bulk of the students who thronged the streets of the medieval university were, undoubtedly, poor. Many were reduced to strange shifts for daily bread. The bursar's accounts of Peterhouse in the early fifteenth century show poor scholars engaged in digging the foundations of buildings, in carrying earth and bricks and in other unskilled labour. The sizars of the following and many succeeding centuries were regularly employed in menial tasks. Favourite medieval stories introduce us to poor students begging on the highways or singing from door to door. The relief of such was always ranked as a peculiarly meritorious field for medieval philanthropy. Noble personages and prelates supported poor scholars in the universities. Edward II maintained 32 boys under their master at Cambridge; and his example was followed by his successor, who erected for his pensioners a special hall of residence, the King's Hall. Wealthy religious houses defrayed the charges of selected students of their orders. Benefactors, even before the college era, endowed loan-chests from which temporary advances could be made on security to hard-pressed scholars. Yet more deserving of university gratitude were the founders of 'exhibitions.'

William de Kilkenny, ninth bishop of Ely, dying in 1256—7, bequeathed 200 marks to the priory of Barnwell in trust for the payment of 10 marks annually to two priests studying divinity in Cambridge. This was the earliest foundation of the type in the junior university. William of Durham, archbishop-elect of Rouen, had, seven years earlier, bequeathed to the university of Oxford 310 marks, to be invested for the maintenance of ten or more masters of arts studying theology.

An all-important step forward was taken by Walter de Merton.

Scholars not belonging to any religious order had hitherto, necessarily, either lodged with townsmen or in some specially hired hostel or inn. Of these last, there were many in both universities. Fuller records the names of thirty-four in Cambridge, several of which were still standing in his day, although with an altered character. Oxford claims a far larger number. These halls were managed by principals recognised by, and usually, though not necessarily, masters of, the university. Some of them were connected with special faculties, as law, divinity, or the arts. But they were mere residential inns, neither chartered nor endowed.

In 1263 or 1264, Walter de Merton founded 'the House of the Scholars of Merton' at Malden, in Surrey, linking it with a company of scholars resident in Oxford, and there supported on the produce of the Malden estate. A few years later, the warden was transferred from Malden to the direct charge of the Oxford group, and, in 1274, under revised statutes, the college of Merton started on its long and brilliant history as a permanently settled, chartered and endowed foundation.

In 1280, Hugo de Balsham, tenth bishop of Ely, imitated in Cambridge the example of Walter de Merton by planting a settlement of 'studious scholars' among the brethren of the hospital of St John; in 1284, the severance of the scholars from the brethren gave rise to the establishment of Peterhouse, the oldest of Cambridge colleges.

The college, it must be noted, was something more than a hall. In the hall, with its officially fixed rental, students of all degrees found some protection against the arbitrary exactions of the townsmen. They were subjected to certain disciplinary regulations. They paid for their accommodation. The college, on the other hand, was, in origin, the endowed home of a limited number of students of a particular class. Further, the college was not a monastery. It had a rule, which borrowed something from the principles which experience had approved in the orders; but it was not monastic. On the contrary, it was anti-monastic: the scholars of Walter de Merton and Hugo de Balsham were directly prepared for service in the world as men of affairs. Finally, the college was not, in the first instance, a profit-making school. Its doors were not open to all seekers after knowledge. Its scholars were members of a close corporation, living on a common stock, men of approved ability pursuing advanced studies under discipline. The disturbing guest and the would-be *perendinant* were, alike, repelled.

This conception comes out clearly in the statutes of Merton

and in the earliest Peterhouse statutes, which were avowedly based upon the Merton rule. The Peterhouse society was to consist of fifteen scholars, one of whom was, as the master, to be the business head. A candidate for a vacancy in the body must be *vir honestus, castus, pacificus, humilis et modestus (quatenus humana fragilitas nostra sinit) et indigens, ac in arte dialectica Baccalaureus.* The field of study for the scholars was determined as including the arts, the philosophy of Aristotle and theology. The majority of the scholars must always be engaged in the diligent pursuit of the liberal arts ; only with the express sanction of the whole body were certain designated fellows to proceed to the reading of theology. Two, but not more at the same time, might study the canon or the civil law, one, the medical art. Each fellow must follow a regular academic course, must prepare himself by hearing lectures, reading and discussion, for a career of activity. The aim of the founder was not the endowment of a life of learned ease ; his revenues were intended, it was clearly stated, for scholars *actualiter studentes et proficere volentes.*

The college conception took rapid root. Before the year 1400, there had arisen in Cambridge six of the present colleges, with Michaelhouse (1324) and King's Hall (1332), which, later, were absorbed in Henry VIII's stately foundation, Trinity ; in Oxford, the college of Merton had rivals in six of the existing colleges, besides Gloucester Hall (now Worcester), which was erected by the aroused Benedictines for students selected by their order, and the dissolved Canterbury Hall.

The foundation of several of these societies is directly traceable to the Black Death (1349). Oxford was half-depopulated, whether by the actual ravages of the plague or by the flight of the students. Cambridge, likewise, suffered terribly. Vast numbers of the country clergy were swept off. It was, partly, at least, with a view to recruiting the depleted ranks of his diocesan staff with well-equipped scholars that bishop Bateman founded Trinity Hall, Cambridge (1350), as a college of canonists and civilians, and, in a more catholic spirit, completed the labours of Edmund Gonville on a neighbouring site. About the same time and, seemingly, in the same spirit, Elizabeth de Burgh, countess of Clare, enlarged the earlier establishment (1326) of University Hall, and the guild brothers of Corpus Christi founded Bene't or Corpus Christi College (1352). The generous founder of New College, Oxford, referred to the repairs of the devastation wrought by the plague as one of his inciting motives.

The attention of the pious benefactor, who, in centuries past, would have endowed a convent, was now drawn rather to the university, and that with the direct encouragement of at least the secular clergy. So Mary de St Paul founded in Cambridge, in 1347, the college of Mary de Valentia, commonly called Pembroke Hall; and Exeter, Oriel and Queen's arose in Oxford beside the first period group, composed of Merton, University and Balliol.

The statutes of these various societies set out particular objects, and differed, accordingly, in minor detail; but, in all cases, the main purpose was the same, and there was no vastly significant departure from the primitive model.

The old hostels had sheltered, and continued for some time to send forth, famous men; but Oxford and Cambridge scholarship associated itself rapidly with the newer colleges. Merton claims, not only Duns Scotus and William of Ockham, who were drawn away by the friars, but also Richard FitzRalph and bishop Bradwardine, the latter of whom is ranked by Chaucer with Augustine and Boethius. Wyclif is variously connected with Merton, Balliol and Canterbury Hall. The great clerical statesmen of fourteenth and fifteenth century England can be mostly identified with the universities and with colleges. If William of Wykeham was no trained scholar, and John Alcock was, possibly, nurtured in a hostel, no men were more alive than they to the advantages of college life. Henry Beaufort studied both at Peterhouse and in Oxford. William Waynflete, who was master of Wykeham's school at Winchester, provost of Henry VI's foundation at Eton and Beaufort's successor as bishop, was, if not himself an Oxonian, destined to rival both his distinguished patrons, episcopal and royal, by his fine college of Magdalen.

In the first instance, the college was but the chartered and endowed house of a small society of *scolares* or *socii*, pursuing advanced studies in a large university. Walter de Merton, indeed, from the very first, provided for certain *parvuli*, seemingly his kinsmen, who, under the care of a grammar master, were to be prepared for entry on a course in arts; in most, if not in all, of the early foundations the door was opened to poor students, who, in return for menial services, were supported on the superabundance of the victuals furnished by the founder's bounty, and assisted in the pursuit of learning. But neither Walter de Merton nor Hugo de Balsham can be supposed to have contemplated the extension which was, ere long, given to the initial conception of the college by the admission, in constantly increasing numbers, of the class of undergraduate pensioners. Still less can they have looked forward to the day when colleges should dominate the university.

Development is, however, the necessary condition of all true life. Already, before the end of the fourteenth century, many of the old inns had become annexed to colleges. It was then decreed that no scholar should henceforth presume, on pain of expulsion, to dwell elsewhere in the university town than in a hall or hostel. This meant the disappearance of unattached students. By the middle of the fifteenth century, the system of admitting *commensals* had become established alike in the poorer and in the more wealthy foundations ; and, when that step was reached, the English universities were on their way to that strange confusion and distinction of college and university which is the puzzle of the continental observer.

To William of Wykeham is due a fresh extension of the educational conception of both university and college.

Throughout England, in all the chief towns, were to be found grammar schools, attached to convent or to cathedral, where boys were instructed in the rudiments of learning. Many of these schools were, probably, established in and around Oxford and Cambridge. In Cambridge, the local schools seem, as was noted above, to have been under the rule of a *Magister Glomeriae*, who, as a nominee of the archdeacon, attempted, for a time, to hold his own against the chancellor. The pupils of the grammar master were mere children. While still juveniles, they were wont to secure admission to the university.

William of Wykeham, bishop of Winchester, the favoured chancellor of Edward III, whose personal literary acquirements papal supporters and the holy father himself had not hesitated to call in question, was inspired to establish in Oxford a college which should outrival the most splendid foundation of the university of Paris. In 1379, he obtained a royal licence for the execution of his project; and, in 1386, after some years of building, the warden and society entered into possession of the magnificent erection of ' Seint Marie College of Wynchester in Oxenford.'

The 'New College' was conceived on grand lines, alike in its architecture and in the numbers and life of its students. It combined the features of a society of learning with those of a collegiate church. A warden and seventy 'poor indigent scholars, clerks' composed the academic society, and were assigned to the usual studies of philosophy, theology and canon and civil law, with a slight intermixture of medicine and astronomy. Ten priests, three stipendiary clerks and sixteen choristers were designated for the conduct of Divine service in the chapel, which was a conspicuous feature of Wykeham's design. All members of the society were to proceed to priest's orders within a limited time. The allowances for the maintenance of the scholars and the upkeep of the college were fixed upon a most generous scale.

Had William of Wykeham proceeded no further, he would have enhanced that reputation as an architect which had won him royal approval and consequent wealth, and would have gained the name of a munificent patron of letters and of Oxford. He took, however, the forward step which marks the man of genius. He conceived the idea of linking his college with a particular preparatory institution, and, by the creation of 'Seint Marie College at Winchester,' became the founder of the first great English public school.

The school, already in existence in 1373, but settled, finally, in buildings erected between 1387 and 1393, reproduced the features of Wykeham's college. There were the warden and the seventy poor scholars, and there were the ten priest fellows, three priest chaplains, three clerks and sixteen choristers. But, whereas the instruction of the junior members of the society was, at New College, entrusted to specially salaried senior fellows, the teaching of the scholars of Winchester was assigned to a school master and an under-master or usher. And the studies of Winchester were confined to grammar alone. From the ranks of the Winchester scholars were to be filled up vacancies in the numbers of the scholars of New College as they occurred, each nominated scholar passing a two years' probation in the university before his final admission.

It was as a direct imitator of Wykeham and copier of his statutes that Henry VI, in 1440—1, founded the allied institutions of King's College, Cambridge, and 'the College Roiall of oure Ladie of Eton beside Windesor.' Half the fellows and scholars of Winchester were transferred to Eton to constitute the nucleus of the royal school, of which William Waynflete, the Winchester school master, became an early provost. The royal school at Eton, rising under the shadow of the palace of Windsor and under the eye of the court, became, henceforth, the school *par excellence* of the sons and descendants of the English nobility. Whilst it owed much to the collegers who passed from its foundation to the ranks of the fellows of King's, it owed still more in fame to the wealthy oppidans, who crowded to share in its teaching. It is not the least among the legacies of great men to the future that they excite emulation. William Waynflete became the founder of Magdalen (1448); archbishop Chicheley, a Wykehamist, founded All Souls (1438).

In Cambridge, queen Margaret was stirred up by the labours of her husband to lay the foundations of Queens' College (1448), where her good work was preserved and completed by Elizabeth Woodville (1465). Robert Woodlarke, third provost of King's College and chancellor of the university, founded St Catharine's (1473). John Alcock, bishop of Ely, who resembled Wykeham in being at once skilled architect and prominent statesman, erected Jesus College round the chapel of the dissolved priory of St Radegund (1496). In Oxford, Richard Fleming, bishop of Lincoln, having repented the Wyclifite errors of his youth, endowed Lincoln College as a special bulwark against heresy in his diocese (1429). When Thomas Wolsey, papal legate and archbishop, suppressed monasteries in order to rival with his linked foundations of Cardinal College and Ipswich the creations of Wykeham and Henry VI, men might have foretold the coming of a peaceful church reform. Kings, noble dames and princes of the blood now contended with prelates and grateful scholars in college building. At Cambridge the Lady Margaret, countess of Richmond and Derby, mother of Henry VII, claimed the honours of foundress, not only of Christ's College (1505), in which was merged Henry VI's grammar foundation of God's House (1439), but of the larger college of St John (1511). Thomas Lord Audley, chancellor of England, under licence obtained from Henry VIII, completed, under the name of Magdalene, the college of which the erection and endowment were begun by the unfortunate Edward Stafford, duke of Buckingham. It remained for Henry VIII himself to combine Michaelhouse, Edward III's foundation of King's Hall and an unendowed hostel in the magnificent college of Trinity (1546). In the same England in which the supporters of rival houses were wreaking mutual destruction on the battle-fields of the Roses, men were thus actively engaged in building colleges. It was fitting that in the monarch who united the contending claims, and in his son, should be found active patrons of the learning of the renascence.

What, we next ask, were the subjects and the courses of medieval academic study?

The early education of the generality of English youths in the Middle Ages was found in a school attached to some cathedral or convent. In the old grammar schools, reading, writing and elementary Latin constituted, with singing, the subjects of instruction. The 'litel clergeon, seven yeer of age' of *The Prioress's Tale* learned in school 'to singen and to rede, as smale children doon in hir childhede.' He had his primer. A school-fellow translated and expounded for the enquiring child the *Alma redemptoris* from the antiphoner of an older class. The prioress, doubtless, here indicates the teaching of the conventual schools of her day. Through *Ave Maria* and *Psalms*, learned by rote, the boy passed to the rudiments of grammar, with Donatus and Alexander de Villa Dei as guides, and Terence and Ovid as providers of classic texts. Latin was the living language of all abodes of learning, and to its acquisition, as such, were mainly directed the efforts of all the old grammar schools. The same course was pursued at Winchester and Eton. In the days of Elizabeth, boys at the public schools were 'well entered in the knowledge of the Latin and Greek tongues and rules of versifying.' But, for William of Wykeham and Henry VI, Greek was not as yet. William Paston, in 1467, desiring to quit Eton, 'lacked nothing but versifying,' and endeavoured to convince his brother of his acquirements by some lame Latin lines. A little more skill in such versifying, some knowledge of Terence, of Ovid and of Cicero's letters, with the confidence derived from constant exercise in Latin conversation, were the equipment with which his best furnished contemporaries went up to the discussions of the university. The nature of the studies which the young aspirants would, thenceforward, pursue may be gathered from the oldest extant university statutes.

The studies of the medieval university were based upon the *trivium* and *quadrivium*. Martianus Capella, a Carthaginian, in an allegory *de Nuptiis Philologiae et Mercurii*, written about 420 A.D., introduces us, with the persons and descriptions of the attendants of the earth-born bride of the god, to the seven liberal arts. Three of these, grammar, logic and rhetoric, constituted the *trivium*; which formed the course of study of the medieval undergraduate. The bachelor passed on to the *quadrivium*—arithmetic, geometry, music and astronomy—his conquest of which was denoted by the licence or degree of master of arts. To these seven arts, the thirteenth century added the three philosophies—natural, moral and metaphysical.

An Oxford scheme of study of 1426 demands: one year's

reading of grammar, with Priscian as text-book; next, three terms' study of rhetoric, with Aristotle, Boethius and Tully as teachers, reinforced by Ovid and Vergil; finally, three terms' reading of logic with Boethius and Aristotle, *Topica* and *Priora* being expressly enjoined. Of the subjects of the *quadrivium*, arithmetic and music require each a year, while geometry and astronomy call each for two. The three philosophies need each three terms. Some of these courses were, seemingly, concurrent, the entire arts curriculum covering, in general, eight years of three terms each. The Cambridge requirements were, evidently, much the same. Sir Robert Rede, in 1518, bequeathed £12 per annum for the payment of three lecturers in logic, rhetoric and philosophy. Of these three, one, whose style as *lector Terentii* reveals his function, was assigned, by statute, to lecture to students of the first and second year on 'books of humanity'; the second lecturer read logic to third year undergraduates; the third lectured to fourth year students and bachelors of arts on books of philosophy.

The educational methods pursued differed in no small degree from those at present in use. Of written examinations, the medieval student knew nothing; his progress was secured by compulsory reading of set books and enforced attendance on assigned lectures; by frequent 'posing' and debate; and, lastly, by the necessity of himself delivering lectures after attaining the baccalaureate. He might, indeed, content himself with 'inception in grammar,' when, on the strength of the delivery of certain discourses on Priscian and of the certificate of three posing masters of his minor art, he passed forth qualified to teach in an elementary school; but, if his ambition soared to higher flights, he might assume obligations to his university which represented labour continued during upwards of twenty years.

The complete arts course was, in general, the necessary prerequisite to the study of theology; but students possessed of the needful permission might pass directly from the *trivium* to the pursuit of civil, and then of canon, law. In Oxford, as in Paris, regents in arts asserted a claim to pre-eminence in the direction of university reading. In 1252, it was enacted that no scholar should receive the licence in theology, who had not previously been regent in arts.

The Cambridge *Statuta Antiqua* set out regulations which were in force about 1400 A.D. The five stages of the arts' student's career, therein indicated, were successively represented by: *admission to the question,* by which, in his fifth year at earliest, after previous attendance at scholastic discussion, he was introduced for formal university testing; *determination,* a far more serious ordeal, involving an active share in a long series of public disputations and the duty of summing up in approved fashion the results of debate; *cursory lecturing* on the *Posteriora*; *inception,* whereby the scholar acquired the licence of master and was regularly authorised to teach; and, lastly, *regency,* a period of active lecturing *ordinarie,* as officially appointed instructor, and of enforced attendance upon various public gatherings for university business and ceremonial.

No scholar might incept in arts in Cambridge in the fifteenth century unless : he had previously *determined*; had, for three years at least, continuously resided and studied in his proper faculty; had attended during three years the lectures of his own master on Aristotle's philosophy, together with any such mathematical lectures as might be given in the schools; had publicly opposed and responded in his faculty in due form in the schools; and, finally, unless he was provided with certificates *de scientia* from five, and *de credulitate vel scientia* from other seven, masters of arts.

Should he proceed, as, if ambitious of promotion, he must, to the study of theology, of law or of medicine, the master of arts must pass afresh through certain clearly defined stages :

None shall be admitted to incept in theology, unless he shall have previously been regent in arts; unless, also, he shall have heard theological lectures for at least ten years in a university; *item,* he shall have heard lectures on the Bible *biblice* for two years before he incepts; he shall have lectured on or in some canonical book of the Bible for a year, for at least ten days in each term; nor shall it be permitted to any to 'enter' the Bible before the second year after the completion of his lectures on the *Sentences*; and he shall have read all the books of the *Sentences* in that University, and shall have remained at least three years in an approved University, after the lecturing on the *Sentences,* before he shall be licensed. Furthermore, he shall have preached publicly *ad clerum* and shall have publicly in all the schools of his faculty opposed and responded after lecturing upon the *Sentences,* in such sort that he may be in very deed of known and approved progress, manners and learning according to the attestation *de scientia* by all the masters of that faculty in the manner aforesaid; and, finally, he shall be admitted when he has sworn that he has completed this set of requirements[1].

Similar detailed provisions guarded the doctorates of canon law, civil law and of medicine. The 'grace,' which, in later times,

---

[1] *Statuta Antiqua,* 124; *Camb. Doc.* I, 377.

became the necessary formality for proceeding to a degree, was, in origin, a *privilegium* of the masters dispensing with some special requirement in a particular case[1].

A comparison of the statutory requirements of the university with the contents of a medieval college library would appear to furnish a sufficient basis for judgment as to the extent of the studies indicated.

Peterhouse is fortunate in still possessing, not only a library catalogue of 1418, but the majority of the volumes therein described. It is clear from its arrangement that, unlike the noble collection vainly bequeathed by Richard of Bury to the Benedictine house of Durham in Oxford, and the great library of duke Humphrey of Gloucester, it was a working library. Making allowances for entries on the roll inserted at a somewhat later date, the collection of 1418 contains over 300 volumes. These are divided into two classes, as being either 'chained in the library' or 'distributed amongst the fellows.' They are further arranged under subject-headings as representing theology, natural philosophy, metaphysics, moral philosophy, astronomy, 'Alkenemie,' 'Arsmetrice' (arithmetic), music, geometry, rhetoric, logic, grammar, poetry, chronicles, medicine, civil law and canon law. Theological works occupy the largest space. Canon law and civil law in combination slightly exceed the three philosophies. Of medical chained books there are fifteen; but, amongst the fellows, for regular reading, logic, poetry and grammar are in greater request. Astronomy is studied; though it is in the chained library where Ptolemy reigns among a company of Arabians and their Jewish translators, together with Bacon *De multiplicatione specierum cum perspectiva ejusdem* and half a dozen recent table-makers, closing with John Holbroke, who was elected master of the college in the same year. Of the other subjects of the *quadrivium*, music, arithmetic and geometry are, under their several proper headings, denoted each by a single tome. A second copy of Euclid, indeed, elsewhere appears, bound up with astronomical works, as do two other treatises on geometry; and there are two copies of the *Arithmetica* of Boethius; but the weakness of the mathematical element is very marked, as compared with the overwhelming force of the philosophy of Aristotle.

---

[1] Friars, being prohibited by the rules of their orders from graduation in secular branches of knowledge, required a dispensation to graduate in theology. The stringent enforcement against them of university regulations provoked heated altercation and, as already seen, led to parliamentary and papal interference: *ante*, p. 351; Rashdall, II, 379.

It is to be remembered that the fellows of Peterhouse were at least bachelors of arts, whose main studies would be concerned with cursory lecturing on *Posteriora*. Of thirteen works on logic, which the library of 1418 contains, we find, accordingly, eight distributed amongst the society. The eight consist entirely of texts of Aristotle, including *Posteriora*, *Priora, Topica* and *Elenchi*, with texts of Porphyry, various commentaries and collections of questions on both Aristotle and Porphyry and the *Sophismata* of William of Heytesbury (fellow of Merton, 1330; chancellor of Oxford, 1371). In the chained library, Boethius joins Porphyry and Aristotle, together with the *Philosophia* of the great Albert, the *Summa* of Ockham and commentaries of Kilwardby and St Thomas. A later fifteenth century hand added to the catalogue the *Summa* of Peter Hispanus and the *Quaestiones* of William Brito (*ob.* 1356). Under the several headings of natural philosophy, moral philosophy and metaphysic, the catalogue of 1418 records no fewer than eighteen volumes of Aristotelian texts, together with commentaries by Averroes, Aquinas, Egidius Romanus (*ob.* 1316), Walter Burley (*ob.* 1345), Durandus and Peter de Alvernia, and the *Summa* of John Dumbleton (fellow of Queen's, Oxford, 1341). Under the same class heading Palladius and Columella introduce agriculture and veterinary medicine; Seneca and Pliny instruct *De Animalibus*; and Capella and Isidore range through all fields in dictionary fashion.

In the lower educational stages of the *trivium* we find, for grammar, authorities in time-honoured Priscian, as edited by Kilwardby, in the *Dictionary* of Hugucio (bishop of Ferrara, *ob.* 1213), the *Catholicon* of friar John de Janua, the *Summa de expositione verborum Bibliae* of William Brito, Bacon *De Grammatica* and the inevitable *Doctrinale Puerorum* of Alexander. In rhetoric, Cassiodorus and Tully are supported by Guido delle Colonne's *History of the Trojan War, Pharaoh's Dream* by John Lemouicensis, and *Practica sive Usus Dictaminis*, a 'Complete Letter Writer[1]' by one Master Laurence Aquilegiensis.

The civilians were, in view of statutory requirements, necessarily provided with all the books of the *corpus juris*. They were furnished, also, with *glosses* of Accursius and comments of Bartholus, Odofredus and Peter de Bella Pertica (*ob.* 1308). The favourite text-writers were, however, Cinus of Pistoia (*ob.*

[1] M. R. James, *Peterhouse MSS.*

1336) and Azo (*ob*. 1200), 'the light of the lawyers,' whom Bologna was constrained to recall from Montpellier. Of *Cynus super Codicem*, as of *Parvum Volumen* (*e.g.* the *Institutes* and *Novellae*), *Digestum Vetus, Digestum Inforciatum, Digestum Novum* and of *Codex*, there were three copies, two of each being distributed to fellows, who borrowed also the *Summa* and *Brocardica Azonis*. For canonists, with the necessary texts of decrees, decretals, *Liber Sextus*, 'Extravagants' and Clementines, there were commentaries of Paulus, of Joannes Andreae (*ob*. 1348), of William de Monte Lauduns (*c*. 1346), of William de Mandagoto and of Henry of Susa, cardinal of Ostia (*ob*. 1271). As English clerks, the Peterhouse fellows had, doubtless, frequent recourse to their several copies of the *Constitutions* of Otho and Ottobon, and, it may be surmised, to *Liber taxarum omnium beneficiorum Angliae*, which lay in the chained library. But their regularly used manuals of canon law were, clearly, the famous *Summa Ostiensis*, which appears in both sections of the library; the similarly honoured *Rosarium* of archdeacon Guido de Baysio, which recalls the Bologna school of 1300; and the ever popular *Speculum Juris*, or *Speculum Judiciale*, of William Durand (*ob*. 1296) to whom Boniface VIII vainly offered the archbishopric of Ravenna. Two copies of *Speculum*, with the like number of texts of decretals, *Liber Sextus* and Clementines, are lent out to fellows, while another copy of each remains in the chained library. The law fellowships of Peterhouse were, evidently, full, the statutes permitting, as has been noted, to not more than two contemporary fellows, the study of canon, or civil, law.

The one fellow allowed by statute to adopt the medical art was pursuing in 1418 the regular university course: he had borrowed Macer, *De virtutibus herbarum*, and the prescribed texts of 'Johannicius' and of 'Isaac.' Chaucer recites the qualifications of his Doctor of Phisyk:

> Well knew he the olde Esculapius
> And Deiscorides, and eek Rufus,
> Old Ypocras, Haly and Galien;
> Serapion, Razis and Avicen;
> Averrois, Damascien and Constantyn;
> Bernard, and Gatesden, and Gilbertyn.

The Peterhouse chained library of 1418 held but thirteen volumes of medicine; but a brief examination of the contents of its shelves enables us to identify at least ten of Chaucer's classical authorities. The ruler of the medieval medical school was, undoubtedly, Galen, whose commentaries upon Hippocrates must be twice heard in lecture by the Cambridge would-be medical inceptor. Other prescribed books were the *Breviary* of Constantine, commonly known as *Viaticus*, the *Isagoge* of Johannicius, a general introduction to physic, the *Antidotarium* of Nicholaus, Theophilus *De Urinis* and the works of Isaac, a high authority on dietary and fevers. Amongst additional authors represented on the Peterhouse shelves, a notable place was claimed by Gerard of Cremona, an indefatigable translator, and by Richard, the Englishman, who is identifiable with Richard of Wendover (*ob.* 1252), canon of St Paul's, the compiler of an encyclopaedic treatise covering the entire field of Medicine. It is no hard task to detect the *fontes* of medieval medical knowledge. Isaac, a Peterhouse librarian scribe informs us, *fuit araabs nacione.* Gerard of Cremona translates one book of Galen in Toledo from the Arabic into Latin ; another is introduced as *ad tutyrum translato johannici filii ysaac de greco in arabicum et a marcho toletano de arabico in latinum.* Medicine, with astronomy, passed to western Europe through the hands of the Arabian and the Jew.

And what, finally, of theology, the crowning study of the medieval university ? There, indeed, the Latin held his own. In the Peterhouse chained library of 1418 an imperfect Chrysostom practically monopolises the representation of the eastern church, with Cyprian as spokesman for the African. A magnificent Latin Bible, the gift of archbishop Whittlesea, is flanked by a host of patristic writers of the western church. Augustine, Ambrose and Jerome are followed by Gregory and Isidore, by Bernard and Anselm, by Stephen Langton, Lyra and Hugo de St Victor. There are the inevitable sermons standing behind great names. There is, too, the *Historia Scholastica* of Peter Comestor, *Magister Historiarum.* But in the list of books distributed amongst the fellows the true character of the theological studies of the university comes out. With four more Bibles, one being specially assigned for daily reading in hall, a glossed *Gospel of St John,* a brief tractate on the epistles of St Paul, two or three books clearly designed for private meditation and Grosseteste, *De Oculo Morali,* there are two additional copies of *Magister Historiarum,* six Psalters, four Latin, one Hebrew and Latin and one Hebrew and no fewer than nine copies of the Master of the Sentences, reinforced by the *Summa* of Thomas Aquinas, the *Quaestiones* of his opponent Henry of Ghent (*ob.* 1293) and

John Bokyngham *Super Sententias.* The ancient fathers of the church here appear only in the shape of extracts in the much used *Pharetra,* a medieval *Familiar Quotations.* The working theology of fifteenth century Peterhouse was the theology of Peter Lombard.

The education offered to the young scholar in the Middle Ages was, essentially, utilitarian; he was trained for service in public functions. A few rules of grammatical expression; some elementary calculations; geometry, consisting mainly of ill-informed geography; music sufficient to qualify for the singing of a mass; and Ptolemaic astronomy, directing to the correct determination of Easter—these, with much skill in argument derived from long exercise in the use of dialectic forms, constituted the ripe fruit of the course in *trivium* and *quadrivium.* The disputants in the schools wasted their energy in a barren philosophy. The few followers of Roger Bacon in the domain of a progressive natural science, more than suspected of alliance with the Saracen and the Evil One, could find legitimate scope for their research only within the confines of a crude medical science which combined the simples of the herb wife with a barbarous surgery. Unless caught in the scholastic net of metaphysics, the medieval student could find substantial mental food only in theology or in law. And, in a field where to trip was to be denounced as a heretic, the theology offered was the slavish repetition of received glosses, the killing of the literal sense of Scripture in the drawing out of the so-called allegorical, moral and anagogical meaning, or, at best, the application of syllogistic methods to the *dicta* of ancient fathers.

Of the Humanities as such, the fourteenth century was strangely innocent. The cataloguer of the Peterhouse library of 1418 assigned a special place to chronicles. He placed under this head Cassiodorus, Valerius Maximus and Sallust, with Vegetius, Frontinus, Aimonius of Fleury and the anonymous writer of a treatise *De adventu Normannorum in Angliam et de jure quod habuit Willelmus bastardus ad regnum Angliae.* Quintilian, Macrobius and Seneca he classed as natural philosophers. Poetry he conjoined with grammar; and, with Priscian, Hugucio and Alexander de Villa Dei he ranked Ovid, Statius and Lucan. When, with them, they bring the *Epistles* of Francis Petrarch, we catch the glimmering light before the dawn. Twenty-two years later (1440), Robert Alne lent to his old friend John Ottryngham, master of Michaelhouse, who had been admitted with him as a fellow of Peterhouse on 5 October 1400, a copy of Petrarch's *De Remediis utriusque Fortunae.*

It is scarcely thirty years ago, when all that was taught in the university of Cambridge was Alexander, the Little Logicals (as they call them) and those old exercises out of Aristotle, and *quaestiones* taken from Duns Scotus. As time went on, polite learning was introduced; to this was added a knowledge of mathematics; a new, or at least a regenerated Aristotle sprang up; then came an acquaintance with Greek, and with a host of new authors whose very names had before been unknown, even to their profoundest doctors[1].

So wrote Erasmus in 1516[2].

It was to men well known to Erasmus that the English universities and English schools owed educational reform. Grocyn and Linacre brought Greek to Oxford; but it was John Colet who introduced to that university a sane and natural method of Scripture exposition, and it was John Colet, too, who took Greek to the English public school. In 1510, as dean of St Paul's, he founded a school in the churchyard of his cathedral, where 153 boys, who could already read and write and were of 'good parts and capacities,' should be taught good literature, both Greek and Latin, and be brought up in the knowledge of Christ. 'Lift up your little white hands for me,' he wrote in the preface to the Latin grammar which he composed for the use of his scholars. The petition has the ring of the medieval founder; but with the so-called Lilly's *Grammar* and with Colet's teaching of the catechism, the articles and the ten commandments in the vulgar tongue began the modern period of English middle class education.

Like England, Scotland had long had her monastic schools, whence ambitious students passed to the university of Paris, or joined the *boreales* of Oxford or of Cambridge; but it was not until the beginning of the fifteenth century that the northern kingdom saw the establishment of the first university of its own.

At St Andrews, which was destined, in 1472, to be raised to the dignity of a metropolitan seat, a conventual chapter of Augustinian canons had superseded an earlier society of Culdees. In 1411[3], Henry Wardlaw, a discreet and learned prelate, himself a doctor of canon law, who had been, not without hot contention, raised to the bishopric in 1403, was inspired to found a university in his cathedral city. He was excited thereto, in part, at any rate, by the difficulties experienced by such of the Scottish clergy as

---

[1] Trans. in Mullinger, Vol. I, pp. 515—6.   [2] *Ibid.* p. 516.
[3] The foundation charter is dated 27 February 1411.

were 'desirous of being instructed in theology, in canon and civil law, medicine and the liberal arts' by reason of the 'dangers by sea and land, the wars, captivities and obstructions in passing to and from foreign universities.' That these dangers were no light matter was demonstrated by the conspicuous object lesson of king James I, still in the English captivity, into which he had fallen when on his way to France, as a young prince fresh from the teaching of Wardlaw himself. The good bishop secured the hearty concurrence of his prior, James Haldenstone; and, in 1413, a bull of Benedict XIII, the anti-pope whom Scotland then acknowledged and to whom Wardlaw owed his bishopric, recognised the new foundation as a *studium generale*. The constitution and discipline of the university was determined by the bishop's foundation charter; which, with the charters of the prior and the archdeacons of St Andrews and Lothian, was confirmed by king James in 1432 after his restoration to his kingdom. The founder constituted the bishop of St Andrews for the time being perpetual chancellor of the university and reserved, likewise, the right of final determination of disputes arising between the university and the town, saving the privileges of the prior and chapter and of the archdeacon of St Andrews. The general government of the university was remitted to an elected rector, who must be a graduate in one of the faculties and in holy orders.

The new *studium generale* had, in the first instance, neither special buildings nor endowment. In 1430, Wardlaw granted a tenement for the use of the masters and regents of the faculty of arts; and other well-wishers, in course of time, came forward with similar benefactions; but the teachers of the university were, for a long time, maintained on the fees of their hearers, and on the profits of benefices which they were authorised to hold under a general licence of non-residence. The 'auld pedagogy' was, in fact, an unendowed ecclesiastical seminary, served by beneficed masters, who found their pupils among youths resident or lodging in the town. The institution was much encouraged by James I, who had, during his enforced stay in England, imbibed a taste for literature in general and for poetry in particular. Under the royal charter of confirmation, the resident members of the university were exempted from every species of taxation. As in Oxford and Cambridge, the privileges of scholars were extended to those who served them.

In 1458, bishop James Kennedy, an able and worthy prelate, who was closely connected with the throne, his mother being a daughter of Robert III, enriched the university with its first college, that of St Salvator; endowing it with parochial tithes 'as a college for theology and the arts, for divine worship and for scholastic exercises.' The numbers of the society were fixed, *ad instar apostolici numeri*, at thirteen persons; a provost, a licentiate in theology, a bachelor in theology, four masters of arts and six 'poor clerks.' The college set up a claim to confer degrees independently of the rector of the older foundation, and supported it by a bull of Pius II, of 1458; but the pretension was speedily relinquished on the intervention of Patrick Graham, half-brother of bishop Kennedy, and the first metropolitan of St Andrews. In 1512, John Hepburn, prior of St Andrews, converted for the purposes of a second college the buildings and property of the ancient hospital of St Leonard, which had been erected in an earlier age for the entertainment of the pilgrims who thronged to worship at the shrine of St Andrews. Hepburn enjoyed the support, not only of James IV, but of the king's illegitimate son, the young archbishop, Alexander Stewart, who was destined to fall with his father, a year later, on the fatal field of Flodden. The archbishop, a pupil of Erasmus, himself took in hand the conversion of Wardlaw's *pedagogium* into the college of St Mary; but his untimely death left the task to be completed, with royal and papal approval, by his successors, the two Beatons and John Hamilton (1553). The college of St Mary, which, at least after 1579, was given up entirely to the study of divinity, completed the three foundations, which remained the constituent colleges of St Andrews down to 1747; when failing revenues compelled the amalgamation of St Salvator's with St Leonard's. The historian John Major, in 1521, himself provost of St Leonard's, marvelled at the *incuria* of Scottish prelates, which had left Scotland without a university until 1411. The Scottish bishops of the fifteenth century made ample amends for their supine predecessors.

In January, 1450, William Turnbull, bishop of Glasgow, obtained from Nicholas V a bull, which recognised the establishment in his cathedral city of a *studium generale*. The bull was locally proclaimed in the following year, when statutes were drawn up and courses of study prescribed.

Yet again, in 1500, bishop Elphinstone of Aberdeen completed the erection of King's College, in 'the granite city,' having obtained papal authority in 1494. The third university of Scotland was formed on the model of its predecessors as a combination of conventual rule with the special pursuit of learning. It acquired

a particular lustre from the person of its first principal. This was
Hector Boece, correspondent of Erasmus and historian, who had
held the appointment of professor of philosophy in the college
of Montaigu at Paris.

The Scottish universities were directly clerical in origin; and
the briefest examination of the statutes of their colleges demon-
strates their thoroughly ecclesiastical character. The Scottish
episcopal founders worked hand in hand not only with monks
but with friars. It is noteworthy that bishop Kennedy founded
a Franciscan convent in St Andrews, where the Dominicans had
been established by one of his early predecessors (1272—9); and
the provincial sub-prior of the Dominicans was, with the minister
of the Franciscans, included among the seven electors to the
provostship of St Mary's. In the result, while the Scottish
university was, in its first days, an ecclesiastical seminary, its
education assumed, with the advent of colleges, the purely conventual type. St Leonard's, which may be selected as a typical
college, was, under its canon regular principal, as a college of
philosophy and theology, a glorified monastic school.

The subjects of instruction comprised grammar, oratory, poetry,
Aristotelian philosophy and the writings of Solomon as preparatory
to the study of divinity. Prior Hepburn forbade the admission
of a student under fifteen years of age; but the university
statutes permitted *determination* at the age of fourteen.

From mere boys, in the Scotland of the fifteenth century, no
serious preparatory equipment could be demanded. The council
at Edinburgh, in 1549, urged the rectors of the universities to
see to it *ne ulli ad scholas Dialectices sive Artium recipiantur
nisi qui Latine et grammatice loquuntur*; and called upon the
archdeacon of St Andrews to appoint a grammar school master for
that city[1]. Other indications assist to show the low standard of
the current Latin. There was no professor of the Humanities in
St Andrews, 'the first and principal university' in the sixteenth
century.

A reforming commission, in 1563, complained of the lack of
teaching of sciences and 'specially they that are maist necessarie,
that is to say the toungis and humanities.' James Melville testifies
that, in 1571, neither Greek nor Hebrew was to be 'gottine in the
land.' When at length, in 1620, a chair of Humanity was endowed
in St Leonard's college, the local grammar master complained that
its occupant drew off his young pupils by teaching the elements

---

[1] Herkless and Hannay, *The College of St Leonard*, p. 160.

of Latin grammar. There was no professor of Greek in St Andrews until 1695. The modern superiority of Scotland in philosophy is traceable, in fact, to a belated medievalism. The Scottish reformation caught the universities of the northern kingdom still directly under church control, the clerical instructors clinging to their Aristotle and their Peter Lombard. The results were temporarily disastrous. In spite of the assertion of Hector Boece that, in early days, the university *excrevit in immensum*, the numbers of no Scottish university in the fifteenth or sixteenth century exceeded the membership of one of the smaller English colleges, such, for example, as Peterhouse. In 1557, there were thirty-one students in the three constituent colleges of St Andrews; in 1558 there were but *three*. Glasgow and Aberdeen dwindled in like fashion. Yet the Scottish universities reproduced the Parisian distribution into four nations under local quarterings. The description which John Major gave of his contemporary Glasgow is, with the variation of the local reference, equally applicable to St Andrews or to Aberdeen: 'The seat of an Archbishop, and of a University poorly endowed and not rich in scholars; but serviceable to the inhabitants of the west and south.'

In one particular the northern kingdom advanced beyond her southern sister. A Scottish act of parliament of 1496 declared that:

It is statute and ordanit throw all the realme that all barronis and frehaldaris that ar of substance put thair eldest sonnis and airs to the sculis fra thai be aucht or nine yeiris of age and till remane at the grammar sculis quhill thai be competentlie foundit and have perfite latyne. And therefter to remane thre yers at the sculis of Art and Jure sua that thai may have knowledge and understanding of the lawis. Throw the quhilkis Justice may reigne universalie throw all the realme[1].

This enactment was enforceable by a penalty of forty pounds.

That net of compulsory education, with which nineteenth century England enmeshed her lower orders, was endeavoured to be thrown over her young nobility and lairds by the Scotland of that gallant monarch, whose courage disastrously outran his generalship on the slopes of Branxton Hill.

---

[1] *Acts of the Parliament of Scotland*, II, 239; Tytler, IV, 25.

CHAPTER XVI

TRANSITION ENGLISH SONG COLLECTIONS

In France, a large number of manuscripts have survived from the thirteenth, fourteenth and fifteenth centuries to testify to the songs that were sung by the gallant, the monk, the minstrel and the clerk. English literature has been less fortunate, and yet there are extant a goodly number of Middle English songs.

With the exception of two notable anthologies of love lyrics and religious poems, these songs were not committed to writing until the fifteenth and early sixteenth centuries. The inference is not to be drawn, however, that they were mainly the product of the late Transition period, since, evidently, they had been preserved in oral form for a considerable time. This is proved by the existence of different versions of the same song, by allusions to historical events earlier than the fifteenth century, by elements of folk-song embedded in the songs, by the essential likeness of the love lyrics and religious poems to those in the two thirteenth century collections, and by the fact that certain songs are of types which were popular in France in the thirteenth and fourteenth centuries, and were probably brought to England at the time of their vogue at home. The songs can therefore be regarded as more or less representative of the whole Middle English period.

Of the folk-song element, a word may well be said at the outset, for, though no pure folk-songs have survived, the communal verse has left its impress upon these collections.

The universal characteristics of folk-poetry are, as to substance, repetitions, interjections and refrains ; and, as to form, a verse accommodated to the dance. Frequent also is the call to the dance, question and answer and rustic interchange of satire. Though no one song illustrates all of these characteristics, they are all to be found in the songs taken collectively.

The refrain is so generally employed that a song without it is the exception. In the majority of cases, it is a sentence in Latin

or English, which has more or less relation to the theme of the
song, as the refrain :

> Now syng we right as it is,
> *Quod puer natus est nobis*[1],

which accompanies a carol of the Nativity.   Frequently, however,
meaningless interjections are run into such a refrain ; thus :

> Hay, hey, hey, hey,
> I will haue the whetston and I may[2];
>
> Po, po, po, po,
> Loue brane & so do mo[3].

Such interjections are of great antiquity, and, in a far distant past,
were the sole words of the chorus.   Sometimes the interjections
are intelligible words, which, however, have been chosen with an
eye to their choral adequacy, as :

> Gay, gay, gay, gay,
> Think on drydful domis day[4].
> *Nova, nova, ave fit ex Eva*[5].

Some of the songs have preserved refrain, interjection and repetition as well, as in the case of the following poem :

> I haue XII. oxen that be fayre & brown,
> & they go a grasynge down by the town;
> With hay, with howe, with hay!
> Sawyste you not myn oxen, you litill pretty boy?
>
> I haue XII. oxen & they be ffayre & whight,
> & they go a grasyng down by the dyke;
> With hay, with howe, with hay!
> Sawyste not you myn oxen, you lytyll pretty boy?
>
> I haue XII. oxen & they be fayre & blak,
> & they go a grasyng down by the lak;
> With hay, with howe, with hay!
> Sawyste not you myn oxen, you lytyll pretty boy?
>
> I haue XII. oxen & they be fayre & rede,
> & they go a grasyng down by the mede;
> With hay, with howe, with hay!
> Sawiste not you my oxen, you litill pretty boy[6]?

Presumably this song is the product of a conscious artist, yet
it is representative of that amoebean verse which invariably
results in the evolution of poetry when individual singers detach

[1] *MS Balliol* 354, ff. 211 *b*, 227 *b*—*Anglia*, XXVI, 254.
[2] *Ibid.* ff. 226 *b*, 248 *b*—*Anglia*, XXVI, 270.
[3] *Bodleian MS, Eng. Poet. E. I.* f. 29 *b*—*Percy Society*, LXXIII, 42.
[4] *MS Sloane* 2593, f. 8 *a*—*Warton Club*, IV, 10.
[5] *Bodleian MS, Eng. Poet. E. I.* f. 27 *a*—*Percy Society*, LXXIII, 36.
[6] *MS Balliol* 354, f. 178 *b*—*Anglia*, XXVI, 197.

themselves from the chorus, and sing in rivalry. Moreover, it is representative of the simplest and most universal type of such verse, the improvising of variations to accompany a popular initial verse or phrase.

Another common form of the amoebean verse is question and answer. This is beautifully illustrated by a song of the early fourteenth century, a stray leaf of which has, fortunately, been preserved[1]. The song is arranged in recitative, but, relieved of these repetitions, is as follows:

> Maiden in the moor lay
> Seven nights full and a day.
>
> 'Well, what was her meet?'
> 'The primrose and the violet.'
>
> 'Well, what was her dryng?'
> 'The chill water of (the) well spring.'
>
> 'Well, what was her bower?'
> 'The rede rose and the lilly flour.'

On the same folio is a quaint poem, which has retained the invitation to the dance:

> Ich am of Irlaunde,
> Am of the holy londe
> Of Irlande;
> Good sir, pray I ȝe,
> For of Saynte Charite,
> Come ant daunce wyt me in Irlaunde.

The call to the dance is also preserved in several fifteenth and sixteenth century May poems.

A poem in which 'the song of a swaying mass is clearly to be heard' is the familiar repetitionary lyric:

> Adam lay ibowndyn,
> bowndyn in a bond,
> Fowre thowsand wynter
> thowt he not to long;
> And al was for an appil,
> an appil that he tok,
> As clerkes fyndyn wretyn
> in here book.
> Ne hadde the appil take ben,
> the appil taken ben,
> Ne hadde neuer our lady
> a ben Hevene quene.
> Blyssid be the tyme
> that appil take was!
> Therfore we mown syngyn
> Deo gracias[2].

---

[1] *MS Rawlinson*. D. 913, f. 1.   [2] *MS Sloane* 2593, f. 11 a—*Warton Club*. **IV, 32.**

Many an ecclesiastical denunciation testifies to the prevalence of this communal singing in medieval England; but so much more potent are custom and cult than authority that women, dressed in the borrowed costumes of men, continued to dance and sing in wild chorus within the very churchyards, in unwitting homage to the old heathen deities.

Some of the song-collections are anthologies taken from the popular songs of the minstrel, the spiritual hymns of the monk and the polite verse of the court; others are purely the *répertoire* of minstrels; and still others are limited to polite verse.

Of the latter, fortunately, there is preserved the very song-book that was owned by king Henry VIII, containing the lyrics of love and good comradeship that he composed when a young man; and there are, in addition, the books which were in part compiled, and in part composed, by the authorised musicians of the courts of Henry VII and Henry VIII. These have preserved types of chivalric verse based upon French models, as well as songs in honour of the royal family, and songs composed for the revels and pageants which were a brilliant feature of the court life in the early decades of the sixteenth century.

The collections of minstrels' songs are especially rich. The minstrel no longer confined himself to songs of rude and humble ancestry, but encroached both on the devotional verse of the monk, and on the songs of the gallant. This readily explains itself, if one is mindful to identify these minstrels with that class of men who had more and more usurped the prerogatives of minstrelsy, the *scolares vagantes*, those irresponsible college graduates and light-hearted vagabonds, who were equally at home in ale-house, in hall, in market-place or in cloister, and who could sing with equal spirit a ribald and saucy love song, a convivial glee, a Christmas carol, a hymn to the Virgin, or a doleful lay on the instability of life or the fickleness of riches. Most of them were men who had taken minor orders, and who, therefore, knew missal, breviary and hymnal; their life at the university had given them some acquaintance with books, their wayside intercourse with the minstrel had given them his ballads and his jargon of washed-out romantic tales and their homely contact with the people had taught them the songs of the street and of the folk-festival; they were, therefore, 'the main intermediaries between the learned and the vernacular letters of the day,' and they tended to reduce all to a common level. If they compelled the rude folk-song to conform to the metres of the Latin hymns, they compensated for this by reducing to these same simple metres the artistically fashioned stanzas of highly wrought spiritual songs, as well as by introducing the popular refrain into lyrics of every kind. When they sang of the joys of Mary, of the righteousness of a saint, or of a prince renowned for his deeds, they received the approbation of bishop or abbot; when they satirised his cupidity, or sang wanton songs at banquets, they called down the bishop's indignation; but, bishop or no bishop, they never lacked an audience.

As the ability to read became more general, and as taste was refined by the possession of books of real poetic merit, the minstrel, even if one who had tarried in the schools, found his audience more and more limited to the common folk; but, even in the fifteenth century, though his wretched copies of the old romances, with their sing-song monotony, might be the laughing-stock of people of taste, his Christmas carols would still gain him admission to the halls of the nobility.

As the minstrel thus trespassed upon the provinces of religious and polite poets, so each of these in turn invaded the fields of others, with the result that the monk adopted the formulary of amatory address for his love songs to the Virgin, and the gallant introduced elements from the folk-poetry into his embroidered lays.

Considering this confusion, for purposes of discussion it is more satisfactory to classify the songs with reference to types than with reference to authorship. Romances and tales have been dealt with elsewhere: though they are to be found in the collections, and were, probably, chanted in humdrum fashion to the accompaniment of a harp, they are narratives, and not at all lyrical.

The carol was brought to England from France at an early date, and there are extant Norman carols that were sung in England in the late twelfth century. In essentials, there is little difference between these carols and some of those that were sung in England three centuries later. They observe the refrain, which is most commonly a repetition of the word 'noel'; they open with an invocation to those present,

> *Seignors ore entendez a nus,*
> *De loinz sumes venuz a vous,*
> *Pur quere Noel*[1];

and their theme is the Nativity and the attendant gladness.

---

[1] Sandys, *Festive Songs*, 6.

It is probable that the composition of carols was widely
cultivated in the thirteenth century, for most of the carols are in
simple Latin metres, and Latin lines are employed either as refrain,
or as an integral part of the stanzas. Such a tradition must
look back to a period when the English composer felt the need of
relying upon the support of Latin metres, and it was in the
thirteenth century, as extant religious poems demonstrate, that
English metres were thus being conformed to the models of Latin
hymns[1].

The metre most commonly employed is the simplest, a one-
rime tercet of iambic tetrameters, followed by a refrain, usually
Latin. Thus:

> Gabriell that angell bryʒt,
> Bryʒter than the sonne is lyʒt,
> Fro hevyn to erth he (too)k hys flyʒt,
> *Regina celi letare*[2].

Sometimes the Latin verse rimes with the English, making a
quatrain, or a Latin line may be introduced into the tercet itself.
The quatrain with alternate rimes is also used, though less
frequently. Other popular metres are the rimed couplet, and the
ballade stanza, which, however, is confined to the longer narrative
carols. Occasional carols are composed in the highly wrought
French metres, but they seem exotic.

The Latin lines in the carols are familiar verses from the
hymns, canticles, sequences, graduales and other parts of the
service in missal or breviary, relating to the Christmas season; and
practically all can be found in the *Sarum Use*.

Of the refrain there are various types. Sometimes it is a
stanza or verse from a Latin hymn, as:

> *Ihesus autem hodie*
> *Egressus est de virgine*[3];

sometimes an English verse and a Latin verse combined:

> Be mery all, that be present,
> *Omnes de Saba venient*[4];

sometimes merely the word 'nowel' or 'noel' in recitative; and
sometimes an invocation to be merry:

> Make we mery in hall & bowr,
> Thys tyme was born owr savyowr[5].

---

[1] Cf. Morris, *Old English Misc.*, *E.E.T.S.* XLIX, 1872.
[2] *Bodleian MS, Eng. Poet. E. I.* f. 26 a—*Percy Society*, LXXIII, 83.
[3] *MS Balliol* 354, f. 178 a—*Anglia*, XXVI, 196.
[4] *Ibid.* f. 165 b—*Anglia*, XXVI, 176.
[5] *Ibid.* f. 220 a—*Anglia*, XXVI, 231.

There is also a very pretty introduction of the shepherd's pipe in certain carols that sing of the shepherds watching their flocks by night; thus,

> Tyrly tirlow, tirly tirlow;
> So merrily the shepherds began to blow[1].

As the Christmas season was a time for festivities and merry-making as well as for worship, it was natural that some of the carols should deal with sacred themes, and others with secular themes; indeed that some carols should confuse the two types. The services within the church gave ample warrant for such a confusion. Moreover, as Christmas theoretically supplanted a pagan festival, but practically compromised with it, it was natural that elements of pre-Christian rites should be reflected in carols.

Religious carols are, for the most part, narrative in content. The Nativity is, of course, the dominant theme, but, as the festival season lasted from the Nativity to Epiphany, or even until Candlemas, the events of Holy Week, and the lives of the saints whose days occur at this season, furnish many of the themes.

It may be that carols were written to divert interest from those pagan songs, with their wild dances, which, even as late as the fifteenth century, made Christmas a trying and dangerous period for the church[2]. Certainly, the folk-song element in carols suggests the probability that at one time they were accompanied by dancing.

But, whatever the origin of carols may have been, it is clear that they were much influenced by those dramatic elements, which, prior to the advent of the mystery plays, were a popular part of the Christmas services in the church; for the episodes dramatised in the services are the ones that most often figure in carols. It seems not a little strange that carols were not more often introduced into mystery plays of the Nativity. One of the shepherd carols, however, is like the mystery in spirit. It introduces the character of Wat, and, with it, homely, half-humorous touches such as are characteristic of the plays:

> Whan Wat to Bedlem cum was,
> He swet, he had gon faster than a pace;
>
> . . . .
> Lull well Ihesu in thy lape,
> & farewell Ioseph, with thy rownd cape[3].

---

[1] *MS Balliol* 354, f. 222 *a*—*Anglia*, xxvi, 237; *Bodleian MS, Eng. Poet. E. I.* f. 60 *a* —*Percy Society*, lxxiii, 95.

[2] Cf. Robert of Brunne, *Handlyng Synne*, 8987 ff., *Chron. Vilod.* 1022.

[3] *MS Balliol* 354, f. 224 *a*—*Anglia*, xxvi, 243.

The themes of secular carols are the feasting and sports of Yule-
tide, customs that were inseparable from the great hall of the
nobleman's residence, where the whole community was wont to
assemble for the Christmas festivities. To be sure, these carols
were sometimes sung at other seasons, for did not the Green
Knight entertain Sir Gawain with

> Many athel songez,
> As coundutes of Kryst-masse, and carolez newe,
> With all the manerly merthe that mon may of telle[1]?

but Christmas week in hall was the proper setting. Several carols
relate to the custom of bringing in the boar's head. The classical
example is the familiar carol,

> The boar's head in hand bring I,
> *Caput apri differo*[2],

but others, though less well known, possess equal interest. In one,
the minstrel relates how, in 'wilderness,' he was pursued by a
'wyld bor,' 'a brymly best.' In the encounter that followed, he
succeeded in refting both life and limb from the beast, in testimony
of which he brings the head into the hall. Then he bids the
company add bread and mustard, and be joyful[3]. In another,
warning is given that no one need seek to enter the hall, be he
groom, page, or marshal, unless he bring some sport with him[4].
In still another, the minstrel speaks in the character of Sir
Christmas, and takes leave of

> kyng & knyght,
> & erle, baron & lady bryght[5],

but not without a fond wish that he may be with them again the
following year. He hears Lent calling, and obeys the call: a
lugubrious summons indeed to the luckless wanderer who must
turn his back on this genial hospitality for eleven months to come,
and depend on the fortuitous goodwill of the ale-house.

Charming, also, are the songs of ivy and holly, which were
sung in connection with some little ceremony of the season. In all
the songs, ivy and holly appear as rivals; and, whatever the
ceremony may have been, it certainly was a survival of those
festival games in connection with the worship of the spirit of
fertility, in which lads invariably championed the cause of holly,

[1] *E.E.T.S.* f. 484 ff.
[2] Cf. *MS Balliol* 354, f. 212 *a*—*Anglia*, xxvi, 257.
[3] *Bodleian MS, Eng. Lit. E. I.* f. 23 *a*—*Percy Society*, lxxiii, 25.
[4] *MS Balliol* 354, f. 223 *a*—*Anglia*, xxvi, 241.
[5] *Ibid.* f. 208 *b*—*Anglia*, xxvi, 245.

and lasses that of ivy[1]. We can fancy young men entering the
hall with branches of holly[2]:

> Here commys holly, that is so gent,
> To pleasse all men is his entent, *etc.*;

singing the praises of the shrub, and warning their hearers not to
speak lightly of it[3]; while young women enter from an opposite
direction, and go through a similar performance with the ivy.
Thereupon, both young men and young women enter upon some
kind of a dance, which resolves itself into a contest in which the
boys drive the girls from the hall:

> Holy with his mery men they can daunce in hall;
> Ivy & her ientyl women can not daunce at all,
> But lyke a meyny of bullokes in a water fall,
> Or on a whot somer's day whan they be mad all.
>
> Nay, nay, ive, it may not be iwis;
> For holy must haue the mastry, as the maner is.
>
> Holy & his mery men sytt in cheyres of gold;
> Ivy & her ientyll women sytt withowt in ffold,
> With a payre of kybid helis cawght with cold.
> So wold I that euery man had, that with yvy will hold.
>
> Nay, nay, ive, it may not be iwis;
> For holy must haue the mastry, as the maner is[4].

This *débat* of holly and ivy, like other songs of winter and
summer, looks back to that communal period, when dialogue was
just beginning to emerge from the tribal chorus.

Related to Christmas carols are spiritual lullabies, for the
simplest of the three forms of the lullaby is, virtually, a carol, in
which, along with other episodes of Christmas Eve and Christmas
Day, the spectacle of Mary singing 'lulley' to the Infant is described. The refrain is all that differentiates this carol from others:

> Lullay, myn lykyng, my dere sone, myn swetyng;
> Lulley, dere herte, myn owyn dere derlyng[5].

In the second type of lullaby, Mary and the Infant talk to one
another. Mary regrets that a child, born to be King of kings, is
lying upon hay, and wonders why He was not born in a prince's
hall. The Babe assures her that lords and dukes and princes will
come to worship Him. Then Mary would fain know how she

---

[1] Cf. Chambers, *The Mediaeval Stage*, I, 251, and chapter III; Ellis and Brand, *Popular Antiquities*, I, 68, 519 ff.

[2] Cf. *Bodleian MS, Eng. Poet. E. I.* f. 53 b—*Percy Society*, LXXIII, 84.

[3] *Ibid.* ff. 30 a, 53 b—*Percy Society*, LXXIII, 44, 84.

[4] *MS Balliol* 354, f. 229 b—*Anglia*, XXVI, 279.

[5] *MS Sloane* 2593, f. 32 a—*Warton Club*, IV, 94.

herself can best serve Him, and He replies, by rocking Him
gently in her arms and soothing Him to sleep:

> Ihesu, my son, I pray ye say,
> As thou art to me dere,
> How shall I serue ye to thy pay
> & mak the right good chere?
> All thy will
> I wold ffulfill,—
> Thou knoweste it well in ffay—
> Both rokke ye still,
> & daunce the yer till,
> & synge 'by, by; lully, lulley.'
>
> Mary, moder, I pray ye,
> Take me vp on loft,
> & in thyn arme
> Thow lappe me warm,
> & daunce me now full ofte;
> & yf I wepe
> & will not slepe,
> Than syng 'by, by; lully, lulley[1].'

The third type is distinguished from this by the melancholy
character of the conversation. The Mother tries in vain to assuage
the grief of her Child, and, when she fails to do so, inquires the
cause of His tears; whereupon He foretells the sufferings that
await Him[2].

A variant of this type introduces an allegory, in which a maiden
weeps beside the couch of a dying knight:

> Lully, lulley, lull(y), lulley;
> The fawcon hath born my make away.
>
> He bare hym vp, he bare hym down,
> He bare hym in to an orchard browne.
> (*Ref.*)
>
> In that orchard there was an halle,
> That was hangid with purpill & pall.
> (*Ref.*)
>
> And in that hall there was a bede,
> Hit was hangid with gold so rede.
> (*Ref.*)
>
> And yn that bed there lythe a knyght,
> His wowndis bledyng day and nyght.
> (*Ref.*)
>
> By that bede side kneleth a may,
> & she wepeth both nyght & day[3].
> (*Ref.*)

---

[1] *MS Balliol* 354, ff. 210 *b*, 226 *b*—*Anglia*, xxvi, 250.

[2] Cf. *ibid.* ff. 210 *a*, 226 *a*—*Anglia*, xxvi, 249; *MS Bodleian, Eng. Poet. E. I.* f. 20 *a*
—*Percy Society*, LXXIII, 19.

[3] *MS Balliol* 354, f. 165 *b*—*Anglia*, xxvi, 175.

All these poems are characterised by a lullaby refrain, and it is the conventional introduction for the poet to describe the scene as one that he himself witnessed 'this other night.' The device certainly savours of the French, but I have not yet discovered a French poem of this character. Nor do there seem to be corresponding poems in Latin or German. The metre of most of the songs falters between the Teutonic four-stress alliterative verse and the *septenarius*; the original type was, probably, English, and later singers tried to conform it to a new metre. Moreover, the word 'lulley,' which is the burden of the refrain, supports the theory of English origin, and this supposition is also borne out by the character of the secular lullaby, which has the same lugubrious tone, with its regret that the little Child is ushered into a world of sorrow[1]. This is characteristically Teutonic.

Merging into the lullaby is the complaint of Mary, of which many examples have survived. The song which blends these two types is one of great beauty. As in other lullabies, the Virgin tries in vain to soothe the Babe to sleep, and, distraught at His grief, enquires its cause. Thereupon, the Child foretells the sufferings that await Him, and each new disclosure calls forth a fresh burst of grief from the afflicted Mother: 'Is she to see her only Son slain, and cruel nails driven through the hands and feet that she has wrapped? When Gabriel pronounced her "full of grace," he told nothing of this.' The medieval world thought long upon the sorrows of Mary, as upon the passion of Christ, and this poem portrays the crushing grief of the Virgin with the naïve fidelity and tenderness characteristic of medieval workmanship.

The refrain of the poem shows that it was sung as a carol:

> Now synge we with angelis
> *Gloria in excel(s)is*[2].

Conversely, another carol, which is concerned with the events at the cross, has, for its refrain, a complaint of Mary:

> To see the maydyn wepe her sonnes passion,
> It entrid my hart full depe with gret compassion[3].

Some of the complaints are monologues; others are dialogues or trialogues. The monologue is usually addressed to Jesus or to the cross, but, sometimes, it has no immediate relation to the passion, and is not directed to any particular hearer[4]. The

---

[1] Cf. Guest, *History of English Metres*, 512.
[2] *MS Balliol* 354, ff. 209 b, 225 b—*Anglia*, xxvi, 247.
[3] *Ibid.* ff. 214 a, 230 a—*Anglia*, xxvi, 263.
[4] *Ibid.* 214 a—*Anglia*, xxvi, 262; *E.E.T.S.* xv, 233, xxiv, 126.

dialogue is between Mary and Jesus, or Mary and the cross[1]. In the trialogues, Mary, Jesus and John converse. John leads the weeping Mother to the cross, she calls upon Jesus, and He tenderly commits her to the care of the beloved disciple[2].

These complaints are based upon Latin hymns and similar writings, upon *Stabat Mater, Ante Crucem Virgo Stabat, Crux de te Volo Conqueri*, the *Gospel of Nicodemus*, the *Meditations of Augustine* and the *Tractat* of Bernard, and, while the English poems display much lyrical excellence, they contribute little to the tradition.

A similar type of poem is the complaint which the crucified Christ makes to sinful man. This is usually a monologue[3], though sometimes a dialogue, remorseful man responding to the appeal of Christ, and pleading for mercy[4].

Other poems which celebrate the Virgin include prayers—some in the form of carols, *aves*, poems upon the five joys of Mary, or upon the six branches of the heavenly rose. Some of these songs are translations, in whole or in part, of Latin poems; others seem to be original. They perpetuate the intense ardour of devotion, the mysticism, the warmth and rich colour of the earlier English songs to Mary, and they heighten the effect by a superior melody.

Apart from the types of religious songs already considered, there are a large number of moral and reflective poems. Some of these are hortatory, urging man to know himself[5], to beware of swearing by the mass[6], to make amends for his sins[7], or to acknowledge his indebtedness to God[8]. Others are contemplative, and reflect upon the certainty of death[9], the fickleness of riches or fortune[10], the prevalence of vice[11], or the worldliness of the clergy[12].

In their most highly developed form these poems are allegories,

---

[1] *Herrig's Archiv*, LXXXIX, 263; *E.E.T.S.* XLVI, 131, 197, CXVII, 612; *Bodleian MS, Eng. Poet. E. I.* f. 34 a—*Percy Society*, LXXIII, 50.

[2] *MS Sloane* 2593, f. 70 a—*Percy Society*, IV, 10; *Bodleian MS, Eng. Poet. E. I.* f. 27 a—*Percy Society*, LXXIII, 38.

[3] *E.E.T.S.* CXVII, 637.

[4] *Add. MS* 5465, f. 68 a—*Herrig's Archiv*, CVI, 63.

[5] *MS Balliol* 354, f. 156 b—*Anglia*, XXVI, 170.

[6] *Ibid.* ff. 214 a, 230 a—*Anglia*, XXVI, 263.

[7] *Bodleian MS, Eng. Poet. E. I.* f. 30 b—*Percy Society*, LXXIII, 44.

[8] *Ibid.* f. 27 b—*Percy Society*, LXXIII, 39.

[9] *Ibid.* ff. 38 b, 48 a—*Percy Society*, LXXIII, 57, 74; *MS Balliol* 354, f. 177 b—*Anglia*, XXVI, 191.

[10] *MS Balliol* 354, ff. 194 a, 206 a—*Anglia*, XXVI, 207.

[11] *Bodleian MS, Eng. Poet. E. I.* f. 60 b—*Percy Society*, LXXIII, 96.

[12] *MS Balliol* 354, f. 156 a—*Anglia*, XXVI, 169.

with conventional introduction and conclusion, and a prelude, which is commonly in Latin. In some of the songs, the allegory is highly articulated. For example, the poet pictures himself as sallying forth on a bright summer's morning in search of sport, with his hawk in hand, and his spaniel leaping by his side. A hen pheasant is flushed, and the hawk gives chase; but, while the sport is at its height, the poet suddenly finds himself entangled in a briar, on every leaf of which is written the warning *revertere*:

> My hart fell down vnto my to,
> That was before full lykyngly;
> I lett my hawke & fesavnt fare,
> My spanyell fell down vnto my kne—
> It toke me with a sighyng fare,
> This new lessun 'revertere'[1].

The summer's day symbolises the period of youth; the hawk, its fierce passions; and the briar, conscience. In the majority of the songs, the allegory is less developed than in this.

Most often the poet represents himself as wandering through a forest on a sunny morning. As he wanders, he hears the singing of a bird, or of a company of birds, and the burden of their song is some moral reflection or some exhortation[2]. The allegory is usually neglected after the introductory stanza. Almost invariably the song concludes with a prayer for succour in death and deliverance from the fiend[3]. The conventionalised nature setting and the allegory of these poems are clearly French, and the metres most often used are the ballade stanza and the *rime royal*.

In the forms in which we have been considering them, these songs were ill adapted to the ordinary audience of the minstrel, and he, accordingly, popularised them by shortening them, introducing a refrain and substituting simple metres, in which the rhythm is strongly marked.

These moral songs shade into another group of didactic poems, which embody shrewd practical wisdom, of the type dear to Polonius. They concern themselves with such homely advice as to hold your tongue[4], to try your friend[5], to look out for a rainy

---

[1] *MS Balliol* 354, f. 155 *b*—*Anglia*, xxvi, 168.

[2] *Ibid.* f. 170 *b*—*Anglia*, xxvi, 180; *Bodleian MS, Eng. Poet. E. I.* f. 38 *b*—*Percy Society*, lxxiii, 57; *Porkington MS, No. I*—*Warton Club*, ii, 1.

[3] Cf. *MS Balliol* 354, ff. 156 *b*, 157 *a*, 170 *b*—*Anglia*, xxvi, 170, 171, 180 *et freq.*; *Bodleian MS, Eng. Poet. E. I.* ff. 24 *a*, 38 *b*, 60 *b*—*Percy Society*, lxxiii, 28, **57**, 96 *et freq.*

[4] *Bodleian MS, Eng. Poet. E. I.* ff. 22 *a*, 28 *a*—*Percy Society*, lxxiii, 23, **41.**

[5] *Ibid.* f. 23 *b*—*Percy Society*, lxxiii, 28.

day[1] and to beware of matrimony[2]. These songs also employ the prelude and refrain, and, incongruous as it may seem, often close with a prayer. Some of them are distinguished by quaint and picturesque humour, as is shown in the following stanzas :

> Quan I haue in myn purs inow,
> I may haue bothe hors & plow
> & also frynds inow,
>   Throw the vertu of myn purs.
> Quan my purs gynny3t to slak
> & ther is nowt in my pak,
> They will seyn, 'Go, far wil, Jak,
>   Thou xalt non more drynke with vs[3].'

The songs warning young men to avoid matrimony belong to the satires against women, a poetical tradition which was one of the contributions of France to Buranic verse. In no class of songs is the *esprit gaulois* more evident. That sly distrust of woman which early insinuated itself into French romances, and which grew bolder and harsher as the ideals of the renascence encroached upon medievalism, in the poetry of the common people found expression in blunt and broad satire. This tradition was augmented, however, by a native English contribution, for the satire which gives evidence of the greatest antiquity of all is strongly alliterative, and observes the repetitions of early communal verse :

> Herfor & therfor & therfor I came,
> And for to praysse this praty woman.
> Ther wer III wylly, 3 wyly ther wer,—
> A fox, a fryyr, and a woman.
> Ther wer 3 angry, 3 angry ther wer,—
> A wasp, a wesyll, & a woman.
> Ther wer 3 cheteryng, III cheteryng ther wer,—
> A peye, a jaye, & a woman.
> Ther wer 3 wold be betyn, 3 wold be betyn ther wer,—
> A myll, a stoke fysche, and a woman[4].

Several different types of these satires are to be recognised, but the style best designed to endear itself to the popular taste was that used in little dramatic narratives of the Punch and Judy school of comedy, in which the poet tells the story of a family quarrel, wherein the good man is invariably worsted by his muscular and shrewish helpmeet. This broad farce finds its

---

[1] *Bodleian MS, Eng. Poet. E. I.* f. 26 b.
[2] *Ibid.* f. 26 a—*Percy Society*, LXXIII, 34 etc.
[3] *MS Sloane* 2593, f. 5 b—*Warton Club*, IV, 14.
[4] *Bodleian MS, Eng. Poet. E. I.* f. 13 a—*Percy Society*, LXXIII, 4.

dramatic counterpart in those brawling scenes in the mystery plays which pleased the rude populace, and, like the scenes from the plays, the songs are not without clever and humorous touches, as when the hen-pecked husband is sent flying from his door, only to discover his doleful neighbour in a similar plight[1]. Does not such a song perpetuate a tradition of the Latin stage, which the *joculatores*, with their rude performances, carried to the Gallic provinces, and eventually bequeathed to the minstrels?

In another class of satires, women are praised ironically, the refrain serving to turn the apparent praise to dispraise; thus:

> For tell a woman all your cownsayle,
> & she can kepe it wonderly well;
> She had lever go quyk to hell
> Than to her neyghbowr she wold it tell.
> *Cuius contrarium verum est.*
> To the tavern they will not goo,
> Nor to the ale-howse neuer the moo,
> For God wot ther hartes wold be woo
> To sspende ther husbondes money soo.
> *Cuius contrarium verum est*[2].

The third type of the satire against women is pretentious and artificial. It consists in proposing impossible phenomena, and then concluding that when such phenomena actually exist, women will be faithful. These poems are drawn out to an interminable length; a few specimen lines may suffice:

> Whan sparowys bild chi[r]ches & stepulles hie,
> & wrennes carry sakkes to the mylle,
> & curlews cary clothes horsis for to drye,
> & se mewes bryng butter to the market to sell,
> & woddowes were wod knyffes theves to kyll,
> And griffons to goslynges don obedyence,
> Than put in a woman your trust & confidence[3].

These poems are scarcely more than translations of the many French poems of the same kind[4].

Of all popular poems, convivial songs, with their festivity and their rollicking spirits, are the most engaging. For eight hundred years students have been singing

> *Gaudeamus igitur,*
> *Juvenes dum sumus,*

and it is to these medieval student songs that the youth of to-day turn as to the perennial source of convivial inspiration.

---

[1] *Bodleian MS, Eng. Poet. E. I.* f. 34 b—*Percy Society*, LXXIII, 51.

[2] *MS Balliol 354*, ff. 228 a, 250 a—*Anglia*, XXVI, 275.

[3] *Ibid.* f. 250 b—*Anglia*, XXVI, 277.

[4] Cf. Montaiglon et Rothschild, *Recueil de Poésies Françaises des* XVe *et* XVIe *siècles*, Paris, 1855—78.

Some drinking songs are daring parodies of hymns, justifications of drinking by the Sacrament, credos of wine, women and song. All these were already venerable in the fifteenth century.

Other songs savour of the ale-house rather than of college halls. These look back to the folk-poetry. Drinking songs were, assuredly, one of the early types of communal verse, and the folk-element is apparent in many fifteenth century convivial songs, as, indeed, in the corresponding verse of the Elizabethans. Such well known refrains as 'Hey trolly lolly' and 'Dole the ale' are of venerable antiquity, and the songs which consist of variations of a common phrase show an indebtedness, of course, immediate or remote, to communal poetry. Thus, such a song as the following plainly took its cue from the folk-song:

> Bryng vs in good ale, & bryng vs in good ale,
> For owr blyssyd lady sake, bryng vs in good ale.
>
> Bryng vs in no browne bred, fore that is mad of brane,
> Nore bryng us in no whyt bred, fore ther in is no game,
>   But bryng us in good ale.
>
> Bryng vs in no befe, for ther is many bonys,
> But bryng vs in good ale, *etc.*[1]

This song, however, can hardly claim so remote an ancestry as another, in which the repetitional phrases are, in themselves, of no significance, and are merely used as framework. This is evidence of remote origin, as the study of comparative literature testifies, and the little Latin courtesy with which the song introduces itself cannot conceal its real age:

> *Omnes gentes plaudite,*
> I saw myny bryddis setyn on a tre;
> He tokyn here fley3t & flowyn away,
> With *ego dixi*, haue good day.
> Many qwyte federes ha3t the pye,
> I may noon more syngyn, my lyppis arn so drye.
> Many qwyte federes ha3t the swan,
> The more that I drynke, the lesse good I can.
> Ley stykkys on the fer, wyl mot is brenne;
> Geue vs onys drynkyn, er we gon henne[2].

A merry song that links the convivial poem to the satire on women is the narrative of the gay gossips who hie them to the tavern, and there, tucked away, discuss their husbands, though not without many an anxious eye on the door[3].

---

[1] *Bodleian MS, Eng. Poet. E. I.* f. 41 *b*—*Percy Society*, LXXIII, 63.

[2] *MS Sloane* 2593, f. 10 *a*—*Warton Club*, IV, 32.

[3] *Bodleian MS, Eng. Poet. E. I.* f. 57 *b*—*Percy Society*, LXXIII, 91; *MS Balliol* 354, ff. 194 *b*, 206 *b*—*Anglia*, XXVI, 208.

Hardly to be distinguished from convivial songs are the songs of good fellowship, of 'pastyme with good companye,' which exhort

> Tyme to pas with goodly sport
> Our spryts to revyve and comfort;
> To pype, to synge,
> To daunce, to spryng,
> With pleasure and delyte
> Following sensual appetyte[1].

Such songs were especially liked by Henry VIII, when he was a youth, and a group of them is to be found in his song-book.

The song of the death dance is represented in several manuscripts by a most melancholy and singularly powerful poem. The insistent holding of the mind to one thought, with no avenue of escape left open; the inexorableness of monotonous rimes; the irregular combination of monosyllables, iambics and anapaests, that strike like gusts of hail in a hurtling storm; all these aid in compelling heavy-hearted acquiescence:

> Erth owt of erth is worldly wrowght;
> Erth hath goten vppon erth a dygnite of nowght;
> Erth vpon erth hath set all his thowght,
> How that erth vpon erth myght be hye browght.
>
> Erth vpon erth wold be a kyng;
> But how that erth shall to erth he thynkith no thyng:
> When erth biddith erth his rentes home bryng,
> Then shall erth for erth haue a hard partyng[2].

And so the poem runs for sixteen stanzas.

Love songs are varied, and they are genetically so complex that they often baffle analysis. They range from the saucy and realistic, though always animated, songs of the clerks, to the ornate and figured address of the gallant, who imitates in his ruffled and formal phrases models brought from over seas. Though some songs have advanced little, if at all, from the rude amours of country swains, and others are merely a transplanting of the graceful and artificial toyings of the court-trained gallants of France, the majority fuse traditions, so that a single song must sometimes look for its ancestry not merely to direct antecedents in English folk-song and French polite verse, but, ultimately, to French folk-poetry and the troubadour lays of which this polite verse of France was compounded. Indeed, English verse itself may have been directly influenced by the troubadours.

The French types which were translated or imitated without

---

[1] Flügel, *Neuenglisches Lesebuch*, 148.
[2] *MS Balliol* 354, f. 207 b—*Anglia*, xxvi, 217.

material modification include the address, the *débat*, the *pastourelle*
and the ballade.

The address is a poem in stately and formal language wherein
the poet addresses his lady, his 'life's souereign pleasaunce.' His
attitude is that of a humble and reverential suppliant, who, though
confessing the unworthiness of the service which he proffers, yet
relies upon the mercy of his lady to accept it. Not uncommonly
the poem is a New Year's letter, in which, failing a better gift, the
poet offers his mistress his heart—to her a little thing, to him
his all[1].

Though the *débat* has a variety of themes in French lyrics, in
English it is restricted—save for the song of holly and ivy—to
contentions between the lover and his heartless lady[2]. These
songs are as unfeeling as the vapid French verse of which they are
but echoes.

Of the type of *pastourelle* in which a gallant makes love to a
rustic maiden there are two examples. One of these *pastourelles*
was sung by Henry VIII and his companions, and, in somewhat
revised form, is still popular to-day:

> 'Hey, troly, loly, lo; made, whether go you?'
> 'I go to the medowe to mylke my cowe,' *etc.*[3]

In the other, a gallant urges a maid to visit the wildwood with
him, that they may gather flowers, and at length she yields to
his importunity:

> 'Come ouer the woodes fair & grene,
> The goodly mayde, that lustye wenche;
> To shadoo yow from the sonne
> Vnder the woode ther ys a benche.'

> 'Sir, I pray yow doo non offence
> To me a mayde, thys I make my mone;
> But as I came lett me goo hens,
> For I am here my selfe alone,' *etc.*[4]

The more primitive type of *pastourelle* in which one shepherd
laments to another the treatment of an indifferent shepherdess
survives in a song attributed to Wyatt, but which he can hardly
more than have revised:

> A! Robyn, joly Robyn,
> Tell me how thy leman doeth, *etc.*[5]

---

[1] *E.E.T.S.* xv, 66—Padelford, *Early Sixteenth Century Lyrics*, xxxiv.
[2] *MS Sloane* 1710, f. 164 a.
[3] *Add. MS* 31922, f. 124 b—*Early Sixteenth Century Lyrics*, 84.
[4] *MS Rawlinson*, C. 813, f. 58 b. This MS is being edited by the writer for *Anglia*.
[5] *Early Sixteenth Century Lyrics*, 10.

Transferred to the religious lyric, it has also survived in a shepherd's complaint of the indifference of the clergy to the welfare of their flocks[1].

Of all forms of French amatory verse, the ballade enjoyed the greatest popularity in England. It was the form in which the gallant most often essayed to ease his bosom of the torments of love. Every phase of the conventional love complaint, every chapter in the cycle of the lover's history, is treated in these ballades precisely as in the corresponding verse in France[2].

Light-foot measures, such as the *lai* and the *descort*, exerted a noteworthy influence upon late Transition lyrics, though English poets were content merely to adopt the characteristic common to all the species—the long stanza of very short verses—and did not observe the metrical peculiarities that differentiate one species from another. This light-foot verse was cultivated to good effect, and furnishes some of the best songs. They are rapid, musical and enthusiastic. Any phase of the lover's experience may be treated in this verse, but it seems to have been most employed in those songs which deal with the parting, the absence, or the reunion of lovers. The following verses, which open one of these songs, will illustrate their grace and spirit:

> Can I chuse
> But refuce
> All thought of mourning,
> Now I see
> Thus close by me
> My love returning?
> If I should not joy
> When I behould
> Such glory shining,
> Sith her tyme of stay
> Made me to decay
> With sorrow pining,
> Silly birds might seem
> To laugh at me,
> Which, at day peering,
> With a merry voyce
> Sing 'O doo rejoyce!'
> Themselves still cheering.
> Absence darke
> Thou dost marke,
> No cause but fearing,
> And like night
> Turnst thy sight
> All into hearing[3].

---

[1] *MS Balliol* 354, f. 156 a—*Anglia*, xxvi, 169.
[2] *MS Rawlinson, C.* 813, contains a large number of the ballades.
[3] *MS Harleian* 367, f. 183—*Herrig's Archiv*, cvii, 56.

A French type, which, while having no complete exponent, has yet influenced several English songs, is the *aube*, or complaint of the lover at the envious approach of morn, a motive which Chaucer used with effect in *Troilus and Criseyde*[1], and which Shakespeare immortalised in *Romeo and Juliet*. In one of the songs, the refrain of an *aube* is put into the mouth of a 'comely queen' (Elizabeth of York?) who, in a 'glorious garden,' is gathering roses—

> This day dawes,
> This gentill day dawes,
> And I must home gone[2].

The *aube* motive is also used as the introduction to another song, in which a lover complains of an inconstant mistress:

> Mornyng, mornyng,
> Thus may I synge,
> Adew, my dere, adew;
> Be God alone
> My love ys gon,
> Now may I go seke a new[3].

One of the earliest phases of the *aube* tradition, that the approach of day is announced by the crowing of the cock, is the theme of a festive little song, which, in other respects, is not at all like the conventional type. Indeed, the light-hearted spirit of this merry song is a direct violation of the *aube* tradition:

> I haue a gentil cook
> crowyt me day,
> He doth me rysyn erly
> my matyins for to say.
> I haue a gentil cook,
> comyn he is of gret,
> His comb is of reed corel,
> his tayil is of get.
> I haue a gentyl cook,
> comyn he is of kynde,
> His comb is of red scorel,
> his tayl is of inde;
> His legges ben of asour,
> so geintil & so smele,
> His spores arn of sylver quyt
> in to the wortewale;
> His eyuyn arn of cristal,
> lokyn al in aunbyr;
> & euery ny3t he perchit hym
> in myn ladyis chaumbyr[4].

The repetitions in this song show that it is of considerable antiquity.

[1] 1465, 1702.   [2] *Add. MS* 5465, f. 108 *b*—*Neuenglisches Lesebuch*, 159.

[3] Ritson, *Ancient Songs*, III, 4, from *Harleian MS* 2252.

[4] *MS Sloane* 2593, f. 10 *a*—*Warton Club*, IV, 31.

A more apparent influence is observable in the case of the *chanson à personnages*. This type of poem finds its germ in the spring rites attending the pre-Christian worship of Venus, when maidens, escaped from the tutelage of their mothers, and young wives, from the exacting authority of their husbands, rushed to the meadows, joined hands and danced and sang of their liberty. In the opinion of Jeanroy, such festivities had become an almost liturgical convention. By the twelfth century, these songs had been incorporated into semi-polite poetry, and the resultant genre enjoyed two centuries of popularity. In the earlier form of the genre, the poet represents himself as listening to a young woman who complains of her tyrannical mother or of her cruel husband, and, sometimes, as even protecting her in an ensuing quarrel. In the later and more refined form, the mother or husband is not present, and the poet consoles the young woman, or even makes love to her, the emphasis thus having shifted from the narrative and dramatic elements to the lyrical. The opening words of the *chanson* are the conventional *L'autre jour* or *L'autrier*, and the opening verses contain a description of May, the scene being placed in a bower or a garden.

Though English songs furnish no complete example of the *chanson à personnages* as it existed in France, there are a score of songs in which the poet represents himself as chancing upon a maiden or a man who is lamenting an unrequited love, or the treachery of a false lover. As in the *chansons*, these poems open with the words 'This other day' and a description of May-time, and place the scene in the 'wilderness,' the wild wood supplanting the French bower, through the influence of the native English songs of the spring to which reference was made in a previous chapter of this work[1].

Whether this modification of the theme of the *chanson* began in France, or whether it was strictly an English development, I have not been able to determine.

Just as other types of love songs were taken over and employed in religious lyrics, so this type of song was transferred. In one song the poet comes upon a maiden deep in the wood, and she is great with child. This maiden does not lament her condition, however, but rather sings for joy, since it is given her to bear a Child in whom *verbum caro factum est*[2].

The *chansons à personnages* shade into the English May poems,

[1] See Vol. I, pp. 360 ff.
[2] *Bodleian MS, Engl. Poet. E. I.* f. 47 b. Cf. also *Anglia*, XII, 236, 254, 263; *Herrig's Archiv.* CVI, 53, 279, 282, 283; *Early Sixteenth Century Poems.* 12. 83.

the refrain of a *chanson* sometimes being taken from popular English verse, as the well-known refrain:

Colle to me the rysshys grene, colle to me[1].

The May poems that follow the English tradition all breathe that blithe, out-of-doors spirit, that vernal enthusiasm for the greenwood and the fields, which consistently characterises spring songs from 'Sumer is i-cumen in' and 'Blou northerne wynd' to 'It was a lover and his lass,' and Herrick's sweet summons to Corinna. Every wisp of a spring poem has this odour of green things about it, this contagion of happy *abandon*. One little song has only this to say,

> Trolly, lolly, loly, lo,
> Syng troly, lolo, lo.
> My loue is to the grene wode gone,
> Now [af]ter wyll I go;
> Syng trolly, loly, lo, lo, ly, lo,

yet how completely it expresses the mood[2]!

Of kindred spirit are hunting songs, songs of the 'joly fosters' who love the forest, the bow and the horn and the keenness of the chase. Who would not fain be present, when

> Talbot, my hounde, with a mery taste
> All about the grene wode he gan cast.
> I toke my horne and blew him a blast,
> With 'Tro, ro, ro, ro; tro, ro, ro, ro!'
> With hey go bet, hey go bet, how!
> There he gothe, there he goth! [Hey go howe!]
> We shall haue sport and game ynowe[3].

It is to be regretted that, for the most part, hunting songs have only survived in the more or less modified forms in which they were adapted to pageants, for they were usually marred in the effort to accommodate them to some allegory, as when the aged foster hangs his bow and arrows upon the 'greenwood bough' and, at the command of Lady Venus, leaves her court in disgrace because his 'hard' beard repels maidens' kisses[4].

The best of the songs written by official musicians of the court are those in praise of members of the royal family. One of these is a spirited recital of the prowess shown by Henry VIII in the

[1] *Royal MS, App.* 58, f. 2 *a—Early Sixteenth Century Lyrics*, 83.

[2] *Add. MS* 31922, f. 43 *b*. For the licentious love songs of clerks, cf. *Anglia,* XXVI, 273, 278; *Warton Club,* IV, 35; *Herrig's Archiv,* CVII, 58 etc.

[3] Wynkyn de Worde's *Christmasse Carolles, Douce Fragment,* 94 *b—Early Sixteenth Century Lyrics,* 75.

[4] *Add. MS* 31922, f. 65 *b—Anglia,* XII, 244. Cf. also *Letters and Papers of Henry VIII,* I, 718, 4622—Jan. 6, 1514—for the pageant in which the song probably occurred.

tourney[1]; a second is in praise of Katherine and 'le infant rosary[2]'; a third is an animated trio in which each singer professes to love some flower, the praise of which he sings, the last stanza making the disclosure that all three love the same, the rose which unites both the red and the white[3]; and a fourth is a prayer with the refrain:

> From stormy wyndis & grevous wethir
> Good Lord preserve the estryge fethir[4].

A few songs that do not come under any of the above classes at least deserve to be mentioned. Thus there are a few riddles, which perpetuate a style of poem popular in the Old English period[5]; a poem in light-foot verse descriptive of a market-day or a fair, where there is a bewilderment of goods for sale, a multitude running here and there, a fisticuff, a swaggering drunkard and a noisy auctioneer[6]; a fragment of a spinning or knitting song (?)[7]; a pedlar's song[8]; and a swaggering soldier's song[9].

Such, in brief outline, are the types of songs that constitute these late Transition collections. These songs are all but unknown to readers of English verse, and they have as yet been all but ignored by scholars; yet they constitute an important chapter in the history of our literature. When they are made more accessible, they can hardly fail of appreciation, for they will be enjoyed for what they are, and the student of literary movements will recognise in them one of the two great streams that unite to form the Elizabethan lyric.

[1] *Add. MS* 31922, f. 54 b—*Early Sixteenth Century Lyrics*, 90.

[2] *Ibid.* f. 74 b—*Anglia*, xII, 247.

[3] *Add. MS* 5465, f. 41 a; *Early Sixteenth Century Lyrics*, 91.

[4] *Ibid.* f. 104 b—*Neuenglisches Lesebuch*, 159.

[5] *MS Balliol* 354, f. 218 b—*Anglia*, xxvi, 228; *MS Sloane* 2593, f. 11 a—*Warton Club*, IV, 33.

[6] *Harleian MS* 7578, f. 106 a—*Herrig's Archiv*, cvii, 59.

[7] *Ibid.* 109 b—*Herrig's Archiv*, cvii, 61.

[8] *Bodleian MS, Eng. Poet. E. I.* f. 26 a—*Warton Club*, IV, 76.

[9] *Add. MS* 5465, f. 101 b—*Neuenglisches Lesebuch*, 147.

CHAPTER XVII

BALLADS

The subject of this chapter needs careful definition. Sundry shorter poems, lyrics of whatever purpose, hymns, 'flytings,' political satires, mawkish stories in verse, sensational journalism of Elizabethan days and even the translation of Solomon's Song, have gone by the name of ballad. Ballad societies have published a vast amount of street-songs, broadsides and ditties such as Mme de Sévigné knew in Paris under the name of *Pont-neuf*; for many readers, unfortunately, there is no difference between these 'ballads' and *Chevy Chace* or *Sir Patrick Spens*. The popular ballad, however, now in question, is a narrative poem without any known author or any marks of individual authorship such as sentiment and reflection, meant, in the first instance, for singing, and connected, as its name implies, with the communal dance, but submitted to a process of oral tradition among people free from literary influences and fairly homogeneous. Conditions favourable to the making of such poetry ceased to be general after the fifteenth century; and, while it was both composed and preserved in isolated rural communities long after that date, the instinct which produced it and the habit which handed it down by word of mouth were, alike, a heritage of the past. Seen in critical and historical perspective, balladry takes its distinguishing marks mainly from this process of oral tradition. Owing to this process, the ballad has lost its dramatic or mimetic and choral character and become distinctly epic; it has, in many cases, even forfeited its refrain, once indispensable; but it has kept its impersonal note, lacks, last as first, all trace of deliberate composition and appeals to the modern reader with a charm of simplicity quite its own. Nearly all critics are agreed that no verse of this sort is produced under the conditions of modern life; and the three hundred and five individual ballads, represented by some thirteen hundred versions, printed in the great collection of Child, may be regarded, practically, as a closed account in English literature. Diligent gleaning of the field in the ten years following the completion of that work has brought little or nothing that is new; and little more can be expected. Here and there a forgotten manuscript may come to light; but, in all probability, it will contain only a version of some ballad already known. The sources of tradition have, apparently, at last run dry. Sir George Douglas notes that the Scottish border shepherds, at their annual dinners, no longer sing their old or their own ballads; what are known as 'songs of the day,' mainly of music-hall origin, now rule without any rivals from the past. Remote and isolated districts in the United States keep a few traditional versions alive; such is *The Hangman's Tree,* a version of *The Maid Freed from the Gallows,* still sung, with traces of Yorkshire dialect, after generations of purely oral tradition, as it was brought over to Virginia 'before the revolution.' But these recovered versions have revealed little that is both good and new.

Yet another line of demarcation must be drawn. English and Scottish ballads as a distinct species of poetry, and as a body, can be followed back through the fifteenth century, occur sporadically, or find chance mention, for a century or so before and then altogether cease. Owing to the deplorably loose way in which the word 'ballad' is applied, not only the references of early historians, like William of Malmesbury, to the 'popular songs,' the *cantilenae,* the *carmina vulgaria,* from which they draw for occasional narrative, but also the passages of older epic that tell a particular deed or celebrate a popular hero, are, alike, assumed to indicate a body of ballads, similar to those of the collections, extending back to the Norman conquest, back even to the Germanic conquest of Britain, but lost for modern readers by the chances of time and the lack of written record. Such a body of ballads may, indeed, be conjectured; but conjecture should not pass into inference. Not a single specimen is preserved. It is, to be sure, unlikely that the primary instinct of song, the tendency to celebrate heroes and events in immediate verse, and the habit of epic tradition, main constituents of balladry, should cease as we cross the marches of the Transition period and pass from the modern speech and modern metres, in which our ballads are composed, into that more inflected language, that wholly different form of rhythm, which prevailed in Old English and, with some modifications, in all Germanic verse. To claim for this older period, however, ballads of the kind common since the fifteenth century in England, Scandinavia and Germany, is an assertion impossible to prove. The Old English folk must have had popular ballads of some sort; but it cannot be said what they were. Singing, to be sure, implies a poem in stanzas; and that is precisely what one cannot find in recorded Old English verse— the one exception, Deor's song, being very remote from balladry. It is true that the subject of a popular ballad can often be traced far back; Scandinavian ballads still sing the epic heroes of 'Old Norse.' Community of theme, however, does not imply a common poetical form; and it is the structure, the style, the metrical arrangement, the general spirit of English and Scottish ballads, which must set them apart in our literature and give them their title as an independent species. We find a relative plenty of 'popular' verse in the thirteenth, fourteenth and fifteenth centuries—songs by a political minstrel of some sort, which had their immediate vogue, were recorded here and there, and soon forgotten—but this sort of thing should not be confused with songs made among the people, passed down by oral tradition and marked with those peculiarities of structure and style which are inseparable from the genuine ballad of the collections. In the absence of texts, conjecture is useless. The earliest recorded piece of English verse which agrees with balladry in all these important characteristics is the famous song of Canute, preserved in the chronicles of Ely[1]. The king's actual part in the case is doubtful, and unimportant. Coming by boat, it is said, with his queen and sundry great nobles to Ely, Canute *stood up*, bade his men row slowly, 'called all who were with him in the boats to make a circle about him... *and to join him in song*; and *composed in English* a ballad (*cantilenam*) which begins as follows:

> Merie sunge the munechës binnen Ely,
> Tha Cnut ching rew ther by.
>
> Roweth, cnihtës, noer the land,
> And herë we these munechës sung....'

The verses are familiar; but their significance is not always noted. The chronicler turns them into Latin, and, with clear reference to popular tradition, adds—'and so the rest [of the song] as it is *sung in these days by the people in their dances, and handed down as proverbial....*' That is, the song was traditional a century and a half after the supposed fact, and it seemed natural to the chronicler that such a *cantilena* should be

---

[1] *Historia Eliensis*, II, 27, in Gale, *Hist. Script.* I, 505.

improvised to the singing of a chorus. Perhaps songs of this kind were in Malmesbury's mind when he apologised for using as material for his history *cantilenae* 'worn by the friction of time'; but the political verse of minstrels like the later Laurence Minot is a more likely assumption; and, whatever the likelihood, the verse itself has vanished. In Canute's case there is a fragment of actual song, of the highest value; for it is not only one of the earliest recorded pieces of English poetry to break away from the uniform stichic order of Old English metres, but it is in the rhythm which belongs to the best English and Scandinavian ballads of tradition. Grundtvig thinks that the quoted lines are the burden or chorus of the piece, which was doubtless narrative in its further course, and told, one may conjecture, of Canute's own deeds. This desire of the warrior to sing the battles he has fought did not pass away with the lost songs. A passage in bishop Leslie's *History of Scotland*, used in part by Andrew Lang for the solution of the problem of ballad origins, declares that 'our bordir men,' as Dalrymple translates, delight in their own music and in the songs that they themselves make about their deeds and about the deeds of their forbears. The bishop's Latin is unequivocal: *cantiones quas de majorum gestis, aut ingeniosis praedandi precandive stratagematis, ipsi confingunt.* Gaston Paris[1], on good evidence, has made a similar assertion about the early Germanic and English warriors, who, before the days when the minstrel existed in a professional class, sang their own deeds and furnished the prime material of later epics. Even in *Beowulf* a warrior is described improvising a song on the defeat of Grendel. There is, thus, a presumption that border ballads, like *Cheviot* and *Otterburn*, owed their earliest form to the improvisation of fighting men who could sing their own deeds; and thus, too, one draws a faint line, mainly touching theme and conditions of origin, from the 'old song of Percy and the Douglas' back to those lost lays that inspired the poet of *Beowulf*.

But this is all. Of the actual structure and form of those old lays nothing is known; and it must be remembered that even *Cheviot* and *Otterburn*, while of the undoubted general type of balladry, are not, in more exact analysis, of the typical construction which one finds in ballads recovered from genuine oral tradition. All that can be said of material gathered from older chronicles, or suspected in older poems, is that it lends itself to

---

[1] In *Romania*, XIII, 618, he explicitly defends the analogy of these border songs with the old *cantilenae* of Germanic warriors.

conjecture, not to proof. The one exception is this song of Canute, which may pass as a genuine ballad fragment.

Short work can be made of other assumptions. In the fourteenth century, 'rimes of Robin Hood and Randolph, earl of Chester,' are mentioned in *Piers the Plowman* as known to the common men of that day. Robin Hood ballads are preserved; the Randolph cycle is lost. But the outlaw literature must have been popular long before that. The story of Fulk Fitz-Warine, preserved in French prose and paraphrased by Leland in fragments from 'an old Englisch boke yn ryme,' gives its hero traits and experiences not unlike those of Robin Hood. The forged chronicle of Croyland says that 'ballads' about Hereward were still sung, in the chronicler's day, by the common people and by women at the dance. The deeds of Waltheof at York, told by Malmesbury, are plainly taken 'from a ballad'—so Freeman declares; but from what sort of ballad? Waltheof, it is true, was sung 'in the warlike songs of the tongues of both his parents'; one of these songs, however, the Danish one, is preserved, and has no trace of balladry about it, but all the art and artifice of the professional scald. Ballads of the outlaw, indeed, would be of a popular and traditional type, as the Robin Hood cycle shows; but political songs, which also had their vogue, were, doubtless, made by the minstrel, who, also, retouched and sang again the rude verses which warrior or outlaw had improvised, taking them out of their choral conditions, smoothing, adding, connecting and making them fit for chant and recitation *de longue haleine*, precisely as the *jongleurs* of early France, according to Gaston Paris, remade the improvisations of an age that knew no minstrel class at all into the *chansons de geste* and into the epic itself. Such remade poems could again be broken into ballads, popular enough, sung and transmitted by very humble folk. For a late example, the Scottish ballad *Gude Wallace* has its evident source in the *Wallace* of Blind Harry; but 'the portions of Blind Harry's poem,' says Child, 'out of which these ballads were made, were, perhaps, themselves composed from older ballads, and the restitution of the lyrical form may have given us something not altogether unlike what was sung in the fifteenth, or even the fourteenth century.' Nevertheless, most of the 'ballads' cited by the chroniclers seem to have been political songs, more or less popular—not what could be called, in strict use of the term, a traditional ballad.

In one case, we are on sure negative ground. Henry of Huntingdon has a fiery piece of description in which he reproduces the story of a battle ; as with similar passages, a 'ballad' is his source ; but here, luckily, that source is known. He is translating a poem, inserted in the Old English *Chronicle*, on the battle of Brunanburh ; and whoever will read this poem, whether in the original or in Tennyson's spirited rendering, can see at how great a distance it stands from any ballad of the traditional kind. Minstrels, moreover, as actual authors of the ballads recorded at a later day, are utterly out of the question. Barring a few wretched specimens labelled by Child with the minstrel's name, and inserted in the collection because they still may retain some traditional note, that 'rogue by act of parliament' to whom Percy ascribed the making of practically all English and Scottish ballads is responsible for none of them. It has been pointed out by Kittredge as 'capable of practically formal proof that for the last two or three centuries the English and Scottish ballads have not, as a general thing, been sung or transmitted by professional minstrels or their representatives. There is no reason whatever for believing that the state of things between 1300 and 1600 was different, in this regard, from that between 1600 and 1900....' Still stronger proof lies in the fact that we have the poetry which the minstrels did make ; and it is far removed from balladry. 'The two categories are distinct.' When, finally, one studies the structure and the elements of the ballad itself as a poetic form, a form demonstrably connected with choral dramatic conditions in its origin but modified by a long epic process in the course of oral and quite popular tradition, one is compelled to dismiss absolutely the theory of minstrel authorship, and to regard ballads as both made and transmitted by the people. This phrase is often misunderstood and challenged, but in vain. All poetry, good and bad, is found by the last analysis to be made in the same way ; and there is no romantic mystery or 'miracle' about the ballad. What differentiates it from other forms of poetry is the conditions under which it is made and the agency by which it is handed down. We may reasonably infer for early times such a making and such a transmission ; but the older product is lost, and we are restricted for our study to the actual and undisputed material at our command.

All English and Scottish ballads agree in the fact of tradition, —tradition, in the main, oral and communal ; and there result from this fact two capital exceptions to the ordinary rules of literary investigation. It is well nigh useless to hunt for the 'original' document of a given ballad, or to compare the several varying versions, and so establish, by whatever means, an authentic text. It is also useless to lean with any confidence upon chronology. Some of the ballads gathered, within a century or so, from oral tradition of Scotland, are distinctly older in form than many of the ballads of the Percy manuscript, written down in the seventeenth century, and are closer to the traditional ballad type than many pieces of even earlier date of record than the famous folio. This renunciation of authentic original texts, and of chronology in the ordinary sense, is generally conceded. A few critics, however, are still of opinion that ballads are, after all, nothing but anonymous poems, and that to trace a ballad to its author is not, necessarily, an impossible task.

We touch here the inevitable 'ballad question,' not to argue about it, but simply to record the fact that weight of authority, as well as numbers, inclines to the side of those who refuse to obliterate the line between popular ballads and lettered verse, and who are unable to accept writers like Villon in France and Dunbar in Scotland as responsible for songs which, by this convenient hypothesis, have simply come down to us without the writers' names. Child, cautious as he was in committing himself to any theory, signed an explicit confession of faith in the ballad as an independent poetic species.

Tradition is something more than a confusion of texts ; a choral throng, with improvising singers, is not the chance refuge, but, rather, the certain origin, of the ballad as a poetic form ; and, while one is not to regard the *corpus* of English and Scottish ballads as directly due to such singing and improvisation, it is thither that one turns for origins, and it is to tradition that one turns for the growth and spread of the versions themselves. Once choral, dramatic, with insistent refrain and constant improvisation, the ballad came to be a convenient form for narrative of every sort which drifted into the ways of tradition. This traditional process has been mainly epic, although oral tradition alone would not and does not force the ballad out of its choral structure, its dramatic and lyric purpose. What slowly reduces the importance and, therefore, the function of these old elements is the tendency of ballads towards the chronicle, the story, the romance. Literary influences worked upon it for these ends.

A close study of the material demands that we distinguish two general classes. One, demonstrably the older in structure, tends in form to the couplet with alternating refrain or burden, and in matter to the rendering of a single situation. These

ballads, often closely allied to Scandinavian versions, are printed
by Child in the forepart of his collection as a tribute to their
undoubted age. A dominating feature here, often recorded and
always to be assumed, is repetition; it takes a form peculiar to
balladry, is found in all these old pieces and has even left its
mark on the majority of the other versions in Child's four volumes.
As, however, epic purposes prevailed, this typically oldest ballad
was lengthened in plot, scope, details, and was shorn entirely of
its refrain. Hence a second class, the long ballad, recited or
chanted to a monotonous tune by a singer who now feels it to
be his property, a kind of enclosed common. Instead of the short
singing piece, steeped in repetition, almost borne down by its
refrain, plunging abruptly into a situation, describing no characters
and often not naming them, telling no long story and giving no
details, here is a deliberate narrative, long and easy of pace, free
of repetitions, bare of refrain, abounding in details and covering
considerable stretches of time. By a happy chance, indeed, this
epic process can be followed into its final stage. We have a
number of ballads which tell different adventures in the life of
Robin Hood; and we have an actual epic poem, formed upon
these ballads or their very close counterparts, which embodies the
adventures in a coherent whole. Between the style of the *Gest of
Robyn Hode*, however, and the style of the best Robin Hood
ballads, there is almost no difference at all; and these, for all their
age of record, may well represent the end of the epic process in
balladry. In metrical form, they hold to the quatrain made up of
alternating verses of four and three measures, which is not very
far from the old couplet with its two alternating verses of the
refrain. The change in structure is mainly concerned with loss of
choral elements, especially of incremental repetition. The well
known opening of *Robin Hood and the Monk* shows both the
change in form and the new smoothness of narrative·

> In somer, when the shawes be sheyne
> And leves be large and long,
> Hit is full mery in feyre foreste
> To here the foulys song;
>
> To se the dere drawe to the dale,
> And leve the hillës hee,
> And shadow hem in the levës grene
> Under the grenewood tre.
>
> Hit befel on Whitsontide...

Then the story begins with a dialogue between Little John and
Robin, passes into the third personal narrative and so tells its tale

with a good plot, fair coherence of motive, character and event, exciting incident of fight, imprisonment, disguise, escape and the proper pious conclusion—

> Thus endys the talking of the munke
> And Robyn Hode i-wysse;
> God, that is ever a crowned king,
> Bryng us all to his blisse!

not unlike the prayer that Chaucer puts into the mouth of the nun's priest when his tale is told. There are ninety stanzas preserved in this ballad, and it has suffered losses by mutilation of the fifteenth century manuscript. Old as it is by record, however, it seems far more finished, familiar, modern, than a ballad recovered centuries later from oral tradition in Scotland, short, intense, abrupt, with communal song for every other line of it from beginning to end, a single dominant situation, a dramatic and choral setting. Just enough epic detail has been added here to supply in tradition what was lost by transfer from actual choral rendering; and, even as it is, the taking by the hand, the turning round, seem little more than the stage directions of a play. *Babylon*, local only by name and place, is familiar in its plot or situation 'to all branches of the Scandinavian race,' and has long wandered on its path of tradition. The reader should repeat or sing aloud both the burden and the stanzas throughout:

> There were three ladies lived in a bower,
> *Eh vow bonnie,*
> And they went out to pull a flower
> *On the bonnie banks o' Fordie.*

> They hadna pu'ed a flower but ane,
> When up started to them a banisht man.

> He's taen the first sister by the hand,
> And he's turned her round and made her stand.

> 'It's whether will ye be a rank robber's wife,
> Or will ye die by my wee pen-knife?'

> 'It's I'll not be a rank robber's wife,
> But I'll rather die by your wee pen-knife.'

> He's killed this may[1], and he's laid her by,
> For to bear the red rose company.

> He's taken the second ane by the hand,
> And he's turned her round, and made her stand.

> 'It's whether will ye be a rank robber's wife,
> Or will ye die by my wee pen-knife?'

> 'I'll not be a rank robber's wife,
> But I'll rather die by your wee pen-knife.'

---

[1] Maid.

He's killed this may, and he's laid her **by**,
For to bear the red rose company.

He's taken the youngest ane by the hand,
And he's turned her round, and made her **stand.**

Says, 'Will ye be a rank robber's wife,
Or will ye die by my wee pen-knife?'

'I'll not be a rank robber's wife,
Nor will I die by your wee pen-knife.

For I hae a brother in this wood,
And gin ye kill me, it's he'll kill thee[1].'

'What's thy brother's name? Come tell to me.' —
'My brother's name is Baby Lon.'

'O sister, sister, what have I done!
O have I done this ill to thee!

O since I've done this evil deed,
Good sall never be seen o'[2] me.'

He's taken out his wee pen-knife,
 Eh vow bonnie,
And he's twyned[3] himsel o' his ain sweet life
 On the bonnie banks o' Fordie.

It needs no deep critical insight to see how near this little ballad is to the choral throng. The characters, of course, can be 'said' or told instead of being presented and acted, and a word of information must be given about them; but no attempt is made, as later epic curiosity would demand, to tell more particularly who and what they were. The situation is the main thing, and it is developed by a method which, evidently, depends upon choral and dramatic conditions. The refrain of the throng is constant; and the action advances not by continuous narrative but by a series of repetitions, in sets of three stanzas, each repetition, however, containing an increment, a new phrase or word to match the new posture of affairs. This incremental repetition is the main mark of old ballad structure; it is woven into the stuff, retained its importance long after the choral conditions which were responsible for it had been forgotten and occurs whenever a situation needs to be expressed in an emphatic form. Only in the long narrative ballads, the chronicles, the pieces that have been submitted to the most urgent epic demands, does this incremental repetition fade away. Moreover, it furnishes the connection with that source of balladry—not of modern ballads—in improvisation and communal composition, with the

---

[1] The rimes in this and the next two stanzas are, evidently, disordered.
[2] Of=by.   [3] Deprived, parted.

singing and dancing throng so often described by medieval writers. Studies in old Portuguese popular song show a corresponding growth of interlaced repetitions, in fixed formula, out of choral iteration in the communal dance[1].

A ballad known in English as *The Maid Freed from the Gallows* still has an astonishing vogue throughout Europe; in Finland, alone, there are fifty versions of it. Now and then, a narrative has been prefixed to explain the situation; but, usually, the situation stands for itself and is, beyond all doubt, original. The setting, of course, varies; now the girl is to be drowned, or carried off by pirates, now, as in the English version, she faces death on the gallows. Who will save her? She appeals to a series of relatives, all of whom refuse to interfere, until a climax is reached, say with the true-love, who is ready to part with all he has and is, so as to save her life. For each of the relatives there is the same stanza of request, the same stanza of refusal, the increments being mere change from father to mother, to brother, to sister and so on, till, with the true-love, refusal turns to triumphant consent. The cardinal facts in this ballad are, first, the ease with which it can be sung to any length, so long as names of relatives hold out, with no artistic effort of composition, after the initial stanzas have once been given, and, second, and most significant fact, the actual use of it for dance and mimetic game in one of the English versions, in a Faroe version and in sundered groups like the Danish and the Magyar. Not only is the connection of dance and ballad firmly established, but, as Kittredge points out, the making of ballads in a throng becomes a perfectly intelligible and even necessary process. Of course, few ballads can remain in this initial stage. They are submitted to oral tradition, and are sung as stories rather than presented as action. More than this, a whole narrative, often a definite occurrence, historical or legendary, or even, it may be, a late form of some old classical tale, will find its way into the ballad structure and so be handed down in the traditional way. The epic process changes this ballad structure, however, only so far as the narrative demands; there is a succession, rather than a juxtaposition, of events, smoother progress, disuse of the refrain, pruning of repetition, and, above all, a desire for better aesthetic values. Otherwise, the narrative complies with the rules of its form. The ballad remains anonymous, objective, simple. From the mass of stories drifting along the same traditionary stream, other

[1] See H. R. Lang, 'Old Portuguese Songs,' in *Festgabe für Adolfo Mussafia*, Halle, 1905, and his earlier *Liederbuch des Königs Denis von Portugal.*

details may join the old situation or the borrowed tale, and make a narrative out of it which has counterparts in popular ballads all over the world. A new event, as in Scottish ballads like *Captain Car*, falls easily into the traditional form, and finds half of its phrases, even some of its stanzas, made to hand. The versions, again, may vary with place and time, but not in any premeditated way. The stamp of popular simplicity remains; the old formulas, commonplaces, epithets, traditional in balladry, occur without fear of restraint by the poet or of exchange for 'heightened' speech; the ballad may resemble literary poems in its matter, but never in its structure and style. Short or long, old or new, it shuns metaphor and all striving for figurative effect. It is simple in the sense that there is no play of fancy in epithet, phrase or word, or in the arrangement of words and phrases. It is not simple in all senses, because it has its own easily recognised style—that ballad 'slang' oftener mentioned than known. It adheres, when it can, to dialogue; it is free from sentiment; and its modifications are due to a tendency working on purely traditional lines. The change can often be seen in a single ballad, where the main situation, choral and dramatic, has been furnished with opening and concluding verses of a purely narrative type. A possible explanation which reverses this process, which assumes the detachable epic details to be original and the choral verses to be an addition, and a redaction to fit the story for dance or game, is not to be considered for a moment. A mass of evidence, partly derived from the study of European ballads at large, partly drawn from the stores of ethnological material, puts such a plea out of court.

We may thus state with confidence the general outlines of ballad progress. What gave the ballad its existence as a poetic species was a choral, dramatic presentation[1]. Refrain of the throng, and improvisation by various singers, leant heavily, as all primitive poetry teaches us, on repetition. To advance the action, this repetition became incremental, a peculiarity of ballads which is radically different from the repetition by variation in Old English verse and from the 'thought-rime,' or *parallelismus membrorum*, established by Lowth for Hebrew poetry. The rhythmic form into which the ballad verse naturally ran is that four-accent couplet known all over the world and in every age,

---

[1] Any study of ultimate origins would have to reckon with old ritual and the survival of myth, sources that have been proved of late for the St George plays in England and for the beginnings of medieval drama throughout Europe.

as Usener has pointed out, in popular song. With the refrain, this couplet formed a quatrain; in later and longer ballads, as also in some of the short 'situation' ballads, the refrain is replaced by a second and fourth line, constituents of the regular stanza, which may be an actual substitution for the refrain, or else are simply the three-accent portion of the old *septenarius*, a conclusion which merely sets us hunting for the popular sources of the *septenar*. However this may be, the question is not vital. Given the structure, the form, of choral and dramatic balladry, one now reckons with its predominant epic contents, due to a process common in the poetry of all races. It is at this point that a regrettable confusion occurs: the sources of actual, recorded ballads, their narrative origins, whether historic, legendary, romantic or mythical, are confounded with the sources of the ballad itself, of the poetic species as a whole. The narrative element in our ballads is, of course, the most obvious mark for grouping them and comparing them with the popular verse of other lands; but to account for English balladry as a whole, we have to rely on the foregoing analysis of its constituent parts. Analysis of theme is misleading for the larger question. For example, there is nothing in Celtic tradition which exactly corresponds to the English popular ballad; such cases as the *Lord Randal* versions in Irish and Welsh must be due, as E. G. Cox points out, to importation. But there are hundreds of points in narrative, situation, motive and what not, where English ballads may touch Celtic tale or song. How far these points of contact concern the origin of a given ballad is to be determined in the individual case. On a different plane entirely stands the ballad itself as a poetic species—a form of wonderful definiteness and stability, flourishing at one time with great vigour in the Germanic and other continental races, and showing such vitality in survival as to retain its hold upon English and Scottish tradition for at least five hundred years.

Turning now to the ballads as a body, their sources both textual and material, and the classification of them, one notes the difficulty with which collectors have to contend on the frontiers of their subject. A few manuscripts preserve what may pass as ballads, because, although sacred legend is the source of them and a carol is their evident form, they bear the marks of popular tradition. Whether these inclusions be always necessary or not, there is no doubt with regard to certain exclusions which still cause unnecessary comment. The famous *Nut Brown Maid*, for example, a spirited and charming dramatic poem long ago laid to the credit of some woman as her *oratio pro domo*, her plea for the constancy of the sex, has not the faintest claim to its position in many a collection of popular traditional verse. So it is, for different reasons, with *The Children in the Wood*; there is no mark of popular tradition upon it. Still another question rises over the counterfeit ballad. By Child's reckoning, *Auld Maitland* is spurious, and he drops it from his list; but Andrew Lang makes a vigorous plea for it. It has the marks of a traditional ballad; but are they genuine? Some of the poorer and later pieces in his collection Child admitted only because of the possibility that they may contain traditional elements more or less obscured by the chances of the broadside press. In general, however, his path has been fairly plain. The oldest ballad, by record, is *Judas*, from a manuscript of the thirteenth century. Another legendary piece, *St Stephen and Herod*, along with a curious old riddle-ballad, may be dated, in their manuscript record, about 1450, the time also of *Robin Hood and the Monk* and *Robyn and Gandeleyn*, which are followed, half a century later, by *Robin Hood and the Potter*, and by the earliest printed copy of the *Gest of Robyn Hode*. From the nature of the case, these ballads, oldest of record, are all far gone in the epic process, or else, like the riddle-ballad, are stripped of choral features; it was reserved mainly for tradition to hold in survival that old ballad structure, and to give to eighteenth century collectors the stretched metre of an antique song as unlettered folk still sang it at work and play. The legendary pieces, however, which have been recovered from oral tradition are never equal to the old manuscript copies; and one of the very few 'finds[1]' since the close of Child's collection shows the disorder in the extreme.

In print of the early sixteenth century comes a long outlaw ballad, *Adam Bell, Clim of the Clough and William of Cloudesley*; and, slightly later, there follow in manuscript *Cheviot* and *Otterburn, Captain Car*—the latter, also, recovered later from tradition—and a version of *Sir Andrew Barton*. Only eleven ballads, as Kittredge notes, 'are extant in manuscripts older than the seventeenth century.' But then came the Percy folio, written about 1650, a strange medley of poems good and bad, with many of the finest ballads interspersed; it was partially known through Percy's *Reliques*, printed first in 1765, but its actual and precious contents came to light only in recent years

---

[1] *The Withies*, printed by F. Sidgwick in *Notes and Queries*, Series 10, No. 83.

and made possible the publication of Child's collection itself. This folio is the most important of all the ballad sources. It is supplemented by the Percy papers—copies made at sundry places in England and Scotland, mainly from recitation; by a number of broadsides and 'garlands,' where the task of culling out real traditional material becomes difficult to a degree; and, finally, by collectors in Scotland, Herd, Mrs Brown of Falkland, whose memory saved several sterling ballads, Scott, the 'old lady' whose manuscript Scott obtained, Sharpe, Motherwell, notorious Peter Buchan and the rest.

Apart, now, from chronology of the record, this material may be grouped according to its subjects, its age in tradition and its foreign or local origins. Oldest in every way, and quite independent of place, are the riddle-ballads which open Child's first volume. They are far simpler than the Old English riddles, and are closely related to those ballads of question and answer made in many countries at the communal dance, and used to determine the choice of a partner or the winning of a garland. One Scottish ballad frames the contest of youth and maid in a little story; the chorus of the throng has become a simple refrain:

> There was a knicht riding frae the east,
> *Sing the Cuther banks, the bonnie brume,*
> Wha had been wooing at monie a place,
> *And ye may beguile a young thing sune.*

This strange knight puts a girl to the test of riddles. 'What is higher nor the tree? What is deeper nor the sea?' he asks, and ends with a challenge to name something 'worse than a woman.' The girl answers all, saying, at the close, that Clootie—the devil—is worse than woman; and off goes the fiend, named and baffled, in fire. Close to this sort of riddle-ballad, very old, widespread, still used in many places for the dance, is alternate request for impossible things. A late form of this ancient sort of ballad or 'flyting' is *Captain Wedderburn's Courtship*, where the maid is finally vanquished; 'and now she's Mrs Wedderburn,' the ballad concludes, with a final change in its infectiously vivacious refrain. Still further from the early type is that 'base-born' but saucy little ballad, *The Twa Magicians*, where alternate changes of form in pursuer and pursued take the place of the 'flyting' by word and wit.

The epic tendency, always working out of situation into narrative, now takes us to a very large group of ballads, which seldom content themselves with the dramatic crisis, but deal in a more intricate plot, furnish the details and even add a store of romantic incidents. This ballad of domestic complications, the tragedy of kin, looms large in all European tradition; borrowing, however, or a common source, is not always to be assumed even where the story is the same, since certain primary instincts must bring about like results wherever men are set in families or clans and human passions prevail. Still, there is, in many cases, abundant reason for identification, and, even, for alliance with more distant branches of balladry and tales. Bride-stealing and its results, for example, were common experience, and the bare fact needed no importation; but a plot like that of *Fair Annie* is found in the *Lai le Freine* of Marie de France, and, although it is no very recondite affair, yet it is stamped by its recognition-motive at the end. A knight from over sea steals Annie, takes her home, makes her mother of his seven sons and then bethinks him to get a lawful bride with shiploads of dower. Annie welcomes the new wife; but her moans are overheard, and the two turn out to be sisters. This, with the ballad of *Child Maurice*, on which Home founded his play of *Douglas* and which greatly moved the poet Gray, with *Babylon*—already quoted—with *Hind Horn*, certainly related to the gest and the romance on the same theme, has, in the recognition-plot, a strongly romantic suggestion; but it is noteworthy that these ballads all tend, either by abundant repetition, or by structure and refrain, to the oldest type, and can be connected with that simplest structural form which is preserved in *The Maid Freed from the Gallows*. The stealing of a bride, as a familiar fact, was an obvious subject of a ballad of situation; and such a ballad lent itself easily to one of two epic processes. Either it was connected with a local legend—flight, pursuit, fight and the death of all parties save the bride—and resulted in an *Earl Brand*, or, in Scott's version, a *Douglas Tragedy*[1]; or else it drew on international matter, on myth, legend, the 'good story' of commerce, what not, resulting in a *Lady Isabel and the Elf-Knight*, or in a leisurely and elegant bit of romance like *King Estmere*[2]. Indeed, these three ballads will serve as types of the local, the half-localised and the unattached. Tragedy broods over them all, but is least suited to the third type; king

---

[1] Out of the original eleven stanzas of the *Child of Ell*, in the Folio, a version of this ballad, Percy made a poem of fifty stanzas for his *Reliques*.

[2] An absurd companion piece of this ballad, whether so designed or not, is *Will Stewart and John*.

Estmere must overwhelm the soldan; Susy Pye (in *Young Beichan*) and Hind Horn must win their loves. These are entertaining verse. *Earl Brand*, however, like *Babylon*, like the Scandinavian versions, is tragic in the matter; although a closely related ballad, *Erlinton*, killing fifteen of the pursuers, spares the father, and lets the lovers go off happy to the greenwood. *Lady Isabel*, too, escapes by whatever stratagem from her savage wooer; and here, of course, are borrowed motives, as in the 'three cries' for help. There is a glimpse, too, of supernatural aid, as, in some versions, that of the talking birds. In a ballad of similar theme, but quite prosaic details, *The Fair Flower of Northumberland*, it is hard to say whether the supernatural elements have been toned down or lost, or else were never in the piece at all. Among other elopement stories of the primitive sort, mainly situation but with a few romantic details, *Gil Brenton*, a sterling old ballad, is worthy of note; the type, however, easily passes into mere sensation, into mawkish and cheap sentiment and into the rout of tales about runaways fair or foul, mainly localised in Scotland. There is even sadder stuff than this. *Brown Robin, Willie and Earl Richard's Daughter* (purporting to account for the birth of Robin Hood), *Rose the Red and White Lily*, *The Famous Flower of Serving Men* and *Tom Potts*, are a descending series with very low fall. The singing-robes of balladry are here in rags, and tawdry rags too. There is recovery of old traditions, however, in the Scottish ballads of bride-stealing or elopement like *Katharine Jaffray*—whether Scott's own doing, or compiled from traditional fragments, in any case the model of his *Young Lochinvar*—and in like pieces of varying merit, *Bonny Baby Livingston*, *Eppie Morrie* and *The Lady of Arngosk*—the last named known in many of its details, both as an event about 1736 and as a popular song, but unfortunately recovered only in fragments. Very different, finally, is the tone of two good ballads, *Willie's Lyke-Wake* and *The Gay Goshawk*, where love finds out the way by stratagem and inspires robust verse of the old kind.

Complications of kin make up ballads of domestic tragedy, a most important group ; and even the inroads of a doggerel poet upon the old material, even the cheap 'literature' of the stalls, cannot hide that ancient dignity. The motive of *Bewick and Graham*, outwardly a story of two drunken squires near Carlisle, their quarrel, and the sacrifice of two fine lads to this quarrel in the conflict of filial duty with ties of friendship—told, by the way, in verse that often touches the lowest levels—redeems the ballad

from its degraded form and gives it the pathos of a *Cid.* The cry
of the dying victor—

> Father, could ye not drunk your wine at home,
> And letten me and my brother be ?

is not impressive, perhaps, as a quotation ; but in its context and
climax it stands with the great things of the great poems. *Andrew
Lammie,* enormously popular in the north of Scotland, represents
another class of homely ballads, more or less vulgarised by their
form, their overdone sentiment and their efforts at literary grace,
but not without appeal and a certain force of tradition. Tradition
at its purest, and an appeal to which few readers fail in responding, characterise the great ballads of domestic tragedy. *Edward,*
for example, is so inevitable, so concentrated, that sundry critics,
including the latest editor of Scott's *Minstrelsy,* would refer it
to art ; but tradition can bring about these qualities in its own
way. *Lord Randal,* with its bewildering number of versions;
Little Musgrave and Lady Barnard, a favourite in Shakespeare's
day and often quoted ; *Glasgerion* (who may be the 'Glascurion'
mentioned in Chaucer's *House of Fame* and may represent the
Welsh Glas Keraint), a simple but profoundly affecting ballad on a
theme which no poet could now handle without either constraint or
offence; *Child Maurice*; *The Cruel Brother*; *The Twa Brothers*—
with a particularly effective climax—offer tragedy of the false
mistress, the false wife, the false servant, and tragedy of more
complicated matter. Wives false and wives true are pictured in two
sterling Scottish ballads, *The Baron o' Brackley* and *Captain Car,*
both founded on fact. *The Braes o' Yarrow* knew another faithful
wife. Darker shadows of incest, mainly avoided by modern literature, fall in possibility on *Babylon,* quoted above, and in real
horror upon *Sheath and Knife* and *Lizie Wan.* The treacherous
nurse, again, with that bloody and revengeful *Lamkin*—a satiric
name—long frightened Scottish children ; and a case of treachery
in higher station, involving trial by combat and giving many hints
of medieval ways, is preserved in the old story of *Sir Aldingar,*
familiar to William of Malmesbury. Finally, there is the true-
love. The adjective is beautifully justified in *The Three Ravens,*
unfortunately less known than its cynical counterpart, *The Twa
Corbies.* True-love is false in *Young Hunting* ; and fickle lovers
come to grief in *Lord Lovel, Fair Margaret and Sweet William,*
and *Lord Thomas and Fair Annet.* Fate, not fickleness,
however, brings on the tragedy in *Fair Janet, Lady Maisey,*

Clerk Saunders; while fickleness is condoned and triumphant in ballads which Child calls 'pernicious': *The Broom o' Cowden knowes* and *The Wylie Wife of the Hie Town Hie.* Better is the suggestion of *The Wife of Bath's Tale* in the popular *Knight and Shepherd's Daughter. Child Waters*, which both Child and Grundtvig praise as the pearl of English ballads, belongs to the well known group of poems celebrating woman's constancy under direst provocation; neither Chaucer's *Clerk's Tale* nor that dramatic poem of the *Nut Brown Maid* pleads the cause of woman with more eloquence. Ellen in the stable, with her new-born child, appeals to any heart:

> Lullabye, my oune deere child!
> Lullabye, deere child, deere!
> I wold thy father were a king,
> Thy mother layd on a beere!

While this ballad has wandered far from the dramatic and choral type, the survival in its structure is marked enough; and its incremental repetition, in several sequences, is most effective.

Ballads of the funeral, echoes of the old *coronach, vocero*, whatever the form of communal grief, are scantily preserved in English; *Bonnie James Campbell* and *The Bonny Earl of Murray* may serve as types; but the noblest outcome of popular lament, however crossed and disguised by elements of other verse it may seem in its present shape, is *Sir Patrick Spens*, which should be read in the shorter version printed by Percy in the *Reliques*, and should not be teased into history. The incremental repetition and climax of its concluding stanzas are beyond praise. Less affecting is the 'good night'—unless we let *Johnny Armstrong*, beloved of Goldsmith, pass as strict representative of this type. *Lord Maxwell's Last Good Night*, it is known, suggested to Byron the phrase and the mood of Childe Harold's song. To be a ballad, however, these 'good nights' must tell the hero's story, not simply echo his emotion.

Superstition, the other world, ghost-lore, find limited scope in English balladry. Two ballads of the sea, *Bonnie Annie* and *Brown Robyn's Confession*, make sailors cast lots to find the 'fey folk' in the ship, and so to sacrifice the victim. Commerce with the other world occurs in *Thomas Rymer*, derived from a romance, and in *Tam Lin*, said by Henderson to be largely the work of Burns. *Clerk Colvill* suffers from his alliance with a mermaid. *The Great Silkie of Sule Skerry*, a mournful little ballad from Shetland, tells of him who is 'a man upo' the lan',' but a seal, 'a silkie in the sea.' Other transformation ballads are *Kemp Owyne, Allison Gross* and *The Laily Worm*. In *Sweet William's Ghost*, however, a great favourite of old, and in the best of all 'supernatural' ballads, *The Wife of Usher's Well*, dignified, pathetic, reticent, English balladry competes in kind, though by no means in amount, with the riches of Scandinavian tradition.

Epic material of every sort was run into the ballad mould. *King Orfeo* finds Eurydice in Shetland ; the ballad is of very old structural type. Sacred legends like that of *Sir Hugh*, and secular legends such as *Hind Horn*, occur ; while *Sir Cawline* and *King Estmere* are matter of romance. Possibly, the romances of Europe sprang in their own turn from ballads ; and *Sir Lionel*, in the Percy folio, with its ancient type of structure, may even reproduce the kind of ballads which formed a basis for *Sir Cawline* itself. Minstrels, of course, could take a good romance and make it over into indifferent ballads ; three of these are so described by Child—*The Boy and the Mantle, King Arthur and King Cornwall* and *The Marriage of Sir Gawaine*. With the cynical *Crow and Pie* we reach the verge of indecency, also under minstrel patronage, though it is redeemed for balladry by a faint waft of tradition. This piece, along with *The Baffled Knight* and *The Broomfield Hill*, is close to the rout from which Tom D'Urfey selected his *Pills to Purge Melancholy*. Thoroughly debased is *The Keach in the Creel* ; but *The Jolly Beggar*, especially in the 'old lady's' manuscript, is half-redeemed by the dash and swing of the lines. Old ladies, as one knows from a famous anecdote of Scott, formerly liked this sort of thing, without losing caste, and saw no difference between it and the harmless fun of *Get Up and Bar the Door*, or the old story, which Hardy seems to record as still a favourite in Dorsetshire, of *Queen Eleanor's Confession*.

With this ballad we come to history, mainly perverted, but true as tradition. *Lord Delamere*, debased in broadsides, *Hugh Spencer's Feats in France* and the vastly popular *John Dory* ; naval ballads like the poor *Sweet Trinity* and the excellent *Sir Andrew Barton* ; Scottish *King James and Brown*, and that sterling ballad *Mary Hamilton* which Andrew Lang has successfully called back from Russia to its place at queen Mary's own court, with twenty-eight versions still extant to attest its vogue—all these are typical in their kind. But the historical ballad, recited rather than sung epic in all its purposes and details, and far removed from the choral ballad of dramatic situation, is best studied in those pieces which have become traditional along the Scottish border. Not all, however, are of the chronicle type. In 1593, a certain freebooter was hanged, and his nephew took good vengeance for him, calling out a ballad; whatever its original shape, one finds it still fresh with the impression of actual deeds; and, in its nervous couplets, its lack of narrative breadth, the lilt and swing of it, one is inclined to call *The Lads of Wamphray* a case of *ipsi confingunt*—a phrase of which Leslie was making use, not far from this date, as to the Borderers and their songs. The dialogue is immediate, and has the old incremental repetition:

> O Simmy, Simmy, now let me gang,
> And I vow I'll ne'er do a Crichton wrang.
>
> O Simmy, Simmy, now let me be,
> And a peck o' goud I'll gie to thee.
>
> O Simmy, Simmy, let me gang,
> And my wife shall heap it wi' her hand.

This was not made at long range. Epic, on the other hand, and reminiscent, is *Dick o' the Cow*—cited by Tom Nashe—a good story told in high spirits; long as it is, it has a burden, and was meant to be sung. *Archie o' Cawfield, Hobie Noble, Jock o' the Side* and others of the same sort are narratives in the best traditional style; Scott's imitation of these is *Kinmont Willie*— at least it is so much his own work as to deserve to bear his name. Still another class is the short battle-piece, of which *Harlaw, Bothwell Bridge* and even *Flodden Field*, preserved by Deloney, may serve as examples. *Durham Field*, in sixty-six stanzas, was made by a minstrel. Refusing classification, there stand out those two great ballads, probably on the same fight, *Cheviot* and *Otterburn*. The version of the former known as *Chevy Chace*, 'written over for the broadside press,' as Child remarks, was the object of Addison's well known praise; what Sidney heard as 'trumpet sound' is not certain, but one would prefer to think it was the old *Cheviot*. One would like, too, the liberty of bringing Shakespeare into the audience, and of regarding that ancient ballad as contributing to his conception of Hotspur. These are no spinsters' songs, but rather, in the first instance at least, the making and the tradition of men-at-arms. A curiously interlaced stanza arrangement, here and there to be noted in both the old *Cheviot* and *Otterburn*, as well as Richard Sheale's signature to the former as part of his minstrel stock, imply considerable changes in the structure of the original ballad. Sheale, of course, had simply copied a favourite song; but the fact is suggestive.

Last of all, the greenwood. *Johnie Cock*, says Child, is 'a precious specimen of the unspoiled traditional ballad.' A single situation and event, it contrasts sharply with a long story like *Adam Bell* as well as with the various pieces, short or long, which deal with Robin himself. From *Johnie Cock* to the *Gest* is a process of great interest to the student of traditional verse. Had the *Gest*, indeed, been made by its humble rhapsode in an unlettered age, the epic process would have had even more scope, and would have drawn upon poetic sources already claimed for deliberate composition and the literary record. As it is, Robin may be proud of his place. 'Absolutely a creation of the ballad muse,' he is the hero of a sterling little epic, and of thirty-six extant individual ballads, good and bad; the good are mainly of a piece with the old epic material, and the bad are indebted for their badness to the corruptions of the broadside press, the editing for garlands and the exhausted vitality of late tradition. Robin has a definite personality throughout, though the degenerate ballads, as in the case of late poems about Charlemagne, make him anybody's victim. Any local hero could be exalted by the simple process of outwitting and trouncing the old master of that craft. One of the latest poems, a dreary compilation called the *True Tale of Robin Hood*, the only piece in Child's collection which is not anonymous, is the work of Martin Parker. But one forgets trash. Robin remains as the best ballads and the *Gest* have drawn him—generous, brave, pious, with a touch of melancholy and a touch of humour unknown to the strictly choral muse. The narrative art of this good verse is very high. No story is better told anywhere than the story of Robin's loan to Sir Richard and its payment; humour is held firmly in hand; and Chaucer himself could not better the ease and sureness of the little epic. Nor does the *Gest* improve in all ways upon its material. *Robin Hood and the Monk* is a sterling piece of narrative. The brief close of the *Gest*, telling, in five stanzas, how Robin was 'beguiled' and slain, and rather awkwardly quoting an unconnected bit of dialogue, should be compared with the ballad of *Robin Hood's Death* from the Percy folio. Here, in spite of eighteen missing stanzas, the story is admirably told. Every incident counts: the testy humour of Robin at the start, the mysterious old woman banning him as she kneels on the plank over 'black water,' the fatal bleeding, the final struggle, revenge, pious parting and death—good narrative throughout. It is clear that a process had taken place in the gradual formation of this cycle which not only brought its several parts into fair coherence, but, also, exercised a reactionary influence upon tradition itself. In any case, with these ballads of Robin Hood, balladry itself crossed the marches of the epic, and found itself far from the old choral, dramatic improvisations, though still fairly close to the spirit and motive of traditional verse.

A word remains to be said on the sources and the values of British ballads as a whole. Common 'Aryan' origin, though it was still held in a modified form by Gaston Paris, can no longer be maintained so as to account for the community of theme in the ballads of Europe. What has been done by scholars like Child and Grundtvig, by Nigra, Bugge and others, is to have established certain groups, more or less definite, which, in different lands and times, tell the same general story or give the same particular motive or detail. To account for these groups is another task. A pretty little ballad from Shetland narrates in quite choral, dramatic form the story of Orpheus and Eurydice. Bugge has traced the same story from a Danish ballad far back into medieval times; its ultimate source, to be sure, is the classical account. Another source, we have seen, is legend; still another is the direct historical event. Evidently, then, the matter of sources is something to be settled for the narrative part of each individual ballad; but, however great the interest of this investigation may be, however obvious its claims and satisfactory its results, it does not affect the specific ballad as a literary form. The structure of the ballad—what makes it a species, the elements of it—derives from choral and dramatic conditions; what gives it its peculiar art of narrative is the epic process working by oral tradition, and gradually leading to a new structure with choral and dramatic elements still surviving, though dwindling, in the guise of refrain and incremental repetition. The metrical form remains fairly constant throughout. With certain other formal characteristics, the commonplaces, the conventional phrases and motives, there is no space to deal here. So, too, with regard to imitations good and bad, we can only refer to Scott's *Kinmont Willie* for one class, and, for the other, to that famous forgery, the *Hardycnute* of Lady Wardlaw.

The aesthetic values of the ballad call for no long comment. They are the values which attach to rough, strong verse intent upon its object. Trope and figure are out of the question, and all feats of language as such. No *verborum artifex* works here. The appeal is straight. It is, indeed, ridiculous to call the ballads 'primitive'; not only have they a developed art of their own, but they are crossed at every turn by literary influences, mainly working for coherence of narrative, which are indirect, indeed, yet sure. Nevertheless, the abiding value of the ballads is that they give a hint of primitive and unspoiled poetic sensation. They speak not only in the language of tradition, but also with the voice of the multitude; there is nothing subtle in their working, and they appeal to things as they are. From one vice of modern literature they are free: they have no 'thinking about thinking,' no feeling about feeling. They can tell a good tale. They are fresh with the open air; wind and sunshine play through them; and the distinction, old as criticism itself, which assigns them to nature rather than to art, though it was overworked by the romantic school and will be always liable to abuse, is practical and sound.

CHAPTER XVIII

POLITICAL AND RELIGIOUS VERSE TO THE CLOSE OF THE FIFTEENTH CENTURY—FINAL WORDS

In a previous chapter[1], something was said of the changes in language and in thought which accompanied the Norman conquest of England, and it was pointed out how short a time, comparatively speaking, was needed for the fusion of race with race. The incorporation of a French vocabulary into the vernacular was, inevitably, a more prolonged operation; or, to speak more precisely, it was longer before that fusion became apparent and was reflected in the literature of the people, the literary or fashionable language being, for many a long year, the tongue of the conquerors. The influence of the courtly literature of the ruling caste in more than one direction has already been pointed out[2]. It is no part of the scope of this work to encroach upon what more properly belongs to the earlier literature of a modern language other than our own, or to tell over again what has already been dealt with in the pages of Gaston Paris, in the volumes of Petit de Julleville and elsewhere; but our interest in medieval French letters must always be more than that of mere neighbours. Thus, the period now reached in the history of our own literature, when the death of Gower points, approximately, to the end of French letters in England, offers an opportunity for mentioning, in the course of a very brief summary, the work of one or two Anglo-Normans whose writings either are intimately connected with English historical events and personages, or have left their impression on the form and matter of the rapidly growing body of vernacular literature. To some of these, special reference has already been made—Philippe de Thaon, whose *Bestiary*[3] belongs to a popular and fascinating type of didactic literature, and helped to furnish

---

[1] Vol. i, pp. 149 ff.

[2] Vol. i, chapter xiii. See also vol. i, pp. 238, 446, 447, 460, 466 ff.

[3] Dedicated to Adela of Louvain, the second wife of Henry I, for whom Benoît the Anglo-Norman monk versified a *St Brendan* in 1121.

material for early English writers on similar themes, and whose guide to the ecclesiastical calendar, *Li Cumpoz*, sets forth what the ignorant clerk ought to know ; Geoffrey Gaimar and Wace, who became the mediums by which earlier English and Latin histories provided material for the work of Layamon; William of Wadington, whose *Manuel* was written, probably, for Normans in Yorkshire, and another 'Yorkshire Norman,' Peter of Langtoft, who were the literary god-fathers of Mannyng of Brunne[1].

Gaimar's *Estorie des Engles* was based, mainly, on the Old English *Chronicle* and, apart from his relation to Layamon, his chief value for us lies in the sections which deal with contemporary matters, in his contributions to the story of Havelok and in his descriptions of social manners and customs[2]. Of greater worth is the life of William, first of the Marshal earls of Pembroke and Striguil, regent of England, a soldier and states-man who died in 1219, after having served, for nearly half a century, more than one king of England with rare fidelity, and whose deeds are worthily enshrined in the poem which bears his name. *L'Histoire de Guillaume le Maréchal*, which was finished in 1226, consists of some 19,000 octosyllabic lines, and its discoverer, Paul Meyer, has claimed for it a place in the front rank of French medieval historiography, and as having no superiors in its kind in the writings of the thirteenth and fourteenth centuries[3].

Garnier de Pont-Sainte-Maxence's *Vie de St Thomas Becket*, a poem worthy of its subject, and of great historic value; Fantosme's *Chronicle of the Scottish Wars* of 1173–4; Ambroise's *Histoire de la Guerre Sainte*, with Richard Cœur de Lion for its central figure ; Old French psalters and saints' lives ; moral tales, like those told by the Franciscan Nicole Bozon in the earlier half of the fourteenth century ; immoral fables ; pilgrimages and gospels for the laity; popular presentations of current science and works on venery, such as those which probably served the somewhat mythical Juliana Berners ; *lais*, as those of Marie de France —all these may be recorded as links in the direct chain which bound French medieval literature to England. To these may be added books of counsel and courtesy, which became models for and directly inspired the popular literature of the native tongue —'the booke,' for example, 'whiche the knyght of the Toure

---

[1] Vol. I, pp. 104, etc., 170, etc., 204, etc., 226 ff., 344 ff., 447, 460, etc., etc.

[2] See, for example, in Wright, T., *A History of Domestic Manners and Sentiments in England during the Middle Ages*, pp. 84, etc.

[3] *L'Hist. de Guillaume le Maréchal*, ed. P. Meyer, t. III, p. cii, Paris, 1901.

made to the enseygnement and techyng of his doughters, translated
oute of Frenssh in to our maternall Englysshe tongue by me,
William Caxton'; dialogues, as those contained in a *maniere de
langage que t'enseignera bien a droit parler et escrire doulz
françois*[1], which help to make clearer to us the social relations
of the fourteenth century; and French versions of the old
romances such as Caxton and his followers popularised, to which
reference has already been made, and which will be further
discussed when the prose of the sixteenth century is under
consideration.

Political verse to the end, approximately, of the reign of
Edward II was glanced at in a previous chapter[2]. In addition
to the two poems in the mixed languages therein mentioned, may
be noted a *Song against the King's Taxes*, written in the reign
of Edward II, in five-line stanzas, the first half of each line, save
the fifth, being in Anglo-Norman and the latter half of each line
and the whole of the fifth being in Latin. Its theme and its
form can best be seen by such a stanza as the following:

> *Depus que le roy vodera tam multum cepisse,*
> *Entre les riches si purra satis invenisse;*
> *E plus, à ce que m'est avys, et melius fecisse*
> *Des grantz partie aver pris, et parvis pepercisse.*
> *Qui capit argentum sine causa peccat egentum*[3].

From the reign of Edward III onwards, English, as the main
vehicle for political verse, apparently ousts Anglo-Norman. A late
Anglo-Norman poem, written about 1338, *Leus veus du hairon,
The Vows of the Heron*[4], has, for its object, the goading of the
young king Edward III to war with France, by comparing him
with what was held to be a cowardly bird. The poem relates
that Robert of Artois, who had his own purposes to serve, caused
a heron to be served at the king's table and called aloud the bird's
virtues and vices as it was carried in:

> *Et puis que couers est, je dis à mon avis,*
> *C'au plus couart qui soit ne qui oncques fust vis*
> *Donrrai le hairon, ch'est Edouart Loeis,*
> *Deshiretés de Franche, le nobile pais,*
> *Qu'il en estoit drois hoirs; mès cuers li est falis,*
> *Et por sa lasquethé en morra dessaisis;*
> *S'en dois bein au hairon voer le sien avis.*

This is too much for the king; and he and his courtiers make their
warlike vows on the heron. The war that ensued, together with

[1] See P. Meyer, *Revue Critique*, 1870, p. 371.   [2] Vol. I, p. 370.
[3] Wright, T., *Political Songs*, 1839, p. 184.
[4] *Political Poems and Songs*, ed. Wright, T., 1859, Rolls Series.

the Scottish war of the earlier years of the boy-king's reign, were sung by Laurence Minot; and the death of the king, in 1377, called forth a tribute[1] the overmastering thought in which was the very old fashioned sentiment

> That alle thing weres and wasteth away.

That the evils of the time were not absent from the minds of thinking men we see by the writings of Gower and by the *Plowman* poems. In these last, there is no room for the light hearted gaiety, the easy-going happiness that causes us to regard Chaucer, though a contemporary, as almost belonging to another world. To the writers of the *Plowman* poems the times were out of joint and more than jesting was required to set them right; their sharp solemn rimeless lines ring in the ear like the sound of an alarm or the first few strokes of the passing bell.

The unquiet reign of Henry IV saw the miserable game of heresy-hunting at work under the statute *De Heretico Comburendo*, and political revolt after revolt in the north. Four years after the burning of William Sawtrey the Lollard, at Smithfield, a lay court condemned the saintly archbishop Richard le Scrope of York to death for high treason and provided that the sentence should be carried out as ignominiously as might be. The virtues of the archbishop are celebrated in Latin and in English verses; and the political and religious 'crimes' of the Lollards are not forgotten by other literary clerks.

Both Latin and English poems against the Lollards and songs against friars, are of common occurrence. One poet sings

> Thai dele with purses, pynnes and knyves,
> With gyrdles, gloves, for wenches and wyves[2],

while another, in a fifteenth century MS, combines Latin and English, beginning

> Freeres, freeres, wo ȝe be!
> *ministri malorum*,
> For many a manes soule bringe ȝe
> *ad poenas infernorum*[3]

and continuing, in violent lines which cannot be quoted, to set forth current crimes. In the Middle Ages, popular singers, 'westours and rimers, minstrels or vagabonds,' who followed their calling along the king's highway, helped, often enough, to fan the flames

---

[1] *Political Poems and Songs*, ed. Wright, T., 1859, Rolls Series, vol. I, p. 215.

[2] *Ibid.* p. 264.

[3] *Reliquiae Antiquae*, ed. Wright, T. and Halliwell, J. O., 1841—3, vol. II, p. 247. See also vol. I, p. 322.

of rebellion, political and religious; it should be remembered to their credit that, consciously or unconsciously, their work was not without effect in the emancipation of the people.

Ten years after the 'Glory of York' had been executed, the victory of Agincourt gave further employment to song writers; but the specimen of their work preserved in the Pepysian MS does not bear comparison with later poems on the same theme. Professional and laudatory verses on deaths and coronations we can leave aside; but the interest of its satire should preserve from forgetfulness a poem on the siege of Calais, 1436. 'The duk of Burgayn,' with 'grete prid' set forth 'Calys to wyn,' and his preparations are told with a rare spirit of raillery. In Calais itself, even

> The women, both yung and old,
> Wyth stones stuffed every scaffold,
> The spared not to swet ne swynk;
> With boylyng cawdrens, both grett and smalle,
> Yf they wold assaute the walle,
> All hote to gev them drynk[1].

In 1436—7, was written one of the most important and remarkable of early English political poems, *The Libel* [or little book] *of English Policy.* The poem begins by 'exhortynge alle Englande to kepe the see enviroun,' and it is an early example of the political insight which recognised that the natural source of the greatness of a small island lay on the sea; its influence on later naval developments can scarce be doubted. English commercial relations with foreign nations are discussed by the anonymous author at considerable length; 'the commodytees of Spayne and of Fflaundres,' and of many another community are reviewed, and oddly enough these things read in rime:

> And lycorys, Syvyle oyle, and grayne,
> Whyte Castelle sope, and wax, is not in vayne;
> Iren, wolle, wadmole, gotefel, kydefel also,
> Ffor poynt-makers fulle nedefulle be the ij.

The Irish question is well to the fore, and there is a Welsh question as well:

> wyth alle your myghte take hede
> To kepe Yrelond, that it be not loste;
> Ffor it is a boterasse and a poste
> Undre England, and Wales another.
> God forbede but eche were othere brothere,
> Of one ligeaunce dewe unto the kynge.

And then the author turns to discuss 'the comodius stokfysshe of Yselonde' brought by the seamen that go out from Bristow

---

[1] *Political Poems*, ed. Wright, T., vol. ii, p. 151.

and from Scarborowgh 'unto the costes cold'; and he harks back to Calais and urges, in language which sounds strangely modern, that there be

> set a governaunce.

> Set many wittes wythoutene variaunce
> To one accorde and unanimité,
> Put to god wylle for to kepe the see.

> The ende of bataile is pease sikerlye,
> And power causeth pease finally[1].

The last political poem to which reference need be made here is a mocking dirge, called forth by the death of the king's favourite the duke of Suffolk, on 3 May 1450, 'a dyrge made by the comons of Kent in the tyme of ther rysynge when Jake Cade was theyr cappitayn...writn owt of david norcyn his booke by John stowe[2].' The poem describes how 'bisshopes and lordes, as grete reson is,' took their several parts in his funeral service, and it deserves mention by reason of the prosodic art shown in the refrain, 'in which the passing-bell slowness of the first half

> For | Jack | Napes' | soul *pla-* |

suddenly turns head over heels into a carillon of satiric joy and triumph with

> *cebo* and | *diri\ge*[3]'

A careful examination of fourteenth century religious poems preserved in the Vernon MS and elsewhere, of the minor verse of the school of Richard Rolle of Hampole, of passages in the religious plays such as those which tell the story of Abraham and Isaac and of the fugitive verse of the fifteenth century should convince the most sceptical of the wealth of early English anonymous poetry, and of its great prosodic interest; it should abolish the practice of regarding verse associated with the outstanding names, and the so-called 'court-poetry,' as the only poetry worth consideration; and it should help us to render tardy justice to periods sometimes dubbed barren wastes.

The note of simplicity of utterance, often combined with

---

[1] The quotations are from T. Wright's text, in *Political Poems and Songs*, but see also the first volume of Hakluyt and *The Libell of Englishe Policye*, 1436, *Text und metrische Übersetzung von W. Hertzberg, Mit einer geschichtlichen Einleitung von R. Pauli*, Leipzig, 1878. Cf. also the poem *On England's Commercial Policy*, Wright's *Political Poems and Songs*, vol. II, p. 282.

[2] *Political, Religious and Love Poems*, Lambeth MS, etc., ed. Furnivall, F. J., E.E.T.S. 1866, new edition, 1903.

[3] Saintsbury, G., *A History of English Prosody*, vol. I, p. 261.

perfection of form, which is struck in such poems as the thirteenth or early fourteenth century lyric from the Egerton MS

> Somer is comen and winter is gon,
> > this day beginniȝ to longe,
> And this foules everichon
> > joye hem wit songe!
> So stronge kare me bint,
> Al wit joye that is funde
> > in londe,
>
> Al for a child
> That is so milde
> > of honde[1],

is found again in the *Sayings of St Bernard* in the Vernon MS

> Where ben heo that biforen us weren,
> That houndes ladden and haukes beeren,
> > And hedden feld and wode;
> This Riche ladys in heore bour,
> That wereden gold in heore tressour,
> > With heore brihte rode[2][3]?

It is carried on by Michael of Kildare, in a hymn written at the beginning of the fourteenth century in which there are movements like this:

> This worldis love is gon a-wai,
> So dew on grasse in someris dai,
> Few ther beth, weilawai!
> > that lovith Goddis lore[4];

it becomes exquisitely melodious in the northern Hampole poems of, approximately, the middle of the fourteenth century, notably in the alliterative verses beginning

> My trewest tresowre sa trayturly taken,
> Sa bytterly bondyn wyth bytand bandes;
> How sone of thi servandes was thou forsaken,
> And lathly for my lufe hurld with thair handes[5],

and in Eve's lines in the 'Coventry' play:

> Alas! that evyr that speche was spokyn
> That the fals aungel seyd onto me.
> Alas! oure makers byddyng is brokyn
> Ffor I have towchyd his owyn dere tre.
> Oure fflescly eyn byn al unlokyn,
> > Nakyd for synne ouresylf we see,
> That sory appyl that we han sokyn
> > To dethe hathe brouth my spouse and me[6].

---

[1] *Reliquiae Antiquae*, vol. I, p. 100.   [2] complexion.
[3] *Minor Poems of the Vernon MS, with poems from Digby MS*, vol. II, p. 521, ed. Furnivall, F. J., E.E.T.S. 1901.
[4] *Reliquiae Antiquae*, vol. II, p. 190.   [5] Horstman's ed., vol. I, p. 72.
[6] *Ludus Coventriae*, ed. Halliwell, J. O., pp. 27, 28, 1841.

It exerts magical power in the beautiful carol from the early
fifteenth century Sloane MS:

> I syng of a mayden that is makeles,
> Kyng of alle kynges to here sone che ches.
> He cam also stylle ther his moder was,
> As dew in Aprylle that fallyt on the gras.
> He cam also stylle to his moderes bowr,
> As dew in Aprille that fallyt on the flour.
> He cam also stylle ther his moder lay,
> As dew in Aprille that fallyt on the spray[1];

it shows itself capable of infinite pathos in the appeal of Isaac to
his father in the Chester play:

> Alas! father, is that your will,
> Your owne childe here for to spill
> Upon this hilles brynke?
> Yf I have trespassed in any degree,
> With a yard you maye beate me;
> Put up your sword if your will be,
> For I am but a Childe
>
> . . . .
>
> *Abraham*
> Come hither, my Child, that art so sweete;
> Thou must be bounden hand and feete[2];

it reveals passion, strong though subdued to that it works in,
in the *Quia amore langueo* of the Lambeth MS *c.* 1430[3]; and it
finds an echo in the poem to the Virgin, printed towards the
close of the fifteenth century in *Speculum Christiani*, beginning

> Mary moder, wel thou be!
> Mary moder, thenke on me.

There are, of course, duller and more sophisticated utterances
than these. Mysticism often acts as a clog and didactic aim
frequently achieves its usual end and produces boredom. But
that happy sense of familiarity with the company of Heaven,
which is one of the characteristics of an age of profound faith,
finds delightful expression in hymns from Christ to His 'deintiest
damme'[4] and, above all, in the religious plays. These last,
which were written to be understood by the common folk, are

---

[1] *Songs and Carols*, ed. Wright, T., Warton Club, 1861, p. 30.

[2] *Chester Plays*, ed. Deimling, H., E.E.T.S., 1893, p. 75. The extant MSS of the
Chester cycle belong to the end of the sixteenth century, but the substantial features
of the passage quoted above are found in the fifteenth century Brome play on the same
subject (*Anglia*, VII, pp. 316—337), with which the Chester play would seem to be
connected.

[3] *Political etc. Poems*, ed. Furnivall. F. J., p. 177.

[4] *Hymns to the Virgin and Christ*, ed. Furnivall, F. J., p. 3, E.E.T.S. 1867.

mirrors which reflect the tastes of the people, in the fourteenth
and fifteenth centuries. An ingenuous audience wished to be
moved easily to tears and laughter; rough humour and simple
pathos jostled each other on the booths or travelling stages on
which were set forth the shrewishness of Noah's wife, and Isaac
submissive to his father's stroke, the boisterous comedy of
quarrelling shepherds and their criticism of the angelic voices.
It was not gold and frankincense and myrrh that would appeal
most to the imagination of the idler in the market place, but a
ball, a bird and 'a bob of cherys,' which the visiting shepherds
give to the Child-Christ, as they address him with

> Hayll, lytyll tyne mop!
> Of oure crede thou art crop;
> I wold drynk on thy cop,
> Lytyll day starne[1].

Truly these writers and actors 'served God in their mirth,' but
they were not allowed to go on their way unmolested. There are
poems against miracle plays as against friars, and sermons too;
and in the mass of carols and love lyrics, whether amorous or
divine, which form a characteristic feature of fourteenth and
fifteenth century English poetry, and which are treated in an
earlier chapter in this volume, there appear now and then the
spoil-sports who think 'the worlde is but a vanyte'[2] and, when
the briar holds the huntsman in full flight, only take it as a
warning to ponder on more solemn things.

Of the purely didactic literature that was intended for daily
needs, a typical example may be seen in John Mirk's *Instructions
for Parish Priests*, a versified translation from Latin of a very
practical kind, concerned with the things that are to be done
or left undone, the duties of priests and what they are to teach
and all such items as entered into the daily religious life of the
people[3]. To this we may add 'babees' books' and poems of homely
instruction, in which the wise man teaches his son and the good
wife her daughter. For those who were soon able to buy printed
books, there were works like the first dated book published in
England, the *Dictes and Sayings of the Philosophers*, whilst
Caxton's *Book of Curtesye*, addressed to 'lytyl John,' and his
printing of a *Great* and *Little Cato* sufficiently indicate the
popularity of precept and wisdom literature. The middle of the

---

[1] *Towneley Plays*, ed. England, G. and Pollard, A. W., 1897, p. 139.
[2] *Hymns to the Virgin and Christ*, pp. 83 and 91.
[3] Ed. Peacock, E., E.E.T.S. 1848.

fifteenth century gives us the *Book of Quinte Essence*, an early treatise on 'natural science,' in which, among other wonderful things, we learn how 'to reduce an oold feble evangelik man to the firste strenkthe of yongthe' and how 'to make a man that is a coward, hardy and strong.' And, in a fourteenth century MS you may run your eyes over medical recipes[1], which vary between cures 'for the fever quarteyn' and devices 'to make a woman say the what thu askes hir.' Woman was ever a disturbing factor, and the songs of medieval satirists do not spare her. One of them ends his verses with the counsel of despair:

> I hold that man ryght wele at ese,
> That can turn up hur haltur and lat hur go[2].

To the fourteenth and fifteenth centuries belongs the figure of Robin Hood the outlaw, who was known to the writers of *Piers Plowman* in the middle of the fourteenth century and stories of whose deeds were first printed by Wynkyn de Worde at the close of the fifteenth century, in the *Lytell Geste*; and with a reference to him this brief summary of 'rank and file' literature must close. He is the typical hero of English medieval popular romance, 'open-handed, brave, merciful, given to archery and venery, good-humoured, jocular, loyal, woman-protecting, priestcraft-hating, Mary-loving, God-fearing, somewhat rough withal, caring little for the refinements of life, and fond of a fight above all things'[3]. In this combination of qualities we may fitly see that blending of Norman and Englishman which helped to make the England of the ages of faith a 'merrie England.' Akin in many ways to Hereward the Englishman and Fulk Fitz-Warin the Norman, he represents, in the ballads that grew up around his name, the spirit of revolt against lordly tyranny, and he stands for the free open life of the greenwood and the oppressed folk. The ruling classes had their Arthur and his knights, their 'romances of prys,' the placid dream-world in which moved the abstractions of Stephen Hawes and the bloodless creatures

---

[1] *Reliquiae Antiquae*, vol. I, p. 51.

[2] *Ibid.* p. 77. A more gallant feeling is shown in the records of the *Pui*, a fourteenth century association established in London originally by foreign merchants in imitation of similar associations in France, *en le honour de Dieu, Madame Seinte Marie* and all saints, *por ceo qe jolietes, pais, honestez, douceur, deboneiretes, e bon amour, sanz infinite, soit maintenue.* In that society, no lady or other woman being allowed to be present at the festival of song, it was held to be the duty of members *de honurer, cheir, et loer trestotes dames, totes houres en touz lieus, au taunt en lour absence come en lour presence.* See *Munimenta Gildhallae Londoniensis*, vol. II, p. 225, *Liber custumarum*, Rolls Series, 1860, ed. Riley, H. T.

[3] Hales, J. W., *Percy Folio.*

of the 'court-poetry.' The people had their songs by the way-side, their ballads born of communal dance and their more or less pagan festivals, at which sons of the soil, maidens and apprentices who had been bidden to

> Suffer maister and maistresse paciently
> And doo their biddyng obediently
> . . . .
> Serve atte the tabille manerly [1]

could, for a while, escape from these duties and enter into a life of their own.

A word may be permitted by way of postscript, not merely to this chapter but also to the present volume. It has been sometimes urged that the fifteenth century, in the matter of purely English literature, is dull and uninteresting ; that it is an uninviting, barren waste, in which it were idle and unprofitable to spend one's time when it can be fleeted carelessly in 'the demesnes that here adjacent lie,' belonging to the stately pleasure houses of Chaucer and the Elizabethans on the one side and on the other. It would rather appear that a century, the beginning of which saw the English Mandeville translators at work, and the end of which saw one of those versions printed ; a century to which may be credited *The Flower and the Leaf,* the Paston letters, Caxton's prefaces and translations, the immortal Malory, lyrics innumerable, sacred and secular, certain ballads, in the main, as we now know them, *The Nut Brown Maid* (in itself sufficient, in form and music and theme, to 'make the fortune' of any century), carols and many of the miracle plays in their present form, can well hold its own in the history of our literature as against the centuries that precede or follow it. At least it is not deficient either in variety of utterance or in many-sidedness of interest. It is not merely full of the promise that all periods of transition possess, but its actual accomplishment is not to be contemned and its products are not devoid either of humour or of beauty.

[1] *Reliquiae Antiquae,* vol. ii, p. 223.

APPENDIX TO CHAPTER II

The following parallel passages from the two Wyclifite versions will show some of the differences between them. Broadly speaking, these differences are greatest in the earlier part of the Old Testament, and are only small in parts of the New Testament. It should be noticed that the order of the books in the Old Testament and Apocrypha is different from that of the A.V., following the *Vulgate*.

EARLIER VERSION.

LATER VERSION.

Exodus xv, 1—5.

¹ Synge we to the Lord, forsothe gloriously he is magnyfied; the hors and the steyer up he threwe doun into the see. ² My strengthe and my prey-syng the Lord; and he is maad to me into helthe. This my God, and hym Y shal gloryfie; the God of my fader, and hym Y shal enhaunce. ³ The Lord as a man fiȝter, Almyȝti his name; ⁴ the chare of Pharao and his oost he threwe fer into the see. His chosun princes weren turned vpse-doun in the reed see: ⁵ the depe watris couerden hem; thei descen-diden into the depthe as a stoon.

¹ Synge we to the Lord, for he is magnefied gloriousli; he castide doun the hors and the stiere in to the see. ² My strengthe and my preisyng is the Lord; and he is maad to me in to heelthe. This is my God, and Y schal glorifie hym; the God of my fadir, and Y schal enhaunse hym. ³ The Lord is as a man fiȝter, his name is Almiȝti; ⁴ he castide doun in to the see the charis of Farao, and his oost. Hise chosun princis weren drenchid in the reed see; ⁵ the depe watris hiliden hem; thei ȝeden doun in to the depthe as a stoon.

Isaiah vi, 1—4.

¹ In the ȝer in which diede king Osias, I saȝ the Lord sittende vp on an heiȝ sete, and rered vp; and ful was the hous of his mageste, and tho thingus that vnder hym weren, fulfil-den temple. ² Serafyn stoden vp on it, sixe wenges to the oon, and sixe to the other; with two thei couereden the face of hym, and with two thei couereden the feet of hym, and with two thei flown. ³ And they crieden the tother (*var.* toon) to the tother, and seiden, Hoeli, hoeli, hoeli, Lord God of ostes; ful is al the erthe of the glorie of hym. ⁴ And to-moued ben the thresholdes of the heenglis fro the vois of the criende, and the hous fulfild is with smoke.

¹ In the ȝeer in which the king Osie was deed ᵃ, Y siȝ the Lord sittynge on an hiȝ sete, and reisid; and the hous ᵇ was ful of his mageste, and the thingis that weren vndur hym, filliden the temple. ² Serafyn stoden on it, sixe wyngis weren to oon, and sixe wyngis to the tothir: with twei wyngis thei hiliden the face of hym, and with wyngis thei hiliden the feet of hym, and with twei wyngis thei flowen. ³ And thei criden the toon to the tother, and seiden, Hooli, hooli, hooli is Lord God of oostis; al erthe is ful of his glorie. ⁴ And the lyntels aboue of the herris were moued to-gidere of the vois of the criere, and the hous was fillid with smoke.

As an illustration of the glosses on the above extract (in the later edition), the following are given:

ᵃ was deed; not bi departing of the soule from the bodi, but in which ȝeer he was smytun of God with lepre, for he wolde take amys to him the office of priest; for fro that tyme he was arettid deed to the world, as Rabbi Salomon seith.

ᵇ the hous; that is, the temple bildid of Salamon; netheless this clause, *and the hous was ful of his mageste* is not in Ebreu, neither in bokis amended.

EARLIER VERSION.	LATER VERSION.

St Matthew vi, 1—4.

¹ Take ȝee hede, lest ȝe don ȝour riȝtwisnesse before men, that ȝee be seen of hem, ellis ȝe shule nat han meede at ȝoure fadir that is in heuenes. ² Therfore whan thou dost almesse, nyle thou synge before thee in a trumpe, as ypocritis don in synagogis and streetis, that thei ben maad worshipful of men; forsothe Y saye to ȝou, thei hau resceyued her meede. ³ But thee doynge almesse, knowe nat the left hond what the riȝt hond doth, ⁴ that thi almes be in hidlis, and thi fadir that seeth in hidlis, sal ȝelde to thee.

¹ Takith hede, that ȝe do not ȝoure riȝtwisnesse bifor men, to be seyn of hem, ellis ȝe schulen haue no meede at ȝoure fadir that is in heuenes. ² Therefore whanne thou doist almes nyle thou trumpe tofore thee, as ypocritis doon in synagogis and streetis, that thei be worschipid of men, sotheli Y seie to ȝou, they hau resseyued her meede. ³ But whanne thou doist almes, knowe not thi left hond what thi riȝt hond doith, ⁴ that thin almes be in hidils, and thi fadir that seeth in hiddils, schal quyte thee.

If a passage such as *Ephesians* ii be taken, the differences between the two versions will be found even slighter than in the above. These extracts are taken from the edition by Forshall and Madden, but its exhibition of the textual evidence leaves much to be desired. It must be borne in mind that many different workers, in all probability, took part in the translation of each version.

J. P. W.